Yizkor (Memorial) Book
of
Horodenka, Ukraine

Translation of *Sefer Horodenka*

Original Yizkor Book

Edited by: Shimon Meltzer

Published in Yiddish and Hebrew in Tel Aviv, 1963

Published by JewishGen

**An Affiliate of the Museum of Jewish Heritage - A Living Memorial to the Holocaust
New York**

Yizkor (Memorial) Book of Horodenka, Ukraine
Translation of *Sefer Horodenka*

Copyright © 2014 by JewishGen, Inc.
All rights reserved.
First Printing: March 2014, Adar Sheni' 5774
Second Printing: September 2019, Elul 5779

Original Yiddish Yizkor Book Edited by: Shimon Meltzer
Translation Project Coordinator: Mark Heckman
Layout: Celia Haupt and Joel Alpert
Image Editors: Errol Ford Genet and Martha Forsyth
Cover Design: Nili Goldman
Publicity: Sandra Hirschhorn
Yiddish and Hebrew Consultant: Josef Rosin
Indexing: Jonathan Wind

Published by JewishGen, Inc.
An Affiliate of the Museum of Jewish Heritage
A Living Memorial to the Holocaust
36 Battery Place, New York, NY 10280

"JewishGen, Inc. is not responsible for inaccuracies or omissions in the original work and makes no representations regarding the accuracy of this translation. Digital images of the original book's contents can be seen online at the New York Public Library Web site."

The mission of the JewishGen organization is to produce a translation of the original work and we cannot verify the accuracy of statements or alter facts cited.

Printed in the United States of America by Lightning Source, Inc.

Library of Congress Control Number (LCCN): 2013922521
ISBN: 978-1-939561-15-2 (hard cover: 572 pages, alk. paper)

Front Cover Credit: Avraham Yeger (see family note on page xviii)
Back Cover Credits: Chana Nadel-Grinberg, Michael Hirt and the Original Yizkor Book

JewishGen and the Yizkor-Books-in-Print Project

This book has been published by the **Yizkor-Books-in-Print Project,** as part of the **Yizkor Book Project** of **JewishGen, Inc.**

JewishGen, Inc. is a non-profit organization founded in 1987 as a resource for Jewish genealogy. Its website [www.jewishgen.org] serves as an international clearinghouse and resource center to assist individuals who are researching the history of their Jewish families and the places where they lived. JewishGen provides databases, facilitates discussion groups, and coordinates projects relating to Jewish genealogy and the history of the Jewish people. In 2003, JewishGen became an affiliate of the **Museum of Jewish Heritage - A Living Memorial to the Holocaust** in New York.

The **JewishGen Yizkor Book Project** was organized to make more widely known the existence of Yizkor (Memorial) Books written by survivors and former residents of various Jewish communities throughout the world. Later, volunteers connected to the different destroyed communities began cooperating to have these books translated from the original language—usually Hebrew or Yiddish—into English, thus enabling a wider audience to have access to the valuable information contained within them. As each chapter of these books was translated, it was posted on the JewishGen website and made available to the general public.

The **Yizkor-Books-in-Print Project** began in 2011 as an initiative to print and publish Yizkor Books that had been fully translated, so that hard copies would be available for purchase by the descendants of these communities and also by scholars, universities, synagogues, libraries, and museums.

These Yizkor books have been produced almost entirely through the volunteer effort of researchers from around the world, assisted by donations from private individuals. The books are printed and sold at near cost, so as to make them as affordable as possible. Our goal is to make this important genre of Jewish literature and history available in English in book form, so that people can have the personal histories of their ancestral towns on their bookshelves for themselves and for their children and grandchildren.

A list of all published translated Yizkor Books can be found at:
        http://www.jewishgen.org/Yizkor/ybip.html

Lance Ackerfeld, Yizkor Book Project Manager

Joel Alpert, Yizkor-Book-in-Print Project Coordinator

JewishGen
Yizkor Book Project

This book is presented by the
Yizkor Books in Print Project
Project Coordinator: Joel Alpert

Part of the
Yizkor Books Project of JewishGen, Inc.
Project Manager: Lance Ackerfeld

These books have been produced solely through volunteer effort
of individuals from around the world. The books are printed and
sold at near cost, so as to make them as affordable as possible.

Our goal is to make this history and important genre of Jewish
literature available in English in book form so that people can have
the near-personal histories of their ancestral towns on their bookshelves for themselves and for their children and grandchildren.

Any donations to the Yizkor Books Project are appreciated.

Please send donations to:
Yizkor Book Project
JewishGen
36 Battery Place
New York, NY 10280

JewishGen, Inc. is an affiliate of the
Museum of Jewish Heritage
A Living Memorial to the Holocaust

Yiddish Title Page of Original Yizkor Book

ספר האָראָדענקע

רעדאקטאר : שמשון מעלצער

פארלאג פון דער האראדענקער לאנדסמאנשאפט

אין אמעריקע און ישראל

תשכ"ד ● 1963

Hebrew Title Page of Original Yizkor Book

ספר הורודנקה

העורך: שמשון מלצר

הוצאת אירגון יוצאי הורודנקה והסביבה

בישראל ובארצות הברית

תשכ"ד • 1963

Translation of the Title Page of Original Yizkor Book

SEFER HORODENKA

Red. SH. MELTZER

Published by

The Book Committee of "Sefer Horodonka"

in United States and Israel

1963

The Book of Horodenka (Horodenka, Ukraine)

48°40' / 25°30'

Translation of *Sefer Horodenka*

Edited by: Shimon Meltzer

Published in Tel Aviv, 1963

Acknowledgments

Translation Project Coordinator: Mark Heckman

Donated Translations

Gertrude Geffner, Ellen Geffner Biderman, Sara Geffner Lewis, Anne Geffner

This is a translation from: *Sefer Horodenka*,
published in Israel in 1963 by "Former Residents of Horodenka and
Vicinity in Israel and the USA."

It is written in both Yiddish and Hebrew (with some old records written in
German); 432 pages.

Foreword to the English Translation and Publication of Sefer Horodenka

Norman Berman and I first thought about translating Sefer Horodenka after an IAJGS conference in the 1990s. Each of us had a copy of the book, but were unable to read most of it. We contacted some of the original authors, who were members of the Horodenker Association in Israel, and contacted heirs to the U.S. copyright holder in order to get permission for the translation. We also used our limited Hebrew, Yiddish, and German abilities to translate or transliterate a few portions of the book -- the necrology is one example -- and inveigled or paid people with better language skills to translate the table of contents and some of the smaller chapters. A few years later, Ellen Biderman took on the task and, in short order, had located qualified translators and paid them to translate the vast majority of the book. This project would not exist but for Ellen's contribution.

Other people who provided encouragement, funds, editing, or translations, include Koka Leah Greif, Tosia Schneider, Debbie Dworski, Yehudis Fishman, Harvey Buchalter, Dahlia Yohai and others who I've left off of this list due to poor record keeping, but whose contributions are nevertheless appreciated.

Note that this translation is not complete. Many of the book's chapters were duplicated in Hebrew and Yiddish, For example, the first chapter "About the Publishing of the Horodenker Book", by M. Fleshner, begins in Yiddish on page 1 of the original book. The same chapter in Hebrew begins on page 17. One translation from each of the duplicated chapters is present in this edition (sometimes from the Yiddish; sometimes from the Hebrew -- it depends on which language a particular translator was skilled in). The duplicated chapters are very similar to one another, but not identical. If, in the future, any of the duplicate chapters are translated, they will appear on the Yizkor Book Projects page

http://www.jewishgen.org/yizkor/gorodenka/gorodenka.html.

But this English edition of Sefer Horodenka is a notable achievement of the JewishGen Yizkor Book Project, the products of which have been enormously popular with genealogical researchers. Thanks go to Joel Alpert and Lance Ackerfeld for their work in publishing this volume.

We all hope you find this translation a valuable aid in learning about the lives of your ancestors and kinfolk who lived in Horodenka.

May their spirits be bound up in the bundle of life!

Mark Heckman
Davis, California, USA
15 Adar 1 5774, 15 February 2014

Preface from the Original Yizkor Book

PREFACE

Horodenka is a little town in Eastern Galicia, which was said to be the administrative centre of a region containing forty-eight small villages.

The history of its organised Jewish communal life begins in the year 1743, although Horodenka is mentioned as a small village as early as 1579. According to historical documents it was raised to the rank of a city in the Seventeenth century when it passed into the hands of the famous Polish noble family Potocki, who owned the entire agricultural area. There are certain documents from which it would appear that a number of Jewish families were already living there in the early part of the Seventeenth century, even before it became a town. Reliable sources, however, make it clear that the Jews of Horodenka became significant as a community only in the middle of the Eighteenth century. Jewish merchants from the city are recorded among the visitors to the International Fair at Leipzig, 1739—1748.

Documents of the half-century 1870—1927 show that the average percentage of Jews in the entire population varied between 33% and 40%, against 45%—55% of Ruthenians (or Ukrainians) and barely 10% of Poles.

On the map Horodenka will be found at the point where the one-time Polish frontier touched on the frontiers of Russia to the East and Rumania to the South. As a result of this topographical position the inhabitants of Horodenka, and especially the Jews among them, were always the first to suffer at the outbreak of war between the above countries.

It should also be noted that although the Poles were a small minority, their historical and political aspirations in this region had the result that they were almost always in charge of municipal institutions and life. On the other hand the Ukrainians, who were usually in a numerical majority, were unable to take over municipal institutions and the mayoralty in the absence of properly trained and qualified political leaders. Nevertheless they developed national aspirations, and various official declarations from the neighbouring country encouraged them to attempt to join the Ukraine, which was under the Tzarist regime and part of Russia.

The Jewish Community had to find a way of living together with the other two national groups and their political aspirations which could not always be understood by their two neighbours. In addition, the Jewish leaders of the city often found it very difficult to maintain a single line of policy which at the same time enabled them to live satisfactorily among themselves and with their neighbours.

As a result there were constant disagreements between

מראה הרחוב הראשי בשנת 1915
די הויפט־גאַס אין יאָר 1915
View on the main street
in 1915.

the various inner Jewish groups regarding the right steps to take as various political problems emerged. It followed that neither of the other national minorities was on friendly terms with the Jews, with results that were clearly felt between 1914 and 1917 during the First World War, when the city was repeatedly occupied and re-occupied by the Russians and the Austrians in turn. In this situation Jewish lives and property were in constant danger, and a virtual pogrom atmosphere was the order of the day.

However, the Jews of Horodenka faced their final tragedy during the Second World War. Horodenka had been occupied by the Russians a few weeks after the German attack on Poland in Autumn 1939. When the Nazis attacked Russia in turn, in June 1941, they occupied Horodenka and remained there until the end of the war. During that period of close on four years they virtually succeeded in their "final solution" by exterminating the whole Jewish population. In this they were gladly assisted by a large number of the local Ukrainians, who as a result have "inherited" all Jewish property in one way or another. According to reliable evidence about 3,000 adults and children were murdered in 1941 and 1942, in the course of three "Actions".

A bare handful of Horodenka Jews succeeded in escaping from the city of their birth and made their way either to Russia or to Rumania. From them it is learnt that no significant resistance was shown by any part of the local population at the commencement of the Nazi occupation. Soon after the first Action, however, Jews ceased to believe Nazi promises and propaganda and began to realise their true position. Several young Jews then joined the partisans who were just beginning to organise resistance activities in the forests on the other side of the River Dniester. Thanks to this handful of men and women, who ultimately reached Israel, U.S.A., U.S.S.R. and Latin America, we know some facts about the destruction and annihilation of Horodenka Jewry and Jewish life.

No matter how much we grieve we cannot bring back our dear and beloved parents, our sisters and brothers and their innocent children, who were deprived of their lives so murderously during the "liquidation" of European Jewry.

In 1945 the first survivors arrived here in Eretz Israel and gave an account of what had happened. Those already in this country who had been born or had lived in Horodenka then organised a Committee with the aims of giving all possible aid and comfort to the newcomers, and establishing a monument for the thousands of Horodenka Jews who had fallen victim to the Nazis between 1941 and 1945. The various suggestions made about the most suitable monument included a proposal for a Memorial Volume to record the story of the Horodenka Jewish community from its beginnings until its end; a history covering a period of 2—4 centuries.

It was decided to adopt this proposal, and so a

התחלת ההדפסה של ספר־הורודנקה
אנהויב פון דרוקן דעם
„ספר האראדענקע"
The Begin of printing the
"Sefer Horodenka"

beginning was made with "Sefer Horodenka", the Horodenka Book, which has been edited, written and financed by sons and daughters of Horodenka all the world over. Some of the articles, it is true, were written by persons who were not born there; but they either lived in the city for several years or married Horodenka men and women, and can therefore be regarded as residents.

We who have survived are the sole orphans and heirs of what was a flourishing community. We do not set out to produce a volume which is exclusive, nor do we aim at a work of outstanding literary value. What we have tried to produce is a joint co-operative publication made by and speaking for the survivors of this small Jewish town, as part of the history of that remarkable Jewry of Poland which existed for so long, until it was finally obliterated from the map of Jewry throughout the world.

In this brief English preface it is not our purpose to repeat all that is to be found in the Hebrew and Yiddish sections. What we aim to do is to give the children of those who came from our little birthplace some idea of the fate of their grandparents and kinsfolk, in order that they may from time to time remember those thousands who were slaughtered by the Nazis during the Second World War, with all the resources of modern science and organisation. And it goes without saying that this "Sefer Horodenka" could never have come into being if all the children of Horodenka who have survived the

overwhelming catastrophe had not made every effort and assumed the necessary responsibility.

It should be borne in mind that this volume, like others of the same kind, has meant an outlay of about $8000, in addition to the difficulties involved in collecting and editing the material itself. It was possible to achieve this result only thanks to an agreement reached between the Horodenka townsfolk in the U.S.A. and Israel. In bringing about this agreement our friends Ruth and Abe Podway of New York played a very important part.

We wish to thank all those who have participated in any form in this volume, and who have helped to bring it into being. Thank you one and all for anything and everything you have done.

We would like all former members of the Horodenka community or from the surrounding villages, and all those who have the names of individual survivors coming from the region, to send their names on to us, in order that we may ensure that all of them have an opportunity of obtaining this volume. For we know that at the proper memorial season each and every one of us will read through the list of Jewish victims who gave up their lives to hallow the Holy Name and the name of the suffering Jewish people.

May their spirits be bound up in the Bundle of Life!

For and on behalf of the Book Committee

M. FLESCHNER

Tel Aviv, Rosh Hashana 5724, September 1963

המסיבה להופעת המחצית הראשונה
של הספר 14.11.1962
צום דערשיינען פון ערשטער העלפט
פון בוך 14.11.1962
The meeting where the completion of the first Part of the Book was announced—
Tel-Aviv 14/11/1962.

Acknowledgements

Special thanks to the National Yiddish Book Center in Amherst, Massachusetts and the New York Public Library for supplying the high resolution images used in this book.

Notes to the Reader:

Also please note that all references within the text of the book to page numbers, refer to the page numbers of the original Yizkor Book.

Note: The original book can be seen online at the NY Public Library site:

http://yizkor.nypl.org/index.php?id=2266

MAP OF UKRAINE IN 2014

Location:

Latitude 48°40' and East Longitude 25°30'
        40 miles ESE of Ivano-Frankivsk,
        32 miles NW of Chernivtsi (Tschernowitz),
        23 miles ENE of Kolomyya (Kołomyja).

Geopolitical Location Over Time

Period	Town	District	Province	Country
Before WWI (c. 1900):	Horodenka	Horodenka	Galicia	Austrian Empire
Between the wars (c. 1930):	Horodenka	Horodenka	Stanisławów	Poland
After WWII (c. 1950):	Gorodënka			Soviet Union
Today (c. 2000):	Horodenka			Ukraine

Nearby Jewish Communities:

Chernyatyn 2 miles W
Yaseniv-Pilnyy 2 miles SSE
Potochyshche 7 miles NNE
Ustechko 8 miles NNE
Chortovets 10 miles WNW
Zalishchyky 11 miles E
Chernelytsya 11 miles NNW
Hvizdets 11 miles WSW
Dzhurkov 14 miles W
Snyatyn 15 miles SSE
Obertyn 15 miles W
Davydivtsi 16 miles SE
Vasyliv 16 miles ESE
Tovste 17 miles NE
Demiche 17 miles SSW
Zabolotiv 17 miles SW
Tovtry 18 miles ESE
Doroshivtsi 18 miles ESE
Bil'che-Zolote 19 miles ENE
Knyazhe 19 miles S
Zolotyy Potik 19 miles NNW
Zastavna 19 miles ESE
Khotymyr 19 miles WNW
Kitsman 19 miles SE
Vashkivtsi 20 miles S
Sokolov 20 miles NNW
Dzhurov 20 miles SSW
Nepolokivtsi 20 miles SSE
Palashёvka 21 miles N
Yazlovets 21 miles N

Banyliv 22 miles SSW
Ulashkivtsi 22 miles NE
Yahilnytsya 22 miles NNE
Vikno 22 miles ESE
Oleyёvo-Korolёvka 23 miles ENE
Kolomyya 23 miles WSW
Koropets 23 miles NW
Vilyavche 24 miles SSW
Rozhniv 24 miles SSW
Nyzhni Stanivitzi 24 miles S
Glinitsa 25 miles SSE
Miliye 25 miles SSW
Ozeryany 25 miles NE
Drachyntsi 26 miles SSE
Lanivtsi 26 miles ENE
Tlumach 27 miles WNW
Borshchiv 27 miles ENE
Kostintsy 27 miles S
Nyzhniv 27 miles NW
Barysh 27 miles NNW
Ustye 28 miles E
Chortkiv 28 miles NNE
Verkhneye Krivche 28 miles E
Kabeshti 28 miles SSE
Rzhavintsy 29 miles ESE
Gorishnyaya Vygnanka 29 miles NNE
Buchach 29 miles N
Pystan 30 miles SW
Otyniya 30 miles W

Note on the Yeger Family from Horodenka

Grandfather Avraham (ben Yoel) Yeger (b. 1885 in Sniatin) married in 1903 to Rivka Lea bat Yosel and Chaya Shor from Horodenka. Avraham and Lea Yeger had five children: Rosa, Yoel, Yosef, Miko and Sheindel.

In 1914 with the outbreak of World War I, when the Russians approached the city, Avraham took his children, Rosa (10), Yoel (4), Yosef (3) and Miko (2) and walked all the way to Vyzhnytsia, Romania to his sister Chana.

A short time after that they had to take the train to Czechoslovakia, where they stayed for two years until Avraham's recruitment to the Austrian army.

For four years the children stayed in an orphanage in Vienna where they suffered from hunger and illnesses. Lea stayed in Horodenka with her elderly grandfather Yizchak Reuven Shor.

After the war the family was reunited with assistance of the Red Cross. Lea opened a small store in Horodenka, which provided a living for the family.

Yoel grew up to be an activist of the Gordonia movement and made Aliyah to *Eretz-Yisrael* in 1930. Rosa and her brother Yosef married Israel Grinberg and his sister Fanya respectively, also from Horodenka. Both couples also made Aliyah.

Miko and Sheindel (born after the war) remained in Horodenka with their parents Avraham and Lea. They were murdered by the Nazis along with all the Jews of the shtetl.

HASHEM IKOM DAMAM!

The three Yeger siblings who made aliyah before World War II lived to see children, grandchildren and great-grandchildren. These families constitute defiance of the goals of the Nazis and proof of our people's endurance in spite of the Nazis.

Message to the world and Nazism is: "**Never Again**"

Written by Avraham Yeger in 2014 in Israel in Hebrew.

Family Notes

TABLE OF CONTENTS

Introduction

About the Publication of Sefer Horodenka

By Moshe Fleshner

Translated by Yehudis Fishman

At last we, the survivors of Horodenka, a small town in East Galicia
are witnessing the publication of the Yizkor Book (a memorial book) for
the martyrs of our town and those who lived in its vicinity. This book
is the outcome of a plan that we carried in our hearts and discussed
for more than fifteen years, but were unable to bring to fruition – until
today.

Welcome Party to R. & A. Podway in Tel-Aviv

The delays did not arise from fundamental differences of opinion.
All of us were residents of Horodenka; we had survived years of
calamity and retribution. We felt that we were still in mourning – that
we were orphans who had lost our fathers and our mothers as well as
our sisters and our brothers. Each one of us felt that something had to
be done to commemorate the martyrs of Horodenka. We wanted to
establish a worthy headstone in memory of our town where we took
our first steps, where we dared to dream of a better future and of a
free world for every human being – a world that would guarantee
freedom of expression to the Jewish people. We felt obligated to
inscribe and memorialize all those who had died, whether they were

family members or friends, individuals or entire families, even if we did not know their burial sites.

Technical problems were the primary cause for the delay in publishing this book. It was clear to us, the members of the committee in Israel, that the book had to be written by Horodenkans themselves – those men and women who witnessed the atrocities and the destruction of the town and who carried the awful memories in their hearts. They are the only ones who could express all this sorrow and desperation. We knew that in order to execute such a difficult task the Horodenkans in two major centers of residence, Israel and the United States, would have to cooperate and create an organizational infrastructure. Last, but not the least, we had to find the financial resources needed to make even the first step toward our goal. And we needed to take care of some basic problems that came up during the negotiations.

First on the agenda was the issue of the language of the book. There were those who thought that it should be published only in Yiddish, the language that most Horodenkans spoke and the language that most Jews in Israel and the United States, including Holocaust survivors, understand. Others objected. They claimed that the purpose of the book was to perpetuate the memories of our beloved ones for the next generations, and therefore the book should be written in Hebrew, the language of our sons and daughters. There were those who expressed their wishes to publish the book in English, for the sons and daughters of the Horodenkans who live in the United States. Thus we concluded that perhaps the book could be published in three languages – Hebrew, Yiddish, and English. Opinions and positions were formed and taken. Everyone stood his ground, trying to convince the others of the strength of his opinion.

A major problem arose at the time when we were deep in the process of creating the book and after most of the material had already been written and all the conflicts had been settled: Should the book serve as a memorial for the entire community and portray a destroyed congregation with a rich social life, or should it be a personal account, where each individual has the opportunity to express their inner feelings and describe their dear and close ones who are gone forever?

We corresponded for a few years with the "landsmanshaft" in the United States regarding the publication of the book, but we could not reach agreement. There were also occasions when qualified representatives from the United States visited Israel and when members of our committee visited the United States. But negotiations weren't useful and didn't break the ice or overcome the frost.

Until "one clear day," a Horodenka couple – Ruth and Abba Podway (Podvoysoker) from the United States arrived in Israel. In Horodenka Ruth was called Rivkah Neigiser. During the years 1917 through 1919, Ruth was a Zionist and belonged to one of the first Zionist-Socialist youth groups, Ha-Shomer, which had been established soon after World War One. Therefore, it is no wonder that she showed "inclinations" toward Israel in general and toward Horodenka in particular. Her husband, according to friends who knew him well before he moved to America, always had a strong sense of justice and was always ready – even if it meant self-sacrifice – to lend a hand and help those weak and weary, regardless of their political views or opinions. In his youth in Horodenka, he was active in the establishment of Yiddish kindergartens and public schools. These schools gave children from families of poor laborers and unskilled workers a Jewish and general education to help them find their way out of their depressed cultural condition.

The American Book Committee in New York
Sitting from right to left: Z. Shpierer, S. Kirschner, A. Podway, Mrs. R. Podway, H. Eckhaus & M. Rosenkranz.
Standing from right to left, second row: L. Spierer, A. Shechter, A. Birnbaum, N. Rosenkranz, M. Podwisoker, I. Fink, Ch. Fiedler, M. L. Ladenheim, M. Nadler & A. Oringer.
Standing from right to left, third row: L. Koch, F. Lichtenthal, N. Reif & R. Bahr.

This modest beginning was the foundation from which Abba Podway and "his right arm," Rivkah-Ruth, grew to become renowned non-partisan social activists. Many changes, no doubt, occurred in their life-style and customs, during all those years when they struggled to rebuild their life in the United States; but to this day, their Jewish-national inclinations have not changed. Those inclinations led to their active participation in many projects and enterprises that were carried out by American Jewry since the establishment of Israel. To that point, their first visit to Israel was with the "Volunteers of the Histadruth Fund" from the United States.

As a result of Ruth and Abba Podway's first visit to Israel, there was a complete turnaround in the relationship between Horodenka organizations in the United Sates and those in Israel. It was now possible to fulfill our obligation to the families that were destroyed in the Holocaust. I would like to express my hope that the cooperation between us will not end upon the publication of this book and hope the friendly relationship between the two organizations will continue.

Immediately after our first meeting with the Podways, we felt their strong desire to do something to benefit the Horodenka people in Israel. During the three weeks of their first visit we talked a lot about our problems and at the end we decided to establish "Kehilyah" – a foundation to give financial help and loans to survivors of Horodenka living in Israel. The Podways personally gave the first donation to the foundation and later gave additional amounts for its growth. Additional funds were also received from their friends and acquaintances, especially from Mr. Abba Kremer. Details about Kehilyah are included in the concise financial report that I presented in one of the yearly memorial meetings for the victims of Horodenka.

The establishment of Kehilyah in 1958 was only the first link in a chain of activities that the Podways arranged on one of their biannual visits to Israel. Their visit in 1960 became a turning point in the publication of the Yizkor Book. They were impressed by our story about the deadlocked negotiations with the "Landmanshaft" people in the United Sates. They took it upon themselves to mediate and help us reach an agreement with our Horodenka brothers and sisters to make the publication of the book possible. The Podways also committed to take care of the financial problems related to the publication of the book in the United Sates. Their initial contribution was more than all the amounts that had been donated by other Horodenkans to date. It is no secret that we in Israel are not wealthy enough to finance a book that costs eight thousand dollars (close to 18,000 shekels) to publish.

When the Podways returned to the United States, they established a committee for the publication of the Yizkor Book. We began a

The Memorial Book Board in Israel

Sitting from right to left: M. Fleshner, Mrs. P. Fleshner, Mrs. K. Greif, Mrs. B. Feder, Mrs. R. Rotman & G. Lindenberg.
Standing from right to left: R. Prifer, J. Frishling, H. Marksheid, M. Stachel, I. Rauchwerger, J. Shapira, Z. Shchory, A. Pilpel, M. Gloger, M. Sucher, N. Bergman, Sh. Sucher, D. Hartenstein, L. Frishling & N. Strum

constant correspondence. Before long, it became clear to everyone that the apprehensions of both sides were very exaggerated and that actually the differences in opinion were not so great. For fear that the renewed effort to accomplish the task would fail again, each side behaved cautiously and therefore we managed to solve the major problems effortlessly.

In addition to correspondence during the past two years, we also had the opportunity to meet with important members of the [Horodenka] committee from the United States who came to Israel as official or unofficial representatives. First to arrive was Mr. Leibala Koch, an exceptional Jew who for years had been a philanthropist supporting a number of needy families in Israel through his private anonymous charitable foundation. (He is far from wealthy and takes no public credit). A few months later Harry Eckhaus arrived. He is a businessman and a member of the committee in the United States. Together we resolved a few problems concerning the publication of the book. I must note that there were members of our committee who could not easily understand the "other side." I do not intend to dwell on details, but it is important for me to mention it as one of the many difficulties and obstacles that we had to overcome. Mr. Eckhaus' visit was also crucial for another reason. The amount of money that he brought from the United States enabled us to begin our task and gave us assurance that there would be no financial obstacles in publishing the book.

A few months following Eckhaus' visit, Mr. Hass and his wife arrived for a visit to Israel. Mr. Hass is a long time member of the Progressive Horodenka Association in the United States and served as its director for a period of time. A reception was given to each of these guests by our organization and by the Yizkor-Book Committee. By the time each of the guests left Israel, they all had become loyal friends of our project and our organization.

Up to this point, I have tried to describe the sequence of events that led to the publication of the Yizkor Book. Now permit me to say a few words about the book itself. The first task was to find a suitable editor. Unfortunately, we could not find the right person among the Horodenkans. With sheer "luck," and I am using the word "luck" in its simplistic meaning and not as a metaphor, we succeeded in getting the poet Shimshon Meltzer to agree to be the editor of the Horodenka Book.

We are confident that we could not have chosen a better editor, as Meltzer is known as one of the best in Israel. We could rest assured that by entrusting him with the editing of the book we would get more than we had hoped for. The close collaboration between him and our members, who are the "true" authors of the book, enabled us to properly plan the memorial for our martyrs that were murdered and for our community that was eradicated.

In addition to his literary talent, Meltzer is, in a certain way, one of the Horodenka people. Not only was he born in Tluste, which is on the outskirts of Horodenka, but a year prior to his emigration to Israel he and his wife lived in Horodenka where he worked as a teacher in the Hebrew School. Therefore, his descriptions of the town, its roads, its people, and its atmosphere are authentic and accurate.

As mentioned above, we succeeded with the selection of the editor. However, the quality of the book is not determined just by the editor but also by the material presented to the editor. Here we suffered a disadvantage, since during the Holocaust Nazi oppressors murdered many of Horodenka's Jewish intellectuals who would have contributed greatly to this book. Their testaments were buried with those of blessed memory.

That dwindling of collective memories is evident in many chapters of the book. On one hand many of the events of the past were not included, since those elders who could tell about them have long since passed away. Thus we lacked information about the different organization and institutions in our town during the years just before the Holocaust. We did our best to collect as much material as possible. We hereby present to the public a book that was written by the survivors of our town, with all its imperfections. The public will read it and form an opinion for better or for worse.

We took upon ourselves the distinct responsibility of publishing a list of the Holocaust victims from our vicinity who were killed in different Actions. Here, too, we faced questions that required the full cooperation of the Horodenka survivors. During the past two years we took every opportunity to appeal to the Horodenkans in Israel and in the United Sates to request lists of their loved ones or acquaintances who perished in the Holocaust. Indeed, we managed to compile a long list based primarily on the recollections of the survivors. Therefore, it is inevitable that there will be errors, inaccuracies and omissions. In spite of this, we felt that it was our holy duty to publish such a list even if it is incomplete.

I feel myself obligated to add some explanations and to apologize to a lot of people who participated in the writing of the material for the Horodenka book. I would like to reiterate what we said and emphasized in every meeting. Each member was free to write about whatever he or she desired, but we were not obligated to publish his or her material unedited. We stated that the editorial board together with the editor would have the final authority to decide what to print. We were also obligated to check all the facts and dates in the manuscripts and to make changes. We did all we could and hope that we succeeded in avoiding mistakes.

In some cases we copied into this book paragraphs and chapters from a variety of sources like chapters from A. Granach's book and a poem by M. Birenboym. We thank all whose permission enabled us to do so.

I would also like to mention the enormous and important work that was done by groups of volunteers in Israel and in the United States. These volunteers spent hours, weeks and months of their free time, neglecting their own personal matters. I would very much like to express my gratitude to these people in the name of the Organizations in Israel and in the United Sates and say: "Yishar Kochachem!" (May your strength remain with you forever!)

The most difficult time was the last few months before the publication of the book. We worked zealously to be able to finish in time. In this period we faced complicated problems that we could not have foreseen. It is quite possible that some of them arose from our

1
**The printers of "Achduth" with the Committe Members at the beginning
of printing the "Sefer Horodenka"**

wish to finish this work in November of 1962, which was within two years of commencement of work on the book. In addition we wanted to include Ruth and Abba Podway in the book's publication ceremony before their November 18th departure to the United States.

I would like to point out that during the last two years, many members of the small committee in Israel helped me, as primary person in charge, in the process of publishing the yizkor book. They are: Nachman Bergman, Yosef Yanker, Tzvi Marksheid, Yitzchak Rauchwerger, Zelig Shchory, Moshe (Monya) Stachel, Gavriel Lindenberg and Itschak Shapira. The last two were also members of the editorial board in which Joshua Streit and Moshe Stachel participated. Additionally, our friend Gavriel Lindenberg was largely responsible for the preparation of the material for the memorial book.

Through the entire process, and especially at the end, Gavriel worked tirelessly preparing the material for editing by typing, doing adaptations, translations and proof reading. People close to Lindenberg and who are familiar with his work complimented him on his ability, his dedication and diligence. I have known him for years and have been working with him in the organization for Horodenka survivors and in the management of Kehilyah. I have also worked with him on this book. I respectfully join them with my own compliments.

Additionally, I would like to commend the hard work and the dedication of the members of the American committee of our organization. I want to bring to your attention these people: Izador Oringer, Mo Nadler, Izik Fink (the secretary of the book committee in the United States), Sam Kirshner, Mendel Rozenkranz, Izik Shechter and Zelig Shpierer.

In light of the important task that we accomplished, it is my pleasure to note that all of our members, who were called upon to assist us in our work, fulfilled their obligation with commendable dedication. I express my deepest gratitude to both organizations in the United States and in Israel. I also want to thank two enterprises for their big help in the printing of the Horodenka Book: "Achduth" cooperative print in Tel-Aviv and United Graphic Corporation Ltd. in Tel Aviv. They guided me in the preparation of the galleys and we benefited from their unusual attention.

It is worth briefly reviewing the actions of the "Organization of the Survivors of Horodenka and the Vicinity" in Israel during the twelve years of its existence. I would like to do so by quoting from a report given at a memorial meeting on December 15, 1957. At that meeting, Moshe Fleshner, the director of the organization read the report and Yitzchak Shapira eulogized the community that was destroyed. A few guests from abroad and a few newly arrived immigrants also attended the meeting. Later they all expressed their happiness that they were once again among the community of Horodenka people.

Report on the Organization's Activities

(Given at the Yikzkor Meeting on December 15, 1957)

By Moshe Fleshner

It is twelve years now that our organization, "The Organization for the Survivors of Horodenka and Its Vicinity" has existed. The active members are interested in achieving three goals. First we want to commemorate the memory of the martyrs of our town by having a Memorial Day each year around the time of the first Action in Horodenka; by planting trees in "Yaar Hakdoshim" (Forest of the

Martyrs); by establishing a memorial tablet in the "Holocaust Cellar;" and by publishing a memorial book in memory of the town's martyrs. Second we want to provide financial help to Horodenkans who immigrated to Israel after the Holocaust. Lastly, we want to establish a relationship between the Horodenkans in Israel and those abroad.

During the twelve years of its existence, our organization has succeeded in accomplishing some of these goals. Once a year we hold a memorial meeting at which Horodenkans meet and remember together their loved ones that were killed in the Holocaust. We established a memorial in the form of a forest "Yar Kdoshem Polin" (The forest of the Polish Martyrs) in the Martyrs' Forest planted by the Jewish National Fund in the Jerusalem mountains. We held discussions with the directors of "Martef ha-Shoah" (The Holocaust Cellar) regarding the establishment of a memorial tablet to be placed among the other tablets that are on the walls in memory of the Holocaust victims of Polish communities. But our main mission – publication of the book in memory of the victims of our town – is still before us. We have not been able to overcome all the obstacles standing in our way. Nevertheless we have not given up and we are confident that a day will come when we will be able to add this last link to the chain of events done in memory of the martyrs of our town.

We have made some progress in extending help to the survivors that have come to Israel. This accomplishment was a result of the visit of the Podway family to Israel last summer. They helped initiate and fund Kehilyah – a fund for the Horodenka survivors. Horodenkans living in Israel and "landsmenshaft" in the United Sates also made contributions. During its short existence, the fund has dispersed loans to new immigrants and to residents in the sum of a few thousand lirot.

Horodenkaer Landsleit attending the annual Yizkor meeting in Tel Aviv

Some of these loans have already been repaid.

We must acknowledge that the assistance given by Kehilyah did not solve all the financial problems for those who are in need, but it did provide assistance to those needing to obtain apartments, etc. We now call upon the Horodenkans who live in Israel to join the fund by making financial contributions to increase its capital.

Our third goal was to nurture relations among the people of our town living in Israel and abroad. We tried to do this by arranging special parties and group meetings during the holidays and during visits of guests from abroad. Many of our members took advantage of these gatherings and had a good time.

Before I proceed with our program, I would like to wish a speedy recovery to one of the Horodenkan elders, Mr. Yosel Bergman who is bedridden. This is the first time that he won't be attending the memorial meeting. In the name of all those present here tonight, we wish him a speedy and complete recovery and express our hopes that we will have the privilege to see him among us at future meeting.

As we do every year, let us remember the members of our organization who died in the last year. I'm asking the audience to respect their memory by standing. There names are: Eliezer Fridler, Mati Shertzer, Uritza Frishling, Henya Rubel (mother of the Langshtein family in Israel), and Feiga Foler. Two family members of our friends also passed away: Ataliya Lindenberg, wife of Gavriel Lindenberg and Shrage Shvartshtein, husband of Haya Shvartz.

May their memories be blessed!

And now I would like to invite our friend, Mr. Yitzhak Shapira, to talk about the people of Horodenka.

Horodenkaer attending the annual Yizkor Ceremony in "Yaar Hakdoshim"

A Sad Walk Around Our Town

By Yitzchak Shapira

Our human brain cannot comprehend nor grasp how it all happened. The Jewish nation has never been spoiled by the nations of the world. We have had our share of pogroms, slaughtering, inquisitions and forced conversions. However all those dwarf against the terrible holocaust that the Jewish nation faced in Eastern Europe thirteen, fourteen and fifteen years ago. World history has never recorded, since creation, such a planned and loathsome murder executed by military commanders and scientists. These supposed representatives of the twentieth century, with treacherous sadism, slaughtered, butchered, murdered and burnt men, women and children. It was done with precision using the methodology that the German Nazis were known for, and with the full cooperation of the human filth in all the countries occupied by the Hitler regime. There is no doubt that a large span of time must pass before the essence of this immense tragedy and catastrophe, which happened under the sun and in full view of the entire world's population, can be assessed correctly.

Hertzl, the founder of national Zionism, taught us that a Jewish State will rise from the adversity of the Jews, and indeed, the State of Israel is today a reality. But is there a shore to this sea of tribulation, this sea of blood and tears that were spilled during the massacre of six million Jews in Europe? There is an old saying that life is more bearable than death, and that every wound is destined to heal. It is quite possible that in the near future, students will read in their textbooks, with horror and nausea, about the lowest depth that human endeavors reached during the war. But we, who are present here today, the survivors of Horodenka, have cut off limbs that are still bleeding. We are part of the large body of masses of Beth-Israel, orphans who lost their fathers and their mothers. Those who are still mourning the death of brothers and sisters cannot quietly analyze these historical events. For us, this wound is a reality, a horrible reality.

Our town, Horodenka, blessed be her memory, was pure and righteous, and even though it was unprogressive compared to some other modern cities, its people embodied vitality and aspirations. Its Jewish residents were of all races, classes and ages and possessed an inner soul, for which the Galician people were known.

I would like you to join me on a short trip in our small town. We will not travel through each street. Rather our trip will take us to the people who lived there and to their places of work. It will be a kind of socio-demographic trip. I would like to ask forgiveness from all the young people here, those who were born after the period that I have chosen to discuss tonight. It is the period that immediately followed World War I, a period that was extremely crucial for our town. It was a period in which nations woke up and demanded their independence. It was a period of revolution that brought awakening to our region. It was the period following the Balfour Declaration when we were occupied first by the Austrians, then the Romanians and Ukrainians, and among them the Podolians, and later the Polish. I chose this period, the years of 1920-1930, because I remember it vividly. I visited Horodenka for a week in 1937. It was a short visit, but I managed to notice that nothing much had changed. I met the same people, and more or less, life seemed to be the same as when I left the city in 1925.

Now I would like to relate my memories of our families who were from various social classes. It is possible that many of the sons and daughters of these families may live differently than their parents, but none-the-less, the ethical values remain the same for generations. The fruit usually represents the tree. When I look here at the faces of these youngsters, I recall what their parents looked like when they were young and how they conducted themselves.

First on our tour of Horodenka, we will pass by the schools. Among them is the Yiddish high school, and most importantly the Hebrew high school, which was responsible for generations of students who spoke and understood Hebrew. Those schools produced the pioneers and first settlers who went to Israel in pursuit of their dreams.

Let us now pass by the "heders" (the little schools). If you close your eyes you will surely remember the different rabbis and the heders of that period. We can remember the "more modern" heders where the Bible was taught with interpretation. There were also conservative heders where the Rabbi waving a belt was the last word together with his counterparts: the Rebetzen with her "hard heart," and her group of strict assistants.

From there, let us proceed to the many synagogues in our town. First let us enter into the primary synagogue that was destroyed in the first invasion during World War I. Later there were efforts made to rebuild it. I remember, and surely some of you remember this huge synagogue with its precious caretaker, Dudi Zelner. All of us heard the pounding of his hammer that woke up the town's people to do God's work. I remember how during Kol Nidre night he watched Pietro, the Sabbath Goy, who tended the crowded Yortzeit candles making sure they didn't bend over or die out prematurely, God forbid.

On both sides of the synagogue there were two areas that were crowded with worshippers saying their prayers and entreaties in competition with those inside the large synagogue.

And close by stood the seminary where a group of important scholars, headed by Rabbi Ashkenazi, my he rest in peace, gathered. Rabbi Ashkenazi was one of the most learned rabbis in Galicia. He was an incredible scholar with a very sharp mind.

And let me briefly mention all the Kloyzen (clubs), old and new, which were named after the different Rabbis according to their associations and religious affiliations. There was Yad Chrutzin and Tzyonistisher Farain, the cradle of Zionism in Horodenka. It was the spring from which we quenched our thirst for Aliyah to Israel. Let me also mention the ha-Hitachdut and the Bond, which inspired the establishment of such organizations as ha-Shomer, he-Chlutz, Gordoniah and he-Chlutz haTzair. There were also the national funds such as LiterarisheTzirklen and the dramatic clubs, including one at the warm and pleasant house of our friend Hesel Suka.

Our town was blessed with a variety of believers and "apikoroses." I remember one of them vividly, but I won't mention his name. He was an avid learner and a sharp scholar, but an "apikoros" by choice. He used to brag about the fact that when he wrote letters of the Sabbath, he started with the words "Today is the holy Sabbath...."

Let me list the many avid students of the Mishnah. I will mention only those who were prominent among those scholars: Hayim Shnitzer, Meir Shlaam, Shlomo Shtreit, and Yehiel Rozenberg. And last, but not least, my father, who first had the title of "Dayan u-Moreh Tzedek" (Judge and Righteous Teacher), and who, after the death of Rabbi Ashkenazi, was promoted to the head of the Rabbinical court.

Our town did not have many religious functionaries because we were not a wealthy community. But we had many who served God faithfully. Let me remind you that during the Days of Awe, Sabbaths at the synagogues, and the three feasts many minyamim gathered in different locations and sang the Zmirot. Again let me mention some names to refresh our memories. Ma'chale Vaves, Shimshale Minitzer, Shlomo-Hayim, also known as Der Nayer Shochet, and his wife's delicious Harazaveh Bretlac.

For those of you who did not attend the "three feasts" to elevate the soul and to hear the Zmirot, let me mention those Ba'ale Tefila (cantors) who filled the synagogues with beautiful voices. I will mention, in one long breath, just a few of a long list who chanted during morning and evening prayers: Moti Sukar, Berl Zeifer, Shlomo Greitzer, Shalom Hirsh Fink, with his wonderful voice, Isaac Meltzer, Yosi Shapira, cantor of the Central synagogue for Kotokivka, and the Schecter brothers, Anchel and Notzya.

I don't want to discriminate against those people who achieved higher academic education and who practiced in our town periodically. We were very proud of them. I am not going to mention their names, but let me announce them by profession: doctors, dentists, pharmacists, magistrates, lawyers, and the judge Rathoizer. There were also world-renowned artists like Alexander Granack and Rana Pfeifer.

Though Horodenka was not an academic town with many scientists, all its Jewish residents were hard working people who labored and did everything possible to enable their children to learn the Torah and the mitzvot. They got up early in the morning to work, both in the summer and in the harsh winter. A few were rich, many could barely make a living, but all of them did their best to educate us, their children, who are here today.

Again I am not going to mention names, but let me give you a list of the various occupations. I am sure that you will recall who did what.

Let me begin with the foods that were sold by our residents either wholesale or retail: herring, petroleum, sugar and salt, flour and sweets. Other people worked in lumber and iron, confectionery and manufacturing, shoes and hats, leather, fur wool, fabrics and upholstery. Other merchants sold soaps, shoeshine, resin for carts, plaster, tar, candles, or books.

I would like to mention now those righteous and devoted Jewish women at the "apples market," and those vendors who sold "kvasnitzes." I remember how they bent over their stands during the summer with no protection from the scorching sun and how they were bundled with layers of clothing during the harsh winters, warming themselves over the "fire top" which was by their feet.

Let me also mention those in our town who had vocations. These included rope makers, meat butchers, blacksmiths with their metal tables, tailors, carpenters including those who built coffins for the Christians. There was also the "Russian carpenter" who was probably as good if not better than the best of the carpenters in Horodenka. Let me mention the watchmakers and the fur makers and finally coachmen with their carts and wagons, the insurance agents and mechanics. These are just a few of the trades of Horodenkans.

And among those with other talents, let me mention the artisans. There was Valul Greinberg, a mechanical engineer who was well known and respected in the community, together with his children. Almost equal to him, Dodi Meltzer, was a first-class artist and painter.

I did not know many builders, but I can see in front of me the image of the respected Baruck-Leib Greidiner.

All those I mentioned above, including their families, are no longer among the living.

Before I complete this review of the people of our town by mentioning those good people living in the surrounding areas, let me mention briefly the financiers and economists. At the top of the ladder those who accumulated property and wealth included Alter and Shmuel Yungerman, Yosel Zeifer, Berl Shfirer, Yosel Zeidman, and Rubel Shlomoh Pa'al. Right behind them were the owners of the quarries and the flourmills, both big and small.

I would like to end this tour with a description of hundreds of Jews that lived in villages around Horodenka. They were observant Jews that labored tirelessly in order to provide food and shelter for their families in the hope that their children would not follow in their footsteps but would rise above the level of education that the village could offer them. They sent their children to schools in the city, to high schools and universities if they were able to pull their finances together. When their children were still young, these parents summoned Yeshivah students from the city to serve as temporary teachers even if only for one or two lessons. I remember these young teachers. I also remember that those Jews who lived in distant villages would invite Jews who were single to come and join them for a minyan. During the High Holidays they would invite Ba'ale Tefilah to conduct the services. I even remember how during harsh weather conditions, those Jews risked their lives to go to town in order to purchase kosher flour for Passover, or to buy the four kinds of branches for Sukkot. And I remember the utmost dedication and devotion they exhibited towards the lulav and the ethrog by placing them on a bed of straw so that, God forbid, the pittam wouldn't break off.

I remember clearly, as if it were engraved in my mind, how all those Jews did whatever they could to keep the purity of the family intact, according to their understanding of Jewish laws. Every Sunday evening, they would sit in their wagons, in front of the Mikveh and wait for their wives who went to purify themelves. It was an act of dedication for one's belief. These were the efforts of Jews to maintain their Jewish identity in those God-forsaken areas surrounding our city.

I have attempted to depict for you the multiple and colorful facets, both economic and cultural, of our community. Members of our large community dispersed to many countries and beyond the great ocean, to North and South America. The sons and daughters of Horodenka even reached Australia. However, the hearts and souls and yearnings of the Jews of Horodenka were directed towards the land of Israel and its resurrection. Horodenkans sent its pioneers to Palestine during the various Aliyot with love, a deep longing, and with a strong spiritual belief in the coming of the liberation and redemption. The Jews of Horodenka believed that during their lifetime, salvation would come to Judah, and the family of Israel would dwell peacefully in its land. But unfortunately most did not live to see the fulfillment of this dream. Their tears and prayers did not help, their shouts and cries to God did not yield results. The Nazi savages gathered the Horodenkans during the first, second and third Actions, in the synagogue or fields, they torturing and murdering them in the most sadistic ways. And God looked down from the sky and saw how we were ridiculed and mocked by the goyim. And in spite of all this, netzah Israel lo yeshaker (your name we did not forget.).

To all the holy and pure men, women, and children that were murdered and burned in Nazi Europe:

May their names be remembered for ever and ever;

May their memory be praised and be written in the book of Life of the Nation of Israel and among the holy ones of the wars of the Hashmonaim, (aseret hajruge malhut), the brave men of Zahal, and the slain of Sinai.

Let their names adorn the resurrection of Israel in its land.

Horodenkaer attending the annual Yizkor Ceremony in "Yaar Hakdoshim"

Upon the Publication of this Book

By Shimshon Meltzer

ITluste (Tolstoe), my birth town, is situated between Chortkov to the north and Zaleshchiki to the south. Officially Tluste belongs to Zaleshchiki where the Starusta, the place where the pub owners went to renew their liquor licenses, was located. But spiritually it belongs to Chortkov, where people drove to seek advice from the Rabbi. They sought the Rabbi's blessings for a good livelihood, a comfortable life and for sons who would always live by the Torah. These two towns seemed to me, a boy of five years, like two distant legends and as two promises for the future. I hoped that when I grew up, I would have the good fortune to see them.

Unexpectedly, the big war broke out and we were exiled from our town. Thus the first big town that I finally saw was neither Chortkov nor Zaleshchiki but Horodenka. The escape took place on foot on a Saturday morning. My brother pushed a loaded stroller with big wheels as we climbed up the hill to Ryzhanovka, And I, the youngest of them all, lagged behind, trying to catch up.

In Ishtichka, which is on the banks of the Dniester, the escapees stopped to rest. Jews wrapped in Talitot prayed in a minyan near the big river and among the towering trees of the forest. Daring young men tried to cross the river by climbing on top of burned logs that moved like fast cats. Those logs had been the pillars that until recently supported the bridge that crossed the river.

Late Saturday night, the retreating Austrian army arrived with its wagons. They tied rafts together to make a long bridge and we all crossed the river. On the other side the rafts were loaded back on the wagons, upside down, to let the escapees hide beneath them. In the chill of the night the caravan made its way in the dark, in swaying wagons, up the hill from the Dniester. When the first ray of sun lit the horizon we arrived in Horodenka.

Three things were inscribed in my child's memory from the sights of those days.

A wagon with a large metal barrel was rolling down the street as it sprinkled water across the dusty road to prevent dust from rising. Miracle of miracle – this was the first miracle of modern technology I ever witnessed.

On Rosh ha-Shanah people prayed in a home. The road to the house went up a steep hill. On the right it climbed up and on the left it went down. I had to be careful of how I climbed or I would stumble and fall, God forbid, down, down, down. Many years later when I was a teacher in Horodenka, I went to look for that terrible hill – but I could not find it. What seemed like a mountain in my childhood, was probably a small hill. No wonder I could not locate it.

The third miracle occurred while our family was staying in a house that belonged to a large family. I was surprised to see that the man of the house, his wife and his children sleeping on the floor next to our family, while no one slept on the two beds in the room. Later I understood the reason why. It has a positive and a negative side. The owner was concerned that we might ruin his mattress and sheets. But, while we were there he wanted us to feel at home, so he and his wife and children joined us sleeping on the floor.

That was my flight from Tluste into the "world" and Horodenka was the first stop. And perhaps it is not a coincidence that after wandering across villages and cities throughout the country, Horodenka was also my final stop in the Diaspora before immigrating to the land of Israel. My wife and I spent only one year there – in fact, only ten months – but we managed to fall in love with that town: its landscape; its surroundings; and its people; especially the young people, and their endless activities; and our students. Those students came to our school in the afternoon after hours in the public schools to learn Torah for the sake of the land of Israel.

It was our first year of being together and, as it is for many young couples, one of the most beautiful. The "snow" song will ever remind us of those days. We had only a small flat with one room but it was large enough for us, a young couple. We had different styles of old furniture, everything was temporary, for only one year. Glass windows surrounded a small balcony. White curtains were put up and everything glowed in the brightness of winter. How pleasant it was.

Our apartment was in Mrs. Schwartz's house, across from the Pobiat house. I used to walk to school from that house not through the main street, but through the kapandreyah, a beautiful small park. (For some reason, none of the writers in this book mention that park, but I feel that I need to mention it because I spent many wonderful hours of reading there.) A chicken coop stood in a hidden corner of that park. Inside that coop was a large eagle with large wings. He was locked inside. One of his wings was broken. He used to extend the healthy wing and wave it up and down, hitting the metal bars as if he was ready to take off. Meanwhile his broken wing was dangling behind and getting dirty with his droppings. I don't know whatever happened to that eagle. I always wondered why the Polish people let the eagle remain in that coop. After all it is the symbol of their country. To me, it always symbolized the Jewish eagle, one of the four beasts described in Ezekiel. And furthermore, there is the eagle that belonged to Yehuda Ben-Time, as mentioned at the end of the Pirke Avot: "Be mighty as a tiger, light as an eagle, fast as a deer and strong as a lion to follow the will of your Father in heaven. And the will of our Father in heaven is that every young Jew will leave the Diaspora and emigrate to the land of Israel."

We didn't have a lot of belongings to take with us from Horodenka at the end of the school year. Everything went into a small peasant cart that took us to Tluste for a short stop before emigrating. Mrs. Schwatz, the owner of the house, treated us to a lavish farewell breakfast. When we left the house we were confronted with our students standing around the cart, crying and sobbing. Many of them had become our friends by then as they were not much younger than we were. The sight of our students crying with their wet cheeks was the best gift we could have gotten. It was the soul that we found in Horodenka.

"Shalom, shalom and see you soon" they shouted as the cart began to disappear up the road. Years later we were fortunate to meet with a few of them that had survived. Those few remind us of that beautiful year of love. Two of the female students still send us greeting cards from across the ocean.

Thus, I became a citizen, or shall we say half a citizen of Horodenka.

Intermittently for two whole years I have labored over the editing of the Horodenka Book. For two years the atmosphere of my adopted birthplace surrounded me. And I was constantly surprised by the quality of the articles that I was getting. As the verse in the Psalm reads: "Your forehead is like a sliver of pomegranate," and our sages explained it as "even those empty people among you are full like a pomegranate with mitzvot and good deeds." This saying applies to Israel as a whole and to Horodenka in particular. Even the simple people among us, those who never saw themselves as writers or scribes and even those with little education, who set out to write their memories for the first time in their lives, displayed their ability to express themselves by about incidents in their lives – incidents filled with feelings and deep perceptions.

I made it a rule not to overedit. However I corrected the language, the grammar and the spelling. I let each one of the stories speak for itself in its own unique way. I also did not delete complete segments that had already been told by others, even though the many repetitions increased the size of this book. I wanted to give each of the storytellers the opportunity to tell about the town, the people, their deeds and their destiny, in his or her own unique way. We don't really know how important our task is and what it will mean in the future. Perhaps it is the last meeting place of all the eye-witnesses to the events of those days, or perhaps it is the last grand gathering of all the Horodenkans who witnessed the building and the destruction of their town. As the editor of this book, I did not have, God forbid, the right to edit and chop these collected stories.

In his introduction, our friend, Moshe Fleshner has already told about the origin of this book and the work of the different committees. He also thanked and blessed all those who financed it and contributed their time and effort to see this book published and indeed they deserve the thanks. Since I was also editing his introduction I found it flattering to read that the Horodenkans were lucky to find such an editor as me. I deleted some of the praises and the compliments, for modesty sake. On the other hand I left a few compliments in order not to deny myself the truth. I couldn't say for a fact that I was the best editor the Horodenkans could have found, but I will affirm that I did the job with dedication and a warm heart as if I were editing a book, which hasn't been done yet, about my hometown Tluste.

In addition, the Horodenkans treated me with respect and trust. The meetings with the editorial committee were more like a gatherings of old friends. I would like in particular to mention the names of two men with whom I was constantly in touch: Moshe Fleshner and Gavriel Lindenberg.

This man, Moshe, was the moving spirit of this book, the engine who kept this complex apparatus in motion, the publisher, the director, the treasurer, the carrier and the courier. It would be impossible to calculate the amount of energy, time and dedication that he exerted to see this book published. Without his effort, I doubt it if would have happened. He was "crazy about it" in the good sense of the word and deserves to be called "the father of this book."

And the man, Gavriel, as distinguished from the angel Gabriel, who always stands on Man's left side – my Gavriel stood to my right to do any labor, light or hard. And in contrast to an angel that does not perform two tasks simultaneously, my Gavriel performed multiple tasks simultaneously. He wrote a tractate to be proud of and rewrote articles written by others. He copied and translated from one language to another, from Yiddish to Hebrew and vice versa, and he did it magnificently. Without his effort, chances are that the book wouldn't have been published on time or in as complete a form as it is.

It is a sad, draining and depressing task to write, edit and publish a book, which serves only as a headstone for a thriving Jewish community that is no longer in existence. But as the Jewish phrase goes: "There's 'luck' in 'unlucky'." Not all the descendents of towns in Europe that were destroyed are so eager to commemorate them in writing, and establish a memorial for Jewish generations to come.

Horodenka was lucky.

Tel Aviv, 8 Marheshavan 1963

The Israeli Executive Committee with the Redactor and the American guests, October 1962
Sitting from righ to left: G. Lindenberg, Sh. Melzer, Mrs. R. Podway, A. Podway and M. Fleshner
Standing from right to left: N. Bergman, J. Yankner, M. Stachel, J. Shapira and B. Mossberg

The Town and Its Environs

The History of the Jews of Horodenka

Dr. N. M. Gelber

Translator unknown; donated by Ellen Biderman

1. General Overview

Horodenka is located in the southeast corner of Galicia, or "Pokucie", as the Polish people call it. The Jews who lived there during the seventeenth and eighteenth centuries also called this area "Reisen." During the years between the two world wars, the town was on the crossroads of three countries: Poland, in which Horodenka was located, Romania to the south and the Soviet Union to the east. Like any border city during the world wars, Horodenka suffered from invasions and changes in regimes. Since the beginning of the twentieth century, control of Horodenka has changed seven or eight times. After World War II, Horodenka became part of the Soviet Union. But by that time the town the Jewish population was totally eradicated.

Welcome Party to R. & A. Podway in Tel Aviv

The written history of Horodenka begins in the sixteenth century. According to documents from 1579, Horodenka was a remote village on one of estates owned by the Polish aristocrat Michal Moszylo Buczacki. The village of Horodenka received the status of a town in the seventeenth century when Mikolaj Potocki, son of the aristocrat Stefen Potocki assumed the ownership of the Buczacki estate. Potocki left the

Roman Catholic Church, which was Polish, and joined the Greek Catholic Church, which was Ruthenian and to which most of the villagers of eastern Galicia belonged. Amongst his estates was the town of Buczacz.

Before his death in 1782 Stefen Potocki handed Horodenka to his relative Jan Potocki who expanded and developed the town. He built churches and a fortified palace for himself and developed the town's economy. He also reconstructed the hospital for the poor that was built in 1754. This hospital continued to provide services until the beginning of the twentieth century.

A. Podway in Tel Aviv at Welcome Party

The middle of the eighteenth century was a turbulent time for Horodenka. In 1739 the Russians invaded the region. They demolished many houses, robbed the inhabitants, and even desecrated the churches and tortured the priests. In the meeting of the Sejm (the parliament), which took place in Vizhnia, on August 22, 1740, representatives from Horodenka, Czarnelica, Tysmenica, and Syniatin related all the atrocities that their towns suffered during the Russian invasion.

When Poland was first divided in 1772, Horodenka was annexed to the Austrian Monarchy. This resulted in many administrative and legal changes. Horodenka became a part of the Zaleszczyki district while during the Polish regime it had been part of the Kolomyja district. Househager, the district governor, is mentioned in the reports from that time as a capable administrator. He was interested primarily in the welfare of the farmers helping them to increase their agricultural productivity and opening new markets for their products. Tobacco and beef were his favorite commodities. As a result,

Horodenka grew and prospered. The Austrian authorities also took care to improve cultural institutions. In 1788 the first public school opened in Horodenka.

Economic conditions improved in the nineteenth century when many people began to move to Horodenka. In the year 1879 there were 8,824 people living in Horodenka, of which 3,159 were Jews. Ten years later, there were 10,014 people living in the city.

As the town grew, its administrative status changed. It was declared a county seat. Czarnelica, Obertin and nearly 50 other villages were now within its jurisdiction.

In 1848 the status of estate owners changed. The Austrian regime forbade the serfdom of the farmers and the large estates were partitioned. In this manner Horodenka changed hands, from the Potocki family to Baron Mikolaj Romaszkan.

The economy of the town was primarily based in agriculture. The main products were wheat, eggs, cattle, and horses. Other trades revolved around agricultural products. In 1870 there were two lime furnaces, nine water mills, a steel mill, three potash kilns, nine distilleries, a beer brewery, a factory with seventy weaving looms, six soap-producing factories, and thirty furriers. That year in an effort to develop the entire area, there was a plan to establish a steamboat line on the Dniester that would stretch from Horodenka to Odessa. However, it never materialized.

Starting in 1870, the authorities took a census every ten years. The following table shows the composition of the population from 1870 through 1921.

	1870	1880	1890	1900	1910	1921	% (1921)
Jews	3,159	3,661	4,340	4,255	4,210	3,048	31
Poles	857	1,741	1,153	1,259	1,332	6,859	69
Ruthenians	4,726	4,547	5,635	6,056	5,650		
Others	82	65	34	43	31		
TOTAL	8,824	10,014	11,162	11,613	11,223	9,907	100

The mayor and an 18-member council ran the city. According to the municipality records from the year 1874, the council consisted of 7 Jews, 5 Poles, and 6 Ruthenians.

2. The Beginning of Jewish Settlements in Horodenka

The first Jewish community in eastern Galicia (which is located in the south-east area of the Reisen area) was established during the 16th century. However, during the 15th century there were a few Jews living in the Halicz region, which included the counties of Kolomyja and Trembowla. These Jews were mostly businessmen. Some leased salt mines, a few were moneylenders to the noblemen, some traded animals, and others imported goods from the western regions. Evidence of the existence of Jews in the area appears in a document written in 1444. A court in Horodenka sent a letter to a court in Lvov inquiring about the procedure for swearing in a Jew in court. The few judges that were around came from Lvov, a metropolitan city that had many Jewish residents. Jewish merchants from Lvov came to markets in Jazlowiczy along with farmers from the region, including some from Horodenka. Documents from that period mention the names of only seven Jews. Among them are Shimshon from Zezdaczow (1450), his son Joshua, and a Jew by the name of Isako from Litch (1439-1441). It is difficult to determine the exact date in which the first Jews arrived in Horodenka because of the lack of official documents. According to Austrian documents from a later period, there were few Jewish families in Horodenka prior to the 17th century when it was declared a city. Many Jews began to settle in the border regions and in Reisen shortly after Podolia was returned to Poland through the Treaty of Korlowitz.

In a document dated October 12, 1743 Mikolaj Potocki, granted the Jews emancipation to live in Horodenka. His father had granted emancipation to the Jews of Buczacz on May 20, 1727. The same type of document was also used in other Jewish communities like Chortkov and Stanislavov. According to the document, Jews were given the right to settle in the town and also the right to engage in various trades, wholesale and retail dealing in all kinds of merchandise, except for Christian religious articles.

The Jews were required to pay tax of one "taller" for each house that faced a street and half a taller for houses that were inside a courtyard. A site was allocated for Jewish burial. In it the Jews could build a guardhouse that was exempt from property tax. The Jews living on the estates of the Potockis were exempt from paying general taxes, especially taxes for the maintenance of the palaces and taxes for cattle with horns. However, Jews were required, like the non-Jewish residents, to pay for road maintenance.

The Jews were under the jurisdiction of the local governor but not the local courts. They had the right to appeal any decisions to the mayor. They were not required to appear in court on Saturday and it was forbidden to incarcerate them in the city jail, except in the case of criminal offenses. It was also forbidden to hold the weekly market on Saturday. Jewish Rabbinic courts had the authority to try and arbitrate cases between Jews. The Jewish butchers were not required to slaughter pigs for the palace; instead they had to pay a special tax to the local owners. They were also allowed to buy houses from Christians and to build breweries and distilleries on the condition that they obeyed the laws associated with such businesses. In addition Jews were allowed to own bars and serve liquor and wine by paying a special rent to the owners of the town.

Jewish craftsmen, like their Christian counterparts, were required to belong to guilds and unions and pay the appropriate dues and taxes. They were not required to go to church, participate in religious processions, or give candles to the church. But they did have to pay for candles for the church.

There is not much information regarding a unified Jewish community in Horodenka before the 18th century. However, from that period on, we know that Horodenka was well organized, taking care of Jewish villagers. Jews made their living trading both retail and wholesale in grain, cattle, skins, and furs. Jewish merchants had good business relationships with Germany during the years 1739-1748. Many Jewish merchants attended the big international fair in Leipzig. In 1739 and 1740 Mosheh Avraham stayed in the home of Feitel Meir. In 1746 Nathan Gershon came with his worker Leibel Hirsh and also stayed at Feitel's home. Nathan came often between the years 1738 and 1748. Volf Zeisel came in 1740. This list indicates that prior to the annexation of Horodenka to Austria, there were Jewish merchants and traders who exported agricultural good to Germany and imported goods from the west.

Wealthy Jews leased property they owned outside of Horodenka. One of them was Shabtai Katz and his son Gershon Rappoport who owned Lantzekron Arandi.

The Jewish community of Horodenka was organized in a manner similar to other communities in Poland. The community was a member of a Jewish regional committee located in Lvov and was obligated to pay taxes like other Jews in Poland. The internal life of the community was also conducted like other communities. Various matters concerning the leadership of the community, taxation and education were in the hands of the community; judicial matters were under the jurisdiction of a Beit Din (Court of Rabbis). The community was usually led by three to five "parnasim" (community leaders) who were also accountable to the government. Following their election they were required to take an oath of loyalty to the king and country in the presence of representatives of the government. The leaders would divide the various tasks among themselves and every month these assignments would rotate. In addition to these leaders, each community also had a committee of "tovim" to deal with various matters concerning the welfare of the community. The parnasim were elected by a specified number of "kashrim" (electors) who were picked in a lottery. The organizations of Jewish tradesmen also had representatives (usually their leaders) in the community government.

It is not clear to what extent the Jewish community in Horodenka was involved in fighting for Jewish autonomy in the Riesen region during the last half of the 18th century. However, we believe that their efforts were as pronounced as those of other Jewish communities in the region.

We can also assume that during this period there were guilds of Jewish craftmen and professionals that were represented at board meetings of the community. The rabbi, the judges, and the synagogue's shamash, reader, and writer would go to plead with the authorities on Jewish matters. They were all paid from funds collected from members of the community. The community as a whole took care of the educational and economic needs of its people. Representatives went door to door and collected money to cover administrative fees and taxes owed to the government, including the special taxes that only Jews had to pay. During the years 1718 and 1719 the Jews of Horodenka paid 877 gold nuggets per capita a year; in 1727 they paid 1200 gold nuggets.

Unfortunately we do not have detailed information about the rabbis and the leaders of the Jewish community during that period except for a single document signed by one rabbi containing the results of Jewish census.

The census was conducted on February 11, 1765 for the purpose of collecting per capita taxes. Komisar Yozef Paradowski and Macej Karwaszecki conducted the census. The Rabbi, two board members, and the shamash from the Jewish community were witnesses. They counted 863 Jews who were required to pay the per capita tax. They also counted 60 children under the age of one. A few villages adjacent to Horodenka were also included in the census with the following results: In Czerniatyn there were 7 adults and 1 child; in Okna, 7 adults and 1 child; in Sarafince, 20 adults; in Horodnica, 13 adults and 1 child; in Potoczysk, 13 adults and 1 child; in Zezwaczow, 7 adults and 1 child; in Niezwicz, 10 adults; in Herasimow, 4 adults; in Luka 8 adults; in Podwerbowce, 6 adults and 1 child; in Tsamkabetza, 4 adults; in Trojca 12 adults and 1 child; in Podwysoka, 8 adults and 1 child; and in Raszkow, 7 adults. In all, there were in the greater Horodenka area 989 adults Jews and 67 children, totaling 1056.

Rabbi Manes Ben Shimshon, the presiding rabbi at the time, signed all documents asserting that all Jews were counted in his Polish name Manis Samsonowicz. Two leaders of the community together with Shimshon also signed. The statement read: "We counted and registered all the Jews, adults and children living in apartments and in the villages adjacent to Horodenka and in between on the roads and we did not miss a soul in accordance with the laws of the Sejm.

Following the laws set by Treasury Department on April 22, 1766 and March 25, 1767, concerning the debt of Jewish communities, Horodenka was required to pay 3 golden nuggets, four grushim and a half-shilling per Jew. The total sum was 3,095 Polish gold pieces.

3. Horodenka during the Shabbetean and Frankist Movements

In the 1700's the Shabbetai-Zvi movement had a large number of advocates and supporters, including scholars and Rabbis. Most of its members lived in the southeast portion of the Riesen region. The Turkish Jews who immigrated to Kamieniec-Podolski during the Ottoman occupation promoted the belief in Shabbetai-Zvi as the Messiah. They spread their belief among the Jews living in Podolia and Reisen. The movement influenced Jews in Horodenka as well. The Frankist movement followed shortly thereafter. According to Rabbi Yaakov Amedin, who in the second half of the eighteenth century conducted a fierce movement of opposition to the Shabbeteans, many Horodenkans were enthusiastic followers of Shabbetai-Zvi. This occurred because Horodenka was situated in the midst of about 10 towns where the largest numbers of the movement's followers lived. These towns included Gliniany, Nadworna, Tysmienica, Rohatyn, Buczacz, Komarno, and Podhaicy.

Rabbi Zvi Hirsh was the chief Rabbi in Horodenka at that time. Later he was also the chief Rabbi in Jazlowicze and Zalesczyki. These two towns were part of the Poniatovski estate. Hirsh's son, Rabbi Meir Margaliot, took over the Rabbinate after his death. He is the author of *Meir Netivim* (*The Light of the Ways*). He became the son-in-law of the famous Rabbi Itzik – also known as "Rabbi Itzik of Horodenka."

In 1752 Rabbi Margaliot competed with Rabbi Hayim Rappaport for the position of chief Rabbi of the entire Reisen region. Bjonowicz and Barko, leaders of the community, decided to divide the duties of the office. Margaliot was named alternate Chief Rabbi and Rabbi Rappaport ran the day-to-day business of the area. Finally the community decided to split the position and give Rabbi Margaliot the title of vice-rabbi even though this was not permissible without the authorization from the governor. This shows how much they respected the Rabbi Margaliot and how difficult it must have been for them to decide among the two rabbi.

Yitzhak Ber, Meir Margaliot's brother, was elected chief Rabbi in Jazlowicz and Zaleszczyki after their father's death. He was one of the main participants in the public debate with the heads of the Frankist movement. The debate occurred in Kamieniec-Podolski. Leib ben-Daniel, one of the leaders of the Jewish community, also took part in the debate. Another debate took place in Lvov in 1759.

Rabbi Yitzchak Ber Margaliot was the last loyalist of the Podolia county committee. He signed, together with Leib ben-Daniel, a proclamation regarding the abolishment of debts in 1763. Rabbi Ber used some of his own money to pay the debt. When it was all said and done, the committee owed Rabbi Ber 2,980 golden nuggets, which included a year-and-a-half of interest.

When he was still chief Rabbi in Horodenka, Margaliot gave a written statement to the Jewish committee in Brody about testimony given to him by the Rabbi of Satanov regarding happenings in Kamieniec-Podolski. He describes the wild parties and raucous behavior of the residents. It is also interesting to note that in Lanscron, a gathering of the Frankists was discovered in the house of Rabbi Labor Riches. According to the testimony given, they were there every night. There were orgies, dancing, and playing around by the Jews of Horodenka. The testimony of Rabbi Bel Bolichavil said:

One night a Gentile farmer drove his cart, which was loaded with firewood, into town. He heard loud music coming from one of the houses and he led his horse toward the house. He knocked on the door and asked the people if they would like to buy his wood. They chased him away and didn't buy anything from him. The farmer continued to the house of the local Rabbi Gershon Katz of Horodenka who had a lease in the town of Lansconia and who used to buy wood from the farmer. The farmer told him about the party in the house of Rabbi Labor Riches and asked if there was a wedding. Rabbi Gershon sent his servant to check it out, but the man could not see into the house because heavy drapes covered the windows. The servant was determined and he poked a hole in the wall, which was made of mud and straw. He was stunned to see men and women dancing together. Upon hearing this account, Rabbi Gershon consulted with the leaders of the Jewish community, the owner of the estate and a judge. They decided to go to the house the following night to see for themselves. The following night the group approached the house cautiously. They quietly poked a few holes in the walls. What they saw inside the house left them stunned and shocked. Jews, male and female were dancing together naked. They were singing while uttering the name of Shabbetai-Zvi and other names of their spiritual leaders. It was on the 27th of January of the year 1756.

Upon seeing the evidence, the property owner, Romanovski ordered those people to be taken to the castle as prisoners. Most of the people in the group managed to escape but Yaakov Frank and eight followers were arrested. The following day, Rabbi Isaac ha-Cohen informed Rabbi Mendel, the chief Rabbi of Satanov about the incident.

Horodenka was also one of the centers of the Frankist movement. The leaders of the movement maintained a relationship with Prince Radziwill who showed interest in religious issues and who visited Yaakov Frank in 1759. In a list of Jews who converted to Christianity after the debate in Lvov, there is not a single name of a Jew from Horodenka. It appears that they remained loyal to the Frankist movement without changing their religion.

In 1766 Aharon Yitzchak ben Moshe, son of a famous family of Rabbis, the Teomims, left Horodenka for the city of Altona Germany as a messenger and preacher for the Shabbetean movement. This is how Rabbi Yaakov Emdins described the situation in his book *Struggle*:

In 1767, a person arrived in Altona from Poland. His name was Aharon Yitzchak, from the famous Teomim family in Horodenka. He came as a preacher of Shabbetai-Zvi. First he stopped at Frankfurt am Mein. When he came to Altona he inquired as to the whereabouts of Wolf Akives. At first many of the members of the community gathered in the house to welcome him with honor, but soon they realized that he was one of Shabbetai-Zvi's followers and they chased him away from Altona with shame.

After being forced out of Altona, he went to Chevering and stayed there with Yosef Nata, a respected member of the community and an agent of the Prince of Hallenburg. From there Aharon Yitzhak proceeded to Hamburg. Soon after there were rumors that Aharon Yitzhak was a preacher of the Shabbetai movement. At first Yosef Neta refused to believe this. However he became convinced when he received a letter from Professor Tichzen in January 1767. In it there was a copy of a letter that Aharon Ytzhak Teomim had sent him. In the letter, Aharon claims that Shabbetai-Zevi in the true Messiah. Here are a few paragraphs from the long and cumbersome letter:

God bestows his wisdom to the wise men. With each generation, in every nation and state and with every language, God seeks man's wisdom and truth – the complete truth of mankind. The knowledgeable Prince Radziwill, who studied in depth all the religions of the world, did not find a single religion as truthful and filled with Godliness as the religion of the king Messiah Shabbetai-Zevi. Therefore he aligned himself with us to fight in the name of our truthful Messiah. His advisors requested that we enlighten those blind Jews of Horodenka, who are dwelling in the shadow of death, by teaching them the religious wisdom of Shabbetai Ben-Zevi. His teachings will heal those with broken hearts and will free those imprisoned by the web of other religions. The prince wants to have those people, Jews and Gentiles alike, live on his estate where they will be protected and safe and will lack nothing. I have been traveling from place to place to preach Shabbetai's wisdom and seek those who believe in him. I have been wandering until I came to this town and met the writer Mr. Weiler to whom I told the reason of my visit.

Yitshak Aharon requested that Weiler introduce him to Professor Tichzen so the latter would, hopefully, help him with his request. The letter shocked Yosef Neta and he immediately wrote to Professor Tichzen:

Dear Mr. Tichzen: I was shocked and frightened by the letter that my friend, Yitzhak Teomim, a member of a family of sinners and wretched people who stand against the Torah from God, sent you. I was enraged, after having him under my roof and giving him my hospitality, to find out that he is a heretic. We must chase after his kind with whatever means we can find in order to fulfill God's revenge against those who disobey God's Torah.

It is not known whatever happened to Yitzhak Aharon Teomim. There is no evidence that he returned to Horodenka and the end of his mission.

Family Names 1789-1791

Leiser Katz	Nachman Silber	Moses Weinreb
Leiser Ordentlichs	Littman Wolf	Koppel Offenberger
Leib Aberbach	Leib Sander	Moses Aberbachs
Herschls Katz	Hersch Sohar	Schaul Aberbachs
Herschs Ant. Moses Tiger	Salamon Staüber	Jeruchim Edelstein
Samson Axel	Schmuel Blater	Mordko Edelstein
Leib Edelstein	Abraham Bräver	Boruch Rosenkranz
Moses Agatstein	Juda Sussmann	Josel Rosenkranz
Jzig Silber	Schlomo Dolinger	Feibel Rosenkranz
Jankel Schnürer	Dawid Weiskern	Hersch Wasser
Abraham Guther	Leib Dolinger	Jankel Wasser
Samuel Wasser	Seelig Haschel	Chaim Zuckermann
Abisch Hochman	Josel Katz	Josel Prehauser
Hersch Offenberger	Salamon Frajer	Chaim Prehauser
Seinwel Silber	Leib Luster	Josias Mayer
Jichil Silber	Joel Kirschner	Berl Katz
Moses Offenberger	Nossen Sturmer	Noa Katz
Obadia Offenberger	Jakob Bruckner	Moses Katz
Moses Jurman	Moses Knöpfner	Hinde Karin
Schomer Fink	Maier Diamant	Borouch Schönbrum
Moses Rath	Herschs Gaber	Schije Reis
Mortko Diamant	Nussen Fuchs	Jankel Sokeler
Chaim Adler	Aaron Rosenkranz	Abraham Sucher
Maier Rosenkranz	Wolf Offenberger	Leib Rosenkranz

Hinde Koltin	Abraham Buchner	Benjamin Dankner
Leib Feuer	Nossen Weinberger	Chaim Emmer
Schmuel Offenberger	Leib Weinberger	Elias Reis
Moses Katz	Schmerl Hartenstein	Schlome Fessler
Moses Katz	Joachim Kanzler	Abraham Ragendorf
Manele Färber	Leib Bankner	Schlome Schaffer
Elias Hollering	Srol Gutman	Israel Schaffer
Hersch Schmidt	Leib Kramisch	Judas Feldmann
Srul Zauber	Dawid Schaffer	Baruch Schruber
Izig Rubin	Abraham Glasberger	Berl Koller
Taube Rubin	Wolf Schneider	Srol Agatstein
Lowisch Korn	Jankel Reismarker	Moses Agatstein
Schmul Glas	Israel Fink	Tod'res Hoffmann
Mathel Guttman	Hersch Igelman	Falk Imbermann
Hersch Geiger	Mordko Glasberger	Mayer Huber
Hersch Schutz	Hersch Neumeuer	Wolff Zuckerman
Samuel-Eerber	Leib Reither	Markus Pfau
Jakob Friedmann	Jokel Färber	Kalman Neuhauser
Kalman Kellner	Chaim Offenberger	Hersch Dollinger
Hersch Bergman	Moses Tuchner	Hersch Liebermann
Dawid Melzer	Moses Bruckner	Leib Stern
Leiser Flügler	Schmul Tannenbein	Juda Libig
Jacob Balbirer	Abraham Austern	Nossen Katz
Leib Feuer	Gute Prüffer	Schlome Glasberger
Abraham Weinreb	Jankew Lanpker	Juda Böhm
Juda Ordner	Abe Rosenbaum	Srol Mass
Chaim Gerson	Jossel Rauchman	Wolff Rosenkranz
Salamon Ruppert	Hersch Schapira	Nossen Zuckerman
Srul Rubin	Jsaak Singer	Aaron Barber
Berl Schleiffer	Laiser Huber	Mortko Reiss
Herr Thronberger	Moses Schwantheil	Seelig Spierer
Rifke Weischin	Mayer Fleischer	Mayer Edelstein
Koppel Bergbauer	Mothle Saz	Hersch Weinreb
Koppel Fruchtner	Jankel Pfeiffer	Manes Silber
Seinwel Friedman	Schlome Schneuer	Dawid Geiger
Oscher Schaar	Schlome Hengst	Chaskel Lerner
Srol Kugler	Moses Töpfner	Ihre Aberbach
Samuel Schneier	Berl Briller	Lazar Eisman
Israel Neuberger	Izig Steigman	Leib Jurman
Leib Feldner	Chaim Guther	Jone Beerman
Leib Hartenstein	Schmuel Fragner	Simon Brauer
Aaaron Wechsler	Leib Rindner	Mordko Saiffer
Moses Kracher	Laiser Brait	Monusch Schubert
Moses Kramer	Hersch Herrmann	Leib Schuhner
Schlome Kramer	Moses Schmukler	Wolff Slattner
Isaias Kramer	Aaron Huttmann	Leib Wieser
Aaron Gutser	Mayer Färber	Izig Ohringer
Izig Orenstein	Jankel Oringer	Abraham Ochsenstern
Abraham Kugelus	Aaron Lezter	Berl Wasser
Dawid Rosenberg	Moses Donner	Nossen Sichig
Hersch Diener	Srol Mager	Moses Edler
Schapse Schneider	Chaim Schmitt	Herz Armer
Nochem Winter	Scholem Agatstein	Mordko Luster
Berl Wohl	Schlome Frischling	Beer Knobler
Zallel Rats	Abraham Pfeffer	Leiser Schneider
Mendel Pulthman	Nossen Platzker	Moses Silber
Abraham Feldman	Jossel Treiber	Abraham Stein
Schmul Strisling	Wollf Winkler	Schmuel Katz
Schabes Imberman	Izig Winter	Moses Dreyer
Hersch Barts	Jankel Aberbach	Salamon Dolmann

Mordko Meerbaum
Abel Weidner
Josef Briger
Schaje Puchler
Izig Kleinbauer
Scholem Kiel
Abraham Bruckner
Chaim Langer
Jossel Junker
Eeisig Sucher
Hosias Schirm
Abraham Leihner
Michel Propstler
Maier Mauler
Daniel Hecht
Maier Schatzberger
Mothie Doppler
Kalman Glasser
Jakob Liderer
Moses Flügler
Hersch Sonnenfeld
Schlome Silber
Maier Bruckenstein
Aaron Schatzberg
Moses Turkner
Simon Predig
Froim Imbermann
Hersch Feuer
Mothie Kaz
Moses Bruckenstein
Eisig Sucher
Schmul Hager
Herz Pechert
Moses Zangel
Izig Gottlieb
Hersch Schwimmer
Hersch Sucher
Jankel Eckstein
Moses Austern
Izig Zorn
Godel Lochner
Leib Guttmann
Srol Goldschmidt
Chaim Stürmer
Ruben Richter
Mayer Riegelmann
Moses Buchner
Moses Maas
Dawid Feuer
Monas Burger
Hersch Binder
Jankel Rosenbaum
Chaim Sissler
Schapse Dankner
Saul Berghauer
Moses Freimann
Todres Kugelmoss

Beril Koch
Izig Glasberger
Abraham Neuberger
Aaron Burger
Simon Gloger
Moses Katz
Litmann Tuchmacher
Joachim Halka
Leib Offenberger
Izig Zuckerman
Yre Reuter
Schmul Jurmann
Hosias Tauber
Srol Tauber
Moses Tauber
Israel Katz
Schoel Katz
Juda Fettner
Gerson Oker
Leib Oker
Oscher Freibeck
Salamon Jäger
Berl Dachs
Schlome Geldner
Simon Herland
Mayer Acker
Kallman Eder
Koppel Menschner
Wolf Latesschneider
Mayer Goldberger
Hersch Kronn
Moses Gettner
Wolf Offenberger
Abraham Brand
Leib Grazer
Mayer Korker
Jossel Walther
Izig Walther
Hersch Prinz
Jzig Brettler
Schaje Steinbauer
Gerschon Schindler
Jossel Fischer
Schaje Hass
Gerschon Schneider
Srul Fuchs
Srul Stigliz
Manele Mass
Dawid Schaar
Leib Leman
Fischel Rittersporn
Jossel Rosenkranz
Beril Beermann
Hersch Schaar
Hersch Bildner
Dawid Wisinger
Gerschon Bildner

Peisach Stepner
Rosa Wilmann
Feibisch Willmann
Israel Landmann
Izig Bildner
Jossel Bildner
Leib Denninger
Samuel Krupfbein
Nochem Fischer
Srol Lampner
Berl Schneider
Hersch Rindner
Nossen Barth
Schmuel Rindner
Hersch Schaar
Hosias Jonas Rosenkranz
Wolf Rindner
Dawid Heine
Hersch Hallman
Leib Rossler
Jossel Ziegler
Mendel Rosenkranz
Joachim Ast
Boruch Splitter
Leib Wasser
Salamon Schmierer
Laiser Wasser
Seelig Flaschner
Joel Sonnenblum
Mayer Pflauminger
Ihre Lutner
Gerson Begelman
Kalman Weissman
Chaim Degelman
Abraham Erdreich
Leib Taubl
Haskel Schaar
Srol Aberbach
Jankel Feihtner
Jakob Schubert
Karpel Fliegler
Isser Bitter
Izig Frohnberger
Simon Kammel
Schmuel Kalker
Juda Fink
Leib Zuckermann
Hersch Hoptasch
Dawid Offenberger
Mechel Feuer
Wolf Aberbach
Wollf Kaz
Hersch Wolkenstein
Schlojme Ast
Lasar Rosenkranz
Perez Schaar.

Archiv des Ministerium des Innern (Wien) IV T 11 Galizien Judenwesen 1786—1792 ad 2639 ad 23276 pr 742
Liquidation.

4. The Beginning of Chassidism in Horodenka

According to the writer of the *New Generation Order*, pages 12 to 26, thirty-seven people were lucky enough to be chosen to study directly with the Baal Shem Tov, the founder of Chassidism. One of those students was Rabbi Nachman from Horodenka, who turned out to be one of his most outstanding students. His name was mentioned in a number of books that were written about the Baal Shem Tov and his students including: *The Praise of the Baal Shem Tov* and *The History of Jacob and Joseph*. His favorite saying was "It all happens for the best." There are few specific details about Rabbi Nachman's life. It is known that he was in Miedziboz when the Baal Shem Tov passed away. He regularly would go to his grave and prostrate himself over it. When Rabbi Nachman wanted to emigrate to Israel, he asked the spirit of the Baal Shem Tov for permission. Then with a glowing face he announced that the Baal Shem Tov ordered him to go to Israel.

In 1764 Rabbi Nachman made Aliyah to Israel. With him were Rabbi Menahem Mendel from Przemyslan and Rabbi Simhah from Zalorzyc, the in-law of Rabbi Shlomo from Dunow, and author of *For the Love of Zion*. The group set sail from Gallatz to Constantinople on the fourth day of Tamuz, 1764. There they waited twenty days for a boat to Israel. On the 18th of Elul, they sailed together with 110 Sephardic and Ashkenazi immigrants to Palestine. On the evening of Rosh Ha Shana they arrived in Jaffa. In Jaffa, the Sephardic immigrants went to Jerusalem and the Chassids continued to the port of Acre. The following day, Rabbi Manchem Mendel and the rest of the group rode their mules to Tiberias where they settled. Rabbi Nachman died there a few years later. His son, Simha, married Fayga, the grand daughter of the Baal Shem Tov and the daughter of Hoddle. From this marriage, Rabbie Nachman of Brassler was born.

5. Under the Rule of Austria

With the annexation to Austria in 1772, there were few changes in the lives of the Jews of Galicia and those of Horodenka. Even after the Austrian occupation, the Jews of Galicia remained organized under the rules that were given to the Jews by the Empress Maria Teresa in 1776. They were still ruled by the main committee of the Jews of Galicia. In 1785 this national organization was abolished. The local matters were still run by the local board members who took care of the business of the congregation, the supervision of the census, the registrations of births, marriages, and deaths, and the collection of taxes. In a small town like Horodenka, there were three leaders at the head of the committee. Actually those board members were very much dependent on the local authorities and had to follow their orders.

In the congregation of Horodenka there was no ordained Rabbi. Rather, there was a teacher who received an annual pay of 104 florins. In 1775, according to documents, the congregation of Horodenka asked, because of the difficult economic situation, to reduce the per capita tax. This request was granted. In 1776, the central authority in Vienna asked for a report about the taxes that a few congregations, including Horodenka, had to pay in the times of the Polish regime to the local estates to enable them to choose their own Rabbis and board members. One of the main goals of the Austrian administration at this time was the cancellation and elimination of Jewish pubs because they saw them as a hindrance to development of the Gentile peasant population. This goal hurt the Jews of Horodenka because many of them leased pubs. There ensued a big struggle. The Jews argued that the authority to lease pubs was given to them in 1743 by the owner of the town, Mikolaj Potocki. This struggle between the local Jews and the central administration in Vienna lasted many years.

One of the most severe restrictions on the Jews of Galicia was the prohibitions and restrictions regarding marriage. For a license to marry, Jews were asked to pay a tax of 3 to 30 ducats, which was a lot of money at the time. Anybody who got married without the license was punished and their property was taken away by the state. Even participating in an illegal wedding was punishable. This restriction unfortunately created a tradition of turning Jews over to the authorities. For instance, between the years 1784 and 1785, the congregation of Horodenka suffered a lot from a Jew by the name of Label Hirschel. He would go to the authorities in Lvov and tell them about the underground weddings conducted by the Jews in Horodenka and the surrounding villages. He also claimed to have information about irregularities in the collection and regulation of local taxes. For his services, he demanded payments from the authorities. However, according to a document dated April 29, 1784, the Governor in Lvov demanded he supply factual material about his allegations or stop his reporting. A report filed by the Governor on May 27, 1784, ordered that he cease reporting underground marriages beginning June 24th through the next census. The local authorities were asked to look out for such marriages and to try and register them and tax the officiating rabbi two florins for each couple. Actually the authorities didn't need the snitching of Label Hirschel because even without his help, 464 cases of illegal marriages were reported in Galicia.

As a result of snitching about irregularities in taxation and collection, Vienna passed an order to supervise the congregations more strictly and to make their board members keep books and report every now and then about the financial activities of the congregation. These books were periodically audited. The board members were made responsible for irregularities and had to pay the difference from their own pockets.

In 1784 it was discovered that Label Hirschel himself was involved in cases of fraud. In order to resolve his problem he promised the central authorities in Lvov information that would gain them an income of 400,000 florin. Because the Governor was interested in this information, an order was given from Vienna to give him money for his snitching and drop the case against him. After he reported his findings in writing, the governor would decide what to do about him and the communities he reported on. Another order from Vienna appointed a committee to investigate wasting the tax money. That was not the end of the story of Label Hirschel.

In June of 1784, he asked to be given the lease for all the Kosher meat in the state. This request was denied. In August of 1784, a group of seven Jews asked to be compensated for the inconvenience his interference caused and were given the money. Label Hirschel is also mentioned as requesting to be paid for having the idea of taxing Kosher meat. His ideas and demands were soon too much for the authorities and in a special order in September 1784 he was told to stop annoying the central authorities and to pay money to the group that sued him for infringing on their rights. In December 1784 he was definitely rejected by the authorities and from that time on, the government documents do not mention him. However, establishing the tax on Kosher meat meant a loss of income for Theodor Potocki, the owner of the estate in Horodenka. He claimed he lost income because the Jews were paying much more money to the central authorities. After a long negotiation, Vienna rejected his demands in an order dated February 26, 1783.

In 1785 the rest of Jewish autonomy was cancelled and all the administrative rights to take care of themselves were abolished. According to the new rules, the taxes were no longer to be collected by the congregation, but rather individually. Every Jew was taxed and the collection was the responsibility of government clerks. Rabbinic courts were abolished. In matters of law, the Jews were under the jurisdiction of their respective municipalities.

The Emperor Franz Joseph II tried, because of his own ambitions, to solve the Jewish problem in Galicia by settling the Jews as land peasants. In 1782, there was an order from Vienna that Jews who were farmers would only have to pay half of the wedding tax and after a short time would be totally released from that tax. Serious efforts to create Jewish farms started in 1785 after the Emperor's decree was published. In the spring of 1786 Novi Sonch founded the first Jewish farm in the village of Dumbrovka. After that a second Jewish farm, New Babylon, was formed close to the town of Burhough. There were a few more little farms that didn't last long. That same government program mandated that 117 of the 1,410 families of Jews in Galicia be settled as farmers. Horodenka was burdened with having to provide for twelve Jewish families that would be settling there. And indeed, by the end of 1794 twelve families had settled in farms around Horodenka. They included twelve men, ten women, four boys and four girls under the age of eighteen. Those settlers received 138 plots of land, nine houses, nine barns, eleven horses, eighteen oxen, sixteen cows, and thirty tools to work with.

In the beginning of the nineteenth century most of these settlers were still farmers. Other families arrived from the towns around Horodenka. They included 129 men, 126 women, 116 boys and 94 girls. All in all there were 465 people. The expense of this experiment of settling farmers came to 200 florins that had to be borne by the individual communities. It took 25 to 40 households to provide the means to settle one family who didn't have their own means to survive. It seems that the Jews of Galicia who did want to become farmers were anxious to get the necessary permits to establish their own farms. In the year 1787, fifty Jews from Zaleszczyki came to the governing body and asked for land across the Dniester. This group owned 25 homes, including 4 taverns, 50 horses, 10 oxen, 76 cows, 20 calves, 17 beehives and a lot of cash as proof that they could farm and be self-sufficient. In 1787 they sent a copy of their request to the Emperor Franz Joseph II, stating:

We have decided to stop being merchants and start being farmers. Because we are being delayed in our request it seems that we will never get our wish or any land to till. We don't know where we should go from here because we have invested all our property in this attempt to farm.

In reply to their letter, the Emperor ordered the local authorities to appropriate land for Jewish settlers, which they did immediately. However they appropriated to them the worst land in the area. The Jews refused to accept those plots and changed their minds about farming. It seems that such requests were very common and that the Emperor was very supportive of them. The local authorities were the ones who put obstacles in the way of fulfilling these plans.

It was very common for the local peasants to complain about the Jews taking over the local grain market, buying everything from them and reselling it at steep prices. The ministers in charge of the county at that time used to send reports to the capital saying that the Jews would buy barley cheap and resell it at a very high profit. He recommended that the right to deal in wheat and barley should be taken away from the Jews. He equated them to the biggest thieves in the area. It seems from other expressions attributed to him that he was one of the staunchest anti-Semites in the area. He blamed the Jews for being stingy and thus being able to cut corners to provide the lowest prices available in the market. He was the one who supported the complaints of the peasants and did his best to take away their permits to deal not only in grains, but also to lease pubs, buy and sell tar, bricks, potassium, liquor, etc.

The Jews tried to intervene with the local authorities and to re-institute those permits. In some cases they were successful. In addition, the Jews of Horodenka, as well as the Jews of Galicia, had a very great tax burden. In 1777 to 1784, the Jews paid the following taxes: Protection and Tolerance Tax, four florins per family; and Property and Occupation tax, four florins per family. Married people had to pay an additional tax. In the year 1784, there was a slight change in the tax structure. The Property and Occupation Tax was cancelled and replaced with the Kosher Meat Tax. The Protection and Tolerance Tax was raised from four florin to five. Also its name was changed to "The Domestic Land Tax." In addition to these taxes, there were special payments that the Jews had to pay for building new synagogues and for consecrating cemeteries (fifty florin a year). Also there was a special levy on building Jewish schools.

In addition to the great tax burden the economy wasn't good. As result Jews often couldn't pay the taxes in time. In 1791 the local authorities demanded that the congregation of Horodenka pay back taxes of 38 florins per family that was owed for the Domestic Land Tax. In a listing of the protocol on July 13, 1792, the leaders of the congregation, Jacob Wasser and Motle Edelstape, and board members Binya Mindankner, Moshe Offenberger and Abraham Sucher stated that there must have been some mistake because the money had already been paid to the government. After a lot of pressure from the Jews and a lot of requests, some of the taxes were lowered. However, after that the local authorities did not trust the Jews to collect the taxes and appointed their own people to do the collections.

To properly collect taxes, the authorities had to make a list of all the Jews in the town. Thus, we have for the first time a complete list of 422 homes according to their German last names that were assigned on February 3, 1785. Taking into account the average of five people per family, the Jewish population of Horodenka was 2,110. In the year 1792, the local authorities in Lvov received another request to try and collect all the money that was owed by the Jews. They went out, and after a lot of pressure, collected most of the money. But it was never enough, and the authorities in Vienna finally realized that because of the economy and because of the levy of taxes, the Jews would never be able to pay back all they owed. Therefore, in 1802, the Emperor Franz

Joseph decreed that all the debts of the Jews would be cancelled and collections stopped.

On June 6, 1797 a new decree came out that made the Jews of Galicia pay a tax on sugar. On October 25, 1798, another special tax was established as a substitute for the local income tax. Also, a value-added tax was collected in case the meat tax and sugar tax didn't bring enough money to the treasury. The system of collecting those taxes was very complicated before 1848. Collections were at the whims of local authorities as much as the central government. It is noted in the archives of Horodenka that one collector of the Kosher Meat Tax, Leiv Kruman, was very cruel to the Jews. They complained about him to the authorities in 1795 but there is nothing in the archives to tell us of the outcome of this complaint.

In 1797 the treasurer of the Horodenka congregation, Rosenberg, embezzled the money that was supposed to pay for the taxes. The local authorities decided that the board members and committee leaders of the congregation would have to come up with the money. The board members appealed to Vienna, but in a decree dated April 12, 1797, the government in Vienna decided that the local authorities were right and that the board members should come up with the money that was embezzled. This burden of taxes created a lot of hard feelings and depression among Galicia's Jews. There are many folk stories from that time about the methods the collectors used and the ways the Jews tried to avoid paying the taxes. This went on until 1848, the year of the revolution.

In the early 1800's the situation of the Jews of Horodenka wasn't any better. In the year 1811, there was a conflict of interest and later an all out war, between the owners of the distilleries and pubs and the owner of the town, the Count Potocki. Citing a contract from 1743, Potocki tried to raise the amount of monies that the lessees were supposed to pay. When the lessees refused to pay any more money, the owner of the town prohibited the manufacturing of wine, beer and liquor. This conflict hurt 92 families who had made their living brewing and selling liquor. Both sides appealed to the authorities and the conflict went on until 1840. Because of this conflict there was also a question of what was to be done with contracts that were old and overdue for renewal. The local internal affairs office in Kolomyja to which Horodenka belonged suggested that the contracts be renewed for three years only. But the authorities in Lvov were against giving contracts for three years and said because many of the pub owners had other businesses they shouldn't get any contracts and that Jews shouldn't be allowed to own taverns and let Christians do the work for them. Because of the interference of the local authorities the Vienna government retracted the leases in 1845 and acceded to the demands of the local owner.

In addition to that, in 1822, there was a plague of fires in Horodenka that burned a lot of the local homes and made many owners poor. After those fires, the heads of the community appealed to the local authorities to reduce the taxes, but they refused, even though the Jews paid five times as much in taxes as the Christians. According to local statistics in that period, every Christian citizen paid 1.17 florins a year and every Jew paid 6.01 per year.

Some relief came for the Jews came after 1868 because the new authority accorded toleration and liberalism toward religious and national minorities. In the year 1852 the Jews were allowed to purchase real estate. Many Jews from throughout Galicia requested licenses to acquire real estate properties. Among them are listed two Jews from Horodenka: Zellig Engel, who owned a grocery store, and Dan Zilbur. They applied for a permit in 1863 and received it a short time later. Zellig Engel also got a permit to purchase plots that belonged to Christians in Christian neighborhoods that were also frequented by Jews.

We don't have statistical data on the Jews of Horodenka in the fist year of the Austrian regime, but do have records from the county of Zaleszczyki to which nine Jewish congregations belonged between the years of 1788 and 1792. In the year 1792 there were 2,969 Jewish families and 3,188 in 1789. This was divided between 6,906 men and 6,925 women, 13,831 people in all. In the year 1869, 3,159 Jews were counted in Horodenka: 1,593 men and 1,566 women. According to the census of 1890 Horodenka consisted of 1,782 houses, containing 11,162 citizens, of which 1,153 were Catholic, 5,635 Greek Catholic, 4,340 Jews and 34 belonging to other denominations. In the whole county of Horodenka, there were 9,990 homes and 52,421 citizens of which 5,207 were Catholic, 40,086 Greek Catholic, 6,979 Jewish and 149 other.

In the year 1900 the statistics for Horodenka were as follows: 1,898 houses with 11,613 citizens of which 1,259 were Catholic, 6,056 were Greek Catholics, 4,255 Jewish and 43 other. In the whole county there were 10,689 houses, with 55,903 citizens of whom 5,641 were Catholic, 43,437 Greek Catholic, 6,708 Jewish and 114 other.

In the year 1921 there were in the whole county 83,970 citizens of whom 7,148 were Jews. In the year 1910 the number of citizens of Horodenka decreased by 400 in relation to the number in 1900. At that time 11.9% were Catholics, 50.3% Greek Catholics and 37.8% Jewish. In relation to the general population the percentage of Jews rose between 1900 and 1910 from 36.6% to 37.8%.

Between the years 1880 and 1910 the percentage of Ruthenian citizens grew from 45.4% to 50.3%. The percentage of Poles decreased from 17.4% to 11.9%. The number of Jews increased from 36.6% to 37.7%. All in all, there were 4,210 Jews in the town in 1910. According to real estate records Jews owned 4,428 hectars of land in 1889 and 5,090 hectors in 1902. Out of fifty owners of real estate in the year 1889, seven were Jews. In the year 1902, nine out of fifty residents were Jews. In 1889 Jews owned 11.9% of the surrounding land; in the year 1902, they owned 9.6%.

6. The Social and Cultural Conditions in Horodenka

According to legislation by Emperor Franz Joseph II, as of March 20, 1785 Jews could create a general school in Horodenka. The Yiddish Elementary School opened in 1788. The teacher at that time was a man by the name of Shimon Borenstate. He was paid 200 florins per year. In the same year, Jewish schools were established in Zaleszczyki, Zeshdatchov, Chortkov, Buczacz, Zyszidaczow and Syniatin. It is interesting to note that a Jew from Horodenka finished the study of medicine in the eighteenth century and was licensed to practice. Besides his job as a doctor, he also served as the state Rabbi of the Ukraine. In 1781 the chief doctor of Galicia, Doctor Yange Kopinski, gave him a document that attested to his knowledge in medicine, especially in botany and chemistry, and allowed him to practice medicine in Galicia. According to Yitzchak Levy, he came to Krakow in 1782 as a doctor and also gave sermons in the synagogues.

In April 1821, the question of traditional Jewish dress was being discussed in the counties in the area. The central authorities in Vienna had taken up this issue in 1788 but came to no conclusion. However in April 1821, a few clerks from the local government in Lvov suggested to the authorities in Vienna that Jews should change their dress to better fit into the general population. The local governor, Fiar von Hower, opposed this view and in May 1821 he reached the conclusion that there is no connection between the way people dress and the possibility of getting them to assimilate into the general culture. But his was a minority vote and the central authorities in Vienna decided to take the opposite action in this matter. This decision caused a lot of turmoil and anxiety among the Jews of Galicia, although a few assimilated Jews from Lvov supported the central government.

The local Jews started swamping the authorities in the central government with requests to cancel the decree, arguing that a sudden change in the ways Jews dress would bring about a lot of trouble. For instance, the fabric to make secular clothes would be very expensive. Among the congregations in dissent was Horodenka. In May 1821 the merchants of Horodenka sent a plea to the central authorities in Vienna asking them to leave the Jews of Galicia alone and let them wear their own clothes. They reasoned that 1) they were attached to the way they dressed since they came from Poland, 2) most of them didn't have the money to buy new suits, and 3) a lot of merchants had a lot of the fabric used to make traditional dress in stock. If change were imposed, they would go bankrupt. Eventually, the issue faded and the decision by the government of Vienna was ignored.

Between the years of 1862 and 1866, there was legislation before the Galician Parliament about city governments. In the legislation that was put before the voters there were a few restrictions and limitations that would have excluded the Jews from participating in city councils. The Jews protested and after much debate, the legislation was amended. In 1878, an organization in Lvov called Shomer Israel, the Guardians of Israel, tried to establish a stronger sense of community by developing a constitution that would regulate all the Jewish congregations making them all members of a national organization. Representatives of Jewish congregations were asked to participate in the Day of Congregations in Lvov on June 18-20 1878. The participants in the conference reached an agreement about regulations and organized themselves in the spirit of Shomer Israel.

Following that conference, the Orthodox Jews declared that any decisions reached at that conference was against their beliefs. Therefore, they organized a union called The Beholders of the Religion headed by the Rabbi of Krakow, Abushima Schriber, and the Rabbi of Beltz. On February 14, 1882, all the Orthodox Jewish organizations got together in Lvov and decided to draw up their own book of regulations. These regulations established, among other things, that the Rabbi of a congregation would be elected for life and would supervise all matters of the congregation regarding education and the teaching of religion. The right to vote and to be elected would only be given to members of the congregation living according to the code of laws, the ShulchanAruch. Anyone not behaving as an Orthodox Jew would be excommunicated.

These ideas, if adopted, would have created a split among the Jews of Galicia, similar to what had happened to the Jews in Hungary. Rabbi Schriber presented the plan of the Orthodox Jews to the ministry of religions and education in the central government. In 1882 the congregation of Lvov protested this plan. Other congregations of Galicia joined the protest. The authorities in Vienna therefore rejected the plan. On March 21, 1890 a book of regulations governing all congregations in Austria and agreed to by the government and Jewish representatives was published. It expressed strong opposition to any attempt to create a rift among the Jews. This book was published as law and started a new era in public life within Jewish congregations.

According to these regulations, a board of governors would decide the matters of the congregation. This community advisory board would be elected for six-year terms. The executive committee would conduct the administrative work of the whole governing board. According to these regulations, in the year 1891, there were elections to the board of governors in all the towns of Galicia including Horodenka. In the years 1891 to 1900 Moshe Pinlesh was the head of the congregation in Horodenka. The following people were chosen in the elections in Horodenka at the beginning of the twentieth century: Yehoshua Dankner, Todus Kugelmas, Haim-Mendel Koch, Schlomo Pell, Monish Schmidt, Yeheiskel Shpierer, Josel Schertzer. The executive committee included: Jahuda Wasser, Josel Zeidman, Schlomo Kramer, Schlomo Avraham Shor. The president of the congregation was Joseph Wezner. Heading the Talmud Torah Yeshiva was Welwel Zeidman and Fishel Wasser headed the Chevra Kedisha or the burial society. The secretary of the congregation was Daivid Zeidman and the Cantor was Josie Shpira, also known as Josie the Cantor.

The income of the congregation was based on a tax that was levied upon each Jewish citizen according to their ability. Before the outbreak of the first civil war, 680 households paid tax. The congregation could also rely on foundations and money that was left to them for charity. Benjamin Dankner left them 20,400 crowns, David Zilber, 4,000 crowns, and Moshe Pinlish, 2,000 crowns.

Besides the big synagogue, the town had Yishivas, various houses of prayer, a few mynion that prayed together, and other local societies and unions. In the 1860s the Rabbi of Horodenka was Rabbi Moshe Teomim, who wrote a lot of responsa literature including *D'var Moshe*, *The Sayings of Moshe*, which explained parts of the *Shulchan Aruch*. This was published in Lvov in 1864. A third volume of the same book that included responsa from him and his son was published in Lvov in 1880.

Rabbi Moshe Teomim passed away in 1888. His son-in-law, Rabbi Alimelech Ashkinasi succeeded him. He was the rabbi of the congregation until he died in 1916. In 1913 Rabbi Ashkinasi participated in the conference of Hamizrachi in Galicia that took place in Lvov. He was elected as a member of the national committee of Hamizrachi and therefore established a movement of Hamizrachi in Horodenka. His second in command was Rabbi Mendel Shpira, who was elected to office in 1903. He was born in 1873 and his father was a rabbi in Jagelnica. There his father and his father's father served as rabbis for over a hundred years. Rabbi Mendal Shpira was rabbi in

Jagelnica between the years 1894 and 1903 before he came to Horodenka.

The second half of the nineteenth century saw the emergence of the Haskala, the Jewish enlightenment movement in Horodenka. Efram Zilber, one of the most educated people in town, was very famous in the area of Hebrew language and literature. He was an expert in ancient and modern literature and wrote reviews and notes to a publication called the *House of the Talmud* that was edited by Isaac Hirsch Wise and Mayer Friedman. This magazine was published in Vienna between 1881 and 1889. He also wrote for the publication *Hamagid (The Herald)*. His book *Sde Jerusalem (Field of Jerusalem)* was published in Chernowotz in 1883. It included explanations and elucidations of the Torah. In 1896 his book *The Flower of the Rose* or *Perach Shashon* was published in Drohpbicz under the pseudonym Ben Paz. It contained commentaries on the Book of Esther.

The "Beit-Hamidrash"

Another famous Horodenka scholar and publicist was the Yiddish writer Schmol Aba Sofel, born on November 16, 1897. He was from a very established family of writers and a relative to the Vishnitzer rabbis. He studied in the gymnasium. He earned a degree in History and Geography at the University of Vienna and later in Chernovitz. In the weekly paper of the Poalie Zion Movement called *Freiheit* or *Freedom*, he published legends from the land of Israel and about Rabbi Ubericher of Bratislawa. He also translated the *Book of Lamentations* and *Job*. In 1921 he published a Chassidic story in the collection *Culture*, that was published in Chernowitz. From 1922 on he was the editor of the *Arbeiter Zeitung*, the publication of the labor

Zionist movement in Chernowitz. He also published a dictionary of Aramaic, Hebrew and Syrian words that were prevalent in the Yiddish language.

In the last decade of the nineteenth century, the Jewish community of Horodenka saw a national revival and the establishment of the Zionist movement, B'nei Zion or the Sons of Zion. In the year 1897, it included 150 members and the chairman was Hersch Schertzer. On December 14, 1898 in the theater hall in Horodenka, the Macabee's banquet was held at which Doctor Mentche of Chernowitz gave the keynote address. Heading the banquet committee was the local postal officer called Gotesman. In February 1899 the B'nai Zion movement had a public meeting at which Doctor Rosenhak from Kolomyja gave a speech about the Zionist congress in Basil and Mr. Kressel gave a Hebrew lecture about the Jewish Colonial Trust. That same organization sent a telegram supporting Dr. Hertzl's efforts. In the years before the First World War, the chairman of this movement was Rabbi Alter Weiselberg. In the year 1907 the first Hebrew school was established. The first Hebrew teacher was Rirachowski who lasted eight months. Another teacher, Hirschpelt taught for sixteen months. Beginning in 1910 there were two teachers, Yehuda Golstein and Yeshiya Itzik Beker. In 1911, there were 84 students in the school. In 1898 a school for Jewish boys was established and funded by the Baron Hirsch. A special building was created that cost 21,475 crowns. This school lasted for fifteen years until the First World War. On average there were 250 to 325 students there every year – most of them from lower income families. The school also gave students their clothes and lunches at a cost of about 2,000 crowns a year.

In addition to the Zionist movement, the Sons of Zion, there were other societies and movements that served different purposes in the town. Important among them was Agudat Achim, The Union of the Brothers, chaired by Itza Ayzi; Agudat Chaverim, the Union of Comrades, chaired by Dr. Yitzchack Baron; Bikur Cholim, Visiting the Sick, chaired by Hirsch Dolinger; the trade and humanitarian organization, chaired by Fishel Wasser and a few others. In 1908 in Horodenka, there were ten credit unions, four of which were Jewish. In the same year a branch of a Benevolent Society from Berlin created a workshop for making hair nets. This workshop employed twenty Jewish female workers.

7. Horodenka – Through the first World War and after

The years of the First World War, 1914-1918, wreaked havoc and almost total destruction on Horodenka and its Jewish inhabitants. As soon as the war started, at the end of September 1914, the Russians invaded eastern Galicia and stayed through the winter of 1915. During the period of this first invasion, there were very few cases of robbery and rape and the general situation wasn't very difficult. In the spring of 1915, the Russians were pushed back across the Dniester and Horodenka came under the Austrian regime once again. A few months later, the Russians again broke through the front line and occupied Horodenka for the second time. This time the Jews were scared of confronting the Russian army. Most of the Jewish citizens therefore escaped from the town together with the retreating Austrian forces. The Russians were furious at the Jews that stayed and took out their hostilities on them. Russian soldiers burned houses and then blamed the Jews as a signal to the Austrian army to come back. Using that excuse, nine Jews were hung in the main street of Horodenka. A month later, the Russians retreated again and the Jewish citizens who hadn't gone very far with the Austrians returned to find their homes burglarized and looted by the army and the local population. A short while later a third Russian attempt to take Horodenka began. This time almost all Jewish inhabitants of the town escaped west. With the support and help of the Austrian countries, especially Moravia and Bohemia, the Jews stayed there until the end of the war in 1918. A small number of the refugees managed to reach Vienna and spent the war there.

At the end of the war, all except for a very few Jews returned to Horodenka and started rebuilding. After the Hapsburger Monarchy collapsed, Galicia was declared a part of the Western Ukraine Republic. With the encouragement of the Ukrainian authorities, national Jewish committees were established in every town and village. Heading the national committee of Horodenka was a lawyer by the name of Dr. Alpert. Representatives of the national committee from Horodenka participated in a conference that took place in Stanislavov between the 18th and 20th of November, 1918. At the beginning of November 1918, Horodenka became a post for one of the Austrian regiments – regiment #24. The soldiers of this regiment started harassing Jews, burglarizing them by day and robbing them at right. They would rob them of their shoes, their clothes and their valuables. They took Jews for forced labor and waited at the train station to rob those Jews arriving in Horodenka.

In addition, during the time of the Ukrainian regime, the Jews suffered from the dire economic situation and from the policies of the central authority. No one could do much about the waves of anti-Semitism. But this regime too didn't last very long. The Polish regime then took control. Galicia belonged to Poland until 1939 when the Second World War started.

A lot of Jews in Horodenka immigrated to the United States along with other Russian and Galician Jews at the end of the nineteenth century and the beginning of the twentieth century. They created the first Landsmanshafts settlement of Horodenkans. They took part in Jewish life wherever they settled and helped create Jewish centers across the sea. They were the ones that weren't harmed by the Holocaust of the Second World War.

The period between the two world wars was a period of blossoming and support for Jewish nationalism and Zionism. That atmosphere was responsible for the fact that a few hundred people from Horodenka made Aliya to Israel and became pioneers. These people who emigrated from Horodenka to Israel and the United States before World War Two are the only remnants of this glorious community that was mostly destroyed by the Nazis along with the rest of the Jewish communities in Europe.

[Page 67 & Page 97]

Great Torah Scholars in our City

Yakov Halevy-Shnitzer

Translated by Yehudis Fishman

As I come to present an overview of the Torah giants in our generation — among whose descendents I am honored to be counted — I want to first of all single out the source from which I obtained this information, and to give credit to my informants. I was the youngest child in our family, and when I was still a boy, I would spend most of my time in the presence of my father of blessed memory, both when studying and in our daily walks. In the days of summer and also in the days of winter, we never skipped our walk after the evening meal. The path was generally regular and took around two hours. During these walks my father would relate to me, among other things, family events, both from his side and my mother's side. It is the essence of these stories that I will try to tell to the best of my memory.

Rabbi Meshulem Wagner, of blessed memory

Rabbi Meshulem Wagner was the son of Rabbi Chaim Wagner, the head of the court of the Shatz community in Bukovina. While still a boy, he became renowned because of his talents and knowledge. As was the custom in those days, children would frequently marry at a young age. So the boy became engaged to the daughter of Rabbi Simcha Veich from Horodenka, a prominent member of the community and a well-to-do businessman. The groom was about 13 years old when he came to our city, and his father-in-law promised him food for ten complete years, on the condition that he would sit and study Torah. It is said that the father-in-law respected and loved the son-in-law so much that he would not let him go by foot to the study house in rainy days, but would literally carry him on his shoulders to the place of Torah.

In truth, his son-in-law did not disappoint him; he became greater and greater and stood out in Torah among the greatest rabbis of that time and in that area.

In those days there lived in Horodenka Rabbi Yeshaiya who was later famous as the rabbi of the city of Yassi, and was called *Yeshaiya'kele Yasser.*

Rabbi Meshulem Wagner "poured water on the hands" (ie. personally attended.-trans.) of this great rabbinical genius. Rabbi Yeshaiya also ordained Rabbi Meshulem into the rabbinate and was profuse in his praise. After the passing of Rabbi Meshulem's father, the rabbi of Shatz, the leaders of this community sent Rabbi Meshulem a letter asking him to come and take his father's place. However, Rabbi Meshulem Wagner rejected the offer, with a phrase from the book of Isaiah: "To bow my head like a reed before people," is impossible for me. Thus he forwent the rabbinical appointment and the inherited legacy and allowed the communal leaders to select another Rabbi according to the desires of their hearts.

After the "ten good years" that he was supported from the table of his father-in-law, it was decided in the family that after Sukos, Reb Meshulem would begin to engage in business and attempt to earn his own livelihood. Reb Meshulem succeeded also in this, and during the winter, placed all his effort in business. However his father and mother-in-law did not look favorably on the change that took place in the life of their son-in-law, because he stopped devoting most of his time to the study of Torah. They waited till Passover; after the Seder night, they walked to the house of their son-in-law. When Reb Meshulem heard the sound of their footsteps together with their quiet sobbing, he went to wash his hands and open the door to see what had happened. After he invited the unexpected guests in, and asked what was the matter, his father-in-law gave his mother-in-law permission to open the conversation. She said, "Is this why we exerted all our efforts and provided for all your needs for ten complete years, according to the bounty of *Hashem* upon us, even providing you with wax candles to be able to learn at night? After all this, look what has befallen us..."

And here, Reb Meshulem jumped up and asked: "If so, what is your wish? Please tell me." The answer was not long in coming: "We want you to go back to full time learning, as was your practice when you were depending on our provisions."

He replied, "If this is your will, I promise to do so right after the holiday." Indeed, he redoubled his efforts at learning, and appeared only sporadically in the store that his wife Chaike ran. At those times, he would give out more in charity than they earned ... Soon he heard his wife grumbling over this strange behavior, and got very upset. So, what did he do? He took out the drawer that contained the money for that day and threw it outside. His wife accepted his reprimand, and from that day on, didn't interfere with his ways and customs.

הנוער הבית"רי
בהורודנקה

ביתר-יוגענט אין
האָראָדענקע

"Beitar" Youth of
Horodenka

Once when he was traveling about on his business to the economic centers of the time, he happened upon the city of Premishlan, and went into the study house of Reb Meyer'l Premishlaner. Reb Meyer eyed him and commanded his attendant to remove the fourth section of *Yad Hachazaka* from the bookcase. He began to read aloud to Reb Meshulem from the end of the thirteenth chapter of the laws of *Shmitah* and *Yovel* (the sabbatical and jubilee years). "Not only the tribe of the Levites alone, but rather each person, from all who come into the world, will dedicate their spirit and understand from their knowledge to be set apart to stand before G-d, and to serve Him .... and he casts off from his neck the many calculations that people seek, behold he is the Holiest of the Holy, and G-d will be his portion and inheritance for ever unto eternity ... and he will merit to have in the world whatever he needs to sustain him, as the *Kohanim* and *Levites* merited..." And the blessing of the *tzadik* of Premishlan was fulfilled in Reb Meshulem.

Another time, he happened upon the study house of Rav Yosef Shaul Nathanson and Rav Mordechai Zev Atinga in Lvov. After they enjoyed sharing novel Torah thoughts with him for over an hour, they asked about his city of origin. When they got his answer, they both were surprised and said that they would have never imagined that "in this southern land," a young man so full of Torah knowledge would be found. So too he visited the study house of the *tzadik* (holy man) and author of the book *Daat Kedoshim*, (Knowledge of the Holy Ones), who lived in Botzatz; he, too enjoyed the spiritual fragrance of Reb Meshulem.

The people of his own city also knew how to appreciate him. When they offered Rav Moshe Teomim a position as the Rabbi of Horodenka, the leaders of the city turned to Rab Meshulem and asked if he would go with them to the city of Yaburov, where Rav Teomim lived, to check him out. Because of his recommendation, they accepted Rav Teomim as the rabbi of Horodenka. However, after a few years, something happened to spoil the relationship between these two righteous men. It was concerning an *aguna* (a women whose husband was missing and a *Halachic* decision was needed for her to be permitted to remarry-trans.) According to Reb Meshulem Wagner, she was not allowed to remarry but according to Rav Teomim, she was allowed. From that day, it was like a mountain had grown between the two of them, and they never made peace.

However, I heard that on the day that Rav Teomim passed away, Reb Meshulem Wagner shut himself in his room, closed the shutters, and cried bitterly. When those who were close to him entered, and were shocked to see him so upset, he replied that with the death of his "rival," he has no one left to debate with. From that they realized that their argument was not of a personal nature, but rather that each one thought he had arrived at the truth through his individual approach.

Reb Meshulem Wagner had two daughters. The older one was married to Yehudah Pasvig, and the younger one married my grandfather, my father's father, Reb Mordechai Zev Shnitzer Halevi. My grandfather was born in Kitov, and was a descendent of Moshe'le from Kitov. He was a true Torah scholar and a wealthy merchant, who did business in iron materials.

My father was born in 1870, and was named Chaim after Reb Meshulem's father. His parents gave him a Torah education, as was traditional in those times. He was educated at the knee of his grandfather Reb Meshulem, and learned Torah from his mouth. When he was still a youth, many exceptional talents emerged in him. At eighteen he was already ordained as a rabbi, and among the great scholars of the generation who ordained him were Rabbi Landaw from

Sadigeira and Rabbi Feivele Shreier from Bohurodshein. The latter added a comment to the ordination document that he was prepared to travel at his own expense to "crown" my father in one of the congregations wherever he would be called to the rabbinate. So too my father was involved with responsa to *halachic* questions among the greatest scholars of his time, including the Maharsham from Borzhan, Rav Steinberg from Brody, Rav Arak from Butshatch-Tarnov, and others. In his youth he stood out through his sharpness of mind and was not intimidated by the illustrious and famous, when he felt that the truth was on his side. More than once he responded as a battling storm, and was even embroiled in a deadly critique against a famous rabbi. He said that the latter made a mistake in something that even beginners should not err in. However, in his old age I heard from his mouth a touch of regret about this. Even in old age, as his strength did not diminish nor his eye dim, he continued to examine the truth in all its aspects. He never made peace with the "layman's approach," as was called the more superficial approach of study: learning Talmud as if one were reciting psalms — this he never could tolerate during his whole life. Speaking of *Tehillim* (psalms), my father was accustomed to chanting them daily; early in the morning before prayer, as he would walk back and forth in his room.

Until this day I will not forget the sweetness of his chanting; I'd be fortunate if I could achieve all the complex melodies that my father used in reciting those lovely verses.

In his youth he taught many students. He would give lectures to the most talented students — those whose heads and hearts were capable and motivated enough to comprehend and pay attention to an in-depth lesson of Talmud with the intricate commentary of the *Baalei Tosaphos*. Among his best students were Reb Dovid Zeidman, Reb Vovie Kimmel, Reb Naftoli Kugler, Reb Nachum Shpund, Michal Naiman, Simcha Shartzer, and others.

My grandfather on my mother's side was Reb Elimelech Ashkenazi.

Rabbi Moshe Teomim of blessed memory and Rabbi Elimelech Ashkenzai of blessed memory

Rabbi Moshe Teomim was one of the most famous rabbis in his generation and the author of several books of responsa in halachic matters including Uriyan Tlisa'i and The Word of Moshe, in two parts. He also wrote a commentary on the Torah called Ho'il Moshe. Rabbi Teomim's family descended from Rabbi Yaacov Lurberbaum from Lisa, who was known by his books, Chavos Daas, Nesivos Mishpat, his *siddur* (prayer book) commentary, Derech Chaim, and others.

Rabbi Moshe Teomim's father, Rabbi Ephraim, was the son of the daughter of Rabbi Lurberbaum. He was raised at the knee of my *zaide* and used to respond to those who would ask him *halachic* questions, "So my grandfather taught ..." The family traced itself back to the line of Rabbi Tzvi Ashkenazi, called the Chacham Tvi, who was born in Open, Hungary, and received the title *Chacham* (wise man) when he was a rabbi in the community of Salonica. After that, he became the rabbi of Altona in Germany and in Amsterdam. There he got mixed up in a quarrel with the rabbi of the Sefardic congregation, which supported the Shabbatean orator Nechemia Chayun. Because of that, his position was taken away. At the end of his life, he came to Lvov and there passed away in the year 1718. His son, Yaacov Emden, who was known by the acronym, *Yaavetz*, (*Yaacov ben Tzvi*), continued his father's battle against the various Shabbatean sects.

When Rav Moshe Teomim passed away, on the fifth day of Kislev in 1888, the city was divided as to which of his sons should be chosen as his successor. His son, Rabbi Naftali Hertz Teomim seemed like the most appropriate choice for the position. However, among the eulogizers of Rav Moshe, was also his son-in-law, Rabbi Elimelech Ashkenazi, who had served as a rabbi in Gur-Hamora in Bukovinia. Rabbi Elimelech's words captured the heart of his listeners, but to the extent that they tended toward choosing him as the successor of the departed rabbi, they bypassed the son. In truth, after much weary give and take, Rabbi Ashkenazi was chosen as the successor of his departed father-in-law.

During the time that he presided in our city until the day of his death on the sixth of Adar in 1916, he was able to raise many students and to shepherd his flock in the ways of Torah. He was a member of the group, *Chibas Tziyon*, lovers of Zion, and he was one of the few rabbis in his generation who supported the attempt to purchase the *esrogim* from the land of Israel, rather than from Korfu, even though the latter were more physically beautiful. He also put his seal, together with Reb Feivel Shrier from Buhorodsheim, on a proclamation praising the use of the Israeli *esrogim* over those from Korfu.

Rav Ashkenazi's house in Horodenka was imbued with nationalist spirit, and love of Zion and the Hebrew language. It was known to me that my aunt, the rabbi's daughter, whose name was Bluma Reize, decided to change her name to the Hebrew version, Perach Shoshan, many years before this custom spread among the Jewish people. The rabbi's daughters were filled with the fragrance of Torah, and they assisted him during times of need by answering questions that were sent to him, or by writing down his original Torah ideas. He left many Torah thoughts in writing, but they were lost in the Holocaust, together with those who were guarding them.

In addition to his greatness as a *Halachic* authority and his talent as a speaker and preacher, my grandfather, the rabbi, also excelled as a melodious cantor. During the summer, he was accustomed to pray in the big *shul,* and in the winter, he would pray in the study house. My older brothers were lucky to hear his prayers and would always try to recreate the songs and prayers that they heard.

After the First World War, when they tried to renew the life of our community in the city, many people looked up to my father, of blessed memory, and offered him the rabbinical seat, as the successor to his father-in-law. At the same time, the communal head got a letter of recommendation from the rabbis Steinberg and Arak, who wrote approximately like this: "Our well-known friend, the righteous Rabbi Shnitzer, is a 'wondrous vision,' in our times, and is worthy of this position, and the merit of the rabbinate belongs to him according to the law of our holy Torah." However, my father rejected the offer, just like his grandfather, Rabbi Meshulem Wagner had. From that time on, our community, as was the fate of many other communities, had no leading rabbi.

After much wearisome negotiation with the heads of the community, my uncle Rabbi Aryeh Leibush, may G-d avenge his death, was accepted as a rabbinical judge, and he kept his position until he was killed in the holocaust together with other holy people in our community. My aunt Blume Raize, together with her husband Rabbi Alexander Ashkenazi, was saved and went to Israel after the war. Their son Elimelech, who was named after his grandfather Rabbi Elimelech Ashkenazi, served as a rabbi for an observant congregation in Sao Paolo, Brazil. He founded a yeshiva there named, "*Kol Torah*" (Voice of Torah) named after the yeshiva in Stanislav, where his father presided. Thus, the chain continued...

[Page 99]

Horodenka in the Years 1890 – 1907

Shalom Kirshner

Translated by Harvey Buchalter

A. Little Horodenka

In 1875 a large part of Horodenka's residential area between the "Proval" and the Street of the Gentiles [Goyishe Gass] was destroyed by fire. ews predominantly resided in that area, and their houses were built close to one another. The fire swept from house to house; not one house could be saved. It was a miracle that the fire did not take a single human life.

Following the disaster, the Mayor summoned the victims and warned them that as a result of the tragedy, residents could not rebuild their houses as close to one another as before. He proposed that some of them should rebuild on the open meadow, and whoever took him up on his offer would receive all of the building materials free of charge. My father, Hirsh Kirshner (of blessed memory) was the first to take the offer and soon began to build in the open meadow.

The meadow was very spacious with side green stretches. Around it were fields planted with many kinds of grain. On one Shabbos, when a group of us took a walk on the meadowland, someone smelled smoke coming from a new house. He then called out, "Hirsh is the first one to smell smoke on the meadow." Thus my father earned the nickname Smokey Hirsh.

With the passing of time, about 70 Jewish families settled on the meadowland, establishing a village or *shtetl*, complete with shops, busy traffic, and an inn. The meadowlands also had its own minyan and it also built its own little shul.

My father was one of the first Horodenkan emigrants to America, in 1889. But a year later he returned. I was born in 1891. I studied in the Baron Hirsh School, and then in the Municipal School, where I completed the 6th course in 1904. I was immediately hired as a transcriber [something like a court reporter] where I worked until 1907. Purely by chance, my parents found out that I was writing on Shabbos. Not being able to withstand the shame of having a son who was a Shabbos-desecrator, they promptly pointed me on the road to America.

There I became acquainted with some of the first Horodenka immigrants: Yonkov and Nuach Reif; Itzak-Saul and Aaron-Yosef Diffier, Yehuda-Yosef and Itzhak Lechner, and Morris Ressler. From them, I learned the true stories of the lives of the original Horodenko immigrants, aside from what I had found out from my father. I remember all the anecdotes that are herein related very accurately. And I take it upon myself to portray them exactly as they occurred.

B. Jews, Poles, and Ukrainians

As in all towns in Eastern Galicia, Horodenka was inhabited by Jews, Poles, and Ukrainians. Although the Ukrainians were the majority, they barely counted in the management of the city. They busied themselves with working the land – on their few acres – or as share-croppers on the land of Horodenka's benefactor, Baron Romaszkan. The Baron seldom lived on his property; he lived mainly in Vienna and his property was managed by his manager, Stepanovich. In the Baron's estate was a factory for processing chicory, in which a great many young girls – thin Jewish girls – worked for the low wage of one crown per day, for ten hours of work.

The management of the city was in the hands of the Poles, even though they had the smallest number of inhabitants in the city. The high-government officials, such as the Governor, the High Court Judge, and the tax collector were appointed by the government in Lemberg. They were all Poles, as was the Mayor, who was voted into office by the residents of Horodenka. The Ukrainians were unaware and not involved in politics. And so, without fail, a Pole – with the help of the Jewish voters – was always voted in as Mayor.

This lasted for many years until the Ukrainian attorney Okunievsky settled in the town. He took upon himself the task of ending this situation. He founded the Narodny Dam (House of the People), which was similar to the Poles' Sokol. He traveled from village to village, enlightening the peasants, showing them the injustice of their lives. In the national elections, he put himself on the ballot and also organized the peasants. After several years of tireless work, they succeeded in electing Okunievsky-supported candidates to the Reichstag. Okunievsky promoted several clerks, court reporters, and transcribers in his department. His most outstanding appointment was a young Jewish man, Karl Fenster.

C. Officials, attorneys, writers, and *ombudsmen*

In the world of Horodenka, Jewish workers did not assume an important role. In the Court of Justice, there was the official Prifer and his adviser, Halzel; the reporters Baruch Merboym, Alter Koch, the brothers Beryl and Feival Tey, and myself. In the high-salaried Interior positions worked Zeidman and Merboym in taxation; in collection, Hecht and Halpern. The secretary of the budget was Saide Offenberger; the person in charge of birth certificates was Zalman Kalmus. Before my time there were four attomeys in the town: the Ukrainian, Dr. Okunievsky; one Jewish one, Dr. Baran; and two Poles. They all employed the same Jewish clerk. The town Notary was a Pole and he employed a Jewish clerk.

Horodenka also had several *ombudsmen*: Leib Merboym, Yudel Wasser, and Moishe Fidler. The ombudsmen used to prepare cases, even once an appeal to the high court. They did it for a much smaller fee than the regular attorneys. Their activity was not strictly legal, but they always found a way of getting around the restrictions. The one most highly regarded was Moishe Fidler. He had a sharp mind for jurisprudence and even Okunievsky often used his talents.

A new, modem courthouse was built in the town in 1902. The new judge was Kalischuk, and the rest of the judges were Poles. All judicial authority of the three towns and 28 villages in the Horodenka vicinity fell within the jurisdiction of the Horodenka court. It was later decided that on a once-a-month basis a Commission consisting of a circuit judge and a clerk would be sent into the towns and the larger villages to hear minor cases.

D. Markets, market places, shops, goods, and sales

The center of the city was the marketplace. It was divided into three sections: one for the peasants who arrived with horses and wagons; the second for the female peasants who used to come with produce to sell; and the third for the Jewish stall-keepers who sold nothing but fresh fruit. In the midst of the third section of the square stood a clean stall where they sold fresh-baked bread and cakes, wool and cotton, and haberdashery items. Around the market place were many stores, and a great many of them served the peasants from the surrounding villages. These folk came to town once a week. There were also grain merchants and egg merchants who came to market with their chickens.

Horodenka also had a sizable trade in livestock: horses, cows, and swine. This market, the Tarhavizeh, was outside the city limits, in the meadowlands. Important merchants from other cities or even from beyond the nation's borders bought livestock for export.

In the meadowland was also the tobacco warehouse, built by the government in 1905. The production and sale of tobacco and cigarettes in Austria was a monopoly of the regime. Special officials always inspected the peasants' harvest to see if the yield corresponded to the amount of seedlings planted, and it they were carrying out an illegal trade in tobacco.

E. Artisans, innkeepers, storefronts, banks

On the subject of merchandise, shops and stalls – all of which are concerned with trade – there was a large number of Jewish artisans of every class including sewing machine operators, shoe makers, cabinet makers, and tinsmiths. A few of them employed skilled workers and made a nice livelihood. Others worked alone, and others never had enough to eat.

Many Jews derived their livelihood as tavern-keepers. On market days the taverns became filled with peasants who came in to drink a glass of maschke [pure grain whiskey] and have some tavern food. They never failed to drink away the profits made from the goods they had just sold. Once in a while "solid citizens" came in to chat and have a glass of beer. In the taverns one could also buy wine and beer for celebrations of all sorts.

In the city there were also *storefronts* that combined as hotels, restaurants, and taverns. Haim-Mendel Koch, Benish Schmid, and Tadrus Kugelmas owned the best-known inns. Out-of-town merchants, salesmen, travelers, landlords and priests stayed there, and sometimes even actors who came with their theater troupe. There you could always get a good meal and you often had the opportunity to play a game of cards. More often than not a prosperous person or a priest went back home from the card game with empty pockets.

As is known, no trade can possibly exist without credit and loans. Thus, there were some banking establishments which arranged credit. There was a Polish bank, the Kasa Ashtennashii, and the Young Man's Bank (the Sportsbank). There was also Moshe KamiPs bank, in addition to a few loan sharks who always took a higher percentage from those forced into having to deal with them. Near the Baron Hirsh School was a moneylender who gave small weekly loans for small businesses, at a low interest rate. Stetanovitch, the manager of the Horodenka Benevolent Society started up a pawn shop, and some called it a " rag- bank!" Here one could put down timepieces, rings, earrings, candlesticks, furs and clothing. One paid three percent per month. The manager and bookkeeper of the bank was a Young Jewish man, Michel Ofenberger.

F. Afflictions and labors

Not far from the center of town was the Magistrate. Once a year, often at Purim-time, a military company assembled and showed off their drills to the young people who were eligible for military service. Jews almost never had any great desire to join the military, to live three long years in Gentile company – not observing Shabbos and having to eat *treif* (forbidden, non-kosher food). Thus, young Jewish men who had to witness the "presentation" began during Chanukah to "afflict themselves:" that is to hardly eat or sleep, to smoke a lot, and to appear before the draft board gaunt and weak, but happy to be able to evade military service. In order to forgo sleep, the "afflicted ones" would get together every evening in the Chortkover Shul (kloiz) and from there, parade around the streets singing and dancing until daybreak. Whoever evaded the draft the first time around still had to present themselves a second time. If they evaded the draft the second year, they had to present themselves for a third time. Only by evading the draft the third time were they finally discharged from any military obligation. Some Jewish men went so far as to permanently deform (cripple) themselves so as not to enter military service. Let it be understood: some saved themselves through bribery, buying off the draft board with great sums of money.

The soldiers who were waiting to be drafted were mustered out at the end of summer, following the harvest; the call-up letters were delivered at Yom Tov, between Rosh Hashanah and Yom Kippur. This created a great uproar in the town. In addition to this, all of the new recruits from the surrounding villages – young men of "innocent laborers" who were wild and always brawling – swiped produce from the Jewish stalls. In short, everything became topsy-turvy.

G. Police and Militia

The police force in Horodenka was administered by the Municipality and was composed of a force of policemen and a commander. The commander was named Marovski. He was a tall Gentile with a long, wide, yellow-white beard. The Gentile police were Benedick, Michakeh, Tschfurdeh – a Gentile of small stature with a clipped beard – and Eike, a former coachman of the Mayor, Raschko. Jewish police and officers were: Israel Polizei; Fridshand and Hershke Kramer. Kramer, some years later on, went to America with his family to join his other children already there. He died in New York. Schloime Dankner was an undercover policeman, a position that gained him little sympathy among the Horodenka Jews.

The activity of the police was limited, because keeping order in the city and surroundings belonged to the militia, which carried out its duties in the name of the national government and the municipality. They carried out their investigations in cases of theft or assault, or even murder, arresting the suspect, preparing the accusation, delivering it to the court, and so forth. They were the overseers, testifying to the legality of commercial ventures, the taverns, and the men's social clubs. They also made sure the Jewish merchants kept their shops closed on Sunday.

A "report" by a militia policeman often was punishable by a fine of from 10 to 20 Crowns. But you could also pay the tine by "sitting" in jail. For each five Crowns, you could sit for one day in jail. The verdict was rendered so that you went "to *sit*" on the Friday before sundown, and that was considered one day. Saturday and Sunday were each considered two days. And so, one could "sit" out the punishment without losing out on a day's work.

JEWISH INSTITUTIONS

H. The Shul and the "Kloiz" (the shul of a hasidic rebbe)

As with all towns, the heavily-Jewish towns had their self-governing institutions. The kehilah (community council) supervised the public affairs of the Jewish population, such as maintaining the rabbi and religious courts; ritual slaughterers and cantors; a synagogue, bathhouse, and mikvah.

Reb Ashkenazi had no sons, but had nine (!) daughters. His son-in-law Chaim Schnitzer was an outstanding scholar and was called Chaiml. Chaiml's father, Mordechai Shnitser, had an inn which was managed by his youngest son, Simcha Shnitser.

The big shul stood not far from the study hall. Its neighbors were the various hasidic kloizen, the men's social hall, the bathhouse and the mikvah.

The shul was immense and built of brick. On the exterior, the bricks were plain and "flat," and the shul appeared somewhat old-fashioned. The entrance was through a huge gate which opened and closed by "Polishim" (side patios) on both sides. The shul did not have a ceiling; the roof was criss-crossed with long, thick rafters from which hung the brass chandeliers. However, the huge building with the aron-kodesh eastward facing and the bimah in the middle, made a grand impression.

In the great shul mainly younger people and business-types davened. The hasidim who belonged to the small congregations didn't daven there. There you could listen to a cantor daven and thus go back home earlier than you could from the study hall, or from the kloiz, where they davened deliberately and with great fervor.

In the great shul the principal cantor, Yossi, used to daven. His family name was Shapiro, but they always called him Cantor Yossi. He had a lovely voice, and for the High Holy Days ,he called upon his own choir. Whoever heard him chant the Kol Nidre will never forget it.

Many of the singers gradually went to America. They included Abraham Feyer, Moshe Dolinger, Baruch-lsaac Shpierer, Antschel Meltzer, Joseph Dolinger, Ellie and Schloime Hus, and Abraham Berkover.

The baal-kiroh (Torah reader) was Shalom-Hirsh Fink. He had a sweet, strong voice which you could hear from the most distant comer of the great shul. His pronunciation of each word and his cantillation was a pleasure to listen to.

On the other side of the shul, steps led up to the women's side. The majority of the women didn't know how to daven and said each prayer and blessing which the farzogerins (the women whose job it was to pass on the prayers she heard coming from the men's side), dramatically called out to them.

Apart from the weekday davening, the great shul was always empty; for smaller minyans it was more comfortable davening at the "gate-house" (alcove to the shul). Even on Shabbos, the great shul did not fill up. But the great shul did fill up when there came to town a Torah scholar, either for a Shabbos, or in the middle of the week. In shul each year there was held a lively prayer service in honor of the coronation of Kaiser Franz-Josef in which the Jewish students from all the schools and practically all the Jewish residents joined.

Aside from the great shul and the house of study where the Maspolim (non-hasidic Orthodox) prayed, the town had a great many kloizen (shuls of hasidic rebbes), each for a different stripe of hasid. Chortkover, Katitchinitzer, Vizhnitzer, Kosover – even the Schatzer rebbetsen had her own group of hasids. There were two Chorkover kloizen, one new and one old. Aside from them there was a Stoliarisch kloiz, the Kinski kloiz – where the teamsters davened – and many kloizenim and minyans in different parts of the town. In the bigger kloizen, one could find a tew young lads or students "oit kest" (talmudic students from the schtetlach who came to town, boarding with families) sitting and learning. In any case, Horodenka was considered to be a hasidic town. A once-in-a-lifetime event was the visit of a renowned rebbe to town. The hasidim waited for their (visiting) rebbes to arrive on the train, met him with wagons, and accompanied by music, drove him to town. And it was the lucky hasid who had the rare honor of the rebbe lodging with him.

Horodenka also had its chief rabbi, rebbe Michele Hagger, one of the three brothers of the Vizhnitza dynasty. The hasids bought him a big, beautiful building on Zolishtecker road near the Baron Hirsh school. It had belonged to the Polish official named Tzuloif. Next to the house was a large park with flowers and fruit trees and even a stable for a few horses and a wagon.

I. Brotherhoods: Bikur-Holim and Cheverah Kedushah

As in many towns, Horodenka had brotherhoods – a bikur-holim, and a cheverah kedushah. The bikur-holim had regular members in town who paid dues monthly or yearly. From time to time, two "guardians" went throughout the town dispensing the funds the society had collected. This was provided to the poor and to those who were ill, giving them a chance to get better!

In town there was a hospital – a long, tall building which stood on the cliffs near the river. The Catholic diocese, under the authority of the "kraiz-fisicus," or the government-appointed doctor, managed the hospital. Right before I left the town, they built a new and modem hospital building in the meadowlands, on the way to Zaleszczyki. Aside from the "Fisicus hospital" were also three other doctors in town: the old Dr. Roschko, who was also the mayor for many years; Dr. Tzaponovsky, and the Jewish doctor, Kanafas. For the less serious cases. Shimshon Rauer was called. He could "place cups" (essentially, bleed) and leeches and could "figure out an illness." In town, there was also a Jewish veterinarian, Dr. Bach.

The brotherhood of Bikhur Holim would hold elections each year during Succos and elect the director, or "boororim" as he was called. The first Shabbos after Succos they held a kiddish in the home of the "booror-rishon" (head, or director). The Shabbos after Succos was dedicated as the Shabbos of the Bikkur Holim. Prior to the festival of Pesach, they would congregate in the great hall of the shul to "drink wine and crack nuts."

Should, God forbid, anyone die, the body would have to be delivered to the chevrah kedushah. The chevrah kiddushah folk watched over the body. They would bring the prepared body to the cemetery, dig the grave, and "deliver the body to the land of Israel (holy ground)." Poor people were buried at no charge to the family, or for a nominal charge. But when a wealthy person died, a "healthy corpse" as they called it, a great deal of money was charged to the family and there was no way they could elude payment!

The chevrah kedushah held elections once a year and celebrated a kiddish on the tirst Shabbos after Pesach. This was their special Shabbos in the great shul. Many people considered it a mitzvah and a great honor to be a member of the chevrah kedushah.

J. The Sweatbath

The state-operated bath house was a one-of-a-kind institution. Friday, late in the afternoon, parents and youngsters arrived at the "schvitz" to soak their weary bones and remove the dust and sweat from the previous week. And returning from the bath – what can be compared to it? – their faces beamed and became illuminated like the colors of the setting sun!

The interior of the schvitz was a world unto itself. From the highest bench, one could hear the shout, "Another ladle-full, another ladle-full." This meant that more water needed to be poured over the hot stones, so that steam would rise. Then they would swipe their scorched bodies with "brooms" (switches). There was also a mikvah in each bathhouse where one immersed oneself for the ritual purification following the "schvitz." Very observant Jews would immerse themselves before the start of Shabbos, before davening, both summer and winter.

Aside from the government bathhouse there was also the privately owned one, belonging to Ellie-osef Schpierer. During the summer, people would go to the limestone wheel of the great mill, and also Sabicks River. Many also went to cool off in the waters of the Tschervaneh River.

I should also remind readers that in the Horodenka sweat bath a tragic event occurred. On January 27th of 1901 the Horodenka Landsmanchatt Society in America received the sad news that the boiler of the schvitz had exploded and that many people perished. We immediately telephoned the grieving crowd in the Horodenka great shul, where rabbis and several congregants "watched over" the bodies of the deceased. We also mailed a letter to Horodenka in which we blamed the leaders of the Jewish community for their negligence.

HORODENKA SCHOOLS

K. The Baron Hirsh School

The Baron Hirsh School consisted of four grades, for boys. It was maintained, as were all schools, by the municipality, but it was solely for Jewish children. The children received their books for free, and even poor children received a cooked meal before going back home. Before winter they received coats and boots, and on Pesach they got suits, caps, shirts and handkerchiefs.

The Baron Hirsh School was in a building on Zalischticker Road, just beyond the rebbe's courtyard. The director of the school also lived there. The first Director was named Berliss, and the teachers were Mazler, Chamedes, Kuzman – Chana and Nora, who were Yankel Feyer's nieces. Later on, Mazler became the director. The director of Hebrew Studies (Religious studies) was Zanvul Weiselberg, and he was also the strictest teacher. For the slightest infraction, he would take out his bamboo rod.

L. The Gentile School

The school which the Jews referred to as the Goyische Shul (Gentile or Christian School) was a six-grade government-run school for Christian and Jewish children. Here, Polish naturally predominated, but Ukrainian and German were also taught. There were three "religious subjects" teachers: for the Polish children, the Polish priest; for the Ukrainian children, the Ukrainian priest; and for the Jewish children, a Jewish teacher named Dretler. The Director was Serafim – a small, crippled Pole. Of the teachers, I remember two, Losinski and Kazenkevitch.

Some Jewish children went to study in the Lemberg Royal School, in the Kolomyja Gimnasia, or in the Zaleshchiki Teacher Institute. Later on, a Polish Gimnasia was founded which was attended by many Jewish children.

For girls there was a separate six-grade municipal school, similar to the one for boys. Several girls went on for further study in Polish seminaries (private schools) in Zaleshchiki or in Ukrainian schools in Kolomyja, where they graduated as teachers. These were Roisa Yurman, whose married name is now Morganstern, Hannah Shpierer, whose married name is now Dufler, and Feige Vildman, the wife of Isaac Shpierer. All three now live in America and are members of the Horodenka Benevolent Society.

The Akerboi School was located not far from the Baron's estate. Only boys studied there, almost all of them Christians. Although in this part of town many Jews managed businesses – both Jewish and Gentile ones – Jewish students were rarely found in the Akerboi School.

M. Horodenka's Typical Characters: the "makaness oreh" (Shabbos host)

Hirsh Dollinger was a good men's tailor who owned a big shop, In addition to his brother Fishel and his four sons and three daughters, he also took in a few boarders and student-boarders, several of whom came to him from poor villages. Both family and boarders filled up the house. Thus, Hirsh Dollinger became an important "Shabbos host.". For Shabbos observance he invited six to eight guests, and he would say that without a Shabbos guest, he did not experience the joy of the Sabbath. Often he would invite a rabbi who was in town to his Shabbos table. His wife, four sons and three daughters emigrated to America where his wife and his son Moishe died.

N. A Warm Jewish Heart

Hirsh Weinberg was an interesting sort who had a soft spot in his heart for every needy person. It's possible he saw more needy people than anyone had ever seen before. He worked for the municipality in various posts. First he was a tax collector; then he was warden in the jail on the courthouse grounds. At the end, he was paymaster who paid the municipal workers on the first of the month. Even though he worked for the municipality, he was shomer Shabbos in word and deed. He davened in the great shul.

O. Dudeye Zellner

Dudeye Zellner was the town shammos ("crier") and also the shammos for the chevreh kadushah, the burial society. As town crier, each daybreak he would bang on the doors and windows to awaken and call the congregants to shul with a cry: "Wake up, wake up, worthy people!" He would waken the sleepers with three knocks, but when there was a death he would give two knocks, and then you knew that on this day there would be a funeral.

As Shammos of the chevrah kedushah Dudeye Zellner would bring the deceased and the casket to the family home and he then busy himself with the arrangements. He appropriated the surname Zellner because as a young man he was a soldier (Zellner means "soldier"). He was left with a few medals from those days, which he always shined like new and wore on his chest.

PORTRAITS OF THE OLD HOME

P. Baking Matzoh

Baking matzoh was an undertaking that lasted from five to six weeks prior to Passover. There were a few families who possessed the "privilege" of handing out the various "honors" (ritual tasks).

The "market" job of figuring out how to distribute the tasks began even three to four weeks earlier. Each bakery needed a "kneader," eight orten" (dough rollers), a "shaper" to fashion the matzoh's round shape using the tooth-cut shapers, a "flour boy," and a "water boy" to bring the flour and water. And finally it needed a good and experienced "watcher." Let it be understood that each bakery searched around to find the best workers without having to pay out too much money for the work.

As soon as the work began, it went full-force – six days a week and eighteen hours per day. Many of the very able housewives would visit the bakeries to observe how the matzoh was being baked, and to tip the bakery workers with "drinking money."

In 1900, a Jewish man from the meadowlands settlement area, Hershel Symes, brought about a revolutionary change. He brought in a machine to roll and cut the matzoh. This produced square rather than round matzoh. The oven was also different, as it was open on either side. From one side the "watcher" placed the matzoh, and from the other side, an assistant removed the baked matzoh. The other matzoh bakers searched frantically for a religious justification to outlaw the machine-made matzohs, but the rabbi who investigated the machinery and the entire baking process declared the matzoh Kosher.

Q. Jewish Weddings

The Jewish weddings in the villages were beautiful, interesting and impressive. The Shabbos before the wedding set the tone as the groom was brought to the shul for the "aufruf." The groom was often called to chant the Maftir and if "he was weak with the Hebrew" it was considered a personal disaster. Following davening, the bride's father invited everyone home for kiddish.

The ceremony of "setting down the bride" was a sad one. The jester" would begin to "sing to the bride" and she wailed away with bitter tears, especially if she had lost one of her parents, or was orphaned. After that, the groom covered the bride's face with the veil.

The chupah was assembled under the sky. The bride called the groom and dared to step on his foot, which was considered a sign assuring a good life with him. After the kiddish was made, the blessings completed, and the groom had broken the glass, the musicians would cut loose with their instruments and play lively dance music, and with "dancing and splashing feet" the crowds carried on in celebration. They performed the "droshe geshank" ("the "bounty of the Law") ceremony, and they finally ended the evening with more dancing and music. Often, the musicians were separately paid, for their listening music, and then again, for their dance music.

In Horodenka there was a band consisting of Kalman Rosenkrantz and his son, Hersh-Koppel, the fiddler; Mendel Oispresser, the flutist; and the three Guttman brothers. Aaron Guttman played second fiddle, Yankel Guttman, the bass, and Leibzeh, the cripple, the "tazin" (a type of percussion instrument). The two Glassman brothers, Saide and Vulf, were truly virtuosos who often traveled to America to play and become well known. Often, when they came back to Horodenka , they gave music lessons to school children. Saide Glassman died in New York. Isaac Klizmer from Samarkovitz also died there.

R. The Rite of Chalitzah

When I was a young boy studying with Abraham-Isaac Ellis, I and some of the other, young boys heard that something was going to happen which hadn't happened for many years: a boy would grant Chalitzah. The news whirled around the town. Wherever people congregated, they soon began to speak of the Chalitzah.

And so what is the so-called Chalitzah? The bet din (religious court) assembles a minyan. The shammos delivers the wooden board on which bodies are laid for burial. Then a white sheet is raised, as one would hang a curtain to separate the corpse from the living. Then the court asks the brother of the deceased if he agrees to wed the widow. If he says no, he must put on a special show with a strap of leather tefillin on his right foot. And she must remove the corpse's shoe and spit three times in his direction. Then the court declares a judgment that the widow is free to marry whomever she will.

Such a case was "tried" when the eldest son of Schickel Kvesher, who was married to Shimele Zabo's daughter, died after a short time. The younger brother granted the widow Chitzah. This is something I will never forget.

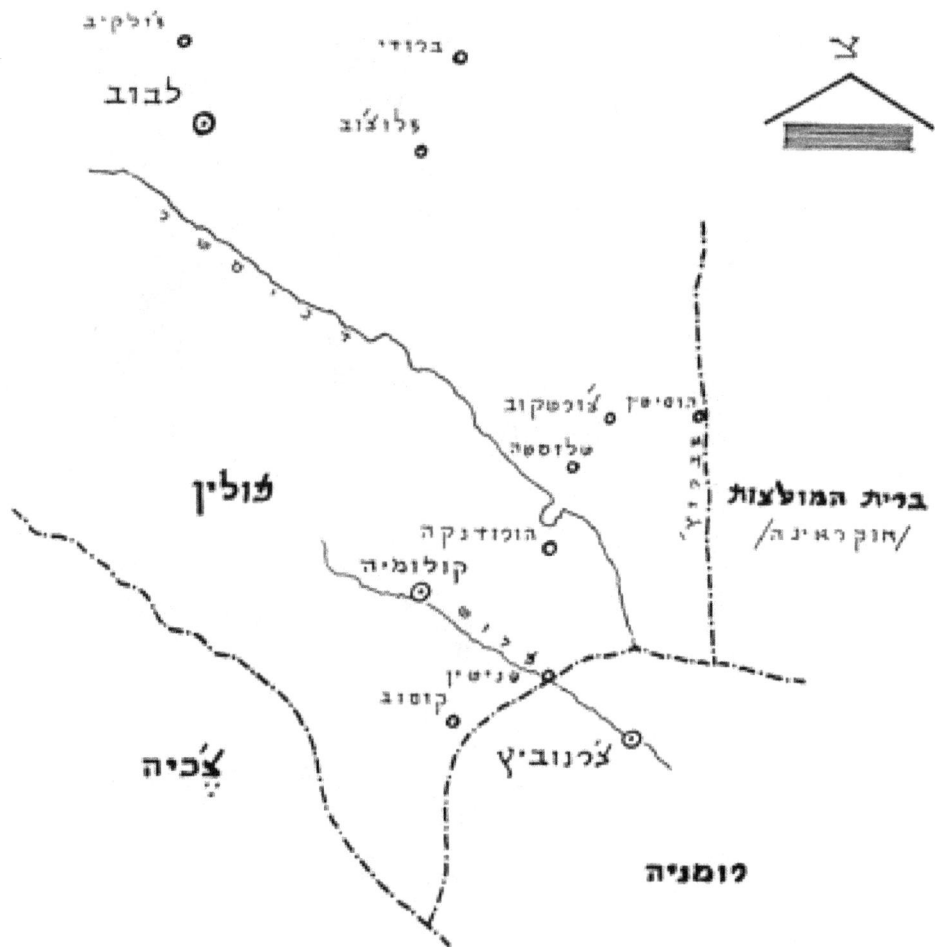

Horodenka and the neighbouring Cities in Eastern Galacia

Horodenkaer Landsleit attending the annual Yizkor Meeting in Tel Aviv

The Presidium of the Yizor Meeting in Israel

Setting from left to right: M. Fleshner, A. Youngermann, The late Sh. I. Lindenberg and H. Sucher. The speaker (standing) J. Shapira and sitting to his right is J. Streit

Horodenkaer attending the annual Yizkor Ceremony in "Yaar-Hakedoshim"

The third class of the Hebrew School with the teachers Mrs. And Mr Metzer 1932-3

Hebrew School with A.Liebster as Master

Celebration of the Balfour Declaration in the Grand Synagogue

Pilsudsky Square

Committee of Karen Kayemet LeIsrael

The Yiddish School 1933

[Page 106]

1895 1960

FIRST HORODENKER SICK AND BENEVOLENT SOCIETY

OFFICERS AND ARRANGEMENT COMMITTEE

NAT REIFF
Financial Secretary

BERNARD DOLLINGER
2nd Vice President

MOE NADLER
President

ABRAHAM BIRNBAUM
1st Vice President

MAX DOLLINGER
Chairman of
Budget Committee

PHILIP LICHTENTHAL
Treasurer

MENDEL ROSENKRANZ
Chairman
Arrangement Committee

JACK BRAND
Secretary
Arrangement Committee

HARRY BAHR

MAX REICHER
Ex President

ISIDORE DOLLINGER
District Attorney
Bronx County

LEO SUSSMAN

WILLIAM REIFF

SAM NADLER
2nd Trustee

NATHAN ROSENKRANZ
3rd Trustee

MAX PODVESOKER
Recording Secretary

65TH ANNIVERSARY

Gus Studio

The Horodenka Landsmanschaft Societies In America

1895   1960
FIRST HORODENKER SICK AND
BENEVOLENT SOCIETY
ARRANGEMENT COMMITTEE

BESSIE LICHTENTHAL   ROSE NADLER   CLARA ROSENKRANZ

DORA DOLLINGER   YETTA REICHER
Trustee   BEATRICE REIFF
Chairman of
Old Age Fund

ADELE SUSSMAN   BETTE BRAND   ESTELLE DOLLINGER

SOPHIE BIRNBAUM   MRS. NADLER

65 TH ANNIVERSARY

Gus Studio

Sholem Kirschner

Translated by Harvey Buchalter

a. The First Emigrants.

When the first news arrived about a new, far-off land where the streets were paved in gold, a group of courageous young men assembled and then departed to seek the so-called golden land. The first group was made up of the following Horodenkan natives: two brothers, Yacov and Nuach Reiff; three brothers, Itzhak-Shaul, Aaron-Yosef and Gershon Duffler; Leib Meltzer; Avremel Schneyer; Moshe-Maness Neigesser; Hirsh Kirschner; Hirsh Fidler; Morris Ressler; Antschul Gradinger; Yehudah-Yosef Lechner; Hirsh Kindenerer; Nuach Bergman; Necha-Leah di bobeh (Brontshtein) and Yehudah-Shaul Kluger. They disembarked in New York in 1889.

They "didn't taste the honey" of the new land. A few became peddlers; most of them became furriers. They stood together with one another and shared whatever they had. They struggled to save a few hundred dollars in order to return to Horodenka and do whatever it took to open a small business and become a worthy, respectable person. This was the dream of each emigrant in those times.

Some of them fulfilled their dream, and after a few years of working in New York, returned to their families and remained in Horodenka. A few went back to New York after a short time. After they spent the money they had earned in New York, they concluded that Horodenka afforded them no opportunity to make a living.

Little by little, more and more young people, driven by the economic conditions, came to New York. The lonely life in a strange place, far from parents, from wives and children, from neighbors and friends, impelled the immigrants to organize *landsmanshaft* societies. In 1895, the first Sick and Welfare Society was founded. It celebrated its 65th anniversary in 1960.

b. The First Society.

The goals of the Society were many and varied: to meet as often as possible in general meetings; to give worthwhile assistance in times of sickness and need; and God-forbid, if someone should die, provide him with a cemetery plot and a funeral. As they all lived in New York at that time, in adjoining streets, they established their own shul with a *minyan* for Shabbos and holidays where they adhered to the Horodenkan customs. The *aliyot* were auctioned off. The third *aliyah* and the sixth *aliyah* and the *maftir* repetition were always sold for the highest price, and on Simchas Torah the shul was packed with men, women and children carrying flags with "lights" (candles attached to the stick) and apples; the faces of the children beamed as bright as the red of the apples! They sold the prayers *Emess ha-Rayess* and performed the "*Ha-Kofess*" (march/processional carrying the Scrolls). Afterwards they bought a keg of beer and then just had a good time. And with God's help, if it happened that a landsman was able to "write" (sponsor the writing/purchase of) a Sefer-Torah, then it became even more festive. Accompanied by music, the Sefer Torah was carried under the *chupah* and through the streets of NewYork and then back into the Horodenka shul where the final letters of the final words were sold, and the crowd thoroughly enjoyed the festive event with schnapps, honey cake and beer.

The membership of the Society came together twice each month when the *landsleit* met to hear the latest news from Horodenka. Elections were held twice a year, and the "politics" of the election brought about heated arguments more than once!

The Society accomplished a great deal in the years of its existence. Primarily, the people who came later on didn't feel as lonely as the first immigrants. They came and saw familiar faces who provided them with a place to stay and with a job.

Deliverty of $2500 to the UJA by theCommittee of the Prog. Horod Society

In the years before the First World War, there were two places in New York where Horodenka people could meet. Shaya Kirschner, Meyer Alinsky's son, and his wife, Golde, Aaron Itzhak's daughter, had a restaurant in the heart of the Jewish neighborhood, on Rivington Street. The *landsleit* – unmarried men and women and those with families still in Horodenka – would come to eat. On Sundays, families would also come, with wives and children to eat a good, broiled steak, drink a glass of cold beer and listen to the latest news from Horodenka. The second place was on Rivington Street where our landsman Mendel Dollinger had a money exchange and a shipping bureau where you could always catch the latest news from our town.

On two different occasions attempts were made to take members away from our organization. The first time was during the Dreyfuss Affair, when the entire world was absorbed in the exploits of Emile Zola. A group of young people from Horodenka founded an Emile Zola Society, but the Society didn't enjoy a long life. A few years later the same young people founded the Horodenka Young Men's Society, which also disbanded because of internal conflict.

In 1912, several of the members of the Horodenka Health and Welfare Society, under the leadership of Mendel Dollinger, left the Society and joined the Jewish lodge, Brith Abraham, but a few years later they re-joined the first Horodenka Society .

c. The Second Society and the Assistance-branch.

In the few years before the First World War, a great many people from Horodenka came to New York. Many of the younger ones had no interest in joining the original Horodenka Society, the membership being older and the direction "conservative" (old fashioned). When war broke out in 1914, the connection between us and our town was torn asunder. We knew that our parents, sisters and brothers were wrapped in the fires of war and were desperate for our help. We all felt we should help them with all of our strength. However, the younger people had no desire to join the original Society. After some deliberation they came to an agreement to start a society for younger Horodenka men and women. On Sunday November 15, 1914, a group of young people met: Sholem Kirschner, Mendel Rosenkrantz, Moshe and Schlomeh Dollinger, Scholem and Yosef Daifek, AlterYurman, and a young man from Warsaw, Yankele Karman. They founded the Progressive Horodenka Young Men's and Young Women's Sick and Welfare Society. The meeting was held at David Daifek's residence.

Soon thereafter we called for a general membership meeting of Horodenko young people in New York, on Sunday November 22, in a hall on Rivington Street. The following members were in attendance: Heskell Fidler, Leib Koch, Schmuel Neiman, Abba Teicher, Velvel Yurman, Isaac Neigisser, Schmuel Yankner, Moshe Weisel, Charley Yurman, Meyer Herman, David Yurman, Pesiah Teicher, Menashe Bomberg, Moshe Kirschner, Alter Sturm, and Max Becker. The provisional officers, who would serve until January 1, 1915 were the following: Scholem Kirschner, President; Mendel Rosenkrantz, Vice President; Schlomeh Dollinger, Protocol Secretary; David Yurman, Finance Secretary; Scholem Daifek, Treasurer; Leib Koch, Abba Teicher and Charley Yurman, Trustees: Schmuel Yanker, Speaker; Haskell Fidler, Director.

In the meeting that was held on Chanukah, December 2, 1914, we, together with the original Horodenka Society and with the Horodenka lodge, founded the Assistance Society for Horodenka war victims. We threw ourselves into this effort with the greatest intensity.

The New York Assistance Committee called a mass meeting of all Horodenka *landsleit* from New York and surrounding areas on a Sunday in February 1915, in the Romanian Shul on Rivington Street. The *Shul* was packed, and soon over $5,000 was collected. The Committee also began to target all *landsleit* who had not yet contributed. In addition, they arranged theater productions to raise money for the fund. As America was still neutral, we had the opportunity to send assistance to the Horodenka war victims and to those who were militarily evacuated as well as for those who remained in Horodenka. This was very difficult work, but it was done with love and sacrifice.

It was indeed difficult to assist our sisters and brothers following America's entry in the war, in 1917. We had lived to see the war's end, and in 1919 we sent Mendel Dollinger as our representative to Horodenka to distribute aid to the war victims. We also provided direct aid to those closely related to us. We also sent "a nice few hundred dollars" to provide to the needy, who otherwise had nothing for Passover.

d. The construction of the *shul*

In 1925, we received a plea from Horodenka to help them build a Yiddishe Shul where children could receive a Jewish education, and also a culture center where they could enjoy their free time and celebrate their *simchas* and not have to go to the Sokol (Polish Center) or to the Norodny Dam. We immediately undertook the task to carry out their wishes. We selected a Board to direct the work. We planned theatrical productions and dances and visits to people's homes to help raise funds. Thus began the work of constructing a Jewish Cultural Center and a Yiddische Shul in Horodenka; we sent over $14,000 to that end. But it was not destined for the youth of Horodenka to have their own cultural center. Not long after it was completed, the nightmarish Hitler years began.

e. Relief work during the Second World War

During the Second World War we again organized the Assistance committee and attempted to send assistance to each person we were successful in locating. But to our sorrow, very few remained for us to help. Thousands of our sisters and brothers were slaughtered and only a few solitary individuals were fortunate enough to survive.

We called a mass-meeting in the commodore Hotel where we quickly collected around $10,000. In addition, we had theatrical presentations to raise money. We sent packages or rations through Hirsh Leib and Yosef Meltzer to all Horodenkan survivors from whom we had received news of their whereabouts. We helped a great many *landsheit* to save themselves from their living Hell; we helped settle them in Israel, in South America, and in New York. Each free hour we gave ourselves over to this work; much of it was accomplished with our self-sacrificing president, Mendel Rosenkrantz. He delivered the ration packs to the post office in his own car. We also sent medicine to the sick; families in New York did this.

The activity of the Assistance Committee came to an end in 1951. Before the Committee disbanded, it gave the United Jewish Appeal a check for $2,500 to build a home in Israel. This represented the balance that remained from our contributions.

f. The activities of the Progressive Horodenka Society

The Progressive Youth Society did not want to be part of the original Horodenka Society and shortly after its founding decided not to admit married couples as members. Thus, married people could join only the original Horodenka Society. Let it be understood that the members who subsequently married could still remain as members. But many young married couples protested against the non-married resolution and would not forget that the Progressive Society had closed its doors to them. To make things right, in April 1928, we decided to allow married couples to join, but only if they were under age 35.

In 1932 we decided to admit new, married members who were under the age of 40, instead of 35. Six years later, in 1938, we decided to admit our children as members with all rights and benefits, for only five dollars a year, in order to afford them the opportunity to become familiar with our work, and for them to become the future leaders of our Society. From that time on, some of them actually held the office of President of the Society, the examples being Peretz Koch, Leib Koch's son; Hershel Fidler, Haskell Fidler's son; and now, Donald Neimark, who is not from Horodenka, but whose wife comes from the Rindner family of Chernelitza.

We continued to have cordial relations with the original Horodenka Society--and we involved ourselves in all the assistance programs. We attend their presentations, and they come to ours. During the first 25 years of our existence we put on a gala ball twice yearly, in May and December, and they were very successful. Every five years we publish an anniversary journal. In 1959 we celebrated our 45th anniversary, and we will celebrate our 50th year anniversary in 1964.

Our activities fall into many different realms. Until recently, the meetings were held twice monthly. Thus, we maintain contact among our members. From time to time we present lectures on current events and we attend presentations, but in the last few years many of the *landsleit* have moved to the suburbs and do not attend the get-togethers as often any more.

Each year in the month of Elul (usually August/September.) we have a memorial gathering to pay tribute to the departed, tragic victims of the Hitler years. A huge crowd assembles to hear the eulogy *(ha-safed)* and the memorial prayer (*al-male-rachamim*) recited by our distinguished rabbi, Dr. Israel Schur.

The Yiddish School 1933

We take part in the work of the "Joint," in the Federation of Jewish organizations in New York, in the associations of ORT, HIAS, in Histadrut, the Jewish Labor Committee and other important organizations to whom we contribute large sums of money. We also became very involved in the work to elect our member, Isidore Dollinger, District Attorney, a post which he still holds.

In 1942, Leibele Koch received the consent of the Progressive Horodenka Society to found a Women's Society which would bear the name of his departed wife, Sarah (Sadie). The organization was founded with the name Ladies Auxiliary, and still exists. Its most important objective is to help Horodenka *landsleit* who are destitute or sick to get back on their feet. The Ladies Auxiliary has about 50 members, mostly the wives of our members. They arrange, with our help, events for Chanukah and Purim for the membership. They become involved in the general assistance work that we undertake. They also help out individuals who come to them directly for assistance, and for other worthy causes. Their meetings almost always take place at the same time as ours.

In 1944 our President-elect Leibel Baer suddenly became ill and died a short time later, at age 50. He was born August 22, 1904 and died April 11, 1954. He was the son of Yohanan Baer, and left a wife and two children, two sisters and five brothers. We the members of the Progressive Horodenka Society and his dear friends were deeply grieved by the tragic event. We arranged a beautiful funeral and established in his name one of our most important foundations: the Leon William Baer Assistance Fund. He was put to his eternal rest in the cemetery of the Progressive Horodenka Society.

The first cemetery of our Society was consecrated in 1917. In 1936 we purchased a piece of property for a second cemetery, and in 1956 we bought a plot for the next generations for $9,000.

g. Alexander (Shaike) Granach (of blessed memory)

In the summer of 1931, a beloved guest from Horodenka arrived – Alexander Granach. We arranged a wonderful reception for him and also an evening event in the Central Plaza Hotel. He was deeply touched by the "masses" of *landsleit*, of stage artists and writers who attended. Two months later he returned to Germany.

Two months later he came back to America and promptly got roles in movies and became very popular on the English-speaking stage. In America he voraciously took to work writing his autobiography. He wrote the book in German and it was soon translated into English. The Progressive Horodenka Society selected a committee to make arrangements to have the book translated into Yiddish. But soon we received the sad news that on Wednesday March 14, 1945, Granach died during an appendectomy procedure. He had become ill while performing one of his better-known roles, "A Bell for Adono" on the English-language stage.

The sad news made a devastating impression on all of his close friends. We immediately began to make arrangements for his funeral; it was held on Sunday, March 16, 1945. The funeral parlor was crowded with *landsleit*, friends, stage artists, writers and journalists. Eulogizers were Rabbis Jochanan Prinz and Israel Schur, Yacov Ben-Ami, N. Nathanson, Margo and Frederick March, Dr, Wachtel, and our

President, Scholem Kirschner. The Cantor, Vinaver, accompanied by an organ, chanted *al-male-rachamim.*

A long procession of cars accompanied the casket to the cemetery. Words of reverence were recited at the open casket by the writer Nachman Meisel and our *landsleit,* Martin Birnbaum and Yitchok Isaac Schechter.

The book committee immediately took up the task of having the book translated into Yiddish. The work was given over to the stage artist and writer, Jacob Mestel, and the book was published by the YKUF, in an edition of 2,600. The autobiography of Granach is a valuable work and his everlasting monument.

h. Three Eminent Townsmen

In 1938, Ben Bonus, a Horodenka "baker boy" landed in NY. He had ambition and talent. He began to perform on the Yiddish stage and today is acclaimed in the world of Yiddish theater.

In 1936, Isidore Dollinger, a young attorney, the son of our landsman Mendel Dollinger, was elected Assemblyman in the State of New York. There he served seven years, and was subsequently elected State Senator from New York. Five years later, in 1948, he was elected Congressman. Eleven years later, in 1959, he was elected District Attorney. The fact that he holds high office notwithstanding, he is a youthful man and a member of both Horodenka Societies. In 1936 he was President of the Progressive Horodenka Society. He is unfailingly willing to help out a landsman with both advice and the means necessary to carry out a task. His only son Edmund and his brother Abraham are also members of our Society and attend our meetings and our *simchas.*

החועדה המכינה של חגיגות יובל הארבעים של האגודה הפרוגר־ סיבית בניו־יורק (1954).

דער אראָגניזיר קאָמי־ טעט פון די פּראָגרע־ סיווע האָראָדענקער סאָ־ סייעטיס פייערן זייער פערציקסטן יובל (1954).

Arrangement Com. of the Progressive Horodenker Soc. to their 40th. Anniversary (1954)

Dr. Benny Gradinger was born in New York, but both his parents are natives of Horodenko. His father is Mendel Nuach, son of Anschel Gradinger, one of the first natives of Horodenko to come to New York, and his mother is Feigeh-Toibeh, daughter of Lazer-Yocov. He completed the *folkshule* and the high school with highest honors and then received his degree as an accountant from New York University (NYU). Later on he received his Masters and Doctorate from Columbia University. During the First World War, in 1918, he served in the Army Air Force and reached the rank of Colonel. He was chief of the Budget Office in the technical-development branch of the Army Air Force. Following this, he became the representative of the Director-General of the Relief Administration, Herbert Lehman. As is known to all, Herbert Lehman became Governor of New York and later Senator, and was a Jew with a "warm, Jewish heart." In 1955, Gradinger was a special consultant to the office of the New York state comptroller. He was a Professor of Finance at NYU. In addition, he manages his own financial firm. He has been a consultant to the Department of the Interior in Washington, and also a consultant to Israel.

He is a member of both Horodenka societies and has held many posts in the Progressive Society. He is involved in all affairs and is always willing to help with both advice and material assistance.

The last visit of Al Granach 1937

[Page 112]

Blue-green Tongues

Leon Yurman

Translated by Harvey Buchalter

A. Little Horodenka

A town languishes in the midst of unending suffering. On the first few nights the Germans abandon the streets and soon the remaining people await the arrival of the approaching enemy – the Russian-Czarist Army. The Dniester River blocks their incursion momentarily; but for how long? The people wait in their attics and speculate. The silence is broken by their beating hearts. And the night falls silently. No sound of a falling leaf, no rustling. Night falls gruesomely silent, with anticipation. Pale-blue beams of moonlight spread as with held breath – dim and quiet. Only in solitary places, between random trees, silhouettes wander about, swaying and flittering.

From somewhere in a hole in the ground or from a cellar one soon hears the lament of a child which is quickly hushed. And stillness returns once again.

The town is abandoned. The dirt roads, empty of people, are laden with anxiety from waiting. Only light from the dark-hued moon. Not a single person is on the dirt roads. Only packs of dogs, abandoned, feral from hunger, run about, a groaning sound emanating from their throats. A voice is heard from somewhere. The town shakes with fear. A hoarseness grows in parched throats. Eyes swell with fear. Whitened lips inform the sound of: "This is what is happening?!"

Moon beams gush snowflake blue light over the leaden roofs. The perfectly round solitary stars gleam with apprehension. And soon a dog appears somewhere along a cliff, dragging along an anguished bark throughout the town. The townspeople shiver; fear grows and spreads its flattened wings over both young and old. It flings the mother's nourishing breast from the sucking child. The dog keeps sounding its lament.

The night is without end!

המקוננת באבע חיה־בייליה׳ס על־יד מצבת הקדושים שניתלו על־ידי
הצבא הרוסי „באשמת ריגול" בשנת 1915.

די קלאָגצערין באבע חיה־ביילעס ביים קבר פון די קדושים. וועלכע
די רוסען האָבן אויפגעהאָנגען אין יאהר 1915. „פאַר שפּיאָנאָד".

Babe Chaye-Bailis, the professional lamenter at the
Gravestone of the victims hanged by the Russian Troops
in 1915, for "alleged Spionage"

The Cemetery

A blood-red sunrise has crept its way out of the twilight. The fields have become smoky – the blackened body of mother Earth with her countless thousands of laments. The dirt roads run vacantly over mountain and valley and become lost in whirling dust in the distance. The wall near the town's mountain peak stands yellowed and "settled in" in the bluish light of the moon. Ravens fly about – the symbols of war. They cut through the air, wait, and then proceed to gather, aware of everything waiting.

The dirt road became alive! Dust whirled in the distance on the Dniester Road. Horses whinnied and reared their heads, chasing and pecking one another with sharp spurs. Nine Cossacks on smallish Tscherkesker horses appeared. They galloped frantically, as fire sparked from their hooves.

Suddenly a dog appeared on the dirt road – a starved cur with a body deformed by human neglect. One of the soldiers – the one with a pistol – spotted him on the run and shot once, twice. The dog crumpled, its feet in the air, and lay prostrate. The eyes of the cavalryman were ablaze.

About four weeks later, a Hungarian rifleman shot the Cossack, also in mid gallop: once, twice. He turned, hitting the ground, rolled over with his feet in the air, and he too lay prostrate. The eyes of this rifleman, too, were on fire.

War roared. An orgy of celebration. Swarms of soldiers. The earth became black and scorched. The broad fields, the "breadbasket of Galicia," was bleeding to death. Memory furnished no example of this.

As far as the eye could see, masses, masses of wandering people. Aircraft flew about. Heavy "36ers" rolled along, dragged along by massive Arabian horses. Light machine guns and also heavier ones. Officers on horseback and cavalrymen. A black mass, blurred by the dust.

One mass riding by. One order: burn and pillage and totally devastate {mach churban} the land!

One mass, a bloody giant. "If not me, then you! Who will remain? Me!"

A mass of soldiers rode in a quick trot to music, to a beat created to liberate the people. Aircraft sputtered overhead. Officers shouted and the mass went forward uniformly. The officers' eyes took in everything beyond the mass of soldiers.

And then suddenly a blast from a loose cannon. And again, stillness.

The top branch of a tree, broken off by a shell, flitted in the wind, barely holding on by its bark. All the other branches were bent toward the ground. But the top branch, the one almost torn from the tree, was still fighting its last battle. One of the fighters saw this. The spark of humanity in him became alive and he imagined himself "human" once again, and he separated himself from the pack, in the process forgetting where he was, who he was. The wind continued to howl. An officer ordered him – he who with silenced lips attended to the flickering crown of the tree – to move away. He refused. So they took him away, and, one discharge from a rifle later, everything went back to "normal." But one of the "masses" sorrowfully bit his lip; the crown of the tree still swayed in the wind!

Heavy and blackened like a rusty hammer, night fell over the town of Horodenka. People shivered, waited. Stillness and solitude, that feeling of a breath held, walked with air-like steps over all of the ordinary people who awaited the arrival of the enemy. And both sides were caught up in waiting: One gloomy and close to being annihilated, its limp hands outstretched. The second, the predator – murderer – that is how they were looked upon – was about to break through the Dniester line, either today or tomorrow. He is here barely 48 hours, and the town is his for that stretch of time, the women and the young girls, the gold and the money!

Their plunder wracked the lives of the subdued masses. Their blood quickened in their veins. In the middle of the night one was awakened and looked around. He would see the thousand upon thousand of submissive souls. He would flee. A second person would then arise. Then a third. The night would become suddenly alive and wracked in blood. Blood! Blood!

Wild cries wracked the night. Awakened from their pretense of sleep by the echoes of the cry, men and women scurried about; even the smallest children, their eyes hollowed by fright, quietly sobbed.

Ay, how the horses stamped about! How they carried on over the stiffness of the night. Hooves flickered with fire. Eyes filled with the inevitability of plunder, glinting in fear, as never before. The night was consumed with shrieks, becoming red with blood. And blood also flowed from beards which had been tom away, now littering the streets. The beards shrieked along the howling streets:

"'Mama, Mama!"

Frenzied cries transformed the town, painting it red in the night. A horror! Save us! "Ha, don't scream, you cripple! I only want to straighten out your hunch back, your crooked back.

"Ha, ha, ha!"

Heavy steps pounded his back, his hunched back. And he was "straightened out." Drunken laughter accented the war chronicle.

The omnipresent, eternal, depressing walls of confinement suddenly motioned. The walled-in spaces suddenly became filled with Jews, old and young ones. And one, a sage. was pulled by his beard – his long, white beard stamped him with Jewish-ness – and was brought forward, half-dead. The constant cries among the captives became stilled; not a word could enter the walled confines.

An old woman was dragged from her cellar and taken to her room . She was stripped bare and put onto the table. A blackjack whistled past and landed solidly on her. Streams of blood squirted up towards the ceiling. Blood whipped about and landed as splotches over the white walls.

"We are dyeing your room, ha ha." She was silent although she spoke a few words later on. And then, sometime later, she fell into total silence.

Grayish pictures, panoramas, showed up: Shoeless soldiers wallowing along the dirt roads; women being pulled about by their hair stoically maintaining their silence. And the night deliberately passing, passing like hot blood pouring from a living organ, a practiced flow, on the bloody 15th of May 1915. The day in which fright and its memory infected our town.

Dawn reflected another bloody day. Pillars of smoke and fire enveloped the town. The marketplace, the heart of the town, was swept by fire and smoke as houses burned, and the sunlight whirled in springtime reds over a leaden horizon.

Wires on the telegraph poles hung neglected – no one knows how long --- awaiting a message from a loved one. Some soldiers wandered about with fixed bayonets among the jungle of loose wires. And others set up tables in the middle of the market place. The day commenced a marketplace of doom. A Cossack galloped like a madman, a naked woman tied to the saddle of his horse. Blood and mud freely mixed together, intermingling on the sandy road.

At the height of the imprisonment, they drove the Jews out, and each fourth one was taken aside so as to take a total of ten; the rest were taken back to the walled enclave. The locks resonated as the doors again enclosed them.

Ten Jews selected to be impaled by bayonets.

The captivity continued. The town burned. Through crooked, old and dirty streets Jews were driven. One once spotted his house and stood in front of it stone-still for a moment, as bayonets impaled countless "guilty" Jews one after another in the screaming dawn of May.

Suddenly there was mass-hysteria, as eyes became fastened to the sight of the telegraph poles. The will to live, with wild-eyed obstinacy, rose up in the core of the Jews' being and faced down the challenge of death. A struggle between life and death broke out between the helpless captive and the Cossack. But still they hanged nine persons, people who had just been alive and who breathed fear and at the same time, yearned for a springtime morning.

One victim came loose from the rope, and before any of the Cossacks had the chance to hang him again, he ran away, but not far enough. Two Cossacks grabbed him near a burning house. His large frame shook as he grabbed both of them and took them into the burning house. Then the deadly flames fell upon all three of them and covered them for all time.

Women were customarily shamed on the tops of tables. In the middle of the day, in the market place and wherever houses burned, the smoke was visible through the clearness of the dawn. And the nine people suspended on the telegraph poles had exposed their bluish-green tongues, which were covered with dust and grime. Nine lifeless tongues. Nine tongues up against the monster – the beast of imperialism which ruins lands, that kills people and releases the savagery that lurks within the human breast.

The day had ground down and had brought an end to the harsh, dark night.

[Page 114]

About the History of Our City

William Offenberger

Translated by Harvey Buchalter

The name "Horodenka" originated in the Ukrainian word "harad" which means "garden." According to legend, Horodenka was built by a Ruthenian duke by the name of Tscharney. He lived in a village not far from Horodenka, which was named after him: Tschnernelitsa. A castle stood there in which the Duke probably lived.

When the Polish king Casimir, *Vielke* (The Great) allowed Jews into Poland, 150,000 settled in the province, which later – after the first Polish census – was called Galicia. According to the census, Maria-Teresa governed the 150,000 Jews, but this knowledge brought no great joy, either to the Princess, or to the Jews.

After Poland, Austria was the greatest Jewish center of that time. The heads of state sought all means possible to decrease the number of Jews. The anti-Jewish mood combined with economic strangulation created a constant environment of insecurity for the Galician Jews. First they were tolerated: later they were driven out and subsequently allowed to return, but under harsher conditions and punishments. The Jews of that time had to exert all of their strength to maintain their unity, their one-ness as a people standing in opposition to the possibility of becoming extinct.

In Jewish society, the Rabbis had the greatest authority, notwithstanding the influence exerted on them by the Kabbalah. Even so, the two strands running through the community, the interior (personal religious life) and the community-based life, formed the illusion of natural autonomy (self governance both as a religious individual and as a community). To the outside observer, they would give the appearance of being under the thumb of the Polish aristocrats.

The Hasidic movement had become established in Galicia. It had its origin in the person of Israel ben Eliezer, Baal Shem Tov. He was born in the area of Kosow in the year 1700, and according to certain folktales, his mother and other kinsmen were from Horodenka. One of his best-known students was Rabbi Nahum of Horodenka who assembled the pages of the Baal Shem Tov's Torah into scroll-form and decorated it as well.

The establishment of the Hasidim caused an outcry in the other Rabbinic circles, generally called the Misnaggdim. There were long years of bitter rivalry between the two religious customs. In neighboring Olomay, it went so far that in 1776, the Rabbis burned all Hasidic writings with excommunication. And they also threatened all followers of Hasidim. Finally the Austrian authorities became involved in the rivalry and the Hasidim gained the right to have their own congregations and their own Rabbis.

Under the authority of the Polish King, Jan Sobieski, Poles and Austrians together fought against the Turks in Seratin, a village near Horodenka. The battles against the Turks had the character of a Christian battle against Islam: the Jews were blamed for having betrayed the Motherland as the Polish army retreated and the Jews were abandoned to the retreating soldiers. There were no actual witnesses, but documents in YIVO point out that these soldiers inflicted a pogrom upon the Jews.

For hundreds of years our ancestors endured a double oppression, first from economic shortcomings and then from the environment of ignorance that surrounded them. And so the small towns nurtured their own culture and their own rituals that are so genuinely reflected in the work of the great Jewish writers. Of the "types" which the great Jewish writers portrayed – wagon drivers and water carriers; *cheder*-teachers and musicians; tailors and shoe-makers; buyers and sellers – all are flesh and blood portrayals derived from East European Yisddisheh life. All of the communities that nurtured Jewish life and customs existed for over 550 years and then were so tragically destroyed by the desolation brought about by the Nazis.

We will eternally remember our loss and will struggle to maintain the rich cultural inheritance, which they have bequeathed to us.

Jewish Educational Institutions in Horodenka Between the Two World Wars.

The First World War brought many changes to Horodenka. The Austrian- Hungarian monarchy ceased to exist. Poland became a sovereign republic and in the new republic the relations between Jews, Poles and Ukrainians in their day-to-day dealings were normal. Jews did not become citizens with full rights, but they enjoyed many freedoms that gave them a chance to catch up after the four years of war.

Thanks to the intervention of the American Jewish Committee, President Wilson pushed through a peace treaty, the Treaty of

Versailles, which initiated new policies. These protected the rights of ethnic minorities in the newly-established nations. This was a never-before-stated ideal; the Polish Jews felt for the first time that their meager rights as citizens were not solely dependent upon the rule of the sovereign, but could be enforced by an international treaty.

This was finally realized in the field of education. Jews could now search for ways to give their children a better secular education, and at the same time, a Jewish education.

In those days the *cheder* was the only Jewish school. Although old-fashioned, it fulfilled an essential role: to maintain the traditions of the Jewish people from the age in which Jewish life was centered upon the *Shulchan Aruch.* For generations the school existed and helped educate Rabbis and scholars who studied Torah day and night. And now, in our day, under the sun of freedom, new ideals have come about and new schools have been founded.

The Hebrew language school was founded according to the ideals of Zionism. Their schools' followers dreamed of building the land of Eretz Israel. They consumed the poems and songs of Chaim Nahman Bialik, joyously celebrated the holidays dedicated to Dr. Herzl each 10th of Tammuz, and helped collect money for Keren Kayemed and Keren Heysod. The largest number of the First Aliyah (ershteh halutzim) were students from the Hebrew school who were infused with its spirit. The older students and the teachers who remained knew that here were educated the pioneers of a great, new experiment.

The Yiddish school, which was founded with the assistance of the progressive Horodenka Farein in N.Y., had a far different aspect. There the children sang and recited Jewish folksongs and Jewish poems written by modern Jewish poets. There they industriously learned and wrote about the work of the great Yiddish classic writers: Mendele Mocher Sforim, Y.L. Peretz, Sholem Aleichem, and others. They knew that they lived in a time when Yiddish literature resonated and the spirit of freedom hovered over all of Europe.

The WIZO Kindergarden

The fervent leaders of the Yiddish school and the Yiddishist community in our city were persons such as Asher Shtreyt, Yehudah Hirsh Sobol, and others who were totally taken in by the ideal of freedom for the masses. And they planted the ideal of freedom in their students and they prepared them to aspire to and struggle for a better and more beautiful tomorrow for all humanity. They inspired all to bring freedom not only for all the Jewish people but also for all oppressed people.

The two aforementioned schools, both of which had deeply rooted but opposite aspirations, were both Jewish national schools in which the children studied in the afternoon, after studying the mandatory curriculum of the Polish school. There were also assimilationist groups, made up mainly of lawyers and officials, who were not interested in learning Hebrew or in Jewish education; they sent their children only to the Polish school.

Whoever aspired to higher education sought out the Polish *gimnasia* and could, at least in theory, study further at the university. But in reality this was very hard to bring about; in addition to the financial difficulties there were also a variety of obstacles, mainly quotas, in enrolling Jews at the university.

School for Yiddish, Pupils and Teachers

The School for Yiddish, Committee and Teachers

In the years preceding the Holocaust, the Orthodox group Agudat Israel founded two schools that strived toward a modem education within the framework of a Jewish-religious curriculum, The Yavneh School for boys and the Beit Yacov school for girls. Horodenka Jews sought ways to acquire a secular, liberal education and at the same time not lose contact with the traditions and culture of their people.

But the horror of Nazism blotted all of this out. They killed the students along with their parents and their teachers. Thus, one of the noblest capitals in the history of our people was obliterated from the earth.

[Page 117]

Our Town as I Remember It

Gavriel Lindenberg

Translated by Yehudis Fishman

The house where we lived in Horodenka stood separate and isolated from the other houses of the city, although it was just a small distance from the market square that was the city's central point. It stood alone in a valley near a river. On one side of the river, the city spread out with a population of mostly Jews, a minority of Poles, and a smaller minority of Russians. On the other side was the big suburb of Kotokivka, whose population was mostly Russians (Ukrainians). The Jews referred to them simply as "goyim," in contrast to the Polish, who were called *Polyakim*. The spiritual center of this heavily populated suburb was a Greek-Orthodox Catholic church, which was in the center of the city and surrounded on all sides by Jewish houses. Every Sunday and holiday, a throng of both young and old would flow to this church, which was quite distant from their homes and was located in the heart of the Jewish section. In those days, when the crowds would come out of the church, the main road of the city would be blocked by the masses who were wrapped in lamb's fur that provided a shield from the bitter cold winters and from the heat of the scorching summers. At times there would be a procession coming from the church and proceeding through the neighborhood to bless the fields in the season of *Tamuz* (July), or to carve out a cross in the layer of thick ice that was on the pond in the season of *Teves* (January). As is customary, they carried many flags on these marches and the sight brought wonder to our eyes. We always watched as these marches made their way through the road next to our house. My little nephew, when he first saw this parade, burst out: "Behold, the flag of the tribe of Judah!" He had received a Jewish education and in his imagination, he connected these flags with the "flag of the tribe of Judah," from the song, "Lift up to Zion, a banner and a flag."

As was mentioned, our house was set apart from the other houses in the city. This was not because of its distance from the city, but because of its topographical position. It was situated in the valley that extended several meters up on one side to Kotokivka, and on the other to villages near the Dneister, like Potochishche, Strel'cheye, and others. The road also led to the Jewish village near Tshomolize. On the other side of the valley, opposite our house and at a distance of a few meters from the front door, there was a mountain with a steep path that led to our house. On this mountain stood a building that in my childhood was a hospital. Nuns draped in black robes would go in and out of it. By its structure, it seemed like a very old building. A thick wall surrounded a wide garden that was in front of the building. This wall was actually built on the slope of the mountain and supported in several places by slanted stone pillars. This gave it an ancient appearance, and reminded us of fortified castles from the middle ages. The wall extended the entire front length of the garden and faced the main road. A narrow path near the wall functioned as a primary road connecting us with the center of the city.

"Sobik's Teich" (The Pond)
Local Forest, Brandy Brewery

Inside the wall was a strange and mysterious world. The only link between that world and me was a gate in the wall into which the nuns were swallowed as they went about their tasks. Besides the gate in the wall, there was also an iron gate that opened periodically to receive a sick person from the neighborhood who was brought in a wagon or to bring out someone who had passed away. Through the gate, it was possible to peek and see a little of what was going on in the courtyard – recovering patients strolling in the garden and a small donkey tied to the water wagon. However, these pastoral sights could not negate the mystery that hovered around the building and the institution.

It is superfluous to point out that the hospital was just for the Christian population. The Jewish people primarily turned to Shimshon, the doctor who was an expert in enemas and cupping. However, he also used the more modern remedies like aspirin and quinine. The more progressive among the Jews turned to the Jewish doctor, Kanafas, or to one of the two Christian doctors – Roshko the Polak, or Tzipanovski, the Ukrainian.

After many years, the veil of mystery was removed from the hospital. Around the year 1910, the Polish Gymnasium was established in this building. I was one of its students. In the nice and quiet corridors now echoed the voices of hundreds of young men, most of them Jews. However, it was not easy for a father to agree to the idea that one's son should go to the Gymnasium on Shabbos, instead of going to shul. (The Jewish students were exempt from writing on Shabbos.) But what wouldn't a Jewish father do for the future of his son? He decided therefore to swallow this bitter pill, so as not to deny his son the prospect of becoming a doctor when he grew up.

Until then, I had only descended to two sections of the hospital wall. But the two other walls were also interesting. The third section faced the big square in front of a Polish church, the Roman Catholic one. In the middle of the square stood a tall statue of the "Mother of the Messiah." It was a wondrous sight to see an old Polish woman approaching the statue and kissing it. Probably the Jews were held back from sleeping in the square and approaching the opening of the church. Near the church was the house of the ruler of the district. A special path opposite the church led to this building where many Jews went to set their affairs in order.

The fourth section of this building was completely different from the other three, which faced the settlement and were situated toward daylight. The fourth faced north, across the river. This was not one of the walls of the garden, but rather a long wall that extended behind the hospital and had no opening, except for a small slot of a window. This wall was built at the height of a mountain, in a place that was very steep. It actually stood on a declining side that was supported by stone pillars built onto the slope.

A pleasant coolness and mysterious dimness rested on this place, even in the midst of a scorching summer day. The mystery in the air increased through the knowledge that behind the stone walls on the top of the mountain was a strange world of sick people and nuns. The narrow area between the slope of the mountains and the river was filled with hills and clefts; only one narrow path followed the length of the stream. The mountain slope never actually touched the river shore. The path was very steep, and only with great care was it possible to cross safely without slipping into the water.

However, once you crossed the lower path and reached the other side of the river, a new world was revealed to you. A broad path extended to the main road and led to the linen factory, which used the river waters. These waters were channeled into a wooden trench that brought them to the top of the giant wheel. When the waters fell on the wheel, they turned it and then shattered into thousands of sparkling fragments.

The mysterious and pleasing dimness that rested on this unique scene behind the hospital understandably contained a lot of romance. The location obviously contributed to this atmosphere. It was nice to sit here on one of the hills with a book in hand, distant and separate from the bustle of the world, to concentrate on reading, or to become absorbed in the predilections of the heart. And so the place was conducive, especially the hidden parts, as a place of isolation for boys and girls, and for hidden activities. The river held many secrets as it passed through these hidden corners. However, its path was quick, and it didn't have time for gossip or for revealing secrets out of school.

Once a year the river saw different kinds of views. Not only this, but the river itself actually became a messenger for a mitzvah. This occurred on the first day of Rosh Hashanah when the city dwellers went out to *Tashlich*. Jews of all ages who were G-d fearing, as well as righteous women, stood and emptied their pockets of their transgressions into the river. The river fulfilled its mission faithfully and carried all their sins into the great sea (according to the prayer) "so that they would not be remembered or counted and never again go up on the heart." Immediately after the high holidays another mitzvah presented itself to the river. On the banks of the river stood clusters of willows, some old and some new. When Sukos arrived, Jewish children would come and take some of its branches to complete the four species of the lulav, to cover the Sukah and to use for *Hoshanos*(five willows that are beaten on the ground) on Hoshana Rabbah (the last day of Sukos).

However, those days of holy use were few throughout the year. During most of the days of the year, the river was used for secular and ordinary activities. Every Sunday, the Ukrainian boys from the village would go down to wash their horses. The third day of the week was the market day. The neighboring farmers would bring their horses from the nearby market square to water the horses. And on every day of the week, the sound of the washerwomen would echo at a distance while they washed their white garments in the river water and beat them with a specially designated wooden implement called a *pralnick*. (By the way, this implement was adopted by Yiddish speakers, and by way of a joke, they would call a big and heavy book called "a *pralnick* book.")

For about three months of the year, the river took a rest from all its jobs, and was alone with itself under a thick layer of ice that covered its face. Not only was its voice silent, but also the whole surroundings were sunk in a winter slumber, under a white blanket. But, as soon as the snows began to melt, and the first sign of green was visible, immediately from the side of the factory, the shepherd boys appeared with their flocks. The main location of grazing space was across the river. More than once the goats actually reached our house. From the city came the only Jewish shepherdess, the shepherdess of the geese, the wife of Nathan Kohut, or, as we called her, "The Kohuteche." Every year, she would appear in the beginning of spring, leading in front of her the family of geese with their many goslings. For entire days, she would sit near our house and guard them. It was a captivating and interesting sight to look at the flock of geese and goslings going in and out of the water. But woe if one of us would dare to come close to them. With sudden anger, the geese would fall upon us and try to finish us off. While we still had breath in us, we would escape to find refuge inside the walls of our houses.

Until now, I have spoken about the river in the singular, by which I refer to its main channel that was close to our house, and flowed in a fixed and steady stream. This is appropriate for a calm river that "accepts the yoke of mitzvos and good deeds"– a river that doesn't waste its waters frivolously and guards each drop so that it should bring benefit to civilization, moving the wheels of the mills to supply people with their allotment of bread. However, there were two other channels whose waters were not harnessed for work. They flowed freely, far from the ordinary stream in the wide part of the valley. These were free to spread out according to their soul's desire, jumping and skipping over the smooth stones that were often in their way. The waters of these streams were exceptionally pure because no human hand touched them, forcing them into narrow, sullied pools. So they flowed one beside the other, along an extended patch of land. Only when the tamed river finished its job of grinding the wheat did it descend from its dwelling place to join its wild brothers, the impetuous and reckless ones, merging again into one stream.

All the businesses that needed a lot of water or sewage naturally concentrated around the river. Two resources could not be found within the city area. Across the streams, inside the borders of the valley, was the city slaughterhouse. From it, the protracted and pitiful cries of the cattle that were being led to the slaughter reached our ears. This building sparkled from afar due to its white plastered roof that was unlike those of most of the city houses, whose roofs were made from wooden shingles.

Not far from the slaughterhouse was a stone quarry that provided the material for building the few stone houses that could be found in the city and its environs. Stone houses were generally considered luxuries, and only prosperous people erected them. Most of the city's houses were built from wood, with a thick layer of plaster. Beams of wood served as the structure that was put together by expert builders. Wooden slabs were stretched out between the pillars. The slabs were made from wood pulp and were plastered inside and out with a thick layer of plaster blended with straw that was prepared from black soil. Over this layer was spread a thin layer of red clay, which was also used for brickmaking, was spread. It took many weeks to dry these clay slabs, and only afterwards was the house plastered and ready for use.

This method of building was influenced by the proximity of our city to the district of the Carpathian Mountains that provided wood for the cheapest of the cheap. The plastering did not involve any expense except for the manual labor and the work of the feet to mix the mud and straw. This method was simple and cheap. In the years before the First World War, this building method with baked bricks came into fashion more and more. The knobs for doors and windows were also improved. In our old house, the windows were closed by two hooks, fastened by rings below the window ledge and above the upper lintel. The door closed on a moving hinge that opened up by pushing on the doorknob. Here one could clearly see the source of the expression the "palm of the lock," since this part did truly resemble a palm. It seems that this form was kept and passed down from the earliest time

In the regular course of years, an authentic building movement did not appear in the city. Still, there were a number of Jews who drew their livelihood from construction. Among those I remember was Zalman Suchar, who was, if I recall correctly, a building architect. He was of small stature and with a slight hunchback, and belonged to the group, "The Youth of Zion." His total opposite was Raphael Sofer, a tall Jew with a pointed beard, who was a certified architect and was hired as a contract laborer. Father would ask his advice in every matter involving changes and improvements to our house. Among those in this profession, I also remember the name of Yochanan Baer, though I do not at all recall what he looked like.

Among the buildings that were built before the First World War, it is important to single out the *shul* in the courtyard of the Rebbe from Horodenka. This was a building about ten meters tall; the top floor was meant to serve as the women's section. Its building stopped with the outbreak of the war. The building's structure remained standing in its desolation till after the end of the war, at which time the entire courtyard was sold to Meir Frischling (who for some reason was called Meir Punkali, perhaps because his origin was Russia; all Russians were called by Jews of Galicia, "Ponye," or sometimes with the added adjective, Ponye *Ganev* – Ponye the thief.) When our family returned from its wanderings in Austria in the year 1919, the building stood empty. My father rented it for manufacturing tombstones, which were then ordered in great amounts to mark the burial sites of those who passed away during the five years of the war. Among the work that we created was a large and beautiful (according to the perception of

Hordenkans) memorial stone dedicated to the holy ones whose were killed by the government and who were put to death by hanging by the Russians in the year 1915. These happenings were the result of a belief that the Jews set the city on fire to signal to the Austrians that the Russians were coming.

There was a complete change in those days – in the years 1919/1920 – in the progress of building in the city. Many houses were destroyed during the war, and there was a need to construct them anew. This was accomplished with the help of the new government of Poland. Building then increased greatly. The builders introduced a newer and cheaper process: bricks of earth mixed with straw were built between the beams of wood that formed the structure of the building. Sometimes buildings were put up from these bricks, even without a wooden structure. As I remember, these buildings were able to stand securely, at any rate, until the year 1925, when I left Horodenka.

Among the houses built out of stone and bricks was the house of our closest neighbor, Eli Yosef Shpierir and his wife, Chava Miriam. Even during my childhood, they were an old, childless couple who were once well off, but who with the flow of time, had lost their wealth. They made a living, with difficulty, by maintaining the bathhouse, which was generally active only on the eve of the Sabbaths and holidays. The building was a too-big, two-story building that seemed very neglected and forlorn. Except for the front wall, all the walls were not plastered and were covered with soot from the smoke of the bathhouse. The building stood on a slope, half way between our house and the road, in such a way that its lower floor with the bathhouse in it, stood entirely underground, in front of the road. The connection between the road and the apartments on the upper level were by means of a wooden bridge ten meters long. This bridge, shaky and worn with age, added its own character to the building. The living quarters contained two apartments, one of which was fit for living or manufacturing. In the course of time, there was a factory for the soap of Isadore Aryeh. He was the son-in-law of Yankel the milkman, who was a farmer in the nearby village and who would appear daily in his wagon providing fresh milk to the area's inhabitants.

For about two years, there existed in this dwelling a shoe polish factory named "Levanon." The polish had a picture of the Hebrew high school in Yaffo, and instructions in easy Hebrew, that was popularly called "Zionist *Globen.*" In short, this was to a certain extent, the manufacturing section of Horodenka, which meshed with the various businesses that sprung up in our house, from time to time, according to the needs of the time, and the demands of the market and its lacks.

The existence of the industrial district was brought about in great measure from the presence of "living waters" in this place. The spring flowed from beneath the ground near the door of the bathhouse; its waters were clear and pure. However, the waters were hard and not good either for cooking or for washing. For those whose were not used to it, it was even difficult to drink. Still, their work made possible the existence of this important establishment.

The Grand Synagogue

From the source of this water, whose accepted name was, "Das Rindel," was an iron pipe that brought the water to our house. The water flowed without interruption, day and night. If we did not use it up, it would immediately flow outside to a ditch and from there to the river. Thus our house benefited from conveniences that were not found in any other house in the city: supplies of water for drinking and sewage. All the other city residents would buy a limited water supply from the water carriers who would carry on their shoulders a yoke with two buckets, or from those who would transport water on wagons. The removal of trash water was simpler. This was cast into the street, in front of the house or behind it. However no damage resulted, since in the summer the water quickly evaporated, and in the rainy season, one bucket of water more or less did not make much of a difference.

The waters of the river were the basis for the main business in our house, which was washing, or, more precisely, the machine for cleaning and ironing white garments till they were stiff and shining. One should know that washing in Horodenka fifty years ago was not like washing in these days. The purpose of washing in our times is to ease the life of the "foundation of the house," (a term for Jewish woman) and to make clean white clothes available to her for her family. However, in those days, it was accepted and agreed upon that the "foundation" of the house was obligated, in addition to her family responsibilities, to wash the white clothes with her own hands, or at least to supervise the washing by the hired washer. It would not enter the mind of a woman to give over her white clothes to a devilish washing machine. If a washing machine had existed in Horodenka, it would have had another purpose, which was bound up with the fashion of those days.

One of the main parts of the male wardrobe was a stiff and shiny collar; many different shapes were designated for this collar, appropriate to the personal tastes and elegant fashions of the wearer. The most selective dressers also wore cuffs, called *mandshetn*. Regarding the dickey, there were those who insisted on wearing a shirt with a stiff and starched dickey – though most were satisfied with a type of a shield called a *forlange* that they would wear over the shirt. In short, there was a wide pillow designated for treating this particular garment. This was the job of the cleaning lady in Horodenka.

It was not the way of a Jew, especially an inventive Jew, to be satisfied with one profession. My father had another profession – that of a sign painter. Due to his natural talent and to the experience he accrued working for a year and a half in New York, he acquired an appreciable knowledge in this field, and produced by his hand an established and perfected service.

Among the signs that he painted, there were two types that could be called professional. The first type was referred to as "eagles." In Austria tobacco was owned by a government monopoly. The farmers were obligated to give all their produce to the government and the processing occurred in government factories. The wholesale marketing was given over to specific tobacco markets, which were called by the name of "traffic," or to selected smaller stores. Each of these stores was obligated to set up a round sign of uniform size with the two-headed Austrian Eagle. These eagles were a significant part of his work, since every tobacco and cigar store was obligated to have this sign by government decree.

His second type of work occurred during a particular season. There was a business crisis about five years before the First World War. Many Jews went into the business of loaning money to the neighboring farmers (with their fields and property as a lien and security) to enlarge their farm to buy machinery, or to cover the expenses of their flight to Canada. This protected a great number of farm workers, among them many farmers from our surroundings. The loan business apparently had a strong power of attraction, and many Jews were trapped in it, sinking their savings into it.

When the latter was not enough, they took out loans from banks for this need. And behold, a crisis broke out in the year 1912. The higher finance establishments of the country felt that the political horizon was darkening and the war was about to erupt. So they began to diminish credit and call back the loan documents, instead of exchanging them as they had previously done. Because of this, many of the merchants reached a situation where they were forced to declare bankruptcy. In this case, the creditor was able to foreclose on all the property of the debtor, to close his business, and to undermine the foundation of his existence. However, there was a straightforward strategy to prevent this situation. Before the declaration of bankruptcy, documents would be brought to the courthouse, which would prove that the property belonged not to Mr. X but to his relative, or – the way it was done in many cases – to his wife. Therefore, he made a complete transfer of his property to his relative, friend, or wife. The creditors though could contest the transfer, and in some cases, they actually did so. Mostly however, they were not really interested in destroying the existence of the borrower, and they were forced to settle with him, and to agree to a partial payment of the debt, and to a protracted payment plan.

The change in ownership of the business office necessitated a change in the sign. However, here too a strategy was needed that made it possible to follow the law as well as keeping the sign with the name of the previous owners of the business. The strategy was that on top of the big sign was suspended a smaller sign that carried the name of the new owner, and under it in small print was the previous address in Polish: "Pshodtom." When the two signs were joined, one could read, in black and white, that the business belonged to so and so, but formerly belonged to another so and so. The new owners were modest, and therefore saw no need for a blatant display of their ownership.

These signs with the *pshodtom* on them were for a certain time the style of business for Horodenka and only a few of the businesses were missing them. The preparations for declaring bankruptcy were made as usual in hidden chambers. However, one had to pre-order the signs. Thus my father became, to a certain extent, a member of the secret circle of those who prepared for this move.

My father's occupation of sign painting brought in good money for the support of the family. However, since he worked in this field only to a small extent and sporadically, he decided upon another venture more suited to the large area around the house and the unlimited abundance of water. So in the year 1907, he opened a shingle factory with two friends, Buni Fleshner, may he be separated for life, and Motti Shertzer, who is currently living in Israel. For several years, the factory prospered, until serious competition arose – a Polish establishment that the Jews referred to as *Der Poviat*. Because of this competition, the factory dwindled until it was completely closed.

Years passed. The conditions of the world war wreaked havoc on all phases of life. Some livelihoods withered and others sprang up. Success shined especially on the diligent, who knew how to explore risky businesses. My father was never included in these, but he succeeded in establishing – at least for the duration of a year – a new kind of factory made possible by the times.

The most popular drink in our place was coffee. This drink was blended with an appropriate amount of chicory that grew sufficiently in the houses of the well off, but was almost zero near the houses of the poor. The main supplier of chicory in our area was the Frank factory, whose product was known by its red wrapping with a green ribbon. (This package also functioned for cosmetics, supplying rouge for the cheeks of the girls of the village and the city). Because of the conditions of the war, there was a shortage of chicory in the country. It entered the mind of Hirsh Birnboym, the close friend of my father, to manufacture a substitute for chicory from roasted barley with an addition of molasses from the leftovers of refined sugar, and a small amount of roasted and ground beet sugar. Immediately an oven was built for drying and roasting. They also set up the machinery for crushing the sugar beets. For grinding, they used small grinding stones called *zhorne* that were moved manually by the household workers. The products were wrapped in wrapping similar to the Frank product, and were very successful in the market.

It didn't take long before the Russians were defeated and the Austrian army took their place. Because of the dwindling supply of chicory, the army too lacked this product, and the factory began to provide the army with large amounts. But the good days did not last. The Austrian army stood its ground only for a few weeks, and as the army retreated, the majority of Jewish residents also left their homes because they were worried about the consequences of the invasion of the Russian soldiers, who came straight from the front. In truth, these worries were not groundless. The nine city residents that remained were hung for no reason, the city center was wrecked and burned, and many lost all their property.

The suburb Kotikovka that lay on the ascending part of the road opposite our house was populated almost completely by the

Ukrainians, with only a few scattered Jews. However, the first houses behind the bridge were Jewish houses. From among the residents of these houses, I recall a few because of the special connection that we had with them. There was the store of Ahron Leib Cohen, where I used to go as my father's messenger when the temptation of smoking overcame him. (There were periods when he was able to conquer this temptation.) There was also the home of Avrohom Cohen, a tall and swarthy Jew. Both of them prayed in the "Zion*Farein*," and therefore stand out very much in my memory. However, the personality that stuck out most in this neighborhood was Noach Shpierer, a very old Jew with a white beard and piercing eyes. He walked like a soldier, energetically, with a straight stature and a protruding chest. It seems that in his youth, he was a man of very strong temperament, with "his hand against everyone and everyone's hand against his." As I recall, in my days, he was involved in many arguments in his place of prayer, the big *shul*. There was a well-known saying that whomever Noach Shpierer offered a greeting, had better hold on to his cheeks with care, out of worry for the consequences of that "extension of the hand."

In the midst of the suburb of Kotikovka was also the home of Yossi Shapira, the *chazzan* of the big *shul*. He had several sons, whom I remember only the first born, who was known by his nickname, Leizer Bogan. On the other side of the bridge near the main road, there were only a few houses. There was the beautiful house of Shmarya Kugelmas. Near this house was the home of Fishel Wasser. To the extent that my memory serves me, it was actually very difficult to call this place any kind of a dwelling. It was sort of a dark cellar with one tiny window, and if I'm not mistaken, one or two goats also lived in it. The house of Shmarya Kugelmas stood in the corner of a narrow alley among whose residents I remember in particular, Baruch Leib Liser. On the other side of the alley near the main street, there was also one large house. Right behind it, on a hill there was a narrow path that led straight to Yehudah Wolf Shuchner's store, which faced the parallel road.

On this hill stood a cluster of houses with a large courtyard in the center. The real estate owner of Horodenka, Baron Romaszkan, owned this cluster of houses, whose residents were Polish. Around this house was a garden. In one part was a vegetable garden and in another part grew fragrant lilac trees that spread out their fragrance with the coming of spring. After a while, a local post office also was established there.

The name of Baron Romaszkan was bound up with a special image that was seared into my memory during the days of my youth. The manufacture of liquor in Austria was a government monopoly and the primary seller, both wholesale and retail, was centered in a special store in Propinatzia. The distillery that provided the liquor for Propinatzia was in the Baron's courtyard. It was usually transported on a wagon harnessed to a pair of oxen whose long horns evoked fear. The appearance of oxen pulling their burden and transporting their precious liquid was a part of the Horodenka scene of my childhood, and it's impossible not to mention it.

On the other side of the road, opposite the cluster of gentile houses, the wall of the hospital spread out, and after it began the houses of the city. The road took a sharp right turn, and when it reached the crossroads, the main road appeared in its full length and ran through the middle of the market square.

The houses around the market square had a character that was unique among the business sections of the rest of the world. One door was next to the other, in the closest proximity, making it possible to use every cubit of precious space for a source of livelihood. As the popular saying goes: "A door in the market is a window in heaven." The exceptions were the first two houses behind the hospital that were built according to the style of the city suburbs. They each had one story with a wooden porch painted white, and around the house, a flower garden surrounded by a wooden fence painted white or blue. One of these two houses belonged to a certain official, and Moshe Kalmus, a clean-shaven Jew of short stature who was involved in land business, owned the other.

Near the house of Moshe Kalmus stood the house of Hersh Leyb Sitz, which was given over completely to the business section around the market. This house also had one story, like most of the houses of the city, but it had two fronts, both occupied by stores that were rented out to different storekeepers. Among these stores I remember two that I want to single out.

One of the distinguishing marks of the Horodenka scene was the open water canals, that spread throughout the length of all the streets between the road and the sidewalk. On one part of the main road, the sidewalk widened and covered the canal under it; on the other roads, the canals were open, and bridges stretched over from the road to the sidewalk. One must admit that these bridges, shielded by railings from two sides, added a picturesque aspect to the city. Together with rows of chestnut trees, they gave a beautiful appearance to the main streets. In the rainy days of summer or fall, and in the spring when the snows melted, the canals were full of water that flowed powerfully to the river. When I was walking with my friends from school, my soul desired to plunge into them with my new boots. They were not worried about the water! So, I entered the canals instead of going on the sidewalk, like civilized people do. This happened many times until word reached my father's ears. He took the opportunity to give me a lecture in the laws of proper etiquette in a captivating manner. As was made known to me afterward, it was the daughter of Zeyde Rindenoy who told my father about the escapades of his son. There is no doubt that this detail reminded me of the owner of this store, who otherwise was no different, that any other storeowner in the neighborhood.

The second resident that I remember well was Meir Frishling the watchmaker. He was one of my father's friends, and daavened with the Zionist minyan. Frequently I went to his store with father, and naturally I felt inclined to check out his work, when he was occupied with those little wheels, alternately taking them apart and putting them back together.

The owner himself, Hersh Leyb Sitz, was known in the city not just because he worked in the city center, but because of his special work. He worked as an unofficial lawyer, what they called, *vinkel shrieber*. People would turn to him to get some legal advice in situations where a professional lawyer wasn't needed, such as writing requests to legal or administrative authorities. His daughter Pepi was the high school friend of my sister, and his son Eyber sat on the same bench as me in school.

The market square was divided by the main street into two sections of unequal size. On the left of the road was the smaller section, which was designated just for human traffic. On market days the farmers' wives primarily gathered there. They brought eggs, chickens, vegetables and fruit to sell. The other section that was much bigger than the left side was split in the middle by a street that was specially designated for riding vehicles. On market days, which took place on the third day of the week (Tuesday), the square was bustling with an abundance of people and vehicles, and was extremely crowded. On other days of the week, traffic was much lighter.

Around the market square, stores were clustered according to their wares. People's primary livelihood was from the money they made on market days. In my childhood, on the right side of the square, there was a special section of booths, called *budkes*. These were occupied by peddlers of merchandise, but they could not compete with the storekeepers. The merchandise sold there were five and dime materials – woolen thread, cotton for knitting socks and sweaters, cheap linen, etc. There were also booths for selling various baked goods.

From the two sides that were designated for booths, houses stood that were primarily filled with stores. However, there were also some homes, among which was the home of Yudel Ekerling, whose business was small bank loans, and who was called the *bankel master*.

Among the stores that were in this square, I recall the store of Maltzi Bergman, which was run by his two grown sons, Yossel and

Shoel Bergman. Their brother, Leibish Bergman, who had fled to America many years before the war, was one of my father's close friends. The members of that family were experts in fishing, and raised fish in ponds. One of the special offshoots of their business was crab hunting, which supplied this desirable food for many royal houses in Europe. This family also owned a brick-making factory.

The houses around the market square were arranged like the Hebrew letter *Ches* (i.e., shaped like a doorway - trans.) At the right end stood houses. One of the beautiful homes on the edge of the market square was the house of Yechezkel Shpierer. This house had one level, but since it was built on slightly elevated ground on several steps, underneath it there was room for several stores. These were primarily designated for the business of exporting eggs. These merchants were known as 'egg packers,' since their main work was to gather eggs in cartons and prepare them for export. I remember only two of them: Pinni Bornstein and Toybe Agatshteyn.

I had a special connection with the house of Yechezkel Shpierer, since among his tenants was my uncle, my mother's brother, Mendel Flor. (One of his sons became famous in the thirties as an international chess champion named Salo Flor, and he visited Israel in the year 1934.) I remember my uncle's home very well. I think it was the same style as most of the dwellings in the market square. In the front, of course, was the store. The inside room behind the store was always in the dark, since it received only a dim light from the window in the door connecting to the store and from a window facing the other room. This room too was illuminated only indirectly from the kitchen window that faced the courtyard. In general, these were dwellings without much sunlight or air and enveloped those who lived there in a rather gloomy atmosphere.

Behind the house of Yechezkel Shpierer was a long row of stores among whose owners I remember very few. My uncle's nearest neighbor was Feivish Muller, who also had a grocery store. In this row was also the store of Chaike Shtreck, a capable and unusually energetic woman, who succeeded in maintaining her position in business even after the death of her husband, who passed away in his youth. An exception to most of the stores in that row, which were groceries, was the store of Yehoshua Pomerantz, who sold holy books, religious objects, and some secular story books, and in later years, Hebrew textbooks.

This row of stores was attached to the big market square that served on market days as a gathering place for the wagons of the farmers who came in from the villages. The merchandise that was sold in these stores met the needs of the ordinary person such as flour, salt, kerosene and matches, and other basic needs. The stores in the opposite row were different in character. Some stores sold leather and boots, and only a few grocery stores like those of Yankel Haber and Shlomo Shtreyt met the ordinary needs of the citizens of the city. They sold a greater and more colorful selection of supplies; some even sold delicatessen.

The row of stores that stood almost in a straight line with the statue of the "holy mother" in the Polish gathering square, opened with the leather store of Binyamin Reichman. Right behind it was a store, which I have difficulty correctly characterizing as it was neither a restaurant nor bar, though a person could always find something there to quench his thirst or quell his hunger. Mainly this was a kind of club where, in a narrow space of four by four, people of all stripes – merchants and middlemen – gathered to complete their business on a light drink with a snack. There were also unemployed young men who came to peruse a newspaper or to while away their free time in playing chess, either as actual players or as observers (kibitzers, according to chess terminology). The conductor of this colorful gathering was the owner himself, Hershel Sucher. He always stood behind the counter, and even more than he was involved with his business matters, he participated in conversations and expressed his opinions like one of the experts on the burning political issues in Judaism or Zionism. He was always immersed in these matters, commenting on everything and offering a *halachic* opinion on every issue that came up for discussion or on the political scene. Now, since the innkeeper was a consummate Zionist and one of the main speakers in the group *Bnai Zion*, his store became a meeting place for Zionists, especially the Zionist youth. There, they would spend their free hours and receive training for Zionist activities and communal service.

Hershel Sucher's store, therefore, was not just a store but also an organization that had a significant impact on the life of the city. From his store on, there were a variety of stores, most of which sold leather and boots. Among them was also the store of Hershel Berman, one of the young Jewish businessmen in the city who was well off and modern. His son Meshulem was one of the select few who were sent to another city to study in high school, even before there was a high school in Horodenka. He would awaken the interest of other young boys when he came to visit for holidays or vacations. He studied in Chernovitz, Bukovina, which was considered a German city, in contrast to the Polish ones that were prevalent throughout the cities of Galicia. In Chernovitz, he boarded with his uncle, his mother's brother. My father mentioned him occasionally and referred to him simply as Fishel Orner, but in Chernovitz he was known as Professor Brener and was one of the heads of the German high school in Chenovitz. At the end of the war, he was appointed the head of the Bukovina testing committee, which was located in Vienna. In the year

1917, when I had to turn to this committee about a testing matter, I received a sealed response from the hands of Professor Brener, and my father identified him immediately as the son of Hershel Berman.

Near the store of Hershel Berman, stood the store of Moshe Shukhner, who was also a leather merchant. His son Asher was one of the outstanding members of the young Zionists group. He was the special chess player of Horodenka, and as was known to me, he was held up as the classic Bohemian, who by his unique life style deviated from the typical nature of the average Horodenkan.

In the center of this row of stores, a wide opening burst forth near the open gates to a space called the "Einfor house," which belonged to Shlomo Avraham Shor. He was a welcoming host who was one of the more important homeowners in the city and was in the camp of the most orthodox. His son Kalman Shor, however, was a young man who shortened his beard and clothes, and was a Zionist who *daavened* in the *Zion Farein*.

I already mentioned the two grocery stores of Yankel Haber and Shlomo Shtreyt, which were an anomaly among the leather stores in this row. However, I can't just mention the names; I need also to elaborate on each of these families.

Several ties bound our family with the Haber family. The first was Yankel Haber, one of my father's personal friends. He was well-off, deliberate, honest and straight, one of the few who was not involved in monkey business. He had the best buyers and everyone knew you could find the highest quality merchandise in his store. The store was not exceptional in its modern arrangements, but there was the maximum cleanliness that could exist in such primitive circumstances. Aside from the top quality, the purchasers were treated to the pleasant faces of the two sellers, Yankel's wife and his oldest daughter Dunyah, who stood out because of her height and in her striking beauty. The younger daughter Bella Haber was my sister's friend in high school, and was frequently invited to our house.

I rarely had occasion to enter the store of Shlomo Shtreyt and don't know what to say about it, but I think that it too stood out for all those good qualities that I mentioned in the store of Yankel Haber. Here, however, the most important thing was not the store, but the family of the store's owner. The father, Shlomo Shtreyt, was not only one of the most important residents and supporters, but also one of the foremost Torah scholars of the city. Certainly, he desired to raise and educate his children in the ways of Torah and *Mitzvot*, but transgressions arose and the times were confused. In the midst of the storm of war, the family was uprooted from its place and arrived in Vienna, the royal capital city. Under those conditions it was difficult to protect the fermenting wine from souring in order to protect the children from straying from the ways of their fathers. By the time the family returned from its wanderings, the process could be described by the verse: "The children struggled in her womb." The father continued to follow his path, but as for the children, not only didn't they walk in the ways of their father, they were even separated in their own ways. The first born, Asher, became an enthusiastic Bundist, speaking in Yiddishisms. Together with his fellow Bundists, Baruch Itzik Shpierer, Issac Fink, Yehudah-Hersh Sobel, Yossel Katz and others, he founded the Yiddish school, joining the network of the school of *Tzishe*. He himself spread Torah to Jewish children, many of them among the poorest of the nation who lost the spark of the old *cheder*, but did not find the way to the revival of Hebrew. In contrast, the younger one, Yehoshua, was an ardent Zionist, active in student groups and political corners, sinking all his talent and energy into Zionism, and above all the 613 *Mitzvot*, in all their detail.

Two by two, the dispute was drawn into the family and encompassed in miniature the three main streams of the passing generations: the observant stream, those who ignored the concept of exile, and those who saw it as a necessary reality. The youngest son Yehoshua remained faithful to the path, and he is now with us in our homeland. Anyway, the polemic ended as it ended, and woe to us that it ended in such a manner.

I would not fulfill my obligation to the Shtreyt family if I did not mention the youngest daughter Feige. For a short time, she was my student in a small group of girls who learned Hebrew and Bible from me around the year 1922. Among those who participated in this group, I especially remember her and her friend Rochel Kvetsher. They excelled in their knowledge with their true longing to acquire the language in its fullness. Last but not least, I remember the glow of their faces. Rochel was the daughter of the carpenter Shikel Kvetsher. I used to go in and out of his factory that made frames for signs, and at times I went in to borrow carpenter tools for my father's work.

Shlomo Shtreyt's house was the last in this row of houses, and only a narrow alley divided it from the row of houses that enclothed the *Chet* of the market square. In the section near the Shtreyt's house between it and the main street, there were several small stores. One was the stores of Paye Grapakh, or as she was called, Paiyakale. On the sign still rested the name of her departed husband, Yonah Grapakh. The store was run by the widow and her daughters and was one of the most successful stores in the city. It had two entrances to parts of the store. The stores in this row were so narrow that only if you joined the two stores could you perhaps create one significant space. Garments and trifles were sold in her store. The store supported not just the widow and her daughters, but also the new family that was created when one of the daughters married a man named Vabel, who came from outside Horodenka.

Near the store of Paya Grapakh was a small store that was not concerned with supplying the material needs of the Jewish settlement, but with providing for the spiritual needs of the new generation. This was the store of Motel Horvitz. This was a long, narrow store; a shelf upon which books were organized by category took up half its width. In the second half, there was scarcely any room left for two men standing side by side to walk. I myself didn't go to his store; I was too young in those days – all of twelve years old – but one of its regular visitors stayed in our house, and so I came across reading material that was sold – or perhaps borrowed – from this store. Rocklass of Berlin were the primary printers of these books. They came out in a popular edition that was cheaper than the best books from Germany and Europe. Among the books that reached our house, I remember especially a thick volume of Origin of Species, by Darwin, and the dramas of Ibsen and Strindberg. In short, this was serious literature that could open the mind, and awaken the thinking of an intelligent person.

Among the group of readers of the library of Motel Horvitz, I had a relationship with a certain group of four friends who drew their spiritual nourishment from this source. This group included two students in the fifth class of the Polish high school, who, though they came to this establishment a few years late, rose above their older peers in spiritual aspirations. The other two were not students, but stimulated their intellectual and spiritual needs by reading and thinking. This four-fold friendship was captured in a picture that showed the four of them in the year 1913, a short time before the outbreak of the First World War.

The one who stood out the most, and was the most talented, was Shmuel Abbah Sofer, the son of Pinchas, the shul attendant, who served in the courtyard of the Horodenka Rebbe. Shmuel Abba was sharp and quick, and his mouth was always full of wise sayings and paradoxes. He attended high school on a scholarship that was usually given to fellow students who had difficulty in their studies. It seemed to me that he was far from excellent, and in general appeared as a cynic who despised ideals. During the war he disappeared from Horodenka, and never came back. From people who came from Chernowitz, I found out that he was a reporter for the Yiddish paper Poalei Zion, and was killed by the Nazis a short time before the city's liberation by the Soviet forces.

The second student in this group was Voveh Shtrum, who is now with us in Israel. He too was forced to provide for his food and studies through teaching, since his father Kmiel Shtrum was not well off and had a large family. The Shtrum family was one of the few who all went to the land of Israel. Most of them were involved in Zionist activities in Horodenka. I should especially single out Noson Shtrum, whose dedication to Zionist activities knew no bounds, and who put his shoulder to every task that most others shirked. People joked that in each of his pockets nestled a container for each Zionist organization: in one, *Keren Hayesod*, in the second, *Keren Kayemet*, in the third, the *Shekel* committee, and in the fourth, the Hebrew school committee.

The third in the group, Meyer Kron, also settled in Israel, but is not in our acquaintance. If memory serves me, his appearance in those days was that of a handsome, Hebrew-speaking young man who came periodically to visit his friend Berl Mosberg. He was not actually from Horodenka, but from a nearby village. Perhaps his connection to working with the earth influenced him in the pioneering effort to make Aliya and attempt to become a farmer in our land. His Aliyah began in the year 1912, but he quickly became unhappy with the conditions in Israel and returned to Horodenka. With the outbreak of the war, he left Horodenka and never came back. Only in the year 1933, with the deterioration of conditions in Europe, did he arrive in Israel from Vienna.

Finally, the fourth in this group of friends was Beryl Mosberg, who ten years later became my brother-in-law. He was the proletariat among the four; from his childhood he earned his living working in our laundry. The work was arranged in such a way that he was free two or sometimes three days a week. He used these days for reading and self-growth. Thus he merited entering this select group of young intellectuals. About four years before the war broke out, he and I made a pact that we would only speak Hebrew between us. We kept this pact for years until it became second nature. Actually, we were practically the only ones in the city who used the Hebrew language in daily life.

My description of these four upright young men conveys a little of the spiritual atmosphere that rested upon the youth of that generation. These young people absorbed their spiritual food from the books in Motel Horvitz's store. This provided them with a window to the great world of literature and creativity.

Before I leave the market square, I want to focus on two related matters: the police and the theater. There were two types of police in Horodenka, as in all of Austria: the gendarmes under the government and court system, and the police who were under the local city authorities. These two were distinct in their clothes and in their weapons. The first group dressed in hats with sharp copper points and was armed with guns and bayonets. When they were on duty, they appeared mostly with bayoneted rifles. Their appearance alone aroused in the hearts of the citizens a desire to avoid meeting them, and how much more so, their weapons. The city police dressed in civilian clothes, but to delineate their authority, they wore long swords that were never drawn from their sheaths but rather served a decorative function. Among the few police who dominated at that time, I remember two: one was tall and dark and named Benedict; the second was short and had a beard that was almost white with age. He was Michael and the children teased him calling him "Michael Tshaporda."

The theatre in my city was very simple. In various street corners they set up slightly elevated wooden beams upon which were set lanterns. Each day toward evening, it was possible to see one of the city police going from lantern to lantern with a ladder on his shoulder to light them. Two or three years before the outbreak of the war, an iron beam was put up in the corner of the market square at the crossroads and a giant lamp was suspended that cast its light over the entire square. But the complex mechanism of the lamp caused the policemen many difficulties, until one of the Jewish advisors of the city council arose and gave some scholarly advice. "Before we struggle in vain to turn the policeman into a mechanic, it's better that we take a mechanic and turn him into a policeman."

This corner where the lamp stood was the most prestigious corner in the market square. Practically every year at the time of the annual fair, a group of actors would appear to set up a tent in this corner. The official title of this theatrical performance was "A Comedy," and the actors were comedians. One of the most notable acts was tightrope walking over the heads of the crowded masses.

Later the market square was split up, with the main street of the city extending a long way – about three or four hundred meters – until the crossroads. There, the path turned right, at the side of the courthouse building, and continued to the train station and to the village of Shtorniatin. The main street turned into the road that led to Syniatin.

On the right side of the main street, which was attached to the market square, was the store of Mordechai Shnitzer, which contained iron and building materials. I remember Mordechai Shnitzer as a short old man who ran the store and handled his goods to the extent that his advanced age allowed him. However the life force of the store was his young son Simchaleh, a young man of average height who was always in a state of perpetual motion. His oldest son Chaim, was seen infrequently in the store; he was the studious one in the family. He was ordained as a rabbi, and was the son-in-law of Rabbi Elimelech

Ashkenazi. Most of the neighboring farmers who came to buy iron implements for their farms did not notice him dealing with the merchandise. With the passage of time, simple farm machinery like harvesters and hand-driven threshing machines was brought into the store.

In my childhood I was familiar with the store and its owners since I went in frequently, as my father's messenger, to buy machinery or merchandise. After the First World War, there were changes in the family relationships. The patriarch of the family, Mordchele, passed away. The business center was burnt and destroyed during the Russian invasion, and the merchandise was moved to the house of Shnitzer, that stood on the other street of the main street, not far from the market square. Inevitably, Reb Chaim had to leave his "four ells of Torah," to be involved with "settling the world," and he took part in running the store with his brother Shlomele, who continued to be the "first violin" in the business. Meanwhile, the children grew up, and the sons of Reb Chaim began to work in the business, together with the older ones.

However, this last statement contains an exaggeration. In truth, the main worker was Chaim's first-born son, Meshulem. The other three sons didn't really work, each for a different reason. Moshe, who was a little younger than Meshulem, had a very leisurely temperament, averse to much activity. On the other hand, Shmuel Abba had overflowing energy, which stirred him to leave his home and city and move to South America. The youngest son Yaakov studied Torah in his uncle's house in Sokol, and came home only as a guest for the holidays. After several years, he was sent to Israel to learn in Hebrew University. Thanks to this, there is a remnant of this multi-branched family even now with us in the land.

After the First World War, in 1919, our family returned to Horodenka as one of the last families to return. We spent a long time in Western Austria, and waited for the opportunity to immigrate to Israel, without wasting time and energy in the chains of intermediate stations on the way. Only when our hopes were dashed did we involuntarily return to Horodenka. Now the Jewish settlement passed through a short time under Ukrainian rule. This period stood out for the deep understanding of the nationalist longings of the Jewish nation. All the Jewish youth, except for those that were caught up in the Bundist spirit, were part of the Shomer branches that were involved in dialogues of Nationalist concerns, and in learning Jewish history and the Hebrew language. At the center of interest were Buber's writings on Hassidim. The youth, who were then removed from Torah and Mitzvot, had a revived interest in Hassidim through the perspective of Buber, and became enthused through it. There were two Hebrew schools in the city, one directed by Illa Libster, and the second by Asher Yungerman; both produced many students. (Parenthetically, Libster was a student of Rabbi Z.P. Chayes in Vienna, who was then engrossed in the study of Aramaic and its grammar. After a while, he went to Paris to learn chemistry and became an inventor. Some say competitors who were jealous of the success of his inventions pushed him out of the field.) In short, there was a spirit of Hebrew in the city, and understandably, Meshulem Shnitzer was also caught up in this spirit. His Torah training, on one hand, gave him an adequate background, and because his interest in Torah was not furthered due to conditions of war, he channeled his interest into the language. Thus, his propensity for Hebrew was more rooted and deeper that that of most of the city's youth. When I came to Horodenka, he was a friend and brother to his neighbor Eliezer Bilder, the son of Menashe Bilder. I was immediately accepted by the group as the third strand. As the saying goes, "a threefold cord cannot quickly be severed."

After some time, in 1921, Eliezer left for Israel. However, a year later he returned due to the harsh conditions in the land. Still, he absorbed much fragrance from the land of Israel and brought this fragrance to us. He himself didn't go again, but his younger brother Moshe went a few years later with a group of pioneers. However he died in the land at a young age.

In the course of five or six years, until I went to Israel in 1925, we three used every available hour for the spirit of the Hebrew language. It goes without saying that we were the first on the scene for every Hebrew activity and were involved in every nationalist action in the city. One of the primary functions was to insure the continued existence of the Hebrew school, which usually existed on miracles and stood with a question mark for almost half of each year, between semesters. After the first bloom of enthusiasm and after the volunteer teachers, Yungerman and Libster, left Horodenka, the future of the

(1919) Hebrew School with A. Liebster as Master

school's existence was placed on the shoulders of the school committee. These members were appointed from among the most dedicated to the Hebrew language. At that period, the one who generally officiated as a teacher was Mr. Korn, who succeeded very well in his job. There were also courses for completion led by Tzvi Pomerantz and myself. These courses primarily focused on Tanach and Hebrew literature. Only at a later stage did we hire two teachers, Sh. Y. Pineles, and Shimshon Meltzer, who became famous later on as Jewish scribes.

Parallel to the Hebrew nationalist Zionist movement, was an active branch of the Yidishist Bundist movement, whose leaders were Asher Shtreyt, Yossel Katz, Issac Fink, and others. The personal relationships between these leaders and their members were very good. As I mentioned, there were occasions when two sons of a family were members of different movements. Only in one area were there common lines between the members of two groups – when the drama group was established in the city. (It is interesting to know that the stimulus for this joint venture came from the need to amass money to put a roof on the big *shul*, which had burned during the Russian invasion. For this activity, both groups volunteered.)

Concerning this topic – the theatre in Horodenka – there were three stages. I knew the first from the stories of my parents from the good old days before my birth. In those early years after their marriage, between 1890 and 1895, a professional theatre group came to our city periodically to bring pleasure to the residents. The company's pleasant and well-received presentations came from the pen of Goldfaden: *Zvei Kuni Lemels*, ("Two Timid Creatures"), *Chinke Finke*, *Shulamit*, etc. My parents, as a young couple not yet saddled with children, didn't miss a performance, especially since my father was "close to royalty" because of his job designing the posters. The songs and the jokes from these performances served as entertainment in our house throughout my childhood. I also remember the second stage, when the theatrical group of Gimpel from Lvov came for guest performances in Horodenka in 1911-12. I was then about ten years old and was permitted to join my parents in attending the performances. In those days, the star of Yaacov Gordon was in ascendancy, with his plays *Di Shechita*, ("The Slaughtering") *Der Vilder Mentch*, ("The Wild Person") *Go-tt, Mentch, un Teivel*, ("G-d, Man, and the Devil") etc. The third stage came in 1919 to 1923, when Horodenka got a theatre group of its own. It performed plays in Yiddish and succeeded in pleasing many theatergoers, who returned from the cities of west Austria to watch the high-level performances of these professional players.

There is no doubt that the first thrust came about through the visit of a native of Horodenka, the brilliant actor Alexander Granach, in

1918. I was not in Horodenka at the time of his visit, but according to the words of friends who were present, his appearance made a strong impression, and without doubt awakened dormant talents. In truth, many talents were awakened, and one of them, Mendel Diner, became a professional actor after he got his first training in Horodenka. His handsome appearance must have helped him in the choice of this profession. After a while, we heard that he appeared on the Jewish theatrical platform in Soviet Russia. After that, however, we didn't hear anything about him for several years. We assumed that he was swallowed up in this broad land, together with other remnants of Jewish culture that disappeared from the platform of history.

Among those who stood at the head of the drama activity and were the first of its members, the following names are etched in my memory: Isaac Fink, Mendel Diner, Hirsh Sobel, Motti Katz, Dunya Meir, Tziporrah Lindberg, Henya Birnboym, and Etel Treysuber. They presented the plays of Gordon: *Der Unbakanter*, ("The Unfamiliar") and *Chasye di Yesomeh*, ("Chasye the Orphan") and that of Hirshbein: *Ba'ym Behrg*, ("Near the Mountain"). The troupe moved away from its fixed setting and performed in the nearby city of Gabozdzitz. Its performances are still remembered very positively by the remnants of that town.

It is also worth mentioning a Hebrew drama group that found its way to Horodenka. My friend Meshulem Shnitzer had an only sister who married a young man named Koch, who I think came from Tluste. The couple lived for a time in Shnitzer's house, and the groom was "an enlightened one" who knew Hebrew. He grew friendly with us and one day asked our opinion about a play he wrote on the topic of Elisha ben Avuya. I can't remember why the author merited the cloak of dramatist, but it is clear to me that these visitors did have great talent, but nothing came of their visit.

Near the store of Mordechai Shnitzer stood a wooden house of two stories with a magnificent front. This was the most beautiful house in the city. It was the pharmacy of Meiron Luria, whose name was emblazoned on it in large, gold-embossed letters. Meiron Luria himself belonged to the assimilated groups in the city, and his pharmacy was open even on Shabbos and holidays, both because of danger to life, and because its owner didn't care about Sabbath observance. In my early childhood, this was the only pharmacy in the city, until the opening of a competitive pharmacy, "The New Pharmacy of the Golden Seal," whose owner was Polish.

Near the pharmacy and the store of Shnitzer, the transportation workers of Horodenka – the wagon drivers and the porters – acquired a resting spot. There were two kinds of wagons: flat wagons for transporting merchandise through the city and wagons for transporting people to the train. I remember two of the wagon drivers, who were by custom known not by their family names, but by their nicknames, Kopel (or Kopale) Zanki, and Berl Boulai. Besides these two types, there was a third type of wagon driver, who didn't show up much in the city, since they traveled between cities, transporting merchandise from the large neighboring cities, Kolomyja and Stanislvov. Their wagons were fortified with linen canopies to protect the merchandise from heat and rain.

The front of the pharmacy faced the main street and the south side of the building faced a narrow alley that led to the big *shul*. The *shul* was a large and tall stone building, a building that remained unfinished for many years. Outside, the walls remained unplastered, and inside you could still see the structure of the roof on its beams, since they didn't have the means to complete the ceiling. Because of the appearance of the shul, one could guess who were the people praying – the simple people, remote from both wealth and honor. The fancier and better off householders *daavened* in the *shteibel* of the Chorkover of Viznitzah Chassidim or in the *minyan* of Yudel Pasvig where the *misnagdim* daavened. Consequently, the big *shul* remained for the ordinary daaveners who didn't belong to the existing movements. They came to *shul* only to fulfill the obligation of praying with a congregation.

In the hall of the *shul*, from right to left, there were two prayer rooms, called *palushim*, that were designated for congregational prayer, but for a more limited group. These prayer rooms were designated for the same kind of attendees who visited the big *shul*. The *shteibel* that stood next to the big *shul* had a different character. Those who prayed here were householders who didn't have a strong enough connection to Chassidim to pray in a particular prayer room or *kloyse*. The study house and the *shteibel* were in the same building, on both sides of the corridor. In this building there exuded a greater warmth than in the big *shul*, both physically and spiritually.

Following the alley, not far from the big shul, there was a long structure that served as the central meat market. In the middle was a long corridor, and from both sides of the corridor were about twenty sales stalls, one for each butcher. This setup served to insure efficient control over the sale of meat, which was the primary source of income for the community cashbox.

Near the central butcher shop was the special property of Horodenka that Alexander Granach described so profoundly in his book, <u>A Man and his Path</u>, the Proval. This was a deep and wide ravine that extended almost the whole length of the city from south to north, splitting it in half. This division had somewhat of a social character. Across the proval, behind the façade of houses with a respectable appearance, there was a sprawling cluster of poor and neglected houses. This section was called *Di Hintergasse* (the lower street). The streets in this section were not paved. In the rainy season it was difficult to enter them, and for two weeks, it was difficult to get out safely. Here the homes of the poor were concentrated – the shoemakers and the tailors, the wagon drivers and the porters, the peddlers and the middlemen who didn't have a permanent location like the merchants at the center of town.

Three bridges linked the two parts of the city on either side of the river. One was on the road near the house of Mendel Reys, or, as he was called, Mendel Getzels. The second bridge was near the butcher and the third was further south on the way that led to the small Ukrainian section. The Ukrainians did not come to the city often since they built their own church that the Jews called, "Nikoliski's church." The proval existed in the city until the First World War when the ruling Austrian army was forced to close it for sanitary reasons. Since there was a state of war, they found a way to conscript hundreds of Jews and non-Jews, who worked a stint of "forced volunteerism," without payment and without time limit.

Celebration of the Balfour Declaration in the Grand Synagogue

In the street around the big *shul*, the house of study and the *shteibel*, there were various kinds of schools that served beginner students to students of Talmud. On this street, one could become familiar with the students and their teachers. Unfortunately, I was largely removed from this experience. I only went to the school of Menashe the Melamed during the first stages of my education. Together with my sister Faige, we learned how to read Nishmas (a Sabbath prayer) from the siddur that was printed in large letters. We knew it by heart better than we knew how to read it from writing. As in a dream, I remember a joint visit of the cheder children to say the prayer of Shema. There is a Jewish custom that the night before bringing a baby boy into the covenant of Abraham our father, young school boys were invited with their Rebbe to say Shema near the crib of the infant and his mother's bed. On that night it is told that there is increased danger from "destructive forces" that plot to harm the well being of the newborn. For this visit, the students would go out en masse with their Rebbe in the lead. When they completed their task, they were honored with nuts, raisins, and sweets.

The beginning of my *Chumash* study as a six-year-old boy was accompanied by a ceremony and celebration that was held on Shabbos in the *cheder* of Menashe the *Melamed*. However, after that, I was exiled from the table of the *melamdim* and handed over to the Hebrew schoolteachers. As my father wanted to supplement my studies in Tanach as it was taught in the Hebrew school -- studies that were rich in quality and poor in quantity, he hired private teachers who either came to our house or taught me in their houses. For over two years, I was the student of Shlomo Heller, who gave classes in Tanach to individuals or small groups. He was one of the more progressive teachers who assisted in translating the commentary of the Ibn Ezra, and paid attention to grammatical principles, though his pedagogical approach was not to translate classic Hebrew into Modern Hebrew. On Shabbos afternoon, I would sometimes visit his house to study *Pirkei Avos* (Ethics of the Fathers.) From among his books, my attention was drawn to a Hebrew book about the wonders of nature. I don't remember the name of the author, but I'm almost sure that this was the *Sefer Habrit* (Book of the Covenant) by an anonymous author.

After I finished my Tanach studies with Shlomo Heller, I studied Talmud for a while with Reb Kalman Shmuel, the son-in-law of Mendel Lesser and the grandfather of our friend Lippe Liser from Kibbutz Ramat Dovid. There, I studied with a small group of three or four students, one of whom was his grandson Lipa. The studies took place mostly at night, especially in the long winter nights. Lipa used to make the other students laugh when he showed wall shadows of grazing goats by creating appropriate hand positions. In short, of the special flavor of learning in Cheder, I tasted only the edge of the fork. Furthermore, I knew the melamdim of Horodenka only by name, and not by their essential character.

The two well-known *melamdim* in the city who were not teachers of the very young but rather taught at an intermediate level, from Chumash studies through Talmud, were Yonah the Melamed whose family name was Leibman, and Yehudah the Melamed from the family of Toyber. However, he was usually called by the nickname that stuck to his family, "Yehudah Bazjor." He was one of the older teachers in the city and many of the students' parents had also been his students in the past. He was known as an impatient teacher who "cast bile" upon his students and threw fear into them by word and deed.

A different sort of teacher was Reb Notah Katz. He also translated his teachings into Yiddish, but his school was more progressive than the others that concentrated primarily on Talmud. Reb Notah put a lot of attention into learning Tanach and used many modern commentaries such as Mendelsohn's Biur, which was controversial in the eyes of the other *cheders*. The students also received something of an education in grammar and in general, a spirit of the new times wafted within the walls of this *cheder*.

The family of Notah Katz was similar to that of Shlomo Streyt to a certain extent, though without such extreme contrasts. The father was a man of the older generation. The oldest son, Motti Katz, was taken to the army straight out of high school, and upon his return, he gravitated toward Zionism. He was a man of action and went to Israel with a group of the first immigrants, who included Asher Yungerman, Eliezer Bilder, Monk Kanopas, Hertzel Veykh , and others. However, the younger son, Yossel, entered head first into the Yiddishist movement and was one of the founders of the Yiddish school, as well as one of its teachers. After the father died, the rest of the family – the mother and two sisters – followed the oldest son to Israel. The younger son remained faithful to the concept of exile, and suffered the lot of the Jewish population in exile.

In one of the corners of this section that included most of the *shuls* and the cheders, the city bathhouse stood. Mainly this was a for a *shvitz* (steamroom-sauna) and bathing was allowed for individuals only on special request. The heat and steam bath was accomplished by a very primitive process. In a specially constructed oven, special round stones were heated for several hours till they were red and glowing. The non-Jewish assistants would periodically spill several pitchers of boiling water on these stones. The water would instantly burst into steam, and the boiling steam gushed out of the stove and filled the entire bathhouse. The seats were placed on stairs, one above the other, and the further up one went, the hotter it got. To increase the pleasure, the attendants would beat and rub the bathers with special bundles of reeds that they would wave higher and higher in order to heat them well.

In the main section of the bathhouse was the heated *mikveh*, from which they drew water for washing during the *shvitz* and for dipping into when the *shvitz* was finished. The washing day was usually the day before Shabbos. However, Chassidim and scrupulous people would take an additional dip on Shabbos morning before prayer.

Besides the city shvitz, there were two other bathhouses with *shvitzes* in different corners of the city: one of Eli Yosef Shpierer, that was made according to the pattern and design of the city bathhouse, and the second of Velvel Greenberg, made according to the newer and more advanced model. The main new feature was that the steam for the shvitz flowed from a boiler, when needed, with a deafening noise. The hot and cold water was sufficient for those who took showers. Many faucets were available in a wide hall for the convenience of the bathers. The hygienic conditions were much more up-to-date compared to the other bathhouses, but the *mikveh*component was completely missing. Those who came to the bathhouse could only wash and had to overlook the commandment of immersion in a *mikveh*, which they could fulfill only in the other bathhouses.

Like an arrow shot between the above described section and the main street, stood a cluster of houses that spread out in a straight row from the alley near the pharmacy of Luria to the crossroads that led on the right side to the area of the Ukrainian Count Pilvarkovi and to the section of the city's Frankist population. This row of houses consisted of several stores, among which I will mention only two that I used to go into at regular intervals. One was Leibele Korn's iron parts, and the second was Yona Kramer's shoe store where we went before the holidays to buy new shoes. This was an experience that added a charm of its own to holiday preparations, and is one of my favorite childhood memories.

On this row was also the store of Feivel Kvassnik, the primary supplier of Kvass, the national drink of Horodenka. Kvass was a sweet drink made of dried fruit that was sold in the summer at many of the stands in the city. It was poured from glass pitchers in which ice cubes were floating, into thick glass cups, and it would quench the thirst of the citizens and their guests. Reb Feivel was a great expert in the manufacture of Kvass, and this cool drink was refreshing and invigorating. On market days, the drink was sold also by traveling merchants who would announce their wares in loud voices. Among them,

Meir Hershele stood out. He had a huge, shining forehead and ceaseless humor, and would proclaim his drink in Ukrainian peppered with rhymes like: "Sweet as honey, cold as ice, whoever drinks will truly live." Meir Hersheleh was literally poor his entire life, and was supported by many temporary jobs, but he bore his lot with a smiling face and words of teasing and jokes – about both others and himself – never left his mouth.

This row of houses on the right of the main street was slightly elevated to several steps above the road. The extremely narrow sidewalk near the water canal allowed movement only with difficulty. In contrast, there was a wide sidewalk on the other side of the road that concealed the water canal beneath it. Over it the main flow of pedestrians was concentrated. It was natural therefore that several important stores would be located there. Nearby was also a non-Jewish establishment that made a big impact on the community life of the city's Jewish population.

A row of stores opened here with ready-made clothing sold by Chaim Shuchner. It was a double store with two doors, and Chaim worked there with his three sons, two of whom were twins, Moshe and Pilah. The more professional Jews of the city did not shop in the store. They generally preferred clothes with a "Jewish cut," that could not be found in these types of stores. The Jewish and Polish officials also didn't need ready-made clothes and didn't like these styles. The Ukrainian village population in that district also didn't use European clothing because their natural garb was linen shirts and pants in the summer, and lambskin in the winter. There remained therefore only shoppers from the poorest of the people who weren't that particular about their clothes, and for whom it was easier to buy a cheap ready-made garments than to look for cloth merchants or tailors. To the latter they turned only in times of celebration, to sew wedding cloths etc. In the years before the First World War, there was another type of buyer of ready-made clothes. The economic conditions and the burden of debts forced many of the surrounding farmers to emigrate to Canada. These emigrants didn't want to appear in their strange national clothing and therefore felt obligated to buy European garb before going out into the big, wide world. Afterward, a period of relief and prosperity came to this store that was practically one of a kind in our city.

Near Chaim Shuchner's store, opposite the pharmacy, stood Yossel Landheim's fruit stall. Yossel was called, as was the custom, by his mother's name, Yossel Mindis. Our neighborhood was blessed with fruit that fell from trees – apples, pears, and peaches – fruit that was sold cheaply and in great bulk, near the stands by the village women who brought them for sale. Since this abundant produce was prevalent everywhere, it was unnecessary to display them and to sell them specifically on the first sidewalk. In that place, primarily rare fruits were sold, fruits that came from other countries: Yellow peaches that didn't grow in our land, grapes imported from Hungary and Germany, and melons sold in slices. These fruits were also used to say the blessing of 'Shehecheyanu,' on the second night of Rosh Hashana. Oranges were also sold and purchased to revive the soul of the sick, or in contrast, to add pleasure during performances by the Jewish theatre from Lvov in the Sokol auditorium. The fruit stalls remained in place until the outbreak of the war in the year 1914. At that time, the roads were damaged and the order was changed and imported fruits undermined the basis of the business. However, the place didn't change its character much, and after the war, David Glugar opened a store for the sale of candy and delicacies. This store had a great appeal for the younger generation who longed to see the world in their own lifetime.

At the edge of this cluster of houses near the alley, was the store of the watchmaker, Shmuel Frishling. He prayed in the Zionist Minyan and was father's friend. His son Artzi – nickname for Aaron – went to high school in Chernowitz. I remember that Artzi Frishling was the first to appear in the streets of Horodenka riding on a bicycle, thus drawing a lot of attention. My special closeness to this family developed in 1916, when we wandered like refugees during the third invasion of the Russian army. Many of our Jewish brothers acquired horses and wagons to prevent their having to flee by foot and to be able to salvage more property. With the partnership of our uncle Mendel Flor, our family was able to acquire a wagon. Shmuel Frishling also traveled with his family in a wagon harnessed to a skinny horse. Since the invasion happened at the end of summer, together we made the trip to Stanislavov through the many encampments in villages and even sometimes in open fields. There was not much food for the animals, and more than once we would joke that Shmuel Frishling would give his horse an overabundance of water, in the place of the food that was missing.

On the other side of the alley stood a two-story building belonging to Reb Velvel Zeidman. He was one of the few upon whom it is said: "He had Torah and greatness in one place." He was materially well off, as well as being a Torah scholar who lived righteously. He was concerned with the needs of the community and was among the group of the most extreme religious who opposed Zionism. He was rarely seen in the streets, and therefore I remember his appearance only in a blurred way, since I saw him only two or three times. In contrast, I knew his young son Froike (Ephraim) well. He was a handsome, well-dressed youth, who hung out with the young Zionists in the city. Since he was conscripted in Lipnik, Moravia around the time of the world war, he was a frequent visitor to our home when we were refugees for a few years. When we got to Israel in 1925, we met him in Jerusalem, and both of us frequented the home of Artziali (the uncle of Ephraim Geller), of blessed memory. He stayed a while in Israel and wanted to settle there, but didn't succeed. In the end, he returned to Lvov to his family, and from then on, I heard nothing about him.

Velvele Zeidman also had a beautiful daughter, but I never got to see her. A report about her came to my ears from a special guest. We needed a worker to turn the ironing wheel for our laundry business. Ordinarily, an older, very intelligent non-Jew named Haritzko, did this work. However, during the days he was absent, either due to illness or his holidays, Jewish workers assisted us. The ones available were Meir Hershele who was mentioned above, and in an emergency, Binyomin Katz, who was nicknamed, "Trombar." He was a very short person with a doubtful smile always spread over his face. He was single and a person of extraordinary simplicity, and the family would often joke at his expense. For example, they would ask him if he would agree to get married to the daughter of Velvele Zeidman, and he would answer with his simplemindedness that he desired her very, very much, but thought that she was not an appropriate match for him, since he could not provide for her in the luxurious manner that she was accustomed to.

The home of Velvele Zeidman was on the second floor; the first floor was occupied by several stores, among which was the store of Chaim Hersh Zeidman that contained cloth and woven goods, the iron supplies of the store of Eliezer Friedler, and the grocery store of Motel Adelshtein. Eliezer Friedler went to Israel on the heels of his son and daughter and son in law Yitzchak Shapira. However, Motel Adelshtein and his wife Matel were killed in the Holocaust with all the Jews of Horodenka. After the Holocaust we found out that their son Yaacov Adelshtein was one of the Zionist leaders of the Jewish community in Czechoslovakia. He sanctified the Divine name by his consistent and courageous behavior during the Nazi regime. May his memory be blessed.

Near these stores stood a building that was externally different than the other buildings in that row, because it was obviously recently remodeled for its new purpose. This building held the organizations of the national Ukrainian movements, and in the front of the building, the "Torhovlah," the cooperative store. From generations back, there was in Eastern Galicia a divergence of roles among three groups; a divergence that no one questioned. The Ukrainians had the agricultural role, the Polish held office positions in the local government, and the Jews handled business. Craftspeople came primarily from among the Jews, but there were a significant number of non-Jewish workers, especially carpenters, shoemakers, and builders. However, beginning in the early twenties, there were early signs of a change in these distinct rules. Jews who graduated from public schools penetrated more and more into liberal administrative groups. The Jews, because of their quick grasp and their proficient knowledge of the German language, which was the native language of Austria, rose in most situations to higher positions than the Polish and the Ukrainians. Also, when they began to dedicate themselves to mastering Polish and Ukrainian, they didn't lag behind the ones who spoke these languages from birth. On the other hand, there was a strong movement to take businesses away from Jews. The practical outcome of this movement wasn't felt much during its first decade; it was hard to compete with the complexity and organization of Jewish businesses. However the propaganda that supported this movement contributed a lot in spreading the poison of hatred for Jews, and to portray them as taking advantage of the populace by their business methods.

In the framework of this movement, the Ukrainian Torhovlah also arose. One must admit that this was a beautifully arranged and clean store. However, by its very nature it was set up for a very limited group of purchasers from among the Ukrainian intelligentsia and didn't meet the traditional needs of the village buyer. Thus the Jewish storekeeper remained, as before, the primary provider of basic, everyday needs.

In the years that preceded the Russian Revolution, the Second World War, and the Nazi Holocaust, the Jews were so involved in marketing eastern and central European products that it seemed that no winds could move them from their position and nothing could upset their place without a general disturbance in the economy. On the basis of this feeling the saying was formed: "Just like the word 'Goy' can't exist without the letter Yud (Y sound), so too the non-Jew can't survive without Jews. (Yud also means a Jew)." It appears that in those days there was a basis for that saying. Even the group that concentrated around the Torhovlah found the need to engage at least one Jew as a middleman between itself and the Jewish neighborhood, probably to prevent direct contact with a large number of Jews. Therefore a Jew was found who placed himself at their disposal for the sake of his livelihood, even though this wasn't the most honorable profession. I don't remember the name of that Jew anymore, but everyone's nickname for him was *cum* which in Ukrainian meant "friend." He would also come to our laundry very often as a messenger from his "bosses," and that's how I got to know him.

Inside the building were the organizations of the Ukrainian National movement, which included in those days mainly only their intelligentsia. On their property was an extremely large hall with a stage for performances – the Narodny Dome (People's house.) In the years before the First World War there were no ties between the Jewish national movement and the Ukrainians. Both of them were still in their infancy stages, and both suffered from the hostile attitude of the local ruling Poles. I think the closeness came in the years 1917-1918, during the short period when the Ukrainians ruled eastern Galicia. It was a fact that the Ukrainian ruler was sympathetic to the Zionist cause, and the relationship didn't split even after east Galicia was annexed to Poland and referred to as the "little Poland of the east." The Zionist youth in the city would organize parties at pre-arranged times, primarily for the purpose of conscripting money for Zionist causes and various community needs. In all cases we were able to use the Narodny Dome.

The Torhovlah was really the last store in this row of business buildings. In one of the buildings behind the Torhovlah was a storage place for selling whiskey -- the "Propintzia," which also did retail business. At the end of the row was the hotel of Monish Shmid. I think I was in this house only one time, in 1922, when an Israeli Shaliach, named Erez, visited there.

The business section that took up almost half the length of the main street extended to the hotel of Shmid. From there on, on both sides of the street were homes, legal offices, and some communal organizations. Only here and there jutted out a store that served the residents of the immediate neighborhood.

The hotel interrupted the row of houses. The houses receded to a depth of about twenty meters, creating a road two meters wide. In the front part, trees were planted under which were benches for relaxation; the other part served as a gathering place for worshipers in the Greek-Catholic church, the Ukrainian one, which was one of the houses on that street.

In the first house lived a Jew called Itzik Elya Leichtmache (candle maker), so named because of his craft of making brass candleholders. These candleholders were a much-needed necessity in the generation before mine, because each home had brass candlesticks in honor of the Sabbath. Each Jewish woman would beautify this mitzvah, and would recite blessings over many candles, according to the number of people in the family. Usually an older grandmother would live in the house, and she would also need several of her own candles. (In times of emergency, they would also use extra candles ensconced in clay candleholders.) One of the beloved activities of the children was polishing the candlesticks before Shabbos until they sparkled and were prepared for festive lighting. Only in the later generation, with the appearance of silver or silver-plated candle holders that were inexpensive and mass produced, were the heavy brass holders pushed aside and became obsolete in most Jewish homes.

Itzick Elya's home was a single house. A narrow alley separated his house and the hotel; on the other side was a small street that led to the city garden. On the other side of the street was Shamai Bakher, who was considered a well-off Jew, though I don't know his profession. He acquired his house at a later time, in 1933, through his involvement in the Zionist movement, and it functioned as a community house. I don't remember if Shamai Bakher's house was attached to the wall of the Greek Catholic church, or if there was another building between them.

It's interesting that the church stood exactly in the center of the Jewish settlement, and not closer to the Ukrainian suburb from where flocks of people headed to the church every Sunday. In truth, even the Roman Catholic Church stood among the Jewish houses, because there was no escape from living in this neighborhood where most of the population was Jewish. This was also less surprising than it otherwise might be, since the Polish people who were Roman Catholic were also citizens of the city. Besides this, its isolation and alienation was not so deeply felt because the central government building was attached to it. This latter building was also very large with a beautiful front, and therefore a Christian section was formed. In contrast, the Greek Catholic church was totally surrounded by Jewish homes, and appeared to be actually captured by them.

The Jewish houses of prayer did not stand at all in the front part of the main street. The bigger ones were behind the main street, closer to the big *shul*. In the streets further away from the center, there were a few small*shuls*, besides the special *minyanim* for Shabbos and holidays. Two such *minyanim* also existed on the main street; one of them, the Zionist *minyan*, was actually located opposite the entrance of the Ukrainian church, on the other side of the street. On ordinary days the two camps – the Jews and the Ukrainians – would not meet. One celebrated on Shabbos and the other on Sunday. However both groups met when one of the Jewish holidays occurred on Sunday or when one of the Ukrainian holidays happened on Shabbos. It would be difficult to say that this meeting brought pleasure to the Jewish group, but I don't recall any disturbance created by one group encountering the other.

The Zionist *minyan* was held in a rented room in the home of Aharon Kugelmas, and was used for prayer on Sabbaths and holidays. On Shabbos after daavening and on weekdays, the room served as a meeting place and a reading room for the Zionist organization, *Bnei Zion*. There it was possible to read the Jewish Zionist newspapers, both in Yiddish and Polish. The *Tagblatt* was the daily Jewish newspaper printed in Lvov. A weekly Hebrew journal called *Hamitzpeh* was printed in Krakow. Occasionally, there was also *Hatzefirah* the daily Hebrew newspaper that came from Warsaw. After 1918, after Galicia was annexed to Poland, the Yiddish *Tagblatt* stopped, and the Yiddish readers had to be sustained by the Warsaw papers -- Heint and Moment. On the other hand, in Lvov there began to appear a Zionist newspaper written in Polish named *K'ville*, (The Moment). One could also find in this meeting room, the newspapers of the world Zionist movement: *Di Velt*, in German, and *Haolam*, (The World) in Hebrew. In the years before the first world war, there were two primary newspapers from the capital of Austria: *Noy Praiya Proso* and *Vienna Zjornal*.

The existence of the Zionist *minyan* and the Zionist organization was burnt into my memory from my childhood. From the time they were small, the children would accompany their fathers on Shabbos to this prayer house. I don't recall any other *shul* that my father prayed in before he had turned to the Zionist *minyan*. My uncle, Mendel Flor, my mother's brother, was also one of the steady attendees there. He had the weekly job of reading from the Torah, or, as it was called, being the "Baal Koreh." These readers were also among the prayer attendants, and only rarely, on the high holidays, would they bring in a cantor from the outside.

In addition, my father served as the cantor and was accepted very graciously as an accomplished "master of prayer." He also had a regular position as the cantor for *Kol Nidre* and *Neila* on Yom Kippur. Among the people praying, there was one who stood out by his pleasant voice; the impact of his sweet prayer remains as one of the most enjoyable memories of my childhood. This was Boni Fleshner, by occupation a bank clerk. He was also one of the three partners of the shingle factory that was in our courtyard. It's also appropriate to mention a talented person who appeared in the Zionist *minyan*. For a long time, a young man prayed with us by the name of Shaul Sucher, a man of short stature with a pointy, golden beard. No one had suspected that he was musically talented, but on one of the days of the festival he approached or was sent to be the cantor, and it turned out that he had an exceptional voice. He didn't indulge in complicated trills, but he pronounced the words clearly. From then on, he acquired a prominent reputation and eventually ended up in Lvov, where he was appointed the cantor in one of the synagogues.

A few houses away from the Zionist Minyan was Weinstein Hall. This was the only public hall that served as a kind of coffee house for the professional intelligentsia of the city. Sometimes it was rented for weddings and parties. In the years following World War One, the Yiddish school resided there, and the place was transformed from a building of leisure activities to a place of Torah

Somewhat distant from Weinstein Hall was the home of Yudel Pasvig, where there was a minyan for Sabbaths and holidays. Yudel Pasvig was the son-in-law of Meshulem Wagner, one of the heads of the few *Mitnaggedim* (opponents to Chassidim) that lived in the city. I didn't know Meshulem Wagner because he died before my time, but it appears that he was related to reb Chaim Shnitzer's family.

The home of the city rabbi, Reb Elimelech Ashkenazi, was also on that main street a few houses due south of the Zionist minyan. He had an ordinary home like every businessman, no better or worse. One can assume that it wasn't too spacious, especially since one room had to be dedicated to receiving visitors, and his family was blessed with daughters. In my childhood, most of them were already married, and two of them were daughters-in-law in the Shnitzer family; one of them the wife of Reb Chaim Shnitzer and the other the wife of his brother, Simcha Shnitzer. Since I was close to the Shnitzer family, because of my friend Meshulem Shnitzer, I was also acquainted with another son-in-law of the rabbi, Israel, who lived in Sokol. This young man had a special charm. He was upright and handsome, and of a noble appearance that could not easily be forgotten.

I know very little to relate about the rabbi as a spiritual leader. He was considered a great Torah scholar and everyone treated him with respect, but I don't know what he did specifically to increase Torah knowledge in our city.

On the other side of the street opposite the Rabbi's home, which was considered the spiritual center of the city, was the finance center. Here were the offices and homes of the city bankers, Alter Yungerman and his son Shmuel. This was a big single story house, divided into two wings for two families. The building was beautiful, with a small garden in front, and a white picket fence around it. Special attention was paid to the echoes of a piano that emanated periodically from the house due to the talents of the family's daughter. Like all the Jews of the city, the family of Shmuel Yungerman left Horodenka during the war, and returned a long time before our family did. When we returned to Horodenka in 1919, Asher Yungerman, the first-born son of Shmuel Yungerman, was the head of the Hebrew school that was founded in the city by his friend Azriel (Illa) Libster. He was also one of the first to make Aliya. In Israel too, he devoted himself to education and to this day is a principal in one of the schools in Haifa.

One of the few houses between the Zionist minyan and the home of Rabbi Ashkenazi belonged to Doctor Kanapas. As the only Jewish doctor in the city, Dr. Kanapas was a familiar figure in every Jewish home, since in those days people stopped relying on magic potions alone, and began to call doctors in times of need. The Jewish doctor was able to speak German with his patients; in his home, Polish was spoken, according to the custom of lawyers, and many Jewish government clerks. In short, this home was, at least according to external appearances, an assimilated house. However, in his old age, the situation changed significantly. His son Monak joined the Zionists and moved to Israel with the first pioneers. Also his son-in-law, the lawyer Dr. Mans, who settled in Horodenka, became an active Zionist who was at the head of the Zionist organization in the city. Eventually he also went to Israel with his family, and settled in the Kibbutz of Shiller. After the Second World War, Dr. Kanapas's widow also joined her daughter and son-in-law in Shillers' kibbutz.

The more distant that each home lay from the business center, the more their external structures were sprawled out and their interiors more expansive. The homes of lawyers and court clerks – some Jewish, some not – were near the courthouse. In one of these houses with a beautiful fenced in porch was the office of Dr. Werber. On the other side of the street was the office of the Ukrainian lawyer Dr. Okuniovski. In this section was also situated the government police office, the Gendarme.

Near Yungerman's house, there were several homes whose residents filled a role in the cultural and social life of the city during different seasons. The first house was the home of the Shapira family – the family of the judge, Reb Mendel Shapira and the family of Shmulik Shapira. These two families were blessed with offspring who were active in the Zionist movement, with the pioneers, and with the Hebrew movement. Among them are included Yitzchak Shapira, the judge's son, and Liba Shapira, the daughter of Shmulik Shapira.

Yitzchak Shapira was among the younger generation trained by the *Shomir* (The Guardian), who were students in Yungerman and Liebster's Hebrew school. He was an activist in government, culture, and even in sports. One should especially point out his involvement in founding *Chalutz*, (The Pioneer) and his part in founding the *Gordonia* organization in our city. When he got to Israel, he settled down in a workers' collective near Tel Aviv, in Tzupit. Also he worked as the secretary of the agricultural center and was a special member of the more important groups of the party of Poalei Eretz Yisrael.

Liba Shapira hung around the Zionist youth of the city and, with her expansive spirit, in her infectious joy, and her pleasant voice, there was no Zionist activity in the city that she didn't participate in. In Israel, she continued her communal activities and her dedication to the labor party. Liba Hoffman Shapira was also known as one of the activists who worked on behalf of the organization of working mothers in the city of Haifa, where she lived.

Near the house of the Shapira family was the house where Hershel Preminger lived with his brother Leizer. Tzvi ("deer" in Hebrew, and Hershel means "deer" in Yiddish) Preminger was the epitome of a Zionist in the period before World War One. I already mentioned that he instituted Hebrew speech in his house. He also established a factory for shoe polish called *Levanon,* whose product appeared in a package with a symbol of the Hebrew high school in Tel Aviv and had instructions for use written in Hebrew.

The third house was that of the Libster family. The father of the family, Abba Libster, was ultra-orthodox, and was one of the staunchest opponents to the opening of Baron Hirsh's school. His oldest son Israel *daavened* with the Zionist minyan and his daughter Mazdi was involved in teaching in the Polish public school. However, the place of honor in the city's cultural scene belonged to the youngest son, Azriel – called Illa Libster. In 1918, together with Asher Yungerman, he established the Hebrew school and developed an educational program that expanded and flourished.

Uri Chaim Shertzer owned the last house on the main street. Its front faced the side of the street that turned right and led to the courthouse building, to the train station, and on to the village of Czerniatyn. Many of my childhood memories are bound up with Shertzer's house, since that's where the first Hebrew school run by the Rirachowskis was conducted. There one could also find the Hebrew kindergarten run by Tziyupeh Shertzer. The owner of the house, Uri Chaim Shertzer, was well known to me and for several years he daavened with the Zionist minyan. He was much older than most of the others who prayed there, and it's questionable whether he prayed there because of ideological compatibility, or because of convenience of location. He usually came to pray accompanied by Shaul, the son of his old age. (He came to Israel during World War Two and his oldest son Naftali also came to Israel). In the years before the First World War, he opened a modern restaurant, and introduced something new – a big jukebox whose music was enjoyed by the guests. The jokers of the Zionist *minyan* used to say that since he acquired the jukebox, he changed the words of the liturgy from "to listen to the song and prayer," to "to listen to the song and NOT the prayer."

The street that turned right from the main street was generally outside of my interest, except for two houses, both of which were associated with Torah learning. One was the house of Alter Zilberg, where the Hebrew school was situated after it left Uri Chaim Shertzer's house. Alter Zilberg was an enlightened Jew and a dedicated Zionist, and for many years he served as a head of the group, "Sons of Zion." He had two grown sons and both of them learned geometry in one of the state high schools; they would come home for vacation. I especially remember the younger one Itzik, who during his military service came to visit his parents in an elegant officer's uniform. He allowed himself to go bareheaded, something that wasn't acceptable in a Jewish home like that of Alter Zilberg. Their home was in the old house in front, and the school rented out the new house of two rooms in the courtyard.

A short distance from Zilberg's house, on the other side of the street, was the home of Mendel Liser, in which I spent many evenings of my childhood as a student of Reb Kalman Shmuel, the father in law of Mendel Liser. Reb Kalman Shmuel was even then – in the years 1913-14 – an older Jew, a widower living with his son in law. He spent only a few hours a day teaching, and in them he taught Talmud to a small group of students, among whom I was included.

The second road branched off the main street and led outside the city to the village of Statzuva, and to the city Sniatyn. This road also was tied to several childhood memories. It led to a wide grassy area called "Toliki," that served as a playing field for the youth of the area and as pasture ground for the horses of the city's wagon drivers. In the years after the First World War, this land served as a central soccer field, which to my sorrow, I had no part in. I remember this grassy area mainly in the years before the world war, from the Shabbos walks that the members of the "Sons of Zion" organized in the summer, before sunset. Often I would accompany my father on these walks and I'd listen to the conversations of the grownups, which in the course of their talks would cross the entire field. Many of the houses on the street had somewhat of a village character. A big courtyard that was sometimes used for farm supplies, vegetable gardens, birdcages, coops, and barns for various animals, small and large, surrounded them. Such a place was the home of the Ofenberger family, whose sons were involved in farming and the city's Zionist youth. The second house in this neighborhood that I recall from my childhood was the home of Abba Kalmus, who daavened in the Zionist minyan and was a friend of my father. He was the one who emptied the large storage bin in his yard and let the Hebrew school use it to celebrate one of the graduation ceremonies.

It was the third or fourth graduation ceremony of the Hebrew school. The first graduation under the leadership of the Rirachowskis was celebrated in the biggest and most beautiful hall in the city, the Polish Sokol hall. This hall was on the street opposite the main street, behind the house of Rabbi Ashkenazi. It was also rented for guest appearances of the Jewish theatre, but it was used primarily for local celebrations of the Polish population, and for presentations and celebrations of Polish students. In this hall, gymnastic lessons for local high school students were held. In it we also saw moving pictures for the first time, which, because of technical faults, seemed to be constantly raining. From all the pictures that were shown, I remember the film, "The Last Days of Pompeii." However, nothing can be compared to the feelings that were awakened in us at the presentation of the film, "Jewish Life in the Land of Israel," which was shown in a festive celebration that took place in the streets during Passover.

Opposite Sokol hall was a two-story building which housed the Polish public school for boys. Most of the Jewish boys who did not attend the public school founded by Baron Hirsh learned there.

The public schools were run according to the educational system of the private schools. The public school for girls was in another corner of the city. All the Jewish girls learned in this school because the Baron Hirsh School was designated only for boys. It existed only till the outbreak of the war in 1914, and when it closed due to conditions of the war, it never opened again.

In this school, I spent four years of my childhood. During all those years the teacher of my class was Mr. Norad. Two of his sons emigrated to Israel. The school's principal was Mr. Mosler. From the other teachers, I remember especially Mr. Zanvil Zilberg, a relative of Alter Zilberg, who was the religious teacher. The studies included the basic principles of the Jewish religion and an abbreviated history of the Jews in Biblical times. We were also taught the Polish version of the Ten Commandments, all this from the syllabus of the Polish school. In Baron Hirsh's school, they also taught chapters from the Bible translated into German. Thus they fulfilled their obligation of teaching Hebrew and of "paying a tax" to the Jewish character of the school. However the Jewish character was preserved mainly because all the students were Jewish. Outside the walls of the classroom, children spoke the vernacular of Yiddish, while the students of the public school were inevitably in a Polish environment. The language of education in Baron Hirsh's school was also Polish, but they also taught German, the language of the rulers, and Ukrainian, the language of the masses of villagers in the country.

This is a good place to tell of one of the first teachers in this school, who in my time was already a teacher in a different city. I knew him only as my father's friend, whom I met on one of his infrequent visits to our city. This teacher was born in Horodenka and was the son of a rope maker, Pinye Shtrikmacher (ropemaker). His father was a short, silent Jew, with a long white beard filled with stalks of flax from his constant involvement in his profession. The son Yankel Fink was tall and handsome, and from behind his gold-rimmed glasses peered forth two eyes filled with intelligence and humor. In his youth he was in the group of the *Maskilim*, but left them and picked up a working knowledge of Polish.. (Most of the Maskilim were satisfied with a knowledge of the German language and chose teaching in public school as his life's profession.) He was separated in a good way from the other schoolteachers, all of whom, except for Mr. Viselberg, tended toward assimilation. He, however, remained a nationalist Jew all his life, and stayed faithful to the Hebrew language. His letters to my father were very rare, but they stood out in their beautiful Hebrew style, and they testified to his deep connection to the language.

The school of Baron Hirsh stood on the city's border, on the way to the village of Sarafince, not far from the city's center. This was a one-story building with four classrooms, the teachers' room, and, also I think, the residence of the principal Mr. Mosler. There was a wide room, which the students used as a playroom during recess. In the middle of the courtyard there was a kind of scaffold, on which some planks of wood were stretched in a vertical position. The children exercised on them, climbing up about four to six meters. This provided an outlet for the youthful energy that bubbled in their midst. There was a sizeable portion of students from among the poor; these students received short jackets and boots for winter and a warm meal before they left school in the afternoon.

Near the school of Baron Hirsh stood the courtyard of the rabbi of Horodenka, Reb Michale Hager. This was a very big building; most of the rooms were designated for the rabbi's private quarters, and only two rooms and a hallway were designated as rooms for prayer. The rebbe was descended from a dynasty of rebbes of Vishnitz, but was not among the most famous of them. Most of his Chassidim came from Horodenka, and only a few came for the holidays from surrounding areas to spend time in his courtyard. A short time before the First World War, they started to build a large synagogue in the courtyard near the house, but when the war burst out, the rebbe escaped with his family. After the war he settled in Chernowitz, and didn't come back to Horodenka. Several years later, the son of the rebbe Reb Michale, Rabbi Baruch Hager, became one of the leaders of the Mizrachi movement in Chernowitz

While speaking about the Rebbe, it's hard to skip over his "shadow," his *gabbai*, or attendant. It's appropriate to mention him

not just in his own right but also and primarily for the merit of his
son. Reb Pinchas, the *gabbai,*was a Jew with broad shoulders, a
prominent stomach, a beard streaked with old age, and wise and
smiling eyes. He was known as a man of humor, and didn't take his
honorable role very seriously. He joined the Rebbe during his
wandering in the days of the World War, and after the war he also
settled in Chernowitz and remained at his post until the end of his life.

I knew his son, Shmuel Abba Sofer, during the years 1912-1914 as
a student in the third and fourth classes of the Polish high school, and
as a close friend of Berl Mossberg, who hung around our house. He
was a tall, skinny kid and got to high school two years late, since
before that there was no high school in Horodenka. But he wasn't
satisfied with the knowledge that he got in high school. He swallowed
every book he could obtain, primarily from the German library of Motel
Hurwitz. His close friends were the Shtrum brothers, his classmates,
and also Mayer Kron and Berl Mossberg, both of who were several
years older than he. He excelled due to the penetrating ability of his
mind and the sharpness of his sayings, one of which I remember in
relation to education. He was accustomed to saying: "A person is
obligated to educate his parents," meaning he must train them not to
be an obstacle to his development. It seems this saying was based on
his personal experience, for he convinced his father to accept his free
life-style, even with his position as the attendant in the courtyard of
the Rebbe. It is near certain that a great portion of the educational
success of the son was due to the merit of the father, as the "student,"
whose grasp in those matters was not so difficult.

Around the year 1917, in the thick of the First World War, Shmuel
Abba happened to be in the city of Leipnik in Moravia, where many
refugees from the war relocated. In this city, there was an
encampment established by some of the troops, to which several
Horodenka folks belonged. For the short period that this camp was in
Leipnik, he would spend many of his free hours in our house, and
sometimes even offered to help me in my studies. Till this day, I
remember how he once explained something in physics to me – the
difference between kinetic energy and potential energy – a fact that
stuck in my memory. After the war, he settled as a scribe in
Chernowitz, in which his father Rabbi Pinchos also settled as the
attendant of the Rebbe of Horodenka. There he also was involved in
communal activity and in scribal work, and earned his full title from
Dr. Shlomo Bikel and Yitzchak Paner.

The second soldier among the people of Horodenka, who used to
come in and out in our house in Leipnik at that time, was Heinrich
Shpierer, the second son of Berel Shpierer, the communal head of
Horodenka. In that summer of 1917, Henya Birnboym happened to

come to Leipnik, when she returned from Vienna to visit my sister who was her devoted friend, and living in our home. Heinrich Shpierer spent a lot of time walking with girls (after asking them permission). In truth, he was an ugly boy, but he would often speak about his imminent death on the Italian front, where he would soon be sent when his training was up. "You'll see," he said, "in another three months you'll open the paper and find my name among the list of those who fell on the southern front." A short time after he was sent to the front, his wealthy father came to Leipnik to find a way to nullify the decree. However, Heinrich refused this by saying that if he got out of going to the front, someone else would be attacked by the bullet that was meant for him – and such a low deed, he's not prepared to do. Actually, it happened as his heart prophesied. A short time after he arrived at the front, he fell from the enemy's' bullet.

The row of the few houses between the Rebbe's courtyard and the building of the Polish meeting house, comprised two buildings, that I had a special connection to – the homes of the Bilder family and the Shnitzer family. This was a connection of two generations. Both Menashe Bilder and Chaim'l Shnitzer were connected to my father with ties of friendship expressed by mutual respect and deep love.

In an absolutely accidental manner, the bond of friendship between the parents passed over to the generation of the children, and I was very close to both Eliezer Bilder and Meshulem Shnitzer. I studied with Bilder for four years at Baron Hirsh's school, but when I went to the Polish High school, our paths separated and I don't recall any other interaction we had until we returned from the exile in Moravia on one summer night in 1919. I remember that he was one of the people who met us in the train station, but I don't think he came to see me, but rather to accompany his friend from the *Hashomer* group, Henye Birnboym. However, when we met, we immediately renewed our friendship, with the mutual longing and expectation for a resumption of a full Jewish life. Eliezer Bilder was a handsome youth, friendly and pleasant to everyone. He was a member of *Hashomer*, one of the outstanding students of the school under the administration of Yungerman Libster, and he stayed friendly with his neighbor Meshulem Libster who was several years his senior. I was accepted as a third member of this group, which decided to use only the Hebrew language as our means of communication.

In 1920, Eliezer Bilder went to Israel with the first group of pioneers. But because of the lack of work combined with an outbreak of malaria, after a year had passed, he gave in to the pleading of his parents and returned to Horodenka. He brought along with him a large bundle of Israeli experiences and a great admiration for the leaders of the workers. Primarily he mentioned the name of Remez

Vashprinztik, may his memory be blessed. He continued on a regular basis to receive the workers' newspapers: The Young Worker and The Collection. Thus we lived to a certain extent in the atmosphere of Eretz Yisrael and were updated on everything that happened in the land. We were especially moved by the discourses of Y. Lupven of blessed memory, and of Ch. Shorer, may he be singled out for a long life.

When I went to Israel in 1925, I left these two friends and their families. Like the majority of families who leaned toward Zionism, they were satisfied with sending representatives: Only one from each family reached Israel: Moshe Bilder, of blessed memory, and singled out for life, Yaacov Shnitzer HaLevi. My friend Eliezer Bilder died in his youth from a malignant disease and the rest of his family perished in the holocaust. The lot of these families followed the lot of the collective house of Israel – not one remained.

From among those who dwelled near the school of Baron Hirsh, I remember two: Yekhezkeil Dul and Tzirel Koser. Dul was a well to do Jew, who made his living in leather and farmers' boots. What distinguished his house from all the others was the large fruit orchard that surrounded his home. His son, whose name I think was Meir Dul, was my neighbor on the bench in the Baron Hirsh school, and during summer vacation he would sometimes invite his friends to the orchard and offer them some of its fruits: blackberries, blueberries, unripe apples, and bitter pears.

Tzirel Koser was a widow who supported herself from a small grocery and writing materials store, patronized primarily by the school's students. I also recall her son, a quiet young man around twenty. I don't remember what his business was, but he could have also been involved with his mother's little store.

Tzirel Koser's store stood in the row of houses opposite the Baron Hirsh School and the Rebbe's courtyard. One of the distinguished residents in this row was the old Polish doctor of the city, Doctor Roshko. There was also the Polish pharmacy called "The Golden Star," that arose as competition to the pharmacy of Miron Luria. In the last years before my aliya, Doctor Kaufman lived there; he was one of the few who escaped the Holocaust and was successful in reaching Israel with his entire family. Here also stood the house of Yonah Veykh, whose son Hertzel Veykh went to Israel with the first pioneers from academic circles. He didn't stay long in Israel and moved to one of the countries across the sea.

The steady row of houses ended around the home of Menashe Bilder, where there was a wide path that led on a slight slope to the building of the Armenian Polish church, or as it was called by the Jewish dwellers, *Di Timchas*. In this area lived the Horodenka landowner, Baron Romaszkan (before the land went to Prince Lubomirski) and one of the respected Polish citizens, Stepanovitz.

Near this church stood a beautiful renovated building with a pretty garden in front, called *The Poviat*, meaning, "the central house." This building contained the management of several economic institutions that were under the Polish community organization. One of these stood out in relation to our family: the large shingle factory that succeeded in ousting from the market the production of shingles in our house by my father and two partners.

Near the village square, opposite the entrance to the Polish church, was a one-story city building called the *Gemina*. This building was narrow and tall and contained space for city departments and also the city police station, and even a temporary waiting room for passersby. Once a year during the last days of summer, this building was used for conscription to the army of his Honor, Emperor Franz Yosef, and afterward, for the Polish army. This was the only opportunity I had to visit this building.

The path that led to the Armenian Church continued past the church to a narrow path that opened up to the main street near the Greek Catholic church and was swallowed up at the end by the trails of the city park. In this alley behind the Armenian church, was the villa of one of the honored wealthy men of the city, who served for many years as one of the communal leaders and was beloved by most of the city dwellers. The man's name was Berel Shpierer.

In his youth, Berel Shpierer was a member of the *Maskilim* – the secularists –who gathered around Chaim Leib Halpern, a person for whom all the *Maskilim* of Horodenka "poured water over his hands" (attended to). I don't know how he acquired his wealth, but I do know that in my childhood, he owned a small bank. One day I found out that he obtained the property from Bornstein and became its landlord. My father was his childhood friend and this relationship continued after he became wealthy. He was considered an adherent of the Zionist movement, but he wasn't a member of the local Zionist group.

Therefore he was trusted by the ruling powers as one who was not suspected of harboring extreme Jewish nationalist positions. He moved up the ranks of the Zionist hierarchy whose slogan was to wrest the zeitgeist, the contemporary cultural outlook, from those ultra orthodox who opposed Zionism. People felt that there was no one in Horodenka better suited to be appointed the head of the community, and so he was chosen around 1911 as the communal head, with the support of the Zionists, the workers union, and other groups who did not support the leadership of Orthodox Judaism.

To the extent that I recall, there was no separate office for the community meetings; instead they were held in the home of the communal head. There also was the community council called the *Koltus-raat*. The secretary was David Zeidman, who was an official in the central ruling house. Functioning as the community secretary was an additional side job for him.

I don't remember if they had new elections after the war, or if the community council just continued its job out of inertia. I only know that even in 1924, the composition of the community council was practically unchanged: Berel Shpierer was the head and my father was one of the council members. I remember this clearly because of something that happened. The oldest son of my sister was born in 1922. When he was about two years old, my sister had to spend most of her time earning a living, and she needed to get a woman who could be a housekeeper and babysitter. As was then the custom she preferred a Christian village girl who was more acceptable for many reasons. It happened that they got a young girl of high natural intelligence. She quickly mastered the few Hebrew words that were necessary to take care of a two-year old. In the course of time, her storehouse of Hebrew broadened to the point where she could explain the songs of Bialik to the child. Thus we had in our house the phenomenon of a Hebrew- speaking Christian girl. Once when the community council was having a discussion about Hebrew language and speech, the head of the council said, partly as a joke and partly with seriousness: "If only I knew how to speak Hebrew like the maid in the Lindenberg house." In any case, especially with regard to spoken Hebrew, there was indeed something to envy....

The tragedy that struck Berel Shpierer when his son Heinrich fell at the front wasn't the only tragedy that struck this family. In 1919 or 1920, the gang of Petylura reached our place. This gang ostensibly came to join the Poles in their war against the Bolsheviks, but actually engaged in murdering Jews and plundering their property. Berel Shpierer, as a wealthy Jew, wanted to avoid the face of evil and escaped with his family in a carriage. On the way, the gang of Petylura overtook him, plundered some of his belongings and killed his oldest son Mitzi, who had completed his studies as a lawyer and stood out in his refinement and exceptional courtesy. The only son left to him was Luci, who was around my age. In the days of the Russian conquest before the Nazi rule, the entire family was exiled to Russia and there he disappeared. Only the son Luci succeeded in escaping Russia; it's reported that he ended up in one of the lands across the sea.

The rest of the path, which crossed through the main street, led to the "Courtyard," the property of Baron Romaszkan that later went to prince Lubomirski. The path continued to the train station called *Yakubuvka*, where those who missed the main train went with the hope of catching the second one. It also led to the villages of Kornev, Raszkow, Semenovka, and to the city of Obertin. On the section of the road that was still within the city boundaries, several families lived whom I want to mention.

The first building near the crossroads was a cluster of large buildings surrounded by a stone wall covered with fragrant lilacs, buildings that I already mentioned. In these buildings many Christian families lived, and before World war One, a post office was also there. Since this was a Christian section, it was natural that the only store selling pig meat was located there. Near there was also, I think, the store of Chaim Hirsh Meltzer, who was one of the participants in the Zionist *minyan*. In the years after World war one, some Jews lived in these houses; the one that stands out is that of the Marksheid family. Rabbi Elimelech Marksheid stood out from all the Jews in the city in his extreme righteousness, but his sons and daughters not only did not follow his path, but also stood out in their extreme philosophical positions. Still, this was one of the families where all the children went to Israel, and because of the children, so did the parents. Only one son, Chaim, came back to the exile after staying in Israel a few years, and he perished with the other Jews in the city.

Near this cluster of houses, which were in general a part of the business section surroundeding the market square, stood the house of Dudi Shtachal, the owner of one of the saloons that served primarily as a meeting place for the farmers on market day. On the other days of the year, they hoped for city guests who might long for a glass of beer. Not far from there was the store of Yehudah Wolf Shuchner, a Jew old in years with a wide and long white beard, who in spite of his age appeared full of strength and worked full time running his grocery store with both wholesale and retail stock. The primary workers in his store were his three sons: Bum Shuchner and his brother Milek (Yerachmiel) who hung out with the young Zionists in the city, and the third son, Zarakh who was completely invested in the store's business.

On the other side of the road, opposite the house of Yehudah Wolf Shuchner, was an alley that led to the butcher shop and from there on the left, to the large synagogue, and – by contrast – to the city bathhouse. The alley deserves mention because of the two houses that stood at its entrance. One was the *shteibel* (a small shul) of the Chassidim of Vishnitz. It was a long building of average length, whose walls were filled with windows, like a porch enclosed in glass. This gave the building an appearance of temporality, in contrast to the Chortkover *shteibel* that was a large solid building of thick walls. The temporality of the former building was perhaps appropriate to the lighthearted character of the Vishnitzer Chassidim, in contrast to the seriousness of the Chortkover Chassidim.

Opposite the shul of the Vishnitzer Chassidim was the home of the Dayan, the judge, Mendel Shapira. I remember this especially because of my many visits to his house as a messenger of my mother, of blessed memory. She acted as a proper Jewish woman, inspecting "with seven eyes" the insides of every chicken that was slaughtered. In every doubtful situation, she would send me to the Dayan to receive his Halachic decision regarding the Kashrus of the suspicious organ or of the entire chicken. Only in rare occasions did he declare the chicken unfit for eating; in most situations, I left his house with a positive answer, as a representative of my mother who waited hopefully for the decision of the Dayan.

Near the Dayan's house stood another house that was etched in my memory from childhood, even though the memory weakened somewhat with the passing of time. In this house lived my Zaide's brother, Izzi Melamed, who made aliya in his old age, in order to die in the holy land. This happened when I was about six or less, and although this was one of my more pleasant memories, it was also one of the haziest of this stage in my life.

The house of Bartfeld stood isolated in the center of town and sprawled between the road to Kotikovka and the road that led to the courtyard. At the end of the street stood two rows of houses, and between them a street that connected the two roads. Among the residents of this street that I passed by innumerable times in my childhood, I recall only the family of Baruch Leib Liser, the father of Avraham Liser from the community of Yifat, and his brother Yitzchak, of blessed memory, who passed away in Tel Aviv in 1960.

According to how it was told to me from the Liser family in Israel, this family reached Horodenka from Russia in mid century. During my time, this Horodenka family had four patriarchal families whose fathers were: Baruch Leib, Mendel, Kmiel, and Yosel who worked in the produce business. In my childhood I knew Mendel Liser, whose father-in-law Kalmen Shmuel was my Talmud teacher, and his son Lippe, a fellow student. Also I knew Herschel Liser, the son of Kmiel, who was one of the Zionist youths in the period before the World War. After the war came a time of Zionist activities for the young sons. Some of them went to Israel, and one of them, Avremel'che Liser, from the community of Yifat, acquired a name as a detector of mines which were set up to destroy the farms in our land.

The first building on the second side of the street was the house of Ben Tzion Strikmacher (rope maker), whose family name was Dinar.

He had an only son named Mendel, who reached adolescence at the end of the World war, and like many of his peers, joined *HaShomer* and the cultural groups that sprung up around it. Among the actors in the drama groups and amateur bands that arose in the years 1919-1924, Mendel Dinar stood out as an extremely talented actor. Somehow, he found his way to cross over to Russia, and actualized his talent as a Yiddish actor. However, from then on, no knowledge of his life and activities reached us.

Ben Tzion Dinar's house stood actually on the shore of the *Proval*, near the spot that met the wide valley through which the streams flowed. On this spot a bridge as wide as the road stretched out over the *Proval*. On the other side of the bridge stood the house of Mendel Rice, who was known by the name of his father, Mendel Getzels.

Mendel Rice's house was a solitary house whose front faced the other side of the road, whose one side turned toward the *Proval*, and the other toward the row of houses that turned straight south. The front of these houses turned toward the *Proval*; at a distance away, and near them was a paved road, without a sidewalk, which assured an easy access, even in the rainy season. Among the dwellers of this street, I will mention Moshe Lampner, whose house was the first in the row, and had a wide gate like that of a hotel. Then there was Zaide the butcher and his wife Sarah *di zeideche*, both of whom had big bellies and no children. Finally, came the family of Simcha Lagshteyn.

Simcha Lagshteyn was the former brother-in-law of my father, the husband of my father's sister Devorah. She passed away in her youth and left behind a little girl named Golda. After the death of his first wife, he married a second wife named Yuta, and had two sons. Simcha Lagshsteyn was far from Torah and enlightenment. He had a quick temper and was blind in one eye, and even his livelihood was obtained with difficulty. Therefore, it is no wonder that the daughter Golda used every opportunity to distance herself from the murky atmosphere in the house, and to come our home to be with her aunt, and especially with her grandmother, my father's mother, where she found a substitute for the maternal love that was missing from her life. She was an outstanding student in a girls' school run by Mrs. Reichnochova, and she excelled especially in poetry readings in Polish and Ukrainian. During the war years, our ways parted. After the war she returned to Horodenka, but our mutual grandmother was no longer alive. Thus the contact between us weakened even before I moved to Israel. I know only that she married a villager from around Horodenka, and presumably her fate was like that of all the Jews of Horodenka.

The street described above was the last paved road of the city. Behind this row of houses was a big cluster of plain cement houses and narrow streets without pavement that were full of mud during the summer. When the snows melted, they filled with puddles and mud of significant depth. This section of the city was called by the general name *Di Huntergasse*, meaning the back street. It is not even necessary to say that its residents, except for a few, were among the poorest of people – laborers, peddlers, and wagon drivers – and other kinds of Jews whose sustenance depended upon a miracle.

The northern border of this section was the road that led to the courtyard of the estate, and the houses on both sides of the city belonged, as seen from their design, to the planned part of the city. The main direction of the road was from east to west, and although the part near the *Proval* made a small turn to the right, afterward the road immediately returned to its primary direction.

In my childhood there stood a new big house built from unplastered red bricks and with a roof covered with shiny, white slats. This was the house of Gedalia Shpierer, a Jew who became rich from business dealings in horses. It seems that in the building itself or near it, a place was set aside for a stable, and the horse business left its mark on several of the family members. Not only did the son Baruch Itzik go out in public wearing boots and riding pants (which by the way was in style even for those who never rode a horse in their lives) but also the young daughter, Sosia, dared to walk in the street in riding clothes with a whip in her hand, and she thereby earned the nickname "Sosia the tomboy." In contrast, the older sister Gitel or Gisela, excelled in playing the violin, and surprised all who heard her whenever she agreed to play in front of an audience. After the First World War, she brought with her a new stringed instrument called a Banjo, and opened up the jazz era in Horodenka. The entire family immigrated after that to America, and I think none of them perished in the Holocaust.

Not too far from Gedalia Shpierer's house, at a short distance from the road, stood the house of Dudi Meltzer, or Dudi Mahler, according to his profession, who was one of my father's friends, but also a competitor in the profession of painting signs. Although he never reached the level of perfection that my father had, thanks to his talent and to the experience he acquired in New York, he was, like my father, also a master of many crafts. The profession that gave him the title Mahler was painting, which included not only plastering the walls of a building, but also engraving different colored designs, according to the custom in those days. Painting signs was subsidiary to painting, though his main livelihood was in a small, cloth making building on the floor level of his house. The moving power of this factory was a horse that was harnessed to an apparatus called 'Kirat,' and the clients were the farmers of the neighborhood who came to squeeze oil from the sunflower seeds.

Next to Dudi Meltzer's house stood the house of Velvel Greenberg, who has already appeared in this essay during the description of the modern bathhouse that occupied a prominent place in the building. The two-story building stood on the edge of the slope that led to the creek's channel. The upper part, on the road's plateau, was used for the growing family; a modern locksmith with a system of machines moved by steam occupied the lower part that was on the slope. This mechanism was used mostly to fix the heavy mechanical equipment that began to be used by the mansion's landlords, such as clumsy threshing systems with a system of complex revolving wheels. A steam machine on wheels that looked like a locomotive, named "Locomobile" turned these on. All year round, especially on the days before the harvest, part of the slope next to the workshop was occupied entirely by three or four machines of this kind. When it was their turn to come out into the air after the repair, four pairs of horses were harnessed to them. These horses finally succeeded, amidst cheers and encouragement and the assistance of about half a dozen people, to take these machines to the flat part of the road, and from there they could reach their destination, pulled by only two pairs of horses.

It seems as if all the talent of Horodenka in the field of designing machines was concentrated in this house. The patriarch of the family, Velvel Greenberg, was skinny and bent over with a short, pointed beard, and was an exceptional craftsman. His four sons also followed in his footsteps. The first born, Udzi, became famous as an excellent craftsman even before the First World War. Besides this, he also stood out in on the stage of the local drama club. The next brother, Yisroel, who was known by his nickname, 'Tzunia,' also excelled in crafts and broadened his knowledge through self-study and immersion in books about craftsmanship. He settled in Israel in 1912, and so too did his two younger brothers. All three were immersed in metal making in Israel. Yisroel Greenberg established a machine factory worthy of its name near Tel Aviv, and also stood out in the field of engraving in a local production plant. He was also one of the first to establish a military industry before the State of Israel was founded. In the days of the Kommemiyut War, Greenberg placed his factory at the disposal of military manufacturers, and it became an important center for the production of weapons and bullets for Israel's defense army. He didn't seek or accept any payment for the use of his factory, even though when the war ended and the factory was returned to him, he had to invest substantial funds from his own pocket to fix the machines and to prepare them once again for civilian operations.

Among the other houses that stood in this row, I remember only three: the house of Nota Boral, the house of Azriel Fleshner, the father of our friend Moshe Fleshner, and last and most beloved – the house of Hirsh Birnboym. Hirsh Birenboim was one of the most unique personalities of Horodenka. He stood out both in his great height and his unique spirituality that had no rival among the city dwellers. In his youth he was one of the group of intellectual heretics that Chaim Leib Halperin led and guided spiritually. Birnboym moved far away from all his friends in actualizing the teachings of their leader, which they did primarily by curtailing every expression of traditional Judaism: shortening prayer, shortening the beard and sideburns, and shortening clothes. Also his life profession as an expert in manufacturing *shnaaps* in one of the distilleries located on the large mansions, distanced him from the Jewish environments and caused him to become closer to the Ukrainian villagers. In their company, he spent most weekdays and even some of his Sabbaths. Because of this influence, he absorbed much of the nature of the peasants, and knew how to spice his words with sayings and parables that were popular among the Ukrainian people. At times, even a measure of coarseness was not missing from them. He admittedly did add a measure of charm by being so audacious as to refer to things in the names that were appropriate to them.

Birnboym was my father's closest friend, and like him was also a Zionist member, without taking an active part in its programs. Like most of the enlightened ones, he was proficient in the German language, and was familiar with the classics of German literature. He also loved to immerse himself in books of natural healings, and acquired a wide knowledge in diagnosing illnesses and prescribing natural remedies.

The friendship between Birnboym and my father extended to their families. The compatible ages of the children in the two families enabled the ongoing continuity of this friendship. This was a bond that spread over two generations. Strong ties of friendship existed especially between my sister, a small blond girl, and Henya Birnboym, a charming, dark-haired girl who was very tall for her age. They shared a bench in their studies, and also shared childhood playfulness. They could be seen together all hours of the day or night. This friendship continued through the years when they both became active in Zionist groups and in professional drama clubs.

Henya Birnboym was "the singer" of Horodenka. She had a pleasant voice, not too strong, but soft as velvet and full of expression – a voice that could penetrate the heart. She was not easily persuaded to perform and it was very fortunate when she got together with Gitel

Shpierer to sing, accompanied by her violin, some of the popular songs that we loved like, *Voiyet, voiyet, baize vintn.*

During the Holocaust only the patriarch of the family, Hirsh Birnboym, remained in Horodenka. According to the testimony of one of the survivors, he was among the first to be executed by the government in the village of Michaltche. The rest of the family members were then scattered to all corners of the earth, in Israel, Europe, America – places where the hand of the oppressor could not reach.

I began this essay with a description of my father's house, and concluded with the Birnboym family, which was closest to us out of all the Horodenka families, and to a certain extent, continues to be so until this day. A short distance from the Birnboym house, the row of residential houses ended. The road that led to the estate, to the agricultural school, and to the airport was surrounded on both sides with a pine tree forest, which was the property of the estate owner. Only a few houses stuck out here and there from between the trees, and I remember only two: the family Freedshand, one of whose sons got to Israel and settled in a Chassidic village called Yad Shalom, and the family of Streezobar, whose daughter Ethel was a school friend of my sisters, and also participated in the drama club, successfully portraying the characters of older mothers and grandmothers.

Near those places, on the right of the road, was one of the natural gems of Horodenka, the big lake called *Sobikas Teich*, that attracted, with enchanted ropes, the most daring swimmers of Horodenka. I, however, to my distress and shame, only heard about it, and perhaps saw it from afar once or twice, but never got near it. However, it had a bad name in the city as a cruel master who demanded each year 'an offering of the life' of one of the excessively audacious swimmers.

My essay is complete, but not finished. I have brought up what remains in my memory of the city and its inhabitants, from those who I encountered in too short of a life span. I was twenty-five when I left Horodenka and immigrated to Israel. One must subtract from this at least the first five years of my childhood and the three years that we were refugees in Moravia. I don't pretend that I succeeded to encompass in my essay all the groups and sectors of the Jewish settlement in the city. There were at least another two important sections that I didn't even touch upon: the ultra-orthodox circles and the workers groups. My connection with these two groups was very tenuous, and the little I know about them is not worth hearing about. However, although this description is unfinished and truncated, it still encompasses a significant portion of the city and its Jewish dwellers. I hope too that I have assisted the readers in visualizing a city and its inhabitants, and perhaps my portrait has even succeeded in transmitting to the coming generations some brush strokes of the city of our birth, a city that was completely destroyed together with other Jewish communities in the exile of Europe.

[Page 137]

Eight Chapters About Horodenka

Alexander Granach

From the book, Ot Gait a Mensch

Translated by Harvey Buchalter

All about Horodenka: The Great Rivalry

The difference between the village of Verbovtsy and the town of Horodenka was greater than the difference between Horodenka and some other large European capital cities. Horodenka possessed all the traits of a somewhat self-confident, youthful, bustling, up-to-date town. At the same time, Verbovtsy was somewhat isolated, quiet, and mundane.

In the village, one made a living from the earth; life was tied to it. In Horodenka, one derived a living from the labor of another, even if the two of you had nothing in common. The village, by contrast, had something resembling an order or arrangement. Everyone knew how everyone else lived and also what he or she earned. One lived with the livestock, the earth, and even with the routine changes in school semesters. In the village, troubles were never in short supply. Imagine if an animal falls down, or if drought devours the earth, or if suddenly, in the middle of spring, a hailstorm attacks and makes a heap of the seeds and blooming plants; or smack in the middle of summer, when fieldwork turns your hands into hot metal, there appears a rain-laden cloud and settles itself into a quiet, "rested" puff, and then BOOM! endless buckets of rain. You don't become gloomy, but rather deeply concerned. Then you peer at the sky and curse the foolish spring that delivers a hailstorm on its own seeds and blooms. Or, you throw your hands up in hopelessness over the "turned around" summer from whose clouds gush rain at the wrong time and in the wrong place.

In the village there lived poor and rich alike. When a hailstorm burst, or a drought appeared, or when a disease spread among the animals, it affected everyone equally. And so one person helped out another, because everyone was a neighbor.

It was totally different in Horodenka. There, you didn't extract a livelihood from the earth, but rather from other people. In the village, you looked toward the heavens and believed that all bounty came from there. In town lived the Polish estate manager Romashkin and the Jewish banker Yungerman; it was them we all looked up to. They could place fortune before a person, or they could just as easily ruin him. They themselves had their managers and brokers who were in position to dispense good salaries to others. One lived from the earnings of another, and so on down the line, to the least fortunate.

Horodenka was also built differently than the village. All around the village, cottages and gardens were laid out helter-skelter, spaced a distance from one another. The "high quality" places and the poor ones were all topped with straw roofs, and all the men wore the same linen shirts hanging out of their linen trousers.

In town, everything was different. One group, those who were bureaucrats, wore short-length jackets with buckled shoes, a starched collar in the *stolyantse* style, a prim hat, and gloves. They rode around in carriages. The others simply ran around barefoot and naked. Horodenka was built in "rings." The first ring encircled the entire town. Here, most houses had straw roofs, with some having tile roofs. This is where the Ukrainians lived. Each day they brought a few potatoes, or onions, vegetables, string beans, lima beans, and chickens to the market.

In the middle ring stood houses with metal roofs and gardens with flowers, as you might see in villas. There lived the officials of the tax collection and justice bureaus, and of the municipality. The next circle encompassed the Jews, "fenced in", as it were, by the rings.

What was the face of Jewish Horodenka? Smack in the middle was the market, surrounded by houses on each side. Further away was the post office, and further still was the Orthodox Church with an onion dome on the roof. It was whitewashed and spotless. In the dome two pigeons made themselves a comfortable nest. Through the market, Kaiserstrasse wound its way and intersected other main streets; the church stood in a "T" of perpendicular streets. In front of the church there hung directional signs indicating east, the way to the Dniester River, through the town of Ostemska all the way through to the Russian border; the West, to Kolomyja, Stanislav, and Lemberg; to the south to Zaleshchiki, which was known in Galicia for its carrots; and the north, to Obertyn, the town of horsemen and thieves. If you happened to ask someone the question: "Are you from Obertyn," he would immediately reply, "You, alone, are indeed the thief!" Along the four directions lay forty-eight villages that comprised the municipality.

Kaiserstrasse cut the Jewish section into two parts, the high streets, and the low streets. The high streets had sidewalks with Belgian blocks which led to the courthouse, the first sizeable building on the west side, and then to the market and the church on Zaleshchiki Street, all the way to the Baron Hirsh School.

The town took the utmost care to keep the high streets immaculate. They cleaned and watered them down. The lower streets were never kept up. There once was a huge culvert there, the *proval*, and all the garbage and sewage was dumped into it. Early in the morning you could find people "doing their business" in the open water. Thus, it smelled from sewage, and if it rained or was very cold, you could choke on the odor.

The tiny homes, *sthtiblach*, stood one next to the other, because it cost less to build on to a neighbor's wall. One house rested against another. It stood and held on to the other like a shivering, swooning person, afraid to stand unaided, alone. Here lived the poorest of the poor: shoemakers, sewing machine operators, carpenters, metal workers, barrel makers, millers, furriers, bakers, and all sorts of draymen and carriers — toiling men who loitered about all day in order to earn five coins for bread for the blessed household. They all waited desperately for Tuesday to come, when Jews and Gentiles from the surrounding forty-eight villages would come together in the market place; they made their living hauling for the Tuesday market.

A portrait: All at once, total confusion and congestion, a rushing about. Then, more congestion, more rushing about, as if the world were turning topsy-turvy. The high- market arena turns into the horse and livestock market, which is usually located on the outskirts of town, on the meadowlands (*toliki*). The stallions had caught a whiff of their mares or of just-maturing foals and whinnied wild songs of courtship in their direction. The poor cows have not been milked today, their udders full of milk; they mourn forlornly for someone to relieve them. The sheep bleat, crying longingly for green fields. But the greatest outcry comes from the pigs. They squeal as if pieces of living flesh were cut from their bellies. In the midst of the cacophony, the handlers and the brokers break into a sweat. They scream and bargain with one another, their eyes popping out of their sockets. They shake hands - a "klop" of one hand to the other — resoundingly. "Okay, okay, we have reached a price." The profit is all of three guilders. The purchaser is ready to take possession of the horse, the cow, the sheep or the pig, but is still anxious to make another three guilder. Another pounding handshake, another deal is made. "I'll meet you halfway," one says to the other. "A guilder and fifty cents more!" They agree on a price of two guilders, and then drink it away with a toast: *Maharitch* (a go-with-fortune toast), *L 'chaim,* and a blessing for the health of the animal.

Trading was on a smaller scale in the state-owned market. There, the poor peasants sold their chickens, geese, ducks, grain, flaxseed oil, and their homespun linen. From there, they'd go to the clothes markets and buy colorful kerchiefs, glass beads, wool to weave into shirts, sugar, salt, pots, matches, or herring. The storefronts are teeming: whiskey is being devoured along with beer, cider, rum; they eat fatty sausages and *kielbasa.* All are happy and somewhat drunk.

People hurry about in a frenzy, some, with frightened, searching eyes. Here a child is lost; there a thief has been caught. A snorting horse crashes into the earthenware pottery for sale. There's a moan, then a scream. A non-stop cussing, and then the sounds of hundreds of wares for sale being shouted out. Merry-go-rounds turn and beckon. And within it all an overpowering sense of poverty emanates from the side streets; it is the need to earn a few cents. Carpenters are trying to sell their storage chests and barrels; shoemakers, their boots, and shoes; furriers and tailors, their suits of clothing. If you go there without cash, you barter goods with the peasants for wheat (grain), chickens, geese, ducks, and eggs. The women give nothing away. They sell challas, cakes, *kuchen,* boiled beans, and *piroges* stuffed with potatoes, cheese, meat, sweet cherries, sour cherries, or blackberries. Everybody seems to be rushing about and shouting. Everything, everybody, wants to get out. People agree on a price, then change their mind in an effort to cheat you out of a penny.

For us young folks, it is a wild holiday. We're happy just being included in the tumult. We carry *kvass* in glass urns to sell. It's sort of a mixture of apple juice, and a home-concocted brew of Feivel Kvasnick, who would smack us in the ear if we didn't sell his brew. We hated him and even made up a song about him:

Feivel, Feivel, give me *kvass*
Freeze it up and kiss my ass.

Ice was added to the *kvass,* so that when it melted it resulted in a colder and more watered-down brew. We sometimes would "eulogize" our product, begging, and even sometimes threatening people to buy:

Fresh *kvass*, it's something nice
It's delicious, and cold as ice.

Or:

Buy our *kvass*
Don't be an ass
It's the latest, it's a treasure
Go and drink it. What a pleasure.

And if threats did no good, I would shout:

Kvass, kvass, ice-cold *kvass*
When you drink it, you'll feel sound.
And if you don't,
Then die like a hound.

The old peasants would cross themselves, go right ahead and buy a glass of *kvass,* and sometimes ask for more, to boot. But in passing, they would also remark that it wasn't necessary to cuss to make the sale. "They're right," I thought, but if I didn't cuss, maybe they wouldn't buy any *kvass,* and they wouldn't get a bit extra either. The cussing seemed to attract business, so I would call out my product, shouting and cussing. Each Tuesday, I earned thirty to forty cents. I gave the money to my dad. He would praise me for doing well, and this made me feel lucky and proud. My older brother, Shabtai, who earned barely a third of what I earned, became more and more jealous, which made me only happier and more confident in my own ability. The town gave birth to the spirit of competition.

One Tuesday my oldest brother, Schechne, arrived home from the village. Toward dusk, he and my dad went to the flour dealer, Sholem Luft, and gave him a total of twenty-five guilders. He decided to open up a bakery. Mr. Luft then extended twenty-five guilders in credit and flour that would be guaranteed by my brother.

The day came when we moved up from the side street and took over the location of Efraim Gloger's bakery, in partnership with Mr. Tzuloif, not far from the Baron Hirsh School. And so, we finally became "bourgeoisie." We used to bake bread and challah, *rugulach* and kaiser rolls. And even though we all helped out in the bakery, there were not a lot of customers in the beginning, and we weren't able to sell more cheaply than the other bakeries. But we were our own best customers. Although my father explicitly forbade us to touch the baked goods, we couldn't resist and each of us "removed" fourteen or fifteen fresh rolls, *rugulach,* and bagels. Each one of us was convinced that he alone was the "sneaky one", but we were all guilty! It was no wonder that business in the bakery began to go bad.

My siblings and I went to the Baron Hirsh School by day, but at night we would wake one another up to turn the pastries and braid the loaves. Something once happened at work that made a great change for my brother and me. He was seven; I was six. He was tall and thin; I was stocky and short. I always had to look up to him and this bothered me. When we both were awakened for work, he took his time getting up and I would spring up like a buffalo. He would moan or cry, and noticing this, I became even more alert. This was when I first exhibited my unique ability: Here I learned to "construct my stance" as an actor; I could "act" as if I was ready to go to work, even if I wasn't. As he failed, I was being praised. He began to detest me, and I took advantage of his helplessness. As he became less and less certain of himself, I became more and more self confident. That's how it was in school, on the street, at play, and even selling *kvass*. May God forgive me, but some of it was my own fault. I had the feeling that I was committing a secret crime, that I was taking away his self-confidence while increasing mine in the process. This was our rivalry. We were no longer living in the village, but within the city limits of Horodenka. With the "street smarts" I gained from competing with other boys, I learned a lesson: the distance from the village to Horodenka is a longer road to travel than the distance between Horodenka and any European capital you could name.

My Rabbi Shimshele Milnitzer, Who was Worthy of Our Love

The *cheder* in Horodenka was a lot better than the one in the village. Our teacher R'Shimshele Milnitzer was a quiet, good person. He never beat us and was very happy when we would simply leave him alone. "A spoiled child needs to be loved," he would always say. And also: "A child with a good head, one who has the potential to learn, is better than a very apt child who resists learning." We were very much like the latter, and this was reflected in our pranks.

Once, we tied his *kopete* (robe) to the chair as he sat down. A second time we tied his shoe to a table leg. He would always good-naturedly shake his head and smile. When he was weary of study, he would nap with his head on the table. Once, we fixed his beard to the table with wax. When he stood up, he said nothing. All he did was make a sweeping motion with his hand on the tabletop. Then he brushed the wax from his whiskers. He never brought up that incident again, until a few days later when he said:

"Children, the other day you played a joke with my beard. I didn't say anything, at the time but not because I didn't resent it. But now that it's over, I fear that I have been afflicted with terrible thoughts that I was unable to voice at that time. I know that I am nothing more than a poor Jew, and aside from this, I have more than my share of troubles. But the Lord of the world graced me with a beard, as He did for every Jew, as if I was indeed a man of means. So, the beard is my consolation. And then you come around and you want to take that pleasure away from me. By turning the beard into an object of ridicule, you would have made me poorer. But would you have made yourself any richer by taking my beard away from me?"

This incident occurred on a Thursday. Each Monday and Thursday he would fast. And because he was weakened, he would speak very softly. We lowered our heads in shame, and he sent us home from *cheder* an hour earlier. But from that day on, he became holy in our eyes, as revered as a Torah scroll, and we no longer picked on him or played practical jokes.

He was the first to teach us the *alef-bais*. The letters looked like little boxes or parts of some tool or like small huts with miniature doors and windows. The letters danced before my eyes and I was unable to see any difference between an *alef* and a *tof*. But the patient *reb* taught me how to recognize the distinctions, and it became something I could literally taste. It wasn't long before I could put the letters together, like putting little boxes next to one another, forming the letters and placing the vowel sounds beneath them. I began to learn *trope*. We couldn't understand a single word, but that's how we learned how to *daaven*, repeat the prayers, and make a blessing.

I was fortunate to be allowed to begin *Chumash* (Bible). The *reb* began to translate from Hebrew into Yiddish and to then interpret. He would tell us about a world of long ago, far away, when the heavens and the Lord of the Earth were so much closer that Moses the Lawgiver, and the Patriarchs Abraham and Jacob, and the Matriarch, Rachel, would talk to one-on-one with God, just as our "big time" merchants in Horodenka would visit with Baron Romashkan or the banker Yungerman.

When you started studying *Chumash*, you marked the occasion with a celebration. On *Shabbos*, they prepared an *anzugel* (a question-and-answer fest). Then the neighbors and relatives would pile up about twenty pocket watches ands chains that they would then fasten to me and the other boy undergoing the same test. They then had us stand on the table and the rabbi, along with my mother, father, relatives, and friends sat around in that narrow room in anticipation and good cheer, awaiting the delivery of my *droshe* (Torah commentary).

Thus began the test. The rabbi stretched out his arms as if he were about to deliver a blessing and said to me "Bow your head and I will bless you."

"Beautiful Joseph. Charming Joseph. Just as Joseph, the Blessed, was favored by God and man, so shall you, my young lad, find favor and grace with God and with all people."

"Amen, Amen, Amen," they all resounded.

Then he began to ask his questions, and I answered him:

Enquirer (E): "Which tome are you studying, young man?"

Me (M): "The *Chumash*, gratefully."

E: "What does *Chumash* mean?"

M: "Five."

E: "Five what? Five bagels for a nickel?"

M. "No. Five Holy Tomes are contained in the *Chumash*."

E. "Which tome are you studying, young man?"

M: "Leviticus" (*Viekra*)

E: "Can you translate *Viekra*?"

M: "And He Called".

E: "Who called? The *shamus* called everybody into the *shul*?"

M: "No God called to Moses to proclaim the laws of the animal sacrifice. A sacrifice is holy, and I am also holy even though I'm only a small child. That is why the rabbi began to study *Viekra* with me.

E: "Study lad, and show us what you know."

Then he winked to the crowd and they all smiled.

So I said out loud, "*Viekra* ... and He called ... Lord God, Moses. One of them was called Moses."

Then I heard from all sides: "*Mazel Tov, Mazel Tov.*" They had cut me off in the middle of my explication.

My mother cried out her fortune and joy (*glick un naches*) and all the neighbors cried along with her. They grabbed and kissed me — against my will!

I was the center of attention. Everyone was looking at me, and I looked away from them. Never had so many people looked at me so approvingly. I knew they all came on my account; it was such a warm, comforting feeling, sweeter than the honey cakes that they gave me to eat.

Even with the episode of beard waxing, we all felt great love for our rabbi, R'Shimshele. We went to *cheder* willingly, even in winter. We studied into the night and returned home with hand-held lanterns. We eagerly listened to the rabbi talk, as almost each syllable and word had its own interpretation, an entire story contained within. He spoke of the true holiness of the Torah, on the meaning of each word, and the underlying purpose for including it. This is how he would begin:

"Schmuen and Levi were brothers." Then suddenly he would say, "What kind of brothers they were! How strong and how big they were, and how powerful! And he was called Levi because once the Philistines were chasing him and he was dying of thirst in the middle of the desert. Then lions attacked him and he grabbed one lioness and swung her and then hit another one in the snout, lifting her high in the air, so that he was able to drink the milk from her teats; then he just pushed her aside. Schmuen could lift up entire mountains on his shoulders and toss them at his enemies. And they had a sister, a beautiful woman. The Philistines attacked her when her brothers were away from home and they defiled and shamed her. So the brothers went off to the Philistine town and used their weapons to kill all the men and they destroyed the city in order to avenge her."

Another time we learned about Yoni and Jacob. And the rabbi began to tell us:

"Yoni and Jacob were starving in Egypt. And so they told Joseph that after Jacob died he should disinter his bones from Canaan and bury them with his father's. 'I (Jacob) failed to perform this worthy task for your mother, Rachel. I buried her on the road to Bethlehem, and I didn't even take her into the town. And you should know that if it rains, or if the road becomes too steep, it will mean "no!" The earth was dry and soft.'

"'I served my tenure with Laban; first seven years for Leah and afterwards, seven years for your mother Rachel. We fled from Laban and he chased and overtook us, and he said that we had taken away his wealth. I became furious when I heard this and said, "Whomever stole your wealth shall starve." And indeed, your mother Rachel had taken his riches with her, and she perished.

'I had buried her in the middle of a field on the way to Bethlehem. Why, you may ask again? I'll tell you. I had a vision and I saw that my people would be in exile, abandoned, and defeated. When they would pass the tomb of Rachel, they would pray and cry and wail, "Mother Rachel, see what has happened to your children?" And Mother Rachel would rise up from her tomb, saying: "Father in Heaven, see what you have done to my children." And God will answer her, "I punish them in this way." And Rachel will then ask, "Why are you punishing them?" And then God will answer her, "I punish them for their sin of dancing before the golden calf." And Rachel will then say, "Father in Heaven hear my words which I will tell you: When Jacob came to take me for his bride, he was big and strong and pleasing to look at. From the first time, we found pleasure in each other's eyes. But my father Laban was cunning and wanted to get rid of Leah, because she was small and ugly, with pimples on her face, and not at all clever. And so when nightfall came, he called Jacob into the dark room and he told him to lie under the bed and call to Rachel, so that Jacob would be fooled into thinking that Leah is Rachel. And so Jacob ended up marrying Leah. And I, Rachel, loved Jacob with all my body and soul and every cell in my being. I didn't wish any catastrophe on my sister Leah. I wasn't seeking vengeance. And You, Great God, Creator of all worlds, are still wreaking vengeance over the golden calf?" I would tell Rachel:

"Go my daughter, bring consolation to your children and tell them: I will never forsake you.""

"'The following morning as the sun came out, two thirds of those in the earth remained in their tombs and only the remaining one third rose up. And Moses went up to the people and said: 'Hear the voice of God. Those who are weak-willed, the frightened and weak-hearted in belief, they shall lie in their tombs, and only the strong and those of strong spirit, the ones who have no anxiety or fear and who are strengthened by their faith and belief, only they will be empowered and rejuvenated. They will be energized with new vigor to continue to wander and be able to enter the Promised Land of Canaan.'"

אלכסנדר גראַנאַך בין „עמך" בביקורו האחרון בעירנו

אלקסאנדער גראַנאַך צווישן „עמך" בשעת זיין לעצטן באזוך אין האָראָדענקע

A. Granach, among his 'Folk' whilst his last visit in Horodenka

Our *melamed*, Reb Shimshele Milnitzer, was incomparable. Only the children of poor folk studied with him, though he had a houseful of his own children. He would have to run around all day, seeking loans, getting what he could for free. He bought bread from the profits of his teaching – as much as was needed. We never calculated to see if it came out even. There is nothing as hypocritical as exchanging goods for Torah study, my father used to say. And according to the loaves of bread that the Rabbi takes from us, our knowledge of the holy texts would grow to where we ourselves would become Rabbis.

Sometimes we would make a festive celebration in the *cheder*. We were anywhere between sixteen and twenty children. Each one, according to what he could afford, kicked in a nickel or two and bought rolls, herring, prune jam, some honey, and a bit of whiskey for the rabbi. Then we would sit with him around the table, literally like grown-ups.

Once we bought him a bit more whiskey than usual for our celebration, and the *reb* became very talkative. So we asked him why he never hit a student, as other *melameds* loved to do. Perhaps, he said, it had to do with Joshua ben Nun and Moses, the greatest scholar and the greatest rabbi since Creation. By his third glass, his face became flush and he said, "Maybe it's best to leave it to the Creator to settle, if it's Joshua or Moses." He continued: "God called to Moses and said, 'Listen, my loyal servant Moses, you have endured so much with my people Israel, and I think it's now time for you to take a break and join in eternal rest with your fathers. Don't you think so, my son?' Moses considered it and replied, 'No, my Lord, no. I need to first lead your people to the Blessed Land. Afterwards you do with me as you wish. But as for now, Greatest Lord, I don't really have much time.' And he left.

"A bit later God calls out to Moses again and tells him. 'Do you know, Moses my servant, the angels in heaven are preparing *shofar*-sounders and lyrists. They keep asking when they will finally be able to commend Moshe*Rebenu* to Him. You know, Moses my son. How much we love you.'

"So Moses again answered, 'Yes, I know that Father in Heaven. But what would you say, Creator of the World, if in the middle of the world's creation someone had taken you away and destroyed your plans of creation? And who, but you, could ever know that once work is started it needs to be completed. So please excuse me, Majestic Lord, because I know that your heavens with its angels will never be shuttered to me. So I'll just hurry along, so that with your help and grace you will show me your plans for coming to know what the future will bring.'

"And he left again.

"A bit later God called again to Moses. This time only Moses alone understood God, and he said, 'I know, My Lord, that the angels in Heaven are impatient and that they are waiting and waiting for a great celebration. And for me a golden chair awaits. But I am serious about doing my service; I'm close to the Land Canaan, and I'm in something of a hurry.'

"And so the Lord of the World in his goodness and grace smiled and said, "Moses, Moses, I will not conceal anything because you have not concealed anything from me. You will be grateful to know that I have always been, and will always stand alongside you, but I must also obey certain laws and judgments of the world. So listen carefully. You have a student Joshua, who has studied with you for forty years. He obeys your commands and does whatever you wish him to do. He is now old and his beard shows gray streaks. He sits and waits, and waits. The time has now come when your student Joshua should become the teacher and leader of the Israelites. Now you know this, my son.'

"And Moses raised up his eyes and said, 'Now I know your solution, You, Lord of the world. What is there to consider? Make him the teacher and leader of the people. Let me go over as his student to witness, to witness from afar, to witness what has become of my work, my mission.'

"And Lord God said, 'Moses, my loyal servant, you have found mercy and grace in my eyes. And I will do as you have pleaded. Go, and I will protect and preserve you.'

And so Moses departed. And the Lord God adorned him with grace and touched him with his beams of light. And when Moses descended to the congregation, there was thunder and lightning. His heir, Joshua, stood up and realized that this was God's calling. And he went to Mount Nabo. And God the Creator spoke to him amidst the waiting throng.

"And when Joshua returned he went directly to the holy place and all saw the Presence of God (*shehinah*) in rays above his head and everyone then knew that God had kissed Joshua on that day. And Moses took him by the hand and asked, "Tell me, Joshua, what did God tell you." And Joshua took his hand from Moses' clasp, turned to depart, and answered, 'Did you, did you, Moses, ever tell me what God had revealed to you?' And so he went into the holy place and the people followed.

"And no one noticed how shamed and crestfallen Moses was as he hurriedly ascended Mount Nabo on a wide trail. Lord God was already awaiting him. And Moses raised his eyes to God and said, 'Here I am My Father and Lord. I have arrived.'

"Now you understand," our Reb went on to say, "why I don't regard you as simply students and small children. You can never fully know who is the student and who is the rabbi. There can come a day when one of you will become the important rabbi and I will remain a mere student. I sit here and you look me in the face as if you were just beginning to go to *cheder*. At first, you'll see I lay myself down to sleep as a child. Then I arise fully grown with a beard; and now I have a house full of children."

He reflected on his own words and then made off in another direction: "At this time in my life, it's too late to acquire a new trade. Sometimes I'm jealous of the carpenters, the shoemakers, the tailors, and bakers. They have no need to stretch their palms out, asking for benevolence." (Our rabbi had to go out each Thursday to procure enough to live one, which burdened him with great heartache.)

"Learn yourself a trade," he suddenly said, "because there will come a time when you will have a beard, you'll find yourself with a house full of children, and then troubles and worries will come – as they did to me – as they do to many of your fathers."

Then he began to sing a little folk tune and began to tell us stories about spirits, devils and lost souls that go "bump in the night" along the shadowy paths, who wallow about between Heaven and the depths of Hell and are then transformed into mistreated dogs, or into a pig or maybe a chicken, and who can never rest until they are "revealed" by a holy man and regain their salvation through holy chants. He spoke of horrible demons and nincompoops, especially the scary little ones, who play jokes on one another, especially when they come into the house late at night and turn everything over or put snuff into your nose, bolt down the doors with nails, or put pricks into the handles of hammers so that they cannot be picked up. Such scary and rousing stories our rabbi used to tell!

And at night when we returned home from *cheder* with tiny lanterns I would pause in the shadows and cry out, "Mischief makers, haunted spirits, demons, show yourself. Come here! Come here! Come here! Come Here! Disappear! Disappear! Disappear! Disappear!" The other children would run away in fright. I would shiver in exaggerated fright, not only for the presence of haunted spirits, but from the power I had to make them appear and the pleasure I felt in fooling them. To think that that I alone was not afraid! This feeling would stay with me, and I would do the same thing the following night so that children would throw "gifts" at me to make me stop — old bones, pieces of iron, buttons which they took from their clothing or from their father's and brothers' suits, so that I would no longer call up the ghosts and demons. But the longer we came to these shadowy places, the more I couldn't contain myself!

How they enjoyed summoning those ghosts! I myself took such great pleasure from scaring myself as well. What a frivolous, innocent brat I was! Once, when we were alone, the rabbi said to me, "I know that you are a lot bolder than the older children. You are also a lot smarter. You should see to it that you protect them, and not make them truly afraid. I would never get involved in your 'little business.' I'll leave that to your common sense." I understood it and didn't do it any more. I still craved do all of those things, but I didn't, out of reverence for Reb Shimshele Milnitzer.

Perhaps My First Role

They used to tell us about a certain Jew, Herr Hirsch (Baron Hirsch) who was so wealthy that the Kaiser bade him come to Vienna, bestowed him with many honors, and granted him prestigious positions. But Herr Hirsch said, "I thank you, Great King, but I cannot assume this position." "Why not?" the King wondered. So Herr Hirsch answered. " Great King, Lord God made me wealthy and you wish to grant me honor and give me important positions. But in Galicia live so many little Jewish children; their poor parents cannot nourish them and clothe them. They do not have even enough to send them to school. And because I have the fortune to stand before you face to face, I have a great request: You should permit me to open schools there at my own expense where the little children can learn and grow up to be smart people, and then become brave soldiers for you." And the Kaiser said. "I like that. I like that very much, Herr Hirsch."

And so Herr Hirsch soon returned home as Baron Hirsch and started Baron Hirsch Schools all over Galicia, including a school in Horodenka.

There was a world of difference between the Baron Hirsch School and the *cheder*. In the *cheder* it was dark and dirty; but Shimshele Milnitzer loved us and spoke to us as if we were his own. In the Baron Hirsch School it was light and very clean; the teachers treated us like little animals and they beat us. But if we studied, they gave us a cap with a shiny brim. For really studying, we received a new pair of pants. And for studying an extraordinary amount, they gave us a suit of clothes. And for being geniuses in the classroom, they dressed us from head to foot, complete with collared shirts and handkerchiefs. We all were serious about attending school washed and clean, even with good-looking shoes. If a child weren't properly dressed, he would be embarrassed because the others would shame him, and then he was sent back home.

The teachers were dressed in the German style and they spoke Polish. If the lessons we had to prepare were poorly executed, or if a question was not correctly answered, the teacher would hit us on the palm of the hand with a ruler. Some did it only for appearances sake, and that hardly hurt. But the Yiddish teacher, Herr Weiselberg, used to smack your hand with the edge of the ruler. This was the first truly bad person I had met in my life. He had a reddish-yellow goatee like Kaiser Franz Josef and loved to look at himself in the mirror and comb his hair immediately after he had beaten us. His face would become as red as a beet. On the table lay the ruler, which was a bamboo stick, and a comb and mirror to groom his beard. More than once he would lay us over the chair and whack us with his sharpened bamboo stick. Children would plead to the walls with forlorn cries and murmurs. But pity the child when Herr Weiselberg noticed him! He ordered him to lower his pants and he "delivered" with the stick on his naked behind. It not only hurt very much, it was embarrassing, as well. Herr Weiselberg was a master at giving beatings. We detested him, and even his children, who attended school with us. All of the teachers hit us, even the female teachers, but Herr Weiselberg hit more than he taught, and this is why we resented him.

But, little by little, we took our revenge on them. In winter we would bring icicles and frozen snowballs and wage war with them. In the spring, millions of beetles swarmed about. We would catch them and at an agreed upon signal, release them at once in class. The teacher, Frau Chamades, would become hysterical and scream. We put on our most sorrowful faces; as if we knew nothing about what we had done and laughed to ourselves. During a change in classes, we filled up her gloves with these bugs. When it came time to go home, she put on her gloves, but as she did so, she screamed from fright, and we giggled with joy. She summoned the principal, Berless, a tall, gaunt man with lead-colored face and turned-up mustache. As punishment, he made us stay after class, but she had to stay along with us!

Only one teacher never hit us. His name was Dreyfuss. When he himself was a youngster, he would bring home his schoolbooks and he would be rewarded with sweets. But Dreyfuss unexpectedly died.

The benevolence of Baron Hirsch made it easier for us to bear the burdens that were inflicted upon us by the other teachers. The wonderful arrangements they made for us to enjoy *Yom Tov*, the delicious bean soup they prepared for us in winter, and the playground in the schoolyard made up for everything else.

Life at home followed a routine because each of us worked; each had something to do. We arose at four in the morning to shape bagels and knead dough. At six, we brought it to the buyers in the market in flat-bottom baskets. At eight, we went to school. I always had tiny bits of dough stuck in my fingernails. I showed this off proudly to the kids at school to let them know that I worked at night, just like the big shots!

My older brother, Shabtai, was always a gloomy guy, tired and needy of sleep, with blood-shot eyes. He played with no one else, just studied in school. And when the teacher would call on him, quietly and uncertain of himself, he would stammer indecipherable words. I was the only one who understood what he was saying. The teachers inevitably embarrassed him, telling him to sit down, and then they would call on me. All I needed to do was repeat what he had said, but I did it in a loud and sure voice. So the teachers respected me ... on my brother's account — my poor brother Shabtai.

We sat in the third row of benches. Next to me sat two light-haired, simple children. They had long blond hair and red cheeks and they were dressed in blue (school-issued) suits and sailor caps. These were the children of the banker Yungerman. Every day they brought different treats to school. Once they brought challah with bits of chicken; another time bread and butter, honey and jelly. And they also brought raisin cookies with butter topped with cherries, grapes, apples, sour cherries, pears, or even strawberries.

Once, during a semester break, I was hungry – as always – and I looked upon the Yungermans' treats and my mouth began to water. I stepped up to the younger one and asked her for a bite.

"No," she honked like a goose and went on eating. I could feel that my face was reddening with shame. From that time on, I began to loathe them both and every other day I dreamed up different catastrophes for them. I brought soot and spread it on their chair seat so they blackened their suits and their notebooks. I put tiny pebbles on their seats and once even a nail, pointed upwards. As soon as one of them sat down he began to screech and everyone burst out laughing; I alone played the innocent one and kept quiet. Another time I even filled my inkwell with ink and placed it on the edge of the bench so that when the teacher called on me I stood up, motioned with my hand, and the ink spilled all over my neighbors' white face, blond hair and sailors' caps. At first, the entire class burst into laughter. Then the smaller Yungerman began to cry. The teacher tried to calm him down, and I made another blameless, but compassionate, face. I thoroughly enjoyed every minute of it, more than I would have enjoyed the sweet raisin cookie with butter. My life consisted of dreaming up practical jokes.

Once I leapt onto the bench with my elbows and delivered such a massive blow to the poor little banker's ribs that I almost knocked down the other kids on the other end of the bench. Another time I stood up "with difficulty" and "accidentally" stepped on his foot so hard that tears came to his eyes. He started to hide from me, fearing my practical jokes.

Then once, during recess, he came up to me. He said, "Why don't you ask me for something?" I said, "If I say yes, will you give it to me?" Then the other brother chimed in, "Just go ahead and ask." And I said, "Yeah, and you had better give it up!"

And I could not believe my eyes. They had prepared a box of treats for me. They even threw in a pen. From then on they would bring me something new to eat every day. It became a joy to go to school. And so the inkwell never again overflowed. There were no more pebbles and nails underfoot, and I no longer picked on them. We became friends and went together to the market in order to steal fruit. We had long sticks with a nail on the tip. When a juicy one turned up, we would use the tipped stick to pick an apple or a pear and then we'd dash away. We were a small pack of bandits who attacked the branches of apple trees. Or during the apple-picking harvest, we would "rescue" the fallen ones preying like a flock of crows on what was left behind. Near the armory we "found" — that is, when no one was looking – pieces of iron and horseshoe nails and we would sell it to that hypocrite Mordechai who traded in scrap iron. We could tell that he knew where it was coming from, but we had no problem cheating him. We always had five or six thieves in our "brotherhood." While a few of us were selling to him, the others stole pieces of iron from his own storehouses so we could sell them back to him once again! So it came to pass that two or three times he bought the very same horseshoe, and the same nails; we always doubled up in laughter when this happened. Seeing how it went, we once stole an old samovar and immediately demanded he buy it. He became suspicious, then looked us over from on top of his pile of junk, and started to take the belt from his pants. So we threw the samovar in his face, kicked up our heels, and quit doing business with him.

Once the Yungerman children's private tutor came to our home and scolded me in front of my father saying that not only was I a thief, but that I was turning the Yungerman children into thieves as well. So my mother threw him out of the house and shouted at him that if he dared come around again, the children would have a curse on them. But when the tutor left, my dad sent everyone out of the house and he had a talk with me. He said, "I believe every word. But I want to hear it from your lips. Say yes, or say no. An honest man, Shimshele Milnitzer, teaches you. And the Torah holds, 'Thou shalt not steal.' As long as you're still not a Bar Mitzvah, the *rebbe* and I are responsible for your transgressions. Admit it. Is it so or not? Now go and decide your punishment. How many whacks should I give you?"

"Yes," I blurted out, ashamed of myself. And I requested twenty-five whacks on the behind.

"So let me do it, my son, " my father said. "You are truly not a thief. Thieves are also liars. Say that you will never do it again and I will withhold the punishment." I promised him. Then my father called in the others and said to them, "Herr Yungerman is a thief himself. He steals from God and from ordinary people and even the entire world.

That is why he is afraid that his children will also turn into thieves. We are, thanks to God, honest people and we have nothing to fear."

At the time I didn't quite understand my good, honest, father. But if there exists a Garden of Eden, he is sitting there and is smiling to himself and thinking about how long it takes for children to understand the basic rules of life.

One Tuesday, before the market opened, a wonderful thing happened. They strung a long wire stretching from Herr Noyman's high-storied store, all the way to the post office. A man, a woman, and a youngster slightly older than me appeared, dressed in colorful tights with spangles. The mother wore green tights. The father was in red. The kid was in light blue. They all ascended a ladder. The mother began to drum and the kid blew three loud blasts on his trumpet. Then the father gave a speech. He said that he spoke all the world's languages, but here he would speak Polish, because the mayor of the town spoke Polish. He went on to say that even though they had received commendations and medals from all the kaisers and monarchs of the world, they themselves had come to Horodenka to perform their acts because of the truly fine mayor. "Now," he says in a high-pitched voice, "I will risk the life of my only child, all for the sake of his artistry." His eight-year-old child was barely older than me, and was to suspend himself on a tightrope stretching across two houses. He demanded no payment beforehand, saying, with tears in his eyes, that if – God forbid – something should happen to his child, what good would the money do him anyway? But if the Lord God would safely deliver the child through the air on the tightrope connecting one house to the other, he, his wife, and child would allow themselves to walk around with an upturned hat for donations. He was convinced that such heartless people who would leave the site after witnessing such a feat would not reside in a proud place such as Horodenka. He was sure that everyone would reward the great artists who risk their lives willingly, who had received commendations from all over the world, and medals, too, from Kaisers and monarchs.

It seemed that thousands of people crowded the market with anticipation. The parents tied two strings to the kid's belt, put a long pole into his hands, to balance himself, and bounced him up to the rope. It became deathly quiet among the spectators; they began staring at the rope. The father was shouting something to his child. The mother wiped away a tear and the kid crossed himself once more.

"Attention, attention: Look, honorable visitors," the father called out in perhaps twenty different languages. "The performance begins."

Above thousands of people, the kid took one step, then another, as if he could intimately feel the tightrope, balancing himself with the pole. He went slowly, shuffling his feet on the rope, step after step, a bit farther, a bit farther on. The crowd watched, muted. He was soon midway along the rope, but then he tilted the pole up and out, and called out in a heart-rending voice, "Father, the wind!"

The onlookers begin to squirm. Gentiles crossed themselves. But thanks to God, the child went further along. He was even quicker than he was before. He balanced himself with the pole and moved even more quickly. After five more steps he had reached the roof of the post office building. The entire market erupted in shouts and shrieks, and danced about in wondrous joy. The father and the mother collected money, and none of the spectators left. Each one dug a little deeper to give up their *groschen* to them.

I was not standing far away from the kid; I literally "absorbed" him with my eyes: a person, a child just like me, had put his life on the line. I looked at him in wonder and jealousy.

On *Shabbos* after our meal I called my brothers and several buddies from the neighbor's house. The long rope remained suspended above the ground. I took my bread-paddle in hand, closed my eyes, gathered my strength and began to put one foot in front of the other on the tightrope. I made my way exactly as he did, step after step, and in the middle I pretended that I was about to fall and I began to scream, "Father, the wind. Father, the wind. Father, the wind."

Neighbors began to congregate. Our bakery filled up. A deaf neighbor asked, "What's going on?" Another one answered, "Don't you see?" And the bakery became so hot you could choke! And we went about and shouted, "Father, the wind." The poor kid probably went crazy!

"Moishe, They-Break-Glass"

There were lots of nut cases (*meshugenah*) in Horodenka. But Moishe the water-carrier was an excellent example of one. He was tall with broad shoulders. He was quiet, always occupied with his own thoughts, and never talked to anyone. If someone asked him something, and they often teased him, would turn his head away so that he wouldn't have to look him in the eye, and he would answer in a harsh, labored voice, as if each word was literally giving birth to the next one. He usually threw in two or three expressions that didn't have to do with anything at all. Once, when I was with some buddies walking past the bathhouse we heard him screaming and arguing with such a choking, possessed-by-demons voice that we thought someone had attacked him and wanted to garrote him. We opened the window from the outside and saw that he was standing in the middle of a half-filled tub, flailing his arms and talking to imaginary beings:

A ladder appeared and reached toward the heavens. And lightning struck everyone's scabby skull. And is that the reason that they break the glass?

It was like his entire face was roaring.

And trees skated in the abyss. And is that the reason that they break the glass? They play the holy texts with their fingers, and etch the blue from the sky... And is that the reason they break the glass? Break the glass?

He expunged it all in one breath. We watched it all, scared out of our wits. We gaped at him. And then we started to mimic him:

On the ladders' scabby head, in heaven grew... why do they break the glass, Moishe? Why do they break the glass? They etch the blue from the holy texts. They break the glass, Moishe. 'Do they break glass?' I said, 'do they break glass?'

As soon as he saw us, he immediately became silent, stretched himself on the ground, as if nothing had happened. We left him and went back to our games.

But from that day on, the whole town called him, "Moishe, They-Break-Glass."

Moishe, They-Break-Glass wore rags, but he looked different than the other nut cases. The rags on his back were clean. In summer and winter he went barefoot; he had fine looking feet. When he became hungry, he took two basins from the bath and earned some money by carrying water that he exchanged for food. He usually brought the water directly to the bakery and got an old loaf of bread in return. But you could never depend upon him, because he brought water only if he was hungry. When his thirst was quenched, he would quit carrying water and go back to poking around the bathhouse, or in some hayloft where he would loll about murmuring to himself.

When children teased and annoyed him, he wouldn't pay heed. But when a grown-up did it, he became crazed, bared his white teeth and his big black eyes literally popped out of his red face. Wise-aleck kids then knew they were headed for a slap from the bony fingers of his arms, which "sailed" on both sides of his broad shoulders.

"Moishe, They-Break-Glass" was not from Horodenka. He hailed from other parts; no one knew where. This was never discussed. He led life his own way. He was, to put it in a nutshell, a true character — like no one else. What could be worse than the town nut case? And so everyone knew that "Moishe-They-Break- Glass" stood out among all the other nut cases.

Once, around Passover, someone gave him a clean shirt and tie to wear. And so, all cleaned up, he went around the side streets, looking good. The townspeople looked at him up and down — in the street, from the opened doorways, through the windows, as if looking at him for the very first time. Women blushed; men regarded him with jealousy; wagon-drivers were jealous of his broad shoulders; the teachers were admiring of his honest face. And no one cared to mock him. They began to whisper that "Moishe, They Break-Glass" may not be "all there," but he is certainly not a nut case. The pious Chana Rochel, the fortune-teller swore that she had seen the visage of God (*shechineh*) shine on his face. Yashe the cripple, the tailor with the diseased lungs, swore on the lives of his seven children that "Moishe, They Break-Glass" can be nothing less than a *lamed-vovnik*.Chaim, the wagon driver, chirped in about his face: one for which the heavens open up! "If Horodenka doesn't treat him with the respect he deserves, he will make so many cuts with his heavenly whip that Horodenka will be erased from the earth itself!" "Wow" another chimed in, "To think you are fooling with a *lamed-vovnik!*"

Truth be told, "Moishe, They-Break-Glass" was a lad from Brody, the well-known city of Galicia near the Russian border. He was engaged to marry Chanah Shrifrin, the house servant of the rich merchant, *Reb* Horowitz. But the sickly Madame Horowitz soon died, and the overstuffed Horowitz began to desire the healthy and strong house servant as a bride and he claimed her as his own.

On what was supposed to be their wedding night, the unlucky Moishe spitefully broke all the merchant's glassware and then ran away to Horodenka where he started to become crazy. He carried water when he was hungry, and slept in the bathhouse or on straw in a stable. Then the children of Horodenka gave him the name, "Moishe, They-Break-Glass." With time, some folks began to regard him as a *lamed-vovnik.*

The Family Shrinks; Poverty Increases

Everything in the world is arranged a certain way: there is even order in disorder. Even in the dishevelment of our family there was a proper way of doing things. My oldest brother helped our father open a bakery with his dowry gift and stayed with us to help. His wife bore a child each year, exactly as our mother had done, and he began to get worry lines on his face and wrinkles on his forehead, just like our father.

On a certain day, our brother Yankel, the practical joker, packed up his trunk and carved a new walking stick from a grape vine. And when our father asked him what it meant, Yankel told him that in the Hungarian city of Mishkaltz a rich but childless man lay dying, and that he had sent for Yankel to be his heir.

"Did he just send for you?" our father asked with a smile. So Yankel answered that someone had told the rich man what a comedian Yankel was. The man sent for him, so that he could laugh one final time before he died. And to prove his point Yankel began speaking like a buffoon, splayed his legs to resemble a tire, rolled his eyes, howled like a dog and chased after us, mooed like a cow and crowed like a hen. Everyone laughed out loud. And when our father asked him when he planned on returning, Yankel took the walking stick in hand and with an unaccustomed wave, said earnestly: "The rich man owns rooms filled with gold. As soon as he's dead and I finish counting his treasure, I'll come back with a pair of horses and carts filled with gifts of gold.

He then lifted up his trunk, said he would return for his farewells, and went off.

He never came back. We never heard from him or saw him again. And if anyone ever asked, we would answer, "We wish him well. He's living off the wealth of a rich guy somewhere in Hungary. He walks around in velvet and silk and counts his gold. And as soon as he is done with this, he'll come home. Then he'll take us there and we'll also get lucky."

And so we waited our entire lives for him to return to us.

The second oldest brother, Avram, once went with the wagon drivers to Lemberg and simply remained there. After some time, he came back home, dressed like a "city slicker," and with gifts for all. He smiled like he was the luckiest man on earth and he asked our father to return with him to Lemberg to see his new bride. He said that he wanted to show the people there that he had good breeding so her father would formally grant him her hand in marriage.

And so our father, feeling very fortunate, put on his *Shabbos* clothes and traveled to Lemberg for the wedding. When he came back he told wonderful stories about Abram's beautiful wife and the great city of Lemberg. "Abram is a cooking-oil dealer and is well respected. He is considered a man of means and everyone listens to him when he speaks. All the people there are friendly and they live in harmony with one another. They all work and make money and have little leisure time, like we do in Horodenka, to gossip and to set one against the other. It's great! Lemberg!"

The graphic descriptions of Lemberg made such a strong impression, that each of us had the secret desire to run off to the big city, where everyone had a job, was friendly to one another and had no time for gossip or one-upsmanship.

And so, thanks to God, four of my brothers "escaped" from their home.

When we opened the bakery, our sister Rochel came back home. She said she had been in Vishnitz with our aunt Toibeh, our father's sister, and there learned how to make women's clothing. In truth, she had made — from cloth, wire, and straw — very beautiful caps. No one had asked her about her friend, Ivan. Everyone was happy that she was now back home and that she had had her fill of the latest fashions. She had "filled out," and was now more beautiful than ever. When *Shabbos* came, the house was full of beaus, who had come ostensibly to hang around with my brothers, but in truth, came to be with Rochel. This made us mad, because we were reproached for going out with the wrong kind of girl. We wanted to uphold the honor of the family, as brothers and as almost-adult men. We also felt some jealousy for the attention she was getting. But she walked all over us. She kept on flirting with them, made come-ons with her fiery eyes of coal, smiled with her snow-white teeth, and the dimples in her rounded, plum-like cheeks. With every bit of foolishness that came from them she laughed coyly, carrying on like a colt. This carrying-on increasingly annoyed us and we could hardly stand her any longer. It got to the point where we could no longer put up with the salacious remarks that the guys made against other girls as well.

At least once a day we heard a boy make a remark about our sister. We felt like we wanted to split his head open! Finally, we headed back home and grabbed our beautiful sister by her braids. But our father got involved, and so we screamed and shouted that we would not put up with having a sister who is a prostitute. Rochel started to cry. Our father warned us that he wouldn't put up with this kind of talk in our home, that our home is "clean" when it comes to that sort of thing.

We didn't talk about it any more. From that time on, Rochel became a different person. She became more cautious and only went out visiting accompanied by our father. And she often sat in our market stall and sold baked goods. But later on we found among her handkerchiefs some hand-written love poems and a piece of cloth with her name and the name of a boy embroidered upon it. She and he had shared a deep love. And so the arguments started anew, but this time Rochel was sent away to live with our aunt in Vishnitz.

Two hired workers also stayed with us. One of them we called, "The Barrel." He was stout and very robust and he earned a gulden and a half, with food and lodging. This meant that in the summertime he slept on the grain sacks and in winter on the hay stacks. That's how we all would sleep. I was very jealous of The Barrel for lots of reasons. After work he could go out for a good time. He had enough money to spend on anything he wished while we, the children of the home, would never be paid regardless of how hard we worked. He had hands of gold. I learned how to work quickly and skillfully from him; within time, I became the most skillful bagel-shaper and roll maker.

The oldest brother in the house was Laibze. He was sixteen years old with golden yellow hair, but he looked much older because he was tall, broad-shouldered, and very rugged-looking. He was the most capable of the children and could speak well when he was only five years old. Laibze didn't worry about how he looked, but he loved to eat well. And so at night, when the others slept, he would cook up the most delicious meals and would share them with me. He was the quiet type; he never quarreled, and would gladly give up his soul for the sake of another. He never carried a grudge. At the time we both lay sick with typhus, we became the closest of brothers. I admired the way he worked hard, and he admired my dexterity. I was the only one who ever knew that on Friday night after the meal was over he visited the bordello, bringing along a gift. Sometimes on weekdays he would send me there with a pair of silk stockings, a painted handkerchief, or chocolate for the little prostitute Salka with whom he was deeply in love. She would send back letters with me, which I would have to read to him because he could neither read nor write. I would also write out his replies, which I composed with the aid of a *brivshteler* (a book composed of canned love letters, poems, etc.). I memorized three entire volumes of *brivshtelers*. I would also steal money from our father and give it to Laibze. This is how we became very close friends.

When Salka got sick she had to be taken to the hospital, and then to another city. My brother grew silent and he began to look bad. Once at night, when everyone was in bed asleep, Laibze cooked up a piece of liver in a pan and then he said that he was going to tell me a secret. But first, I would have to steal at least two gulden for him. I did it. On Saturday night he informed me that I should meet him at the courthouse. This made me extremely curious. I came to the agreed upon place. From there we went into the city. We then sat down by the river, and he began to speak. He said he could no longer remain at home, that he too must leave. We both broke down and cried and he promised that he would always look out for me and said it was probably better that he, the older one, left home first.

We kissed one another and I was left, silent and alone, on that spot. He looked around several times, tipped his hat, and moved on so that he became smaller and smaller until he was nothing more than a tiny spot, and disappeared.

I came home, feeling that my world had ended. At night I went to the bakery and resumed Laibze's tasks: kneading the dough for bread and challah. When our father arrived and saw that Laibze was gone, he said only this:

"My dear children are like the wild birds. They barely sprout wings when they take to the air with barely a word for their father, without a *zeit gezunt*. Well, maybe that's just the way it is..."

I felt ashamed that I couldn't reveal everything to my father, but I was able to do Laibze's work capably; I also thought about him all the time. Half a year later a post card arrived from him. My father put on his glasses and read it aloud: "My Dear Father: I haven't written to you until now, because you never taught me how to read or write. But now I have met a very fine young woman who writes for me. I work in Stanislav for the baker Saibald and, thanks to God, am feeling well. I am hoping to hear from you. Your loyal son, Laibze."

My father removed his glasses, put them away in the case, and two enormous tears dribbled down his beard. It was the first time I had seen him cry. This is how our family became smaller and smaller, as our poverty became larger. We had already gone through my brother's entire dowry and so could no longer keep the bakery going. We became bankrupt.

Even though I was still a underage, I stopped attending school and put myself out as a laborer for another bakery, coincidentally for our bakery's former owner. We were better off that way: being all of ten years old I was an independent person and I felt I could even support a family. This feeling was very useful to me when I became an adult.

My Brother Schmuel, the One with the Wonderful Imagination Returns Home

Several years after Schmuel's disappearance, when we still lived in the village, some Christian folks from the village said they had seen him at the horse market. That evening my uncle Lazar came to by to announce the good news that he had talked to Schmuel at the market place and he was returning home. The house soon filled up with Schmuel's chums. Elkanah, the merchant, also showed up. Everyone wanted to hear the news that Schmuel would bring, about the world outside. We waited and waited deep into the night, but Schmuel never showed up.

On that same night the best horse from Yiz Federkiv's stable disappeared. She was a three-year-old mare. The town was in turmoil. Then at a horse market Yiz Federkiv recognized his mare, now in the possession of Mendel Shpierer. A quarrel ensued. Mendel swore he had purchased the horse from one of Granach's sons, who was going to bring the dealer the proper papers.

"Without them, you do not have a right to the horse," Federkiv complained. And so a new battle began. Our elder brother, Schachne, who was probably trying to maintain the honor of our family, went to a tavern with the horse dealer and Yiz Federkiv. After several glasses of beer they agreed that all three should share in the loss, and so Federkiv was given back his mare.

Years passed. We were now living in Horodenka and the story of the mare was long forgotten. Then Schmuel suddenly appeared. He was now twenty-one years old and was obliged to appear for his military service. He was dressed in a fine fur coat with a slanted collar and wore creased pants and brown boots, just like a cavalry officer. On *Shabbos* he put on a black tie and shiny shoes and he carried his leather gloves in his hands so that all could see the rings on his fingers. He would not go out into the street without his braided riding crop. He wore his green officer's cap a bit to the side so that his long, blond ringlets would show. He would not let a Yiddish word escape from his lips, speaking only German, breaking it up into two syllables ("Dai-atch"). Mother begged him to at least speak Yiddish to her, so that she could understand what he was saying.

"No, Mother, he complained, "no Yiddish. I come from Mislovitz where they speak only "Jehr -man."

On Saturday night we all waited for Schmuel to come back home. It was dark in the house, but no one dared put on a light. Father didn't stand on ceremony and tore into Schmuel right away:

"Listen up, Mr. Know-it-all: I didn't say a thing while you ranted and raved in that stupid German of yours. I didn't say a word when you tried to cheat everyone with your crooked schemes, saying that you're a millionaire. I never even asked you about you being a horse thief. But if you think that you can go about in red trousers and a fur coat and shiny shoes, thinking that you have the world by the tail, you're making one huge mistake! I'll go ahead and beat the daylights out of you with your braided crop so that you'll stop babbling in German about forget about your counterfeit millions. And now I'm about to get your Aunt Henia and you'll immediately ask forgiveness for what you did to her daughter."

Schmuel started to make a howling sound. He threw his head about every which way, beat himself on the chest, even tied to pull his tongue out of his mouth and his hair from his head. Then he became speechless. We became transfixed watching him. Someone put on a light; father gave him a piece of paper and a fountain pen. With a shaking hand Schmuel wrote that he had had become mute and that they should immediately send for a doctor. In an instant, we forgot about our aunt Henia with her daughter and what had happened in the wheat field, and we sent for the doctor to come.

Dr. Kanafas poked him here and there, stuck something or other into his mouth, and massaged his temples. Meanwhile, outside a crowd was pushing and shoving. They all wanted to see the fine-looking Schmuel, the millionaire, the one who God had just "paid," punishing him by turning him into a mute. The doctor asked for two gulden in payment and declared that because Schmuel was a wealthy man, no harm would come to him. Nevertheless, he visited every day and said he would write to an important professor in Vienna about him to find out what he would advise in this case. It's possible there was a blockage in his throat. The doctor came back the next day. This time he said Schmuel should stay in bed and drink schnapps and pepper, so that he would perspire heavily. Then he broke through the crowd and went off.

Schmuel groaned and tossed and turned the entire night. He was burning up. It was a pity to look at him. The next morning he was ashen-gray. We dressed him and we took off with him to see the Rabbi.

The Rabbi's house was packed with people. Father told the Rabbi what had happened; he stared fixedly at Schmuel. Finally, he had something to say: "Schmuel ben Ahron: As God is my witness, my task is to make sure that our prayers for you will succeed."

Tears appeared in Schmuel's eyes.

"I see tears in your eyes," the Rabbi said. "This is a sign that you have taken our words to heart. I now know that you have once again become pious and true. Folks, it's time to begin: let us pray with a full heart so that our prayers will reach the Lord of Mercy."

The people began to pray fervently, and when they came to "*Shma-Israel,*" they suddenly heard Schmuel's voice. "*Shma Israel Adenoi Elahanu Adenoi Ehad.*"

"*Mazel Tov, Mazel Tov.*" The Rabbi interrupted the praying and told the folks to remove their *tallis* and *tfillim*.

Schmuel became totally confused and acted as if he was still mute. But the Rabbi said: "My son, we have all just heard that you know how to talk. But if you want to try to convince yourself and everyone standing here that you are still mute, well, let it be. The fact of the matter is that your parents and the entire community which has always been behind you, now knows, that Thanks to God, you can now speak and that you are out of peril."

We all sat around the table filled with honey cake, glasses of whiskey, and egg *kichlech*. The Rabbi gave a glass to Schmuel and they made a blessing: "May the Lord God give your tongue the power to serve you as it serves every good and pious Jew."

"Amen, Rabbi," Schmuel exploded with joy. Everyone else drank up.

Years passed. I was already in Berlin. Schmuel, on his way to America, went out of his way to see me. He didn't know even a single word of German.

"So, the German? What's with that," I asked him." You used to be a complete German."

"I was a *Milovitzer* German," he answered with a smile.

Everyone Fights With His Own Weapons

My father, my brother Shabtai and I now worked in Wolf Becker's courtyard bakery. My father was paid for the work that all three of us performed — and were worked harder than horses. We began on *Shabbos*, following *Havdalah*, and we worked hard both night and day until Friday afternoon finally came, and we got only a few hours sleep each day. On late Friday afternoon we went to the bathhouse. Friday night we slept at home; *Shabbos* was our only day of rest. After *Havdalah* it was back in the bakery until the arrival of the next Friday afternoon.

I was considered a good laborer. I quietly kept the thought in my head of running away from home. On the holidays, many young workers came back home from their jobs in different cities. They were all nicely dressed, and they told us that everywhere else was nicer and better than in Horodenka. My friend, Rosenkrantz's brother, came back from Czernovitz. He was dressed in a blue striped suit jacket with flowing collar (*Stoyantzer)*and a colorful necktie. And he wore shoes of soft calf leather, with rubber soles. This made him quite an attraction in Horodenka. You didn't just walk about in rubber soles; rather; you "waltzed" upon them. They were both beautiful and practical. And when you wore them down, you could buy brand new soles for a few coins and your shoes are like new again! My friend and I always followed him around. I was jealous of him not only because of his shoes, but for everything else: his wonderful good looks, the way he which he charmed the girls, the locks of hair that dropped onto his forehead, and of course, his great smile which he "brought back" from Czernovitz. All Horodenka was in love with him.

After the holidays were over, he went back to Czernovitz. But I couldn't put his rubber-soled shoes out of my mind. They seemed to wink at me; they beckoned to me. "Make up your mind! You too can have a pair of shoes equal to his! But this won't happen here in Horodenka!"

One *Shabbos,* after the evening meal was over, my buddy Rosenkrantz and I put on our *Shabbos* clothes on top of our weekday clothes, and we took off, walking to Kalomjya. Our hearts were pounding like hammers. As it began to get dark, we passed the village of Verbivtzi, and we decided to spend the night with our aunt Feigeh. I was afraid to approach my older brother and ask for a place to stay because I knew he would get angry and tell us to go back home.

We rose at dawn, packed our pockets with green cucumbers, and continued to make our way. We continued on for perhaps a half hour, when we suddenly heard my Aunt Feigeh call out to us.

My Aunt Feigeh never smiled. She was totally without emotion, and bereft of personality, resembling the soup she used to cook — warmed up, I should say, not cooked. She prepared soups from everything imaginable. We conjured up the thought that she even concocted soup from the wash and from old rags. And she always had something to heat up from yesterday, or from the day before. When did she really prepare anything fresh? We gave her the nickname, "The Leftover Aunt" because her leftovers were served up again and again. Now she was chasing us, taking our baskets and turning them upside down. She was convinced that we had stolen eggs from her. I was so embarrassed in front of my friend, that I was not able to forgive her for that, and I feel this way even now.

After a half-day walk, we arrived at the town of Gvatadzetz, which was quite a bit smaller than Horodenka. Our morning was free. So we sold our *Shabbos* clothes and bought some bread and cheese, some milk and butter. With our hunger satisfied, we went further on until we reached Kolomyja. I went directly to one bakery, then on to another, and for the first time in my life I had occasion to use the code word *Oisschitz* to which the young workers responded with *Lemschitz.* The bakery workers used to move about constantly, especially in the summertime. They barely got by in the winter. But in springtime they all seemed to come out of the woodwork. The delivery wagons were full of young bakery workers who greeted one another with *Oisschitz* and *Lemschitz* and that showed how kindly they felt toward one another.

The bakery lads treated me like I was one of them. They fed us and put us on the road to the village of Yablanov, where they were in need of a young bakery worker such as me. They hired me for twenty gulden a year, with food and lodging. This meant you slept on the sacks of grain, ate twice a day, and got two extra coins each day "to buy something to put on a piece of bread," for a snack. I was more concerned with being able to buy all the nice things I wanted for Pesach, first and foremost the rubber-soled shoes.

My friend Rosenkrantz was hired in Kolomyja as a *komi* (probably a metal-finisher or polisher) in a metal shop. He wasn't paid as well as I was, which was a higher-status job.

Yablanov is not far from Kolomyja, right near the Carpathian Mountains. The peasants who live in that area are called *Chutzulez*. After working for a night, I went into the marketplace to buy a snack. I spied a man with broad shoulders getting down from the driver seat. He turned around and I realized it was my father! I rushed up to him and he took my hand and said to me in a quiet voice, "Go, my, son, finish what you have to do. I'll be here waiting for you."

I was done in five minutes. Together we sat down on the wagon, which he had borrowed from a neighbor, and we rode back home. Father knew I was happy being with him. We spent the entire time talking about the Carpathian Mountains, about my uncle, about the rich black earth in this place, about the poverty of our town, and about the wonderful children my brother Schachne had. Father even told me that he was planning to travel to Chortkov to see the rabbi. He talked about everything, but not about my running away from home.

Once I came home, I immediately went to work for Yashe Baness. He had once worked for us, and then we both worked for Wolf Becker. As a baker, he was in a class by himself. He married and became an independent person. He was a dependable man, and we liked one another. He paid me a gulden each week, including food and lodging. I gave all of my earnings back to the family.

A lad from the town of Obertyn worked alongside me. No one knew his real name, so they called him the "Obertyn Rat." He was older and a bit bigger than me — a skinny guy with a leathery, brown-green face that was wrinkled, like that of an old man. He had a tiny little mouth, like that of a mouse. He drooled when he ate and when he spoke, and he was truly sallow looking, like a rodent that had become sickly. He would never laugh, and he had no use for anything in our town, not the houses, not the people living there. He found fault with me, and would always tattle on me to the boss. He would sidle up to the wife of the head baker and volunteer to clean house, to help out in any way possible, even to watch after her children. She would listen to every word of gossip he spread and would thoroughly enjoy hearing how I, the son of her husband's former boss, must now work for him.

Once, in the late afternoon, we finished our work and went to doze behind the oven. "The Rat" began to annoy me with accusations that I over-dressed and acted like someone important and that I chased after the girls. I kept still. He started to tease me, saying that I'd never grow up, that I'd remain small forever. I become angry:

"Listen, Obertyn Rat, if you don't cut it our and let me be, you'll get it!"

"What can you do to me, you fat kid." "I can bash in you ratty chin!" "Your hands will dry up before that ever happens!" "And I'll make your miserable face spin round!" "Your old man will have to do it because you can't!"

I didn't wait any longer. I delivered the first blow right into his jaw.

He knew how much I loved my father and that I had attacked someone with an axe when he was beating up my father. So he didn't dare hit me back, but said in a cold-blooded voice: "Let the Devil take your father!"

Another vile curse was waiting to leave his lips. He went on: "May the Devil take both your father and his father!"

And so I hit him again and it started all over, this time faster, mechanically. First came a blow, then came a cry of pain.

Me - a blow to his jaw. Him - "Your old man."

I became tired of hitting him, but he kept it up: "Your old man." And I hit him again. Would he let me keep hitting him all day long? I wished it would stop. But I was thinking that he's also hitting me back, but with words. His words seem to give him strength. They became his weapons.

I became so impatient that I would have let my fists have their way into his sticky, filthy flesh, which was like a mess of worms. But suddenly, I had a change of heart; I felt remorse. How would I have felt, if I was all by myself in a strange city with a face like his — with its mouth so distorted — and somebody was hitting me again and again without letting up as I was hitting him.

I stopped hitting him. I closed my eyes and tried to imagine what it would feel like to be a stranger in this town, so alone and unfortunate and helpless.

My hands were dirty and moist from his saliva. I began to quiver as if I had a fever. I turned my face to the wall and cried endlessly.

Once I had a chance to still my emotions, I began to feel deeply ashamed. The Obertyn Rat still lay perfectly still, his eyes wide open, expressionless. I picked myself up, left the bakery, and never returned to Yashe Baness.

For an entire week my right hand felt stiff from the beating I had given him. I had the notion that I would never be able to get his saliva off my skin, no matter how many times I washed. And all that time I kept thinking about a six year-old orphan boy who used to follow us around begging. All of us kids would beat him up. "If you keep beating me up," he would whine in his childish voice, "my father will come and strangle all of you." We let him be for a few days, and when his dead father didn't come, we returned to beating him up. "My father was a *schoichet* (ritual slaughterer)," he would cry, "and if you keep beating me up, he'll come back from the Other World with his killing knife and rip our your guts." We didn't bother him for several more days, but then we went right back to it. This time the orphan sternly warned us, "When you hit me, I'll do awful something to you." And you had to somehow believe him. If he wanted to do something particularly evil, we felt he could do it, because we felt that he could really hurt us.

For sure, everyone arms himself with his own weapons.

How People Fell in Love in Horodenka

The Glager family lived in Horodenka. We called them the *Yorochemnikhes*, after the given name of the eighty-year-old grandfather, Yerochem. The old guy always had a smile on his rosy-red face, which is how I remember him. His tiny sparkling eyes came piercing through his long, bushy eyebrows, and his thick, yellowish-white beard grew longer on one side than the other, as if the wind had blown it from one side of his face. He had eight sons, seven of them who were on their own; they were all glaziers and carpenters. They were respectable folk, tall and sturdy and all Horodenka took notice of them, especially the youngest one, who was slim, but with broad shoulders. He was a bold lad called S'rol-Kuneh. The brothers constantly quarreled mainly because their wives were jealous of one another. It seemed that an entire year could go by before they spoke. But if one of them came to blows with a stranger everyone of them wouldn't hesitate a second to help him out.

But they were as eager to help out anyone else in the town who was in need as they were to come to one another's aid. S'rol-Kuneh was the one who was the ringleader. He made friends with handyman-types, the paupers, horse-handlers, and *draymen*, (carriers) who would follow him blindly. He and his friends would poke their noses into the homes of the poorest people in the town and then threaten the rich folks to fork over money to help them out. The rich folk detested him and told malicious tales about him to the municipality, but the paupers adored him. On Thursdays, the poor people would go from house to house asking for charity. S'rol-Kuneh and his buddies would follow them from a distance and ask them who had given charity and who had not. Once, the rich miser Herr Ofenberger dared to chase the rabble of poor folk from his home, shouting at them as they fled, that he had no fear of the vagabond S'rol-Kuneh, and that he was through giving charity. This happened on a Thursday. The whole town was abuzz! On Friday night, quite "by accident", Herr Ofenberger's house caught fire and disappeared in the smoke. Everyone knew this was the work of S'rol-Kuneh and they were all very happy, even though it wasn't talked about.

On Saturday morning a crowd gathered around the burnt-down house. S'rol- Kuneh and his buddies also stopped to look. "This is like a sacrifice to The Almighty," S'rol-Kuneh roared, with just a hint of a smile on his face, knowing that this really wasn't an appropriate remark to make on *Shabbos*. He felt that God Almighty had given him permission to do this in order to punish Herr Ofenberger's hard-heartedness against poor people.

Ofenberger was insured for the fire, but from that time on, he began to give charity again, and in amounts larger than before. He started making pleas to the municipality to send more new and better-trained police to Horodenka. Among them was a patrolman with a turned-up mustache that stretched almost to his eyes. When he glared at someone with a stare that beamed through the mustache, people lowered their gaze in fear. He loved to arrest anyone he didn't like and he then proceeded to beat the living daylights out of him. He was a frequent visitor at Ofenberger's. After he had a glass of whiskey, he would "purchase" several items and say, "Herr Ofenberger, now there will be law and order here." Oenberger would usually reply, "God has granted it, Herr 'Order-bringer.'" And because of that, the entire town called the patrolman "Herr Order-bringer."

Once in the marketplace, S'rol-Kuneh started a brawl with someone and Herr Order-bringer arrested him. S'rol-Kuneh's buddies wanted him released immediately, but he himself didn't want it to happen. Instead, he calmly stretched out his hands so that the handcuffs could be put on, and said, "You're doing the right thing. There's got to be order in Horodenka, and there will be order!" So they took him off and the entire town broke into such an uproar, that they were forced to release him on the second day. And as usual, no one talked about it afterwards.

One night, two weeks later they took away Herr Order-bringer's gun, tied him up, snipped off one side of his long mustache, and deposited him, as they would a large sack of trash, on the hospital grounds. His rifle with the polished stock, his knife and sheath, his handcuffs and his metal hat with the large bluish-black feathers were all brought to the municipality, with the following message attached:

"To the Royal Municipality of Horodenka: Last night we encountered this patrolman drunk in a ditch. Admittedly, he besmirched the reputation of the Kaiser's authorities. We have taken the patrolmen to the hospital grounds. And his weapons and his helmet are being sent to the municipality. Long live the Kaiser! -S'rol-Kuneh Glager and Friends."

Efraim Glager, from whom we rented the bakery, had a son who was older than me named Moishe-Mendel. We attended *cheder* and then regular school together, stole cherries, hunted for horseshoes, and schemed in thousands of ways. We confided in one another, shared our thoughts about what we knew, what we liked and disliked, and what we were interested in finding out. And we indeed wanted to know everything. The thing we wanted more than anything was to become very strong. As naturally as we would eat a piece of rye bread and butter, we would flex our muscles to see if they had grown bigger. If we had a chance to enjoy a good marrowbone, we became convinced that our own bones would overflow with marrow. If we ate a chicken-neck, beef kidneys, or liver we never had any doubt whatsoever that our own hearts, kidneys and livers would become stronger. We also realized that strength without knowledge and understanding is not enough. So we started to go to restaurants to buy cows-brains, either boiled or stewed, in order to increase our intelligence.

Back in those days in Horodenka we had a park complete with trees, flowers, shrubs and bushes; with fountains and benches and bowers and all the things that a park should have. We used to call it the "Strolling Garden." On Saturday and Sunday, and on afternoons and evenings, you could find young men and young women strolling about. At first, groups of young men or groups of young women walked about, distantly exchanging greetings or jokes. Then couples started to walk about, so that we started saying, "So-and-so is going with so-and-so," or "He and she are speaking to one another." And when "he and she" went around speaking to one another for some time, people in the town would say they are "going out together" or "playing at love."

Most of the "going out" was done on Saturday. On *Shabbos* most of the employed men went to *shul*, not because they were so fond of *davenning,* but to meet up with one another. Afterwards, they would go to a small tavern and grab a bite to eat and toast one another's health. Everyone would enjoy himself and talk about things, throwing in a word or two about a certain young lady, and then they made their way to the Strolling Garden. There they awaited the young girls who used to make clothing or worked as house servants and such; they quickly broke up into strolling pairs. There the plots of novels and lines of poetry were brought to life. Even new lines and lyrics were created about the "apron maid" or about "yearning love."

And there were also some minor tragedies. It could happen that a girl from the better part of town, from "a better element" had "let herself be taken down" or let "false love get the better of her" by a good-looking young artisan.

Immediately the parents would get involved and "start building the *chuppah*," sometimes so quickly that there were scandals.

All of this was new in Horodenka. The old-timers could only shake their heads. "In the good old days we didn't carry on like this: everything had its proper place." This was really the first generation that had forgone the use of a matchmaker. If a young man wanted to be considered for a marriage, he would have to "go out" with a girl, "speak to her" or even "play at love." So, in the Strolling Garden sighs and moans of love always were whispered, as if they were the players in a melancholy drama.

And stories of love were indeed played out so that it could make you roll your

eyes! One was the well-known tale about the lovesick young man whose rival locked him up in a dark castle. And in his misery, he threw himself from the tower, only to land at the feet of his beloved. They fled together, shedding tears of joy.

A second story tells about a young baron, who in spite of his high status falls in love with his own housemaid, which causes them to be driven from the ancestral home. They run off and live as beggars through days of terrible weather, until they fall down in a storm and cannot even get up. And at the very last moment as they are about to breathe their final breaths, a postman revives them and tells them the good news that the baron's grandfather has died and left his entire inheritance to him. In the end, they return home and the poor, downtrodden servant maid becomes a baroness.

The house servant for Herr Kofler was a smallish, pretty young girl named Rebecca who came from the town of Oistzeaschke. She was poor, simply attired, but very lively. Her dress drooped loosely over her thin, fourteen-year-old body, but also enhanced a soon-to-be shapely young woman. She had skin as white as snow, silky brown hair, large black shiny eyes, big round cheeks and two small "loaves" in her blouse.

I made my early delivery of bread to the house wearing my usual delivery-boy outfit that consisted of white pants and an apron with my sleeves rolled up, and on my head my torn cap that contained my flour-sprinkled hair. She would greet me with her laughing voice: "Look, Mr. Torn-cap had delivered some might tasty *rugelach*," or "fluffy rolls," or "crusty Kaiser rolls!" This is what I heard every morning, "Mr. Torn-cap, Mr. Torn-cap" and if I were to hear anything different, it would have broken my heart.

I began to really keep my eye on her, and even followed her around, from a distance. Her friend, Herr Kofler's other house servant, once led me to believe that they had talked about how I followed her around, and so I figured I might as well be seen "by coincidence" walking past their house. She and her friend would coyly look back at me from the open window. This is how it went for some weeks, without words, but with the beating of my heart. Once I said — for all to hear — to my friend, "You know what... this is a great time to take a walk in the Strolling Garden." And then Rebecca said, loud enough for all to hear, "I think I'll rest for a while, and then let's take a walk in the park, okay?"

And both of them disappeared from the window. And so we waited. Finally they both left the house and went straight to the Strolling Garden. Once there, we walked in a circle, but in opposite directions. As we passed one another, we looked at each other coyly, but never said a word to one another. My friend said that it I needed to break the ice with her, and he was right. But every time I passed her, I became tongue-tied and couldn't open up my mouth!

After a few hours of this she said — loud enough for me to hear — that it was time to go back home. We also went back. We got there after they arrived, all the time listening to the drum roll of our hearts. The girls appeared in the window, and a dialog of sorts developed. We didn't even make eye contact. I spoke to my friend and she spoke to hers.

"When you show that you're interested in a girl," I say to my friend, "even if you never speak a word to her, she should understand your intentions."

"If it's that obvious to you," she told her friend, "why be so secretive about it?"

"It no secret, as everyone can see. It's obvious to everybody that I'm in love with someone."

"It's not enough that everyone can see it. Sometimes you have to say it." My heart is warmed by her response.

"You will hear from me very soon. Someone will have to speed it up," she laughingly says to her friend, "because next week we're off to

Zaleshchiki, and there just might be a different "someone" under a different window."

Both girls burst out laughing. As for me, my throat is dry; my heart is beating like a drum. I shout to my friend, "If someone is going to go to Zaleshchiki, that's where I'm going! There, I'll prove my intentions."

"That's good. We're leaving on Wednesday. That's when we'll see if men keep their word or not." I felt like my head would explode.

"Good. I'll follow you there on Saturday."

We all became quiet. I began to think about Wednesday, and about how she said "men." I gazed up at her, and took in her long, white neck, her silky reddish-brown hair and her two coal-black eyes, which were twinkling in the dark. For the first time we gazed at it others eyes, and for the first time I saw that she had a tear in her eye. I also felt like crying, but I wasn't sure why.

"I still have so much to do," she pointed out to her friend, and then looking at me once again, but this time with a bit of anger in her voice, said, "Good night, Mr. Torn-cap."

She disappeared from sight. I felt like a cripple, not able to move from the spot. But all at once she opened the window. She was now wearing a sleeveless nightshirt, without an apron.

"I hope," she said with a cute little laugh, "that I didn't insult anyone by calling him Mr. Torn-cap, even if it's rather appropriate. Good night."

"Good night," I answered her, with thanks in my heart, "Good night."

She had already closed the window and I went back home very contented. That night I dreamed that Rebecca and I were strolling in the park. We were going far away, all the way to Zaleshchiki. She was wearing a sleeveless blouse, and I could spy upon her bare, shapely arms. Her blouse was also low-cut so that I could make out the blooming roundness of her young breasts. We were playing with my torn cap, until we became hungry, at which time we ate the crusty, seeded *rugelach* and the salted bagels which I had baked, and we laughed, laughed all the way until we arrived.

On Wednesday, Rebecca left for Zaleshchiki. On Friday, when my father sent me off to buy postcards, I took the money, and after dinner I left home. My friend accompanied me to the outskirts of town. The sky was very cloudy. I sat down by the ditch and laced up my shoes. My friend gave me his best fountain pen as a going away present and then we swore eternal friendship and made our last goodbye.

I was more than a half hour on my way when it started to rain, and it was raining hard! But a piece of iron in your hand could stop the rain! So I swore to myself that if I could find a piece of iron on the way, it would be a good sign; if not it would be a sign that I should go back home. And right there in front of me was a half horseshoe, as if someone had placed it there for me to find. It was truly a good sign, and I hurried along.

By nightfall I arrived in Serafinitz, a village in between Horodenka and Zaleshchiki. I went into a tavern that was full of Ukrainian peasants. They immediately started to question me: "How old am I? How long have I been on the road? What do I think of the world situation? Why do the Turks wear red fez? And if it's true that Chinese men have one long braid, and if others have one eye in the middle of their forehead." I was able to figure out an answer to each of their questions and they were so pleased, that one of them invited me to supper. But how was I supposed to go eat with him, if they didn't keep kosher? He treated me in the tavern to four rolls and a piece of herring and a pint of beer. My head started spinning and I slept it off right there.

It was cold that night. I got up at dawn and started out again. The birds were singing their morning praises to God and I, a twelve year-old, small, and scared, was wondering alone in the big, wide world. God only knows what they were thinking back home. I really should have said goodbye to my father, but how could I have told him about Rebecca? And what would Rebecca say when she laid her eyes upon me? I kne what I would tell her: "Men are loyal, and they would not stand under another window with a different girl." Suddenly I heard someone call to me. I stared into the distance and I saw a tall man who beckoned to me with a cane. I became alarmed and started to walk away faster, but he was on my trail! I realized that this was not good, and I broke into a trot. But he ran after me. I was going so fast that I felt my heart was going to burst! I as dripping perspiration and I felt dizzy. Who knew how much longer he would be after me until he came up and killed me. Thousands of stars were blinking in my eyes. I could not run any longer, and I fell down.

I lay there quite a while. When I came to, a tall, sweaty gentile with an agreeable face was standing over me.

"You can run like the devil, you little pigeon," he said with a smile, wiping the sweat from his brow.

He picked up his pack that he had carried on a long stick. My fear returned. He took out a loaf of black "peasant bread" and started chatting with me. I started to eat, half from hunger; half from fear.

"It's a pity," he said with a grin, "that we can't enjoy a good bit of booze right now."

I kept quiet.

"Why were you running?" he finally inquired.

"Why were you chasing me?" I asked him back.

"I was chasing you because you were running. Aren't you going to Zaeshchiki?"

"Of course I'm going to Zaleshchiki."

"I already know that. I heard that last night in the tavern, and so 1 figured that because I'm going to the market there, that we could travel together."

We finished our meal and returned to the road. The *shaigetz* spun many lively stories, and I told him some of my own, and so together, laughing and a bit weary, arrived at noon in Dzeaneschke, a town on the outskirts of Zaleshchiki in which a brand new iron bridge was built over the Dniester River in the middle of the town. There we said goodbye to one another as if we were good old friends.

I really liked this beautiful, clean town that the Dneister surrounded like a ribbon. The folks there looked like us, and spoke like us as well. I planted myself in front of a bakery window in which wonderful pastries were displayed. A skinny guy with a blond beard and a smile on his face came up to me and said, "I see you're not from around here. I've never laid eyes on you before."

I explained to him that I'm a "bakery lad" and that I'm from Horodenka and that I was looking for a job.

"Welcome, welcome," he said and gave me his hand. He said, good-naturedly, "By your looks, 1 can see you're more than a half-way capable lad."

He led me to a tavern where he bought me a bagel and a *schnapps*. 1 would rather have had a glass of milk, but why argue with him about it if he wants to give me a job! He asked me how long I had worked and what jobs I was able to do.

"Try me out for a night, and you'll see what 1 can do," I answered. He liked me.

"You're not a boastful one, that 1 can see," he said and led me into his bakery.

Four lads worked for him: the seventy year-old gentile Antush; a middle-aged guy with a long beard, named Rafael; and two not-very-friendly young lads. I was the fifth one. The boss remained there overnight to "help out," but in truth he wanted to see how I would perform the various jobs that he had given me: preparing a Russia-style braided bread; shaping the loaves; making dough to the right consistency. When I made the Kaiser rolls and the *rugelach,* he beamed with pleasure. Back home I was a genius at this. In the morning, when I brought samples of my baking into the store, he said to me: "Let's have a drink and we'll get to know one another better." We went off.

"I know," he says to me in the tavern, "that I can hire you very cheaply until Pesach begins. But I won't even bother asking you what you think you deserve. I'll give you what I pay Rafael, the one with the long beard, and he's the father of three children. You will get a gulden and a half per week, including food and lodging, until Pesach. Agreed?" I gave him my hand, feeling like I was the luckiest person in the world.

I imagined what Pesach would be like back home. Me, all dressed up in blue striped suit, new shoes with rubber soles, and with lots of presents for my brothers and sisters — since I was a big brother to them — a grown-up man living in a strange city, where I had gone to chase the girl of my dreams.

I became lost in thought. My new boss, Menasche Strum asked me, "So, what are you thinking about?"

"About my home," I answered a bit shyly.

"Go ahead, get a good day's rest so that you begin to feel at home here, okay?" And truthfully, I began to feel at home here.

[Page 160]

Our Town In 1929

Moshe Fleshner

Translated by Harvey Buchalter

For a person who wishes to place a value on the memories of his native town, a place in which he spent no more than a third of his life, the following question comes to mind: What genuinely connects you to the small *shtetl* where you were accidentally born? What emotions connect you to the town, even more than to *Eretz* Israel, where you have lived for so long – where you grew to be mature and independent and where you impressed everyone with your prowess in overcoming the problems which are placed before every young man without a trade or experience, the ability to achieve the loftiest goals - to build a family life and intertwine himself in the building of *Eretz* Israel.

And ponder this: the 18 years which you spent in the *shtetl*, the years that determined the course of your development, the place you received your education, as both a Jew and as a *mensch* – you cannot ever renounce itsprofound effect upon you. And even if you forget actual events that today you would look upon differently, you strive to not allow your thought processes to alter that memory. And so the following question comes about: Are you not committing an injustice (to yourself) by forgetting about those beautiful times? Is the thread that connects the past and the present indeed that fragile? And so you come to the conclusion that you must not dismiss, in spite of all that has passed, that little bit that you still retain in your memory.

And now, as our compatriots have taken it upon themselves to create a monument in tribute to our long-ago home in the form of a *yizchor* book which will bring to mind all that we once had and what we have since left, each one of us feels the obligation to re-tell, a task very much like the obligation to recite *kaddish* in tribute to the lost loved ones, those in the mass graves.

The first and most pressing duty falls to those who were witnesses to the barbaric torture and death that brought down our people. Upon them lies the obligation to tell the upcoming generation what the *kulturmenschen*(Nazis), who were worse than wild beasts, did to our parents' generation. And if that is told in the book, then it becomes the most important part of the Book of Memory. But at the same time, a reconstruction must be made of our town and of the Jewish life it contained and the way a town – its fullness of life and its history – is woven into the history of Galician Jewry: the way in which that creation formed the lexicon that portrays Jewish life.

I do not know if the memories I will present will adequately portray the history and folklore of Horodenka Jewish life in the era between 1914, when the First World War broke out, and 1925, when I left for *Eretz* Israel. However, I hope that the Memory Book will generally contain descriptions and sketches that will give an accurate picture of Horodenka of long ago. Keeping in mind the duty and despair to do my part to fulfill my obligation to the anthology of the Book of Memory , I will do my best to share my memories of that time.

a. Childhood

The childhood years of a Jewish boy were certainly no different from those of a Jewish boy in other towns or areas. The first schooling he received was in the *cheder* and in the Baron Hirsh School. Jewish education was essentially traditional, and from the beginning, *Chumash*, Bar mitzvah preparation and various other areas of study were taken up by the *cheder* and upper-school students. After each term, and during the semester itself, we had to be tested. On Shabbos, usually late in the afternoon, the family would come together and the rebbe would have the young boy recite the Torah portions he had learned from the rebbe.

After the age of ten, a boy would have to begin to wrestle with the problem of where to continue his studies. He may have wanted to go to the gimnasia like so many of his friends, but his parents might not have wanted that for him, mainly for religious reasons. But little by little, with the example set by others, the parents usually changed their minds.

As time went on, the *cheder's* role was diminished. Children were sent instead to the Hebrew-language school. Generally speaking, the rise of a Jewish national consciousness brought about a diversity of viewpoints concerning the best way to educate children following the First World War.

The Circle for Literature Activities - 1923

In the First World War, the evacuation by the military of children and the elderly to places unknown, far from their neighbors, made a deep impression in my memory, as well as the memory of the first airplanes flying over our town during the Rusisian invasion.

The first Russian invasion lasted about half a year, after which the Kaiser's army returned. The Jews were very happy, but not for long. The Russians re- mobilized and the Austrians suffered one defeat after another. They soon realized that war was more than an idle diversion, and so they began to draft both older and younger men, so that fathers and their sons, age 17 and over, were taken to the front. The younger children were forced into making a living and became the lifeline of the family. And then came the second and then the third Russian invasion. The Russians broke through the Dniester River front, took over Eastern Galicia, and made their way to Pshemishl. With the capture of Pshemishl, they were hoping to bring the war to a close.

At the time of the second and then the third invasion, Jews, almost without exception, retreated with the Austrian army. Those who were lucky enough were able to get hold of a horse and wagon and loaded their baggage, the barest necessities. The others struggled with packs on their backs, to the roar of the artillery.

No one who was part of that awful pilgrimage will ever forget it. Children lost their parents and parents their children, and not until weeks later searched them out in one of the camps in Tschien or Merrn. I recall how we traveled at night from Olomay to Hungary in a fully packed open wagon, and suddenly it began to rain! It rained the entire night and only in the morning did the autumn sun shine and defrost the icy wheels. At our first stop in Hungary, representatives from the government and the Jewish community began to assist the poor refugees and to give some hot food to the children.

As we progressed, caring people saw to our needs, until we came to our place of rest, where we would remain for the harsh years of the war. The three years we stayed in Behmann, not far from the German border, need to be told in a separate chapter. At first it was hard, but then we became accustomed to the strange environment. But with time, the living conditions became normal and when the time came to go back home, many families were in no great rush and were not anxious to be the first to return home.

The Jews in the towns and villages neighboring Behmann gave a fine and warm welcome to the refugees. The heads of the Jewish community did a lot to lighten the load of the refugees and this made quite an impression upon the gentile community. The Jewish community helped us to enroll in school, in arranging for Bar

Mitzvahs, and inviting Shabbos and festival synogogue – goers to their homes. All of this was essential to our well-being, as most of the families had their fathers in the military and the community workers were deeply concerned that the children's education would suffer from neglect.

Pilsudsky Street

b. Boyhood Years

The refugees who returned found the town totally destroyed. The houses and shops that remained standing were without windows and doors and everything that was once inside was now gone. Several of our Christian neighbors hid our household goods and they later returned them to us; for others, help from the police was needed to bring about their return. The Polish government started a fund to rebuild the town and provided supplies and money, and so the town was rebuilt and things returned to normal.

With the rebuilding of the town, a new era began. Young men now became free of the burden of supporting their families and were able to lead their own lives once again. Several retuned to their studies; others attended school in the evenings. There were several students in town who had completed the *matureh* (basic course of study) but hadn't decided what to do with their lives and worked at refurbishing public buildings.

The activity of the youth then took on a new form that had been unknown in Horodenka before the war: the beginning of youth organizations. They had a Zionist flavor, but they tried to give their members a general education as well. They showed them what subjects to study, how to prepare themselves, and they formed different clubs and circles, such as literary societies, clubs for sports, and a drama society. The drama society was formed thanks to the generosity of our fellow townsman, the great stage performer Alexander Granach, whose magnificent talent awakened the ardor of the town's youth. He gave first-hand instruction to the first group of young actors in the drama society.

I certainly cannot give a complete description here, in a few sentences, of the role Hershel Sucher played in the Zionist life of Horodenka. I will only say that he was the embodiment of a through-and-through Zionist, and was a model for all of us on how to achieve the Zionist ideal. He also set an example by personally doing the tasks that he had called upon others to perform; thus he came with his family to *Eretz* Israel. He also was active in the Horodenka *landsmanshaft* society there. He died in Herzliah in 1959, to the sorrow of all of us for whom he served as an example through his activity and single-mindedness to the cause.

The youth organizations were very active in their various groups for the cause of *Keren Kayemet* and *Keren Hasyod*. They distributed coin boxes (*pushkes*) for *Keren*

Committee for "Keren Kayemet Leisrael"

Kaimus, collected funds by hosting many festivities, and presented evening events and programs whose proceeds were targeted for the Jewish National Fund. Concerning political orientation, most of the youth adhered to the Zionist-Socialist view which also had the largest following in the *Halutz*(pioneer) Organization. The older Zionists were all *Tzoanim Holaim,* or as we would call them, *shtam* Zionists. The first group of *Halutzim* came together in 1919. They hired themselves out to be fieldworkers for the Jewish estate-managers in Galicia and thus prepared themselves for work in *Eretz* Israel. It wasn't easy to acquire work, because the idea of young Jewish boys from the city taking on the rigors of field work was preposterous. Finally, the managers were persuaded and they took us in. The days we worked in the field became a profound experience for us. But it also spelled failure for some of us: those who were unable to do the back-breaking work were forced to return home, and this left a bad feeling in all of us.

The first group of settlers (*olim*), all of whom were gimnasia graduates, left Horodenka in 1920. In the summer of 1920, the second group, of which I was a member, departed. By just pure bad luck, we were delayed in Pressburg, where we had to secure visas from the English consul; the Society to Aid Emigrants to *Eretz* Israel had the job of assisting us in this regard. At that time, the Society was heavily influenced by the extremely religious *Shalumi Amuni Israel* and our group did not take kindly to them. We went round and round for a while, and finally they had their way and they convinced the English Consul to refuse to grant us the visas. Somehow we made it to Vienna, with hopes of getting our visas there, but at the same time there was Arab unrest in *Eretz* Israel and the Mandate government temporarily halted *aliyah* to the land. A few of our comrades then remained in Vienna and learned a trade; they came to *Eretz* Israel a few years later; others talked themselves into turning around and they consequently returned to Horodenka.

It should be understood that our *aliyah* was temporary halted; that is, until the political situation could be resolved. Meanwhile, other catastrophes befell us. We were considered military draftees. To receive an exemption, you had to get an exemption certificate from the military. This was not easy and full of red tape. Finally, it all cleared up, and in 1925 I left for *Eretz* Israel with one of the largest groups that had ever left Poland.

I will not write about the difficulties of adjusting to the new environment, which challenged everyone, not only those from Horodenka. I only want to say that in coming here, our goal was to become one with the community in *Eretz* Israel and not call unnecessary attention to our Horodenka origins. This feeling sustained us until 1945, the year in which we could do no less than organize a *landsmanshaft* society for the purpose of helping our remaining landsheit who had saved themselves from the devastating Holocaust.

c. My final visit to Horodenka

My final visit to Horodenka, a visit to family members, was in February 1929. Together with me on the ship were a few Jews who had abandoned *Eretz* Israel and were making poor excuses for leaving by blaming the land, not themselves. A few years later I ran across them again. They had returned to *Eretz* Israel after having searched and failed to discover the easy life away from the land.

I was not the only one awaiting passage in the port of Constantinople. During the endless wait, we realized how far we had distanced ourselves from Diaspora life and how difficult it would now be to return to our former lives. There, it was very hard for us to convince the young people to leave behind the good things of Horodenka for *Eretz* Israel. At that time, many of them could have come here. They would have removed themselves from the tragic end that befell them.

Europe at that time was enduring a harsh winter and the voyage from Constantinople took four days, instead of the usual two. It was scarcely possible to go from Olomay to Horodenka and I had to travel on Shabbos to Zabldov where my brother Chaim lived. Finally on Sunday night we both landed in Horodenka.

In Horodenka I saw many changes for the good. New buildings were erected, and now there were more markets, automobiles and busses. The economic conditions in the town had also improved with the fine work of Finance Minister Grobski. During the short time I was in town, I attended a few meetings, mostly about Zionism and conducted in Hebrew. I still remember how the Zionist circles were surprised that I had participated in the May Day Norodny Dam demonstration, which was staged by the Bund. They were unable to understand, "how does a Zionist become involved in May Day?"

As I have previously stated, the purpose of the visit was a personal one. It was to be with my family and to celebrate my wedding with Pepi Berman, to whom I had been engaged. Her extended family, mainly her mother (from the well-known Tschermovitzeh family, Brenner) could not come to terms with the idea of not only allowing their daughter to travel alone to *Eretz* Israel, but also for her to be if she would be brought under the*chuppah*. My sister's wedding was also to be performed at the same time, and this was the result of my promise to go back to Horodenka and "make a peace treaty" with the entire family – primarily my parents, for whom this would be the great and everlasting event of their lives. The ten weeks of my visit were, looking back, one extended *yom tov*.

But the holiday ended and the day of my departure arrived. All the relatives came to this solemn event. Aside from my beloved parents were my brother Chaim and his wife and relatives from my mother's side, the Latner family. From my wife's family were her sister Dusieh and her husband, and also all the relatives from both their families who had lost all of their wealth in the first Grozamer stock crash of 1941. And I will forever bear the heartache of not being able to influence all of them to come to *Eretz* Israel and consequently save themselves. In truth, I was not the only one who tried unsuccessfully to get relatives to make *aliyah;* but as I reflect upon it, it is a poor consolation.

Five months following my departure from Horodenka my contact with my wife became very tenuous. During this time she received documents allowing her to join me in *Eretz* Israel. In the five years of World War II, our contact with Horodenka was completely cut off, and we were constantly distressed about the state of our relatives who were left in the Nazi hell-fires. But no one could possibly imagine the extent of the tragedy, its awful reality.

The deeply-held commitment we had to help the few remaining persons who had saved themselves brought to the fore all the *l*andsheit from the towns large and small in *Eretz* Israel. Thus was formed our *Argun Yotsai Horodenka Ve-Ha- Gviveh*, whose activities will be described in a separate chapter.

[Page 164]

A Visit to Horodenka in 1934

by Max Bahr

Translated by Harvey Buchalter

It is possible that I am one of the last to see Horodenka before its destruction, having just returned there after spending ten years in Latin America.

As I traveled by train through Berlin, I strongly felt the Nazi presence. Military forces were everywhere, especially on the trains. In Poland you could feel the presence of Hitler's propaganda. In Galicia, where there was a majority of Ukrainians, most eagerly awaited Hitler's arrival so that they could feel free to murder the Jews and plunder their property. At that time, many Horodenkan Jews wanted to abandon Poland to go either to America or Israel. But their daily suffering prevented all but a few from doing so. All doors everywhere were shut.

I recall traveling by coach to Sniatyn to visit my father. It was a quiet, early morning. I recall how we traveled through the village of Serafinitz, and how the murderous Ukrainians wanted to stop us by reining their horses into our path. But our coachman was cleverer than they were, and he tore off in a gallop, avoiding them.

The Ukrainians shouted after us, "Just wait, you dirty Jews, when Hitler comes we will get whatever we want from you."

And he came, indeed. I can see it now: The murderous gangs of Germans, Ukrainians, and Poles falling upon our weak brothers and sisters – old and young alike – killing them without mercy. And that is why the ancient cry of every Jew explodes from my heart: "We shall never forget!"

[Page 164]

The Villages Around Horodenka

Dov Mossberg

Translated by Yehudis Fishman

In a general way, I am considered a son of the city of Horodenka, rather than from the surrounding areas, since I spent most of my youth in that city and returned there after the First World War. However, I was born in one of the surrounding villages called Semenovka, and I spent my childhood years in another nearby village called Stetseva. I have memories of the home of my father and grandfather, who were both villagers most of their life. Now that the chapter of the history of Judaism in Galicia has been sealed, the chapter about the Jewish villagers and settlers and how they struck roots in a strange environment among the Ukrainian population, is worth recreating with some of the impressions and experiences of a young Jewish village boy.

The district of Horodenka encompassed forty-eight villages, and in them the Ukrainian population was about twenty thousand people. In almost all of these villages there lived several Jewish families, who with great strength in their souls uprooted themselves from the city centers to seek their livelihood in the villages. However, it wasn't easy for Jews to give up the conveniences, security, and warmth of being with the city folk to take upon themselves the loneliness and alienation of living among a primitive and envious folk. This isolation intensified the feeling of exile and they acquired the taste of exile within exile. However, only a select few were able to continue their lives year after year to maintain the genealogy of the Jewish villager, who represented a special type of person in the chapter of life of Jews in exile.

The first Jew to come to the village was generally someone who rented a saloon. This way of earning a livelihood was harsh and bitter and demanded constant interaction with the non-Jews who gathered there during their holidays. They often became intoxicated, and more than once, fistfights broke out among them. There were also threats directed toward Jews, whom they hated intensely. The loneliness that oppressed the Jews during weekdays was intensified sevenfold on the Sabbaths and holidays. On those days, the villager was forced to forgo being able to pray in a congregation, to hear *kedusha* and *barchu* (prayers which can't be said alone-trans.) from the cantor, and had to be satisfied with an "orphaned" and grieving prayer.

And who can describe the great pain of raising children in the village! There were two possibilities open to the individual Jewish villager in educating his children, and both involved great expense: to send his children to a nearby city to attend the *cheder* there, or to hire a teacher, that he would be willing to pay, to come to his home. Under these harsh conditions, the villager had to be satisfied with a very minimal education for his children – to be able to read Hebrew from the prayer book. The father had to watch with a painful heart, as his son grew up to be an *am haaretz*, an ignorant person. We also cannot minimize the effect of the non-Jewish environment to which both their sons and daughters were drawn. More than once, this attraction ended up tragically, with children changing their religion, leaving their parents' home, and casting a stain upon the entire family: fathers did not want to forgive the child who betrayed her family.

Sometimes an outside Jew would drop into this special environment. He might have been a wanderer going from city to city knocking on the doors of philanthropists. I still recall one who was graciously made welcome in the home of a Jewish villager, and honored with a wholesome meal and a place to stay over. The entire

household would then try to get close to him and drink his words with
thirst. Sometimes he would bring regards from the host's relatives or
friends, whom he came across in his meanderings.

Other times, he would just convey news and information about
what was happening in nearby villages or in the "big wide world."
Often the traveler would be a Torah scholar, who transmitted a God-
fearing air. In the middle of conversing with him, the host might
remember something from his childhood learning, and would hold
tight to a brief teaching or story from the guest that he had never
heard before. In the morning, after prayer and breakfast, the traveler
would go on his way with a generous donation from his host, who
would bless him for the pleasure that the guest provided from his visit.
He considered this visit to be "live regards" from the larger Jewish
community to which he belonged and with which his soul yearned to
connect.

However these visits were relatively rare and the rest of the days of
the year, the Jewish villager remained in his sad state of loneliness.
Only when the Days of Awe came would he leave his house and
property, and entrust, or perhaps practically abandon his property to
the hands of non-Jews – the house with its furniture, the field whose
crop had not yet been gathered – and travel with his family to the city,
to spend the holy days together with all the house of Israel, to pour
out his conversation before the creator just like everyone else and to
absorb the atmosphere of the *shul* that was so far away during the rest
of the year. And when the holidays were finished, he went back to his
village, cleansed and purified from materiality, and filled with hope
and faith that his prayer had been accepted, and that the new year
would bring only good on its wings, for him and his family and for all
Israel.

This description of the lonely Jewish villager was actually known to
me only by hearsay. During my childhood, there were about 30 Jewish
families in our village of Stetseva. This was just enough to mitigate the
harsh loneliness. Most of the families in the village were related to
each other by marriage. On Sabbaths and holidays they would gather
for communal prayer, with a *minyan*. They did not travel to the city for
the Days of Awe, but, because they want all to fulfill the directive of
"The glory of the King is in a large populace," two adjoining groups
would gather together for one *minyan* and they would summon a
cantor with a distinguished appearance and a pleasant voice, to help
them celebrate the holiday in all its details.

The relationship between the Jewish villager and the general
population was decent enough. In spite of the vast difference in
religion, in their way of life, and in external appearance, neighborly
feelings existed between them, which were based on shared daily

experiences. These connections were closer among those Jews who were actually involved in working the land. This joint activity and their common concerns even forged a common language. Though these similarities were not enough to uproot mistrust or to diminish the embedded hatred toward the Jew, it was enough to enable proper neighborly relations during stable times.

There was one special village near Horodenka, the village of Chernovitz. Most of its residents were Jews, and most of them were engaged in farming. This city also stood out for their communal activities; for a certain period after the World War One, they even had a Hebrew school.

The landowners occupied a special place among the villagers. In all the neighboring villages, a substantial amount of land belonged to one family, generally a wealthy Polish family who worked the land with peasant villagers who were supervised by a foreman. Sometimes the land was leased out to the tenants who had to pay a portion of the crops to their landlords. This was a residue of the lifestyle of the feudal system, when the land generally remained with the rulers, and the farmers got a very meager portion of the produce, usually just enough to sustain life. In the beginning of the twentieth century, the farmers were free and independent and owned their own portions of land. Still the primary landowner retained his position.

Since most business was in the hands of the Jews, all the landowners needed Jews. Many Jews thus succeeded in winning the trust of the Polish landowners and were involved in their daily business dealings. Many Jews took supervisory jobs. With the passage of time, many plots of land were transferred to wealthy Jews, and the class of Jewish landowners arose. Most of these lived in the village, in an estate that was in the courtyard of the farm. But there were also those who lived in the city and ran their farm through supervisors.

Also in Stetseva, the village where my father lived during his last years and where I spent my childhood, there was a Jewish landowner named Yehudah Cohen, a very learned and educated Jew. His brother Dr. Cohen was a lawyer in Horodenka, who also stood out for his knowledge of Hebrew and his Zionistic leanings, unlike most Jewish lawyers who were usually assimilated. Only in the years after World War One did groups of Jewish intelligencia get involved in political life.

Beside Yehuda Cohen, there were several other Jewish landowners in the villages around Horodenka: Yossel Zeidman in Serafince, Bezner in Potoczysk, Nota Goldberg in Strel'Cheye, the Baron family in Semenuvka and Rakovets, and the Ruble family in Kornev. One of the citizens of Horodenka also joined the landowner class in the last years before 1914, when he purchased the estate in Czerniatyn. This was

Berel Shpierer, who reached a level of affluence in a few short years, and was for a time also the communal head in Horodenka. He was a modern Jew, and in his youth was a member of the *Maskilim* group in the city. The Zionists, who supported his choice, also accepted him. The other estate holders did not participate in communal matters. They didn't turn to Zionism but also were not assimilationists. In the years after World War One, these estates sometimes served as training camps for pioneers.

The differences between the village Jews and the city residents were great. The village Jew in his coarse and simple garments, with his primitive customs and lack of culture, often served as a target for sarcastic darts thrown by the city Jew, who emphasized his superiority at every available opportunity. However, these Jews were bound with every fiber of their being to the collective Jewish nation. They rejoiced in community happiness, and were the first to suffer when a troublesome time came. They had a special merit, these folk who survived by picking food from the ground, and most of them physically fulfilled the historic destiny: "By the sweat of your brow, shall you eat bread."

[Page 166]

The Village of Serafinitz

Abraham Bergman

Translated by Harvey Buchalter

The town of Serafinitz took the form of the printed letter S. The length from one point of the village to the other point was six kilometres. Therefore, the town was divided into two "points." The southern point, which we called "The Other Point", transversed the Kaiser Strasse, which linked Horodenka with Chernovitz, the former capital of Bukovina. The second point, which was called "The Point", went up toward the Tschervaner, a well-known spring, climbing two hundred meters up one side of the hill to the other side. As a result one part of the village bordered closely upon the outskirts of Horodenka.

The population of Serfinitz was exclusively Ukrainian and was made up of one thousand families at the beginning of the twentieth century. The Ukrainians, who were mostly involved in agriculture, were fervent nationalists and also had some intelligent folks amongst them. In the short duration of their independence after the First World War, they exhibited a great deal of animosity toward the Jewish citizens of the village. In those times, the soon-to-be famous outlaw, Tchakovsky, also known as "Harim," was in charge of the region of

Horodenka. He sought to arrest all Jews from the village, blaming them for engaging in espionage. The reason for this was that Jews gathered to *daven* the evening prayers. They were imprisoned for several weeks, under this charge.

Among the forty-eight villages in the Horodenka region, Serafinitz stood apart from the others in its fervent anti-semitism. It was the focus for organizing the paramilitary group *Sitsch* which carried out underground operations with the goal of uniting "Little Ukraine" with the Great Ukraine within the Russian domain.

Among the Ukrainian populace there lived approximately forty Jewish families, and among them the well-known Zeidman family, who were the so-called "aristocrats" of the village. Their estate was in the middle of an enormously large field, with two inns, two mills, and much livestock. The livelihood of the Jews consisted of the following occupations: estate stewards; foremen or overseer; or bookkeepers. A few families made a living by leasing out use of the mills and the inns; some even worked as farmers, working the land alongside the Ukrainians. Some supported their families with little shops, trading in grain and livestock, and in *luft gesheften* literally making deals as middlemen between the town's Jews and gentiles. The Jews of the town were mostly middle class, but there were a few families who didn't have steady work, and they had a rough time "making *shabbos*" (earning enough money to provide for the *shabbos* table).

In the stretch of land fronting the "aristocrat's" residence was a small synagogue in which the Jews from both "points" gathered on Shabbos and Yom Tov to pray, study Torah, and chat about the state of the world. The Jews in Serafinitz were very pious and the rabbi could interpret with all nuances of a page of *gemara*; no stereotypical "country bumpkin" Jews lived in Serafinitz. In spite of living in a gentile environment, the Jews went about the streets on Shabbos in *talis* and *streimel*.

Before the First World War, several dozen Jewish youth emigrated to America. Later, in the years following the war, young people became more involved in charting the course of their education; teenage and young adult students became inflamed with the ideals of Zionism. Some of them went on to *Eretz* Israel as pioneers. At the same time there awoke in the youth the yearning for building community, being together as one and advancing a common culture. They organized evening presentations and made connections with the youth in the neighboring villages and towns. The quality of the evenings was exceptionally high.

The first Jews settled in Serafinitz at the beginning of the 1900's. The first was Abraham Zeidman, who was an important fish dealer. He and others established the commercial life along the river. In the beginning, he lived alone in Czernovitz. Later he helped several Jewish families from the village of Bobin, in Bukovina, to move there with their households. Among the first were the families of Reif and Hoffman.

Following Abraham Zeidman's purchase of the Serafinitz property, other Jewish families settled in the village. They were mainly his relatives, with the same last name. Finally, he himself settled in Serafinitz. He was a very pious Jew, a Torah sage, a knowledgeable Jew and a good businessman. He arranged for his son, Yossele, to marry Rochel, the Berezaner rabbi's daughter. Yossele, although also a learned man, was more at home in the moden world.

After his father's death, Yossele Zeidman lost his inheritance. He had three children, two sons and a daughter, but he didn't derive any pleasure from any of them. His daughter, Devora died young after a failed engagement. The youngest son, Alter, against the wishes of his father, married an Italian Christian woman in Vienna before the First World War. He owned a clothing factory, but was unfortunate in this line of work. He constantly depended upon his father's assistance, and when this was once refused, he committed suicide in desperation. The oldest son, Moshe, was not destined to go down the right road either. He lived a spendthrift life which caused problems constantly with both his father and his wife. His mother, who was descended from a rabbinic family, fell victim to the misery he caused.

[Page 167]

The Village of Korniv

Mordechai Lagshtein

Translated by Yehudis Fishman

The village of Korniv was located twenty kilometers from Horodenka. It was one of the villages that was found of the city and belonged to the district of Horodenka. This collective included the villages of Korniv, Rokovitz, Nezvisko, Semenuvka, and others. In each one of these villages, there were several Jewish families, for whom the city of Horodenka served as both an economic and cultural center. At appointed times, and especially on market day, which took place every Tuesday, villagers would travel to the city to renew their supplies of merchandise in their small village stores, or to sell products for household needs. More than a few families supported their sons involved in the city, so that they could receive a basic education in both secular and Hebrew studies that they couldn't acquire in the village. This practice caused a stronger connection with its neighboring city.

In most of the villages in eastern Galicia, a substantial portion of the village lands belonged to one family, the estate landowner. Over the course of many years, many estates passed over to the hands of Jews. In the environs of Horodenka, there are a significant number of Jewish landowners: for example, the family of Baron in Rokovitz, the family of Rubal in Korniv, Bozner in Potochische, Goldenberg in Strel'cheye, Zeidman in Serafinitz, Yehudah Cohen in Stetseva, Berl Shpeirir in Stcherniatzin. The Jews found their place in the village, also as lessors of estates and farms, lessors of saloons that generally belonged to the master of the estate. So too they functioned as advisors and administrators of work and businesses on different estates.

Among the Jews in the village of Korniv one man stood out. Reb Eliezer Rubal, an estate owner and the father of the large, extended Rubal family. On his estate, the majority of the village Jews found their livelihood for many years up to his last moment. During the period of the Russian conquest in 1940, Reb Eliezer was exiled to Siberia together with his entire family, and there he died in the year 1942, in the city of Samiplotinisk. I alone, his son in law, succeeded in escaping from Siberia with my wife, my son, and my sister in law Chana. We returned to Poland at the end of the war, and from there we made Aliya in 1950.

The center of Jewish life in our village was the *minyan*, a temporary synagogue for Sabbaths and holidays, where the Jewish villagers met for communal prayer. These meetings naturally preserved the tie among the Jewish villagers. There they would consult with each other about their affairs, bring up their concerns, and discuss the education of their children. The location of the *shul*, until the First World War, was in the house of the Rubal family, the owner of the estate. Afterward, the *minyan* moved to the family of Blukopf.

From an economic perspective, the Jews in our village were not that different from the Jews in the other villages. Even though the village atmosphere affected them, the work of the land did not serve as their primary source of livelihood. They were separated in the sense that each one saw it as an individual obligation and honor to dedicate at least a portion of his time to work the ground and harvest the crops with his own hands. This attitude helped significantly to lift up their image in the eyes of the farmers, the natives of the village.

One should point out that each family tried with all its power to acquire a secondary education for their children, as an introduction to higher education. Therefore, the children of Horodenka were sent to other cities to complete their studies. On this topic it's proper to single out especially Rabbi Nechemia Lagshtein, the *Cohen*, who enabled his two sons, Shlomo Zalmen, known as Zunia, and Mordechai, to receive a higher education. They both became lawyers in Horodenka in the years before the Holocaust, and both were active Zionists.

In general the impact of the Żionist movement was not so noticeable in the city. The mature ones were immersed with all their might in concerns of making a livelihood, and the maturing youth were mostly found outside their city. Many years before the First World War, messengers of the Zionist movement reached our village, and tried to encourage the village Jews to acquire plots of land in Israel, for the sake of settling the land, at the latest possible date; however, they did not succeed in sufficiently arousing enough interest and talent to transform the thought into action. After the Balfour Declaration, when there was a diligent emigration movement to Israel, there was one family, the family of Yossel Shwartz, of blessed memory, that focused its efforts and sent its oldest son, Zelig Shwartz (now called by the name Shechori) to Israel, as a pioneer of the entire family. However, not many years passed before this multi-branched family, the father, the mother, the married daughter and her husband, the sons and the daughters, all immigrated to Israel and settled there. This was an outstandingly organized Aliya, but to our sorrow, there were not many like it in the communities of the diaspora. This was also the only family among the Jews of Korniv who was completely saved and did not taste of the Holocaust and its upheavals.

According to what the survivors of the Underground told me, the Jews of Korniv remained in their villages till the last action against the Jews in the month of Elul 5702, (September 1942). My brother, Shlomo Zalmen, of blessed memory, was among them. Even though he had the opportunity to save his own life, he refused to separate from his fellow villagers, and he was deported together with them to Horodenka. There Avraham Shtondik and the two sons of Wolf Lagshein, Aharon and Meshulam, were designated for death. The rest of the village Jews were sent in train cars to the death camp of Bolztz, together with the remaining Jews of Horodenka.

Pilsudski Square

[Page 168]

The Village of Daleshova

Dr. B. Lagstein

Translated by Yehudis Fishman

The village of Daleshova, one of the villages in the district of Horodenka, was home to forty-eight people. Most of these villages were near the Dniester River, and only a strip of thick forest separated them from the river. The dwellers of these villages were primarily Russians who spoke Ukrainian, while a small percentage of them were Poles who had assimilated among the Russians and forgotten the Polish language.

Among these villagers were scattered several Jewish families, and there were some villages where the number of Jewish families reached multiples of tens. In Daleshova, before the First World War, there were ten Jewish families who had inhabited the village for many generations. After the war, however, only five families remained; the rest of the families scattered to nearby cities, and a group of them fled, immigrating to America. The Jews of the village were mainly involved in farming, and some of them in business – for how could a Jew separate completely from business and not go every Tuesday to market day in Horodenka? In general, poor village peasants, who were forced to work as day laborers in order to eke out their living, did the actual work of the fields that were owned by the Jews. They were very jealous of the Jews who lived a relatively more comfortable life, without having to work so hard.

Almost every day, Jews from the neighboring cities would come to the village. Their livelihood came from visiting the village on a daily basis to buy and sell; afterward they would return to their homes at night. The place that they lodged in the village was called the *Kalmanke*, where they could obtain *tallisim* and *tefillin* for prayer, and where they could obtain breakfast after daavening.

The woman, who was known as *Di Kalmanke*, was Baila, wife of Kalman Katz, and oldest daughter of Fruma and Yosef Shneur. Yosef Shneur was a wealthy Jew, who had no sons, but did have three daughters. He wrote a *sefer* Torah that, before his death, he directed to be given over to his learned son-in-law, Kalman Katz, who would say his *kaddish*. So the Torah remained in the house of Kalman Katz, where every Shabbos many Jews from the neighboring villages would gather to pray. After the death of Kalman Katz in 1915, the Torah remained in the hands of the *Kalmanke*, and when we had to leave the village because of the Russian invasion, the Torah was transferred to one of the farmers to guard until we returned to the village. When we returned to the village after the war, the Torah was restored to the *Kalmanke*, and she immediately had it checked, as prescribed by law. From that time on, people began to gather again in her house to pray on the Sabbath, as in the days when her husband been alive. Pursuant to her request, the Torah stayed as an inheritance in the family of her daughter Raize Bidar, whose husband fell in war; she remained a widow with two daughters. These two widows, the mother and daughter, ran the very large farm with great skill.

The Jewish youth in the villages were generally wholesome children who received their education in the central cities or in more distant cities, and weren't much different than city children. However, I must point out that there was always a palpable barrier between the village and the city youth, both in school and on the street. The villagers would wait with longing for vacation, where they would meet up with their peers from their own village and from nearby villages. When the school season would end, many of them would return to their villages and would be occupied, like their parents, in farming and in business. In each of their hearts was implanted an abundant love for the village of their birth.

Most of the youth belonged to the Zionist movement, and they longed to move to the land of Israel. In the evening, they would gather for activities and clubs with friends from the city, who in the village had been involved in training teachers of young children. These teachers were close to the village children, and knew how to reach them. Many of the village youth went out for training, but only a few of them merited to move to the land of Israel, and they scattered to all parts of the land.

The Board of the "Bank Ludowy" (People's Bank)

The Opening Ceremony of the Yiddish School

Institutions and Organisations

[Page 169 & Page 190]

Jewish Institutions in our town

H. Sucher (S. Yischar)

Translated by Dalya Yohai

Kindergarden of the Yiddish School 1932

Community Organizations in our town

Until the year 1918 – the year when World War I ended – the community operated under Austrian law. The Polish law established after that was different, but under both systems the local police and governor of the county had the final say. They always made sure that the head of the Jewish community and other elected officers were people they could trust. During the last ten years these people served as officers: Moshe Filnch, Yosef Bezner, Shlomo Shtreyt, Berl Shpierer and Alter Diker.

The activity of the community concerned regulating the religious needs such as the Rabbi, the Dayan (judge of religious matters), Kosher laws, the bathhouse, and the cemetery. The community taxed its members and from these revenues the community operated.

Executive committee of the Bund

The Presidium of the Yiddish School

The budget had to be approved by the local governor. He made sure the money went for the stated purposes and also for charity. I remember that when I was an officer and the Zionist movement was trying to get the community to fund Keren Hayesod and Keren Kayemet, the governor only approved it after three times.

The Zionist influence in Horodenka started at the beginning of the century. One of their slogans was, "to conquer the communities." They started the politicization process of the Jewish community. They presented their candidates for election and made sure they won. In the past the rivalry was always between the different schools of Chasidim in our town (Chortokover, Vizhnitzer, Kosov and Ottynia). The majority of the town belonged to either Chortokover or Vizhnitzer. These two schools always had disagreements when it came to approval of Rabbis or other such issues.

Before the Zionist movement, Haskalah, a Jewish enlightenment movement that was spread in town by Haim Leib Halpern and Leybish Meltzer, influenced many young people in the community. These people were persecuted by the Chasidim because of their liberal views and opposition to orthodox ways. However, their system of schooling was the same as those of the religious Jews. The followers admired their teachers and treated them like Rabbis. They would meet and discuss ideas and literature – especially works by Goethe and Schiller. This way people got some European education, which although not very deep, nevertheless influenced the life of the community, especially when it came to marriage prospects. Many young ladies preferred to marry somebody who had a wider education than that of an Orthodox Chasid. Actually it is interesting to note that the main followers of this liberal movement were young girls. This might have been because they had more time available as they didn't study the Torah and also because their fathers were more tolerant in the hope that it would help them to get a good husband.

As I said before the first followers of Haskalah were literally prosecuted by the Chasidim. Leybish Meltzer moved to another town. Haim Leib Halpern, who was teacher, also had to leave town and became a storekeeper in Rodolpaskoft – a German village near Syniatin. He died young. However on his deathbed he said he wanted to go back to Horodenka to die among Jews. Before his death he "confessed" and said that Uriel da Costa was wrong to oppose traditional Jewish religious beliefs. He obviously saw himself as a follower of da Costa's "enlightened" doctrines. The Chasidim saw this last confession of his as a big victory and believed claimed that he became a believer on his deathbed.

One of the strange incidents of the time was the existence of a "visionary" in our town. I didn't know him personally and only heard about him. His name was Michalanski. (He was probably Russian, since our names were mostly German) Before he started seeing visions he was a simple guy. After he started seeing visions he became a Rabbi and had followers. Then he got involved in a scandal and ran away.

We had in town some societies that dealt with charity. Chevrat Talmud Torah gave scholarships to poor students. Yehosua Shtreyt and WelWel Zeidman ran it. Yehoshua Shtreyt remembers the students coming to his father to be tested. Among the students were some real talents like Hirsh Priffer-Blutah (he became a chemist and was the son-in-law of Shlomo Shtreyt.)

In town we also had Chevra Bikur Cholim that helped poor sick people. These societies were funded by charity and donations. The other societies, Yad Charovtsim and Agudat Achim, were self help groups and later on became the merchants union that adopted modern methods of financial self help.

The Baron Hirsch School

The economic and cultural situation of the Galician Jews was very poor at the time. There was need for a movement from the outside to help bring about change. And the school of the Baron Hirsch did that. The Baron had two goals: to expose Jews to the outside world and to help the students and their parents. The students got clothing and books once a year and a hot meal daily. There was also a charity budget that gave the parents small loans so they could send their children to the school.

The school had only four grades. If somebody wanted to continue their education they had to go to the public school for 5th and 6th grades. The school was for boys only. Girls could only go to public schools. After graduating from the school the teachers made sure the students learned a trade. Some of them studied agriculture at the school of Slovudka Leshna near Kolomyja and some of them later emigrated to Israel or Argentina.

The Hasidic movement objected vehemently to the Baron's school. One Saturday, I remember, some Hasidim, including Mordechai Molkorev, going from synagogue to synagogue and demanding that the fathers of children who went to the Baron Hirsch School leave the service since these schools were missionary schools. They claimed the Baron didn't mean good for the Jews and that he was a missionary and wanted to eradicate us. But the parents didn't listen to them and sent the children anyway. I was one of the first stidemts of the second year. My father suffered terribly because of the fanatic atmosphere but was independent enough not to pay attention to the intimidation. Slowly but surely the very Orthodox started to change. I remember one of our neighbors who was giving me hard time the first year of the school, later wanted my help taking his child to the school.

The school had great impact on the life of the younger generation. There was an understanding that life couldn't remain as before. People started thinking about immigration to the States and other countries. And that's how the big Horodenkan colony in the States started.

The Zionist movement captivated some of us. The school helped us to see reality through different eyes, opened our horizons, and created a momentum for change. I think that the school's impact is not appreciated enough today.

Unfortunately, in the school there was an atmosphere of assimilation. The first principal Berles, always stated in front of the students that it was important to dress and speak like the Poles. He influenced us. Many of us changed our habits. When evening classes opened the influence increased.

But not all the teachers were like that. I remember two Zionist teachers; Yankel Fink and Zeynel Vizelberg. Vizelberg was a religious teacher who taught Chumush in German translation. He was a friend of the Zionist movement and every Saturday prayed with the Zionists. Yankel Fink was from the town, the son of Pinie the rope maker. He was the first to become a certified teacher. The others were just people who knew something about the outside culture and wanted to be teachers. Over time all the teachers were required to be certified. Yankel Fink left Horodenka and in later years came to visit very rarely.

These schools were originally for the poor among us but wealthier students joined too (they didn't get the financial help) because their parents preferred that they be among Jews and not in the public schools with only Poles.

After the Baron's death the school's administration started to limit their activities. The first schools to close were those in areas with good public schools. The school in Horodenka closed just before World Was I. Thus concluded this chapter of our history about the great cultural and financial help that the Baron Hirsch gave to the Jewry of Galicia.

Veterans of General Zionists

[Page 172]

The Yad Harutzim Assosiation

Mendel Berkover

Translated by Harvey Buchalter

There were many different kinds of artisans in Horodenka, but an artisans' association (craft guild) which would help the craftsman maintain his livelihood did not exist. In either 1907 or 1908 a Horodenka-based association was formed, called Yad Ha-Rutzim. The association's premise at that time was to come to the aid of sick craftsmen, as well as serving as a Bikkur Cholim. In the beginning, many businessmen joined the association, and its first president, who was also one of the founders, was a well-known person, Kurel Fenster. The spark to start the association was lit by the following people: Kurel Fenster, Velvel Greenberg, Moshe-Manes Neygiser, Nateh Lehrer and myself. In the beginning, the association had thirty to forty members. Aside from the president Kurel Fenster, the secretary was Haim-Hirsh Shor (Ben-ltzhak-Reuven Shor). Moshe-Maness Neygiser hosted the first meeting. After that, we rented a place from Yonah Leibman, where we wrote the by-laws and set up rules for membership.

As stated, the goals of the association were the same as for a Bikkur Cholim: to seek out members who suffered illness and to help care for them: provide them with enough money for their week-to-week expenses: pay doctor bills and pay for prescriptions. This was certainly a great help for them, because artisans usually had no savings. In the case of sudden illness, they were usually left without the means to recuperate and go on with their lives.

Two years after the founding, the members who were not craftsmen dropped out of the association. They were Yankel Laster, Nateh Lehrer, Saideh Offenberger, Binyamin Diker, and others. They founded a businessmen's association with different goals from those of the Yad Harutzim.

After the First World War, the association came back to life. The president at that time was Velvel Greenberg. In the years 1930-1932, the association disbanded and many of its members joined the Bikkur Cholim association, whose president was Yossel Geller.

[Page 172]

The Bund in Horodenka

Rebecca Katvan-Kot

Translated by Harvey Buchalter

One of the most beautiful pages of Horodenka's history was bequeathed to us by the Bund. The Bund was a political party of Jewish workers and "folksmentschen," which had a wide-reaching effect on the cultural and political life of Horodenka. The Bund in Horodenka began its activity at the end of the First World War. It participated in all political demonstrations as well as being represented in the Seim and in the Jewish Council by Hirsh Schechter. The Bund's agenda was the formation of a working-class consciousness among the Jewish workers. It organized two craft unions of cabinet makers and sewing machine operators, struggled toward the acceptance of an eight-hour day, and also regulated working conditions. It also became involved in improving "emergency procedures" in the workplace.

In the Bund's meeting place, there was a large library with a reading room where lectures and discussions were held on various subjects. There were a variety of cultural and political circles and a well-organized theater group under the direction of Yehuda Hirsh Sobel, which presented readings by Yiddish writers. The income from the presentations was reserved for the Yiddische Schules. There was also a sports club for youth. Each summer many children went away to a "summer camp."

The most essential thing the Bund accomplished was the Yiddish-language afternoon school for girls and boys. There one learned how to write and read in Yiddish, and studied Yiddish literature and Jewish history. Among its most important accomplishments was making accessible a "heimische" (comfortable) environment, where children would receive a modern curriculum to awaken and elevate the spirit. I will never forget the teacher Asher Shtreyt who made sure that each child who studied with him would become a worthy human being in both word and deed. He was both a great teacher and a great friend. Aside from his teaching, he gave many lectures on political and literary subjects.

The Yiddische Schule had a separate library for children which was filled with works in Yiddish and works from writers around the world. The schule also had a theater group and two or three times a year the children put on presentations with singing and dancing. Even small children from the school's kindergarten participated.

About ten years before the Holocaust, they built a large, modern building for the schule with the help of our landsleit (countrymen) in America. In soliciting help from the American committee (Iandsleit) the work of Isaac Fink is noteworthy. He was one of the founders of the schule and also one of its first teachers. In Horodenka the so called "building cooperative" sold shares of stock, and whoever bought a share became a member of the building co-op. The members were from every stripe of Jewish society, and not only members of the Bund. Even Alexander Granach, in his last trip to our city, donated income from his performance to the building co-op.

The Bund Committee, under the chairmanship of Asher Shtreyt, strived to develop a corps of good "heimische" teachers for the schule. They chose three of the sharpest students and sent them off to the Vilna Yiddish Seminary. One of them was my sister Etel Katvan who graduated with honors and was one of the best teachers in the city as well as the entire region. She was admired by people in other communities as well. In the Soviet era she had an important position. Sadly, she did not survive the war. In 1943 she died of malaria in Tadzikistan, where she suffered from hunger and the effects of the terrible news regarding her family back home in Horodenka.

The Yiddische Schule was capable of delivering all services to the community, but its life became shortened. The dream was shattered by the Red "bafrier" (liberation forces) in 1939. Afterwards came the dark, murderous years of Hitler when the children were slaughtered along with their parents. And today, when one reads about the Bund and the Yiddische Schule, it resonates like a wonderful tale of long ago, which is no more, and will never be again.

In his last years Asher Shtreyt was the chairman of the Bund in Horodenka. He came from a very pious family. His father was Schlomeh Shtreyt, a distinguished Jew, and at one time head of the Council (rosh-ha-kahal). The first time I met Asher Shtreyt was when he was my teacher in an evening class in the Yiddische Schule. He taught us with his whole heart and he made me want to learn all there was to learn. He alone was a "living encyclopedia." Everything you could ask him was immediately explained so clearly that it would remain etched in your memory. The class that he taught was so popular that it had to be divided into two sections. Asher Shtreyt had a kind word for each child and a warm, fatherly smile. He was a very fine speaker and was sought after by every group.

Soon after the invasion of the Russian Army, Asher Shtreyt was arrested. But he was released within a short time got a position as a German teacher for the Russians and became principal of the Yiddische Schule. During the time of the Nazis, Asher Streit went into hiding for a long time. As it was told to me, he went into hiding with Moshe Shifter and his wife (from the Ladenheim family) and they were all slaughtered by Ukrainian low-lifes shortly before the liberation. Asher Shtreyt wrote a book of his memories from the Nazi captivity, but it perished with him.

Hirsh Schechter came from a Hasidic family of ritual slaughteerrs and singers. Hefirst learned how to sing in the Yiddische Schule, and after that became one of the outstanding comrades in the Bund and all the other organizations he belonged to. He was knowledgeable about the laws of Poland, business matters and such, and the Party always heeded his advice.

Thus, as a very modest person he would always say that he was not suited to be selected to serve in this or that commission, but once he was appointed he was the most engaged person. And sitting all day amongst his timepieces - he was a watch-maker - he would prepare his material for the meeting that evening. He had a sober, common-sense outlook which was not readily gladdened by a "quick victory" nor brought down by a sudden defeat.

In his final years he was the Bund's representative in the Kultusrat in Horodenka. By no means would he agree to be part of the Judenrat (Nazi's Jewish Council) and he was among the first casualties.

Yehuda Hirsh Sobel was a man of immense energy. For a time he was a teacher in the Yiddische Schule, but he mainly was involved in theatrical activity. He was among the first to be involved in theater in Horodenka, and in the later years he was the director of theater circle composed of older adults. He also was in charge of holding the tryouts for all the presentations of the children in the Schule. He perished along with the rest of the Horodenka Jews.

Nachman Agatshteyn was, as his father before him, a tin worker by trade. Upon first laying eyes on him, he did not make a good impression. But as he began speaking, he was able to convince those who listened to him. He was active as a leader in the youth movement of the Bund. He had a phenomenal memory and could instantly recall any historical event. He fell to a German bomb in the Russian city of Uman.

Toibe Bernshteyn was a good-hearted girl. She studied voice and led various branches of the youth organizations. Krantschia Shteyner was also a leader in the youth branch where she studied singing and dancing and tried out for performances. Both lost their lives in the horrific Nazi years.

[Pages 175 & 196]

The Abraham Reisin School

Eizik Fink

Translated by Dahlya Yohai

The Abraham Reisin School was created after World War I by the Jewish Labor movement. After the end of the Austrian rule, from November 1918 to August 1921, the Ukrainians ruled Horodenka. Later it became part of Poland and remained so until the beginning of World War II.

When the Ukrainians took over as rulers, they behaved rather well toward minorities, like Poles and the Jews, with regard to cultural and national matters. It was officially stated that if a Jew wanted to petition the government or present any document to a governmental agency, he could do so in Yiddish. In fact, one Ukrainian official approached Nathan Melamed to inquire if he could instruct him in reading and writing Yiddish. Naturally, nothing came of it; there were enough Jewish officials who were well versed in Ukrainian, Polish and Yiddish.

In November 1918, the War was over. Austria was no longer in control. The town was full of soldiers – from 18 to 60 years old – who had returned from the war. Each of them had his own horror story, retelling how he had escaped death. Those who came back from the Italian front had the most fantastic stories. As Moshe Manes Nagisser used to say: "The soldiers who came back speak a lot because the drum hit them on their head and confused them totally..."

Later on, people started to awaken. Members of the organization "Forverts" started their activities. They rented a place to hold their meetings. They decided to make an effort to restore Mrs. Weinstein's "hall."

When Mr. Weinstein started the construction of the building before the war, he intended that it be used for the Jewish people whenever a need arose. The Poles had the "Sokol" hall, the Ukrainians their "Narodny Dom (National Building)." Even before the war when Jews needed a space for any community activity, it was very difficult to get one. When we approached the Poles, there was always the same response: "The hall is taken for the night needed." We had to resort to contacts and persuasion to get the space. The Narodny Dom actually was available at most times for a reasonable price; but when we needed to get a permit from the Poles for the event, they always refused and suggested we wait for the Sokol to become available. So it was always a real struggle. That is why we decided to use Weinstein Hall, which was already half built.

For Horodenka in those days, it was actually a modern building. The bricks came from Kolomyja and the builders came from Czernowitz. The original plan included central heating, but it had not been completed before the War. It had only four walls and a roof. Even the floor was missing. That is why Mrs. Weinstein looked at us like we were lunatics when we said we would like to use it. The installation of doors and floor was possible since we had carpenters among us. But the question remained how to heat such a big space. It was a hard task. Then somebody suggested taking a big metal barrel, filling it with stones, and poking a hole in it to make a furnace. The metal workers did the rest, connecting pipes through the hall, and sure enough we had some heat quite quickly after we started the fire.

Simultaneously there was a great deal of activity and organizing by the Forverts. We organized a choir under the direction of Baruch Itzik Shpeirer. Then we established the library that grew steadily because we raised money for it. When we wanted to organize the evening studies we had a problem. The girls didn't want to study with the boys. They were usually less advanced than the boys and were embarrassed because of that, although it was not really their fault. The boys had learned how to read and write in the Baron Hirsch

School until it closed, and from teachers like Nute, Yona and Mordchai. Those girls who wanted to study and had fathers willing to pay for it had private tutors; but the majority of girls, especially from workers' families, had no opportunity to study. Therefore, evening classes were organized for older girls initially while the boys attended more advanced classes of Jewish literature and political science. This situation continued for a while until the younger children grew up and we had the same level for girls and boys alike.

The Abraham Reisin School was created to provide secular Yiddish cultural education and was supported by local fundraising. From time to time the Jewish community gave us some money thanks to Berl Shpierer, the president, who was a progressive man. We got some help from the "Joint [Distribution]." We didn't get any help from the Horodenka emigrants in the Sates during the first years. The first fundraisers of the Landsmanshaft (immigrant organizations of different communities) brought some money for the poor but didn't help the school.

The situation changed only some years later, when new emigrants from our town moved to New York and joined two organizations: the Horodenka Organization to Help the Sick and Progressive Horodenkan Young Men's and Ladies' Society. They then started supporting the school from time to time.

The Polish government gave us a hard time, claiming the building was not suitable for a school. But the directors organized a building cooperative whose goal was to build a new and modern building for the school which would also accommodate the other institutions of the Labor movement in town. This was a huge task and the people who took it upon themselves didn't realize how much work it involved.

On June 24, 1924 Israel Schneiderman and Abba Podowisker bought Shalom Luft's property for $500 in order to build the Yiddish school. In September 1925 the land was bought officially and was recorded in the books as belonging to the cooperative building union. Immediately after that we tried to raise money for the school through donations and other activities. We also appealed to our friends in the USA who helped generously. A committee was created in the States to help our school. The committee started its activities in 1926 and continued until the city was destroyed.

We continued fundraising to get money from all the citizens of the city and created the alumni organization that had annual dues. We also presented some plays that raised money for the cause. During the years 1926-1931 we had $3,650 for the building. The building cooperative in Horodenka managed to raise 25,735 Zloty ($864).

Dr. Eineigler, the famous journalist and activist from Lvov, wrote about us in his memoirs: "As far as I know, there was in Galicia only one secular Jewish school - the one in Horodenka. The school had its own building and did a great job. Unfortunately, I don't remember all the names of the teachers and many of the activists but I know it was an oasis in the desert and it is worth remembering and commemorating their work. I also know that the people from the Landsmanshaft in the USA sent money to support the school."

ACCOUNTING OF FUNDS 1925-1931

	INCOME		EXPENSES	
Year	Dollars	Zloty	Dollars	Zloty
1925	520	295	520	82.65
1926	2,165	7,932.65	2,164.37	7,899.52
1927	1,400	6,406.86	1,028.33	6,444.22
1928	–	61.87	268.29	60.18
1929	–	1,549.56	102.70	1,551.25
1930	329	10,309.90	329	10,319.28
1931	100	180	76	422.702
	4,514	26735.84	4,488.69	26,779.80

I want to mention that the first teachers in the school were Yehuda Hirsch Sobel, Yosel Katz, and myself. In 1923 I left for America and Asher Streyt took my place. Later on we had some teachers who were alumni of our school and who had completed their studies in the Yiddish Seminar in Vilna.

Foundation of the Yiddish Youth Home 1926

[Page 178]

Memories of the Yiddish School

Pesia Blatt

Translated by Harvey Buchalter

When I think about our dear, familiar Horodenka, the town that once was about her sweet Jews and her beautiful youth, the thought brings me back to my childhood, the years that stay with a person his whole life. And anguish presses upon the heart so that the beautiful dream cruelly dissolves into nothingness. The quiet, benevolent hope that we carried within us each day lies buried beneath our Horodenka dwellings, demolished under a pile of ashes. This is all that remains of our home. And so, I honor the request to relate my memories, to recall my home and the *Yiddische Shule*, which was for us, the children of working people, our second home. It was the home in which we found happiness and carried out the life of our childhood world.

Yiddish School – Teachers and School

I still see before me the grand two-story brick building that majestically stood out from all the others, near the Rinick. Before the memory of the house begins to fade, I hear the sound of my father's hammer at work. I run quickly, in the cold, wintry day, and collapse, frozen, into the school. A pleasant feeling of warmth and comfort surrounds me. The boisterous songs of the Jewish workers greet me, and before too long my voice joins in with the voices of all the other children. We forget about our poverty, the lack of sustenance and the abundance of worry, and we are delivered to another world, filled with ideals and hope.

I remember the happiness we shared when we prepared to celebrate spring festivals. B. Shefner attended one such celebration. We welcomed our guest with song, greeting him in the name of the children. He warmly shook my hand; his eyes were bursting with happiness: our holiday spirit took him under its spell.

Memories also come back to me of our dear teachers, Etel Katvan, Krantschia Shteyner, Yehudah-Hirsh Sobel, Yurman, and others, who instilled knowledge in us and a longing for a better and more just world, with a love for our own people and for each and every person in the world.

Where are you all now, my dear Horodenka Jews? Where are you, our dear teachers? Where are you, Horodenka children? Where are my school companions? Your song has not been silenced for all time, but your belief in humanity has become a bitter disappointment.

Allow these few lines to be like the drop of a tear on your unknown graves. Allow them to renew the honor of their memory for the sake of the remaining Horodenka brothers and sisters who grieve for our annihilated home.

Horodenka, the town where I was born; Horodenka where I lost those dearest to me — I will never forget you.

[Page 179 & Page 192]

The first Hebrew school

Gabriel Lindenberg

Translated by Dalya Yohai

I listened for three hours to the devastating stories of one of the survivors from the Ghetto Kolomyja – stories from the day the liberal Hungarian regime left the area because of the German occupation to the day of the last "cleansing" when the rest of the Jews in the area were killed. When he finished his story, he mentioned the names of two dear people that reminded me of my childhood, a period when the revival of Hebrew gave us hopes for renewal of our nation. I shivered when he said that Ben-Tsion Eyzman and his wife Tsiupa Scheryer were among the last Jews that were brought from Horodenka to the Kolomyja Ghetto.

Tsiupa Scheryer was the first Hebrew kindergarten teacher in Horodenka. I have no idea where she learned her Hebrew as it was 1907 before we had a Hebrew school in town. Maybe it was from her husband. Ben-Tsion Eyzman was a modern scholar whom I liked very much in my youth because of his inner and outer beauty. The memory of his wife is very dear to me and is connected directly with the beginning of the Hebrew movement in Horodenka. I was not among her students though. When the Hebrew school was created I was already a "young man" of six, who studied in the Cheder of Menash Melamed. I didn't continue there because of the revolutionary act of a few parents who decided to educate their children in Hebrew.

My father was very active in this cause as my sister and I were among the first students in this school. And to his credit, I have to say, he continued with this mission for many years despite the expenses that were involved. Hundreds of students studied in this school for the seven years of its existence. It closed in August 1914, when the war started.

Most of the students left the school without any real knowledge; for them it was more like a new fad. But my father was one of the few that really wanted a complete Hebrew education for his children. Nevertheless, even this little Hebrew study that hundreds of children in Horodenka got was important in the long run. It created a base for the renewal of the Hebrew movement after the war, when the hopes for creating Israel started to rise in the aftermath of the Balfour declaration.

The external appearance of the first teacher who was brought into town was a good introduction to the new way of teaching. It was not only that he was Russian – his name was a typical Russian name – Rirachowski – but his face was also very Russian. He had a big name, no beard, a mustache, and looked very much like Shaul Tchernichovsky (a Russian Hebrew poet). His wife was a Hebrew teacher also and she also didn't look like our women. She was tall and beautiful. I especially remember her beautiful masculine handwriting that we had at home in a notebook. She would copy the songs we learned in school: "El Hazipor," "Hayalkout al Haschechem," "Choshov Achim Chovshov" and more. This couple was able to create a vibrant Hebrew school in only one year and to bring new life into the "beautiful language – the one that lasted forever." Until that time Hebrew was only known to the orthodox Jews and some others. At the end of the year there was a show that demonstrated what was achieved during the school year. The whole town was very excited about it.

Although the school was a great success these teachers couldn't hold their job for long. It was too much of a change and they were too far advanced in their behavior and looks for our town. Somebody who was more traditional looking replaced them. The next teacher, I think, was Hirschfeld.

The school also moved from Uri-Chaim Shertzer's flat to Rabbi Alter Vizelberg's flat. He was an old-time Zionist and a learned and respectable Jew. It is possible that there was an interim address but I don't remember exactly.

Once the school was established it grew and prospered. At a certain point there were two Hebrew schools in town competing with each other. After a while they joined together. The teacher in the second school was a local man, Yeshiya Itzik Beker. I was not a student of his but I remember once he substituted for my regular Bible teacher. During the war he moved to Karlsbad and continued his teaching there. Karlsbad attracted many Zionists leaders not only as a vacation spot but also as a place for meetings and conferences. It became a spiritual center for the Jews of Czechoslovakia. When the Nazis took over Czechoslovakia in 1939 he moved to Israel.

Another teacher in Horodenka was Yehuda Goldstein. Unfortunately I don't remember all the details about the number of students in the different classes or even their names. But I remember that in the higher grades we were only three or four students. The teacher Goldstein taught in the school longer than any other teacher. And even with the financial crisis that the school was experiencing they always tried to pay him in order to keep him. He left town only when the war started. When he was the headmaster the school had some serious problems and there were many absences. But the parents' council insisted on having a open test in front of the public. I especially remember the last test before the war in the big barn of father Kalmus that was decorated appropriately for the event. My sister Ziporah was the star of the day because she passed the test of "Daf Gamora." It was a paragraph form the book Mevo Hatalmud. It was remarkable as an example of "Milta Dela Schicha" (memorization).

As I said before, very few students spoke Hebrew other than in school. Even in my family in which there was big support from my parents who even sang the Hebrew songs we learned in school, we didn't get to speak the language. The only people in town that spoke Hebrew in their daily life other than the Hebrew teacher and the Preminger family were my relative Dov Mosberg and me. We made a decision to speak only Hebrew with each other and we did so for three or four years until 1939 when the war started. Dov Mosberg was a young man and a member of "Zion's Youth" when I was still a child. But the only person that was a real fanatic about the Hebrew language was Zvi Preminger. He spoke Hebrew with his family and also had a Jewish maid that learned Hebrew so she could speak to the children. (Most of the maids in Jewish homes were non-Jews.)

He was a member of the B'nai Zion organization. He was a regular in the minyan of this group where my father also prayed. I used to see him on Shabbat with young people talking about politics, Zionism, etc. He was vibrant and had a sharp sense of humor and people like him a lot. He was active in the school council and also was the librarian of the Hebrew library. The library included maybe 30 Hebrew books from the Tovshia publishing company and was located in a small cupboard in the office of the group. He had the key and I often checked out books. But not many others used it.

I remember something else about Preminger that was really unique. In 1910 he lost his job as a clerk in the Ekerling Bank. He decided to open a shoe polish factory. He studied the trade and came up with a good project. Here he found a way to express his passion for Hebrew. He named the factory "Lebanon." On the boxes was the picture of Gimnasia Herzelia (the first Hebrew school in Palestine). Other than the name that was printed in the local language, the rest of the label was in Hebrew. He thought it would be a hit among the Jews. But it didn't happen. He had to close down after two years.

When I came to Israel in 1925 I heard that he had arrived sometime before. He moved there alone and tried to find a job as a stenographer in Hebrew – a system he invented. But here too he was not successful. Finally an offer to hire him came, but it was too late. For a long time I didn't know his whereabouts. In 1946 I heard then that he lived in Haifa and barely made a living as a storekeeper. The man was forgotten and was not even mentioned in the list of Horodenka's survivors and was not invited to the first Horodenka survivor's conference we had.

That's the typical fate of somebody who is ahead of his time.

[Page 180]

Beit Ya'akov School for Girls

Blauma Feder

Translated by Dalya Yohai

From the big family of the Torah schribe Eliyahu Goldstein, I'm the only one to survive and come to Israel.

In the year 1935 when I was very young, Mrs. Sara Sneider came to Hordenka to open the Beit Ya'akov school for girls. She had foundered this type of school throughout Poland.

Beit Yaakov School

The Orthodox liked the idea and the school was created. The active committee for the school consisted of Rabbi Moshkovitz, the cantor, the butcher Yehoshua Dorf, and my father, Eliyahu Goldstein. The head of the committee was Herschel Sucher (Yiskar).

The school had a progressive atmosphere. The girls studied bible stories as well as Hebrew and Jewish history. Some biblical plays were performed, like Achashveros with Dvora Geffner and Youta Kugler as the main characters. Other plays included "Joseph in Egypt" with Gold Sharf; "The Sacrifice of Isaax" with Chana Grapakh and others with historical themes like "Matathius and His Sons" and "Hannah and Her Seven Sons." The girls in school were very active culturally compared to those attending the other schools in town. Unfortunately it didn't last long. After the war started it became much more difficult to have cultural activities. And after the Nazis took over, most of the youth perished. Only a small number of us survived like Lucia Prifer, Priva Frishling and me.

Let my little lines here be a tombstone to the people who died. "TANZVA" (Let their souls rest in peace.)

Beit Yaakov School

[Page 181 & 196]

The Shomer Organization

Menachem Strum

Translated by Dalya Yohai

In the summer of 1918, towards the end of World War I, General Keransky ruled Russia and declared the country a republic. Ukraine was no longer part of Russia and had signed a peace accord with Austria. The Jews of Horodenka started returning to their ruined and burned city from the places they had gone to during the war. These places included Bohemia, Morovia, Austria and Hungary, especially Vienna, the capital.

The "Namer" Group of HaShomer 1919

After a while the city revived. The stores of Izrael Fleshner and
Chaim-Zerach Tzawak were filled with women coming to buy food for
Shabbat. The meat market was busy with women buying either real
meat or only the inexpensive parts to make a cholent for Shabbat.
Again the public baths were open and Jews were going to them on
Friday afternoon. It looked like everything had returned to life as it
had been before the war. The Jews of Horodenka were once again
living the lives their parents and grandparents had lived for
generations, negotiating with the local farmers, buying produce and
cattle and trying to make a living. At the same time the rivers of blood
still were running in Italy and France. But in a little while these
battles ended as well. The small nations of the former Austrian Empire
– Czechoslovakia, Hungary, Poland and Ukraine – were getting their
freedom and independence. At the same time, the Ukrainians started
giving the Jews a hard time and there were many signs of rampant
anti-Semitism in eastern Galicia, including Horodenka.

On the other hand, there was a big renewal among the Jewish
youth. The Balfour Declaration in 1917 had a lot to do with this. The
Shomer organization opened offices in many towns and villages. Their
aim was to educate the youth about emigration to Palestine. In
Horodenka, Benish Noyman, the son of Michael and Vavotschis, was
the main leader. His lectures drew people from all over. First to join
were the students who had just graduated from high school and didn't
have anything to do. Later the girls joined as well and we started to
have different groups. I joined but didn't like my group. I decided to

create my own group with my old friends from the Cheder: Moshe Marila and Moshe Fleshner with whom I had played behind the fence of Ivan Koshovtuiyuk; Michali Pilpel with whom I used to play buttons (a child's game) next to the butcher shop and the public bath; and Motel Birnboym, my playmate for the "Kitke" next to the "Taplitza." The son of Baruch-Lev, Yom-Tov Greidinger; Yosel Mindiyes Ladenheim; and Aharon Kugelmas were also in our group. We become an independent group and called ourselves The Tigers.

All the Shomer students studied Hebrew with Asher Yungerman, Libster and Greif. We also had courses in Jewish history, literature and the geography of Palestine. Every Saturday we had public readings of the Bible with our tutor Mendel Diner, the son of Ben-Zion Shtrikmacher (the rope maker). At the same time blood was being shed among the Poles and Ukrainians, and the Poles and Bolsheviks. In addition, the progroms against the Ukrainian Jews were staggering. We all felt that there was no place for Jews in this part of the world anymore.

On April 24, 1920, the San Remo Peace Conference reaffirmed the Balfour Declaration and we started really hoping that we would have our homeland very soon. The Chalutz (Pioneer) movement started its activity in Horodenka. I, with Moshe and Motel were among the first to join. We decided to prepare ourselves to move to Israel, disregarding our parents' objections.

We were divided into three groups. One worked in Schertzer's lumberyard, the second worked to build a fence for the old cemetery (which was knocked down during the war) and the third group went to work at Nusia Baran's farm in the village of Semenivaka. We belonged to the third one.

The adults thought we were lunatics. They didn't believe that anybody would be able to go to Palestine. They listened to Hershel Sucher (Yiskar) who was the head of the Zionist movement and gave money for the Karen Kayemet, but didn't see the possibility of leaving and moving to Israel as a real one. We worked hard the whole week on the farm. On Friday afternoon we returned home for the weekend. Every weekend we were scolded and yelled at, but nothing could change our minds.

Some weeks before the end of the season, Moshe left. He joined the group that worked in the cemetery. I remember the days Motel and I went after dinner to sit on the hay bales, watch the moon and talk like good friends. We were very happy. One day I got typhus. I was taken immediately to my parent's house. I was sick for weeks and Dr. Kanafas was my doctor.

It was August 8, 1920, around the time the first group was supposed to go to Israel. Everyone in town was very excited. Horodenka was sending the first pioneers to Israel. We were leaving behind everything we knew: brothers and sisters; parents and relatives; the synagogue; the houses of study; the public baths and the "Proval" (ravine) which was next to it; the old and new cemeteries; the well of Yirmiya; the little brook of Chervona, which powered the mill of Moshe-Leib; the pond of Sovik; the Plaza of Horodenka; "Wysokithe Hory," tall mountains outside of town; and the Tolika, the large meadow on the other side of town. All these places were part of so many childhood memories. Now we were going to the old-new homeland, to open the road to many others who would come after us. Our parents lost their resentment and we became a source of pride combined with sadness and worry.

At dawn on the 8th, many met us at the terminal to say good-bye to the first new pioneers. Cries and blessings were heard all over. Then the train arrived and the ten guys and two girls left. At the second train station in the town of Yakubuvka, other Jews came to say goodbye. And that was the last contact between us and Horodenka.

More groups of pioneers were organized and moved to Israel one after the other. After ten years the Jews of Horodenka could be found all over Israel, in Kibbutizim, towns, and small villages. The Aliyah went on until 1939 when the Nazis started their massive killing. And now 26 years after the first Aliyah we stand here and ask ourselves: Is it true or just a dream that Jewish Horodenka was completely destroyed and there is not one Jew there, and even the cemeteries stand vandalized and destroyed? Is it a nightmare or what?

I wish it were a dream, but unfortunately this is the horrible reality. Our town doesn't exist anymore and we'll never see the faces of our beloved that were killed by the evil.

[Page 182]

The Activities of the Hitachdut

Yehoshua Shtreyt

Translated by Dalya Yohai

The Hitachdut branch in Horodenka was founded in 1923. However, we also need to know the background of the events during 1919 –

1923 that led to its formation. We, the youth of that time were influenced by World War I and were eager to "play war." The Shomer organization gave us the opportunity to go back to the youth and innocence we had missed because of the war. We were organized in Shomer in age groups with various names such as Lion, Tiger, Freedom, etc. We met in the little forest by the rabbi's home or in the surrounding hills for discussions and games.

We learned about Herzl and the other people who advocated Socialism and Zionism, including Moshe Hess, B. Borochov, and A.D. Gordon. We also heard stories about the Zionist movement and its actions in Palestine and abroad. The events that took place in Israel after the Balfour Declaration gave us hope and idealism for the future. We wanted to be part of the builders and the dreamers. We read the book Yizkor about the Shomer members who lost their lives in Palestine and cried for them. We also felt a desire to go to Israel and take our place in the events that were unfolding.

When a group of our older friends left for Israel, we felt sadness and jealousy at the same time. The farewell party took place at the home of Shmuel Yungerman; among those leaving was our beloved teacher Asher Yungerman.

But we had hope that soon enough we would be joining them. Soon after their departure we started working the land behind the home of Haim Schnitser (the son-in-law of Rabbi Damta). With no instructions and no proper tools we worked this piece of land just to enjoy the feeling of physical work. We were mocked by the townspeople for this work, but continued nevertheless in order to be considered "pioneers" preparing to go to Israel.

It is possible this work caused our feelings of alienation from the "Zion Farayn" Club. This was an organization of older Zionists that met in the home of Yodel Pasvig, where there was an ark with the Torah and where they conducted services on Shabbat and the holidays. And although we participated in activities such as fundraising and Tzedakah projects, we experienced a rebellious wind, and the older people in our group founded an independent Zionist movement for youth.

The feelings of the young Zionists were not happening in a vacuum. At this time leaders of Hapoel Hazair (A.D. Gordon, Yosef Shprinzak, and Yosek Aharonviz) organized a conference of the Hitachdut in Prague. This became a pivotal event for the Zionist-socialist labor movement in Europe. Its mission was to educate and prepare the young people to make Aliya and work in Israel.

Our elders, Elizer Bilder, Gavriel Lindberg, and Meshulam Shnizer, asked the group to examine our relationship with Zion Farayn and to establish an idealized based for the new organization that would fit our needs.

In 1923 we rented the first space for the Hitachdut chapter. It was in the house of Mr. Yaakov Emzig. We elected a committee and started organizing independent activities like workshops, lectures and a library. At the same time some delegates from the Zionist center in Lvov came to town. These included Fishel Verber, Dr. Nathan Melzer, Dr. Kopel Shwartz, and Dr. Zvi Heller. They brought some relief from the grind of everyday life since the visits were always festive with lecture and banquets.

Especially notable was the visit of Dr. Kopel Shwartz who was the chairman of Hitachdut in Poland. The young people greeted him on adorned horses at the Yakouvuvka train station. Youngsters then accompanied his carriage, in the same way that their parents surrounded the carriage of famous Rabbis when they came to Shabbat in town.

And we still remember one thing that he said, the opening sentence of his speech: "I don't know if history is creating our personality or vice versa." Now that I'm writing these notes and have some historical perspective, the answer to this eternal question is almost clear: the people like Kopel Shwartz and his friends created an amazing historical period, full of debate and action that brought us our country.

From where did we get the will and the ability to create this revolution? The answer has to do with how the younger generation was encouraged to undertake a "personal revolution" by teaching them that work is the basis of existence and that this ideal has to be achieved not in Poland but in Israel, the new home for the Jews.

And this was the background for the creation of the Hachalutz movement in Horodenka, a year after the Hitachdut was created. We were looking for places to train the youth from our town and from neighboring towns. In the summer of 1924 two groups went for training. One went to Potochiska to the farm of Bezner. Among them were Yizhak Shapira, Nachman Bergman and Ephraim Geller. The other group went to Chernelitsa to the farm of Mr. Tereza Petrovitch. This group included Gavriel Lindberg, Noutzie (Yizchak) Shechter (the shochet's son) Zelig Shor and me.

With sorrow and frowning, we were accompanied by the town people before we left. They felt sorry for our families because we were going to be like the goyim and work with our hands.

When we got to our destination, we were put in a hut and slept on beds of hay that were on the floor. In the morning the manager of the farm came to pick us up and directed us in our work. We did all the possible agricultural work and tried to excel.

I can't describe the experiences of those days --- work during the day and song and dance at night. On Shabbat we didn't work and usually discussed ideology and plans for the future. This was our intellectual and spiritual food. We tried to understand the difference between a small group like ours and bigger groups like a kibbutz where everybody joins to work and live together.

In September, around the holidays, we came back to town, physically strong and with a real desire to go to Israel and work for the nation. Enriched in experience and ideology, we came back home and prepared more youth to follow us. At the same time "Gordonia" was created. This was the scouts' branch of our movement, but other members will tell that tale.

In the year 1925 it was time for us to go to the test and to see if we were qualified to make Aliyah. This took place in Chortkov, so we didn't have to spend money for a trip to Lvov. A couple of months later the group indeed made Aliyah. They got to Israel at the beginning of 1926, the year of the economic depression. But despite that, most of them stayed in Israel and only a few came back home to Horodenka, a little bit ashamed.

Those who didn't make it to Israel continued their public work in Hatachdut and Gordonia. Over time they organized in diverse areas such as sports, co-operatives and more education. The Co-operative Bank was created and it helped and sometimes saved the small merchants by giving loans during hard times. They also established a dairy cooperative, which gave jobs to some families. This cooperative initiative was the real revolution, as through it the Jews started learning how to take care of themselves in a cooperative manner.

At that time the "Bund" was the only Jewish party in Poland. But in the thirties a dramatic change took place and many different people joined Hitachdut. It stopped being only an ideological party, but drew people who wanted a better life by moving from Poland to Israel. A direct result of that change was the establishment of the first workers' union in town.

One of the main occupations in town was exporting eggs mainly to Germany. Many workers sorted eggs and packed them for shipping. They were the first ones to form a union. The government suspected that they were communists but it was explained to them that our movement was about educating them towards emigration to Israel. The movement swelled, and it was decided to form another group with the name "Ha'oved" (the worker) and prepare the members to move to

Israel. In our town we had older members and we educated them with simple lectures.

We had many different activities for all ages and in all subjects including the history of the Zionist movement, the history of Socialism, the history of the labour movement, etc. Saturday was our activity day. Especially popular was the Shabbat evening parties, where we had panel discussions and later singing, eating and humorous sketches. The highlight of the evening would be a "krentzchen" or dancing to the tunes of our friend Shmuel Shekhner (the son of the Kleyzmer Mosh Babitzky) who played the violin. We would dance the Hora and other types of dances. One dance in particular, the "Kaprosh" has its roots in both the Hasidic and Polish folk traditions. Our friend Monya Shtachel was an expert. He was our leader and led us during many winter nights to sweat and fun, sometimes for four to five hours in a row. We had some nights... it will never come back.

Like most youth in our generation we also did sports. Bernard Offenberg initiated the first Maccabee club; his brother Heindez continued the club. In Avram Offenberg's yard we put gymnastic equipment and after using them we would go to Toliki, the big fairgrounds for the cattle, and play soccer. We loved soccer and had matches with local Polish groups. We played against groups from Kolomyja, Sniatyn, and Chortkov.

I remember our game when the Polish students from Sniatyn lost to our group and a big, violent fight started. Some Jewish cattle merchants on their way saw us and intervened; otherwise it would have developed into a dangerous situation.

In 1926 a Ha'poel center in Warsaw opened. Others followed all over Poland. All the Jewish groups mentioned above were the organizers and patrons of Hapoel clubs. In our town we had one and we mainly played soccer. Efraim Geller was excellent as the goalkeeper; when he moved to Israel, he continued to play with Hapoel Jerusalem. The youth saw soccer as an opportunity to express national pride and stay in good physical condition.

The Ehodyah branch also produced some good actors and musicians. We also helped to change the political face of the town to a more progressive one. The traditional politicians like Moseh Pinales, Yesef Bezner, Shlomi Kremer and Berl Shpierer were first replaced by the orthodox group and then by those who were losing their faith. The government didn't want liberal Jews to be the leaders because of their fights for legal right for the Jewish population. Those who were part of that story will probably tell it themselves.

My memories are about the time long before the tragic end of the Ehodyah branch in our town. We heard about their extensive activities during the time before the Holocaust. Some of our friends helped smuggle Jews across the Polish borders. Two of our friends, Yitzhak Zin and Shmuel Lester, died while refusing to accept Nazi orders; others were partisans. Other witnesses will tell their stories. God avenge their blood!

[Page 184]

The Gordonia Movement

Nachman Bergman

Translated by Harvey Buchalter

In memory of my friend Schmuellaster who was murdered in Horodenka, in the middle of the town, for not revealing the location of a Jew who had fled from the Nazis

After the First World War, *Hashomer* was founded in our town. I was still a young boy and although I didn't belong to the organization. I remember that there existed an organization with that name, and I recall its leaders, Benish Noyman, Mendel Diner, Moshe Ofenberger, Eliezer Bilder, Beryl Shtrum, Henye Birnboym and Tovah Marksheid. I also remember the teachers in the Hebrew language school from that time: Schmuel Greyf, Ellie Libster, and Asher Yungerman. May all of their lives be a blessing. Two or three years later, I also became involved in things, but by then the *Hashomer* no longer existed. At that time the *Halutz* (Pioneer) Organization started up; it gave its "brothers" the same nationalist education as the *Hashomer*. But in addition to that, it invested them with a worthy goal: to learn how to work in the fields and thereby prepare themselves to travel to Eretz Israel and work to build the land. Our group called itself *Ha- Ichar* – Workers of the Earth – and was composed of the following chaverim: Itzhak Shapira, Ephraim Geller, Leibe Shapiro, Melcha Schlamm, Schmuel Weynroyb, Itzhak-Eli Liser, and me. For the entire summer we could be found at dawn already at school, where we rapidly learned Hebrew. We always expected that the new *chaverim* who hadn't yet learned Hebrew would also learn how to speak it.

By the end of the summer, at harvest time, we intensified our search for work as harvesters and we joined Hasksharah (preparatory training for agricultural emigrants to Palestine). It wasn't so easy to find work as a harvester. The estate managers in our area were inclined to hire peasants from the Carpathian Mountains. To involve little Jewish boys in such work – why, this was something that didn't even remotely occur to them. The first to consent to give us a try were actually the Christian managers from Hantcharov and Tyshkovtske. Later on Yossel Zeidman, the Jewish manager from Serafince, agreed to give us some work. He would say that it was hard to put Jewish kids to work because it hurt him to see them work so hard. But later on he emphasized that with the Jewish boys he would have a *minyan* to *daven* with every day. In Horodenka at that time there existed a group of the Socialist-Zionist Party, Ha- Sokadot. With a push from their chaverim, we founded a branch of the youth organization, Gordonia. The group was composed of these *chaverim:* Moshe Bilder, Schmuel Laster, Bela Stalchel, Leibe Shapira, and me. The Horodenka organization of Gordonia was the third founded in Galicia, after ones in Lemberg and Stanislav. Our group worked with great energy. Within a short time we reached a membership of 450 chaverim, thanks to the assistance of the Bund and the Yiddishche Shule. Within time, we broadened our activity and we pushed for the founding of *Gordonia-farein* (local chapters) in the neighboring towns and villages of Sniatyn, Zaleshchiki, Zablatov, Obertin, and Tysmenitsa.

I had such a pleasant surprise in Tschartavitz. Among the 3,500 residents of the town were about 140 Jewish families – all were involved in farming, as were their neighbors, the gentiles. All were Jewish nationalists and Zionists, and all of the youth and some of the adults knew and even spoke Hebrew in their day-to-day life. They willingly took up our offer, and there was soon formed an active group of Gordonia. The groups elected a central committee; Horodenka became the focal point of all of them. The Horodenka-based group of *Gordonia* met in the rented apartment of Rachel Pasvig. Our major activity was directed toward fulfilling the goals of the old *Hashomer* and other nationalist youth organizations. We also formed small groups that had Hebrew names such as Arie, Kaffir, Nesher, Yaov, and each group devoted itself to reading and talking about Zionism and socialism and to learning Hebrew. The Godonia also concerned itself with exercise regimens for its members. In summer, on Shabbos mornings, people would gather in the meadow and each conversation that took place was about the noteworthy events of the past week and about plans for the coming week. Then they would do a series of exercises and play several games. This appealed strongly to the youth, and perhaps fueled the desire to show off for the spectators who came to watch.

Among its other pursuits, the Gordonia also undertook projects which typified the Jewish "nationalist" spirit. One new undertaking was the newsletter, the "Joumal, " an undertaking in which each comrade could submit some views on the organization's activities and argue back and forth. The articles were gleaned from the experiences of others, or were simply their own thoughts and musings. Within time, we began to put out a "wall-newspaper," to be posted on kiosks, etc. for our comrades. The papers were hand-written until we found a comrade who printed (by hand) so well and so rapidly that he took it upon himself to "publish" an entire hand-written issue. This comrade was Meyer Bumberg, of Blessed Memory. He was a short fellow with a rather weak constitution, but he was a great mathematician and also wrote beautiful songs in Hebrew. Later on, when we put out brochures that were written by our comrades, Meyer Bumberg wrote them by hand; these were later copied by a Hectograph. Some examples of the brochures and the aforementioned broadsides were brought to Eretz Israel and given to the archives of the labor movement.

I would like to emphasize that the organizing of the Gordonia movement, in both the city and the neighborhoods, received vital assistance from a kinsman of mine, Mendel Dul. He was a teacher in the Polish gimnasia in our city, but because of that, was not at liberty to become involved in the Jewish-nationalist movement. But he always evinced a warm interest in nurturing the Gordonia movement. He spent each Friday night with our family and was always eager to instruct me and have me glean whatever I could from his advice on how to be a good teacher. Today he is a teacher in a high school in Haifa.

Unhappily, only a few of the comrades from Gordonia made it to Eretz Israel. In the year 1929 a group of comrades arrived. They should have been the core of a large kibbutz to be named Gordonia G. In the group were the following members: Moshe Bilder, Yosel Yankner, Abraham Latner, Monya Knoll, Moshe Kamil, Schmuel Bumberg, Yehuda Friedler, Esther Hartenshteyn, Yoel Yeger, Eliezer Luft, Baruch Yurman, and Moshe Shikler. They settled in Kfar Ahron, but in time almost all of them abandoned the kibbutz.

And so to conclude, a final episode, not an entirely happy one, from those times. One of our comrades, Meyer Dicker, without my knowing about it, undertook forging certificates in order to give a few of our comrades the opportunity to go to Eretz Israel "above" the quota. After a few tries, his scheme came apart and they arrested him before he used a forged seal that he had set up in Stanislav. He was brought back to Horodenka; they also brought me in to testify. With a great deal of effort, his kinsmen freed him from prison, thus giving him the opportunity to flee to America.

[Page 185]

My Journey to Eretz Israel

Yoel Yeger

Translated by Harvey Buchalter

In the year 1914, at the outbreak of the First World War, I was a four year-old child. Weeks after the outbreak of the war, the Austrian military retreated and the Russians come in. My mother was adamant about staying in Horodenks with her elderly grandfather, Itzhak-Reuven Shor, a "worthy Jew," a prosperous man and a great scholar who had raised her from childhood and for whom she was like a daughter. My father took his four children – my older sister, my two younger brothers and me – to Vizhnitza where my uncle, Moshe Pistener lived. A while later, when it became apparent that the Russian occupation would last longer than anyone had expected, the Austrian authorities sent us to the Czech Republic where we would spend the entire duration of the war.

In the last years of the war, the Austrian military conscripted older men and my father was called up. We children, now left entirely without parents, were sent on to Vienna, to a "kinder-heim."

When the war was over, we still did not know where our parents were. Luckily, my mother and grandfather had stayed alive in Horodenka and through the Red Cross had inquired where we were. In a similar manner my father found us and we all were reunited in Horodenka. I will never forget the first Kiddush. My father and grandfather both wept with happiness to sit together with the whole family at the Shabbos table.

The city was mostly in ruins. Each day the population grew as more families returned from exile. Our family was one of the lucky ones and was able to rent a small place in the city. From a half-kitchen we fixed up a small grocery store, which hardly measured up to the large, fancy store that my great-grandfather, Itzhak-Reuven Shor, had had. Other families, on account of their poverty, could not afford a place to live. So the Hungarian government constructed a barracks – lodging of ten barracks joined together – and crammed several families into each room. For several years, the barracks remained a fixture in the city until all of the residents ended up with decent apartments.

Jewish society centered around various Zionist groups, including the Bund. One group's membership was drawn mainly from merchants and the middle-class; another (primarily the Bund) from among craftsmen and artisans. There was also a small group of doctors, lawyers, and officials, who were almost assimilated, but their children started to join the circles of Zionist youth. With time, their parents became Zionists themselves.

My father was always a full-fledged Zionist. I went to the Hebrew-language school, and was a member of the youth organization, Gordonia. But when it came to the questions of Haksharah (training prospective agricultural worker for Eretz Israel) my father, as well as the other parents, was opposed. In the year 1928, I was the spark of a group that wanted to join Haksharah and so I traveled with two comrades to look for work among well to do Jewish landowners in the Gvozdieta area. But we ended up coming back with nothing because everyone was afraid to give "real work" to Jewish youth. Finally, we came across a Jew who owned a large estate near Stanislvov and who was willing to employ us. He hoped that when we would help make a minyon for prayers when we came to his estate.

As all the parents were against our joining the Haksharah movement, we had to sneak away from the house to do so. We did so after Passover. From our experience in the estate, we learned that the Jewish boys not only worked harder, but also better even than the experienced Gentile workers. On Sundays when we plowed without them, our output was 25% more, even though we plowed with the worst horses. The good horses were allowed to rest on Sunday.

Afterwards, when we had worked six weeks, we decided to go home for
Shavuos. Our employer did not want to give us a vehicle to travel in, so we had to walk home.

On Shavuos, we went to the large Polish manor in Horodenka where a group from HaShomer Hazair was working. On the day of our visit, one of the peasants who worked together with our friends threw a pitchfork and hurt one of our comrads. The situation was very tense. So we barricaded ourselves on the second floor of a building. Several comrades were below in the kitchen, but were unable to bring up any food. So another comrade and I took the large, hot pot filled with rice and milk and, with great effort, were able to make our way past the peasants who guarded the door. Our other comrades and two girls followed us up. Before the peasant workers realized what was going on, we were already upstairs! In the process I burned my hand and foot resulting in two large burn marks.

You should know that the two peasants would not admit that we had outwitted them. So they proceeded to bolt the door shut. We quickly realized that we would not be able to leave and bring in help from the outside. So we tied several sheets together and dropped them from the opposite window. The small and nimble Teitelbaum went down the sheets and informed the police and the rest of our group. Two hours later the police chief arrived and ordered us to empty our revolvers (the peasants had told them we had revolvers.) So I showed him the toy pistols that I had in my possession. The chief laughed out loud and drove the peasants off and freed us from captivity. And so this recounts the first time I became involved in a self defense.

After spending the summer doing field work, we traveled to Nadvarnaya to work in a sawmill. There we "didn't lick any honey" (didn't have an easy go of it) with our Gentile "colleagues." The farm belonged to a Jewish corporation and at least 3,000 workers were there, among them "pioneers" (halutzim) of all stripes: ordinary pioneers; members of Bais-Orim, Hapoel Hamizrachi and Hashomer Hazair; and our group, Gordonia.

On a pleasant winter night – I was just coming home from my second work detail – they called me back to assist. There was a group of pioneers who had gone to the third work detail when they were attacked by some peasants. One of ours, Lippeh Kanner, today one of the important police officials in Tel Aviv, was shot in the hand as he defended himself against them. I realized that if I was to remain working in the sawmill, we would have to settle the feud with the help of the police. I always traveled the back streets, because in the center of town you had to cross a bridge, under which a band of peasants lay hidden, waiting, making the sounds of a wounded person, to entice us to go there and help him out. At some point the police came and scattered them and arrested several of the "bandits. " Then we were able to go peacefully back to our jobs.

Soon, after winter ended, the first of our group traveled to Eretz Israel, in March, 1930. I remained a few more months in Horodenka, but knowing what was going on in Israel in 1929, I resolved that when I would get to Israel, I would join up with the Haganah.

On the 15th of July, 1930, I disembarked in Jaffa, and as they had well-advised me, I had brought along a revolver and 50 bullets. But getting into the Haganah was not so easy. First, in 1933, during the unrest in Jaffa, my fellow workers often did not appear at work. When I spoke to them when they returned they told me about the Haganah. With their help I too became a comrade in the Haganah in 1933. I remained in the Haganah until 1948, when I became a "legal" soldier in the Jewish Army.

[Page 187]

Theatrical Activities

Yeshoah Shtreyt

Translated by Harvey Buchalter

The theatrical life in our town began after the First World War. At that time, comrades from Hashomer would prepare for Shabbos staged recollections of the "Kann," which was a recitation composed of singing and readings. Comrades Mendele Strum, Micheleh PilPul and Yom-Tov Gradinger together with Henyah Birnboym put together a lively and humorous newspaper; they also presented plays based on characters from the stories of Sholem Aleichem.

The impulse for the youth to put on real theatrical productions was inspired by the visit of our fellow townsman, the famous lyrical poet Alexander Granach. He participated in a presentation, and naturally became the star attraction of the event. He recited *Di Geister* by Ibsen, and also put on a one-man show, *Der Baal-Agolah (The Wagon Driver)* with Roza Lazer, Mendel Diner and others. We, the younger members of Hsahomer, organized the event.

A bit later on, before the comrades of the first group of pioneers went on to Eretz Israel, we began to put on "professional" productions in the theater of the Koso Astendashi (the Polish national theater in Horodenka). I will never forget the wonderful experience I had when Hebrew-language teacher Asher Yungerman initiated me into the theater through the production of *Gut, Mentsch un Teivel (God, Man and the Devil)* by Jacob Gordin. Our play featured Roza Lazer, Etil Stizover, Henyeh Birnboym, Fantsye Weinstein, Yoel Shechter, Adete Vasser, Vareh Strum, and Beryl Strum. The starring role was played by Moteh Katz who showed a talent beyond words on the stage and became so widely regarded that, when he came to Eretz Israel, he joined up with the workers' theater group, "'Ohel." There he received very favorable reviews and truly became an outstanding actor. There was also Mendel Diner, who also demonstrated outstanding attributes on stage. He wanted to make a professional acting career, but we never learned whether he did, as he went on to Russia and little was heard about him after that.

The Bund in Horodenka also developed, among its other activities, a matchless dramatic presentation with their own actors and actresses. Weinstein's living room (salon) was a center of cultural life, and the comrades of the Bund presented unforgettable offerings. Residents recreated and identified with the presentation's content.

People would arrive in large groups and they helped out by lending furniture and theatrical props for each performance. The Bund had as members talented stage performers such as Etzie Greenberg, Isaac Fink, Asher Shtreyt, Mansche Briler, Mendel Diner, Fantsye Weinstein, and others. They also had good directors such as Baruch-Isaac Shpeirer, Pasche Klinger, Asher Shtreyt, and Yehudah-Hirsh Sobol. They offered some of the best presentations that an amateur troupe with nothing more than its own resources could offer.

For the common folk, each presentation was something of a lifesaver. I remember that even my mother, whose thoughts were occupied with the shop and its trade, and with Shabbos, the sacred time for davenning and reciting the Psalms and reflecting, would become passionate and live along with each play. Once, upon returning from a performance with Alexander Granach, I started imitating the wagon driver. My mother was so taken by it that she always begged me to do it over and over. Another time, when the Bund staged another presentation, my brother Asher wouldn't let me go with him to the theater. My mother intervened and took him aside. Toward the end of Shabbos when he customarily came around for a bite to eat and said, "You should take Shaike – that is what they used to call me – to the theater." And that's exactly what happened. And so Asher brought my father's dress hat and a Gemara to me and said, " Take this with you and give them my name and they'll let you in." And just like that they let me through the entrance into the hall, which is how I got to go to the theater.

Later on, a new generation evolved, new stage performers appeared, and the "Golden Chain" took on a new aspect. [The Golden Chain is the name given to the flowering of Yiddish culture in Eastern Europe between the two wars. – trans] The usual crowd stopped attending our theater. Several different traveling troupes came to our town to perform for a month at a time to packed houses in the Norodny Dam. This included the Glimerz, Barizes, Latovithches, and Stein troupes among others. Whatever their level of talent, they draw large audiences. However, the old crowd of Bund theater-goers became less and less enthusiastic. But we youngsters were always grateful that we made it through the doors with our forged tickets and disguises.

As we grew up, we learned the theater trade. We began to take part in the performances of Machiros Yosef [works put on by the Hebrew-language school-trans.]. We also performed in so-called literary-evening presentations such as the one commemorating Chanukah, where we recited Chuga Zuckerman's Macabbi Leider. Later, we staged full presentations and revues.

The idea of putting on a revue without our own resources did not originate in Horodenka. A certain very important man from Olamay settled in our town and opened a bookstore and lending library. He was presumably a huge fan of the theater and the light opera, and he also had the ability to direct. With his help we put on a revue called "Chinese" whose musical numbers we will never forget. During this time we had a true Bohemian in Horodenka, the incomparable Asher Shechter, who truly loved theater and light opera. Both the youth and their elders rushed in to perform, if he directed the performance. Thus we revived "The Dead Man" by Scholem Ashe, whose cast included Israel Sucher, Moshe Fleshner, Isaac Reichberger, Joshua Shtreyt, Rivkeh Rauchwerger, Libeh Shapira, Ginkeh Lerer, Dasnie Ofenberger, and others.

This work was also performed in Gvozdets, and it recalles a story which must be told. Because we had to rehearse in Gvozdets' hall, we arrived – all 20 of us – in Gvozdets on Friday evening and booked lodging in the hotel owned by Ursa Schlamm, a brother of Meyer Schlamm. It should be known that we observed Shabbos with everything that was needed to do so and we even had some of our own whiskey to enjoy along with our fish. But when Sunday morning came and it was time to pay the hotelkeeper, our funds couldn't cover our costs, and we had to pay out of our own pockets in order to save face and to get ourselves out of the situation. And about this, there was no dispute: even though we had to travel to other places to perform, it still didn't sit well with us that our work didn't yield us a profit; rather, it gave us deficits which we had to make good on.

But the unsuccessful excursion to the neighboring *shtetl* didn't prevent us from again becoming active in the drama arena. We still loved to perform, and even more than that the directors wanted to direct, and the public really never tired of seeing us perform.

[Page 189]

Shalom Aleichem Club

Shlomo Yiskar

Translated by Dalya Yohai

There were many reasons for the enthusiasm for theater in our town. First, it was better than walking the streets. There was a need to fill the free evenings with some spirited content. Each of us believed that we had a dramatic talent and we only needed the opportunity to develop it. The Shalom Aleichem Club was the answer. It was a place for all the arts, a non-partisan place, where everybody who wanted could participate.

Shatsberger from Kolomyja was the founder and the director of our club. The chair was Mark Cohen and other active members were Morits Pilpel, Bum Ofenberger, Moshe Diner, Meir Bumberg, Shlomo Sucher and others. We had lectures on literature and the theater; we read *Di Literarish Blater* (a respectable literary journal) that was published in Warsaw by Nachman Meizel. We also had sing-alongs.

The first play we performed was *Tevya Ha'cholev*. I was Tevya; Heytsye Reichman was Golda, his wife; and Rivka Rotman was the daughter Chava. Etel Vakhtel, Ilya Pilpel, Chaim Marksheid, and Moshele Weynshteyn were the other actors. The play was a big success. At one point the audience was so tense that people started yelling at the actors. The stage and the set were particularly good. Another successful play was *The Yeshiva Bucher* by Kabim and also directed by Shatzberger. Israel Sucher wrote the music and the songs. I was the Yeshiva Bucher and the Rabbi's wife was Henya Katz. Rivka Rotman, Yitzhak Liser, Yekutiel Meynhart, and others also participated.

This play had, like those in big theaters, understudies for the main actors. After the tickets for the premier were sold, one of my relatives died and Gutman (the son-in-law of Royza Kalmus) jumped in and took my role very successfully. But later on, after the week-long *shiva*, we did the play again with me in the lead; the hall was totally full again.

The plays of the club generated enough money to enable us to continue with our activities. Unfortunately, the political parties wanted to have some of the income for their own activities and this forced us, at the end, to close the club.

Nevertheless, the dramatic activity in town continued and the money raised was used for important causes. The Bund drama club donated the money they made to the Yiddish school and for other community projects. The American Landsmansahft also organized parties to support the school.

Many years have passed since then, but we will not forget plays like *Herzele Me Yuchas*; *Chasia Di Yetoma,* and *Der Yisddisher Kenig Lir*, produced by the Bund.

We, the members of *Hitachdut,* performed *Di Brider Lurie* and *Der Duches* by Alter Katzizne and *Haotzar* by David Pinsky.

In other towns and villages in Galicia there was theater as well, but I don't exaggerate when I say that in Horodenka it was done with extra devotion and love.

It is possible that our own Alexander Granach, who was very successful in the theater outside of our town, was the impetus and reason for others to want to succeed as well. Two of note are Mendel Diner, as was mentioned in Yehoshua Shtreyt's report, and Yisrael Sucher who went to Berlin to be with Granach, and was helped by him to be accepted to the Young Theater in Warsaw under the direction of Dr. Michetz Viechert. Even in the opera in Vienna, Horodenka was represented by Rana Feifer-Laks who sang there many years. The young generation in Horodenka didn't know about her, but our people who heard her sing said with pride "She is one of us – one from our town."

That's how the muse was in our small town; but the Nazis came and killed the spirit and the rest. I hope these lines will be a memorial to this song that was part of Horodenka's experience, but was cut short in its prime.

[Page 200]

Hashomer's Ball

Henya Birnboym

Translated by Dalya Yohai

It is very touching to see grass coming out of ruins. I am amazed by the force of life coming back to cemeteries and find that it represents the victory of life over death! Horodenka was burned during World War I, when the Russians took over. There was no Jewish life whatsoever – only ruins and demolished chimneys.

But everything ends – the war as well. And when this happened, people started rebuilding the town during the day and sleeping in the cellars which were not completely demolished at night

We lacked everything – clothes, materials, food, etc. There were no jobs either. Fighting still erupted in some places around us and, from time to time, we were subjected to new rules and new terrors. We tried to hold on and do the best we could.

The soldiers brought with them some army supplies such as shoes and uniforms. We would get them and dye them new colors. But most precious were the army blankets. We kept them in secret. We were afraid the army would take them away because after all, it was their property. Often it happened that a person would be stopped in the street and the authorities would take his shoes or coat leaving him in the bitter cold. And still he would feel lucky that there wasn't a more severe punishment.

From all over the country we heard news that the Poles were much worse off than we. The soldiers sometimes amused themselves by cutting off half of the beard of an Orthodox Jew. And they didn't mind if the skin went with it. Other Jews were forced to sweep the floor with their beards and to lick the floor with their tongues. The authorities did nothing about this. They just treated it as funny pranks.

In Lvov, the population was without water or bread. They had no windows in the houses in the middle of winter. A Jew had to bend down like a blade of grass that bends in a storm in order to save his life.

But little by little, life came back to the ruins. People were able to get materials. We soon saw some windows in houses instead of the wooden boards. Spring was in the air and there was hope for renewal.

One day a young boy came to town. He was thin and dark skinned. Benish Noyman had come back from Vilna with his parents. He was a member of HaShomer in Vilna and he was so enthusiastic and genuine in his passion that he managed to infect us all. He was quite young at the time, 16 or 17, but nevertheless managed to excite young and old alike.

This activity was extremely important. It infused us with a nationalistic sentiment that had been dormant in all of us – the sentiment that comes from saying "Next year in Jerusalem." But this time it looked like it could become a reality.

Benish talked to the youth and explained very convincingly that they were the future men and women of action. Some of the adults had real problems accepting this huge change of attitude. Nobody prayed or wore yarmulkas. Nevertheless, they couldn't argue with Benish, so convincing was he.

It is difficult to explain to those born in Israel what this meant to us. We were able in HaShomer to taste the future. We could sing and dance and argue freely. We were taken seriously and we had a goal and a dream. We didn't feel alone and oppressed anymore. We had the hope of tomorrow!

We started with one group that became the model for the other groups. The place we rented in town became a center of activity for the whole community. We had a library. Some youth who had finished high school during the war but didn't have the opportunity to continue their studies, volunteered to teach the younger children. And soon enough we had a Hebrew school.

אחת הכיתות הראשונות של בנות ללימוד השפה העברית בהנהלת עזריאל (עילא) ליבסטר (1919)

איינער פון די ערשטע העברעאישע קורסן פאר מיידלעך אונטער דער לייטונג פון עזריאל (עילא) ליבסטער (1919)

A Group of Pupils of the first hebrew Courses with their Teacher A. Liebster, in 1919.

Azriel Libster, Asher Yungerman and Eliezer Bilder were the main forces behind the successful school. And I want to thank them here for their effort on behalf of myself and hundreds of other students.

It was not an easy task. Most of the youth didn't have any formal
education because of the war. The teachers had to teach both Jewish
history and general studies. We discussed different subjects and,
when the weather permitted, we had our lessons on the grass. Some of
the time was devoted to singing. We reconnected with songs from the
past and this added to our cheerfulness. We also planned a show for
three reasons: 1) to raise some money, 2) to show our achievements,
and 3) to reach the public.

I remember very well one of these evenings. The program was very
diverse and was done only by us – the youngsters – with no help from
the adults. We miraculously had some money to dye our shirts green
and we all wore them. The hall was full of people. Nobody wanted to
miss this rare event. We had put a lot of effort into this. We had to get
a permit from the authorities which was really difficult, but once we
got it, we had the green light.

Benish was the first one. He congratulated everybody and was
greeted enthusiastically by the audience. He spoke with warmth and
fervor and everybody listened to him carefully.

The mood was very festive. Benish created a good rapport between
the audience and the players. Everybody congratulated him for his
speech and we were full of admiration. How could one of us express all
that was in our hearts so successfully!

Then it was time for our big show.

I remember the brother and sister Sucher. It was very touching to
hear them sing: she with her innocent face and devotion and him next
to his sister, proud and humble at the same time. They were both
singing about the dire conditions and the hope for the future. Their
sweet faces were beautiful and full of faith. Their singing was full of
warmth and emotion. The audience thanked them from their hearts.

Then Mendale came to the stage. He was chubby with dark eyes
and was a very talented comedian. Sometimes he read for us the
writings of Shalom Aleichem or other comic writers in the center on
Shabbat. Now he was on stage, reading to everybody. In no time we
were rolling on the floor. He was such a good mimic. He was very
confident and did a great job. And the audience was roaring in
laughter. He was trying very hard not to laugh himself. He managed to
finish and then bowed to the room – his face all red against his green
shirt.

The rest of the program was full of songs and games. But the best
part was the funny pantomime of Mendel Diner. He came to the stage
dressed like a mom, with an apron and head wrap, and started
making latkes with kids and a baby around him. The whole act was so

funny that the entire hall went crazy with laughter. Everybody was roaring, laughing and applauding. This community, so worried about its daily life, was laughing a hearty, healthy laughter together. It was very liberating and uplifting.

Mendel Diner, the son of the old rope maker, became the most famous person in town. In the days after the show everybody was "making latkes" and we all sang and stayed very much in the cheerful mood of that evening.

Many new members joined us after this show. We received many more books for the library and people were not so indifferent anymore. The green shirts of Hashomer were seen more and more in our town.

[Page 203]

The First Pioneer Group

Asher Yungerman

Translated by Dalya Yohai

הפרידה מקבוצת העולם
הראשונה (1920)
דער אָפּשייד פֿון די ערשטע
עולים קיין ארץ־ישראל (1920)
Departure of the first
Group of "Olim"
to Erez-Israel (1920)

At the end of World War I, people started coming back to town. The youth that had managed to finish high school during the war organized themselves and met at the house of Hershel Sucher (Yiskar), who was the Zionist idealist in town. Slowly but surely we decided that it was time to act, go to Palestine as the first pioneers, and start the process for others to follow as well. We were 15 but only ten could go. We were between the ages of 19 and 22.

In August 1920, we separated from our families and friends and started the journey. Most of the people in town came to say goodbye and many of them looked at us with admiration and some with jealousy. It was a new era. We were not elderly people going to our ancient homeland to be buried; we were the best of the youth going to work and renew the land.

The journey lasted a month. On September 6, 1920, we came to Jaffa. We stayed there for a couple of days and then we were sent to Rosh Pina to work in an English military camp. We dug and built new roads and the "experts" among us built wooden houses. For six months we lived in a tent. Sometimes after a long day of work, the wind would blow through and the rain would wet us completely. But nobody complained. We were happy to be there and to participate in the work. In the evenings we danced the hora and Mr. Kena'an echoed our songs. After that period some of us found jobs in the farms of Rosh-Pina. We were the first Jewish farm workers. Before we came, they had usually hired Arab workers.

קבוצת העולים הראשונה (1920)

די ערשטע גרופע עולים קיין ארץ ישראל (1920)

The first Group of "Olim" (1920)

It was a time of severe work shortages. Some of us – about half of the group – couldn't take it and decided to go back home to finish their studies. Only two came back; all the others were killed in the Holocaust. May God avenge their blood.

[Page 204]

The First Pioneer Group

Menachem Streyt

Translated by Dalya Yohai

The first pioneer group that was organized to go to Palestine in 1920 included Moshe Fleshner, Reuven Reys, Nachum Katcher, Yosel Yurman, Eizi Eyzman, Yom-Tov Greidinger, Yehoshua Schweger, Shlomo Geffner, Motl Birnboym, and Menachem Strum. When it was time to go, Motel Birnboym gave his place in the group to his sister, Henya Birnboym. Tova, the daughter of Melech Marksheid also joined us. We were in all ten young men and two women. Henya Birnboym was our chairwoman and the administrator was Yosel Yurman. On August 8, 1920 we left Horodenka and went to Bratislava (Pressburg).

Unfortunately, there was severe unemployment at the time in Eretz Israel and the British Mandate stopped immigration altogether. Seven hundred of us were stranded in Bratislava. Two months later we on continued our way to Vienna.

In the meantime, our group spirit was depleted and upon arriving in Vienna the group separated. Some went back to Horodenka; others went to the States. Only three of us, Yosel Yurman, Yom-tov Greidinger and I decided to stay in Vienna, learn a trade, and wait until it was our time to go to Israel. Tova Marksheid joined another group and went with them later on.

It was not easy to stay in Vienna. I contacted Libster, my old chemistry teacher, and with his help found a job as an assistant to a Jewish painter. I managed to find housing where I stayed there until the end of my apprenticeship. After situating myself I started looking for my friends who were still in Vienna. I found Yosel Yurman, and helped him to find housing. He started working for a jeweler. A third friend joined us and studied plumbing. We didn't miss any opportunity to enjoy the cultural riches in Vienna and went to operas, museums, etc. We tried to make our unexpected stay a constructive and beautiful period in our lives.

In the course of the two years of our stay, two more friends came. But they were not planning to go to Eretz-Israel, rather they had left Horodenka to make it in the big world. Michali Pilpel, the son of Yankl Pilpel came first and then Motel Birnboym. We all lived in the same building and managed to all get a special room in a dormitory. Altogether there were 200 of us there and our group was always mentioned as exemplary.

Around August 1922, I finished my studies and went back to Horodenka to say a last good-bye to my family. The Zionist organization had organized a lecture to promote Karen-Hayesod. I managed to leave the party my parents were giving me and go to that event. When I arrived at 3 o'clock I found Moshe Fleshner and Rosa Yeger working on while and blue banners. The Ofenberger sisters and Moshe Karp were ushers. At 5:00 sharp the event started. Mr. Freshl opened and then Zvi Yiskar. I only remember that he asked those present to give money to Karen-Hayesod. When he saw little enthusiasm in the audience he spoke directly to the young girls asking them to contribute money from their dowries. He advised them to go to Eretz Israel where they would find husbands and get married without a dowry and fancy clothes. We then sang Hatikva. Many of us contributed and they collected a couple of thousand dollars.

The "Shiller Group of Hitachdut 1933

Maccabee Football Team 1923

When I was in Horodenka I also visited our friend Yosel Yurman. (there were two of them in town, so we nicknamed him Tares Shwatshenku) Yosel, who was our administrator and who had tried so hard to get our passports and permits to go to Eretz, was now very sick. He was completely paralyzed and couldn't even talk. He had gone back to Horodenka and contracted the flu and never recovered.

With a heavy heart I left my friend and his desperate mother. When I was in Vienna a couple of weeks later, I heard about his death.

[Page 211]

Gordonia's Summer Camp

Bella Shtachel

Translated by Dalya Yohai

Even today, 27 years after my move to Israel, my heart is full of memories of my hometown, Horodenka. She is alive in my heart even more now that she has been destroyed. I'll tell now about the Gordonia organization, in which I spent all my free time after school, and about the Yiddish school in our town. They may seem very different from each other, but actually they complemented each other.

I remember the small room, nicely decorated by Shmuel Lester Zal, where we met. He worked hard to give the room a nice feeling and covered the walls with slogans and educational proverbs. The room was too small to accommodate everybody as our passion and enthusiasm were very high. Our songs and dances disturbed the neighbors and one day they even complained.

Gordia 1930

During the meetings we spoke with the youth about Israel (we called it Palestinografia) – its topography and geography; HaShomer, and the second wave of immigration; and about the three bases of our movement based on the doctrine of A.D. Gordon: pioneers, work and democracy. After every workshop we sang and danced until late at night.

Once a week, on Shabbat mornings, we had sports and field games. We went out of town to a field called Di Toliki and played and exercised until the afternoon.

The Gordonia movement did a lot for the children ages 10 to 12. Many of them went to Israel and today they are good citizens.

Summer Vacation of "Gordia"

From time to time we published a newsletter about happenings in our organization. Meir Bumberg edited and Shmuel Lester designed it. (The two of them died in the war.) Meir Bumberg also designed a poster. He worked many nights to write it by hand and in large print.

In 1932 I went with a small group of boys and girls, aged 10 – 12, to Mikhal'che, a village on the Dniester River, to spend our summer vacation. We called it the summer colony. I had to teach these youth about personal hygiene, from brushing teeth to taking showers every day. Some of them had never used a toothbrush before. We taught them how to live in a group, and about discipline and responsibility. When we came back, their parents were very happy to see their kids healthy and strong. Some of them had even put on some weight. This was a good advertisement for us and many parents started sending their children to our meetings, even those who objected at the beginning. We served the whole area and even the small villages around.

In Horodenka we had a Yiddishe school called "Yiddish Avraham Reizen Shule" where we could learn to read and write. The school was supported by the American Joint Committee and was created by the Bund. They taught mainly the poor kids, some of whom lived in shacks called Barakan Lager. The school gave them school supplies free of charge. There were also prizes for the good students. It was a good place for these kids and had a nice atmosphere. However, the Poles often teased these kids as in the morning they went to a regular Polish school. Even their teachers didn't respect them because of their religion. The studies in the Yiddish School were in the afternoon. First the school was in a rented building, but later a beautiful building, as nice as the Polish school, was built for the school.

In one case I remember, Etel Katvan was sent to a teacher's seminary in Vilna. She was an excellent student and became a teacher herself.

[Page 212]

Ehodyah – The Academic Youth Association

Moshe Shtachez

Translated by Dalya Yohai

In the 1920s, the finance minister Gravsky made the Jews' life really hard. Many lost a lot of money and felt that this was the beginning of a real earthquake. These feelings of insecurity brought many middle class Jews to Israel between 1924 and 1926. Only the depression of 1926 in Israel stopped this wave.

The students were especially worried since the institution of *Numerus Clauzus* (closed number) turned later on to *Numerus Nulus* (no number), which meant a restricted number of Jewish student could go to universities: Eventually the schools were closed to Jews altogether. Even the ones who got accepted suffered abuse from the Polish students and sometimes even physical torture. In this situation, many youth started considering moving to Israel. I was a student in Lvov in 1928 to 1930, and belonged to the academic Gordonia. When I came back to Horodenka in 1930 I started a branch of Gordonia, called Ehodyah, in our town.

"Ehodyah" – Society of Zionist Students 1932

The Ehodyah branch in town was comprised mainly of the sons and daughters of merchants and craftspeople in the community and some working youth.

The youth who went to high school were in a different social class and couldn't join that branch. That was why we created a different organization for the academic youth and started teaching them about the pioneer Zionist ideal. I had many conversations about this with Sala Yungerman and finally we did it.

Only 20 youth joined us and we called ourselves Ehodyah. I have to mention that the group functioned very well and was well integrated socially and ideologically. Later on some more high school students joined. After I moved to Israel in 1933 the activities expanded and some more members moved to Israel. It is important to remember that the move to Israel of most of the members saved their lives.

[Page 213]

The Zionist Youth

Kuka Yiskar-Greif

Translated by Dalya Yohai

The General Zionist Organization had a branch in Horodenka called *Hatikva*. It had the power to and reputation for influencing the Hebrew school and the different funds.

The youth in Horodenka were responsive to the Socialist-Zionist movement. Over the years, however, we saw some more Orthodox organizations like Beital and the Orthodox Zionist movement arise as well. The older generation wanted the youth to be Zionists and aspire to make Aliyah. In 1933 there was an idea to create a new Zionist youth movement but only the very young became part of it, because others in the community were already affiliated elsewhere. The organizers were: Bruno Reif, who died in 1935, Chaim (Munio) Yiskar, Tuvya Korn, Adema Emzig and myself.

Youth of the General Zionist Organization

After Chaim's and my aliyah, Breis Reyckman and Shalom Dermer (his cousin) joined the branch. Through the years the leaders were: Reuven Prifer, Zvi Reys, and Nouska Vakher. They all made it to Israel after the end of the war. The ones who didn't make it were Hailke Zilber, Chmerel Herman, Nina Auerbach and Zichornam Livrachah. These leaders were quite young, 12-14 years old. Their impact was not in ideology, but in infusing in youth the love of the land of Zion and Israel. There was a special atmosphere in the group – one of dedication and friendship. It was always full of song and discussions. We all spoke in Hebrew and our slogan was *"Hazak VeEmatz."*

After Chaim and I went to Israel, there was an active correspondence between Tel-Aviv and Horodenka. They were very jealous of our move to Israel.

Time passed and the war stopped all plans for the future.

During the Russian occupation the branch went underground. They continued keeping in touch with each other and even spoke in Hebrew. This went on for two years that were uneventful compared to the years of Nazi occupation. It is important to tell the story of the branch working with the refugees that came from Romania and Hungary. Tuvya Korn, Reuven Prifer, Zvi Reys, Clara Hartenshtein, Mania Kugler, Sara Frankel, Nina Auerbach and others created a soup kitchen.

Mr. Israel Kugler, a Yudenat member, volunteered to help them despite great danger to himself. He went to the villages to collect food donations from the local Jews, thus helping the youth's endeavor tremendously, both as a model for good work and for its practical value as well. When the Germans ordered them to close the orphanage, the youth took the orphans to the soup kitchen, cleared a room for them, and took care of them. This was not easy since some of them were still babies.

Tuvya Korn was the head of this project and the leader of the branch. He was the older son of Binyamin Korn, the teacher and the director of the Hebrew School in Horodenka and a pioneer of Hebrew in town. They spoke only Hebrew at home. Tuvia was delicate looking, mild mannered, a good and dedicated friend but also firm in his beliefs and very influential in the community.

Before the first action, where there was a feeling of the Nazis would kill the orphans, he refused to leave them and stayed with them until the bitter end. He said, "Their destiny is mine."

[Page 215]

The WIZO Branch in Our Town

Hava Meir-Orner

Translated by Dalya Yohai

In the thirties, the youth of Horodenka were organized to prepare for Aliyah. The *Halouz* organization was very active and even among the adults there was a sense of activism; people belonged to national and Zionist parties. In this atmosphere, the women too started thinking about organizing themselves. In 1934, we decided to establish a non-partisan group. We wanted all the women to join. Frida Frishling (deceased), Donya Rosenbaum (deceased), Bella Bergman (now in Australia), Mrs. Alpert (now in USA) and others started the WIZO [Women's International Zionist Organization] and started supporting *Karen-Kayemet* and *Karen Hayesod.* We created a kindergarten for poor kids and helped them with homework. We also fed the youngsters. The children in elementary school benefited much from our work. We could see that they were becoming better students. We organized parties and events to raise money for the national funds. On Shabbat, we had lectures and entertainment. We also organized parties for children and created a children's theater in Hebrew.

"WIZO" Branch

I remember very well the first "Mother's Day" celebration in 1934. Mrs. Alpert, Mrs. Rosenbaum, and Mrs. Frishling helped put it together. The members of WIZO all helped the teacher, Mr. Berger, prepare a special program with the Hebrew school students. The party opened with a speech by Mrs. Rosenbaum who explained the work and goals of *Hakerem Hakayemet Leisrael*. At the end she called upon the audience to contribute to the fund by giving presents for Mother's Day. Later the children presented a play with dancing. Afterwards there was some food and dance music for all. We raised a lot of money – much more than we had expected.

After I left Horodenka, the group continued its activity. Many of them are now in Israel. Those who couldn't go were very sympathetic to the Zionist ideas. The Germans killed many of the WIZO women in our town. But we will always remember them.

[Page 216]

The Zionist Movement In Our Town

Gavriel Lindenberg

Translated by Dalya Yohai

The Local JNF Committee 1924

a.

The *Hibbat Zion* movement was mainly a Jewish-Russian organization. The harsh treatment of Jews under the Tsar led to an understanding among Jews that they had to move to Israel. However, the Austrian Jews were in a different situation, as that government was relatively good to the Jews. In Galicia there were economic problems, but there was also a sense of freedom that Jews could go everywhere and do anything. The Austrians also didn't get involved in the inner workings of the Jewish communities.

But when political Zionism began to rise, things changed. The Austrian Jews felt very proud that Herzl came from Vienna, worked there, and wrote in German, which was understood by the intelligent Austrian Jew. Thus a lot of enthusiasm developed among the Austrian Jews for Zionism. The reaction of the Russian Jews was a little more repressed and skeptical. Their Zionist movement had similar goals; so they treated the new movement with reservation.

b.

In Horodenka, the Zionist movement had a big following and grew even larger as the younger generation matured. This generation was ready to invest in this organization after their parents abandoned the chains of old traditions.

A branch of the Zionist movement in town started immediately after the first Zionist Congress. In documents cited by Dr. Gelber in his article about our town, there was mention of a Zionist movement as far back as 1897. In the first years after Herzl died there was an annual memorial service in the great synagogue with a lecturer from one of the big cities. Many Jews attended and there was an impression of a dark veil over the city on this day. The *Zion-Farayein-Bnei Zion* was a combination of a club and *minyan* that prayed together on Shabbat and holidays. For many years this took place in the apartment of the Kugelmas Family. The head of the family, Avraham Kugelmas, was an old widow who was supported by his sons, Ahron and Eizi Kugelmas. They were butchers and had some wealth. They were also part of the group. Their apartment was in the center of town next to the Ukrainian church. One room was used for the *minyan* on holidays and Shabbat. It was a ritual that united them.

On other days the apartment was a club for the members and filled with Zionist newspapers in Yiddish, Hebrew, and German; there were also some regular local papers in German. There was the *Latiberger Tagablat* in Yiddish, *Di Walt,* the official newspaper of the Zionist movement in Germany, *Ha'loam,* a Hebrew weekly, *Al*

Hamizpeh, published in Krakov by Sh. D. Lazar and two German-Viennese newspapers: *Di Noye Krei Presse* and *Viener Journal.*

The leaders were two elders Alter Vizelberg and Shmuel-Yitzhak Lindenberg, and two youngsters Hershel Sucher and Hershel Preminger. At that time they had several activities like fundraising for *Karen Kayemet,* such asbuying the Zionist *Shekel* and buying stock for the treasuries settlements. They had some interest in Zionist activity in other places and a little bit of interest in Israel. Only two or three families dreamt of actually going to Israel. This dream could only be realized when everything worked well.

c.

A couple of years before WWI in 1910 or 1911, *Zeirei Zion* opened in Horodenka and all the youth aged 18-22 joined. They had had a hard time with the old club of *Bnei Zion.* They rented a special place and decided to create their own club. Before they could establish themselves, the war started and the youth were the first to be drafted. In August 1914, when the war started, all Zionist activity stopped. Some weeks later the town was captured by Russia and was totally cut off from other Jewish centers in the west. In the spring of 1915, the city was released from Russian captivity, but some months later was again recaptured by the Russians who then started a fire in the center of town and hung nine Jews. The occupation lasted until the end of the war in 1918. Most of the Jewish residents left town and went west as war refugees. They got some aid from the Austro- Hungarian government.

During that horrible time nobody was even thinking about Zionist activity. But it is important to note that the encounter with the Western Jews had a big influence on the youth of both places. For the Zionists in the West, it was their first encounter with deeply religious Jews and they were influenced by their Jewish values. As a result, they often became committed to learning Hebrew. The Eastern Jews learned how to organize a youth movement and were introduced to the values of the western society.

d.

The Balfour Declaration and the Sam Remo decision to create a Jewish State made the Zionist movement a movement of action and established a real goal for the Jewish youth: to train themselves to move to Israel and become pioneers. When people came back to town after the war *HaShomer* was established. Beinish Noyman was the founder. The educational agenda of the group was to study the history of Israel, the geography of Israel, and the Hebrew language. At this time, Ila Libster and Asher

Yungerman opened the Hebrew School again. Among the leaders of the group were Beinish Noyman, Eliezer Bilder, Mendel Diner, Menachem Strum, Tova Markseid, and Henya Birnboym. After a period of two years in *HaShomer,* the group moved up to the *Ha'Chaloutz* movement. Some of them went to Israel; those who stayed back home joined the Socialist Zionist Party *Hitachdut,* which was founded in 1923. This group included Yitzhak Shapira, Yehoshua Shtreyt, Moshe Fleshner, Nahuman Bergman, Eliezer Bilder, Meshulam Shnitzer, and myself

e.

One of the main activities of the youth movements was to help raise money for Zionist funds. The helpers were the fathers, Zionists who believed in the Zionist goal, and other Jews who thought that building Israel was a matter for the whole nation and not only the Zionists. The treasury arm, *Karen Hayesod,* called on all Jews to help, as they needed a lot of people to do the actual work.

There were different ways of fundraising. To fill up the "blue box" of the *Karen Kayemet* there were appeals at weddings and other parties to raise money. Bonds were sold in the synagogues at the end of Yom Kippur, flowers were sold at memorials and on holidays like Lag BaOmer. There were visits to the homes of donors and organizing parties. All the revenues went to the Hebrew school in town or to various Zionist funds. The parties were a combination of fun and work. They also gave the youth an opportunity to socialize and dance. On Hanukah and Purim there was a collection of cakes, wines, and little trinkets; later they were sold or raffled. These, with selling tickets, were the main source of income. There were some expenses, obviously, but usually there was enough left over to support the cause. These events kept the party activists busy.

f.

In between the two Zionist groups *(HaShomer* and *Ha 'Chaloutz)* was the Zionism *Klalyim.* It had the privilege of having two new members – transplants who came to live in town and were extremely active. Both eventually went to Israel to live. One was Yaakov Krashez (who has died) and the other, Dr. Leon (Yehuda) Mensh.

Yaakov came as the son-in-law of Yipel Ekerling. He was tall and handsome. He knew perfect Hebrew, which was quite rare at the time. He also spoke English and was learning Arabic as preparation for his move to Israel. He was very active in town for eight or ten years and then made *Aliyah* around 1930. He first opened a restaurant in Tel Aviv but was not successful. Then he moved to Netanya and worked as a clerk. He died quite young.

Dr. Leon Mensh came to Horodenka as a young and talented lawyer, the son-in-law of Dr. Kanafas. He became a real leader and it was a new development to have people with academic degrees involved with the rest of us.

He was born in Lvov in 1890 and there attended law school. He studied with Professor Stanislav Gavsky, who was a fierce anti-semite. So Dr. Mench, in protest, moved to the University of Krakov. He became a doctor of Law at Prague University.

From his early childhood, he was involved with several Zionist movements: Zion Youth in Lvov with Dr. Biker, *Hakoach,* and the academic group, *Emunah,* which revolved around Jewish culture. This group also practiced fencing for self-defense. In 1913, he was among the founders and instructors of the Jewish Legion in Lvov that was supported by the Austrian Army and had around 250 Jewish youth. The purpose of this organization was to help with the war against Russia that was already on the horizon, but the latent purpose was a Jewish self-defense force.

In the nine years of his stay in our town, Dr. Mensh developed many activities. He was the chair of the Zionist *Klalyim* and was the chair of the Jewish group in the local government that had 18 members. He also founded the Jewish Cooperative Bank and helped establish the Jewish merchant organization. In 1935, he moved to Israel with his wife and lived in Kvizat Shiller. He still lives there today and is very active as usual. He also developed painting as a hobby. During World War II and the years after, despite his age, he volunteered successfully for the Israeli Defense Force.

g.

Between the two wars from 1919 to 1939, 250 people from Horodenka moved to Israel. Naturally, those were the ones who were very active in the Zionist movement. Even after they left, there was no lack of Zionist activity; other young people came to do the work. The ten years before the Holocaust were years of blossoming activity that our town had never had before. *Gordonia* had hundreds of boys and girls and *Hitachdut* was also very active (for older youth). The leaders of the Zionist *Klalyim* were very talented and devoted. Among them, I remember Mr. Zvi (Hershel) Yiskar, and Dr. Mensh. Attorney Dr. Zalman Lagstyn was active until his death.

Other branches were added, like "the Zionist Y outh." Its members included Kooka Yiskar, Haim (Munya) Yiskar, Reuven Prifer, Zvi Reys and most important Tuvya Korn, the son of the Hebrew teacher Binyamin Korn. Tuvya was the founder of the orphanage in town and died with the young children because he didn't leave the children when the Germans took them to the camps. *Beitar* (the revisionist group) also had a group in town and Miko (Shmuel) Yager was one of its leaders.

h.

The jewel in the crown of the local Zionist activity was the establishment of *Bet Haam* in a large building that was purchased from Shamai Bacher. In this way we solved the problem of a suitable place for the different activities. In one building, everything was centralized. This was a major endeavor, in term of money and organization. This demonstrates the positive forces in our town and to where we would have gone if the Germans hadn't killed everyone.

i.

The Hebrew school in town is another amazing chapter of Zionist activity. It was founded in 1907 by a group of parents who felt that there was a need for education in Hebrew and in order to revive Hebrew as a spoken language. Until World War One, the teachers in the school were the Rirachovskies and the kindergarten teacher Zivfa Shertzer. Then came Mr. Hirshfeld followed by Yehuda Goldstein. He was the first one to stay for a while and the students and board of the parents appreciated him very much.

Another teacher at that same time was Yeshuya Izik Becker who had the honor of teaching Hebrew to the Zionist leaders in Carlsbad, where he later was a war refugee. After World War One, local people who were also good teachers revived the school: Shmuel Greyf, Ila Libster, and Ashe Yungerman. Afterwards, Libster to study chemistry and Yungerman went to Israel. Binyamin Korn then came to live in Horodenka; he was previously a teacher in one of the villages. At the same time there were also Hebrew courses for older people (especially women) taught by Zvi Pomeranz and myself.

Binyamin Korn stayed and taught until the destruction of the town. He was a mild man and couldn't lead the school, so teaching in school was given to younger teachers who came from out of town. From 1930 to 1932 there were two teachers who were later to be well known in Israel: the critic Shimon Y. Pinales (Panveli) and the poet Shimshon Meltzer. After they left to Israel, the poet-teacher Yitzhak-Aryeh Berger came and worked until his death at the hands of the Nazis. He managed to inspire his students to express themselves in beautiful Hebrew in prose arid poetry, and published the work in papers that even got Israel. They attest to the high level of Hebrew in our school. These are the only remnants from our Hebrew school in Horodenka.

[Page 219]

The Songs of the Desperate

Yizhak-Aryeh Berger

Translated by Dalya Yohai

<u>in the evening</u>
Thanks for the end of the day, so dark and gloomy,
As it sneaks and disappears into the night,
Finished with this gray existence
And what am I, to expect anything?

The grandfather's clock is counting its minutes silently
The lamp is eating the last drop of oil
And we, what should we look for in the sun.
If we are left to the mercy of every drunk and whore.

The street is thawing, puddles everywhere
The river flows wide with lots of laughing water
Only the human mouth should be silent.

And why should I believe in false promises
When my shoes are torn and dusty
And my life is passing as fast as lightning.

<u>in the morning</u>
My years are passing as fast as lightning
Every town will swallow me and my shaky steps
And there is no one soul around
Who will listen to my frozen blood and being.

In playgrounds, kids are playing and saying
Thanks to father and mother, waiting for salvation
Their singing goes to the heavens
And disappears like their youth.

Every throat is in danger
And the poison is everywhere
My brothers in their exile are degenerating.

Poverty is like a tree with many branches.
There is no hope for our generations
And every prayer says: some dark bread please,
And nobody knows if the cry for help will help.

Memories and Descriptions

[Page 242 & 223]

The Shabos seminar of Shlomo the baker

Dr. Hersh Blutal-Prifer

Translated by Yehudis Fishman

Images and Types of Horodenka Personalities

It is well known that Jewish workers are not generally counted among the Torah scholars, and Jewish scholars are not usually counted among those who join the ranks of workers. However, there were some exceptions to this rule, and one of the exceptions was Shlomo the baker, who held in his house a kind of 'Shabos seminar.' As Shabos would wind down each week several Torah scholars would gather in his home to study Torah just 'for its own sake.'

His name was Shlomo Rosenberg, but few people knew of that. In Horodenka, not many Jews were known by their family name. Almost every Jew had a name added on the basis of who he was. For example, the teacher of young school children was called Moshe Pupik, Moshe, the stomach; Menashe the Goy, was the teacher of older children; and Mordechai Pupik was the name given to the brother of Moshe Pupik. Shmuel the wagon driver was called Shmuel Burlak, the villager. He was a tall Jew whose shtreimel (fur hat) always sat tilted on the side of his head. He would constantly relate how he used to stand guard in the Shoenburn and actually saw the emperor Franz Yosef, whom the Jews of Horodenka called Ephraim Yossel. (They called the German emperor Wilhelm, Velvele.) The teachers Moshe and Mordechai were very heavy men, and so were called Pupik. Menashe the teacher was not a big Torah scholar, but still he had several dozen students from the ages of three to six. They said that he didn't even recognize all his students. One time he saw a young boy lying by the wayside in a puddle and asked him, "Boy, what are you doing here?" The boy said to him: "Rebbe, I study with you." "Ah, so," said Menashe, "you study with me? If so, give me some money."

Other Jews in Horodenka had adopted names of unknown origin. For example, there was Nyuchtche, Baruch Shmanyeh, and Yehudah Bazshor. Yehudah was a teacher and his brother was Chaim Bazshor. Their family name was Toyber. Chaim Bazshor was a furrier, but didn't have patience for this kind of work, and got involved with business. In the summer he sold fruit and during the other months of the year he would sell fish. He was a loud Jew, a socialist, and knew how to deliver speeches. He was the head of the speakers in the 'Plosh' (the auditorium of the shul) and would fight against injustice. His understanding of socialist matters was strange. My brother-in-law, Asher Shtreyt, may his memory be blessed, was a Bundist, and Chaim Bazshor would always say about that: "The son of Shlomo Shtreyt, Asher, behold he is a socialist, so let him come and take my daughter for a wife!"

Yehudah (who was blind in one eye) was a Torah scholar and a teacher. He hated the smell of garlic – so his students would rub garlic on his desk. On Rosh Hashanah, he was the shofar blower in the house of study. One of my teacher's names was Moshe Fligler; we used to call him Moshe Mutzikl (colt). For my knowledge of Chumash and Rashi, I must give thanks to this Reb Moshe. It was with him that I began also to prepare a 'leynen,' that is to master a page of Talmud through my own power. When a young man would want to learn, the teacher would teach him with total dedication. He would offer to teach me even during the holidays in the afternoon.

Horodenka also had a "king" and a "prince." The king and his son the prince were tailors. I do not know why they were crowned with those names. Since their dwelling was burned in 1918 during the First World War, they lived with other families in the old Horodenka hospital. A few years before the war, the Polish Gymnasium had been there. Afterwards, they called this house "the fortress of Sheinbrun."

Just as they called Shlomo Rosenberg Shlomo the baker because of his work, so they called other Horodenkans by their profession. For example, there was Zelig the baker, Leizer the baker, Yossel the baker, Velvel the baker, Shalom Hirsh the tailor (who was also the Torah reader for the shul), Asher the carpenter, Yossel the blacksmith, and Yossi the chazzen (the chief cantor of Horodenka). Others were not called by their profession: for example, Hirsh Doligner and Hirsh Masler were both tailors. The caretaker of the shul was called Yossel Boikie (his family name was Folger). They named the undertaker Bundzior. He was an aged Jew who also supervised the "eiruvin" (the Sabbath rope-fences to permit carrying in a public domain) to make sure they remained intact. He put up his own tombstone during his life, inscribed with the traditional text, including the words, 'Ish Tam V'Yashar,' (a simple and upright man.). The only thing that was missing was the day of his passing. Then there was the chazzan of the Bais Medrash – the house of study – Elisha, whom they called Elisha Baas. His name was Elisha Fleshner, but they always called him Elisha Baas, because of his voice.

A special Horodenka character was "the coughing tailor," Shlomo Pretzlik. His family name was Morgenbeser. He was a chassid of Rabbi Bahur from Kolomea. In the winter he was a tailor, and in the summer he was the attendant of Rabbi Bahur. I would write down the teachings of the Rabbi during the winter. In Horodenka, Rabbi Bahur would lodge with Moshe Shpierer, in a house with a wide gate. These Chassidim were workers who usually held their services in the shul of the carpenters. On Shabos afternoon, many young men, myself among them, would come to the Rebbe's table to hear his wisdom. Shlomo Pretzlik would often go into a coughing spell, and the Rebbe would ask his Chassidim: "Whom should Shlomele give his cough to? To the non-Jews?" "No," said the Rebbe, "he must give it to the priest. Why? Because in the Torah it is written, 'V' hissgalach.' This means, 'V'hiss' – if he has a cough – that goes to the 'galach' – the priest. Immediately the attendant, who was a Jew with a white beard, would bring in the kugel, and the Rebbe would say: "I have an attendant who is completely winterized: His beard is as white as snow, and he 'fresses'." Fress has a double meaning in Yiddish: It means winter frost and it also means eats a lot!

In general the young men who sat around him were clean-shaven. The Rebbe noticed this and began to relate: "My uncle Meir – his reference was to Rabbi Meir of Przemyslany – once went to a cemetery. An Ashkenazic Jew, who probably had yohrtzeit, approached him, and asked: 'On every tombstone, the letters: Tav, Noon, Tzadik, Bais, Hai, are written. What do they mean?' My uncle Meir answered him: 'Ti Na Tzo Bordu Holish –Why do you shave your beard?'"

One of the first students at Shlomo the baker's Shabos seminars was Yitzchok Aryeh the blind. He was blind in one eye. Unwillingly, he was a tailor, but according to his nature, he was a "man of spirit." He had a house full of children but didn't always have enough food for Shabos. One day he made a deal with my father-in-law to fill his sacks with flour for challah and bread in return for doing various sewing jobs. On the following Thursday, he did not have the nerve to get more flour from my father-in-law, so he just walked back and forth in front of the store, till he saw my father-in-law sitting in the store. Immediately, he went in and put his sacks before my father-in-law, with the same sewing proposal... Yitzchok Aryeh did have a copy of the prophets and writings with the commentary of the Malbim, and this alone is enough to testify about his character as a spiritual man. He had a small house with a ground level room and a room in the basement; he himself lived in the basement. In the winter, I would come to Yitzchok Aryeh to study on Friday nights, and in the summer on Shabos mornings, before the morning service. When I came on Friday nights, the whole family would be sitting by the long sewing table and singing Shabos songs to "the heart of heaven." One would think that here lived a wealthy Jew with his family, all were enjoying the pleasure of Shabos. The truth was that the challos baked by Yitzchok Aryeh's wife (a small thin Jewish woman) were made from the borrowed flour.

Hershele from Ostropolier once said that the hardest day in his life was always Thursday. When he was still in his mother's womb, she would travel to the house of the wealthy to bring them flour for Shabos, in order to earn flour for herself for Shabos. Sometimes his mother carried the flour on her stomach, and so he was forced even in his mother's womb to bear the burden of earning a living on Thursdays. Then, when he was a child among all the other boys in Cheder, he was required on Thursdays to know the entire Torah portion, so that the rebbe wouldn't pinch his cheeks and thighs. When he grew and became a young man, he was forced to carry and deliver the flour to the homes of the wealthy. And after his wedding, he was forced on every Thursday to bring Shabos supplies to his wife... This was the lot of a large proportion of the Jews in Horodenka. Shabos supplies referred not only to the challahs, but also to bread for the rest of the week, because on Friday, they would bake for the whole week. They would place the loaves of bread in a row on top of the oven's chimney, one loaf of bread for each day of the week. This resembled a daily calendar that one would tear off page by page. This was also a kind of rationing: as it says in Ethics of the Fathers, "You shall eat bread in measure, and don't eat today that which is designated for tomorrow."

In the summer, I would go once or twice a week down the stairs of Yitzchok Aryeh, and as soon as he would see me, he would say, "I'm begging you, Hershele, please teach me a chapter of Neviyim (Prophets) with the commentary of the Malbim, so I can learn and listen together with you and not interrupt my sewing."

Another student of the 'Shabos seminar' of Shlomo the baker was Tall Hersh, a tall Jew without children, who, on Friday afternoons would sell roasted seeds (of yellow melons) for cracking open on Friday nights. He was also the Torah reader for the Shabos seminars at the afternoon service. The seminar itself had a minyan, but for Shabos afternoon services, they would go to pray in the big shul. It was almost dark, and there wasn't enough light in Shlomo's house, so they needed to go to the big shul with its tall windows.

There were additional students: The son of Zelig the baker, the son of Mendele Lampner, the furrier; the son of Paye Grapakh, a Jew who sold onions and garlic in the market place; the son-in-law of Shlomo the baker (the husband of Rochele, his daughter) and I, the little one. We would learn gemara with the commentaries of Tosaphos and the Maharam, and also the commentary of the "Ohr Hachayim" on the

Torah. I remember when Tu Bi'shvat fell on the Shabos of the Song
(the Torah portion of Beshalach) we celebrated with a keg of beer and
with the fruit of Israel (in total contrast to the weather outside us: high
and cold snow, that would 'break bones'). At twilight, we went to
daaven the afternoon service, and the snow crackled beneath our feet.

And now a few more words about the advanced school in
Horodenka, I mean to say – the greatest Talmud teacher in the city,
Kalman Shmuel. Very few students of bar mitzvah age merited being
his student; this privilege did fall to me. At six o'clock I went to school.
In the morning we learned Yoreh Deah (a section of the code of Jewish
law) with the commentary of the Shach (Rabbi Shabsi Cohen). I
studied the laws of salting and rinsing meat. I admit that I only
properly understood the principle of "absorbing and emitting" years
later when I studied colloidal chemistry...After prayer, we learned a
portion of Talmud with the commentary of Tosafos, and in late
afternoon in the summer, or after the evening services in the winter,
the students would prepare the "laynen," the independent study of a
Talmudic page. We would review the Torah portion of the week on
Thursdays in the late afternoon, or following the evening services in a
hurried manner. We did not learn all the books of the prophets with
Kalman Shmuel.

The small city of Horodenka brought forth from its midst a famous
comedian, Alexander Granach, and an opera singer, Irena Pfeffer, two
special professions that were extremely rare among the Jews of
eastern Galicia.

Woe to those who are lost and can no longer be found.

The Board of the Hebrew School

הלהקה הדראמטית — מועדון ע״ש שלום עליכם
דראמאטישע סעקציע — „שלום־עליכם־קלוב״
The Dramatic Circle "Shalom Aleychem"

[Page 244]

Self sacrifice for the fulfillment of a mitzvah

Yitzchak Shapira

Translated by Yehudis Fishman

The Mikveh (ritual bath)

It was a winter night and the stars were shining bright. The heavens were blue and the earth was covered with a thin blanket of snow. The frost formed designs on the windows of the illuminated houses that lit the way for me to the town bathhouse. I went the long way by the butcher shop whose wide gates were locked and barred at this hour. Its many cells were filled with frightening cow and sheep meat. A sharp and fishy smell filled the empty air and became sharper the closer I got to the "probal" that was outside our city. Deep down underneath it, water flowed from the gutter of the butcher shop and the nearby fountains. After that night, I always felt great fear when passing the locked butcher shop, and I hastened my footsteps to cross the bridge.

Upon reaching the mikveh I found tall village wagons hitched to teams of horses by the side of the street. The horses were lazily eating their spelt from sacks tied to their heads. On the platforms of the wagons sat the dozing drivers. They were wrapped in hairy cloaks, their feet stuffed into the straw in the wagons to keep them from the cold. So they sat for hours, waiting for the women to return from the bathhouse, so they could direct the women's steps back to the village.

נציגי העדות בטקס קבלת-פנים
למפקד הצבא הרומני המרשאל
אורסקו (1919). מימין : הדיין ר'
מנדל שפירא וד"ר באך.

די פֿאָרשטייער פֿון דער שטאָט
ביים קבלת-פנים פֿאַרן רומענישן
מאַרשאַל אַווערעסקו אין יאָר 1919.
רעכטס — דער דיין ר' מענדל
שפירא און ד"ר באך.

Local representatives meet the Roumanian Marshal Averescu in 1919. From right — the Dayan M. Shapira and Dr. L. Bach.

The superintendent of the bathhouse was Fishele Krutz. His wife and helpmate was the 'tinkeren', the woman who supervised at the time of dipping. That night they both stood at the entrance to the mikveh with a shortness of spirit and heavy hearts because of the complaints of the women within. These women were sitting in wooden tubs with the warm water getting colder, as they waited to dip in the mikveh according to the letter of the law. Each month these women came from the villages near and far to become purified in the mikveh. However, this time the mikveh was not completely filled, and the women waited and waited, and even if they had to, would have spent the whole night in this condition.

Upon entering the hallway where the mikvehs were adjacent to one another – the cold one and the warm one for the purpose of dipping – the warning call of the tikenren came out to the women: "Itzik'l the the judge's son is coming!"

Immediately the women covered themselves up in the cloths that were over the baths, and in grumbling voices, they followed my steps to the side of the mikveh: "This time maybe a little less water would suffice..."

My father had given me a key attached to a string. I took it out and used it to open the lock of the cover of a wooden frame fastened over a visible indentation. This marked the amount of water that was necessary for a valid mikveh.

Here I need to explain to those who are not familiar with the laws of immersion. At a distance of several hundred meters from the bathhouse, there is a spring of living water near the well known as a 'rindel.' These waters were drawn by both Jewish and non-Jewish water drawers and sold to Jewish homes. A part of this water was diverted to the washhouse into cold pools, and from there to a large pit, to warm the water. Then a small stream, a thin flow, was drawn into special clay pipes that went beneath the mikveh. Here there was a plug that was opened once a week, on the night following the Sabbath after Havdalah, to bring a flow of fresh water for the duration of the new week.

מראה הרחוב הראשי לאחר
הפלישה הרוסית. — 1915.
די הויפטגאַס. נאָך דער
רוסישער אינוואזיע. — 1915.
View on the main street
after the
Russian Invasion — 1915

Peitro, the strong non-Jew, had many jobs. He did most of them in a state of half drunkenness. He was the 'Shabos Goy' for everything – from lighting the furnace in the winter, to guarding the candles for Shabos and holidays in the shuls. At certain times, when he wasn't drunk and could walk on two feet, he was the central distributor of the waters of the 'rindel' to the Jewish houses. Loaded down with a pole and with two wooden buckets, he poured the waters for all who asked. His primary livelihood came from fixing up the baths in the bathhouse every day of the week, and serving the shvitzers with cool water, without which no one could stand on the top steps. Sometimes he would assist them by flicking the straw brooms made from oak. When the shvitzer was stretched out on the bench with his back up, Pietro, like a professional, would wave the heated brooms and bring his back to a glow. Then the shvitzer would sigh and groan from pleasure.

Every Motzei Shabos, Pietro's job was to empty the mikveh, if it filled more than the needed amount, so hot water could be added as necessary. This mikveh was used for the immersion of women all the days of the week. Also religious men would go each morning before prayer, and especially on Friday after the shvitz. But it happened at times that the spring waters were low, and the mikveh could not be filled during the night or even the day after.

On these occasions, my father would go several times a day to inspect the amount of water. He felt bad that the kosher Jewish women, who came from far away places to be purified, had to wait several hours before being permitted to immerse in the proper amount of water. During these days of going back and forth, I would assist my father, while learning from him, even though I was still young and hadn't reached the obligatory age of fulfilling the mitzvos. I recall how great was my happiness when I could inform him that the waters had reached the indentation...

At these times, significance grew in my own eyes. I felt an indescribable satisfaction as a redeemer and announcer of the mikveh waters, without completely understanding the objective of the mitzvah, and its purpose.

Russian War Prisoners clearing of demolished Jewish Homes 1915

The Esrog

The days of Awe approached in the year 5676 (1915). We returned to our city of Horodenka, after her liberation from the Russian conquest (that took only seven weeks). This time we felt we should not go too far from the city, because the enemy might not hold their position for a long time. Most of the Jews in the city fled across to Syniatyn, Vishznitz, and the other cities in Bukovina. The Prut River placed a barrier to the advance of the Russians.

The Jews that remained in the city suffered terribly from the conquerors. We returned to a part of the city that was destroyed and burned. Without rhyme or reason, the conquerors wrecked a house here and a house there. The houses that remained whole were scorched like firebrands snatched from a fire. For some reason, the conquerors took out their anger on the great shul, but they couldn't destroy it. The roof, that was made out of wood, the benches, the Holy Ark, and the Bimah, with the bookcases, all went up in fire, but the tall walls and the two 'Polishin' that were in the entrance remained standing. They accentuated the giant layer of stones that were cemented in a square like the Western Wall. Also the archways of the doors and windows remained as they were.

The Russians dug in across the Dniester near the city of Ustechko; our side fortified themselves in dugouts on the other shore near the village of Semakovtse. The Austrians brought over to this front one of the most famous cannons called 'The Fat Bertha,' or '42.' When the cannons passed through the city, the ceilings shook from its weight.

Each morning, the thunder of the shelling to the other side awakened us. Each morning a balloon flew up from our side to oversee what was happening on the other side of the Dniester in the camp of the enemy, and perhaps also to guide the shells of Fat Bertha. In vain, the Russians tried to shoot down the balloon. The Jews of Hododenka were proud of their air space. The vibration of the glass in the windows and the shaking of the houses from the rumble of the artillery seemed to us, the children of the city, as a lullaby... The parents engaged as usual in business with the non-Jews in the neighborhood, and they worried about the city's facilities, including those regarding the congregation and religion.

Close to the high holy days, the shul goers did not stop talking about the upcoming major problem – the lack of the four plants necessary for the holiday of Sukos. The Jews who extended their business travels to Lvov and beyond, were begged fervently to search for any kind of an esrog. My father – like the other rabbis in our vicinity – has been involved with selling esrogim from the land of Israel and from the island of Corfu. He found an old lulav that was dried and yellow, and he decided that it was permissable to say the blessing over it. He also obtained myrtles in a wondrous way in Kolomea, and willows of the rivers were plentiful everywhere the streams passed by. But the main thing was still missing – the esrog.

All the effort was in vain. All hopes fell apart and a heavy fog descended upon the city. Despair gripped many of the faithful of Israel. What would the congregation do without an esrog? Suddenly, on the eve of the holiday, a murmuring whisper went around at the time of prayer. It was known that across the Dniester, in the territory of the Russian occupation, our brother Israelites succeeded in obtaining esrogim from Russia, and that the city of Tluste had obtained a beautiful esrog. Immediately the wise men of the city congregated with my father, of blessed memory, at their head, came up   with   a   plan. They found a daring non-Jew from Kotikovka, who agreed for a large sum to take the risk to cross the Dniester. He would have to travel within the Russian lines to Tluste, with a letter from my father to their Rabbi. On the night of the holiday, the non-Jew went on his way, accompanied by blessings and prayers for success in his journey.

On the morning of the first day of Sukos, Jews waited in their talesim (prayer shawls) but did not want to taste anything from the festive meal. They felt that perhaps G-d would have mercy on them and the non-Jew would appear with the longed-for esrog, and they would be able to say the blessing over it. (This is normally done in the morning before eating). However, the day passed, night arrived, and he still did not come. The next day, we woke up early and waited with yearning souls for the appearance of the non-Jew. We completed the prayers of the second day of the festival with our eyes bulging from our sockets, and still the non-Jew was missing.

Suddenly, it was as if the heavens began sparkling and the city brightened. A cry of joy spread from one end of the city to the other: The esrog arrived and it was in the house of the judge, my father, may his memory be blessed! Groups of minyanim gathered before our house. The congregation kept growing. Hundreds of people, men, women and children of all ages – from young school children to students of Talmud to those studying rabbinical writings – all gathered at our house.

My father guarded the esrog that was wrapped in linen and placed in a specially- designed silver case. With the counsel of those who were close to him, he decided to move to the big shul. Its wide hall was still standing (even in its desolation from the time of the fire) and could accommodate the entire holy congregation, who were willing to give up their lives for the sake of the mitzvah of holding the lulav and esrog.

Prominent community members left before father to clear the way amidst the crowd. My father went between them carrying the esrog and the lulav. They were decorated, in accordance with the law, with green willows of the brook and myrtles fastened in a beautiful holder of woven mat. And I, the youth of ten years, trailed after him, holding on to his gartel. (woven belt worn for prayers). Thus we arrived at the shul.

Father got up on one of the wooden benches that were near the northern side of the wall. Before the eyes of the whole congregation, he took the esrog out of its case, and held it and lulav correctly, and began the blessing. Tears streamed from his eyes and from the eyes of all the Jews, who answered Amen to his blessing. With a pleading voice, he begged the large congregation not to squeeze the esrog with their fingers, to clean their hands first, not to break the Pitum, (tip of the esrog, which if broken, invalidates the commandment) G-d forbid, and not to hold the esrog longer than the blink of an eye – as long as it takes to complete the blessing.

At five o'clock in the evening, he was forced to return the esrog to Tluste. That was condition on which Jews had agreed to lend the esrog to Horodenka and to allow our congregation to fulfill the mitzvah this one time, on the second day of the festival.

Father tried to rush the blessers, but all his requests were in vain, for the group just got bigger and bigger. There was no possibility for an orderly line. The pushing was beyond measure. There were cries and shouts. Hands were spread out from a distance. Each one wanted to precede the other in the performance of the mitzvah. Father did not let the esrog out of his hand, not even for the most respected Jews, though ordinarily, it was difficult not to fulfill their requests....Those reciting the blessing were forced just to shake the lulav and to touch half of the esrog that remained in father's hands. Those who blessed first were pushed and shoved wildly by the others, who envied them as those who found the greatest treasure...

For two and a half hours, they passed this way like rows of sheep, before my father, who clasped the esrog in his hand. All their faces were glowing from a divine delight and elevated spirit, for having been able to fulfill this mitzvah. And when we left the shul, crowds of women, who did not dare push their way into the shul, were waiting for us. They too begged for the privilege to make the blessing. My father had decided that in times of emergency, the women were exempt from this mitzvah, but all his decisions were for naught. He was forced to put the esrog in my hand – in order for him to avoid touching the hand of a woman. For an hour I stood surrounded by pure and holy Jewish women, who longed to perform the mitzvah. With copious tears, they continually murmured the blessing for shaking the lulav and afterward the blessing of Shehechayanu. Father tried afterward to use wax to clean off all the stains that clung to the esrog from the hands of the blessers. The non-Jew went back on his mysterious route, known to him alone, to restore the precious fruit to the Jews of Tluste.

During, the rest of the days of the festival we had to be satisfied with the lulav alone...However, on Hoshana Rabbah (the seventh and

last day of the festival of Sukos) the city was astonished when the non-
Jew reappeared. He had brought with him a slightly damaged esrog
from the city of Tluste, where the people knew of our despair of being
without an esrog. They had obtained a second esrog in Chortkov for
their sister city of Horodenka. This time, the crowding was less. The
blessers promised on the spot to pay for the large expenses of
obtaining the esrog. As a result some of the people declined the
opportunity to fulfill the mitzvah this second time, especially when
they had to dish out money right away. But most of them gave with a
generous hand and a willing soul. May their merit protect us and all of
Israel.

Page 247]

Rabbi Nachman from Horodenka

By Shimshon Meltzer

Translated by Yehudis Fishman

When he came to Tiberias, may it be built for the glory of G-d,
The first Tzadik who drank from the divine well,
From the well of the Baal Shem Tov, from the fount of Chassidus –
He, not by himself, he came not alone,
But with a great gathering of followers.
He did not investigate nor seek out much,
He only rented a courtyard and right away lived here –
Is he not the Tzadik, Rabbi Nachman from Horodenka?

And the group lived separate and fenced in,
In that large rented courtyard,
And was occupied with whatever it was busy with.
However, the whole day it neither stopped nor ceased
From pleadings and requests, from Torah study and prayer,
And there was heard the sound of song at the end of each praise,
And each night in the neighborhood here there was singing
In the courtyard of our Rabbi, Nachman from Horodenka.

And our brothers, the good Sefardim, they knew but a little
About the righteous man who desired and longed
To live in the courtyard of that neighborhood,
And since that year was in drought,
And the creations were given over to trouble,
And each heart was downcast, and each soul was bitter,

Who would come to investigate, and who would pay attention here,
About the dwelling of our Rabbi, Nachman from Horodenka.

But after the season for rain came, and stronger
Became the danger of hunger, and the heart of all was broken –
No drop of rain descended from the high heavens,
And the world stood burnt and naked,
The iron heavens whitened by dryness,
The ground was cracked and burning,
And upon all fell fear and terror,
Israelite, Ishmaelite, humans and animals together,

Our brethren, the ancient congregation, the good sefardim,
Prayed pleasantly, as was their charming way,
And abounded with song and joy to the creator,
That he have compassion on the world and bring down the rain.
And opposite them, to make a distinction, was the whole congregation
of Ishmael,
Who went each day to their mosque to pray,
But there was no sign, no indication, no wind, no rain,
Only the gust of the intense heat that withheld the rain.
Suddenly one day, it was not known how,
The news spread out from all mouths as one,
That in this city was a righteous and holy man,
And if he would beseech and pray for rain,
G-d would listen and accept his opinion,
As He listened to Choni the circle drawer, in his time....
Is not this the righteous one who dwells here
In this court, Rabbi Nachman of Horodenka?

So a select and significant committee went
To that high and fenced in courtyard,
And begged the holy Rabbi Nachman
To please request, beseech, and inquire...
For they had truly heard, and it was known
That he knew the prayer for rain, and its secret.
At first, he refused...How would he endanger here
The humility of our rabbi, Nachman of Horodenka?

However, after they returned the next day,
And begged so profusely – he understood that he was chosen
To be the mouth of the Jewish congregation in Tiberias.
So he cast his sight on the parched land,
And sighed a sigh which breaks the body,
And they understood that he would no longer refuse.

Thus Rabbi Nachman responded and announced
That he would pray with the Chassidim in the cave of Rabbi Chiya...

Immediately, the entire city took its stand,
For all – Jews and Arabs – desired to see them –
Rabbi Nachman and his Chassidim,
How that group went out to gather
And descend to the designated cave
Of Chiya and his sons, Chizkiya and Yehuda,
And each and every one of them, man, woman, and child stood
Close to the old wall with the gate.

Behold they watched with wonder and surprise,
That the group which was coming with sighs,
Were dressed as on a complete winter day –
On their heads were hats of fox and tiger fur,
And their bodies were wrapped in wide caftans,
With each corner scattered right and left...
And with pure silver buttons was hereby singled out
The caftan of our rabbi, Nachman of Horodenka.

But more and more like an unanswered riddle,
The community with its eyes wrapped around feet.
On each foot and boot
And each pair of leggings hugging the knees....
And the community staring at its own foot-sandals
Worthy of a drought, open and light...
And it looks at the feet of the other walkers – boots
Heavy and tall, to be anchored in water!

It looked with surprise on all that it saw,
From over the old, high wall,
A group of Arabs, the most distinguished of the city;
Laughed one to the other and continued to point
sharply on the great burden
with which the Jews had burdened themselves so much in the heat.
They mocked the caravan that was meandering with difficulty,
And between those who stood was also Mohamed the Pasha.

This man Mohamed, it's worthy to point out,
He ruled with straightness and moving righteousness,

In his days, the city of Tiberias dwelled securely,
However, when he saw the barren land
And these Jews with their shoes,
Their boots ... he saw in this mockery,
And said in anger and heavy breath,
"These Jews are sure that the rain will come down.

See, look there, and think about their garments,
What will be if it doesn't rain?
If the heavens are still held back,
Their prayer won't help – these cursed arrogant ones?
If in vain they got dressed, these Jews hastened
To transform this burning hot day to a winter-like day,
So pay attention, the congregation of Allah,
To these words of truth that I will say to you:

They are going to pray to the G-d of Israel,
If only their G-d will accept their prayer,
And it will be when they return from that cave,
Dripping from rain, and trembling from cold,
Then we will go down to them, and give them great honor,
And we'll carry each of them on the shoulder,
Till we bring all of them to their house in the courtyard
And as a surrounding wall, we will protect their lives.

However, if G-d refuses to receive,
We will know that Israel is a people of arrogance.
We will know that their prayer was full of pride,
And therefore G-d refused to receive.
And when they return from that cave,
And the drought continues... trouble will come to them.
For we will all come together to the courtyard,
And we'll cut off the head of all of them with a sword!"

Rabbi Nachman, the servant of the faithful G-d,
Did not wait there long, and when the time came
And that holy group went up
To the mountain, with Rabbi Nachman at their head,
They entered the cave of the righteous Rabbi Chiya,
And remained there as much as he needed to remain;
They prayed in the cave the afternoon prayer...

In those days, such holy Seraphim!

They stood in prayer with shudder and trembling –
But also with hope, joy, and song!
How shall we describe here the details.
Who is the person that can say, 'I know them'?
If we merited, we would be with them to see them,
In fact, maybe we would be just like them...
How can we say it, how did the cantor say, 'Who causes the wind to blow'?
And the wind began to blow and expand.

Behold, a cloud arose like the palm of a large man,
And thick clouds poured out after it,
And pulled them in herds
Running and rushing from behind the mountains.
And thunder burst forth like a flying snake
And it shouted and echoed and drummed –
The Creator was opening the windows of heaven,
And the rain poured and spilled and gushed!

And the assembly of Israel with the assembly of Ishmael,
Was struck with wonder and dumbfounded, and amazed and moved,
As pouring rain burst down on them.
They stood silent in their spots; none moved...
They stood and watched with wonder and surprise...
How a group of holy ones came from the mountain,
Even though the rain was pouring and gushing,
The group appeared to approach with a shining light.

Suddenly on the wall on high,
The whole group started to move in place,
Because Mohamed the Pasha leaped and jumped
And descended and began to run to meet those who were coming,
Right away, every strong and honored one among the Arabs,
Rushed after him, running together...
And the whole nation saw how they came to them,
And before the Jews, bowed their knees.

The Pasha grabbed and hugged the legs
Of our Rabbi Nachman and carried him in his arms.

And so saw and did all the rest,
So not even one of the Chassidim remained walking.
For they carried all of them like Torah scrolls.
Shining in the rain and glowing in the light.
In the descent, in the valley, in the elevation and also on the mountain
–

So the Arabs returned them to the courtyard.

And the whole nation of Israel and the whole nation of Yishmael
Was struck with wonder and were dumbfounded and amazed and moved.
Because this day was so great and honored above days,
And on it was sanctified the G-d of Israel among the nations –
And how good it would be if our story could be completed
With the news of the poor one (Messiah) riding on a donkey!
For in the desirable time, the time that G-d supervises over us,
Why is it, truly, that Mashiach is not coming?

They tell in Tiberias, it should be rebuilt for the glory of G-d,
That there flowed that day abundant kindness from the well of G-d,
And that time was ripened for the complete redemption...
However, at the time that Rabbi Nachman was being carried
In the arms of the Pasha... a button came off
From the caftan... Where? There was no solution!
And because of that button, the silver button,
A certain sadness was aroused in someone's heart.

And since a certain sadness came down,
because of a single, solitary button,
The awakening of that moment was blemished.
The approaching redemption was held back...
One single solitary button...it was defective...
The rain came down and flowed to the sea...
And if only in this generation, the blemish could be fixed here –
May the merit of Rabbi Nachman stand up for us!

[Page 249]

With the Chassidim of Vizhnitsa

By Shlomo Sukar

Translated by Yehudis Fishman

Horodenka was a joyful city. Her narrow streets echoed with songs to G-d and to creations. And I want to begin my words with the verses of a song that I sing whenever I recall my old house.

I remember those years when I was a child.
Before me float the pictures where my crib stood.
And when my heart begins to draw me after unfamiliar fortune,
I sing the melodies that I heard in my childhood cradle.

I want to bring up here on paper a small packet of memories from those days past, from the life of Horodenka that was but is no more: How the Chassidim of Vishnitz spent a complete week with their rabbi. In Horodenka were also the Chassidim of Chortkov, but I did not live with them, so I can't describe them. But concerning the Vishnitzer Chassidim, I practically grew up with them.

The matter was like this: My mother, Rivka Sukar, may her soul be wrapped in the bundle of life, herself descended from Vizhnitsa. She knew Torah and Talmud like one of the men, and this only from listening to how Zaide, meaning her father, taught his sons. The Rebbe did not want to talk with any woman, but with the daughter of Leibish Bikel, he was ready to converse for a whole hour. She got married for the second time to a wealthy Jew, Rabbi Meir Frishlig, may his memory be blessed, a produce merchant who purchased from the Horodenka rabbi, Rabbi Michele Hager, may his memory be blessed, the courtyard with two buildings. The Rebbe stipulated at the time of the writing of the deed:

1. There should be a Vishnitzer shul there the entire lifetime of Rabbi Meir.

2. Anytime a rabbi who was a descendant of the old Vishnitzer Rebbe would come to be in Horodenka, he would lodge in the house of Rabbi Meir.

As for the Rabbi himself, no conditions were necessary.

The Vishnitzer Rebbe had seven sons, and after he passed away, each one of them became a rebbe in his own right, in a different city. It's obvious that the first born son inherited the position of his father in Vizhnitsa. The second became Rebbe in Otynya near Stanislavov, the third in Zaleshchiki, and the fourth in Horodenka. More than this, I don't recall. But the fact that there were seven sons, this I know, because they would relate among Chassidim a certain episode. One woman came to the elder Rebbe to ask for a blessing for children, and afterward she went to the Rebbetzin, tapped on her belly, kissed it, and said: "O sanctified holy ark, you brought into the world seven Torah scrolls..."

We can learn from the following story how much the Jews of Horodenka loved their Rebbe. The episode occurred after the First World War in 1920. After the Jews of Horodenka were able to reestablish their livelihoods, they began to rebuild with great effort the Vishnitzer shul on the street of the big meat markets. As was said above, Rabbi Meir Frishlig had already purchased the courtyard of the Rebbe. Rabbi Baruch Leib Ofenberger and Reb Motye Sucar, two supporters of the Vishnitzer shteibel, came to my mother Rivka, peace be upon her, and gave her the news that the Vishnitzer Rebbe was ready to come to Horodenka for Shabos. Coming for Shabos meant automatically from the Thursday before to the Wednesday after – practically a whole week.

It goes without saying that my mother had to cook for the Rebbe and all his attendants. It also goes without saying that the big room had to be cleared for the Chassidim, and a smaller side room for the Rebbe to meet with his Chassidim. This was referred to as 'Praven', and for the sake of our children, who surely don't know the term 'praven,' I want to explain that the Rebbe would receive each Chassid individually for a short conversation, or a piece of advice and encouragement. The Chassid would present the Rebbe with a 'kvitel', a short note on which he would write a request involving material or spiritual matters – salvation, healing, or livelihood in general. Besides the written matters, the Chassid would add oral words, and pour out his whole heart before the Rebbe, and the Rebbe would strengthen him with good advice and blessings. At the time of 'Praven,' the Chassid would place some 'redemption money' at the edge of the table as a gift to the Rebbe. Usually, this was a few coins, according to the ability and generosity of the heart of each one. And to the attendant, they would also leave a certain sum, for the writing of the 'kvitel.' Even non-Jews would sometimes come to the Rebbe to ask his counsel and blessings. (But from their money, the Rebbe would not benefit, but would rather divide it among the poor.) For example, the head of the district of Agufsovitch would be a frequent guest to the Rebbe.

Anyway, we said that the Rebbe was ready to come. The Chassidim weren't lazy, and they tried and succeeded in getting the poritz to lend them a carriage with four horses. With great honor, they escorted the Rebbe with his two attendants from the house on the crossroad of

Yacubuvka through the length of the entire city. It's understood that one of the Chassidim took upon himself the task of wagon driver, and the gentiles were standing on two sides of the city and gazing upon this scene in wonder... Who would think and imagine that bearded Jews would be grooming four horses hitched to a carriage? Near the house, many Jews entered dressed in Sabbath clothing, and received the face of the Rebbe with a reverberating tune: 'For the sake of the fathers, save the children and bring redemption to their children's children...And the nations will know that the Jews have a King...'

How fortunate was I, that I succeeded in pushing my way to the Rebbe, to receive his face, and to be able to touch and kiss his delicate hand, his silken hand. At the time of 'Praven,' I also received an amulet – to the children he used to give amulets. This amulet was a simple Roman coin, but the Rebbe would whisper a blessing over it. The children would sew it into a small linen sack, and they would hang it around their necks, and it would protect them from all evil. It appeared to me, that at that moment, that I made a contract with the master of the universe, forever and ever...

Besides this, the honor and the emotion of daavening together with the holy Rebbe for shacharis, mincha, and maariv (the morning, afternoon, and evening prayers) that was no small thing. I made up my mind to also to go before Shabbos to the mikveh, at the same time as the Rebbe, and I remember clearly the whole procedure that went on there. Each Chasid felt that it was the greatest mitzvah to jump into the mikveh right after the Rebbe came out. They would jump in one after the other. It was really dangerous! But to the credit of the holy Rebbe no one got hurt...

The prayers for receiving the Sabbath were always performed by the Chassidim of Vizhnitsa with great enthusiasm, especially when the Rebbe was present! Some would wait until the Rebbe finished reciting each chapter of the prayers; we waited more than five minutes for the Rebbe to finish saying the 'Shema,' and more than ten minutes till he finished the Amidah. And everything was done with great honor, and absolute silence.

After daavening the Chassidim spread out quickly, each one to his family and his table. Afterward, they quickly returned to 'the Rebbe's table,' to be able to grab the 'Shirayim' (holy leftovers). One of the attendants was also a good cantor, and he brought with him a complete treasure house of tunes. After each course – after the fish, after the soup, after the meat, and after the dessert, they would sing impassioned songs. After that, they would measure them on the feet; in other words, they departed in step with these tunes, in a circle dance.

Not only would the Chassidim of Horodenka come to the table of the Rebbe, but also the Chassidim of Kolomea, from Gvozdets, and even from Delyatin. Among them were also Chassidim who were 'beholden in thanks to the Rebbe for all their wealth.' They tell that the rich man from Delyatin used to be a confirmed miser. Only because of two silver Austrian crowns that the Rebbe gave him as a gift and advised him to begin doing business in jewels did he become a very wealthy man and a prominent miner of precious stones. All this came to him from the blessing of the Rebbe, and he saw the Rebbe as the 'second partner' in all his business. Each year he would send him a half of his profits, besides gifts in honor of Pesach, and in honor of Rosh Hashana. When the Rebbe would come to visit the cities of Galicia, he would also come and bring a very big 'redemption gift.' Now, during the Rebbe's visit to Horodenka, the rich man from Daltin would come and set up a barrel of beer for the Chassidim, and boil up a container of about fifty kilo of beans. There was also another kind of beans, black and tasty ones that were called 'knaipers.' After they tasted the beans that were sprinkled with salt and pepper, they really desired to drink a little beer. The Chassidim would taste one cup, and then another, and after drinking sufficiently, would sing and dance till the light of morning. The joy would especially be great when the Rebbe himself would come into the circle and dance together with the Chassidim. At that time, it seemed to the Chassidim that the gates of heaven were open for them.

Near the table, on Shabos afternoon, a new portion began, the portion of 'kugel.' Each woman from the Chassidic families would send 'in honor of the precious guest,' a delightful kugel, each one more praiseworthy than the other, and they would sink all the talents of an experienced homemaker into these kugels. Some were noodles, some were braided, and some were filled with raisins, almonds, and types of jam. The Chassidim were looking forward to the minute when the Rebbe would push away the full plate, after he himself tasted a very small amount. Immediately would begin the pushing and grabbing, and the plate would be emptied in one split second. The plate itself would miraculously be left intact from under the hands of the Chassidim. Not, G-d forbid because they were so hungry or ravenous, but because they wanted to fulfill the mitzvah of 'Shirayim'. It goes without saying that after the new kugel, would come a new tune and a new dance filled with enthusiasm.

To the 'table of the Rebbe,' would come some of the young men of Horodenka, who were no longer praying, but they were, as they would say, 'children of good fathers,' meaning that the chassidic spark still flickered in them (and until this day, there are hidden Chassidim like these. When they come together here in the land of Israel after thirty years, they still cannot resist a chassidic tune.) These young men listened to the tunes and held on to them in their ears. And afterward they brought them to the meeting of the 'Union of the Workers of Zion.' They would sing the tunes non-stop at the joyful parties there, and would arouse happiness and merriment in the hearts of their friends.

Thus there would come every second year, one of the sons of the old Rebbe of Vishnitz, to lodge in Horodenka. I would be forced to relinquish my bed and to wander for a complete week, but I would always do this with great joy. I and my brother Israel, peace be upon him, were both afflicted by the same thing, meaning, we both loved Jewish theater. We once began at the table of the Rebbe a certain niggun that we latched on to in 'Gllimer's group.' It went: 'Over and over, sing again, Israel, over and over, sing and have no fear...Over and over, sing again, Israel, in honor of the holy Creator.'

Immediately after the Rebbe heard this song, he turned to Reb Zalmen, his cantor, and said: " Learn this song; we shall sing it and give it a fixing...It doesn't matter that the tune originated from the theater..."

Yes, the Rebbe gave a fixing to our tune in the midst of his Chassidim, and we gave a fixing to Chassidic tunes when we sang them among our friends, and afterward transported them to the land of Israel. And not only in one kibbutz are these songs sung until this very day. Yes, yes, Horodenka was a happy and joyous city...long, long ago.

[Page 251]

With the Chassidim of Chortkov

Moshe Stachel

Translated by Yehudis Fishman

1. Bar Mitzvah

The matter happened in the scorching days of summer, in the year 1913. On the Sabbath, toward evening, I left my house for the shul, to daaven Mincha. I dragged my feet slowly, like the way of small children. My brain was filled with thoughts of angels, in the form of giant birds, who enter in caravans, ready and prepared to escort the Sabbath queen. A mirthful laugh awoke me from my thoughts. I lifted my head, and behold, two tall bearded Jews, dressed in shtreimels and capotes, strong in body and cheerful in face, were coming to greet me. They were Yossi Chazan and Yankel Pilpel. Their merriment clung to me, and I began to follow them. They started in the direction of 'Munstarski Kut.' On the way I saw that from time to time, they would increase their mirth with a bit of liquor from out of bottles that were hidden in their chest under their capotes. And so they arrived, with me right behind them, at the courtyard of the Rebbe from Horodenka. I was almost overcome with fear. Such a large throng of Chassidim, I saw only once before in my life. In the giant courtyard was noise and confusion. Flaming faces, shtreimels tilting to the side, unkempt beards, waving hands, and sounds as if a hundred people were speaking at once. And all this in a frightening rhythm, till it was difficult for me to distinguish individuals who were familiar to me. Afterward, I found out that Rebbes were there from near and far who came to celebrate the Bar Mitzvah of Baruch'l, the son of the Rebbe.

Suddenly there was silence. A whisper passed through the crowd: "The Rebbe is coming, and with him, Baruch'l." The whole giant mass began to move backward, to make a place for them. As if by a hidden sign, someone began to hum a tune. At first it seemed far away, but afterward, it got closer and closer, until clear words could be heard: "Siman Tov Umazal Tov,"(a good sign and good fortune) and the 'mezinkl geit,'(the youngest one is coming). And so it was, over and over, each time stronger and stronger. Arms were twined together, hands were placed in their belts, and the whole assembly went out in a strong, enthusiastic dance. One tune followed upon another without end.

הדיין ר' מנדל שפירא והחזן יהושע אש בבית הכנסת הגדול.

דער דיין ר' מענדל שפירא און דער חזן יהושע אש אין דער גרויסער
שיהל.

The Dayan Mr. M. Shapira & Chazan Mr. Yehoshua Ash
at the Grand Synagogue.

My head was spinning. I stood near the fence, with my small forehead stuck to it, and didn't notice that the sun was already setting. I had a waking dream. Instead of Jews with payes, beards, and shtreimels on their heads, I saw a giant black cluster with a flame burning on its head, and it was moving higher and higher into the sky. Cherubic angels were surrounding it and singing in powerful voices that pierced the skies: Hashem said to Jacob, "Do not fear, my servant Jacob." And from then on, that Chassidic tune clung to me, and accompanied me like a shadow, and did not leave me until this day.

2. The Honor of the Torah

There was a custom in the old Chortkover shul, that on Shmini Atzeres, they would daaven mincha and maariv, go home to eat the festive meal with one's family, put the children to sleep, and go back to Hakafos. However, my father, of blessed memory, gave in to my continued pleading and took me with him. At a very late hour, they began the Hakafos, in order to include in the mitzvah and the joy, not just the regular daaveners, but also those who came from other shuls.

The joy grew from minute to minute. Jews who were busy all year around with worries of a livelihood, forgot their worries, and could no longer recognize them. A lightness of mind, a certain joy rippled over their faces. The honor at the Hakafos was given according to ones lineage and importance. It's unnecessary to say that they did not forget to honor the "helpers of the poor," those who were worthy because of their general position, who in their joy, did not hesitate to donate in honor of a Hakafah, a shofar or a megilah wrapped in a talis, instead of a Torah scroll, for they were not worthy of a sefer Torah. The invitation was announced with a special emphasis, and to the mass of people, an exaggerated description, as if to emphasize the opposite. That evening, everyone was designated as 'a great philanthropist,' or at least, 'our teacher and rabbi.'

Thus, the hakafos continued for a long time, till the list of daaveners finished, and the energies of the announcer and the inviter were finished. Also the children joined in and completed the seventh hakafah, together with the honored daaveners. They returned the Torah scrolls, and left only one out to read three portions. Everything ran according to custom. They called up a Kohen and a Levi, and the turn came for the Aliya of a regular Israelite. Then something happened: Among the daaveners were two brothers, Anshel and Binyomin. The following day of Simchas Torah was the yarzeit of their father. As is known, every child wants to bring merit to his father in the world of truth, through an Aliya to the Torah. And they both longed to be called up for, 'Shlishi,' the third Aliya. The Baal Korei called the name of one of the brothers, but the second one who was closer to the bimah, ran up first, and said the bracha, "asher bachar banu." (Who has chosen us) The other brother meanwhile reached the bimah and also began the bracha, but stopped in the middle when the congregation screamed out, "a bracha in vain!" And with ashamed anger from the mocking stares of the congregants, they attacked his brother with tightened fists. Immediately, a fistfight broke out, with the children of the embarrassed brother joining in. All this took place in the presence of the open sefer Torah..." How valuable and important is a sefer torah," I said in my childish brain..."if a Jew is ready to stretch out his hand against the beard of his brother..."

My father of blessed memory, grabbed me on his arms, protected my small head with the palm of his hand, and took me out of the tumultuous shul. Fresh air, from a newly fallen snow, that had just descended, surrounded me and put me to sleep in the eyes of my father.

3. A new tune

For the memory of my rabbi and teacher, Rabbi Menachem Mendel
Shapira

From the days of my childhood, I was drawn to after the Chassidic
Niggun. I didn't miss any opportunity to hear or collect a new niggun –
especially in my second home, that of my teacher and rabbi, the rabbi
of our city, Rabbi Menachem Mendel Shapira. In those years, I was
accustomed to visiting the rabbi each day, to hear Torah from his
mouth, together with his son, my friend, Yitzchak. As time went by, I
became in all respects, as one of his family, in all matters.

During the holiday, when the Rabbi daavened in the left section of
the large shul, Yitzchak and I were the established choir. Out of
appreciation to the rabbi for his sweet and pleasant prayers, those
who daavened in that section would prepare a feast during Sukos with
food and drink in the rabbi's house.

It's obvious that I never missed out on this celebration. First the
honored ones, who prayed in that section would enter, followed by
many Jews who loved a party. Not only the drinks, but also the food
was abundant: Kugels and cakes of all kinds, not to mention all kinds
of drinks. The festivities would generally begin after noon, and would
continue till evening. The rabbi's whole family, under the direction of
the pious and humble Rebbetzin, would do the serving. Her ways were
unostentatious. I remember with love and concern for me. She always
asked me if I happened to be hungry, and did not forget to honor me
with the esrog jam that she made each year. Almost half the city
would come to the rabbi's house all the days of Sukos, just to say a
blessing over that jam.

The meal was spiced with words of Torah from the Rabbi, and with
stories from the guests, and of course, with plenty of singing at the
end. The old and weak man, Shimshale Milnitzer, would bring an
abundance of songs and prayers. More than once do I recall his
"Melech Rachaman," and "V'hasi'ainu" from the Shmone Esrai prayers
of the holiday. The words had a special taste in his mouth, with his
shaky voice that was still sweet and pleasant to our ears. His singing
was on the level of "All my bones will speak..." We also heard "'Bai Ana
Rachitz" from the mouth of Mochole Vovos. We didn't even skip the
Frankish version of "Echod Mi Yodai'ah," from Shmulekl Shapira,
whose appearance represented the essence of the holiday. Meanwhile,
Chaim Aharon finished consuming all the leftovers from the table.
Then the rabbi turned to his son-in-law, the husband of his oldest
daughter Feige, with a request to add something of his own.

He was a 'silken young man', somewhat different from those who we were used to here in Horodenka. Together with his Chassidic walk and wardrobe, there was something a little modern, a little cultured, that was generally rare in our city. He acquiesced to the request of his father-in-law, and began to sing a verse from "Lecha Dodi." The verse that began, "Mikdash Melech." His song was like his demeanor – cultured and with a special flavor. This was a special song that was unique of its kind, which I heard for the first time. Something brought me to an elevated spirit. Forty years have passed, and I no longer recall the external form of that refined and humble young man. However, from time to time, in the moments of release from daily worries, I still here the tune of "Mikdash Melech..." and then I remember all those good Jews who used to be, and are no longer. Some of them have gone to 'their world,' like the way of all flesh, and some were killed by the hands of the inhumane ones. Woe to those who are lost, and are no longer found.

4. The Judge Rabbi Menachem Mendel Shapira, May his Memory Be Blessed

When Rabbi Mendel Shapira was nominated for the position of judge in our city, there arose, as usual in these circumstances, an argument between those who were in favor, and those who were opposed. The opponents among the Chassidim of the Chortkover Rebbe, sent a committee to the Rebbe with the to dissuade him from holding that position, even though Reb Mendele himself was counted among the Chassidim of Chortkov. But the conclusion was the opposite of this. The Rebbe abounded in praise of the position and decimated all the arguments of his opponents. Regarding the argument that the appointee was too young for that job, the Rebbe answered, "With the help of G-d, he will live a long life, and become aged..." On another argument that he is not steeped in Torah to a sufficient degree, the Rebbe replied: "It is written, 'Beautiful is Torah with the way of the world...'" So the opposition to the choice of Rabbi Mendel Shapira was pushed away, and he was chosen to be the judge in our city.

I knew him in the beginning of the thirties, when I learned Torah from his mouth, together with his son Yitzchak, may he be separated for life. Many years before that, in the days of my youth, I would listen to his prayer as the cantor, when he prayed in the old shul of the Vhortkover Chassidim. As I remember, there was none among the daaveners in the kloiz who were not inspired by his prayer. After the First World War, we went to daaven in the Polish section near the large shul, and there his reputation emerged as one of the most exalted cantors in the city. He remained a faithful prayer messenger on behalf of the multitudes of the children of Israel, and they always praised his sweet prayers.

I want to add another dimension about the nature and character of the judge. This was from the time that I used to go in and out of his house. Once on a Thursday a woman came to ask a question about a chicken being treife or kosher. The judge examined the chicken and decided it was treife. After the woman left, he explained to me in detail why he decided as he did. After a few weeks, I happened to be in the house of the judge, when another woman came in with a question similar to the previous one. This time it was on a Friday. The judge again examined the chicken, searched deeply into the law books, checked the chicken again, and after great deliberation, decided it was kosher. When he saw a look of astonishment on my face, he explained the difference in the reasoning between the two situations in which I was a witness. The first case, he said, was on a Thursday, and it occurred to a wealthy woman, who could easily buy another chicken in the honor of Shabbos. Therefore he did not have to enter into complex deliberations to find a way to permit her to eat the chicken. However, in the second case, an extremely poor woman came on a Friday. If I had decided that the chicken was not fit to eat, I would have caused a great financial loss, as well as great emotional distress to a poor family, and would have obliterated the Shabbos happiness from her home. Therefore, I felt it my obligation to examine and search for a way to declare the chicken to be kosher, and I was very joyful when I found that teaching.

These words gave me much material for thought, and only then did I understand the words of the Chortkover Rebbe: "Good is Torah learning together with the ways of the world."

Thus was branded into my memory, the portrait of my teacher and rebbe, Rabbi Menachem Mendel Shapira.

[Pages 254 & 234]

What I heard and saw

Moshe Stachel

Translated by Yedudis Fishman

An ethical lesson from the model of the Czarina

When we still lived in the house of Moshe Finels, the Likhtental family also lived in our neighborhood. The father of the family, Fivel, was known by the name of Fivel Kvasnik, because of his involvement in making Kvass (apple liqueur), which became famous throughout the entire neighborhood.

Fivel married off his daughter to a youth, a very God fearing person, called Elimelech from Marksheid. His religiosity was sometimes beyond human understanding. Once the Shabos candles began to bend and were about to fall causing a danger of fire. Even the tested method of putting the Shabos challos around them did not help. When one of the candles fell and set fire to the tablecloth one of the children tried to put out the fire with all his strength. The head of the family rose and decreed decisively, "Let there be a fire, but the Shabos shall not be desecrated!" Fortunately, someone thought to call the non-Jewish maid who worked in our house; she extinguished the fire.

This Fivel Kvasnik was also my "Kvatter" (one who carries the baby in to his bris). As a result he saw it as one of his tasks to supervise my education properly. He discharged this duty by testing me every other Shabos. Between the hours of three and four, I was tested in his house, and as a reward, I would receive a piece of honey cake, a fragrant pear in the appropriate season, a sweet drink, and as dessert, a cup of Kvass, that would restore the soul. In the face of such a reward, I tried not to disappoint him. Thus this routine continued for several years.

I would not fulfill my obligation with regard to the Kvatter, if I didn't mention what my father, of blessed memory, told me about him.

Fivel Kvasnik was not among the wealthiest men of the city. Still it was possible to find in his cellar a barrel of real wine (not raisin wine). Each day, after lunch, he was accustomed to bring up from his cellar a cup of the best wine, and to have a leisurely drink with his meal. It once happened that one of his friends found him in a "state of dissolution" and criticized him: "Is it possible? Right in the middle of the week, without any special reason, that a Jew should be sitting and drinking wine? This practically borders on gluttony!" And then Fivel gave a very resourceful reply. Calmly he removed his money purse from his pocket, took out a twenty crown paper, placed it before his friend, pointed to the picture of the past queen of Austria, Maria Teresa, and asked: "Do you recognize this young woman?" "Yes," came the answer, "this is the wife of the emperor." "Is it true that she is beautiful?" he asked again. The reply came, "It's true, and to whom should belong a beautiful woman, if not to our emperor, may his glory be elevated." And then came Fivel's incisive response: "You answered correctly. The woman is extremely beautiful ... and still, her value exists only when you can enjoy her ... meaning, money is only valuable to the extent that one can enjoy it." This describes my Kvasser maker.

A businessman who was a member of "the diligent hand"

From that time period, I remember another event. In our city, which never lagged in the absorption of new ideas, the organization called the "Diligent Hand" was established. This was an organization of workers that provided assistance particularly in the area of vocational advancement. My father, may his memory be blessed, was an official member of this organization. One day, he brought home a group picture of the members of the organization. A neighbor came over and asked, "What's going on with you, Reb Yedidya, to be found among the workers; is not your place among the business- men?" My father replied to him. "Is my work less difficult than theirs? Does their labor bring less benefit than mine?" For a long time, this picture occupied an honored place on one of the walls in our home. It disappeared with the rest of the household items, when we left our house during the First World War.

A new teacher whose soul was bitter

In time after we moved to a private house, my teachers changed and I obtained a completely different 'farherer' (tester).

One day, at the beginning of the term, I was brought into the cheder of Yonah the Melamed, Yonah Leibman. The procedures in this cheder were different from the ones that I was used to. It was a little more modern, as shown by regularly scheduled recesses between classes and also in the accelerated pace of studies, resembling that of the public school. The teacher, who suffered from some kind of chronic illness, was always bitter and depressed, and poured out his anger on our heads. He had a weakness for giving disgraceful appellations to those who lagged in their studies. Thus he called the two brothers, Mendel and Niemke Friedman, whose father was a carriage driver, by the names Tate Hai and Mame Voi. The students responded and referred to him as "Yonah Gadzulya," apparently meaning Yonah the Ganif, (the thief), because he would often give us significant beatings that were not always justified. May God forgive him for his deeds; we already forgave him long ago.

As I mentioned, we had regularly scheduled recesses between our classes. During them we would go into a booth wrapped in a climbing vine that stood in the courtyard. We would sit on the circle of benches and play different games, or exchange buttons or other objects. One of our favorite games was Shimshon Hagibor (Samson the Strong). We would all stand on the benches and appoint someone to be Shimshon. Usually we picked Niemke-Voi, who was stronger than all of us. He would stand in the corner of the Sukah, and after he quoted the verse, "Strengthen me this one time" from the book of Judges, he would powerfully shake the corner pillar of the Sukah, and we would throw ourselves from the benches to the middle of the Sukah, acting out the breaking of the temple of Dagon on top of the reveling Philistines. It was clear that whoever rushed to throw himself down would be squashed by the others who fell upon him. One time I felt that someone was pushing me away causing me to fall on the top of the pile. This was the strong hand of Shimshon-Niemke. Afterward, he took me aside and explained to me the meaning of his actions. "You have to know how to adapt; you are weaker than the others and pushing can hurt you more than the others." From then on, I benefited from the protection of Niemke in many circumstances.

This was a "love that was dependent on something specific." Each Monday, I always knew the weekly Torah portion clearly. I was chosen over other good students to review the portion with the flagging students. Among those were the brothers Mendel and Niemke. Their hearts drew them to go to the river instead of reviewing the measurements of the length and width of the tabernacle. In thanks for helping the teacher, I also received certain privileges. It was possible for me to release "my" students, from class earlier than the official time, by certifying that they had reviewed the material and were sufficiently knowledgeable in it. I must admit that this wasn't totally truthful. It seems that the teaching, "One has to know how to adapt," helped Niemke as much as it helped me.

In the cheder of Yonah the teacher, I got to know someone who would remain my good friend over the course of years, Shmuel Abba Shnitzer. We would visit each other frequently, and so I was fortunate that Shmuel Abba's father, Rabbi Chaim Shnitzer, was my second "farherer." (tester of studies). Here I did not receive any reward for my diligence; the reward for studying Torah was, this time, Torah itself. More than once, he would explain to me matters that even my teacher would consider hidden. In their home, I also got to know for the first time a totally new way of life. In contrast to most of the people in the city, who were Chassidim following different Rebbes, the members of the Shnitzer family were obvious misnagdim (opponents of Chassidim) who could be singled out in our city. They were one of the most honored, as well as wealthy, families in our city, but the Chassidim could not forgive them for separating from their community.

"Please don't wake up early to immerse in the mikveh"

Following the first world war, after all the shuls in the city were burned, Rabbi Chaim gathered a portion of those who used to daaven in the shteibel (small shul) and dedicated a room in his house for them to continue the customs of the shteibel. Among the daaveners in this new shteibel was Shmuel Shpan, an extremely observant Jew. One

Shabos before daavening, he came running into the shteibel and proclaimed, "Jews, an obscenity has been done in our city! When I returned early in the morning from immersing in the mikveh, I saw with my own eyes the 'Piakernik'- the carriage driver, Yaponchik, riding on his horses to water them in the potiyak (the source waters for the mikveh)!" The entire congregation lifted up their eyes to Reb Chaim, to listen to what he would tell them. With calmness and deliberation, Reb Chaim answered them, "Reb Shmuel, my advice to you is don't get up so early to dip." Everyone understood the hint, except Reb Shmuel himself....

Since that time, many years have passed. Many of the statements of the personalities I met, stuck with me – except for the teaching of Niemke, who tried to teach me "to learn to adapt." This teaching, I did not succeed in internalizing.

[Page 256]

What Used to Be

Kuka Iskar-Griff

Translated by Dalya Yohai

It is a custom in our country to ask each other where we are from. When asked that question, I answer, "I'm from Poland – from a small town you never heard of!" Still if they insist I say "from Horodenka – did you hear about it?" Most people say, "Yes, Horodenka, sure! We heard about that town. It's near Kolomyja, near Zaleszczyki. I have a good friend who came from there, a real nice fellow despite being from Galicia!"

Strange, but this is usually the response. I don't know why, but many people know exactly where Horodenka is and many have connections with our town.

In fact, a colleague asked me, "What is your connection to your town after so many years in Israel? Why do you now have feelings for this place. Tell me about it!" What could I tell her, or for that matter, anyone who has never visited Horodenka?

Sobil's Lake

There were three churches in the town – the Polish Catholic, the Provaslavic Ukrainian and the Armenian. They were in a triangle and were in the heart of town. At the same center were the town offices, the Jewish institutions, the schools, and the Hebrew school.

The Catholic Church was very beautiful and many stories and legends were connected to the church. On one of the towers were four huge clocks that rang every 15 minutes. You always knew the time, and the rings accompanied us throughout the day. It woke me up every morning because we lived across the street from the church. It is strange, but mainly Jews lived around the churches. There was another bell, with a different sound, on the tower of the Boys School; but it rang only for emergencies or fires.

There were some streets branching off the main street that was like the main artery of the town. They led to Dvorska, Shpitlana, and Kotikovka. There were names that described the different areas in town: the proval area, which was like a wadi; the *shul* area where the big Synagogue was; the Potok area surrounding the River; and the Tchervone area, a place filled with history from the Ottoman Empire. The story goes that there was a big battle there, and so much blood was shed it turned the water red. Other areas include the Toloka area (the big park) and last, the pride of the town, the Zvkrovania (a sugar factory) which was a beautiful area. We used to call these areas by their old names, although they had other official names. I remember the trees and lilac bushes that grew all over town. The policemen played drums to gather an audience whenever there was a new order or instruction.

In front of our house (which we inherited from our grandpa) and in front of our neighbors' homes, all the way to the stores of the Grapach family, there was a market. The farmers parked their horses and carts filled with vegetables, fruits, chickens, and eggs. It was a beautiful sight, very colorful, especially the women's dresses full of embroidery and ribbons. The transportation in town was by horse and cart and travelers used the doroska, a carriage that went only to the train station and back.

Electricity came to us a little late. I still remember, like in a dream, the kerosene lamps, especially the one on our ceiling. We used to polish it once a year for Passover and other special occasions. I saw the first bus in Horodenka. It was parked next to the bar of Kalmus; I don't remember it's form but I'm sure I'll never see a more beautiful bus in my life.

The first radio that I saw was at Dr. Kaufman's. It was a radio with headphones and my father tried very hard to explain to me how it worked. When I was seated in Hebrew school and we sang Hebrew songs, I believed that our songs were going through the air waves to Israel! Every Saturday night we congregated – the older female students of the Hebrew school – in the kitchen of Hilda Burg. We said some prayers, original ones, asking God to bring all the world's Jews together in Israel in our time. We always finished by singing *Shavua Tov, Yerushalaim Ir HaKodesh,* and *Halleluya.*

Were there many towns where girls did this? Our eyes looked towards Zion from childhood, even before we heard bad words from a *goy.* And who can prove to me that this innocent childish prayer, that came from the bottom of our hearts, was for nothing? *Kol Israel,* the Israeli radio station, continues to play *Shavua Tov* to this day on Saturday nights! Maybe we were the carriers of this song and the ones who helped start this tradition.

In the mornings we all went to the Polish Public School and studied to acquire information. We spent only two hours in the Hebrew school, but there and only there we studied, lived and breathed easily. In the Hebrew school we were ourselves – free to live our real lives. Because there, although we were different from each other, we were all united by our common goal and aspiration to live in Israel one day and in the meantime to be the living bridge that connects the past with the future by studying Hebrew and the history of our nation.

The Hebrew school was our spiritual home that we loved and shared. And it is not by chance that its location was in *Beit Ha'am,* the adults' meeting place and the location of the Zionist library. The meeting place was also used as a synagogue during Shabbat and the holidays. It encompassed all the different areas of our lives and in it we could express all of our Jewish feelings.

And what plays we put on during the holidays!! The holiday started long before its actual date because we prepared with skits and plays. We were very successful in these endeavors because in them we were able to express our true feelings and longings. We not only studied the stories of our ancestors, but we loved them, felt them, understood them, and wanted to be like them!

Not long ago I met a friend from Horodenka. In the conversation he told me, "Do you remember how dark your parents' apartment was?" I got really offended. "What are you talking about?" I said, "It's not true." He blushed and said, "Think about it, there were no windows in your living room!" "True, true," I answered, "you are right, but until this moment I didn't realize it. I never felt the darkness. We had so much internal light and warmth, goodness and understanding, open mindedness and bright ideas. I never felt the darkness."

And it was not only me. Many people came to my parents' house to find the light. I still hear the discussions and conversations. People from all walks of life came – from the Zionists to the Bund people to the communists.

And my friend was actually right. Even the wealthy families neglected the apartments. All the doors facing the street were locked at night with strong shutters that had metal bars with huge locks. But the back door to our house and to many others was quite unsafe; even a small child could open them. My Aunt Feiga, my father's sister, was worried about that. When she spoke to my father about that he replied with a smile, "Why fix it? We are going soon!" I think that this reply was typical and the essence of our life. Everything was directed towards the future, to the new home that would be built in Israel.

The only pictures on the walls were in the bedroom. Two big frames –one of a page from the "Golden Book," where my father was registered and, in the other one, a certificate from the *Karem Kayemet* for planting tress in Israel.

In the living room, over the mirror, was a big picture from Petah-Tikva, a town in Israel. My friends and I often pretended we were walking in the picture, thus being in Israel.

I remember, one Passover we got a Matza package from Israel. I think Itzhak Shapira sent it to my father with a bottle of wine from Karmel that we got every year from Mr. Shmuel Itzhak Lindenberg. The package charmed us all. Who ever saw such beautiful Matzas?

Square and white and packaged so nicely with a symbol and Hebrew writing.

In our town it was different. Every head of a household ordered ahead the quantity of Matzah he needed for the family and then came himself to pick them up in a pillow case that was folded twice. Our heart beat with excitement when we tasted the first Israeli Matza and drank the Israeli wine. After everybody tasted them, my father looked at us, smiled and said, "Do you understand? It is not only for us." And soon enough the door opened and people came in and took a piece. It was obvious to everybody that it could not be only ours. It was a real festive occasion, a ritual of getting together, of companionship, because it came from our *Eretz* Israel. By the way, we ate together a lot. On holidays like Simchat Torah, people came over after the prayers for Kiddush and to eat Holuvtchis. Every year we discovered that my dear mother was the queen of Holuvtchis.

There was one day a year when we, the girls, were in control of the Jewish street. It was on Yom Kippur. On that day, we saw with pride our parents and brothers going to the different synagogues in their best clothes and we, the girls, stayed behind to watch the homes. So we walked around in small groups took and care of the babies. We fed them, washed them, and walked with them. We passed the time conversing, telling stories and legends and the oldest among us (aged 18) even fasted.

Today there are playgrounds for children. But we didn't have any and didn't feel deprived. We had everything. We took care of ourselves. Two children hold hands, spin around, and you have a carousel. When we wanted a swing we went to Rosa Ofenberger. Her father had a lumberyard. On the width of a long piece of wood, we put small pieces and there was a swing. And for a slide we went to the roof of the ice room in the Sobel's yard. Our mothers' didn't understand why our panties were so black and torn, but we had great fun. And in the winter, during the snowy days we had lots of fun. Yes, we had time for fun and games. Busy in the morning in public school, in the afternoon in Hebrew school, and also belonging to a youth movement or a sports club, we still had time for fun. Nobody traveled in fast cars, but in a carriage and a horse. We didn't have plumbing in the houses; but we bought water form the water merchant. Taking a bath was a complicated matter. And washing the laundry was a real ordeal. But still we had time for everything – to eat at the same time, to have an interesting conversation, to meet with friends for crafts and hiking. Nobody ran or hurried and still they got everywhere on time. And we never forgot a good word, a smile, having friends over and good conversations. Everything was done in a relaxed manner and with longing to do the same in Israel.

We, the people who made it to Israel, needed only to find work. We didn't have to change anything with our spiritual life because we lived in Israel like in Horodenka.

One day the city council decided to move the municipal market from its original place to another side of town. Instead of the market, they wanted to create a park – the castle of Pilsodyky. They decided to pull our the old trees that grew on the sidewalks. But the trees didn't want to move! They didn't agree to be uprooted! It was a bitter fight. They needed to bring in machines to deal with the trees. They tied big metal chains around the old trees where so many birds nested. There was a huge noise and after a long battle, they managed to pull them out.

A group of students on our way from school stood there sad and crying. My father was standing behind me. He put his hands on my shoulder and said, "Don't be sad, my daughter, it's nothing. If they could do it to us, they would do it with no hesitation." This image in alive is my heart like an open wound.

So the sentiment is not for the physical town, not at all – but for the Jewish life that we had there. For what was there is still alive in our memories.

[Page 258]

Nationalist activity

Yitzchak Roykhverger

Translated by Yehudis Fishman

The days of our childhood and youth happened in a time when national aspirations were awakening among the people of our town. Each year on May 3, the Polish people celebrated their national day with a parade, sports activities, and by wearing wonderful costumes. They made speeches, had meetings and sang their national anthem. The Ukrainians too had their own national organization and on their national day they would get together, ride horses, have a parade and wear their national costumes. During these celebrations we would stand on the side and talk. We were very envious of these people. When was our national holiday? When would we be like the rest of the people? We only had religious days to remember our national pride –

days of mourning, like the ninth of Av and days like Chanukah that celebrated past courage. But these had to be celebrated inside our houses so people who were not Jews would not notice. We did not have parades. We did not have a national anthem. We did not have national pride.

When the war that started in 1914 we forgot these thoughts. During the time of the Russian occupation, the Jewish population was under a lot of stress, humiliation, anxiety and fear. In 1916 during the "great escape," most of the Jews ran away and the city became practically empty of its Jewish citizens. They scattered throughout the Austrian Monarchy and remained there as refugees until the war was over. In 1918, as the war ended, those refugees returned home to find their houses broken, destroyed and robbed. They had to put all their energy into rebuilding their homes. In the beginning a few families had to live together in one apartment. But, eventually, with the support and help of the government, most of the houses were rebuilt.

The youth that came back from the countries of the west where they had been refugees were very different from the youth that left before the war. They were greatly influenced by the Russian Revolution on one side and the awakening of nationalism throughout the small nations in Europe on the other side. There was a special awakening and joy following the Balfour Declaration that gave hope to the Jewish people that they would have, like any other people, a land in which they could live in freedom and practice their culture and religion. Under these influences, a local branch of the Hashomer youth movement was created in Horodenka. This group helped youth to learn about their heritage, and with the resources available to them, to plan for their future and the future of the Jewish people. I too was a member of one of the groups created by Hashomer – a group called the Tiger Group. Heading the group was Elieza Bilder. Its members were: Schreyer, Sukar, Obenrice, Geffner and myself. This was where we learned the history of the people of Israel and the Zionist movement. This was also the place where we read the writings of the fathers of the Zionist movement: Dr. Hertzl, Max Nodoy and Ahad Ha-am. We also learned Hebrew in the Hebrew school run by Mr. Grife Libster and Ashe Yuniman.

After two years of Zionist organization, in 1920, the first group from Horodenka made Aliyah. It was a dream come true, a beginning of the messianic era. But this was a small group and the majority of us stayed and remained active in Horodenka. Our main activity was in the various Zionist unions. These clubs changed their shape from time to time, but their mission remained the same: to raise the consciousness about nationalism and to sponsor national fund raisers.

In 1925, the Culture Circle was created and headed by Dr. Druker. The brothers Berl and Bauer Kugelmas who were high school graduates also participated. This is where we read plays in German and Yiddish and argued about the content. A short time later, from that same group, the Horodenka Amateur Theater Group was created. The members of this group were: Moshe Fleshner, Josua Shtreyt, Liber Shapira, Donya Offenberger, Ali Pelpe, Israel Sukar, myself and others. We used to have our little productions in the hall of the Naradney Dome. It was very exciting and we got a lot of positive reactions from the audience. We also performed in the adjacent towns of Grodydich and Turlitchna with a lot of success. One of the groups that met to study bible and literature was called the Group of Proverbs. Its name was the acronym of the first names of its participants: Moshe Schnitser, Yitzchak Roykhverger, Shalom Lisar, Lipa Lisar and Joshua Shtreyt. Side by side with the Zionist and cultural activities, we found time to be active in sports. We turned the warehouse of Abraham Offenberger into a gym and created the first soccer group, Macabe, in Horodenka. We practiced in the Toliki practicing grounds. Horodenka became an example to a few towns in our neighborhood. They imitated us and created similar movements and activities.

[Page 260]

Some memories of childhood

Haim Yiskar

My story begins in 1920, right after the end of the First World War. When we came back to Horodenka we found that our house had been destroyed, as were most of the houses. From the people who did not leave during the Russian occupation we learned that our house went through two phases of destruction. First they took the furniture away, together with a big library that belonged to my father and a model of the temple that was built by my grandfather's brother, Uncle Yoshi, who was an artist. During this phase, the peasants in the area destroyed household dishes and tools. During the second phase the local regiment of the Russian army turned our house into a bakery. When they ran out of wood from the forest to run the bakery, they started burning the floor panels of our home. But this was the fate of most of the houses in the town.

Our house was next door to the Catholic Church. The front room was a little store from which we sold candy and sodas. We prepared the sodas in the back room using the water from the best well in town. The water from the well was brought to us by the water hauler called Benjamin, the good Benjamin. Whenever he was hauling barrels of water he would tie a little cup to his belt and let people who were thirsty have a drink.

Before we managed to finish fixing the house another disaster came. The army of Petliur, a Ukrainian Cossack, came in to help the Polish army against the Bolsheviks. The people in our town became anxious and started escaping or hiding behind locked doors, in cellars, and in attics. They were hiding from the Hidemuks, Petliur's anti-Semitic soldiers. Whoever dared to go out into the streets was usually hurt by those soldiers.

The memories from the First World War and the atmosphere that remained in the town afterwards influenced children's games. We used to organize war games in our neighborhoods. Each area took the name of one of the main countries that participated in the conflict. We had wooden swords. An ex-soldier released from the Austrian army for mental reasons used to train and lead us in these play wars.

The general school in which we learned was inclusive of all three nationalities in the town: The Jews, the Poles, and the Ukrainians. It was located next to the building of the Polish cultural center in which there was a sports area and a park. This was the boys' school. The girls' school was on the other side of town. The principal of the boys' school was a short, old Pole, with the nickname of Moisha Lebel. Most of the teachers were not Jewish. The religious teacher, however was a Jew: Mr. North. There was always hostility and tension between the groups. The Poles and Ukrainians always united against the Jews. In the afternoon we used to go to Hebrew school and learn the Hebrew language. The teacher was Benjamin Cohen. Not only did he teach us Hebrew, but also he insisted that his family speak Hebrew at home. His son, Tuvia, later became the leader of the Zionist youth in town.

While I was going to Hebrew school, I remember only one funny story. We were learning about Peretz Molenski, the Hebrew writer. Influenced by what we studied at school, I went out and drew the profile of Molenski on the wall of our neighbor's house. A police officer saw the profile and, thinking it was a drawing of Trotski, and therefore unlawful revolutionary activity, arrested the owner of the house. The man asked some of the community leaders to convince the local authorities that he did not know who drew the picture or who it was. Only when I clarified that the drawing was Molenski was the man released from prison.

[Page 261]

A Bunch of Memories

by Leon Spirer

Translated by Harvey Buchalter

Fifty-eight years is clearly a long time in the life of a person; even the forty years in which I find myself in America is also not a short time. Still, I can recall everything I experienced in the city of my birth, Horodenka.

My memories begin in the year 1910, when I was five years old. We lived on the "high" street where generally more Christians than Jews lived. My father, Israel-Mordechai Shpierer was by trade a builder (boi-meister). But in 1910 he had already been in America for a while. He was a generous man to our mother and a loving father to his children, but he had not foreseen the need to take us all to America prior to the First World War. And so we survived five harsh years of loss and sorrow.

My first teacher (melamed) was Moshe Rugendarf, from whom I learned *Humash* (Bible) until *Veyekra* (Leviticus). I remember on the Shabbos following Succos, a neighbor of ours, Yochanan-Matai Stezavertz examined me on the *sidra* in his house. Thereafter I studied in the Polish state school, the so-called Skola-Menska, which was opposite the Polish Sokol (social club). My older brother Selig at that time studied in the Yiddische Folkschule, which was in the Baron Hirsh School. My sister Basia was then a grown-up girl. She was the only daughter in the household and knew enough to go to America shortly before the outbreak of the war. Our seven-year-old brother Velvel, the youngest child in the household, unfortunately died in 1914, the same year the war started with the Russian invasion of Galicia.

The happiness that we had at home disappeared as our father left for America. With the death of our youngest brother and the outbreak of the war, a sad and difficult era began. This was also a hard time for all of Horodenka Jews. The mobilization that drafted the fathers and the grown sons of many families quickly began. With the Russian invasion we had to endure an entire seven months of Russian-instigated pogroms. The Austrian army then returned for a few months, and during their second retreat, just about the entire Jewish population accompanied the army to the other side of the Prut River, beyond Syniatin, toward Vaskovitz, which was on the way to Vizshnitz.

Meanwhile the Russians in the city burned the majority of the Jewish houses, including ours.. After a while, we again returned to Horodenka. By the time of the third Russian invasion, in which the Russians occupied the entire Eastern portion of Galicia, the Austrian government organized the transport of the fleeing Jewish population to the western lands of the Austrian Empire.

Our family dragged itself along with the transport until we arrived in Vienna, the Austrian capital, tired, broken-down, hungry, and sleepy. From there, they sent us on to Behmann in a German Village where we lived with Aaron Dicker's family, seven persons in a room. My brother Selig was already in the army and I studied in a German school for the three years we lived there.

In the year 1919, as the war was ending, the newly-established Czech government gave us the opportunity to return to Horodenka. The journey lasted scarcely two weeks. Coming back we encountered a Ukrainian regime in the city and in all of East Galicia. A short time later the Poles took back the reins of government and life improved and returned to normal.

My father (of blessed memory) died in New York in 1918, and my mother died in Horodenka in 1923. We, their three children, find ourselves in America. We all aspire to educate our children with the Jewish spirit. We belong to all of the progressive Horodenka groups. One of my brother's sons was chosen to be president of the Progressive Horodenka Union in 1963. And our finest hours are spent in the company of pleasant Horodenka compatriots.

[Page 262 & 194]

The Polish High School

Shalom Yaron-Youngerman

Translated by Dalya Yohai

A.

In 1921, parents of children who had finished elementary school had a problem. The Polish high school had closed during the war (1918-1921) and the political situation was not very stable. The military occupation started with the Ukrainian leader Petlyura, then the Romanians, and finally the Polish. The civilian regime was initiated and nobody at that time had any energy to think about a school. And we didn't really have enough children to form the first classes of a high school. The older kids studied out of town or took their exams privately. In the year 1921 it was finally time to take care of the high school situation. The economic situation was also a factor. During these years the economy got better, especially for professionals who were the ones who wanted to send their children to school. They also had the money to do so.

In September 1921 the first two classes opened. It was obviously a Polish school although 90% of the students were Jews. The school was located in the "Sokol" building and the teachers came both from the community and from out of town. Most of the teachers were Jews. The next year, two more classes were added and the school moved to the old school building that was used before the war. There were ups and downs in the school's development. Only during the fifth year of its existence did the authorities certify it. That was also the year when the first students graduated.

The high school was founded by Jews and they were its main supporters. The majority of the students, teachers and parents' council members were Jews. But the school was Polish in all aspects: not only because that was the language that was used, but also because of the political and national affinity. The parents were all Jews who had broken from the traditional Jewish ways – consciously or because of personal reasons (mainly people who worked for the government). But the school also had to be Polish because there was no other way, since a Jewish school would not get recognition from the authorities.

We had two other high schools in town: A Ukrainian school and an agricultural Polish school. The first one was not an option for Jews and the second would not admit us. For that reason the Polish high school was really the only option.

B.

Jewishness was not terribly important to us. We obviously knew we were Jews and that there was a "Jewish Problem" and anti-Semitism. In many homes there were still traces of traditional Judaism: Shabbat candles, Kosher kitchens, fasting on Yom Kippur and preparation for Bar Mitzvahs. Some of us had relatives who moved to Israel and the Zionist newspaper Chwila was in circulation in most homes. But for years there was nobody to take care of our Jewish national education. There was the Hebrew school in town but we were completely estranged from it. And the same was true about the Zionist organizations in town.

I have to mention through, Dr. Frida Rotenshtreich (the wife of Dr. Levi Rotenshtreich, a lawyer who became later very active in Lvov). She was the only teacher who taught us some Jewish history and some Hebrew. But she left town after two years and there was no other person to continue this work with us.

C.

When we were in the sixth grade, there was an awakening of our Jewish identity and sentiment. We learned from reading Chwila that there was a Zionist youth movement in Galicia. Among the founders was Yitzchak Stiger, who later on was accused of trying to assassinate the Polish president Narovtovich.

We contacted the organization in Lvov and got some information. At that time Dr. Ila Libster was in town. He was a chemist and very knowledgeable in Jewish subjects. (He also taught Hebrew in the Hebrew school of Horodenka). When we asked him to teach us, he accepted gladly. For almost a year we assembled in private homes and studied about Zionism. We read the writings of Pinsker, Achad Ha'am, Herzl, A.D. Gordon and Buber. We argued and asked questions. New horizons opened to us and Israel became an integral part of our thoughts. All this activity was done in secret and nobody else knew about it. If the principal found out he would probably have expelled us from school. This man, the principal, was a fanatic Polish patriot of Ukrainian background and was extremely loyal to the government. He didn't have any idea about Judaism. Once he learned a student was a Zionist, he would always sarcastically call him a communist or a Zionist. In these circumstances, obviously everything had to be done underground. Even our teachers didn't know about our activity.

At that time, learning about Zionism didn't have any political meaning. Over time the circle widened and we developed clearer opinions. After two years we could say if we were gravitating towards the Labor party, the Revisionist Party, or to the Party of Zionist Klalim. Later, some of us dropped out and became apathetic to the cause. But those years, 1927-1929, marked a clear change in the attitudes of our youth towards the movement. The seeds that was sown then were planted deep and brought fruits later on.

D.

In 1932, The Union of Zionist-Socialist Academics created the school of the Union members in Eastern Galicia, called Gordonia Akademait. It was a pioneer movement among the students. The two factions – Labor Hitahadut and Poalei Zion – united. and the new name given to the movement was Ichodia (which means union).

Many of us were among the first pioneers who went for a preparation course in Schodniza. The first people moved to Israel in the year 1934. Most of them went to the Gordonia group in Kibbutz Kfar HaChodech and some went to other spots.

But only small a number of our youth connected their lives with Israel. Most of those who stayed behind perished in the Holocaust. The ones who moved to Israel are to be found in Kibbutsim, or working as teachers and academics. There is no question in my mind that the activity of that year was very significant in their being alive and in Israel.

[Page 263]

Two Encounters

Nachman Bergman

Translated by Dalya Yohai

1) An unexpected encounter with the Polish interior minister

In 1930, when he became the minister for interior affairs of Poland, Sklapkovsky decided to make progressive changes in the country to benefit the citizens. One of the changes was to make a daily time for the mayor to meet with without making prior arrangements. You could just come, stand in line, and see the mayor.

The minister himself used to travel in the country incognito to check if the new orders were being carried out properly.

Around the same time, we had a new clerk at the post office and people started saying that something was wrong with her. Often times money would disappear and we were asked to pay more money for postage. I was at the post office one day and I gave her money, telling her that I counted the amount and it was sufficient. As soon as she took my money I heard one coin falling on the floor. She then claimed that there was not sufficient money and that I needed to pay more. I persisted and asked to get into her space to check for the coin that had fallen. She refused and I asked to speak to her manager. This also didn't happen and there was a big argument. All of a sudden, a policeman appeared and wanted to arrest me for making a disturbance. I tried to explain my position to the policeman, when a tall man with a nice fur coat came to my rescue and told the policeman that he thought that I was right or at least I should be able to prove my point. The policeman replied that he was just doing his job and that there was no need for a Jew supporter to get involved. The man opened his coat and identified himself as the interior minister and demanded to get into the clerk's booth to inspect it as I had demanded.

We got in and found a bag hanging from the window with lots of coins inside – all the money she had been able to collect during the day.

The post office manager fainted. And soon afterwards most of the other clerks were fired. The manager himself was sent to a remote area where he became manager of the local train station.

Before he left, the minister thanked me for being persistent and courageous and doing my civic duty.

2) An encounter with a Russian soldier

In the winter of 1915, the Russian Army retreated from Horodenka. The Jews were full of fear and terror of the Cossacks who broke into their houses, beating, shooting, assaulting women and looting all the valuables. Women stayed in the cellars and the men lowered supplies. We had a family from Romania staying with us at the time.

One day two Cossacks came home, saw my father wearing his fur coat and boots and commanded him to give it to them. The men in the house (including me, seven years old) ran out and started screaming. The Cozacks promised to return that evening.

We feared they would return and we were terrified.

The same day all the retreating Russian troops were passing by our town. My father went out and invited a group of Russian soldiers to our home. There were three of their officers in the house and the others stayed in the yard. We had an instant connection with the three in the house and we told them about the incident with the Cossacks. They calmed us, telling us that there was a strict command not to assault citizens and promised to protect us as long as they stayed. The Cossacks eventually returned but the Russians chased them away.

One of the officers was very nice to me and gave me some sugar, hugged and kissed me and played with me. At night he asked to sleep with me, explaining that he had three children of his own back home – one of them my age – and wanted to feel at home. My family tried to discourage him in a gentle way and he gave up trying to sleep with me.

They stayed in our house for a couple of days and really helped us however they could. When they left, they said they were sure we'd meet again when they returned, but the Austrians took over our town after that.

Many years later, in 1932, on my way to Israel, on an Italian ship I recognized the captain to be the same Russian officer who wanted to sleep with the Jewish *boychick*. He also remembered. I spoke to him and it turned out that he spoke good German and Italian. When I asked how he could as a Russian, be working on a fascist ship, he answered, "You don't ask questions like that. You do what you can for the money!"

[Page 265]

Jews and non-Jews in Searfince

Nechah Hoffman-Shein

Translated by Yehudis Fishman

If one would ask me, when I experienced the sensation of exile – a feeling that accompanied me during the entire period of my childhood and youth – I would say that it was practically born in me. This feeling flowed from the atmosphere, where the Jews lived in Ukrainian villages in general and in the village of Serafince specifically. It's possible that in the same period, there were other villages in Eastern Europe whose residents were wholesome and simple and related to Jewish existence in their midst as a natural thing, even though it had different and strange elements. This was not the case however, in the villages of Galicia, and especially in the village whose residents were already given over to the spirit of nationalistic and socialistic stirrings. Their youth strove to acquire knowledge, and so the high school and university students would return to the village and implant a nationalist awareness and consciousness of exploitation and injustice. The most direct example and the one that appeared to the eye as a model of the theory, was the Jew. The village of Serafince, which had the largest percentage of intelligencia of all the Ukrainian villages, acted as the center for this awakening, and impacted the whole area.

The Jew of the village was no longer the type of villager we find in literature, and who was still possible to find in my time in the Russian Carpathian villages of Moldavia or Transylvania. There were still Jewish villagers who were occupied – in addition to Jewish observances – in farming, and they still felt themselves attached to the material and spiritual perspectives of the village. They didn't much question their positions, and they fulfilled the Jewish commandments within proper bounds, and no more. However the Jew in our village was not in essence a Jewish villager, and, to the extent that I can recall, none of them were at peace with themselves. They didn't see the village as their natural locale, not only because of the difficulty in observing the commandments there, and the constant need to battle the outside influences against their uniqueness, but also because of their deep, soulful longing to live another kind of existence, in a Jewish community. This longing accompanied them all the days of their lives, and doubled their sense of exile.

The days of my childhood and adolescence were accompanied by a feeling of jealously, on one hand, and of longings that were unclear to me, on the other. The jealously was toward the non-Jews and their way of life. How good it seemed for them! How clear, and how natural! How everything about their life seemed integrated: their language, their landscape, the seasons of the year, the holidays, their clothing, their work – everything flowed in a natural way like a peaceful river. In all their activities there was nothing to defend or explain. This was true for all of them. They functioned as a unit, and in an atmosphere that was all theirs – in their customs, their various work phases, and how they spent their holidays. I envied them from the moment I could think for myself; I too wanted to be like the rest. I didn't want any of the complexity of our differences, and I wanted to be together with the majority. All the while I kept being told that we were "something different entirely."

I remember how they used to march each spring morning with containers on their shoulders, going off to work in the fields, with their powerful song penetrating the air. How their song poured out across the fields, and the multicolored garments of the women fluttered like flowers over the green expanse and the black earth. How they went to church on Sundays or holidays. How a wedding appeared in the village, and how they danced every Sunday afternoon on the grassy square near our house. How all their involvement with their work was transformed into a festival, and how even going to the river to wash clothes was a sort of leisure time activity. The village didn't seem to know any mourning, but rather every place that they gathered there was happiness, and even their *stipha*, their funeral meal, was like a celebration. At first they were serious and somber but after they ate and drank to their satisfaction, happiness burst forth from their hearts. Even in their personal, internal experience, there was a commonality. Everything seemed revealed to everyone, with everyone's participation and with a similar character for all methodical and peaceful, and with the rootedness of a plant growing organically from nature, from the landscape. How I envied them, with their complete feeling of belonging. How the soul of a Jewish child yearned for such an experience – to be with everyone and like everyone.

At home they tried to implant within us elevated feelings. They emphasized morning and evening that we were different – better, more elevated than the *goyim*. What was theirs was non-kosher, disgusting, and despised. Let us assume that this was true. However, what did we see in our environment? With all our elevated status, everything seemed to me depressing and ordinary. Holidays should have been a sign of importance, understandably to a young girl. Yet this image was not satisfying, because it was not accompanied by the smells that the street and the neighborhoods added. What could the Chanukah candles tell me when they were buried within the house, during the time that the street was filled with song and jubilation on the non-Jewish holiday? What did the matzos at the seder say to me, in contrast to the festivities of the Easter parade, when colored flags flew in the air and songs of choirs and musicians were heard? How seductive was that for a young girl! And in the house meanwhile they would tell me, "Don't play with the *shiksas*, the non-Jewish girls, with their colored eggs, and don't taste their giant Easter bread, and don't go into their homes which are absolutely non-kosher."

Therefore I yearned from the dawn of my childhood for a different world, in which I too could be "like everyone else." The village was very close to Horodenka, and had an ongoing relationship with the city. We had many relatives there. Every new wind also reached us. In the village there was more time to be absorbed in books; there was a great desire to study – perhaps in order to not deteriorate like the townspeople and not to become 'boorish villagers.' There was a strong desire on the part of parents to send their children to the city to study. How much effort was needed for that! They would send us to school every morning in a wagon or snow sled, and more than once we would have to go home on foot. In truth, the distance was only five kilometers, but for a child this demanded no small effort. In addition to this, there was also much fear about meeting troublemakers as we passed through uninhabited areas.

I visited one school in the city after the First World War, at the period when new winds were already blowing there. All kinds of 'isms' competed among them, and the village boy paid attention to the only one that entranced him the most – Zionism. When I was about ten years old, I remember going to a celebration of Zionist youth, and for the first time in my life, I heard a Hebrew song sung in a group. The song opened with the words, "With my plow I inherited all my wealth," and a handsome youth, Eber Sheetz, explained its meaning. The song told about a Jewish farmer who plowed his land in a Jewish village, in a land that was all ours. At that minute, I thought: There everything was like in Serafince, but everything belonged only to Jews. There is where I want to be. This was my entire dream – a village in which everyone was Jewish!

Even in the city, I was not happy. That's not how I wanted to see communities of Jews – rushing around and running after a miserable livelihood, running and still remaining confined in their small space. I wanted broad spaces, like in our village, with people like my father, who would take me on his horse and lead me in the open space on the *Toleki,* along the length of the river. I wanted separate houses, like our house in the village, with its large garden, in which was always found vegetables or fruit to be proud of and to enjoy. It was possible to pull out skinny carrots by their roots, to clean them off on the hems of my apron, and to eat them there on the spot. It was possible to pluck unripe apples and to chew them until the teeth were on edge, in spite of father's strict prohibition from doing so. I wanted a cellar like there was in our house that contained everything good, where from the winter fruit protected by layers and layers of straw, one could select the softest and juiciest pear. I wanted also to search in the barrel of pickled cabbage and to find the sour pickles that I loved. I wanted to help my mother to churn the butter, and especially to drink the tasty buttermilk, in which many pieces of butter floated. I wanted to satiate my eyes on the golden chicks as they first burst out of their shells, to feel in my hands the delicate heartbeat of these creatures, and to protect myself from the brooding hen that tried to peck me. I loved the tumult around the threshing machine, and the *kalakah,* the gathering of the volunteers for husking corn – young men and women – who did their work with song and laughter and a jovial atmosphere that remained in the courtyard till late at night. In the house they cooked *voroniks,* cheese dumplings, in huge pots, to honor the corps of volunteers. The meal was arranged on temporary tables outside, at a late evening hour. At those times of spontaneous happiness, the loneliness of the village Jew was forgotten, or at least mitigated to a certain extent.

My father was one of a kind among the Jews of the village. As a farming expert with a great deal of experience, he made a positive impression on the non-Jews with his expertise, his upright stature, his majestic position astride an even-tempered horse, and his military service – he was one of the cavalrymen of Emperor Franz Yosef I. No, I did not like the nearby town. I wanted a village, but one that would be entirely mine, ours, without the non-Jews.

Why did these non-Jews hate us? Was it only because we were different? Was it because, "You killed our Jesus?" You see, our *shikse* Paraska who worked for us for thirteen years, and to whom my mother was like her mother, said to us, "You see, the Jews killed him." "Why?" I asked Paraska. And she replied: "That's the way the Jews are." I asked my mother if this was true that we killed Jesus. And she said, "I'll give her a good what for, to that Paraska!" However, she added, "When we go by the statue of Jesus, we need to spit three times and say, ' It is an abhorrence,' but make sure that the goyim don't see you...."

From that time, I was accompanied by a fear of the one suspended on the cross, and would go on a longer, roundabout path, in order not to see his face – and also in order not to spit. After that, I certainly began to become acquainted with anti-Semitism, when I heard the speech of my young non-Jewish friend, my twelve-year-old neighbor, Ivan Koztchenko. He explained to me the injustice of the matter, that Jews, even though they don't work, eat white bread, while the non-Jews work and still only have course bread. I tried to correct this injustice, and because my friend was always hungry, I would take bread and challah out of the house, and give it to him. I liked to watch and see with how much appetite and haste he consumed whatever I gave him. In this debate, I would say to him that his arguments don't apply to my father – who worked on the land and not in business. So he would answer me, "You are the exceptional ones, but all the rest are merchants and liars." I wanted to correct his perceptions about us, and I would bring him honey cakes and apple cakes, but nothing helped. He kept his opinion that Jews were evil.

When we grew up, we would return from the city from our studies, and would again meet. Then my opponent was using more sophisticated language to convey his thoughts, and he even made some new points: the Poles were oppressing them. "Every nation needs to be free on its land!" He said, referring to his own people, the Ukrainians. And I said, "Correct, Yantzu, and I too think like this," but I had in mind that we Jews would be a free nation in our own land. So he agreed to my Zionist idea with real enthusiasm.

The longing to leave the village was the desire of every Jewish youth. There was only one way – to learn! In Galicia that meant getting a higher education. To learn work or a trade was considered despicable. This approach of the Jews in exile struck deep roots even among the Jews of the village. It was better to "walk with a cane" and to be involved in a petty and despised business, called *bintelech* (shoestrings) than to learn carpentry or locksmithing. Oh G-d, How did we arrive in our years of exile to these concepts?

The generation that preceded me, the generation before the First World War, found an answer to the crisis of the village Jew: emigration. Many of the youth left for America at that time, as long as the gates of immigration were open. When I recently visited America, I met a large group of people who had fled from our village. From them I found out what things were like in the village before their immigration. There was a great depression, both financially and spiritually. They were totally uprooted and emigration was the only anchor of salvation for them. However, even in America they paid a dear price until they became integrated in the new land. The lack of any trade spoiled things for them.

After World War One, Aliya to the land of Israel replaced immigration to America. The village youth were among the first who longed for training and Aliya. However, they did not always succeed. Their parents did not always agree, but little by little they understood and made peace with it. One of the motivating factors of their acquiescence was their desire to keep their sons and daughters away from the Goyim, and to see them as Jews among Jews. They used to say, "We were the last generation to resist the influence of the goyim, but you will no longer succeed in doing so." They saw their religion continually weakening, and they knew that in Israel they would at least remain Jews. Therefore they no longer resisted when they saw their children falling away from them little by little. I saw my parents in this situation. I saw my mother – how her heart always seemed broken each time one of the children went to Israel. She knew she would never see them again, but she dared not oppose them. All she did was hang on the wall another picture of the missing child, and say in a smile flowing with sadness, like the well known song: "I have paper children on the wall."

These parents, mine as well as others, did not live to join their children in Israel. The cruel wave passed over them. They did not live to see with their own eyes how the dream of their children materialized. They did not live to see their grandchildren freed from those concerns that oppressed us in our childhood. They didn't live to see their grandchildren sprouting from the scenery of their own land, just like the goyim in whose midst we lived, able to blend the spiritual and natural setting into one whole. And they never were able to see how their children held their heads up high – how the miracle happened!

Some people who were saved from the ghetto of Kosov told me how the last Jews of Serafince were transported from there. It was a difficult winter, with horrible famine. The plague of Typhus raged in the ghetto. My father, who was then seventy-four, was very ill and, it seems, not so complete in his mind. He somehow escaped from the ghetto and walked till he got to the Romanian border. There they grabbed him and brought him back while he was continually mumbled, "I want to go to my children in the land of Israel...to my children...in the land of Israel..."

Can it be that in the face of these holy sacrifices we can know how to appreciate the fortune that the rise of the state of Israel bestowed upon us?

Farewell to the late Josel Bergman before his Departure to Israel

[Page 267]

The Village of Serafince

Nachman Bergman

Translated by Yehudis Fishman

Images and Types of Horodenka Personalities

Near Horodenka, at a distance of about an hour's walk, nestled the village of Serafince. There I spent a substantial part of my childhood with my aunt and uncle, Fishel and Roise Rosenroykh, of blessed memories. This was a typical Ukrainian village. One of its residents was a representative in the Landstag in Lvov during the period of the Austrian rule. In a later period, most of the Ukrainian intelligencia moved from this village to the center of Horodenka. The dress of these villagers was different from those of the other neighboring villagers. In the seventeenth century the Turks conquered the village, and a remnant of those times remained in the garments of the villagers. Most pronounced was especially the Turkish turban that women would

wear under their headscarves. The daughters of this village stood out
in their beauty. When a group of women villagers were sent to a dance
festival in Vienna, most came from this village. The residents of
Serafince were very well off. Their land was fertile and very productive.
The relationship of these villagers to Jews was very good, and they
were also friendly to those in other villages. Anti-Semitism was not
openly felt, but it happened more than once that the village
troublemakers threw rocks at the Jews who crossed their paths.

As in the most of the neighboring villages, here too there was a
Jewish landowner, Yossel Zeidman. He had many fields and he hired
some disabled villagers to work them. Because of this, he was to a
certain extent a ruler in the village. His fields were operated according
to modern methods, in contrast to the primitive methods that were
widespread in the villages. There, farmers often used the same
equipment that had been used forty earlier. The estate was like a
miniature palace and was surrounded by a large courtyard that
contained buildings for the machinery, as well as a big yard with fruit
trees. The relationship of the farmers to the landowner was one of
honor and respect, and even love. Only through the younger
generation and the Ukrainian intelligencia did a feeling of jealousy
develop, and thus a lack of respect.

The landowner, Yossel Zeidman, was a handsome man and had a
demeanor that aroused respect. He had two sons. One of them, Alter,
who studied in Vienna was a scholarly person and if I recall, also had
an academic demeanor. He was greatly beloved by his father. When he
came home each year for his summer vacation, Yossel would walk
through the fields without getting involved in the management of the
farm. The other son, Moshe, was the manager of the farm. He was a
popular person who was plain in his ways and got along well with
people.

All the managerial positions in Zeidman's estate were in the hands
of Jews, and from them I will mention just three: Gershon Veitzling,
Leibish Hoffman, and Hirsh Giniger, of blessed memories. There were
others whose names I don't recall. They served him faithfully and
earned his complete trust. The villagers also related to him in an
honorable way. Besides the Jews who were managing the estate, many
other Jews were supported by buying and selling its produce and
serving in other ways as middlemen.

My uncle Fishel Rosenroykh enjoyed a special relationship with
Yossel Zeidman. They studied together in *cheder* and remained friends
all the days of their lives. When I came to visit my uncle when I was
still a young boy, I would also spend time on the estate and would
often arrive there riding on the big dog Hector, the landowner's dog.

The Jews of the village lived among the Ukrainians, far apart from each other. They supported themselves by selling produce, including eggs and other products of the farm. Some of them made a living from small supply stores. On holidays and Sabbaths, they would gather for a *minyan* in the estate home. Aaron Leib Lagshteyn, a modern Jew and a scholar, would serve as the cantor. His prayers were burned into my memory because of his pleasant voice and his beautiful pronunciation of the words. From among the Jews of the village, I remember the families: Giniger, Yurman, Hoffman, Bergman, Rosenreich, Vitzling, and Shechter. They were all killed at the hands of the enemy. Before the Holocaust, only a few of the young villagers went to Israel or fled to America and thereby survived.

[Pages 268 & 240]

Laughter and Tears

Kuka Iskar-Greif

Translated by Dalya Yohai

It doesn't hurt

My father and Berl Shpierer, a wealthy man from Horodenka, were in Vienna listening to a lecture by the socialist Adler. After the lecture, my father asked Berl, "Tell me, how do you feel after a socialist lecture?"

"I'll confess, Hershel, maybe it is a little shameful to be so rich nowadays. But believe me, it doesn't hurt, even now!!"

Luck follows him

During World War One, Berl Shpierer and other wealthy people were exiled to Siberia. Our dance teacher started talking to us about going to Siberia. When we asked him why, he said, "Shpierer has had luck following him all his life. We have to go to Siberia like him because maybe then luck will follow us as well!

Better Vienna at home

Avraham Cohen, the blacksmith, lived in Horodenka where he was born, but his family remained in Vienna after World War One. He came back because he could make a good living. When his children begged him to come and be with them in Vienna and wondered how he could prefer Horodenka to beautiful Vienna, he responded, "It's better to live in Horodenka and long for Vienna than to live in Vienna and longing for home in Horodenka."

Isn't a man allowed to talk at home?

The grain merchants used to give their money to the rich people to invest during the quiet season. One of the rich men gave them trouble and they had a hard time getting the money back. When they complained he used to say, "It's not my fault, it's all because of Yoske, my son."

Once when one of the merchants came to ask for his money, Yoske said to his father, in the presence of the merchant, "Promise him, but don't keep your promise." The merchant lost his temper and started yelling, "Who do you think I am, that you can treat me like that. Every day you promise to pay me tomorrow and you never keep your promise." The rich man replied, "What's the problem? Why do you yell? Can't I talk in my house and say whatever I want?"

He is not going to be involved

About the same person there was another story: When Yoske was five the rich man used to sign his name on bills that came from Lvov. When he didn't pay his debts for a while his creditor came to Horodenka personally. When he came to his house he asked for Yoske. The father called for his son and yelled at him, "Come here, you brat. This man says he has bills and checks signed by you! I want you to know that I'm not gong to intervene and help you out with even one dime!"

The healthy simpleton

A pale and poor scholar came once to our town and told people in the synagogue that he was sick, but a scholar. One of the citizens, a scholar himself and full of compassion, invited him to his home and told him, "You'll sit in my house until you get better and we will be able to study in the meantime." When they sat to study and he saw the extent of the stranger's knowledge, he exclaimed, "You are not a sick scholar, but a healthy simpleton!!"

A *Despite'nik* in heaven

A resident of our town (I can't remember his name), a wise and devout man, prayed every morning. One day a secular Jew asked him, "Wise man, you're known to a be smart man, do you really believe that the supreme judge us in Heaven?" Answered the devout Jew, "I'll admit, I don't know if there is God up there, but I know there is a *despit'nik* there that I have to worry about and my prayer, if it doesn't help, can't harm me!"

Doesn't look like a Jew

In 1920 the Ukrainians entered Horodenka, and as usual, started harassing the Jewish population and took their clothes and shoes. When they attacked Lipa, the shoemaker, he stood up straight, combed his hair, trimmed his mustache and asked them in juicy Ukrainian, "And do I look like a Jew to you?" They apologized and left him alone!

He gave his "assets" to everybody

When Lipa the shoemaker died it was a day of laughter and sadness. This is how he wanted it. It was really a day of mourning because he died quite young and left a widow and children. He was also a very personable man, liked by all. But we all laughed when we heard about his will. He wrote it the last minute before his death, in front of witnesses. He had a sense of humor until the end. The will read: "My two sets of underwear, I give to Tomkoviz, the Mayor; the ripped socks to the president of the community, and the good pair to my children...." It went on and on in this manner.

It's not the same Antshel

Antschel Riechman, the head of a big and vast family, was not a rich man. Before World War One, when he tried to get into the Rabbi's yard, the *gabay* would raise his hand and signal to him: There is no place for somebody like you here. After the war he became rich. When he came to the Rabbi's yard and saw the *gabay* standing at the door he yelled to him: "*Gabay, gabay*, it's not the same Antschel."

A specialist for addresses

My grandpa Zeide Breithchess was one of the first to let his son (my father) go to the Baron Hirsch School. When the Chassidim asked him why, he said laughingly, "I decided that my son will say my *kaddish* with an Ashkenazi accent." When my father got to the second or third grade the Chassidim were not upset with him anymore because he was well known and even respected. They said, "When this kid writes an address, the letter gets even to America."

This is honesty

Meir Shlam was known for his wisdom, his Torah knowledge and even his high mathematical ability. But he couldn't provide for his family.

At the end he became an accountant for a wealthy man, but that didn't make use of his vast knowledge. Some people asked him, "Where is the justice here, you know so much and are so devout, yet you hardly make a living and your employer, the rich man, is a simple man and benefiting from your knowledge." Shlam replied, "That's right and that's as it should be. Can you imagine how difficult it would be for him if he was in my place, with his knowledge?!"

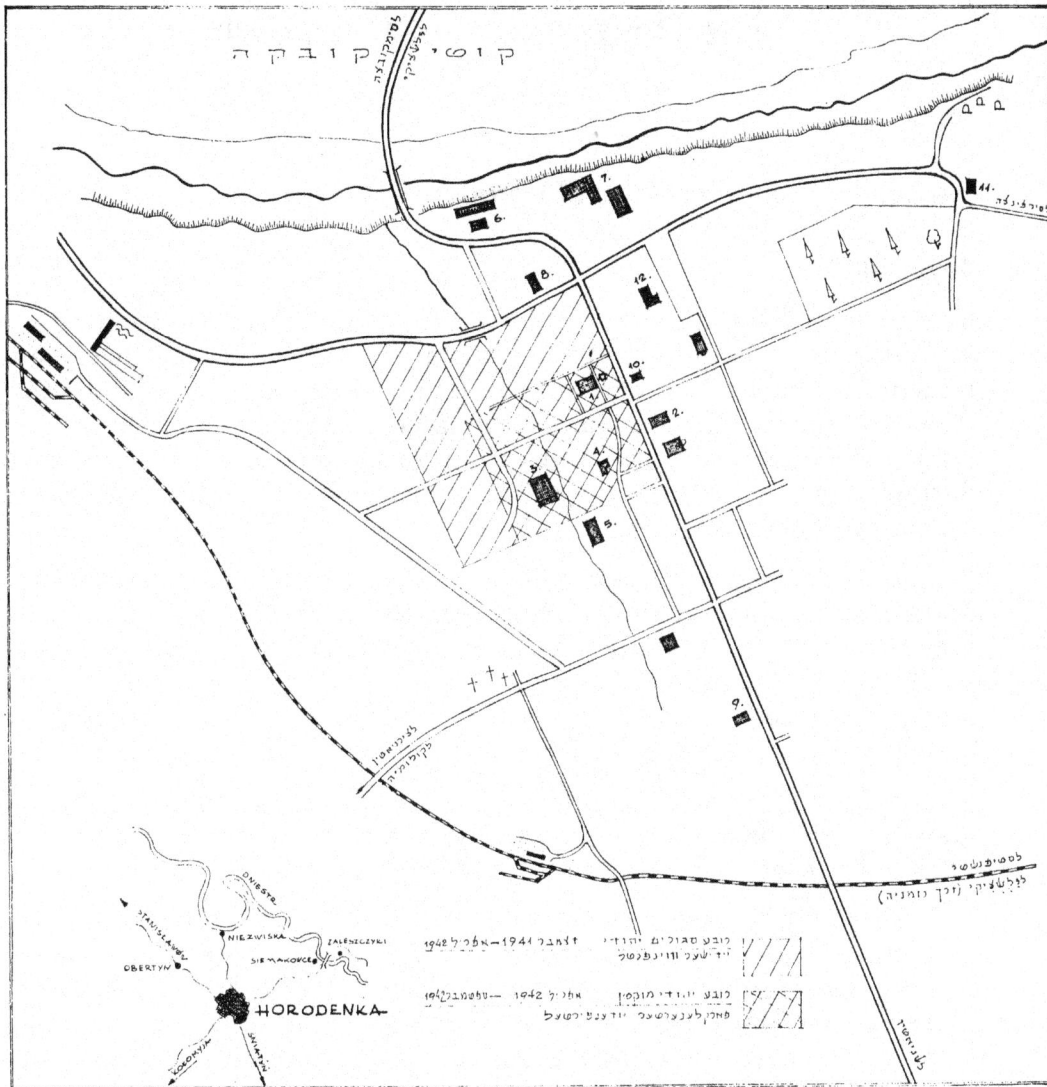

Design of Horodenka 1939—1944

English	Yiddish	Hebrew
1. The Grand Synagogue.	1. די גרויסע שיהל.	1. בית הכנסת הגדול
2 Hebrew School.	2. העברעישע שול.	2. בית ספר עברי — בית עם.
3 The Yiddish School.	3. יידישע שול.	3. בית ספר אידי — בית עם.
4. Jewish Coop. Loan Soc.	4. יידישע קאָאפּעראַטיווע קאַסע.	4. קופת מלוה יהודית.
5 Sokol Building	5. פאָלקס־הויז.	5. בית עם פולני — קולונע.
6. Polish Gymnasium.	6. פּוילישע מיטעלשול.	6. בי״ס תיכון פולני.
7. District Offices.	7. קרייז־פאַרוואַלטונג.	7 מרכז השלטון הנפתי.
8. Municipal Offices.	8. אָרטס־פאַרוואַלטונג.	8. מרכז השלטון המקומי.
9. Ukrainian Gymnasium.	9. אוקראיִנישע מיטעלשול.	9. בי״ס תיכון אוקראיני.
10. Narodny Dom.	10. אוקראיִנישער פאָלקסהויז.	10. בית עם אוקראיני.
11. Talmud Torah.	11. תלמוד־תורה.	11. תלמוד תורה
12. District Saving-Fund Offices.	12. קרייז שפּאָרקאַסע.	12. קופת חסכון נפתית.

Designed by Yehuda Eisman.   ●   געצייכענט פון זכרון דורך יהודה אייזמן   ●   הוכן לפי הזכרון על־ידי יהודה אייזמן

The Destruction of the Town

[Page 273]

The destruction of the Jews of Horodenka

Meyer Sukher

Prior to World War II, Horodenka was part of Russia. As soon as the war between Germany and Russia broke out, the Germans immediately began bombarding the cities under Russian occupation. After two weeks the Russians evacuated the area. As the Russian Army moved out and the Hungarian Army moved in a three-hour skirmish took place in the streets. Three Jews tragically were killed during this encounter.

The Hungarian Army was now in control of Horodenka and for the moment all appeared quiet. However, one Sabbath morning, three weeks later, the first ominous signs appeared. Trains carrying large numbers of Hungarian Jews, all densely packed together, passed through the city on their way to the Concentration Camp in Transnistria.

The Jews of Horodenka hurriedly organized a makeshift kitchen to sustain them and also to provide for the small number who had managed to escape the clutches of this round-up.

On Tisha B'Av, a few weeks later, the first German division entered Horodenka and immediately showed their colors. They invaded the synagogues and threw the Torahs and holy books out into the streets to be trampled to bits. Then they caught several Jews and tortured them. At the same time their Ukrainian collaborators, notorious anti-semites who were the Nazis' civil administrators, began robbing the Jews of their possessions. As the Hungarians were still nominally in charge, the Ukrainians bided their time until the German Army took over completely. Shortly thereafter, the Hungarian army left, leaving the Germans in control. The evil oppression against the Jews which preceded the "final solution" was now felt.

First, the Nazis uprooted the Jews of Horodenka from their homes and crowded them together in the worst part of the city – 1/3 of the area that had previously accommodated them. The Nazis then appointed a "Yudenrat," a Jewish Council, which was supposed to represent the Jews. In addition to the other things which made life very difficult for the Jews, they forced the Yudenrat to furnish luxurious apartments for their officials, stripping the Jewish homes for this purpose. When these officials left town, they robbed the homes of their possessions and sent the "booty" to their residences in Germany. The Yudenrat then had to refurnish the houses anew.

The Jewish communities in the area were deliberately and completely isolated from one another by the Germans so that they had no way of knowing the scope of the German destruction. Therefore the Horodenka Jews still hoped that somehow they might survive the war, not knowing that the plan to totally destroy them was already in progress.

Victims on their last journey

For six months, the Jewish community of Horodenka struggled to live under these conditions. On December 5, 1941 the Germans initiated their "First Action" which led to the eventual total annihilation of the Jews of Horodenka.

The Nazis organized a special Murder Squad for this purpose. These squads operated from city to city in the occupied countries. In Horodenka the Jewish people were ordered to assemble, under the pretext that they were to be inoculated against typhus. The Nazis marched the Jews out to Semakovtse, a nearby town, and in the adjacent forest lined up and slaughtered half the Horodenka Jewish population – 2500 souls.

Dr. Shneyder, a well-known local physician, was among those who believed the Germans were sincere about administering the injections and convinced the Jews of this. The Nazis wanted to free him but he refused, preferring to die with his people.

By mere coincidence, a small group of about 1150 Jews were saved from death in the First Action. I, the author of this article, was among them. At the last minute the Nazis received an order from the military to exempt the Jewish craftsmen, bakers and carpenters. Out of sheer desperation I claimed to be a baker and got Aron Glaser, a well-known Horodenka baker, to vouch for me. They locked us up in the foyer of the Shul and the following afternoon freed us to work for them. That is how I managed to survive at that time.

A number of wealthy Jews bribed their Ukrainian neighbors huge sums of money to hide them and their families. They were delivered into the hands of the German when the Germans threatened to kill anyone found harboring Jews. Of course the Ukrainians kept the bribes.

All the members of the Yudenrat were slaughtered in the forests. A tiny minority managed to escape and save themselves – for the time being at least. However this was the beginning of the end.

To flush out the remaining Jews, the Nazis now proclaimed that they would no longer bother the Jews. Somehow they convinced the approximately 1500 Jews who had hidden themselves to come out into the open. They were now confined to a tiny Ghetto area – three to four blocks long – and a new Yudenrat was appointed. All the entrances and exits to the Ghetto were sealed off. Only the bare necessities were provided – and even those were cut. Those who worked for the Germans outside the Ghetto were closely regulated – their arrival and departure times strictly watched by the Jewish guards who were severely punished for the least infraction of the rules.

Four months passed. On April 13, 1942, the Second Action took place. The Germans rounded up 450 Jews whom they intended to murder. However they implied that one could remain alive for an enormous bribe. Somehow the Jews scraped together whatever they still retained and turned it over to the Germans. In this way 375 Jews were able to ransom themselves as "productive elements" for a little while longer.

Unfortunately, in the Second Action 75 elderly Jewish men and women were taken to the Town Square and the Nazis executed them without pity.

Five months later, on September 2, 1942, the Nazis forcibly assembled the remaining Jews and all others they could locate and transported them to the Concentration Camp in Majdanek to an almost certain death. Nevertheless, 400-500 Jews still managed to conceal themselves from these German sweeps. The Germans were evidently aware of this and now instituted their Third Action six months later in order to be able to declare Horodenka and the suburbs completely "Yudenrien," free of Jews. A few remaining Jews fled to the outlying towns and villages, but the Nazis, with the help of the Ukrainians, made a successful sweep of the area, capturing and killing them

Those few that did manage to escape joined and fought with the Partisans. One such person was Asher Shtreyt, son of Shlomo Shtreyt, who was later killed in the fighting between the Germans and the Partisans.

Through sheer miracles a small number of Horodenka Jews managed to live through the war. Most of them now reside in Israel and America – five live in Europe and are hoping to emigrate.

As far as I know, there are no longer any Jews in Horodenka.

[Page 275 and 365]

My Walk Through Seven Levels of Hell

Reuben Prifer

Translated by Harvey Buchalter

(1)

Until the war broke out between Germany and Russia, the Jews of Horodenka, like all the Jews in the area, got used to the conditions that had become common in the town. Many were reconciled to the idea of living under Communism; others wanted to wait the war out and then see if they could resume their normal lives. People heard a lot of rumors about the German occupation of the western part of Poland, about the life of the Jews there, and about the persecutions, but nobody really thought it would reach the Jews of Horodenka. We believed this first because of the Ribbentrop-Molotov agreement, and second, because many believed that Germany wouldn't start a war with the Russian "bear." We in Horodenka thought that the Russians had a lot of power in this area and that this would frighten the Germans.

On the first day after the war broke out, we were all bitterly disappointed as we watched the Russian power fell apart. Tanks, cannons, airplanes, and soldiers could not hold their position. By the first day of the war, the Russian retreat had already started.

I remember that on the morning the war broke out a few friends
and I decided to hike around the few villages in the area. We left the
house around 6 o'clock going toward the village of Yasenov. This
village had just finished building a very modern airport. When we
reached the place, a few airplanes flew above us and started bombing
the airport. They also started shooting on the village with machine
guns. We were shocked and hid in the caverns alongside the road. By
the time they were done, the whole new airport was destroyed.

(2)

Panic and all kinds of rumors, including those of wide-scale treason
and destruction of the whole Russian military power, accompanied the
Russian retreat. In the last days of their regime the Russians had
started behaving as some of us expected. We heard about cases of
robbery and murder, officers shooting soldiers, telling them to stop
retreating. Our village lived in great fear. And that also made it very
difficult for us to decide if we should join the retreating Russians. Most
of those who decided to do so remained alive. But the majority decided
to stay in town and await what was coming next. We didn't have to
wait long. As soon as the last little groups of Russians retreated, the
Germans started invading the towns. Soon we found out that it wasn't
actually the Germans who were invading the town, but the
Hungarians who had been put in charge of conquering western
Ukraine. There was a short battle inside the town between the
retreating army and the Hungarian army. A lot of people were killed on
both sides. After a few hours, though, it became quiet. The Russian
army totally retreated and the Hungarian army controlled all the
entrances to the town and began to impose its own law and order.

(3)

The first days weren't so bad and the Jews of the town thought that
they could live with this occupation. But soon after a few Jewish
houses were robbed and Jews were mugged and kidnapped to do all
kinds of forced labor, they realized that this would not be a peaceful
occupation. The hope was that the worst that could happen would be
that the Jews would be taken away for work.

Right after the Hungarians entered Horodenka, a few Ukrainian
elements in the police force started organizing. They were nationalistic
and anti-Semitic. They added their own rules against the Jews to
those of the existing regime. The Jews also started organizing and the
first Jewish Judenrat started contacting the Hungarians. In that way
they tried to counter the Ukrainian powers and their wish to take over
control of the town and the Jews.

(4)

Hungary was allied with Germany, and because of the location of Horodenka, our area was placed under Hungarian occupation. The Hungarians decided to transfer some of the Hungarian Jews from their area to Horodenka, claiming that they were of Polish origin. They thought that it would be easier to take care of them in Horodenka. And so it happened that a lot of Jewish refugees started coming through Horodenka, young and old, women and babies, barefoot and tired and hungry. And they would just be marched to a destination unknown both to them and to the people who made them march. The Hungarians allowed them to stay a little while in the town and rest, but they were forbidden to remain in any specific place. And so it happened that these people started roaming among the Jewish houses asking for food and shelter. The situation of the Horodenka Jews themselves wasn't that great at the time because at that time there were also a few hundred refugees from Romania. They had not been allowed to join up with the Russians and couldn't return to Romania either. The situation of these refugees was terrible and they wandered around for a few weeks among the houses asking for food. At that time there was no organization to take care of them.

Tuvia Korn, the oldest son of the Hebrew teacher Korn, proposed that a group of the Zionist youth movement establish a soup kitchen to feed the refugees. When they brought this up before the Judenrat, they were very supportive, promising to help with the food, while the Zionist youth organized the work. This was a time when the Judenrat was still in communication with the Jews from the surrounding villages. They could not collect money, but they could bring in supplies for the kitchen. Kvetsher's house, next to the Polish gymnasium, was dedicated to this purpose. The people from the youth movement started collecting tools, utensils and furniture to turn it into a soup kitchen. There were a lot of problems but the enthusiasm of the people overcame the difficulties.

When the number of Hungarian refugees increased and we needed to feed more people, the Zionist youth approached the Judenrat and demanded a bigger house to expand their work. The Judenrat approached the German authorities who had replaced the Hungarians, thus putting Horodenka under the auspices of the district of Krackow. According to the new rules, the Zionist youth got a new two-story home, the house of Michael Kamil. It was very big and comfortable and could accommodate feeding up to 400 people three meals every day.

Among the Judenrat members who were in daily contact with the people who organized the soup kitchen was Mr. Israel Kugler. He was the first and strongest supporter of the project. He could always find more food when everybody else was short. He collected donations from the rich people of Horodenka and the villages. This demanded a great physical effort because people who went to the villages had to return before nighttime. And although they had passes from the Germans, it was still a very dangerous operation. But he persisted because he liked the Zionist movement and the Zionist youth. As a Judenrat member, he was very supportive of the idea of educating the orphans in the Hebrew language; thus the orphanage and the soup kitchen were managed in Hebrew.

When Mr. Kugler realized that the Germans were planning the destruction of part of the town (although nobody could conceive that they were really planning the destruction and murder of all of the Jews), he got members of the Zionist youth together and gave them his signed will, authorizing them to inherit and sell all his property and to transfer the money to the land of Israel. A few members of the Zionist youth were named as his heirs. After the will was written and signed, a few copies were made and buried inside bottles in safe places where they could be found after the war was over.

Among the people who helped with the orphanage and the soup kitchen, eventually giving their lives while doing so, were: Tuvia Korn, Josef Kokh, Munio Schecter, Josef Reys, Shlomo Korn, Berl Hoffman, Zvi Reys, Reuven Frifer, Lusia Vacher, Nina Auerbach, Clara Hartenshteyn, Savka Shoyderer, Mania Kugler, Sarah Frankel and Malka Friedman. The work was very difficult and although these people were young, they still had to work in shifts. Nevertheless they continued to work.

(5)

One day, the authorities decided to remove the Jewish children from the general orphanage that had been established during the Soviet regime. In accordance with their racial laws, they threw out the 13 Jewish orphans, ranging in age from two to five years. The Judenrat asked the Zionist youth group to provide for the care of these children in our homes. We did not know how to begin, since we had no experience in taking care of children, but we knew we had to make the necessary arrangements.

Dr. Charasch, the son-in-law of Simcha Schnitzer, took in the children for a short time until we succeeded in collecting beds, linens and even toys. We then moved the children to the second floor of Mr. Kamil's house where the soup kitchen for refugees was operating. In addition to our regular duties in the soup kitchen, we thus undertook the additional work of caring for these children. A few refugee women also helped us. In a few days we overcame all the difficulties connected with the care of the children, as well as running the kitchen. It all simply became a daily routine. It is fitting to note that the operation of the kitchen, as well as the education of the children, was all conducted in Hebrew. All members of our working group were well versed in the Hebrew language. We all had completed the Hebrew school of the Talmud Torah.

Needless to say this work was voluntary and the only reward was seeing the children grow and develop. Unfortunately, this lasted only a very short time. In the first action on December 4, 1941, the Gestapo captured 2,500 Jews in our city, among them the thirteen orphans, together with those of our staff who were on duty at that time. They all met their death in the village of Michalcze-Siemakowcza and lie there in the mass grave of our people.

(6)

The first action almost destroyed all of the Jews of Horodenka. There were very few homes and families that had no one who were taken away that time. Mostly, whole families were taken away to be killed. People that did remain alive were children without their parents or parents without their children. It is very difficult to describe the mourning and crying in the streets. When people met each other they started crying on each other's shoulders. And only after a few days could they put the pieces together to see who had been spared and who was taken to die.

After this first action, the town was quiet for a while. People were stunned and could not plan anything. Most of them thought they couldn't survive and that they would lose their minds or commit suicide. But their determination to live took hold and soon enough people started organizing again, putting together new labor groups and sending workers to replace those who had been murdered. Soon after that there was a new decree. A ghetto had to be organized. And the Judenrat was contacted to decide which streets and which houses should be included. A few streets were allocated for the ghetto. They allocated for houses the new part of town, from the Jewish school to the area where the old huts had been torn down. The borders included Schtelshetska Street to the house of Fleshner to the other side of the bridge leading to Kotokivka to the Polish church and the gymnasium.

(7)

In the first days after the ghetto was created people somehow managed and found enough housing. But before long the Germans started pushing Jews into Horodenka from the villages in the area. A lot of the people who were already settled in the available homes refused to let others come in. There were a lot of arguments, but the Germans left no doubt that the people had to accommodate everyone. The Judenrat and the Jewish police took care of law and order and managed to settle arguments between people. Life became very difficult because people were crammed into small apartments.

(8)

During April 1942 there was a new action organized — a smaller but crueler one than the first. The ghetto was left with less people and less whole families. By then people understood what was happening. Even those who had previously believed that the Germans didn't intend to destroy all the Jews lost their illusions. People were desperate and tried to cling to every idea that would help them survive. The Germans knew how to exploit this mood and started organizing groups of people according to their importance.

At the beginning they gave them very convincing names like the "group of doctors," the "group of bakers," the "group of general professionals." They made the Jews think that groups of important people would be spared. This made a lot of people try to bribe their way into one of the better groups. A lot of scheming and cheating occurred in this process. But as people soon found out, nobody was spared; not even the people from the "good" groups.

(9)

In September 1942, in a third action the Germans took away most of the people from those elite groups.

(10)

In the period between the first and third action, those elite groups started organizing. My father, Israel Priffer, managed, through his good connections with the Ukrainians, to become part of a group under their auspices. Each member of this group had permission to walk around the villages within an assigned area and buy skins of domestic and wild animals for the Germans. My father was assigned an area that had five villages. He made contacts with the Jews that lived there. In the course of his work he started to establish places where people could hide if things got worse. After a short time my father got permission to take his family out of the ghetto and to transfer us to a nearby village. That is how, a few days prior to the second action, our family moved to a village with another family. Surrounded by people who hated us, we tried to survive the war.

(11)

At this time the Germans started building a new bridge across the Dniester River, between two villages that were very close. They organized a work force of Jews. However, after the bitter experience the Jews of Horodenka had had working on the Dniester before, most of them were afraid of doing this work. Even worse, the work was not very far from the mass grave of the people who had been murdered in the first action.

It happened that included among the first group were four members of our family and a few other young Jews from the villages nearby, who wanted to live outside the ghetto. We worked in an open camp. We got enough food and the work itself was decent. The Germans who ran the camp were neither Gestapo nor officers, but rather professionals, engineers and technicians. They were only interested in building the bridge. The relationship between some of the workers and the Germans was very easy and comfortable. For instance, one day a supervisor got a message that important people, accompanied by the Gestapo, were coming to see how the work was proceeding. They decided it would not be good for them see Jews working and decided to send us on a boat down the river on that day. One of our supervisors joined us, we thought, to keep an eye on us. But when asked, he said. "I'm going with you because I can't stand these swine." However when as part of the third action by the Germans, an order came to assemble us at 7 a.m. for the Gestapo to pick us up, all this friendship was gone. And even though some of them had tears in their eyes, they still helped the Gestapo put us on heavily guarded carts to prevent our escape and drive us back to Horodenka.

(12)

The third and last action almost destroyed the whole ghetto and lasted three days. Finding Jews and concentrating them in one place wasn't as easy as before. A lot of Jews built bunkers in their houses and although very primitive, this made the Germans work harder. Despite all this, most of the Jews were gathered in a big barn near the train station. There were Jews there who were arrested on the first day and others were arrested only on the third day. Nobody had anything to eat or to drink. After a few hours on the third day, they took everybody out, men and women separately. When the men arrived at the train station, the women were already in the train compartments. I thought that there were at least a thousand men there. We were all made to stand in lines in front of the train while the Germans walked between the lines hitting, torturing, swearing and spitting at us. They gathered 80 young men an hour, including my brother Beryl, and took them aside. We watched and saw how they put everybody in cars that were made for animals, with one small window, covered with barbed wire. Two hundred people were in each compartment. We heard the cries and the screams in the ones that held the women. It is very difficult to describe even today how horrible it was.

After everybody was in, one German told us, "You're lucky. You're not going with everybody else. You are going to work." And although there we were only 80 of us, we could hardly breathe and some died on the way to the labor camp. A lot of people broke the small window while the train was going and jumped out. Bullets from the Germans killed most of them.

We were in the last compartment and were taken to Kolomyja. Some of us wanted to jump, but we decided to wait and see what would be done to us. And the further we went, the more compartments were added to the train. Most of the cars were left at the train station in Lvov while the rest went on.

(13)

Soon the train stopped. The doors were opened and they made us leave the cars. We were marched to the camp of Yanovska. The group grew to several hundred as they gathered young able-bodied people from every town they went through. We were ordered to sit and wait until the Gestapo showed up. Their leader, Pukita, started giving us a lecture, telling us that although we were in a labor camp, which was actually a prison camp, the most important thing was for us to work because the Germans appreciated good work. He said, "I know you are very tired from the road and very hungry. Today you will not work and soon enough you will have food." While he went on talking, people started bringing water and giving it to the people in the first rows. The ones sitting in the back rows were so thirsty that when they tried to get to the water the same Putika took out a gun and started shooting at these people. This was his way of telling us that there would be discipline in the camp.

Life in the camp inside Lvov was not very easy. Thousands of young Jewish men from all over Galicia met their death there. The first days in camp the young men from Horodenka kept in touch, but soon we each had to find our own sleeping place and our own bunk. Also the Gestapo organized us into groups of workers so that what little connection we had with each other was lost. Most of us were put, however, in a group that worked desecrating the tombstones from the Jewish cemetery in Lvov, turning them into pavement for the road. This group was doing very humiliating, physically hard labor and had very few survivors. People who were sick were shot and those who were not shot died while they were working.

(14)

I will now attempt to describe the Yanovska concentration camp within the city of Lemberg, in which young and strong men from Galicia were brought to their death. The camp was built at the very end of

Yanovska Street on three hills. When we arrived there was only one two-story house. It was surrounded by three rows of electrified barbwire and guard towers with soldiers armed with machine guns. There was not a single solitary corner that was not being watched. Even the most private places were watched. Even if two people spoke to one another, they were "found guilty" with a burst of machine gun fire. Not a single bullet was ever wasted, for the goal of this place was not labor, but the chance to abuse young prisoners.

On the first day, we young men from Horodenka kept to ourselves. But as nightfall came, we had to separate and seek out a place to rest our heads. As noted, the camp was not totally completed and the only structure was inhabited. The order was given that we had to find a spot indoors. So we began to poke around and luckily found spots under the "stacked" beds, five or six, one above the next. We had to crawl beneath them, and so we spent the first night of many nights in dust and dirt.

The next day, at four in the morning, we had to appear at assembly, grouped according to work tasks, to do calisthenics at the order of the Gestapo. That was the routine, both summer and winter. Each morning we assigned the new arrivals into work details. Many were assigned to existing groups. Those who didn't make the cut were then moved into new groups. Thus, our Horodenka group was split up. We could see one another only at night, and even that was difficult because we were always occupied with some work. A few work details were taken outside the camp, which was much better, even is the work was usually harder. There really wasn't any specialized work in any of the camps. Even those who had easier work to do were under the thumb of the Gestapo night and day, and so they lasted only two or three weeks.

Many of the Horodenkan youth were assigned to a group that worked at removing the tombstones from the Lemberg cemetery and using them to pave the roads. The work was incredibly hard and depressing. Almost everyone who was assigned to this work collapsed under the pressure. My brother, Baruch Prifer (of blessed memory) was also in this group. Even though they knew they could claim an injury or illness, they also knew what the Germans did with them: they were simply sent back to work. My brother Baruch worked for a week with a broken leg. On the week before Yom Kippur I could not convince him to get up and report to work. That night, when I returned from the work detail, he was no longer there. They made known what had happened to him.

(15)

I was one of the Horodenka lads assigned to work in Lemberg's Pflee-Platz. Fortunately, our group was made up of hard workers. Our overseer — he was named Folotov — had good connections and so our group received better treatment than the others. Some attempted to escape from their details. Escape was not too complicated for the "outside" workers; the complications came later on: where to find a hiding place in Lemberg or in the ghetto, and where to go from there. Escape was also a liability for the remaining comrades. When we came back at night we were counted and it was readily apparent if someone was missing. If one escaped, those remaining were automatically responsible for his work detail. And everyone knew the punishment. Israel Blatt had escaped from our group, even though he had decided not to try it until he had come up with a good plan about where to go. Our overseer, Folotov, was an upstanding fellow. He summoned all the Horodenka lads together and told them he would have to account to the guards in the event of an escape. He would have to say that he himself was not liable. He then chided us, saying that those in the ghetto would certainly rather work for him, rather than work within the ghetto. Finally he said he would "look the other way," about Israel Blatt's escape. But at dawn the next day, Israel Blatt was captured and brought into the camp. The man's horror and the horror of those who witnessed his death cannot be described.

(16)

Each day, as we returned to the camp and met up with people from other work details we would talk about who was still alive. We were not only kept busy all day long, but at night as well. Once, sometimes twice at night they would sound an alarm and everyone would have to rush outside dressed in less than five minutes, file into work details, rush to the rail yard to unload wagons of building materiel for constructing barracks — materiel taken from Jewish homes. Many perished in this night-labor. The Gestapo stood on both sides of the road. If a worker took too much time or couldn't unload fast enough, he was shot in his tracks.

The increasing number of "raids" in the city meant that more young people were brought to the camp, but the actual number of prisoners in the camp scarcely varied. It averaged about 5,000 people. In the camp there were also Poles in a separate fenced-in area. We had contact with them. Their tasks were easier; fewer of them were killed. Once a week they received packages from the Red Cross. Our food ration paled in comparison: 90 grams of bread each day; black coffee in the morning and soup at mid-day; at night, sometimes soup, sometimes coffee.

The work details that slaved within the camp and were forced to live off the rations barely survived for two or three weeks. Here and there, outside the camp, more was available, and sometimes we were given something to eat at the worksite.

In the horrendous surroundings, people held out — survived — longer than you can possibly imagine. Even when a typhus epidemic broke out following the first snowfall, many showed their will to live. They even attempted to escape. And the more that died, the more were brought in from the "outlying regions," those who had remained after the ghettos in the cities and towns had been liquidated. Former members of the Judenrat and the Jewish Police were in this category. But no matter what, the actual number of inmates in the camp never varied.

(17)

In winter we would return "home" from work, in the dark. We didn't have time to socialize much, and so the friendships among the Horodenka comrades came to an end. From time to time, in the morning during assembly, you could see a familiar face. Usually, it was hard to recognize someone. Towards the end, only four Horodenka lads remained in our work detail: our neighbor, Aver Tiker; Dovid Glager, Baruch Reiff, and me. At night we caught up on the latest news from the newest arrivals, or we talked about escaping so that we would not have to die this way, as we saw others die. But the desire to escape wasn't always evident. You could be captured and then sent on to another camp, or even in the best of circumstances, to the ghetto where raids were still taking place. This reality is what held us back. But as the typhus epidemic spread — and I was one of the first to become sick — we saw before our eyes a new way to put an end to life. We four promised one another that we would try to escape. Preparations took a lot of time. In the meanwhile, I recuperated from typhus. My fever fell, but I became swollen. And in a day or two I would not be able to stand up. So I decided to flee right then. As I told my comrades my plan, they decided we should attempt our escape.

(18)

On an early morning in winter during a heavy snow we slipped out of the camp and escaped, each of us in a different direction. We had arranged where to meet in Lemberg at the agreed upon time or maybe even later that same night. Only two of us showed up, my neighbor Aver Ticher and I. Dovid Glager and Baruch Reiff didn't come; we were convinced they had been captured. It became apparent that Dovid Glager had been captured, but Baruch Reiff, as we were later to learn, was not able to find the meeting place. He went to the right of the train station and hid inside a supply wagon, succeeding in making his way to my parents in the Tluste ghetto. A short time later he went to Horodenka to search for some family member. He was captured in Istischke and perished there.

During his first night in the Lemberg ghetto, Tiker went to see his brother and I went first to see to Izzy Veykh, who was from Horodenka. He lived in Lemberg. I had his address. But I had a bitter disappointment: I located where he was supposed to be, but that very same night he was attempting to smuggle himself out by using Aryan papers, so he was unable to help me. He could only give me a bit of money and an overcoat to conceal my camp-prisoner outfit. Aver Tiker and I wished one another the best and separated. But he was not blessed with any luck. Despite his good intentions and planning, he was in for a big letdown. He too had searched for his brother, but when he found him, he was afraid to take him into his household. His brother lived in a room with another family. He felt that if a runaway were discovered, the assisting family would be murdered. So he gave Aver Tiker a bit of money and some clothing. The two of us remained in the ghetto, but without the opportunity of going into a home to warm up and have a glass of tea. No one would sell us anything for money out of fear that we were escapees from the camps. And so, the Jewish Police, which was very well organized in Lemberg, arrested us that very same night and kept us in the "prison" in the headquarters of the Judenrat. This was far better than falling into the clutches of the Gestapo.

Aver Tiker, who slept on the ground near me began to spike a fever and we realized he was coming down with typhus. That morning, after a long debate we took him to the hospital in the ghetto. I remained alone "behind bars" because I didn't have an address or even an acquaintance in the ghetto. I met up with some Jewish police who wanted to take away my overcoat, in order to determine, they said, whether or not I was an escapee from the camp. We almost came to blows, but fortunately the commander of the Jewish Police ordered me to be released.

(19)

With a great deal of effort I succeeded in making my way to Tluste, where the ghetto still stood and where my parents lived with my aunt, Hannah Toybe. The Tluste ghetto was one of the last remaining ghettos and there Jews from the surrounding towns and villages were gathered. A few Jews from Horodenka successfully smuggled themselves out, crossed the Dneiper, and thus ended up in Tluste. I say "smuggled themselves out" because when the Horodenka ghetto was liquidated all the remaining Jews were ordered to the Kolomyja ghetto. The tactic of the Germans was as follows: to concentrate the Jews from the entire area in one central place so they could be easily killed all at once. But the Jews understood this tactic; they feared going on to Kolomyja. Truth be told, the same fear was rampant in Tluste. With great effort a few Horodenka Jews succeeded in coming to the Tluste ghetto before it was closed. That is, enclosed by a wall. There was no question as to where you would live: you could live just about anywhere. The Germans were not that concerned. From time to time they pulled raids that produced many now-empty flats. Making something of a living wasn't that difficult because you could travel around and trade with the Poles and Ukrainians in the area. A few lads from Tluste were brought to the Yanovska ghetto in Lemberg and I found out from them that there were still a few Horodenka folk in Tluste. In one of the Tluste raids Velvel Glager was killed after he had shot a German officer. Glager had been in Tluste with some members of his family.

(20)

Back in those days in Tluste there was a German named Poti. He was the superviser of grain provisioning for the German army and was responsible for a few farms in the area. In one of the farms, in the village of Lisovtzeh, the Germans experimented with growing a plant named "kagsageeze" from which they extracted rubber. But to do so, they required workers. The Poles and Ukrainians were commandeered and many young people were shipped to Germany to work, but even if they were forced under duress to work, many refused. So Poti turned to the Judenrat with an offer: to make a work camp in Lisovtzeh with a few dozen Jewish lads. He would swear that nothing adverse would happen to the Jews who worked there; a few in the Judenrat were convinced that Poti meant it, and that he would keep his word.

But following the bitter experience in the German "labor camps", no Jews could be found who would join this labor detail of their own free will. And so the Judenrat depended upon me. (I had become healthy in the meantime; also, there were no raids at this time)They put me in charge of recruiting for the damned labor camp. They proposed that if I went there, thirty or so more lads would follow my example. They thought it would be a shame to let the opportunity slip by, because Poti's intentions were good, and you had to show him respect and loyalty. They depended on me, because I was the first to escape from the Yanovska camp, which had the reputation as one of the worst in Poland. They regarded me as a "miracle worker" who breaks out of camps; they looked upon me as one who had been to Hell and made his way out of it.

I mulled over the offer, went out to Lisovtzeh to look over the camps, and decided to go there with my brother, Abba. Actually, a group of twenty lads left with us from the Tluste ghetto. In contrast with the other camps, life in the Lisovtzeh ghetto was normal and good. The general supervisor of work was a Jew named Katz who had remained in his position from the time when the farm was still in control of the Jewish landlord. But when we showed up for work in the morning along with all the Gentiles, Katz had not considered that we had no experience in farming, and so he issued an order that we should work exactly like the Gentiles worked. The Gentiles were treated humanely. Most of them were Poles, and we soon became acquainted with them.

(21)

One morning, on the road to Tluste, there appeared several vehicles with Gestapo and Ukrainian militia from the Tluste district. We know that they would soon begin the work of liquidation. An hour later we heard a volley of shots coming from Tluste. The shooting lasted an entire day. As evening came, the murderers traveled through the village again, and we feared that they would enter the camp. We really didn't work that day. We ran to the nearby forest; no one remained in the camp. But the murderers were otherwise engaged or had some other orders not to molest the inhabitants of the camp.

After this incident, more people started coming to the ghetto. Sometimes a few dozen came, sometimes a few hundred, making it very crowded. Poti was given permission to establish more camps such as this one on other farms in the area, and they soon filled up. Whether in ours or in the new camps, entire families would show up, including children and the elderly. Soon the members of the Judenrat also came to the camp and pleaded with the Germans to allow everyone to enter the camp. They showered Poti with gifts and he promised to do it, assured that the Gestapo would not find out. But intention didn't match outcome. The Gestapo began to search the entire camp, and each search "cost" a few victims.

(22)

The lay of the land of the village of Lisovtzeh [Lisivtsy] and of the camp was favorable for us. The village lay in a low valley by a river and on the other side of the river fields spread out for a few kilometers. There was only one road leading to the village, with a hill on one side from which each wagon or even a solitary person could be seen. More than once it occurred to us to flee to the forest before the Gestapo might come. They wouldn't search for us there, knowing that they could be seen and perhaps killed. They were always on the lookout to catch someone.

The person in charge of the farm was a German named Franke. I must say that he treated us well, perhaps because he was so deeply involved in performing his tasks that would not get done without our labor. Once, at harvest time, he depended upon us to remain at work to complete the grain threshing. Night work was very risky, because you could not see if anyone was approaching. He realized this and assured us that no one (the Gestapo) would ever find out. We believed him, but at daybreak we realized that we were surrounded by Ukrainian police. It was still dark and a few of us took advantage of this and started to run to the forest. The soldiers chased after us. Seventeen of us were murdered and the remainder taken by the Gestapo to a site in front of everyone in the camp; they were ordered to dig graves.

Meanwhile, one of those who had escaped came to the foreman Franke and told him what had happened. He immediately – he was not fully dressed – mounted a horse and rode to the site with a revolver in hand, and with a gallop and a shout convinced the Gestapo commander to abandon the plan. And so all of us remained alive. This was unheard of! But this was how he was able to "accomplish" this: he was a cousin of the Governor General Franke of the Krakow District, and so the Gestapo commander certainly took this into account (when he reversed his own decision).

At dawn the next day those who had fled to the forest returned, including my brother and me. After this incident we gained some confidence. In truth, we had dug seven graves. We had become convinced that Franke stood for us "like steel and iron."

(23)

We had an additional opportunity to talk about how good and stalwart Franke was. A typhus epidemic spread throughout the camp and people began to get ill and die. The entire village knew about it. But he wouldn't acknowledge that he knew. Soon he himself fell sick from typhus and was confined to the hospital. A delegation of townspeople tried to convince the Gestapo to liquidate the Jews and the typhus at the same time. The Gestapo and the townspeople went to Franke's hospital bed to get permission for the "action." According to what we were told, he shouted at them, telling them that he personally knew all the Jews in the camp, that none of them was sick, and if indeed an epidemic should break out in the village, it would come from the Gentiles who live like filthy pigs, and thus they should be liquidated, not the Jews. Thus, he deserved a second round of thank-yous.

Two days later his wife arrived in the village, they packed up his clothing and they returned to Germany. Later on we found out that he never got better from his bout with typhus. He soon died. He had also begun to speculate who would take his place; many of us were on pins and needles wondering what kind of person he would turn out to be.

Meanwhile all of the remnants of the ghettos in the nearby towns were liquidated, leaving our camp as the only one reserved for Jews in the entire area. Truthfully, there were a few Jews hidden by Gentiles. There were also Jews who survived in the woods in "bunkers" they had dug from earth, but they more or less lived in worse conditions than I did.

There weren't only young people in our camp, but also children and the elderly. I myself brought my parents into the camp. By that time my father was very sick and could scarcely walk around. If not for our connections with the Gentiles in the village, we would not have made it. When my brother came down with typhus and was unable to remain in the camp, I would take him to the woods for three or four days or plead for him to spend the night indoors for a night or two. The fact that he survived these conditions without either a doctor or medicine was truly a blessing from Heaven.

(24)

A short time later an old German came, wearing a military uniform. But he was not Gestapo. He announced his name was Badenburg and that he was taking over the running of the farm and the camp. A delegation of the townspeople soon visited him and attempted to find out how he felt about the Jews. He didn't disappoint them. He circulated a declaration that said as long as Jews remained, their days on Earth were numbered. When we found out about this, we decided to send him a statement regarding the importance of this agricultural enterprise in which we labored and how much we supported it. But there were no volunteers willing to deliver the statement personally to him. Finally, Moshe Schulman from Tluste, who was our spokesman for a long time, took it upon himself to meet the new man in charge. Schulman returned from his conversation with Badenburg with a contented look, saying that he had found the German different from the way the others had portrayed him. So we then welcomed him, and he inquired about everything going on in the camp, telling us he had to flee Russia in the middle of the night, empty-handed. He gladly accepted the gift that Schulman had brought; curious to know exactly where he stood (with the inmates). We knew that if the German accepted it, it was a good sign because he would then be obliged to give something back in return. And so life went on in the camp. We lived in fear, but at least we kept on living.

Towards the end of January Badenburg was issued an order to pack to pack up all the materiel, load it onto wagons and have trustworthy helpers haul it to the large farm in Tluste and there await further orders. Badenburg realized he had no trustworthy helpers other than the Jewish lads. He asked me to choose ten brave lads to go with him to Germany under his protection and there remain until the end of the war. I offered up his proposal to my comrades, and because our day-to-day life in the camp was so uncertain, we decided to take advantage of the opportunity and provide him with the required company. I myself couldn't go because I did not want to leave my parents.

A short time later the group went on to Tluste. Badenburg had put in his word for them, but he could not understand why I had not taken advantage of his generosity, and this saddened him, but he continued to conduct himself well with me, nevertheless.

(25)

Meanwhile, matters were accelerating within the German regime. In February 1944, the Germans in Tluste received orders to make their way back. They didn't have time to remove everything they had prepared. All the wagons that Badenburg had brought were left behind and our comrades took them to Listovtzeh.

We were very happy with the chain of events, but not for long. We didn't know how long the retreat would last. But this was the main point: what would follow the retreat? Meanwhile, we remained in the village, in fear of the Polish natives and the thieves under the command of Bendera. He was a Ukrainian Nationalist, a sworn enemy of the Jews, but also an enemy of the Russians and Germans. He fought against all of us equally for an independent Ukraine.

We knew we couldn't defend ourselves against the Bendera forces because of their great numbers and armaments; they were supreme in the villages and forests. Thus the camp workers resolved to go to the Tluste farm at the head of the road to seek the protection of the German soldiers against an assault by Bendera's forces. We would re-position ourselves to protect against a cross-fire, but it soon became apparent this would not be the case because the Bendera crew had no intention of going to a place where German forces would be waiting for them! In a Jewish labor camp in the village of Golovchyn'tse (which would not reconnoiter in Tluste) there was an assault and many Jews were killed and wounded. We found out about it the next day and so a group of us went to the town, but we could do nothing but bury the dead and assist the thirty wounded people to Tluste. The Ukrainian bands surprisingly allowed us to do this and didn't stand in our way. We put the wounded in a large barracks within our camp and

encouraged them to do the best they could. Among those wounded
was Yurman, whose uncle was a fur dealer in Horodenka. Among the
dead were people from Horodenka, but I cannot recall who they were.

(27)

Among the Germans who were retreating from Russia were no police
or Gestapo, only soldiers from the Wehmacht. Because they didn't
know for sure if we were Jews, they greeted us warmly and even
shared their medications with the wounded among us. But luckily,
they didn't remain for long. When one group left, another one arrived,
so they didn't have time to figure out whom we were.

This lasted for almost a month until things quieted down. From
time to time a car went by, or a motorcycle or a tank; they never
stopped. We were very hopeful that a truce would be enacted because
the Germans were fighting hopelessly on every front. We placed
sentries on the hilltops to prevent a surprise attack by the Bendera
gangs. I stood sentry on the spire of a church a short distance from
the camp, with two comrades: Muni Wenkert and Max Hellman from
Zaleszczyki.

On March 24, 1944, in the morning, we spotted a tank that
stopped at the outskirts of the town. It began to shoot volleys in the air
above the town. The tank then turned around and quiet resumed for a
few minutes. Soon more tanks arrived and they all began to fire
volleys. We felt that the spire of the church would collapse, but in
truth they weren't firing on the buildings, but rather above them. Then
a row of tanks entered the town. From the spire we could make out
the Red Star on the tanks. Soldiers lounged atop each tank.

As the tanks entered the town, the Russian soldiers alighted and
positioned themselves in the streets. You should know that we didn't
run, but flew to spread the news in the camp. And as the soldiers
approached, we embraced them. They were amazed because the
townspeople were not as happy as we were to see them. When they
rode through the towns and villages no one went out of his way to
welcome them. And when they found out we were Jews, and that we
had somehow remained alive, many of them had tears in their eyes
because they had never seen anything quite like this before. The
regiment's commander was Jew, and so the others were aware of the
"Jewish Matter."

(28)

But a great tragedy was about to unfold. As the soldiers roamed the
streets, about twenty-five German aircraft appeared out of nowhere
and began to shoot and bomb us. This lasted for two hours. One

bomber was shot down and fell upon the barracks where the wounded lay; they all perished in this holocaust.

As soon as the bombardment had begun I ran into the camp. My father had been in the barracks, but he had gone out to see the tanks, and so he saved himself. The two comrades who stood watch with me were also wounded. Muni Wenkert was wounded in the leg. We thought he was only slightly wounded but on the way to the military hospital he died. The second one, Max Hellman, had a serious stomach wound, but he recovered and today lives in America.

[Page 286]

In the time of murder

Chaim Karl Kaufman

Edited by Ellen Biderman

Translated by her father

In the first half of July 1941, the Hungarian army entered Horodenka. The day after they entered they put up a hanging post in the center of town in front of Chaim Mendel Kop's house. On it a sign declared a state of war, listed the rules of the emergency, and threatened to hang anyone who broke those rules. The Ukrainian citizens, who were mostly anti-Semites, became emboldened after the entry of the Hungarians and started persecuting the Jews. In the first few days, one of the Jews who lived in the suburb of Kotikovka was murdered. In the village of Nezviska, in the Horodenka district, local people herded together a group of Jews, put them on a raft and drowned them in the river Dniester. At this time, the rule requiring Jews to wear a yellow star on their clothes took effect. People who worked in medical services also had to wear a band of the Red Cross.

In general, one must say that the Hungarians didn't like the Ukrainians and did not share their determination to destroy the Jews. The Hungarians, like the Poles, wanted this whole district to be part of Hungary, while the Ukrainians thought otherwise. The Hungarians thought it was enough that Jews wore yellow stars and were made to work in forced labor jobs. The Hungarians killed only one Jew, Mendel Politzi, because he refused to work. Dr. Ivar Sitz related this.

Under the Hungarian rule, a city council was put together in which only Ukrainians served. Sivi Maier was a teacher in the high school and his deputy was a teacher named Dorshinski. They also organized the Ukrainian militia headed by a notorious anti-Semite by the name of Tchaikovsky. After the Russians liberated Horodenka, Tchaikovsky was tried and hung by the Russians.

The Hungarian military headquarters were placed in the Polish High School. The chief of the headquarters lived in the house of Dr. Schneyder and his adjutant lived with my family. At this time the Romanians started persecuting the Jewish citizens, forcing them to leave their homes.

Many of the Bukovina Jews who lived on the border between Romania and Galicia joined the Russians in their retreat and arrived with them in Horodenka. When the local Hungarian authorities found out that the Romanian Jews had entered Horodenka, they ordered those Jews arrested and returned across the border. The Ukrainian militia who had originally transported the Jews across the Romanian border into Galicia carried out these orders. At the border the Romanian guards did not want to let the Jews cross back in and shot at them. From the other side the Ukrainian militia started shooting as well. In this manner hundreds of Jews were killed and buried on the spot – right at the border. When representatives of the Jews in town tried to intervene and stop this massacre, the Ukrainians blamed the Hungarians for giving the order. The Hungarians denied this, blaming the Ukrainian militia.

One of the local Ukrainian clergymen, Bebed, was a friend of mine. When he found out about the deeds of the Ukrainian militia, he started preaching against them in church. He reminded his parish that in 1919 the Poles had started by persecuting Jews and ended up killing Ukrainians. At this time another 120 Romanian Jewish refugees were arrested and were about to be sent across the border. When the Jews of the city found out about this, a delegation headed by Dr. Sitz, Dr. Lichtman, and me presented itself to the chief of the military headquarters and asked that the order be rescinded. The Hungarian general claimed that the order for the arrest and exile had not come from the Hungarian headquarters and that the Ukrainians were lying when they said it did. He also promised to work things out with the Ukrainians. The Jewish delegation was sent from one place to another and finally met with the head of the Ukrainian militia, Tchaikovsky. After many hours of begging and promises of bribes, he agreed to issue a letter that would release those Jews. But as fate would have it, the minute he was going to sign the letter, Hungarian soldiers burst into the militia offices, slapped Tchaikovsky and ordered that all arms belonging to the militia be turned over to the Hungarian military authorities. The Jewish delegation was released from the office after explaining why they were there. But it was too late to save the 120 Jews that were sent to their death on the Romanian border. Later we found out that the Ukrainian militia was disbanded in this manner as Hungarian revenge for the Ukrainians' killing of two of their soldiers in a fight.

This was also the time when the Hungarian government started deporting Jewish citizens who had no proof of citizenship. They were deported with nothing and were made to walk from their homes to labor camps in the Kamenets-Podolski area. On their way they passed through Horodenka. The Jews of our town shared their food and tried to help them any way they could. We organized a soup kitchen in which these refugees got free meals and free clothing, even though it was a very hard time for the Horodenka Jews themselves. I arranged with three Hungarian soldiers to get the leftovers from the slaughterhouses to cook for these refugee Jews.

At the end of the summer of 1941, the Hungarian army left Horodenka and was replaced by the German army. Eastern Galicia was redivided into new districts and towns. And so it happened that towns like Tlumecz that previously belonged to the district of Stanislav became part of the Horodenka district. The first governor of the county was a German of Austrian ancestry by the name of Winkler. The local Gestapo chief was named Doppler, a Nazi and an anti-Semite who was one of the first to help establish Hitler's regime. Doppler brought his mistress Mrs. Neiderman with him. Under Winkler's order a committee of local Jews was established with three members: Dr. Hessel, Dr. Ivar Sitz, and me. The governor approached the committee members and told us that from this day on the Jews would be second-class citizens, but if they were honest and obeyed orders, their lives would be guaranteed. And so it was.

Except for forced labor and the taking away of certain civil liberties, nothing was disturbed and life went on as usual. After a few months, however, a new governor from the SS by the name of Hans Hack replaced Governor Winkler. He was cunning and greedy. He dismissed the local committee and established a local Jewish council whose members included, among others, Dr. Hessel, chairman, Dr. Sitz, Israel Kugler, and Izye Geller. This committee was in charge of all matters pertaining to the Jews of Horodenka and the area. Dr. Schneyder and I were put in charge of cemetery matters and medicine.

During the first days of his regime the new governor put out an order requiring the Jews to hand over within 48 hours all their gold (except for wedding bands), diamonds, foreign currency, furs, and even coffee. Everyone who ignored that order would be sentenced to death. The Jews obeyed and transferred all their belongings to the local authorities without receiving any receipts. After a short time another decree was issued requiring all Jewish men from the age of 14 through 60 to register in the local ministry of labor. Jews that registered were forced to do all kinds of hard labor. For example, Jews were forced to attempt to build a bridge over the Dniester River. In that attempt many Jews drowned.

Together with the office of the governor of the district and the Ministry of Labor there was also the military headquarters headed by Major Feidler. Feidler was a Berliner, but he was anti-Nazi. He once told me that if the Nazis won, he would commit suicide. One of his jobs was to supervise the work that was done for the army. Every day he would select a certain number of workers from those who were registered for forced labor. His attitude toward his workers was very humane and therefore most of the Jews tried to work for him. In one decree he placed my dentistry office under the auspices of the army thus directly protecting all the workers from Nazi persecution. It is said that when the first actions started, he refused the SS order to give them cars that would transport Jews to the valley of death.

A special story was the matter of the orphans – the Jewish orphans from Hungary who were deported to Horodenka after the Hungarians entered the town. During the Hungarian regime, these children, 18 in number, were put in a Polish-Ukrainian school that was established in the time of the Russian regime. Christian nuns who took care of all the orphans approached the authorities and the Jewish community committee to have the Jewish orphans removed from their shelter and placed under the care of the Jewish community. They said there wasn't enough food to take care of the orphans. The Jewish council, who knew how bad off the Jews were, tried to avoid the issue and refused to take on the Jewish children. But after Governor Hack came to power, he responded to the nuns' request and ordered the Jewish Council to take the Jewish orphans out of the general shelter. The children were removed to the house of my father and put under the supervision of Israel Kugler. Their daily care was given to a group of adolescents headed by Tuvia Cohen. Because my father had good connections with the local miller, he managed to get five sacks of flours (moved in the dark) to the new orphans' home.

In October 1941, the establishment of the Jewish ghetto in Horodenka was announced and all the Jews were removed from their homes and put in the small alleys and crowded places on the western part of town. My office and that of Dr. Schneider were moved to the house of Schmuel Becker.

In November 1941 a delegation of Jews from Ottynia arrived in Horodenka and asked the chairman of the local council to try to arrange the release of a few hundred Ottynia Jews who were arrested and transported to an unknown place. Dr. Hessel as the chairman of the group went to see the governor. The governor told them that if the Jews of Ottynia gave him two kilograms of gold (about four and a half pounds), 10,000 gold pieces, and a few diamonds, he would try and release the imprisoned Jews in a week. As a token of his good intentions, Governor Hack gave the delegation legal passes to return to Ottynia. A few days later the delegation came back accompanied by Dr. Hessel to give the Governor all that he had demanded. Eight days later they came back from Ottynia and told Dr. Hessel that the imprisoned Jews had not been released. When Dr. Hessel approached the governor with this information he looked very surprised and promised to get in touch with whoever was in charge of those prisoners and try to win the release of the Jews. He asked the delegation to return to Ottynia.

The situation went back and forth like this for a month. Finally, the delegation from Ottynia went back and finally found out that the prisoners had been led out into the forest right after their arrest and shot and buried on the spot.

At the end of November 1941 Governor Hack invited Dr. Hessel to see him and told him that he knew from very reliable sources that a new action against the Jews in Horodenka was about to start. He added that for three additional kilograms of gold, diamonds, and other valuables he would attempt to stop that order. Dr. Hessel relayed the message to the council and they decided to collect all the gold and valuables needed to try to stop this action of destruction. The governor took the bribe and let them know that all the ghetto residents were going to get inoculations against typhoid.

All the Jews were ordered to gather on December 4th by the Yiddish school to get the shots. To make this whole operation easy, he gave the Jewish council members special documents that allowed them to go back and forth between town and the ghetto walls. He also determined that Dr. Schneyder, Dr. Veytsberg and his wife, also a doctor, would administer the shots. When the German Major Fiedler found out about the plan, he and the mistress Mrs. Neiderman warned me not to believe Hack. They told me that they had found out from a reliable source that the action would take place on December 4th and the story of typhoid shots was just a cover-up to get all the Jews together in order to transport them. I relayed the message to Dr. Hessel and the other council members, but most of them tended to believe Hack's promises to save the Jews from destruction. Yet despite the desire to believe Hack's promises, a few doubts started rising in the minds of the council members. Dr. Hessel suggested that Dr. Schneyder try to find an excuse not to administer shots on that day. Dr. Schneyder rejected the idea and said he didn't want anybody else to take his place if indeed somebody was going to suffer and be killed.

On December 3, 1941, Fiedler told Schneyder and me that the expected action would indeed take place the next day and that he would like to protect us from being arrested and murdered. Therefore he planned to send military police to our houses at night and have us arrested and jailed until the action was completed. He fulfilled this promise, and that night military police arrested Schneyder, me, and our families and imprisoned us in the cellar of the house of Shimon Pilfl that was serving as the headquarters of the military police. Dr. Schneyder himself was on duty in the hospital that night. I warned him not to leave the hospital before confirming that the danger had passed. Dr. Schneyder indeed promised to do that, but the next morning he left with Dr. Veytsberg to go and take his place in the area where the people were supposed to get their shots. There they were all transported by the Gestapo to the big synagogue and from there, the site of their murder by the Dniester River.

That morning, December 4th 1941, the Jews went to the Yiddish school to get the shots. After about 2,500 people were gathered the Gestapo and Ukrainian militia surrounded the place, arrested everybody and led them to the big synagogue. At the same time they raided the ghetto and all the Jewish homes outside the ghetto. They arrested, beat, and cursed the Jews before bringing them over to the big synagogue. The place was already crowded. People were kept there all day long without food or water until the next day, a Friday. Tens of children and women fainted and nobody could help them. The cruelty reached its peak in this case.

Among the people who were held in the synagogue was Leib Leibman, son of Jonah Leibman, the teacher, together with his wife and their little daughter. The daughter fainted in her mother's arms and the mother pushed her way to the entrance to let the girl breathe some fresh air. A Gestapo man saw this, grabbed the child and burst her head on the wall of the Ark and killed the mother on the spot. All this happened while Leib Leibman was watching. Through shock and sorrow, he was paralyzed on the spot.

On Friday, December 5th, representatives of the local German authorities came to the synagogue with a list of some of the "helpful" Jews including Dr. Schneyder and asked that they be released. These Jews, except for Dr. Schneyder, were taken out of the big synagogue, put in the corridor and later released between the villages of Semakovtse and Mikolayuvka, about 13 kilometers from Horodenka. The last person to be caught was Motya Mordechai Sucher. He hid through the action in the attic of the synagogue Vizhnitsa Chassidim. He left this hiding place when he thought the danger was over. However, he was caught, put in a truck, and driven to the place with the other Jews.

Trucks taken from the sugar plant in Horodenka were used to transport the Jews to the river. Some of the drivers were Poles who drove slowly in order to let some Jews jump from the trucks and get away. Among the ones that got their chance and jumped were Dr. Hessel, Israel Kugler and others. Dr. Hessel managed to get Aryan papers. However on his way to Stanislav one of the Ukrainians recognized him and handed him over to the Gestapo. The Gestapo soldier took him off the train and made him undress. When he realized that he was a Jew, he shot him on the spot.

In the killing place there were two big pits that were prepared in advance. Next to the pits was a big tent for shade. When these pits were dug a week before the action there was a rumor that this was the grave for dead Jews. When the Jewish council members approached Governor Hack and asked him about the rumor, he said that this was a lie and the pits were dug to keep some calcium and paint for the work on the bridge. The Jews believed this and never asked again.

When the trucks arrived at the pits, the Jews saw the officers and Gestapo armed with machine guns and submachine guns. They were sitting in the shade by a table laid out with food and drink. There was an orchestra playing. The Gestapo then ordered the Jews out of the trucks and into the shade. They then had to get undressed, except for their underwear, and go into the pits. As soon as they stepped into the pits they were shot by the Gestapo. And so the bodies of thousands of dead and dying Jews were piled up in the pits. A few people were not hurt, stayed alive and managed to get out of the pit in the darkness of the night and return somehow to the ghetto. Among the living dead was Drazairlle, Mrs. Rupp, the daughter of Yechil Roseberg, Nettie Reicher, Dvorah Glatzer, and Zippora Eyzman. Most of those who survived were killed in the next action. Very few stayed alive.

From those who lived, two reported incidents should be mentioned. When the Jews left the shaded area after they took their clothes off, Dr. Schneyder was among them, but he was still wearing his shirt. One of the Gestapo saw this and started screaming, ordering him to take the shirt off. Dr. Schneyder took off his shirt and hit the Nazi on his face telling him, "If you think a shirt is worth more than a person's life, take the shirt." He was shot on the spot, before he even managed to go down into the pit.

In another incident, Dr. Ivar Sitz and his wife were holding a little girl in their arms while walking to the pit. They overheard one of the Gestapo telling his friend, "Look, what a cute child. It's a shame that such a beauty should be killed." When he heard this, Sitz approached the Nazi and begged him to take the child and give her to my family for some money. The Gestapo agreed but his partner refused to make the deal and they killed the child with her parents.

All through the massacre, officers and Gestapo were sitting by the tables, eating, drinking, laughing, and amusing themselves. The sounds of the orchestra mixed with the sounds of the machine guns and screams of the victims. The following day, ten of peasants from the area were recruited to cover the pits with dirt. They reported that even a day after covering the pits with dirt, one could still see some motion.

Governor Hack's greed knew no limits. He used lies and tricks over and over to get all the valuables and gold from the Jews into his own pockets. He continually made false promises of release and help to delegations who came to beg for the lives of Jews.

After that first action and murder, the Governor assembled the representatives of the Jews, expressed his sorrow about what had happed and blamed the Ukrainians for putting pressure on the Germans to reduce the number of Jews in the area. He promised that from then on there would be peace and quiet and that there would be no danger to Jewish lives. Under his command a new Jewish council was appointed headed by Morris Pilfl. The Jews were order to re-register and the Jewish council was assigned the duty of giving those with registered documents permission to return to their homes.

Major Feidler told Mrs. Schneyder and me, who were still hiding, that the military police would register us and get our documents. But when the police came to the council to get the documents for our two families, the council chair told them that Doppler, the Gestapo chief, forbade them to give out the documents unless they personally saw us first. After a few days without documents, my wife decided to go to the council personally to get the documents. She was arrested and the rest of our family was also arrested when we came to inquire about her whereabouts. While we were being arrested one of the officers approached us and said that if we gave him the gold that, according to rumors, we had buried, he would arrange our release. We negotiated and finally I agreed to give the officer his gold. Indeed, after they dug out the gold from our backyard, we were released and sent to another house to hide. Major Feidler found out about this and tried to gain our release from the hiding place. He approached Gestapo Chief Doppler and demanded I be allowed to resume my work as a dentist. Doppler agreed and ordered me to reopen my office and clinic in 24 hours. I did and thus managed to keep my family and Mrs. Schneyder alive.

Also during this time, Mrs. Kaufman made friends with Doppler's mistress Mrs. Neiderman. Through her she found out when the next German actions would take place in the ghetto. She also got work permits for a few of her friends including my family, the son of Yaakov Weiner and his son, and the son of Dr. Grenzeyd. These permits protected people from the Gestapo. Through these connections with the mistress of Doppler, Mrs. Neiderman, the remaining Jews were able survive for a while as best they could under German occupation.

In May 1942 Major Feidler left Horodenka and was transferred to Crimea. He took Mrs. Schneyder and her daughter with him. They disappeared in Crimea and have never been heard of since.

In the months of May and June 1942, there were separate actions every now and then. Ten and tens of Jews were caught and transported to labor camps where they died of hunger or torture.

In July 1942 Doppler left Horodenka and was replaced by a new and even crueler Gestapo chief call Feddich. Feddich came to me for treatment for a bridge for his teeth. I prolonged the end of the treatment because I knew that once he was done, Feddich would kill me.

In September 1942 there was a rumor that in a week there would be another action. In order to get the victims to concentrate in one place, there would be a new order to re-register for labor permits. I tried to tell the Jews not to go and re-register. At the same time I tried to get hiding places for my family and me. I finally managed to convince one of the German officers to hide me because me owed me a favor. The next morning the Jews of Horodenka and the area came to the registration office to get the labor permits. After a few hundred of them were gathered, Gestapo cars came and surrounded them, put them on trucks, and assembled them in the courtyard of Count Lovamisky. From there, they were all sent to the concentration camp at Belzec. Most of them died in the trains on the way from hunger and heat. Among them was Itzchak Schecter.

A short time later they announced another registration. This time the Jews understood the implication and did not go near the office. When the Gestapo started searching the houses many escaped the town and hid in the forest on the other side of the Dniester. Even there Germans and local people caught them.

I postponed the end of the dental work on Officer Feddich as long as I could while I arranged a safe hiding place for my family and me. At the end of November 1942, I escaped together with my family to a village and we hid in a bunker in the backyard of one of the peasants. After we escaped from Horodenka, only seven Jews remained in town; of them only one survived, Dr. Tafft, previously a doctor in the town of Chernilitsa.

We hid in that bunker from November 27, 1942 to March 27, 1944, the day that the Red Army entered Horodenka. All in all one must say that the behavior and attitude of many Jews of Horodenka throughout the Holocaust was remarkable. Except for one sole case, they did not lose their human dignity; they stood with honor through all the suffering and the dire tests to which they were subjected by the Germans and their helpers.

[Pages 293 & 381]

In Horodenka and Tluste

Etyl Frieberg

Translator unknown

Before the first action, the hangman of the SS came to our town several times to prepare it. The people from the Judenrat tried to postpone the action by paying them money and trying to bribe them with gold and silver. But the day came when nothing could help. The SS took the money and didn't leave the town. One could tell from the activity in the offices of the Judenrat, which was right across from my apartment, that something extraordinary was going to happen.

A few days previous to the action many in the town received postcards from people in other towns in the area warning that if they were called for a celebration not to go. When I saw all the activity and preparations, I contacted my husband who was visiting his cousin in the suburb of Kotokivka and told him to try to stay there and not return to town. For myself and for my other two cousins I prepared a hiding place with one of the peasants who was our friend. But when we reached the peasant's house he told us that he could not hide us and we would have to go back home. I had no choice but to take my two children and go back home. When I reached the cooperative dairy, Asher Shtreyt, who lived nearby with his wife Bronye, called to me and asked me to hide in their apartment. I wanted to reach my home that was around the corner, but Asher warned me not to go out on the street because it was very dangerous. So we stayed all night with the Shtreyts sitting on their beds, waiting.

Early in the morning we found out that Ukrainian police had surrounded the town. They wouldn't let the peasant women who brought milk and vegetables from their villages to town enter Horodenka. The Shtreyts' apartment was on the top floor. We hid in a very small room that was nearby. The SS people went from one house to the next and asked the people to come out. When they reached the Shtreyt house and screamed "Open up," Shtreyt's wife got scared and answered, "I'm coming," and went out with the two children, Hershel and David. We stayed in the darkened room and the SS thought there was nobody else in the house. Then Asher Shtreyt left the room and went to the tower on top of the dairy building.

When evening came after the dairy workers went home, he called us and told us that from the top of the tower he saw everything that had happened in town. Besides the people who were taken away in cars and trucks, he saw about 400 people being marched to their tragic end.

Following his advice, we all went up to the tower and hid there all day and night. The following day, Friday morning, the town looked like a big cemetery. There was nobody alive except for the Ukrainian police who went around putting yellow stickers on the houses of all the Jews who were taken in the action.

I wanted to find out what happened to my family and I dared to go down from the tower. I told the people who were staying there that I would give them a sign if I saw that the danger was over. Then they could leave the tower.

I found my house locked up as I had left it. I went to the Judenrat office but it was empty. I couldn't find any survivors. In that same house there had been the orphans of the refugees from Hungary that my son Reuben helped care for. One could see there the leftovers of the German plot to make the Jews think that nothing was going to happen. One day before the action, the local governor brought a sack of apples for the children of the orphanage. When I entered the place, I found the tables laid out for breakfast with pieces of bread and butter and pieces of apples. The children never had a chance to taste the fruit. They were taken out early in the morning and led to their death.

I ran over to the house where the tailor Mendel Noach lived. I tried to reach the house of one of the janitors who once had worked with my husband and who we considered to be a friend. I was hoping to hear from him details about what happened. As I was walking, I met Malka Speer who told me that the action was over and that members of my family perished together with most of the people of Horodenka. I went back to the dairy house and I signaled to the people who were hiding there to come down because this action was over.

In a few days the other Jews who were hiding came out and started walking in the streets. The German authorities put out a decree that everything would be normal again and people should go back to work. Men had to go to work unshaven with no sign of mourning. They also started counting the people who remained alive.

Their murderers bought the clothes of the people who were murdered to the city bathhouse. They made the survivors wash and iron them so they could be packaged and sent to Germany, clean and ironed. The wives of the German officers employed some of the Jewish women as seamstresses to sew clothes and underwear. These workers were promised that if anything else happened, they would be protected. But, in fact, these were the first women taken away by the German hangmen.

After the first action the remainder of my family moved to the village of Zimakovich where some of my father's relatives lived. One could do this only with a special permit from the authorities. I remember that the Germans employed one of our friends as a driver. He came to our home to congratulate himself for getting a license for us.

A short time after we left town, very close to Passover, the second action occurred. Rumor reached the village and we left our house for a few days to hide in the fields because we were afraid the Germans would search the houses in the villages also. And we were not wrong. When we came home, a Ukrainian policeman was waiting by each Jewish house giving orders to return to Horodenka and gather there. But the people who were running the estates and who had the authority to keep workers to do the fieldwork agreed, for payment, to accept new workers and demand that these workers stay in the village. And indeed that is how a lot of Jews were saved. More than once a place that needed only 100 workers accepted 500.

Work in the fields was very difficult and the Ukrainian workmen made it even more difficult for us. They gave the Jews the worst jobs and enjoyed humiliating them. Food was a problem too. We were very hungry; even the peasants were hungry. At night we tried to beg for food from some of our peasant acquaintances, but they locked their doors in our faces. During the harvest we would gather some sheaves in the fields and use them to make some flour and broth.

At that time we heard a rumor that a Jew who was a very efficient worker could get a certificate that would allow him to survive longer than others. We were promised that Merboym from the Judenrat could get that certificate for us.

My husband and my daughter dared to go into town in a roundabout way and try to get the certificate. The Polish officers that were serving in the SS took my husband away. They also almost beat him to death. He came home sick and injured. For two weeks we hid him in the fields and tried to get him better. In the meantime my young son, 14, went out to work in his place so he wouldn't be missed. That is how we passed the summer of 1942.

When work in the fields was over, we should have gone back into town. But instead, some of the people in my family got jobs as workers building the bridge over the Dniester. Others hid in the nearby forest.

In the days of the third action, some of the builders of the bridge were arrested and taken into Horodenka. From there they were transferred by train to death camps. Among those who were arrested were two of my sons. They were sent to the labor camp in Lvov. We were finally made to go back to Horodenka. We arrived there on the day that another action was taking place. Those who were arrested were taken to the ghetto in Kolomea. I was arrested also but I jumped from the cart and stayed in Horodenka. Then we decided to leave town, one by one, and to meet in the forest by Tsimakovich. Our wish was to reach one of the towns across the Dniester that was relatively peaceful and not harmed by the Germans. With the help of my brother who was still working on the Dniester Bridge, we managed to cross the river. We hid during the day and at night we would march. We finally came to Tluste. My married sister lived there and she gave us a room in her apartment.

The people of Tluste had the illusion that the Germans had decided to discriminate in favor of those towns on their side of the Dniester and that their fate would be different from the fate of the others. We who were experienced in the German tactics did not trust that perception and we prepared a bunker under the house of my brother-in-law.

And indeed it didn't take a long time until destruction reached Tluste. During the days of the actions, 36 people were hiding with us. The Germans rushed their work there because they felt that the war was going to be over soon. Thus they tried to turn Tluste, in a short time, to Judenrein – free of Jews. After that we could not leave our hiding place. We then had to go into the Lisovska labor camp that was run by the Germans, but not by the SS.

These were the days that the Germans started retreating. Together with them, the Ukrainian groups were also retreating. And these groups tried to kill every Jew that they met on the way. The Jews that were still alive in the labor camp went into the courtyard of the Tluste estate. The estate manager, a German, managed to station soldiers there to protect them against the Ukrainians and also helped to protect these Jews.

After the last of the Germans left Tluste, the town was transferred to the hands of the Ukrainian police. Because the Russian army was so close, they didn't dare to do anything to the Jews. A few hours before the Russians actually reached town, they escaped and left us alone. The first to reach us was a Russian patrol with three tanks. Our men went towards them, but the Russians were suspicious and asked them to raise their hands. When they realized these were Jews they were very surprised because they knew about the destruction everywhere else. They told us that all the way from Stalingrad to here they did not meet one Jew who was alive.

[Pages 296 & 373]

How I Survived

Yehoshua Vermut

Translated by Dalya Yohai

A. The Holocaust

During the first and largest pogrom in Horodenka, in December 1941, I was out of town. After the events of 1939-1941, I left town with my family. We lived in Kolomyja where we experienced the many persecutions. I lost all my relatives and, by a miracle, stayed alive. I hid in different bunkers the entire time. In August 1942, I decided to return to Horodenka and find a way, along with those Jews still in town, to stay alive.

In Horodenka, I found the Jewish population to be under huge stress. The Germans wanted all the Jews registered. They demanded that everybody come to a certain place to have their work permits signed. People who didn't get them signed would be executed. The *Judenrat* got the message to bring everybody for the signing and also was promised that nothing would happen to those that showed up.

Because of the experience of the First and Second Actions, there was a lot of tension. The *Judenrat* decided that it needed to act in a way that, if something happened, they wouldn't be considered responsible. The two days before the chosen date, many people went to the *Judenrat* to hear their options: to go to the *zamenplatz* (the designated site for registration), which would mean certain death, or not go, which would also mean death. Everyone stood there, desperate and frozen but nobody knew what was the right action. Everybody felt that total destruction was coming.

At the last minute the *Judenrat* decided that everybody should go and they also decided about the specific order. Only a small number of Jews decided not to go. They prepared food for a long stay in bunkers. I was among them. The others — especially the young who could work — came on November 7, 1942, at 8 o'clock in the morning, believing that this time everything would be O.K.

After the people gathered, the place was surrounded by German and Ukrainian militia, all armed, and everyone was taken to the trains that then took them to the camps and the gas chambers. Only 80 people who were declared professionals were released. Only they could stay in town; any others were to be shot if found.

The people hiding found themselves in a terrible situation. They couldn't get out because they would be shot and staying in hiding was also impossible. The only solution was to run away. But where to? The non-Jews didn't want to hide us. The border to Romania was heavily guarded and every day the Germans brought back Jews who tried to cross it. That's why there were so few who decided to take this course of action.

At this time, we got information that on the other side of the Dniester, in the areas of Butshash and Tluste, there were many Jews who were not in ghettos. We couldn't believe that 50 kilometers away from us there were free people; so we set out to check the situation. It turned out to be true. It was the plan of the Germans to draw all the hiding Jews to this area in order to catch them all at once.

Every night some people came, although they knew exactly what was awaiting them. Some arrived safely and others were robbed and arrived with nothing.

After two weeks, 200 people — all from Horodenka — were in Tluste and 120 in Botshatsh. My friends and I went to Botshatsh. We were in constant touch with the others and also raised money for the people who had been robbed on the way.

Three months later, the Germans started to find us. We decided to organize ourselves for battle, because we knew that one way or the other we were condemned. We felt that the least we could do is get some revenge. It was very difficult to get ammunition. A gun cost 5000-7000 *zloti,* which was a lot of money a the time. We wanted to local *Judenrat* to help us. They didn't like the idea, but somehow, we managed to get money to buy some guns. At the same time, we sent some people to check out the forests in anticipation of the day we would have to leave town.

However, an unexpected Action took place and all our plans were abandoned. Some people who had the guns were able to kill two Germans and three Ukrainians. Only a small group of people survived the Action; we all went into the forest. There were three groups — 40 people in all, including eight people from Horodenka.

B. In the Forests

At the beginning, it was hard for us to imagine how we could survive without a roof over our heads and no food. But in the first days, we realized that being free without the barbed wire fences and the constant fear was far better than our previous situation. We just had to figure out how to manage.

The first days were difficult. First, we had rain for a whole week and we didn't know how to organize our supplies. Later, we put up tents and then built some bunkers. We organized a kitchen and had three meals a day. We got our supplies from the surrounding villages. Every night some of our people went out and brought back food for the day.

We had only a few revolvers, but we realized quickly that we needed automatic guns. Somehow we got five. All the other Jews who were not armed and who were hiding in other forests regrouped around us. Before that, their situation was very bad. They were frequently robbed and beaten and usually left naked in the middle of nowhere. In these cases, we got them clothes by appealing to the elders of the village where these incidents had occurred. They usually gave us what we needed.

In the first months, we didn't know about the Russian partisans. Then two girls from our group accidentally met with some of them and brought them to us. We had a festive lunch with them and they told us about the War. They stayed with us for a long time and thanks to them we managed to get more guns. We weren't lacking anything: we got clothes, usually German uniforms, and had a radio with batteries. We also managed to get timely information about current events.

It wasn't long before the rumor spread that there was a large, armed force of Jews in the forest; nobody dared to go into the forest. From time to time, however, the Germans would come to do searches. In the summer, it was not too bad because it was really difficult to find people hiding in the thick of the forest; we could easily move from one place to the other. But in the winter, our tracks showed in the snow, so we had to move from place to place outside of the forest.

Because of these events, the Russian partisans decided to move closer to the battlefield. We decided not to do that. We knew that the local population would inform on us to the Germans. Every night we walked 20 – 30 kilometers. This plan paid off. When the Germans got information about us, we were already far away from that plce.

When it became very cold and windy, we started staying with farmers — usually Polish — for a day or two at a time. They would let us stay because we paid them well. We had eight to ten hiding places within a radius of 150 kilometers. For security we would surprise them, stay overnight, and the next day be gone.

In the winter of 1943, the Ukrainians, already seeing the German defeat coming, wanted to get rid of the armed groups. They gathered the local population and told them that we were the only witnesses to the destruction, and thus it was necessary to find us and kill us before we told the Russians about the Ukrainian cooperation with the Germans.

Since they knew that we came to the villages at night, they put guards in every village to watch for us. We learned about this and tried to stay in the fields, avoiding the villages or the roads. Nevertheless, we were in a difficult situation at that time. More than once they discovered us in our hiding places — the traces in the snow revealed us. But we always defended ourselves with the guns. Every time they discovered one of us, he'd be shot on the spot. But when we used the guns, they always ran away.

In January 1943, when we were next to the river, 30 kilometers away from Horodenka, we decided that four people from our town should go and check if there were any Jews still hiding with the villagers. If there were, we'd take them with us into the forest.

It is difficult to describe how we felt when we approached the place where we were born. We knew every stone and every tree. It reminded us of our former life, when we were free with families and friends like normal people. When we approached the local people that we knew, barefoot and wearing German uniforms, they didn't recognize us. When they realized it was we, they got frightened and wanted to us to leave immediately.

Unfortunately, we didn't achieve anything. We found out about some hiding Jews but couldn't make contact with them. In addition, nobody wanted us to stay with them. A local villager, thinking we were Germans, took us in a cart with two strong horses to a nearby village. From there we walked back to meet up with our friends.

The last months before the liberation, our security was very compromised. The Ukrainians organized big, armed groups known as Bendrovitches, who wanted badly to catch us. The roads were full of them. Our wanderings from place to place became almost impossible. At the same time, the Ukrainians started killing the Polish population, finishing off entire villages. One night, we got an interesting offer. We were staying with Polish friend when a Polish delegation came and asked us to help organize a Polish resistance against the Ukrainians. We accepted the offer. They appreciated our courage and gave us a beautiful welcome. In turn, they promised to protect us and help us in any way. We mentioned how many of the people helped the Germans kill our brothers and sisters. They replied that every nation has its bad element, but most of Polish people felt sorry for the Jews!

It is interesting to note that we found the Polish people to be unarmed, but the Ukrainians had a lot of ammunition.

We spent some time in the Polish villages. Many people from hiding in nearby villages joined us. They treated us very well, as they had promised, and had a big dinner for us every night. We went about our business at night and in the day stayed in hiding. Only on Sunday would we go out with our automatic guns to guard the church where everybody was praying. Before we came to the village they had been afraid to go to church for fear of raids by the Ukrainians. They priest told them: "Today we can pray in peace because there is a power outside the building, guarding us from all evil." We stayed in the Polish village until the liberation.

[Page 301]

A Confrontation with the Police

Yehoshua Nudelman

Translated by Dalya Yohai

I was one those who found refuge in the forests, after the destruction of the Butshatch Ghetto. This saved my life. I would like now to share more details about this period.

I myself am from Chernelitza, but had close contacts with the people of Horodenka because of my activity in Gordonia-Hit'achdut. My father and I used to lease the forests in the Chernelitza area and use it for cutting and selling wood. In Kopachintsy, a small village near Chernelitza, my family owned and cultivated a forest. So I became a forest specialist and knew the paths in the forests. I also had maps, especially of forests around Potok-Zloti. After the destruction of the Butshatch Ghetto, I joined the young people who fled into the forests. There were four from Horodenka and I was the fifth from Chernelitza. There were also others from other cities in the area. The Horodenkans were: Yehoshua Vermot; Israel Zilber; and the brothers Yakov and Yochanan Bernstein, Pini Bernstein's sons.

During the destruction of the Ghetto I was gone. I was working for the Germans as a forest specialist. (I still have a certificate with a formal German seal.) One day I got an invitation to come to Butshatch with my tools. On the road I met a dentist from there and he told me it was a trap; that the Germans had once invited a doctor and dentist in this manner and had then killed them. I left the carriage, telling the Germans I need to get another paper, and fled to the forests.

When I met the other hiding in the forest, they asked me to join them and be their leader since I knew all the paths so well. Even before this, I had helped other Jews to hide in the forests, but they were all discovered and killed before they got to their hiding places. I was glad to join the Horodenka group and to work together to save our lives.

This was in October 1943 and so we needed to last through the hard winter months. And we did. I can say with no arrogance that it was thanks to my knowledge of the forests and the people who supplied us with food, helped us with laundry, hid each of us for a couple of days, and treated us very respectfully. I also managed to get some weapons.

I want to relate here about a battle we had with a German and Ukrainian troops. It was February 28, 1944. The day before we had been hiding with the Domkevitz family who lived in a forest on the banks of the Dniester in the area of Chernelitza and four kilometers from Kopachintsy. It had snowed hard that night and we decided to stay one more day and to move during the night. Somehow the police discovered we were there and a whole troop came to look for us. When we saw them, we locked the door and hid in the house. They called for us to come out and when we didn't respond they started to fire. We answered with gunfire and a battle ensued for an hour. Luckily we had enough ammunition — we had 100 bullets — and could hold out for a while. At the end we decided to run out of the house. But we tricked them. Five of us continued to fire and the other five, including me, we behind the troops and opened fire from the back. When they fired at us, the other five left the house. In the battle one of the German soldiers was hurt and they decided to retreat and leave us alone. Their plan was to come back with more people. We took advantage of that truce and quickly left. We even managed to take our belongings. The daughter of the house, Marsia joined us. The parents were not home at that time, so they were not accused of hiding Jews.

A couple of hours later, the troops returned but couldn't find us. They took the other children out of the house and burned it to the ground.

After this incident it was harder to hide anywhere because the troops knew about us looked hard for us. We moved to the other side of the river and continued to hide and move in the forest. We stayed in Potok Kloti a couple of weeks until the Russians liberated the whole area.

[Pages 302 & 328]

How I Survived

Moshe Blazenstein

Translated by Dalya Yohai

When the war broke out between Germany and Russia, I was in Lvov. The first or second day of July, I went back to my mother's place in Kolyanki, 15 kilometers away from Horodenka. The same day, the Hungarian army captured Horodenka and as a reaction, a Ukrainian militia that began attacking Jews was created. In another village, Nezvisko, they killed all the local Jews – 60 of them – and threw them into the river. More than once you would see whole families floating in the water; often they were bound together with barbed wire.

Two weeks later, around July 15, 1941, Hungarian Jews started coming to Horodenka on the way to Ukraine. Many of them stayed in town or in neighboring villages. The Germans in Ukraine killed some of them; many who stayed were murdered by the Ukrainians along with the local Jews.

In Horodenka, the Jews were forced to wear yellow stars and they were forbidden to leave town.

The first Action was on the 4th and 5th of December, 1941. The Ukrainian militia herded all the Jews into the big synagogue and from there they were taken to the village of Mikolayuvka where they prepared a big pit next to the Dniester, not far from the "Pension." They put a wooden board on the pit. Five people at a time were ordered on it. Then they were all shot and fell into the pit. The German Gestapo did the killings and the Ukrainian militia stood guard. Some fell into the pit still alive and then ran away at night. I myself saw a child coming out of the pit and running away. This was on the first day of the Action. The same day they killed Edward Greenberg in the street when he tried to run away from the militia.

On the night between the 4th and the 5th they started to do the "professional" selections. They needed welders, carpenters, and other occupations. My brother Yehuda-Chaim saved himself by registering as an egg packer. On the 5th, in the morning, they rounded up 600 remaining Jews and walked them to Mikolayuvka. The Ukrainian militia again was responsible.

On these two days, 2400 Jews perished. Before the killings they were asked to get undressed down to their underwear. The clothes were taken to the Pension. Among the dead was Dr. Shneyder. After the Action, the Gestapo came to the Judenrat and asked for a confirmation of the number of the dead and also asked for 10,000 marksto pay for the bullets that they had used.

After the first Action a ghetto was established in Horodenka. There was an order that all the Jews from the neighboring villages move into the ghetto. The ghetto lasted until April 1942. It was guarded by the Jewish militia.

I was sent to build a bridge on the Dniester. A German company, Gustav Raga, Tiff und Huchbau, ran the project. Fifty Jews worked for them. We lived in a house in the forest (which belonged to Fizik, the son-in-law of Prishling). We were paid with lunch (usually burgul) and minimum wages. Every day I had to pass by the communal grave because the Germans now lived in the Pension. Sometimes I'd find documents, such as graduation certificates from high school, which belonged to the dead. Some of the Jewish workers got better jobs as welders or cooks.

A Hungarian Jew was responsible for the storage room. The others worked as haulers of the pillars, which were sunk into the river and secured with stones to create the base for the bridge. Some of the stones we brought from a nearby mountain and some came from headstones taken from the Jewish cemetery in Uscieczko.

To tell the truth, the German workers under the engineer Weher treated us O.K. Once during a storm, we were pulling a raft on the river. I was extremely tired, as I hadn't slept all night. There were 200 people in one room including woman and children. When the engineer Weher saw me like that he said, mercifully, "This one is ripe to be killed...."

In April 1942, there was a second, smaller Action in Horodenka. 140 Jews were killed, among them Avraham Ziedman from Kotikuvka, who was in the hospital. He was shot in his bed.

In July 1942, they started to liquidate the ghetto in Horodenka and all the Jews were ordered to move to the Ghetto in Kolomyja. This was a terrible ghetto. People were dying in the streets from hunger and every morning a cart passed to collect the bodies. The ones that stayed alive were finally removed to Belzitz.

Some of the Horodenkan Jews ran away to Tluste, instead of going to Kolomyja and some of them were able to survive. Only a small group stayed in Horodenka. These were the sorters of stuff that was left behind.

September 6, 1942, they started the complete destruction of the Jewish quarter. They put everybody in one of the yards and also took 25 day-workers from the bridge. They told them to come for registration; I was at the time a night laborer and that's how I stayed alive. In the morning on the way back from work I saw the 25 people being taken away in carts, my brother Binyamim included. Engineer Weher saw us coming back and ordered us to go behind the building so we could remain safe.

In Horodenka they put the Jews in the storage shed of the yard and left them with no food or water for two days. When women and children asked for some water they threw them some beets (meant for animal consumption). That's what the people had to suck on. A couple of times the Germans came with bags and asked for gold and valuables. Some preferred to give them money.

After two days they took the Jews out and asked them to line up by fours or eights holding hands. They then took them to the train station. There they put the youth together in one group and the old, the women, and the children together in another. The youth were given a loaf of bread and taken to the Yanovska camp in Lvov; the others went to Belzitz, the death camp. They were taken in wagons with barbed wire on the windows. When it got dark somebody took the wire down and some of the passengers started to escape. The guards shot in the air, but couldn't do anything else. This how my brother Binyamim and his wife got away. They wandered two days in the fields and then went back to Kolyanki and hid at the place of a neighbor, Kazimersh Yashtshur.

After this happened, I worked two more months at the bridge. After our friends were taken away, the Germans treated us like we were non-existent. I think that they felt responsible for this crime. Other than that, as I noted before, they treated us quite fairly.

From time to time, I would go to Kolyanki to get something to eat and to visit my brother. On October 6, 1942, I was on my way as usual to Kolyanki and when I came back I noticed that there was no smoke coming from the chimney in the camp's kitchen, as was usual at this time of the day. I also saw some disorder in front of the camp. So I hid in the forest and a farmer collecting mushrooms told me that they took my friends in carts to Horodenka. I went immediately back to Kolyanki and started hiding. A Ukrainian named Hanet Osadtchuk took me to his house. In the day I hid in the cellar and by night I slept in the hut near the stove. This man had only one room that was both the kitchen and bedroom. He treated me like an angel — especially in light of the fact that I coun't pay him. I repaid him with some stuff that was not worth much. They brought me food in the basket they used to bring potatoes from the cellar, so nobody would have any suspicions.

Usually a four year-old boy brought my food and it is worth noting that he was able to keep the secret.

Once they told me that my older brother, Yehuda-Haim, was sick and hiding in one of the fields with his wife and three children and that he wanted to see me. My brother Binyamim went to see him and slept there one night. Some days later Binyamim got sick and the *goy* sheltering him asked him to leave because as he was sick he would not be able to run away if need be. The *goy* would then be found out and killed.

Binyamim came to me and my good *goy* accepted him, but only temporarily. I brught him to a women neighbor, but she too was scared. Another neighbor sent his dog against him. The day after he came back to me, I asked Hanet to let him stay and I promised him wood. He agreed. He was in the barn during the day and in the house at night. Hanet sent his son to a Jewish doctor that lived in Siemakowce with his wife and small child. He was young and originally from Stanislvov. I wrote him a letter describing my brother's symptoms and he sent back some medicine, saying it was typhus.

In the meantime, Hanet's oldest son also became sick, followed by his wife and the young child; the whole house became a hospital. Eventually Hanet himself got sick and we had to leave his home. We went to the forest. This was the 23rd of January 1943. Outside there was the big frost. My brother started getting better and the *goy* named Ivan Sanduk took him home for some days. I got a high fever too but didn't succumb. Another Ivan Sanduk took me to his house and I stayed there five days and then I went to other houses. Altogether I hid for three weeks. Then I had no place to go. In the meantime I learned that Hanet died; I blame myself to this day. Then Ivan Sanduk and his family died too. I mourned them like they were my relatives.

My brother Binyamim was also roofless at that time. One day I went to a desolate barn and I found him there. We decided to go to the forest. This was February 13th, 1943. In the day we hid behind the rocks in the forest and at night we found a desolate hut and slept there. After two weeks we noticed that we were seen and began sleeping in the forest again.

We ate mainly potatoes that we stole from farmers' cellars. In the summer it was easier. We ate fruits and vegetables from the fields. The biggest problem was the mushroom season when all the villagers came to pick. We had to move from one place to another at that time.

In Kolyanki there were other Jews in hiding. Among them were Rachel and Avraham Guttman, Naftali and Josef Esnfeld and Rivka Eider. Naftali died of hunger and cold. The Guttmans hid at one of their neighbors. However, another neighbor went to the militia to report them. They found Rachel in the barn but didn't find Avraham. She had one foot paralyzed and couldn't walk. They took a cart and brought her to a mountain called Okopi, where horses were buried. They finished their bottle of wine, then shot, killed her, and buried her there. Somebody said that although she was crippled, she tried to escape, but they didn't let her.

In the fall, Avraham Guttman came to the forest. The same day it snowed and we couldn't stay under the trees. But we didn't have another alternative. So we went to the rocks. This was quite close to the road and the guard noticed us and went to the militia. We ran away and left everything behind including shoes and coats. We ran shoeless in the snow and managed to disappear. We slept that night under another rock and the day after we dug a hole like a bunker.

This was a simple hole in the ground; it was so small that we couldn't even manage to lie or sit in it together. We covered it with branches and leaves. Again, in the summer we managed with food and then started stealing potatoes again. Because of the lack of vitamins, my brother became blind at night. I had to guide him. I have to confess that I was trembling in a strange cellar, stealing potatoes. But my brother was more secure. Looking for a hiding place, I always took into consideration the security element. That's why the bunker was located in the middle of the forest on a hill. It proved to be a good decision. We saw often from our hiding place how the obvious places were searched for hiding Jews; but nobody would think that we were in the depth of the hill.

In the summer of 43-44, we started hearing rumors that the Russians were close. In December 1943, Avraham Guttman visited us again. He was hiding with a neighbor who was supplying him with food as well. We told him to give up the "comfort" and come stay with us. He had some sheepskins and he promised to bring them for us to cover ourselves with. We planned to enlarge the bunker, but he went back and never returned. Later, we heard that he was found in the barn. They took him to Horodenka and shot him in the cemetery.

As I mentioned before, Yehuda, my brother, had typhus. When he recovered he ran away with his wife and three children to Tluste. There, his oldest daughter Luci was killed in an Action. They returned to the forest and hid behind the rocks in the field between Horodenka and Kolyanki.

I was told that he used to come at night to one Peuter Yashtochok to get some cooked potatoes. At the end, somebody told the German police and they went, in January 1944 (two months before the liberation) and caught and killed them on the spot. The bodies were taken to Horodenka.

Of all the people hiding in Kolyanki, only Yosef Ensfled and Rivka Eider suvived. But they ran away and the militia was looking for them. They found Yosef at night in the Dalshow forest and killed him on the spot. Rivka was younger and stronger and managed to survive until the end of the war.

In February 1944 there was a deep snow and it was dangerous to go to the village to get food because we would leave footprints in the snow. We still had two kilograms of wheat, so we made flour by grinding it between two stones. We were able to make a soup everyday with one tablespoon. This is how we ate for six weeks. When the snow melted and we dared to go to the village, we almost couldn't walk.

This was the last time we went to the village and this time we were not lucky. Binyamim went down to the cellar to get potatoes and a dog came and started barking violently. The farmer's son came, but when he saw us he retreated. This time we had gone earlier than usual, around 9 o'clock, something we never dared to do before. But since we felt the presence of the Soviet army we became more daring. We left the yard immediately, but managed to get some potatoes. The day after we saw the guard looking for us behind the rocks.

We felt the Soviet Army getting closer and indeed on March 23rd, 1944, we heard an engine and saw a plane with a red star fly very low along the Dniester. We were ecstatic. But still we didn't dare to go to the village until two days later when the Soviets were already there. I was long-haired, I hadn't shaved the whole year. The whole winter I wore one shirt and didn't have the chance to wash it. We were covered with lice and all the villagers came to stare at us.

But this was not the end. A couple of days later, a German troop came to the village. There was a battle between the Germans and the Soviets. We hid in a cellar and the battle was 100 meters from our hiding place. That same night the Germans left. The next day we went to Horodenka and found there a couple of Jews who had managed to hide there or come back from Tluste.

I ran away to Czernovitz. My brother Binyamim was drafted by the Soviet Army and they sent him to the front. That same year he died of a German bullet.

Horodenkians visit the "Yaar Hakdoshim"

[Pages 307]

The Ones Who Saved Us

Peretz Vizling

Translated by Dalya Yohai and Harvey Buchalter

I am far, very far away from my home, my place of birth. Here, things are good; I feel safe and free. But still it is hard to forget my home from long ago, as well as my "home" for the years of the War, 1939 – 1945. It's hard to forget my close friends, neighbors, and all the people I knew — all of whom were so tragically murdered. It's so hard to forget the burdens, the troubled times, and the shameful events we saw before our eyes. How hard it is to forget and not assign blame for the murders committed within the confines of our town, to blame the local residents — those who played such a huge role in the murder of all those dear to us.

On the other hand, it is impossible to forget the few good farmers who risked their lives and hid some Jews, protecting them ferociously. They were extremely patient for a long time, and took care of "their" Jews until the day of liberation.

With one of those families — in a Polish farmer's house — my family went into hiding — my wife, our baby boy, and me. We were there for 500 days. This poor Polish family — husband, wife, and a 20-year-old son — helped others as well at the time of the Actions. We can say that 13 people survived because of them!

During the first big Action, they let 13 people come into their house. They hid and fed them, and then let them go when the danger was over. And they were not people they knew. They did this altruistic work in return for no favors. In the year-and-a-half my family was there, I saw them quickly aging because of the worry; they had terrible fear of being discovered. The day of the liberation, they needed to leave their home and run away from the Ukrainians who wanted revenge on people who hid Jews. I helped them move into town — but the gangs set fire to their house and the father of my friend (an 80 year old man) was burned alive. He had known about us, and in many times of danger he ran to the fields with my son. And for this sin — of rescuing a Jewish boy — he was punished and burned alive. To this day I am heartbroken that I couldn't help him out.

But even in town we were not secure, despite the presence of the Russian Army. Thus one night, we stole some Soviet vehicles and drove 40 kilometers to Poland. With the help of my brothers, my family immigrated to the United States, but our saviors stayed in Poland in

Upper Shlezia. Our good-byes were very emotional, especially for our son Gustav. We cried as well, but we were comforted by the thought that we would be able to help them from the States — and maybe even bring them over.

Unfortunately, nothing worked as we planned. Everything we sent them, including money, was claimed by their relatives who gave them a hard time for what they had done.

It is important to tell more of this amazing story of rescue by a local Polish family. And it is also important to know who were the ones who helped to take Jewish lives.

In our town of Horodenka, almost touching the Romanian border, together with the neighboring villages, there lived approximately seven thousand Jews before the War. Of those who remained alive, only a very small number, scarcely 25, were hidden by Christians, most of whom did it for large sums of money and material goods. A few dozen Jews also escaped to Russia and Romania in the midst of the Holocaust. Others escaped to the other side of the Dniester River, and some joined the Partisans. It is not necessary to ask if more might have been saved. Many more could have been saved, because in our region there was a German civil, not a military presence.

At the beginning of the war between Poland and Germany, our town was occupied by the Hungarian Army. They were not totally innocent, but they were human. When the Germans took over, the town had a *Kreizehoptman* (minister of the county) and some German clerks. The police force had 15 people, two of them members of the Gestapo. They didn't intervene in our lives and actually sometimes helped Jews. For example, when Ginka Lucas, Neta Lehrer's daughter, was put against the wall awaiting execution with her two lovely children, two Gestapo agents gathered them up and took them to their home. The local German headquarters employed 40 people, mostly Austrians, who made a lot of money for hiding Jews or taking them out of the area to Romania.

The Polish Militia also behaved quite fairly. The minister, the agricultural inspector, and the head of the labor department acted as the mayors. They were not very good people, but over time, the *Judenrat*, consisting of the dentist Kaufman, the lawyer Tav, and Meir Koch, found a way to talk to them and influence them on our behalf,. The real enemy was the assistant to the minister *Obersturmbenfuhrere* Dopler. He oversaw the Ukrainian militia, the Polish police force, and 20 – 30 Gestapo members who came to lead the Actions in town. The Ukrainian population conducted killings and lootings, and also was instrumental in finding the hidden

Jews. The inteligencia participated as well. This included the priests and teachers like the principal Dereshinsky, who organized meetings where he told the people to take every opportunity to get rid of the Jews. He was one of those who from the first instructed and incited the rabble. In the villages, he often promised the mob the mountains of gold if only they could promptly rid themselves of the Jews and that this was the appropriate time to do so. The people listened to them and responded enthusiastically.

Dereshinsky, the principal of the school and main inciter of hatred against the Jews, had held an honored position in the Soviet regime, until 1941. As far as the Nazis were concerned, he was an important nationalistic figure because of his fervent pro-Hitler stance and his title of Security Chief. He was a second Josef Goebbels in our midst. And now, as far as the Soviets are concerned, he is a Soviet Patriot deserving of important offices of authority. In spite of what either the Soviets knew or didn't know about his true identity, or if they knew his deeds under the Nazis, he continues to lead a charmed life. He took over the grand estate and all of the adjoining property of the Jewish wholesale merchant Berl Shpierer, who was sent into the depths of Russia by the Soviets, and perished there. There were many of the likes of Dereshinsky amongst us. They cried out. "Why are you putting up such a struggle? You can plainly see you're all going to die." These, the "two-faced," wanted to kiss and make up following the liberation, shouting "ba-ahu," thanks be to God, that you have remained alive. To even bring up their memory is too emotional for me. I still remember all of it. I, too, would have wanted to live as everyone else lives — to laugh as everyone else laughs — but it caused me too much pain to see these people live freely and laugh, knowing that it was only yesterday, or perhaps tomorrow, that they would forget the murders they committed.

Not many people helped the Jews. Even after the annihilation of the rest of the Jewish population in September 1942, there were Jews who were in hiding having been helped by Poles, Ukrainians, some Germans, but mostly Armenians. Most of them did it for a lot of money and assets. The decent people among them kept the Jews, but sometimes were tired of living with the fear of the Jews being discovered. The crooks took the money and handed over the Jews eventually. In some instances, relatives let the Gestapo knew about the hidden Jews.

Among the first casualties were the "poor-folk" who didn't possess anything worth "selling." Next were the Jews who were unfortunate enough to believe they'd be saved, upon being hidden by the [Ukrainian] peasants and essentially "signing over" all of their possessions, which the peasants swore to hide for them. These "trustees" knew from the first how they would get rid of the Jews so that the few rags they possessed would become theirs. If the "rescuers" didn't slit the throats of the Jews, they had their neighbors do it; then they shared in the "wealth."

Josef Hirsch Reichman and his wife, perhaps the richest couple in the town, lived in a village with a Ukrainian family who hid them well. One sister (in the family) and then another wouldn't so much as give them an onion to eat. The peasant soon became tired of "their Jews" and turned in them in to be shot, taking their possessions. The youngest son of the schoolteacher Nard was hidden by his servant for more than a year under the bed. And because she either couldn't or wouldn't help her brother do fieldwork, he turned her in. Both the little Jewish boy and the servant were taken from Serafinitz to town. The servant cried and begged them not to shoot the little boy, to shoot her instead. And the murderers heeded her request, shooting both of them.

Much attention was paid to the peasants' frequent bouts of drinking, carrying-on, and their spending sprees which brought unwanted attention and made their actions suspect. There were special investigators and intelligence officers, who spied on them in order to see what and how much they purchased, or who was buying German-language newspapers for "their" Jews. Many more Jews would have been saved if they (the Jews) had been more circumspect in deciding who their "rescuers" would be. They should have never looked up an "old friend," be he an acquaintance or friend from school or business, because he would have been paid off by the agents. Rather, they should put their trust in the poorest of the peasants. And an even surer bet would have been the dwellers of the criminal underworld, the card-players (gamblers), petty thieves, or the suspicious characters. They never once stepped foot in a church, never picked up a newspaper, but they realized the following: If they succeeded in this "little piece of work" (sheltering Jews) America would pay them handsomely. They possessed more wisdom, more refinement, more pride and were less easily scared. As townspeople, they were not our favorites. But our Jews were too cautious, too afraid of these types, instead seeking more established, more intellectual ones instead.

Surprisingly, most of the saviors were poor Polish and Ukrainian families who helped with no expectations at all. They did it just from the goodness of their hearts. Many more of us would have been saved if we went straight to them instead of going to the wealthiest for help.

The family who helped us was really poor. Not too far from my fields and mill there were six other families who owned mills. Even though they didn't always live harmoniously with one another, the mills provided them with food and a steady income. In addition, there was also an old peasant with three sons and two daughters; one of the daughters ran our household. The peasant, "the boss," made a living by working the fields with a pair of horses.

In 1939, when the Soviets took me far away to perform some work for them, I was not able to take care of my fields. Before leaving, by accident, I met "the boss" in town one day. "Why don't you work my fields," I said to him. "Take over my land and my livestock, so that you can be in charge. Go to work, and if you make something extra, put it aside for me." We immediately agreed upon this and both of us left very satisfied with the arrangement. During the Russian occupation, I was very busy and didn't see him; he became wealthy because of my fields.

When the Russians were retreating I was far away from home, on the other side of the Dniester. I was not able to come back because of the destruction of the bridges on the river. My wife spoke to many farmers about helping us, but to no avail. The *Gaspadarsh* [boss], the man who worked my fields, came to ask about me and heard where I was. He took his horses and brought me home, dressed like a Ukrainian peasant so nobody could recognize me. He wouldn't allow me to pay him anything.

A couple of days later he came again and told me that he and his wife would be very happy to be able to express their thanks to me. "You," he said, "helped me when the Russians were here. Now it's my turn to help you. Since I've had your fields, I've become a wealthy man, and now I want to thank you and your relatives."

He started bringing food to my family and my sister's as well. (It was forbidden to transport food at the time.) Then he remembered that the lawyer Blum from Sniatyn, had helped him once, and he started to bring him food too. When the ghetto was created he became an expert smuggler.

At the time of the first Action that lasted two days, Thursday and Friday December 4-5, 1941, this family had 26 Jews in the house. 2500 Jews lost their lives in this Action.

The farmer came as an angel on Wednesday, although he used to come on Sunday, and took 26 Jews, including my family with him. He put everybody in his cellar; his wife cooked and he and his son brought us food — potatoes and cornmeal, and milk for the children. He was very happy and said it was a festive day for him to be able to do this. Twelve of these 26 Jews are alive today and they will never forget him.

After the Action he took us back to our homes. One day his wife complained to him that some of the Jews didn't thank them and he said to her, "If these Jews were not alive today, would it be better?" And he continued to smuggle food to the ghetto.

Some time after the first Action, I asked him if his family would be able to take my son in. Two days later he came and said yes and they even had an excuse for the neighbors. They would say that he was the wife's sister's son from Kolomyja. I had a big fight with my wife about taking our son away from her, as he was still breastfeeding. But, that night the farmer took the baby, covering him with a rough looking coat, and left at midnight. Two weeks later, my son still cried for his mother; then he got used to it and stopped. They burnt all of the child's clothing and toys and cut all of his hair. He let him creep around the floors barefoot and dirty, so that he would look like an authentic peasant's orphan child.

I knew our rescuers were taking pains to guard our child. This was especially true during the summer work in the field, when it was necessary to be particularly careful, as many day laborers would spend the night. They had to watch him all day long. The child even wore "bandages," concealing the fact that he was circumcised. But it was worse at night. The child could uncover himself when strangers were about, so they decided that one of them would wake up in order to hold and "cover" the child should someone want to see him or play with him. They had a huge job to do. I truly felt for them, and also shared their fears that times could not get any worse for us Jews.

At the time of the second Action, on Monday, April 14, 1942, my wife couldn't stay with them because she feared that our son would recognize her and reveal himself. So she hid this time with another person who had worked for me in the past.

By the summer of 1942, it was obvious to everyone – they could hear, see and feel it in the air – that death was our fate. There was no way of saving us, only a miracle would work — a miracle that could come only from the other side of the ocean, from America and England. Only they could give us a reprieve from the gathering forces of destruction, if only to give the unfortunate Jews a bit more time. Our savior hinted that if it had not been for the presence of the child, he might have been able to hide us from the murderers as well. But if we were all together, it wouldn't be safe. On top of everything else, he lived in constant fear of his wife's relatives, one of whom was a thief and a murderer. If he were to bicker with her, it would have opened the door for betrayal, and then everything would be lost.

The period between the second and third Actions, when we were living in town, we had a daughter. My wife begged me to keep her at least 6 months and then give her away, but unfortunately she didn't survive. It looked like we were not destined to come out of this without paying a terrible price.

At the time of the third Action, September 7, 1942, which went on for a few days, the Germans were looking into the houses to see if any Jews were hiding; they found my daughter. She was with an elderly couple who lived in a small room that belonged to my family, since my father's day. They asked us to give them the baby and they promised to look after her if we gave them the deed to our hut. They said that they loved the child and would take her with them into the fields in the event of another roundup of Jews. The child was now taking nourishment from a bottle. They promised to guard the child well. I believed them and gave up not only the ownership of the hut, but of the entire house as well. But the day of the Action they wanted to go and loot the houses of the Jews and they left her alone at home instead of running away with her to the country. The neighbors had told the Gestapo about the Jewish baby in the house and they came to kill her. First they played with her, she smiled at them. But then one of them left to take Luksenburg to the meeting place and the other took her, put her on the floor and shot her. One of the neighbors told me the story. He came to the stable where I worked. I was one of the Jews to be left alone because I worked.

Word went out that on Monday, September 7, 1942, all workers and remaining Jews were to report for "registration." This went on for four days. In addition to the thirty Gestapo agents who had come from Kolomyja, the Ukrainian militia, and the Polish Criminal Police, eighty percent of the Ukrainian populace from the town and nearby villages poked around and searched in the town, villages, fields, and forest looking for Jews. No one could be sure of the number of Jews captured because many had escaped by crossing the Dniester; things seemed rather calm in the Tarnapoler region. Many escaped from the wagons that carried them off. Several hundred were captured later and taken off to the Kolomyja ghetto; some were able to escape to Romania; some two hundred were able to find refuge. I took heart from their success.

Approximately one thousand of those captured were separated from the rest and put into a stable on a Horodenka estate, and given nothing to eat for four days; then the murderers put them on a train and took them away. The few who remained, famished, delirious, but fortunate, if only for a short while, were eighty "useful" Jews that the local murderers had asked be spared until "their own" (the Ukrainians) could learn the trades and professions formerly performed by the Jews. They were not truly fortunate, though, because they were all taken from their families who were either exterminated or hidden in a cellar or trench. The "useful" Jews didn't dare try to have their families alongside them; they were all forced to live in one barrack so that it would be easy for the murderers to gather them up in the coming three weeks.

Until September 7, 1942, I had worked as a field hand, something of a foreman, for the murderers and was able to reside in our home. Afterwards, my house was confiscated and I was forced to live with one of the other Jewish field hands. Their intention was to "isolate" us in this way, so that we could be more easily found and rounded up.

At the time of the "registration" I had a plan: if I didn't go to the "registration" and a roundup was instead declared, I would climb to the stable's loft and stick myself into a corner. Instead, one of the drivers (a Gentile) who wanted me to live for at least one more month took me to the "registration" (with the understanding that nothing would happen to me). But as the proceedings unfolded, more Jews realized that this was a roundup, not a "registration." Then two automobiles appeared with two murderers inside. The Ukrainian militia, under Inspector Brash, joined with the *Judenrat* officials to gather up the Jews who now knew they had been deceived. I would rather have served ten years of hard labor than to have witnessed these ten minutes from my perch on the wagon: the desperate, tragic Jews, and the actions of one of the *Judenrat* police who whipped one of his underlings for having let a Jew off too easily. I watched the murderous Ukrainians and Poles laugh at our plight. The so-called friend of the Jews, Dr. Bialy laughed his high-pitched laugh at how he was able to deceive the Jews into being caught in a trap. I was obsessed by these ten minutes for four entire days, which was how long the roundup lasted. I felt a little less afraid, because I knew that if my "co-workers" wanted me dead, they could do it first thing in the morning.

The first three days of the Action my wife was hiding again at my former coachman's house (she was there for the second Action as well). On the fourth day, he came to tell her that the Germans were now looking in the farmers' houses to find hiding Jews and it was known that she was hiding in his house. The farmer's wife suggested she go and hide in the garden. But in the garden were Ukrainian boys who helped the Ukrainian militia look for Jews. She didn't know where to go and started walking into town.

Although she had been there during the first roundup, it was at night, and they had traveled there by wagon. Seeing only unfamiliar faces all around, she became disoriented once she got close to her destination. As she approached, the *goyishe* neighbors' threatening looks meant death. Another time she came close to the "holding area" for all of the detained Jews. A few times she found herself in the middle of the ghetto, near the synagogue, not far from the stable, but paralyzed by fear, she didn't approach. *Shkotzim* ran after her to see if she was a *zhiduvkeh*, a Jewish woman who was out alone. After several hours of fruitless wandering she made her way to the outskirts of the town, to the train station. Tired, hungry, and thirsty she sat down and burst into tears thinking that her child was probably dead by now, begging God for one last glance of her only son and her husband.

The farmers were now leaving the fields. She quickly wiped away her tears, as almost all of them cursed, "There goes another Jew." Her strength was almost gone and she didn't know where to turn. What consoled her was the thought of "our rescuer" miraculously arriving, and as if heaven had delivered a miracle, she noticed him standing only a short distance from her. He had come thirteen kilometers across the railroad tracks, past a town and a village. He motioned to her to follow him at a distance. She struggled to follow him until they arrived at our old field. He had her sit so that she could see all that was going on around her. He brought her a piece of stale bread and some water and told her to wait until late evening; he would return after his relatives, his neighbors and even the child would be asleep. He did indeed come for her late at night, bringing her some warm milk. He brought her to his house. She was able to quickly glance at her sleeping child, but then the dogs began to bark. The "rescuer's" son, who was standing guard outside to make sure no one was spying on them, told her to go to the stable attic to hide in a corner that had been prepared. He told her that the following day an even more secure hiding place would be made ready. You should know that my wife had a greater fear of mice than of Gestapo agents, and so she spent the rest of the night in a state of total and complete fear in the hayloft, alone in a stall, aware that mice were all about.

The next morning "our rescuer" went to town to see how I was doing. He didn't find me, but they told him I was still alive, and that another roundup was in progress.

When I found out in the morning that my wife left her first hiding place, I became so desperate that I lost my mind. I blamed myself for leaving her alone. The German I was working for volunteered to go and look in the place where Jews were arrested to find her — but he came back empty handed. Only at noon, our savior came back with a letter from her telling me what happened to her and where she was. He was very sorry about the people he know that were killed and was glad to help some other families to find a hiding place including Heynikh Neyman and his family, and the daughter of Menash Bilder and her husband (called Grinberg). He promised to help move them to Tluste, where the local Jews were living in relative security; and he kept his promise.

After all that, my German employer got me a written license from the *Lands Comissar* to be able to walk free — my wife and I — under the condition that we live with the other Jews and that my wife be the cook. She came back and we lived together in the Tsoyderer house. He had a special permit as a farmer, but we spent most of the time in the stable where I worked. The cooking job didn't last long because they started kidnapping the last Jews that were around. I saw and felt that it was the last month for us – that they were going to kill us soon.

The *Lands Comissar* got rid of his Jewish coachman (Spigel) and I was working very hard. I was not traveling with the boss and thus had to collect the furniture from the deserted Jewish homes and also to carry stoves for new roads. It was hard work for 18 hours a day. The work drained me and I couldn't decide what to do. The *Guspodarsh* had transferred some families to Tluste, but on his last trip some Ukrainian thugs robbed and beat the Jews, chasing them to the other side of the river half naked. He himself was beaten and ordered to go back to his house. So we cancelled the plan to go to Tluste. With the rest of my money, I managed to get my wife Arian papers, so she could travel with them to Lvov, Warsaw or even Germany. But she postponed her departure every day. She didn't want to live without us.

One day the *Kreislanowirt* (the person responsible for the county's agriculture) had a conversation in the presence of his secretary Genia. As I came in I saw that something was wrong because of her face. The inspector poured a wine glass for each of us and said to me, "I will be able to employ you only one more week. I'm going on vacation and my advice to you is to hide wherever you can, but don't trust the Ukraisians. If I can still hire you after I return, I'll do that."

He gave me 20 *zlotas* (enough for 20 cigarettes) for my hard work in the last months and left the room. His secretary told me later that he cried after he left the room.

The feeling that overtook me and the impression this meeting made upon my wife cannot be put into simple words. We stayed awake the entire night. We made all sorts of hare-brained plans. It was evident that when morning came my wife would have to flee, to be hidden by "our rescuer," if he would take her, and that I would stay behind and make the best of it. And after the eight days were up, I would find a hiding place among people I knew in town, and so wait out the official's return from furlough.

Our "rescuer" came to see us almost every day, often walking the twenty six kilometer distance, to see if we needed anything from him. One day, I told him of our plan — that my wife would have to travel that night to his house. He would pick her up with his wagon and then find a hiding place for her. He was very satisfied with the plan because he had previously thought that we had been afraid to go to his home. He said that many others had expressed this fear, because it was known that his family had a reputation for being thieves and murderers. He said, "I will dig a hole for the both of you, because I now know you will also come." This kind and worthy farmer didn't ask how much it would cost to hide us, or for how long. Rather, he rejoiced in being trusted to help us out.

That same night my wife arrived in his wagon without incident. That day he had made a hiding place for her in a haystack. I remained alone, without a home or a family, miserable for eight days and nights, obsessed with being betrayed by someone. I stayed with several known and trusted Christians. But I was still disappointed because my other good friends, Poles and Ukrainians — whomever I asked for assistance — all made the same poor excuses, saying that I should either sit in a field somewhere or in a burnt-out empty house, or in a basement. They all said they would bring me food from time to time.

During this stretch of time, I drove around the *Lands-Comissar* who had always liked me. He asked me where I lived and if I was set for winter. On the seventh day he summoned me again. He asked me drive to the railroad station and pick up a load of potatoes and take them back to my house for the winter. My house, my home, no longer existed, and I was not in need of a load of potatoes. He felt slighted, and then suggested that the Ukrainian militia might be sent to arrest my wife and me. But before anything else happened, the cleaning-maid arrived and said, "The pharmacist, Passman, was just rounded up. A police officer and the manager, Buchovski, are also here. They're going to throw him into the cell at the ammunition center."

There was still a bit of daylight and I was able to see Buchovski, with the key in hand, followed by the Land Commissioner. Bringing up the rear was the poor pharmacist, stooped over white as a sheet, still in his white outfit. I stopped what I was doing, darted away through the field, and went to the home of the driver, Sarakovski.

Later on the watchman, Paraska, one of the other drivers, came and reported that right after the pharmacist was locked in his cell, they came looking for me in the stable. That afternoon, at five o'clock, they returned, but I had pleaded with Paraska to tell no one where I had gone.

The driver (Paraska) took me in as his houseguest. But on the second day, he began to feel a bit wary and stated that a safer place for me to hide would be with his brother-in-law. He said that the Land Commissioner had inquired about me again, threatening to beat him up if he didn't reveal my whereabouts.

When night came, I went with him to his brother-in-law's. I lasted there for a week before he threw me out. I had pleaded with him to allow me to stay one more night, because Paraska, had promised to bring over my sister and her child from Kolomyja. (Her husband had been taken away that week; she had pleaded with me to save her.) But it did no good; I realized that if I didn't make my getaway right now, they would hurt me. Even though it was very late at night, I knew it was the time to leave.

For the next eight days "our rescuer" arrived bringing milk, butter and cheese, flour, and greetings from all who knew me. Each day I would send him back with the letters I had written to the Christians I knew in town, telling them I was on the opposite side of the Dniester River, asking them to take me in and provide me with a hiding place.

There was a fellow named Mika who owed me a favor from way back. Dispirited and fearful, I made my way through the back streets always concealing myself when anyone came close. Thus, I was able to reach Mika's house. He immediately escorted me to the attic, because a washerwoman was at work in his house. I was feeling very cold, but my "soul felt warm" and I felt hope because my new "hiders" told me I could stay with them as long as I wished. In truth, they did much for me. They paid attention to my needs: they fed me well and comforted me. But it was not to last for long. They didn't do as much for me in the second week as they had done in the first. By the time the third week came, I knew I would have to leave.

During this time, I asked my sister by mail what I could do to help her and I informed her how I was doing. I even dropped hints as to my location. Meanwhile, my good friend Brash came back from his furlough. The dentist Kaufman and his family were still "free" within the boundaries of the town, even feeling a bit secure because he was working on the Land Commissioner's false teeth! We sometimes ran into one another at night. I pleaded with them to find out what was on the official's mind, but I was not to get an answer from them. Immediately after he fitted him with his false teeth, they all fled to a village hiding place provided by their old servant. Their hard work paid off: they survived and ultimately made their way to Israel. It was foolish to believe that me, a lowly driver, would be considered "useful" when the last Jewish doctor and dentist were no longer necessary.

My last best hope for a hiding place for my wife, my child, and me was with our worthy "rescuer." Our destiny would be to either starve or be saved together. That night, dressed in clothing to conceal my Jewish identity, I traveled alone through the town by wagon. (Our "boss" wanted to be sure we didn't travel together. If he were captured with me, his whole family would be implicated and then killed.) I moved about like the worst sort of criminal, along back streets and through fields in order to avoid the most dangerous zones, especially through the Polish village of Losyach. After three rough hours of driving, I finally arrived at "our rescuer's" home. Aside from my little boy, everyone else was awake. They awaited me, praying that I would safely arrive.

"Our rescuer's" son was in the field some distance away. He wanted me to walk with him through the fields so that the neighbors would not be able to see where we were headed. My wife and I spent the night and the next day in an "opening" of a haystack, barely able to discern daylight. After spending the night this way, we decided to dig a hole for ourselves because the haystack was barely tolerable, and secondly, because we were too likely a target to be searched out.

It was very difficult. We three, the "boss," his son and I, dug throughout the night; the horse hauled the dirt away. But we were able to finish only half the job. So we had to spend another day in the haystack, risking capture and being sent on to Germany. Fortunately, early snow began to fall early that morning and completely covered the freshly-dug earth and the wheel ruts. The "boss" wanted to delay our next move for one more day: first, the snow was still falling; second, they wanted us to travel by night so that we could get some sleep by day. But this was not possible. A pig from a neighboring village was missing and our "boss'" brother was being accused of stealing it. We were certain that they would come in search of the pig in the morning, because the village militia didn't do this sort of thing at night.

We dug the entire night, easily performing the work of ten people, but it was still not deep enough to lay down boards for a floor. We finally dug through the moist soil until we hit the water level. At four o'clock in the morning, December 15, 1942 we were finally able to descend into the pit. Above us we could hear footsteps. The pit was so cleverly fashioned that it was impossible to take notice or to find it even if a massive search was launched.

The pit was actually within the confines of the house. After we dug it out, we covered it with a false floor and made a kitchen area on its surface. The entrance to the pit was a small opening on the outside wall. In winter it was covered with straw; in summer, with turf. Each night the opening was uncovered so that we could go out into the fresh air, stretch out bones a bit, take care of our bodily functions, and have a hot meal. Early in the morning we could have some milk, bread and water, and then descend into the pit, the dank, dark hole, for sixteen to eighteen hours "stuck and bricked-in" so that no one would notice we were there. For the first few days we felt fortunate because we were all together again as a family, and more than anything else, near our dear son who was still in the rescuers house. Living in constant fear had worn us out. Before, we hadn't had enough sleep; we felt as if our bodies would fall apart. But now, all we did was sleep all day long.

After some time had passed, we were afflicted by the dark thoughts and wonderings about what might have happened to our relatives who resided in town, hiding here and there. Ever since the pit was dug, I constantly worried about their fate. And even our "rescuer," who had always helped them in any way he could, was now fearful of leaving the safety of his house, afraid that he would be arrested. Truly, without him we would have been lost. As time went on, our bodies began to suffer badly: we had toothaches and aches in our arms and legs from having to sit so long in unaccustomed positions.

And then our lot became even worse than before. Things were not only going badly for us, but our "rescuer" and his family were also suffering miserably. They constantly had colds; they felt worn out from having to live in fear both day and night of being arrested. Soon a brother-in-law who had known about our child came to live with them. At every waking hour he ranted at them for keeping the child because this was putting all of their families in danger. He said they should do to him exactly what other farmers were doing with the Jewish children they had promised to keep safely hidden: take them into town and abandon them, or kill them and then bury their bodies. When we heard this kind of ranting and raving, we felt our "rescuer's" wife and son would become angry and discouraged and would try to figure out how to finally get rid of us. I would then sit with them and promise them that my brothers in America would help them to become rich one day. The good "boss" would then continue his old ways of helping us, and things would quiet down once again.

The worst times for us were when the "boss" had to leave home. We felt uneasy, insecure in the pit because we always had to keep an eye out to be sure the entrance was well concealed. And it seemed that our son only made matters worse and they were becoming less patient and careful for his safety. One sister-in-law wanted to verify if he was a Jewish boy or not. She became very angry with them and made serious accusations. But the "boss" and his wife were truly angels. For the two years that she came around, they watched over our child, stopping her from grabbing the child and literally slitting his throat.

Once, in March, 1943 the "boss" was not at home. His sister in law endlessly scolded them about the little boy's presence. So the other family members hatched a plan to counter her. One night, when I entered the house, I noticed a high level of anxiety and anger. They told me that although they loved the child very dearly, it was becoming impossible to keep him given the attitude of the sister-in-law. They said that the child was becoming increasingly hard to handle because he didn't listen and had a mind of his own. They pointed out that my mother and sister, both in Tluste, could take over care of the child. Therefore, the best thing would be to send the child to them. But we knew that if we sent the child there, he would be lost to us forever. I would rather have perished then and there rather than take the chance of having to give my child up to the murderers. Meanwhile, the murderers on our side of the Dniester were coming over to the other side to do their share in the liquidation process. We grieved because there was no end in sight. I convinced the "boss" to supply my mother and sister with some food; I desperately wanted to hear some news about how they were doing, and I harbored the thought of joining them. He departed, carrying food for them, But he returned in two days with no news HB because the bridges over the river had been destroyed and it was impossible to get across.

That night, in the stable, he consoled us, saying that he would never "give away" the child. He said it was his duty to assure the survival of us all. You cannot even begin to imagine the sense of gratitude I felt toward him. My wife and I cried with happiness because fate had brought us such a good, kind person in our terrible time of suffering. We kissed him, and he cried as a deserving father might cry; he calmed our fears. He also talked with the members of his family and soothed their fears and their anger and they subsequently became kinder to us. They promised to take better care of our son. In those three days we aged ten years. My wife made a vow at this time to fast for two days each week, for a year. This lasted until the day of our liberation.

Our son was growing up. He went around covered in filth, in torn clothing, barefoot — even in winter, in snowfall — but he was still a smart little kid, and very handsome. Even the German murderers would carry him about lovingly and give him gifts of money. The other farmers felt compassion for him because (as they believed) his mother was in Russia and he was such a poor little child. They would say, "He's just as smart as a Jewish kid!"

The beggars who were still living in our old house, the same ones who had our daughter killed, still had nothing and so went around the area. They even traveled the twelve kilometers to the home of "our rescuer." This happened in July 1943. They immediately recognized the child from before.

That evening, our guardians told us about their presence. They were pained and fearful. They felt that now everything would come to an end because the beggars would certainly inform on them. The "boss'" wife said that the beggars said nothing. They simply stared at him, smiled, took the pittances they were offered and left the premises. The wife's brother scolded her for sending them on their way. He would have beaten their heads with sticks until they were dead and then buried their bodies. And no one would ever find out. Even the "boss," when he returned from the fields, scolded her for not detaining them until nightfall. He too, would have murdered them, and not even a little bird would let out a peep over it.

We were considering how best to take our child and hide him. One plan was to start a rumor that the beggars were enemy spies who should be immediately arrested. I thought it would be better to bribe them with gifts from my household and with promises of safety so that they would not reveal anything to anybody. The worthy and patient "boss" followed my instructions, with the stipulation that if anything were to go wrong, he would "do what needs to be done." The beggars were very happy about the bribe, promising to not reveal anything. The "boss" returned home satisfied, and every week he delivered food to the beggars. He even made moonshine for them from sugar cane he had stolen.

A few months later another bad thing happened, bringing with it fear and anxiety. The same sister-in-law who had previously argued with the "boss" undressed our little boy when she was alone with him. She was now convinced that he was a Jew. She began to threaten that she would reveal this information, and once again we thought that all was lost. We again began to hatch plan after plan to save ourselves, and we even began to wish our son would not continue to live.

The sister in law's husband, who was the "boss'" brother, also became angry, wishing that his wife would just go ahead and inform on the boy, but three conditions prevented him from doing so: first, he loved the child a bit; second, he too feared the Germans and preferred to be a low target for them so that he wouldn't end up a forced laborer in Germany; and most importantly, came the news that Italy was "out of the war" and that the Russian army was approaching. And even though his wife had told him about the child's Jewishness, she grabbed him in her strong hands threatening to strangle the living daylights out of him, bury him and flee alone into the woods if he divulged this fact to anyone. The child's parents could be important people in England or America, and if the Soviets were to find out what we did to him, we would "be goners," she said.

She then became quiet. She knew her husband would keep quiet. At about eleven o'clock in the morning, our dear rescuers let us know that "the sister in law would keep her mouth shut." Still, this did not quell our fears. It wasn't until they told us how she had threatened him. All of a sudden, two potential enemies were silenced, not to mention the good news about the advance of the Soviet troops. Even though our rescuers now tried in every way possible to keep us alive, my health was getting worse day by day. The damp ground, the lack of fresh air and adequate space had made us sick. Everything we touched was wet and mildewed. My wife's hair was beginning to turn white. The straw "floor" was always wet and moldy. Our heartbeat was becoming irregular; our bones became brittle; we suffered terrible toothaches and we stifled the pain with alcohol until they seem to crumble. Our eyes hurt from the filth and the lack of light. Our heads pounded day and night. We knew we couldn't ask more from "our rescuer" than he was able to give, nor did we wish to anger him in any way. But the worst part was the news, particularly the bad news – which the "boss's" wife always delivered first – about what was going on all around us in the villages.

The Rsenboym family, two sisters and a brother, were captured in their hiding place in a Polish home. They were beaten and tortured to death. The Polish man ran away from home and his family was put in prison. The Kvetsher family was discovered because of a suspicious baker who wondered about the amount of bread that the Polish family was buying. The Ornshteyn family, husband, wife and two children, were attached together with barbed wire and were taken like that through town. Many of the Polish citizens ran after them, spat on them, and watched while they were executed. The brother-in-law of our *Gospodash* was among the watchers and came home late.

The Hoizknecht family from Horodenka thought it could find a place to hide in the meadow after the initial roundup. The woman of the house and her two children, a boy and a girl, had fled there. The man was found dead three days later. After all the roundups were done, they succeeded in escaping to the other side of the Dneister River, but they were grabbed along with others in a subsequent roundup and most were shot and dropped into a pit. The son had been previously chosen to cut the hair from the heads of the dead. He was able to extract his mother, whose hand was broken, and his sister, who had been shot in the foot, from the pile. He was able to pull them to a spot in the woods near Yasenov. There, they were able to stay alive for three months, hiding by day and begging for food at night. The local murderers were informed of their presence. They proceeded to capture them, taking them to the cemetery and shooting them to death.

Not a week went by when we didn't hear such news. We listened to these stories in horror, and it took its toll on us. The "news" — newspapers, broadsides, and general announcements — all recounted the final judgment of those who would dare hide Jews — death and forfeiture of all belongings. This inspired the deepest fear in the local farmers. Rumors circulated that all of the Ukrainians in Poland would be exiled to Russia, their places taken by selected Germans and those who had been disabled in the War. A special edict was issued stating that identity cards would be required by all, even children, certifying that they were Christian. In addition to this, surprise visits were conducted. The murderers visited us a total of thirteen times. Once they came with long staves, searching everywhere, tapping the walls, the floors, the attic, the basement, and the stables, poking at the hayloft. They even poked the earth in the vegetable garden to verify if Jews were hiding in pits. We knew, because we had discussed this with "our rescuers," that if the murderers came, that they would notify us by tapping the "floor" three times when they arrived and twice when they had left. We would then dress very quickly and extinguish the lamp, hold our breath and wait for the murderers to come. It was a piece of luck that they never found us.

Not far from us, Itzeleh, a Jew from Toporovtse, was cornered. He used to visit us at night for something to eat. He had been hiding in a hayloft. He told us that when they poked him with their sharp staves, he was able to contain a shriek. Itzeleh wasn't quite normal any more: he would run through the fields like a lunatic, screaming loudly at God, blaming Him for taking away his wife and children. The peasants and sheepherders would give chase, but they were never able to lay their hands on him. He spent his days in a foxhole, creeping out of it at night to search for food. He held America responsible for his sufferings. From my hiding place, I once saw and heard the "boss" talking to his wife about him: "Itzeleh is here and he's hungry. Go give him something to eat." She said there was no food. He said, "Give him the leftovers that you save to feed the hogs. Just give him something." And he grabbed the last piece of bread, a pot of sour milk, and other leftover remnants of food and took it to Itzeleh. The fact is that Itzeleh is still alive today. He survived the terrible epoch, got married, and now resides in Czernovitz.

Our rescuers were typical poor farmers. Thirteen surviving Jews, now dispersed all over the world, were rescued by this Christian, his wife, and son from the murderers and the local anti-Semitic thugs. If Itzeleh's shirt needed to be washed because it was lice-infested, "our rescuer" would give him one of his own, or perhaps one of mine. He worried about Itzeleh's well-being. He cut his hair and trimmed his beard, knowing that he would never be paid back in any way, even though Itzeleh had once taken him to court over money owed for payment.

The last weeks before the liberation, we were almost on the verge of total exhaustion. Our saviors started feeding us with chicken, eggs, honey, and cakes. When needed, he went to the doctor to get us medicine, telling the doctor it was for his wife. Being afraid of informers, he needed frequently to submit to the demands of neighbors and work for them or sometimes give them different items from his home. When his wife complained about it, he consoled her and promised her that soon the situation would change and liberation was close. This went on until the 24th of March 1944, the day of liberation.

Allow me to describe the great day of our liberation. My wife and I were overwhelmed with happiness. I laughed and cried, shook and trembled. Mt wife acted as if she had lost her mind. She ran around, not being able to stay in one place at a time. The "boss" had to quiet her down, since calm was necessary at that moment.

As we heard the sound of nearby gunfire, we went to the entrance of the pit. Perhaps, as some had said, the Germans were burning the homes as they fled. It would have been dangerous to remain behind because the smoke might have choked us. Countless peasants, both on foot and in wagons, carried loot from the sugar mill and the ammunition dump that the Germans had not taken with them in their retreat. My rescuers also wanted to get in on the action, but we cautioned them not to do so.

Their son was always on the lookout for the latest news. When he came running toward the house in the afternoon, we knew that the Messiah had come! Their son came to the entrance of the pit, followed by his parents, blurting out the news that the Soviets had arrived in town! All three embraced us and we all cried in happiness. The son had spoken to the Soviet soldiers; he had seen the defeated Germans, with their heads hanging low, dirty, and unkempt, but he saw not a single Jew. He advised me not to travel to town, but I couldn't contain myself and went there two days later. At nightfall, he took me to the home of my two trusted friends, the ones who had hidden me for three weeks at the war's onset. These worthy Poles knew our hiding place. They would keep newspapers and have them sent to us. They consoled the "boss" by giving him hope for the future.

We were overwhelmed by our good fortune. But our sadness was also very profound. I was consumed by worry over the fate for my dear sisters, my mother, and sister-in-law; overcome by anguish for my friends and all the people I had known. I had known almost every Jew in town. I had gotten along well with all of them. The Soviet soldiers' lack of warmth and concern for us was palpable. If a Jewish soldier came by, one with a good Jewish soul, he empathized with us. If we pointed out one of the locals who had murdered our people, he tried to make it right. If only he could. All the other soldiers were indifferent or outright anti-Semitic. The only difference was that they were not murderers. A good and fine officer, a non-Jew, helped me send my first airmail letters to my brothers in America. He advised me to seek safe haven in Moscow, a strange city where no one knew who I was. He further advised me to live there as a Christian. This caused me to feel great sadness. And if not for the experience I shared with my rescuers, I would have felt that everything I had lived for was nothing but a waste, a sham.

The first Jews I encountered were the dentist Kaufman and his wife and two sons. I was so overcome with happiness upon hearing that they were still alive that I ran to them that night, having pleaded with a Jewish soldier to guide the way since it was still not safe to travel alone. We had known and loved one another for years. They had done everything they could for other Jews while they had lived with the Germans. They had given away everything they had. They had been jailed as criminals. But they had saved themselves by escaping to the home of their old servant. I found comfort in their company.

Little by little, twenty Jews showed up, arriving from the villages, from the fields and forests, from the other side of the Dniester. They were all in terrible shape, worn out in every way possible. Two families, the Frischlings, had successfully hidden in town and thereby saved themselves.

We, the "chosen" survivors, enjoyed our happiness only momentarily. Things were turning bad on the front. The Russians had retreated from beyond Stanislav and were now fifteen kilometers from our town. The Germans had launched an artillery offensive which pushed the few remaining Jews back to Czernovitz. We barely made our way back to our rescuers. But once there, despite the so-called liberation, it was impossible to remain, even if we had gone back into hiding: roaming bands of Ukrainian thugs were killing Soviets, Poles, and Jews and burning everything in their wake. Traveling at night was perilous. For two nights we sought refuge in a vast field, but the bandits were still close by. We fled to Sniatyn, not far from Czernovitz. But it was unsafe there as well. On the way back to Horodenka, I met the only remaining Jew who survived in Horodenka, successfully hidden by a Polish family. His name was Michal Heyman. His feet were still swollen from being "stuffed" in a cramped hiding place. He told me that his rescuers had to move out twice. They had to carry him away in their wagon.

We had to take back our child from our rescuers. He cried endlessly day and night because he wanted to go back home to his "mommy and daddy." They were saddened that he was leaving, but consoled us by saying he would quickly get used to us again. There was nothing more for me to do. My feeling of gratitude was endless, and mere words could never express the extent of it. This was the first thing I could do for them: after I had met a high-ranking Jewish officer (who brandished medals from the Battle of Stalingrad), he agreed to excuse him and his son from the required work details then in effect. When we took the child away, he made us promise we would always be attentive to his needs.

The situation in town was becoming worse. We tried to convince our rescuers to abandon everything and find refuge elsewhere. They heeded my advice and fled that night, only to be assaulted by bandits along the way. The younger family members were able to run for cover, but the older ones, the father of our rescuer who had done so much for our son, was captured and burnt alive, as everything around him was destroyed in the inferno. I had previously tried to find a place for him in a shelter for the elderly-infirm, but the family could not let him go. We were overcome with grief at his death. I was able to find a good place for our rescuer to live. I worked for the Soviets in an ammunition magazine. I also arranged for his son to work there.

If we were to remain, it would be amongst the resident murderers, in a state of constant insecurity, alone when loved ones lay in mass graves or in meadows or fields worked by farm animals, amongst horses and dogs, where tombstones become paving stones for the sidewalks — with the lettering facing up — and amongst the Soviets who were all evidently anti-Semites who allowed the Ukrainian militias to plunder and round up Jews. All of this is still a fresh memory.

This, all of this, was not why I had survived. Neither did I wish to abandon our rescuers, because I knew the Soviets would not let me cede ownership of my property . Thus, we left, leaving everything behind, for Krakow. We stayed in a refugee camp for a few weeks along with thousands of others. I wandered about aimlessly, taking in everything, noticing all the evidence of anti-Semitism.

From there, we went to Upper Silesia. I began to do something I had never done before: deal in contraband merchandise. My rescuers had received a letter from my brothers in America. We knew we would soon see them and everything would get better for us. I had spent more time worrying about my wife and son than actually providing for their welfare. But I knew I had to provide for my rescuer. I secured grain, two cows, a horse, swine, and fowl for them. But it was so little compensation for all they had done. I gave them everything I had.

But the day of reckoning finally came then we had to bid farewell to them. With my brothers' help, and the help of the Jewish Worker's Committee in Silesia, we obtained a visa to travel on to Sweden that listed me as an agriculturalist. I arrived in America as a "visitor." If I had had the opportunity for my rescuer to accompany me to America, I would have grabbed the chance! They had earned the right. They deserved this honor! And I would also declare to all our fellow Jews, and non-Jews, as well, the following: Whoever truly wanted to save a life could have done so! I sent them whatever assistance I could from Sweden; we sent them help from here as well, but it is never enough. My desire is to bring them here so that I can support them and eternally show them my gratitude. My son should always be able to call them "mommy and daddy, and know that they are as much his true parents as we are, because they saved him from certain death.

We are finally free. We are now safe and secure. But our rescuers are suffering: their neighbors and extended family members are jealous because they receive packages from us. They are all unflinching anti-Semites who feel cheated because some Jews had been rescued. They take some of the things we send to our rescuers. They curse the rescuers saying that no decent Pole would ever think twice about not saving Jewish lives that Poles such as these do not deserve to reside amongst them. They say Poles such as they should be buried. The rescuers now survive in fear in their own fatherland, surrounded by native enemies.

If only I live long enough to have the chance to bring them here to live with us so that we may properly thank them on our behalf, and on behalf of the other Jews they saved from certain death.

חורש
קדושי הורודנקה

[Page 322]

With The Russian Army

Moshe Schuchner

Translated by Dalya Yohai

On June 1, 1941, nine days after the Russians started retreating, there was a great fear and depression in Horodenka. I never saw anything like it. At the same time, we started hearing that the Germans were approaching and about other towns and villages that were under their occupation. We didn't know where they were coming from and nobody knew what to do —to stay or to go with the Russian army. We saw on the faces of the Ukrainians what could be expected from the Germans. They [the Ukrainians] walked in the streets, happy and celebrating our helplessness. They even said it quite clearly that they hoped it was judgment day for the Jews and a day of revenge for them.

Many of us started realizing that the only solution was to go with the Russians toward the East. The Russians were willing to help anybody who joined them. They asked the Ukrainian farmers to use their carts to help with transportation. Each of us could take only a few personal belongings because most of the space was saved for transporting food. The Jews who had carts could join easily. Mendel-Shmuel Gotlief and his family came with their cart and we packed in it all the shoes we had in stock from the shoe cooperative in town. People who ran away felt very heavy-hearted about leaving. We left without any knowledge of what the future would bring and what would happen to us.

After traveling some way, we looked like Gypsies. At first, we hoped we would be able to return to Horodenka in a month or two. But we lost this hope after seeing that the retreat was taking forever. Among us, there were people who regretted leaving; some Ukrainians also told us to go back since all of Russian would be conquered anyway. But most of us didn't listen and continued with the army.

On the way, we were attacked a couple of times by German planes; but nobody died. Toward the evening, we arrived at the Zbrutch River. We crossed the bridge that was once the border between Russia and Poland. With us we had German prisoners under heavy guard. At night we heard planes again. They discharged parachuters who landed next to the place where the prisoners were being kept. There was a big battle between the Russians and the Germans with lots of dead on both sides. In the chaos the prisoners ran away. Our camp — the refugee camp — was far away from there, but still we suffered casualties. We then started running eastward to get out of danger.

Many of the Ukrainians used the chaos to disappear as well. We were left a little band of refugees without any food or supplies.

I arrived at Viniza with 10 other refugees, two carts, and no food whatsoever. I met there the Gotlieb family, the two sons of Wolf Ticker, and the youngest daughter of Gutman, the Kleizmer. I continued on my way with the Gotlieb family. On the way, we met Itzi Pettner, the oldest son of Efrain Pettner. He enlisted in 1940 and was serving as a commander in the Russian army.

We traveled around 800 kilometers and got into Russia, almost 100 kilometers from the Dnieper River. I was so exhausted that I couldn't continue and they left me behind. The day after, I recovered and continued with the army until we reached the military base. There I enlisted!

[Page 323]

How I Saved Myself

Yatke Kiehl-Piekarek

Translated by Harvey Buchalter

In 1939, as the war was just beginning, Horodenka was taken from the Russians. The lot of the Jewish population wasn't too badly off. There were eight children in our family, six sons and two daughters. In 1941 three children were preparing to get married: my sister Raiza, my brother and I. My sister and I did indeed get married, but my brother was not destined to say his vows, for in August 1941 the Germans advanced upon our town, worsening the lives of the Jews.

On December 5, 1941, the first "action" occurred. The Germans assembled all the Jews in the Great *Shul*. Then the elderly were loaded onto trucks and driven to Semakovitse. The younger ones, both men and women, were marched there on foot. Graves already had been dug; they were then shot.

After that action, few Jews remained in the town. The Germans then created the *Yudenrat* (Council) and declared that the Jews who were left would have to pay for the bullets that had been used to annihilate the Jews who had just been taken away.

The sense of fear was palpable. After the first action, there were two smaller actions. Thus the Germans were able to decimate the

Jewish population. I remained with my family and by the end of the summer of 1942, we left for Tlusle, where Jews were still living undisturbed. But this didn't last long. Two weeks after our arrival in Tluste, close to the High Holy Days, the very same SS criminals came and began to make the Tluste region "Jew-free" (*Judenrein*). They assembled us in the town square. My husband and I were there, along with my husband's sister and her husband and their three children. They took everyone to the train station, pelting us with their fists unmercifully along the way.

At the train station they loaded us as if we were cattle into filthy boxcars. We traveled for an entire day without knowing our destination and without any hope whatsoever. With us were the following persons: Elke Glager and her sister; Yossel Landerheim's wife and children, and many other Horodenka folk. All cried out to God Almighty to perform a miracle, to strike the Germans with lightning or bombs. But no miracle occurred, and so we traveled along, endlessly.

Then a thought came to my husband. He had a pocketknife with him, and he began to pry up the nails in the boards of the wagon. Others started to do the same. Some people in the boxcar didn't approve of this and they began to scream: "You are making sure we will all be shot! You are bringing about bad things for us!" But those who were removing the nails paid them no heed and went back to work. Thus, they succeeded in ripping off a few boards and then they began to jump through the holes in the bottom. I was then eight months pregnant. Nevertheless, I also jumped and thereby saved myself from certain death. It was evening time, and I found myself all alone. I began to go back, running rather than walking. On the way, I encountered Tansi Schuchner, her sister and young boy. We were now a group of four. We came to Terebovlya. We went to a house and knocked on the door, but they didn't let us in. We had no luck at all; we slept in the open air. In the morning we went back to the same house and they gave us something to eat and drink. They also told us that a new assault was in the works, and that was why they hadn't opened the door.

I had wanted to meet up with my husband and his family, so we continued on foot. We spent that night in another town. In the morning, my husband appeared! He had also spent the night in this town, in a nearby house. He related that he had also been in Terebovlya, in another part of the same house where I had spent the night. Our happiness in finding one another cannot be described. We again departed. Each town that we encountered had a few remaining Jews.

In Kopychintsy, the Jewish Council provided us with a place to stay. Then we went back to Tluste. On the way, *goyim* assaulted us.

We slapped one of them in the face so hard, that he ended up bleeding all over me. We barely escaped with our lives. I sometimes lost touch with my husband; each time we encountered German soldiers or others who would harm us, we would scurry to the fields to hide. With great effort, we succeeded in returning to Tluste.

In December 1942, I gave birth to a sweet, bright little girl. There was still constant military action going on around Tluste. I once ran away with my child in hand, bullets flying scarcely above my head. I ran off to the fields and stayed there for three days without even a bit of water. My husband crept about looking for me among the dead. When I returned, alive, we were truly in heaven. I once received a telegram from my husband's sister saying that she was in Terebovlya, but from then on, I no longer heard from her.

After a short time, they liquidated the ghetto in Tluste. Abraham Schneiderman's wife encountered me, along with Busieh Steiner and other folk from Horodenka. They told me that they were going to return there. They said good-bye to us and it saddened me greatly that I had to remain there atone with a small child. There was a labor camp in Tluste. My family and I ended up at the camp. We did field work there, always suffering terribly from hunger and cold. In 1943, my own child was "'liquidated." We stayed in the camp until 1944. At that time, the Germans retreated, abandoning us. Soon, the first Russian tanks appeared. Everyone celebrated, kissing and crying with happiness. But then a squadron of German airplanes flew overhead and began to bomb the camp. I fell down alone, sick, solitary, and broken. And then I spent a long time in the hospital in Tscharkov where they removed shrapnel from me; symptoms of this still remain with me.

In 1946, I married a fine man in Poland, and now we are living in Israel, in Haifa. We live a free and decent life. But I will never forget the years of my bitter experience.

[Page 324]

Escape to Romania

Zvi Reiss

Translated by Harvey Buchalter

Following the second wave of assaults in April 1942, the remaining survivors began in earnest to devise a survival strategy. The Germans had begun to divide the Jews according to their vocation (or according to the bribes that were paid) and everyone began to guess which of the groups would be the "fortunate ones," the ones who would be able to stay alive until the end. The groups weren't just composed of Horodenka folk, but from those who remained alive from the whole region. People from one region didn't necessarily know people from other regions. Thus, it was difficult to organize a plan. Each had to concern himself with his own plight, and that of his family, if he still had one. Our family, my father, my brother, and I began to search for a way to save us and remain alive to the end — the end of the war.

One of our perilous options was to cross the Romanian border, but his was full of difficulties and extremely dangerous. Also, a great deal of money would be needed and one could never know what would happen if you succeeded in crossing, or if you could hide once you got across. So we left the door open to all possibilities. After the second wave of assaults, we received news that several had succeeded in coming to Czernovitz with the help of border smugglers and with lots of money to bribe the border police. But this route was treacherous because all of the Ukrainian villages on the way to Czernovitz were already "free of Jews" (*Judenrein*); the peasants worked hand in glove with the German police who posted rewards for those who would come forth and betray hidden Jews.

During the summer, we occupied ourselves with thinking and planning. In September 1942, the third and decisive military assault occurred in Horodenka. Following this one, the town would be free of Jews *(Judenrein)*. My family and I were at this time outside the ghetto in my grandmother's house, outside the city limits, on the road to Serafinitz. There we made ourselves a temporary hiding place. The military action lasted for three days, unlike the previous one, which had lasted only a day or two. We didn't have any food for a long while. After the third day, we had to get out of the shelter in order to find food and find out what was happening in town. We found out from the peasants that Horodenka had been declared free of Jews. We still had a strategy, but we knew that we would have to get to Czernovitz. Because there was no time to find a border smuggler, and knowing that even with one, the route was uncertain, we decided to try our luck and penetrate the border, relying only upon ourselves. In that same night we fled from Serafinitz and slipped through the border to Romania.

The group which had been hidden in the shelter (and which crossed the border) were seven souls: my father, Fishl Reys; my six-year old brother, Smireh Reys; and myself, along with my four cousins: Leisa, Rochel, Hirsh and Abraham Ladenheim. In considering the border, we chose a spot on the Romanian side on a hill approximately two kilometers from our point of departure. And so we broke up in order to cross one-by-one. The border was guarded and always patrolled with spotlights, and so we had to cross by crawling along toward the appointed meeting place.

Although we all crossed the border, not everyone met up at the appointed place. My father and my brother, who had taken off together, got lost. We waited for them two hours — two precious hours. I went around everywhere in search of them, but I saw nothing tin the darkness, nor did I hear anything. So I made my way back to the meeting place in order to go on. We arrived at a field where there were *kukurudzes* and we thought we could remain in hiding for the day. But early the next morning, the peasants who came out to work noticed us and went to the village to call the Romanian police.

The police allowed us live. They rounded us up and delivered us to the police in Bararutz, beating us along the way. There we suffered the punishment of Romanian "interrogation." They made us strip naked and one by one marched us to the interrogator who also beat us. As they returned us to our holding cells, they took off with our clothing, all except the bare necessities, leaving us with absolutely nothing.

We begged for one thing only at the interrogation: that they not send us back to Poland. After being jailed for a day, they agreed to honor our one request. They would not send us back, but rather take us to Czernovitz. We found out later that this was indeed a stroke of luck because we were the first ones that had been caught and detained. The groups that were captured after us were all shipped back to Poland and were then given over to the Gestapo.

We walked from Bararutz in three days, escorted by Romanian police. At each station, we were "interrogated" the Romanian way, accompanied by a beating.

In Czernovitz we were jailed in the *osterplatz* (square) and the "interrogation" began anew. But this time, it was more humane. They even asked us if we had any complaints about the way the police treated us in Czernovitz. We answered the only way we really could, that the treatment was good. We remained in jail awaiting the decision of the regime about what to do with the Jews who had been detained, those who had fled Poland. With us were approximately fifty detainees out of the thousands who had attempted to cross the border, most of whom had been unsuccessful.

The treatment by the police in Czernovitz was humane, thanks to the concern and intervention of the l*ehiloth* (Jewish community council). Even though the country had suffered greatly in the war, twelve thousand Jews still remained in their homes, out of total of seventy thousand before the war. The Kehiloth provided us with food and clothing and they appealed on our behalf (to the government) that we be allowed to work. Still we didn't know what would finally happen to us,

A few Jewish detainees who became ill were taken to the Jewish Hospital, without guards, under the eye of the hospital management. After I had been in jail for a week, I spiked a high fever and they took me to the Jewish Hospital as well. My cousin Leiza Ladenheim had been taken there earlier. While I lay there with a high fever, I found out that by order of the Romanian regime all detainees were to be taken back to the Polish border and handed over to the Gestapo. The detainees who were in the hospital were not taken away because the police ordered that the sick not be disturbed until their health improved. This provided a way out for the fourteen hospital patients. The hospital staff went out of its way to make sure we would not get well too quickly, that we should be under medical care and not under the thumb of the Romanian police. The hospital staff, Dr. Landay (he is now living in Israel) showed unselfish concern for us. In addition to the hospital staff, the members of the *kehiloth*, and especially the Jews from Czernovitz, extended themselves to us in every way. They spent all of their waking hours with us in the hospital. At the High Holy Days they took us to Jewish homes, Dr. Landay always risking himself by allowing us to leave the hospital grounds.

The detainment camp lasted only a short time before the Russian front advanced to Romania. Two weeks earlier, the Romanian police hadreleased us and provided us with documents allowing us to go wherever we wished. But it should be known that this was essentially a cover-up: all they wished to do was put on the appearance of having conducted themselves benevolently with the doomed Jews.

[Page 326]

How We Saved Ourselves

Shaindel (Sophie) Yungerman Alfert

Translated by Harvey Buchalter

As soon as the Russians retreated from Eastern Galicia in 1940, the Hungarians arrived in Horodenka. The town was then relatively quiet. The Hungarians ordered the Jews to perform the forced-labor task of building the bridge in Siemakowcze. In the performance of this task, one Hungarian officer stood out for his cruelty and sadism. Around the town and in the villages, pogroms against the Jews had already started. The Ukrainian peasants had viciously murdered entire families or had run them off. Because of this, all Jews in the villages had to abandon their homes and flee to the towns.

A few weeks later, the first Gestapo arrived and declared the establishment of a Jewish Council (*Judenrat*). My husband, Dr. Alpert, didn't want to serve on the Council because he knew he would have to cooperate with the Germans. But other members of the Jewish intelligentsia worked with the Council.

Shortly afterwards, the Gestapo in Horodenka warned the Council that a pogrom would start unless they were bestowed with "expensive presents." Two members of the Council, Dr, Schneider and the dentist, Koyfman, went around collecting the "gifts'" for the Gestapo. The also visited my daughter, Rena, who without thinking, gave them a precious ring with two diamonds in it. By doing so, she had hoped to save some of the Jews of the town. But a few weeks later the Gestapo came back and forced the Jews to abandon their homes and move into the ghetto. To bring this about, they closed several streets around the Great *Shul*. They were cordoned off and guarded by the Ukrainian police. Only a few Jews received permission to live outside the ghetto — mainly those who worked with the Germans. But even they were still not fully protected from all of the persecution which the Jews inside the ghetto were condemned to suffer.

As the first wave of assaults was taking place, we went into hiding with a Polish neighbor. We were hiding in the attic, on straw, when we heard the German police ask if there were any hidden Jews. The woman answered that there were no Jews hiding with her. Twenty-five hundred Jews perished in the first wave of assaults. All of them, men, women, and children, were brutally removed to Siemakowcze. Once there, they were shot, their bodies falling into freshly dug graves.

A few weeks later, another pogrom was enacted against the Jews. But this time they knew beforehand and hid, so that the persecutors nabbed only one hundred and fifty — shooting them all inside the Great *Shul*.

When the third wave of assaults came, at Passover 1942, we went into hiding with the Polish teacher Vartanovitch. On the last day, when the assault had ended, someone informed on us and the Ukrainian police chased us from the attic and took us to the place where Jews were "assembled" to be sent away. As luck would have it, the transport had already left, so they released us. The teacher's wife was arrested as an example to others of what would happen to those who hid Jews. She was paraded with the captive Jews all around the town. My nephew Weissinger bribed the Ukrainian home-police to return her home. After the assault, my daughter and her husband Aaron Weissinger and son Mundek escaped to the other side of the Dniester River, toward Azieran, where Jews could still live freely.

My husband and I, along with our small grandson, Leon, soon left for there. In Horodenka, all that remained were about one hundred Jewish families of doctors and artisans who worked with the German police. In Spring 1943, Horodenka was declared *Judenrein* when the last Jewish families were chased to Kolomyja, and then, in various sites, liquidated. Among them were Sigghe Zeidman and his wife, Felah, who was a nurse and who had worked for the Germans in the hospital. My sister, Anna Zeidman, was also murdered while she attempted to save herself and her small grandson by getting out of Kolomyja with Aryan documents. A Christian recognized her at the Kolomyja train station and informed on her. For using Aryan documents, she was executed. My oldest sister, Giselle Bartfeld, held out in Horodenka until 1943. After that, she was recognized and then arrested. At that time, there were no longer Germans in Horodenka, only the Ukrainian home-police and the native, so called folk-Germans. The folk-Germans took my sister to the Jewish cemetery and there beat her to death with sticks. Christians who witnessed it told me how in her pain she cried out that Hitler would lose the war and that his accomplices would be painfully murdered.

When we crossed the Dniester and came to Azieran, there was total panic and great sadness among the Jews. A few days earlier the German police and the Gestapo fell upon the Jews and drove them all to one site, shot some of them there, and packed the remaining ones onto trucks and sent them off to a faraway camp. Shortly afterward, Azieran was declared "free of Jews," and the few Jews who remained had to go over to Bartshub where another ghetto had been established. For a few months, we lived together with the other Jews in the ghetto. A few were taken to the work camps at Lisoowce, while a few escaped to the woods, where they were often hunted down and murdered by the peasants. This is what happened to my dear son Mundek: In the ghetto and in the camps a typhus epidemic broke out, and Germans liquidated a great many of those who fell ill. My husband, Dr. Alpert, also died this way.

Through all of these horrible experiences, a very few succeeded in staying alive. And so I remained alive, along with my two remaining sons. Now we live in New York.

[Page 327]

The Murder of the Jews of Serafinitz

Yitchak Hoffman

Translated by Harvey Buchalter

One goes with a heart laden with grief to the graves of our parents. Still more grievous is the disinterring of the graves (revealing the memories – trans.) and tearing at the wounds, still unhealed, never to be healed. Herein, I will relate the holocaust of the forty families of the village of Serafinitz, from which only two or three solitary persons were saved.

1939. This is the year of the first wave of German assaults upon Poland and the beginning of troubles for the Jews. The Russians, eager to take back a piece of the Polish "inheritance," quickly march into Galicia, and what the Poles and Ukrainians were unable to carry out in the space of years, the Germans accomplish in one day. They fashion a pauper from the Jewish community. The little shops are closed; all property is nationalized; the rich Jews are exiled to Siberia or some such place in Russia. The remaining Jews have to seek whatever work still exists. A portion of the Serafinitz Jews abandons the village and goes to the town of Horodenka. Our hearts are anguished as we witness the ground being slipped beneath their feet. And yes, the Russians call this "liberation." But the "liberation" is short-lived. A year later, other 'liberators' arrive. This is the German army which begins the process of liberation anew, and not with the finesse of the Russians. They take on an additional partner, the Ukrainians, and that is when the troubles really begin.

As soon as they tossed the Jews from their homes, they forced them into backbreaking work, goaded by beatings and terrorism; forbidding the selling of food to Jews; not allowing Jews on the sidewalks; forcing them to wear a white band on the right arm. And finally, cold-blooded murder. I will never forget the 4th of December, 1941, when 2,800 Jews were forced out of Horodenka to Mikhal'che in one day, and there, in the middle of the forest, buried — buried alive in a mass grave.

Thereafter, as the greater part of the Jewish families of Serafinitz went willingly or were forced to go to Horodenka, four or five families remained behind in Serafinitz as "useful" Jews. I was in this group, and I survived all the suffering that is possible to endure. I saw death come more than once before my eyes. More than once I shouted, "So, this is the end." The fear of death engulfed me day and night, but when the will to live is strong, you stay alive.

When the Germans came into Serafinitz to see what was happening, there were only seven families: Bergman, Hoffman, Reif, Singer, Ekerling, Geniger, and Reys, and also two sisters from another Bergman family. The rest were already in Horodenka. The first casualty from the Serafinitz Jews was a girl from the Ekerling family who was taken from them very quickly. She was found a few weeks later lying in a field, dead. On the 4th of December, 1941, the Geniger family was murdered in Miklal'che along with the two Bergman sisters and the Ekerlings. The family members who remained lived together and worked for the Germans at the border-crossing station — the women as housekeepers; the men as wood-choppers, restroom cleaners, and other hard and dirty work. This lasted until August 1942. In the month of August, all the Jews were assembled, "concentrated" in the Horodenka square near the train station and transported to Belzetz. A small portion of them had attempted to flee to Romania on several different roads, but only a very few were successful in getting across the border. The others were captured by the Germans and shot.

[Page 328]

The Tragic End of the Korniv Jews

Aryeh Lagstein

Translated by Dalya Yohai

In the village of Korniv, in the county of Horodenka, there were 20 families, mainly involved in small businesses or agriculture. The main farm also belonged to a Jewish family – the Rubels. They were known for their wisdom. Some of the younger generation held academic titles. There were also Hebrew speakers among them and the village became a center for Zionist activity.

The two oldest families were the Lagsteins and Rubels and they were connected by marriage. These families were very influential in the village.

As one of the small group of survivors from Korniv, I would like to talk about some of the earnest people in the village:

Dr. Shlomo Zalman Lagstein was a successful lawyer, an economist and agronomist, a fine and beautiful soul, learned in the Bible and very devoted to the Zionist idea. He took care of his fellow Jews until the last moment of his life. In terrible times he went to the

Gestapo's commanders and spoke on behalf of his brothers. A couple of times he succeeded in saving them; but not for long. The destruction man chine worked in time and in 1942, during the last "action" in Horodenka, he went with his fellow brothers and sister to Belzetz. Even during those days he continued writing his book *Pax Vobicum*. In it he wanted to tell about the horrors. But this manuscript died with him. Very deep in my heart is his memory engraved; he was unique among the Jewish Polish community.

Aaron Lagstein founded the Buslia in Kornev and the other villages around. He also founded the *Hit'achdut* movement and *Poalei Zion*. He was also a member a *HaChalutz* and was prearing to move to Israel. But he was murdered before he could realize his dream. He was killed in Horodenka during the first "action."

Yedel Bercher was a good hearted, innocent man and always helped anyone in need. A couple of times a week he would come to Horodenka and bring dairy products; he always asked everybody what they needed. He was killed in Botchash in the of the Actions.

Among the elders, Rabbi Nehemya Machen Lagstein was a real scholar and a devout man. His home was used as a synagogue. Sometimes on holidays and Shabbat he officiated with a Bible. He was a respectable figure.

Rabbi Eliezer Rubel was the owner of the farm in Korniv. Despite his status he was one of the community. He and his family were involved in community life and participated in Zionist activities. During the was he was exiled to Siberia and died there.

[Page 329]

The Fate of a Picture

Mendel Dul

Translated by Harvey Buchalter

I have been asked to set forth some memories of Horodenka, and I beg the indulgence of my former students from Horodenka if my present perspective makes me now see certain things differently than I did before. Over three dozen years have gone by since those times, and each of you has experienced them in your own way, and none of the details have been lost.

I lived in Horodenka for five years, from September 1924 to the end of 1929. I was a mathematics and religion teacher in the *gimnasia* there. This was the beginning of my career. I lived in the residences of my students and, along with their parents, was immersed in the ups and downs of their lives. The town was as dear to me as the town of my birth, and even years after my departure, as I would randomly run across a former student or an acquaintance from Horodenka, my happiness was equal to the happiness of someone who runs across a dear friend from bygone days. When I began my tenure, there were ten-, twelve-, or perhaps fifteen-year-old children, who, in the course of five years, developed physically and emotionally. They went from being small, quiet little children to mature young adults with both a worldly outlook and broad horizons. Many of them continued their studies after completing the *hoich shul* and moved all over the world. Many now live in Israel and have very important positions and are useful citizens. Sarah works as a nurse; Sala, Gedalia, and Kalman are attorneys; Fala is a diplomat; Yehuda and Atek are engineers; Imek is a physician; Milos is a well-known urologist; Olis is a chemist; Max and Mashke are pharmacists; Necha is a community activist, and so on. I frankly didn't recognize some of them. The little children of the old days had become fathers and mothers themselves. They experience the joys and worries of their own children, and perhaps even with their children's children. I now recall two fragments from my store of memories.

The year is 1928. It is somewhat hot outside, but we dOn't feel it in our classroom. The old building housing the Horodenka *gimnasia* has a large open space in front, with many old trees and in the rear, the rocky, sloping meadow. The seventh grade class is divided into two sections: roughly twenty Jewish students go to the class devoted to studying religion, and eight Christian children remains. (This is meant to satisfy the priest and also the predominant ethnic group.) When the bell clangs both students and teachers knows that the break has come to an end. Silence reigns in the classrooms. A young teacher enters the religion classroom. She has black curly hair. She glances at the students and says, "Today we are going to study the story of Joshua." Each student is at a different level. The students whose Hebrew reading skills are weak protest.

But those who had gone through *cheder* are anxious to read. Kalman quickly opens his Bible. His bright face beams with joy. "Yes, yes," he says, "I want to read." "Teacher, I want to read," Yehuda shouts.

And the always eager Sala opens his eyes wide, raises his hand and looks at the teacher. Even Emek, who secretly reads books on his own during the lecture, tears his eyes away from his book and looks alternately from his teacher to the other students. Davka reads first. His final few words are delivered with a resounding voice, and then he sits down once again.

"Teacher," asks Sigmund who was raised an orphan by his uncle, a religion teacher as his father, an attorney, lived in Zaleshchiki, "will Israel rise up to be the light of the world, as the prophet foretells? And if so, will we live to see it?"

"Yes," Sala answers him convincingly, and reads the text.

"Yes," says Yehuda. "We, our generation, hope to see it happen in our lifetime, and the prophecy will come to pass."

The class becomes animated; a lively discussion ensues. Even those students who resist reading the Bible listen quietly to what their comrades are saying. They don't hear the bell clang, which indicates that the class is ending, that the "break" is coming to an end. The *shamas* Brevovski claps his hands to give notice that the teacher in the next class is waiting for his students.

There, in front of the class, stands the Latin teacher Bongarten, who every one calls "Ficus." He demands, "Why did you keep them for so long? You were probably telling the entire story of the Exodus."

A year later in the display window of Stefanovitch's bookstore there hung a photograph of all of the students and teachers in the eighth grade. For an entire week, parents, relatives, acquaintances and random passers-by, both Jews and Polish, went to look at the photo. This was the first ever class-photo, and it created quite a sensation.

Look at it, one student would say to another. The one in the Slovakian shirt is Emek, the one with the stiff collar and necktie is Sala, and the one in the middle is Maska. But our class picture next year will be even better, they would say.

The year is 1943, barely fifteen years later, in Berzin. The Jews are concentrated in the ghetto. There are epidemics, round-ups, hunger, and deprivation; each day results in more deaths. Only a few individuals reside outside the ghetto. In the two-story house of the Ukrainian Social Club, in the large meeting room, an official presides. He is a Karaite, and can prove this with his documents. (Karaites are a sect on the fringes of Judaism. They reject the Talmud, and evidently were not "counted" as Jews.) His superior officer, Paslovski, is satisfied with his work. All of the directors — there were three of them — know that he is a good worker, and a mathematics instructor. But every day they look him over very carefully to see if he could possibly be a Jew. And the boss tells him from time to time that his wife is also a teacher and that she comes from Horodenka. Another time he tells him that a certain Dr. Grubin, a Pole, used to work for the German Red Cross, but was soon found out to be a Jew from Vizhnitza, and that his real name is Dr. Rubin. He fled, and as he tells the story, he looks me up and down to see what kind of impression it has on me. In fact, every day he would tell me stories such as this, especially on the days that round-ups took place. He would speak to me this way, as the streets ran with Jewish blood. Sometimes I let my mind wander.

Once I started to think about being in my old classroom. The children are studying when suddenly I hear the familiar voices of *daavenning* ... This is how I went about my work.

Once, after a dawn round up, he came into the office very happy to tell me that he had found a new place to live, a small one-family house with a vegetable garden. He had taken over the residence of Baumgarten, one of the Jews appointed to oversee affairs in the ghetto, who had been killed several days ago. Baumgarten had two sons, one of whom had been a teacher in Horodenka, and among the books in the house was a school yearbook from the Polish *gimnasia* in Horodenka. In it he read that there was a teacher of Jewish religious studies that had the same last name as I had, but with the name of Mendel. He was a Karaite with the name of Maximilian, and ... a mathematician. He also discovered a photograph there, but, he said, the religious studies teacher in the picture did not resemble me.

The fate of a picture!

Two weeks later I resigned from this post and found another with the Polish Relief Committee.

The War came to an end. I was no longer useful to them, neither was my wife and child. Now I live in Haifa. And the first picture of my class in the Polish *Gimnasia* in Horodenka remained in Berzin with Paslovski.

[Page 331]

My Father

Martin (Motl) Birnboy

Translated by Harvey Buchalter

And I will never know
Where your final cry was silenced.
Not which horrors of your final hours
Brought you
To your death.
The messenger of death brought me the letter.
And something tore me up inside.
And with weighted weariness, I closed my eyes.

I had no tears.
So many Jews, so many Jewish fathers taken.
How can I weep for one alone?
Alone, I capture you in imagination for one last time.
To see you, for the last time,
With a smile.
On the train station in Horodenka,

And now, perhaps,
If your yahrtzeit falls, or has come and gone.
But you never taught me the Kaddish customs, the Yahrtzeit rites,
You invested belief in people, a boundless civilization.
Your faith invested in Everyman.

You were proud.
A proud Jew with worldly tastes,
The worldly life was your ideal.
Your sustaining breath breathed life into our home.
You were smart, and up-to-date and clever.
In old Horodenka,
Your words caused others to think,
Your thoughts dwell in their memory.

Where did your insights stem from?
This life battered you, orphaned and poor.
Still you opened your eyes to the world.
Poor, through war and pogrom.
Through hunger and want.
You made your way through life,

Like the waters of a wide stream, a whirlwind carries your thoughts.
Connecting you always to your shtetl, with thoughts of love.
And though you strayed from its heart, you ran.
Then you returned.
And promised at the end that you would rather die here.
A poor Horodenka Jew.

I choose today to celebrate your yahrtzeit.
And I feel your presence in my salty tears.
And I see you hands preparing to write, as I do now, hunched over.
When in the First War, they murdered our mother, taking from you
Your only one, your wife.

After the funeral, at home
You quietly sang a sad melody.
Your lips, hidden beneath a black moustache, twitched.

Outside, the wind and snow lapped the house.
I will never forget your final lament.
A lonely, wrenching cry.

Entrapped within the conflagration.
As she was, you are now, as well.
If you were not more than tinder for the fire.
If your being was not the blood and song of the fire.
If you had not seen all the witnesses themselves go up in smoke.
The ashen hands of Germans incinerated all.

None were left.
In tiny Horodenka.
Not the feuding housewives, not even the gravediggers.
Only the black fertile soil will commemorate you.
This ground, now free, incinerates its shame.
And rids itself of German steps.

Your shtetl dark and bright.
Your song, your Horodenka.
The care-free Tchvervaner.
Your meadows, your river.
As I remember you.
They will be remembered.
And Spring will remember you.
The Jews from my town.
And Autumn will cry. Autumn.
The Autumn will cry incessantly for you.

[Page 332]

My last visit to Horodenka

by Hilda Burg

In August of 1941 I was far away from home in the town of Kolomea where I had settled down with my friend Ilana Schindler. We were both working as teachers. We had lost our families and saw the world around us falling apart. We decided to go back to our hometown, Horodenka, hoping to spend our last days on earth with our families. We took the train back home with a heavy heart, knowing the Holocaust was there. We weren't even sure that we could reach Horodenka. We had no papers, but we tried to stay calm and to mislead people who were watching us by talking and chatting all the time.

Miraculously we reached Horodenka with no problems. In the darkness of the night we marched from the train station to our home.

It was a very pleasant evening. There was a very nice wind that seemed to say: "Hilda, you're home again in the place of your mother's warm home. This is the same Horodenka, the same familiar streets in which you walked once singing and chatting with your friends." I thought, "You may be very lucky, maybe that terrible hand did not reach and hurt our town." I hoped that my reaching Horodenka with no problem was an omen that nothing had happened to the town.

The omen wasn't true. As I walked home I tried to think about the ways in which I could enter the house without scaring my mother. When I last saw her she was so helpless and so small that she looked like a little child. That was the reason I came home. I realized that this time we would change our roles and that she would need me as her protector. I was sure that the last days of the war made her weak and left her even more helpless than before.

While I was walking home I started to doubt that I'd find my mother in the place I'd seen her last. In the past few months so many things had happened that everything seemed endless and hopeless. So many losses, so much humiliation, so many tragedies – the misery in each of our lives was enough to fill the lives of hundreds of people in regular times. Thinking that way, I felt myself getting older by the minute and I was getting more and more tired. Then I stopped thinking about the danger that was lurking around me as I walked in the middle of the night on forbidden roads, breathing air I was forbidden to breathe. I only thought about the fact that I was still alive against the will of the enemy, almost against my own will.

What had started out as a nice evening when I arrived now became a nightmare. We started noticing other shadows moving in the dark – some of them pushing, some of them being pushed towards an unknown destiny. Those who were pushed did not resist. They were led like sheep to a slaughter. They did not scream. They did not lift their hands to protect themselves. They were stunned. And only every now and then my ear would hear a moan, a sign, or a cry.

We realized what was happening: everyone was getting ready for the "action" and there was nowhere we could retreat or hide. We had to keep walking, so we did. And while we were marching we could see the shadows of the people disappearing into the night – the night that may have been for some of them, their last night on earth – the night of destruction. But for us, that night was a friend. It hid us from the enemies in the area so we could go on.

As I continued walking I was getting anxious and thinking: how did we dare to do what we did in the last 16 hours? To go 200 kilometers by train, to walk for an hour in a town full of enemies without being noticed? To go through the "action" without being caught? But we continued on. And then finally I reached my home, the home where I'd left my mother when I saw her last. My heart was beating strongly. I knocked on the door but the voice that answered me was not my mother's voice. She wasn't there anymore. She never again would need my help and protection. Without my knowing, she had gone with the others who were taken away. I was struck by my misery and by my sadness. I sat on the doorstep, covering my face and my eyes, without even crying tears or moaning. She was the third of my family that I lost and the last one. Each one went to a place from which there is no return; and each one took a part of my life with them when they went.

[Page 333]

Letters From Hell

Dr. Hirsh Bluthal-Prifer

Translated by Dalya Yohai

From August 1939 on, I lived with my family in Holland. In September 1939, World War II started and Horodenka became part of Soviet Russia. We had more and more difficulties maintaining contact with our relatives there — especially after Holland fell into German hands. The postcards we exchanged had to go through double censorship: Russian and German. They became shorter and shorter, exchanging only short greetings and some news. After the occupation of Holland by the Germans, our relatives worried about us more, because we were under Hitler's shadow. In September 1940, my mother-in-law, Chana Shtreyt died. She was lucky to die in her bed surrounded by family.

There was terrible news about the Horodenka Jews, and letters, written in codes (i.e. with words having double meanings) started to arrive in February 1942.

From a letter on February 1, 1942, written in German and sent under the alias: Asher Schleimazel (Asher the fool), my brother-in-law Asher Shtreyt wrote: "Bronye, Hershele, and David (his wife and two kids) are in Heaven. The family of murderers took them on vacation." My wife couldn't understand the message and asked him to explain again: On March 6, 1942, he answered, "I am surprised you didn't understand: Bronye, Hersch and David are dead in *Gan* Eden with thousands of other Jews. Only half still remains."

The letter from February 1, also had news about the birth of a daughter, Chana, to my sister-in-law, Feyge. On April 18, he writes again: "This week we had again a visit from Mr. Shochet [murderer]. It happened that uncle Chaim [life] didn't leave us except for little Chana [she was murdered in her crib]." Then he told us about the ghetto in town and then added: "I almost went into Mr. Murderer's hands, but managed to get away. I can't give you more details now because of my mood. I hope Uncle Chaim doesn't leave me, although Mr. Fear is still with us. All our brothers went to our dear mother except for some. Aba, Feyge, Shmuel and Metale are doing well. I hope to hear from you, if not, remember, our revenge will come!"

From my brother Barukh I got a card on April 15, also sent under another name, Yishmach Moshe Greenshotof. He wrote: "Twice we were very close to visiting our mother [she died in 1912] and came back. Maybe there will be another opportunity. And we don't know if we will be back. Gitl and Beynsh Halpern also moved...." All these cards went through German censors, but did arrive.

From Asher, on May 5, 1942: "I came back from work and found your card of April 17th. I guess you got the information about what is going on here. I still am in shock. I can't explain what's going on in our hearts. Even Job or Dante were unable to come up with this kind of situation. Let's hope that this will be the end of it. Feyge, Shmuel and the girl are all well. Only little Chana fell victim and went to Bronye and the children [were murdered]. God knows were I get the strength to live..."

After May 1942, the cards were full of complaints about the terrible hunger and included requests for food. Asher wrote on May 14, "The suffering is more than possible to bear. If the Germans come to kill us, we are ready, since it is better to die from a gun than from hunger. I want already to go to my dear Bronye and the children. There is no point in staying here to do the work."

In Holland, we had difficult times too. After May 1st, we had to wear the yellow start and we couldn't go out after 8 o'clock. We could shop only between four and five in the afternoon. However, even when we couldn't get anything because the market was closed, we still made a big effort to send food to Horodenka. In a card from June 29, we got a confirmation from Asher that they had received our parcel. They said it helped a lot and to send more, if possible.

In a card dated August 5, Asher wrote, "It's been a long time. I don't have the patience. We are expecting Mr. Yeshua [G-d] to come and visit. Mr. Pachad [fear] is still here and the *mashchitim* [murderers] still come from time to time. We can get food since it's harvest time, but we don't have money and everybody's starving. Every night I see Bronye and the children in my dreams and I feel better. I am healthy to go to work daily. In my spare time, I write my memories. I see your brother Barukh everyday at work. I hope I can soon tell you about the destruction and of our "friends" who took [murdered] Bronya and the children."

On August 2, I sent a card to Horodenka to Asher's address, but it was returned in September with a note: "Unknown – left." This was at the time when all the Jews from town were forced into the ghetto.p> In a card dated August 9, my brother Baruch wrote: "Aunt Gittel [ghetto] lives on the street of the big synagogue. We live in a shared apartment and we have to pay rent. Before Passover, I went to the village [he had worked as a farmer in the village] and was able to get some food. What's next, I don't know. We are afraid that we are going to join our uncle Yenkel [who was murdered]. Who knows when I will be able to answer you again.."

Then another card came from Asher dated September 12, just before *Rosh-Hashana.* "In our quarters, we had a nice *shochita* [killing]. At this time our family is with Uncle Chaim [life], but it looks like the place will be with *achenu* [our brothers]. I will go to Volochisk [Romania] or Potochek, so I don't have to part from Uncle Chaim. Feyge and the family went to Kolomyja and dear Chaim is still with them. Almost all of our dear brothers went to Bronye and the children. *HaShochet* [the k iller] was going crazy here. Dear Hersh Leif [our cousin Mendel Prifer] and his oldest daughter went there. My memories, I will leave here. When the War is over and you survive, you'll have a taste of the sweet revenge on the enemy. Greetings from those who survived."

Then we got a card from Baruch and his wife, dated October 2, 1942. They wrote from the village of Ozeryony. They ran away to this village hoping that it would continue to be quiet, as it was in an area across the Dniester River. My brother wrote: "We got your card from August 24. Some days after that Mr. Pachad [fear] came to visit Horodenka and stayed five days. Many from our family and friends went with him, including our cousin Hersh-Leif and his oldest daughter. We came here empty-handed and we feel weak from hunger and in exile."

The information about my brother's move to the other side of the river, I also got from Asher. He wrote: "Try to avoid the storm, and if you are called, don't go." He didn't know that we already got a letter to go to Westerbrok, where they were organizing the Jews from Holland. Every week they would send two to three trains from there to Auschwitz to the gas chambers. After the war we learned that my sister-in-law Shlomo's older daughter was sent to Auschwitz from Nice in the southern part of France, even though this area was not under Nazi rule.

גלויות מתוך גיא ההשמדה — קארטלעך פֿון דעם גיהנום

הגלויה מתאריך 1 בפברואר 1942 מאת אשר שטרייט הי״ד אל בני משפחתו בהולנד
א קארטל דאטירט דעם 1'טן פעברואר 1942 פֿון אשר שטרייט צו זיין משפחה אין האָלאנד
A postcard dated Febr. 1st 1942 from Asher Streit — who was murdered by the Nazis —
to his family in Holland, containing the first information about the extermination of the
Horod. Jewry.

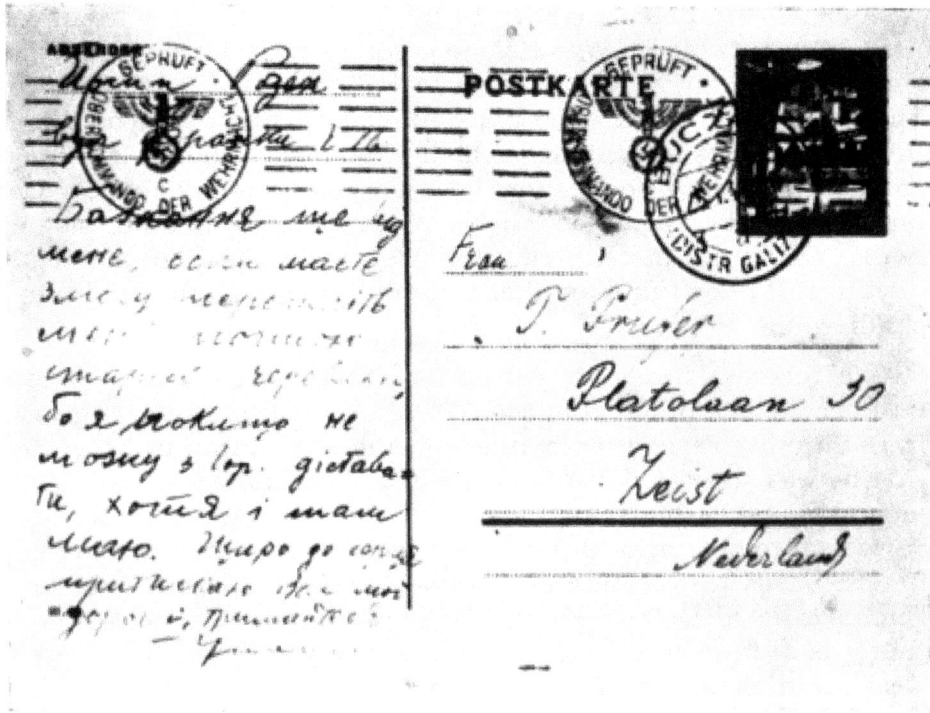

הגלויה מתאריך 25 בינואר 1943 מאת אשר שטרייט הי״ד אל בני משפחתו בהולנד

א קארטל דאטירט דעם 25'סטן יאנואר 1943 פון אשר שטרייט ז״ל צו זיין משפחה אין האלאנד

A postcard dated January 25th, 1943, from Asher Streit to his family in Holland.

Asher's card dated October 14 had terrible news about our family. Asher wrote: "I didn't go to Kolomyja for the last five days, but today I learned that there was a *shochita* [killing] there and Aba, Feyge, Shmuel and the girl left the place, probably forever. Maybe this is for the best. It looks like the whole area of Stanislav County is going to be emptied of Jews. I don't know how long I will stay with dear Chaim, but it looks like not much longer. When I get to the other side of the river, I will write more. Write, too! Be courageous. We are ready for anything! If I don't find another solution, I might go to Bronya and the children.

We received two more cards, both from Horodenka — one from October 21, the other from the 29th. Asher told us that he got a card from Shmuel, Feyge's husband, from the work camp in Lvov. He said that he was separated from his family and probably they were not alive anymore. Asher himself was one of the last remaining Hordenkan Jews sent to Kolomyja. But he managed to run away. He didn't know if he should go to Romania or Buchach. We got a card from him from Buchach dated December 2. He wrote: "Your card from November 6, that was sent to Horodenka, came to me only now. I've been here three weeks and already have had six opportunities to reunite with Bronye and the children. Your idea about them being still alive is very strange. [I had written to him, to comfort him, that maybe they had not been killed.] A week ago there was a *shochita* here. Two thousand went to Bronye. I have no strength to describe my latest experiences. Please try to go someplace where you won't get Bronye's illness. From Shmuel, I don't have any information, although I sent him money twice. Maybe he went to Bronya and the kids. I'm staying here with my brother-in-law and hope to get work in the village. Then we will solve the problem of food and there might be more of a chance that dear Chaim is staying with me."

My brother Barukh wrote to me from Tluste twice, December 20, 1942 and January 24, 1943. This was the last card that I got from him. He wrote: "We got the card dated January 4, 1943 and we are very happy to hear that you are healthy. We are changing our address, not voluntarily, our *zsures* [ones giving us trouble], are changing it. Our town is free of Jews and even Hersh-Leib's sons are not alive anymore. From all of them, only Mendele, is alive and is with me. Hersh-Leib also left. I want to let you know that we had a little daughter and she is three months old. I didn't think I would be able to write you this card. Thank God for that, I hope God will bring us a good new year and you will be able to respond."

Asher Shtreyt wrote us two cards, on December 25 and January 21, from Botchach. In the last one he wrote: "Can you imagine my joy. I came back from my work, sorting rags, in the village, and I found your card from December 17, 1942. My whole life depends on Tony [his sister] and your words. 'Be strong,' comforted me. I don't know long I'll be with dear Chaim, but I am sure you will stay with him, if only for revenge. There were two weddings here, but I wasn't able to go. From Aba, Feyge and Shmuel, there is no news. My brothers are saying that there is hope and we'll be saved soon. I wish it so. Your brother and his wife are still in Tluste. He packed his stuff to join Bronya, but at the last minute, they let them come back from death."

On the 25 of January, Asher wrote again from Buchach — this time, not in German, but in Ukrainian. He said: "I am writing to you from the village where I work as a collector of old wood. In town, the atmosphere is tense and every minute I expect to join Bronye, my dear Bronye. I am trying to stay away from town."

The last card was dated February 12, 1943. He wrote: "I got your card of the 12th of January, 1943. I was really lucky to be able to get it. Our people are not allowed to work out of town, except for some people with "the number 25." This fact is telling me the end is near, because it is impossible to live in town even one hour. A week ago two thousand people went to Bronye. Who knows if I can write to you again. God help us, so we can see each other. Here and in Lvov we have the same situation as in Horodenka. It is very difficult to stay with Chaim."

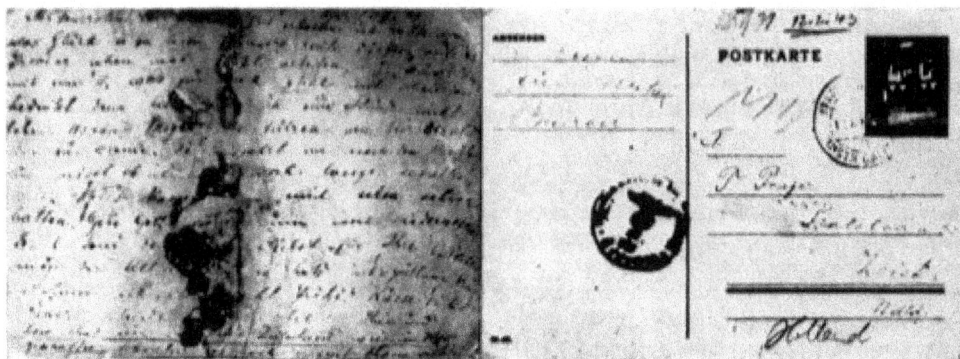

My brother-in-law, Yehoshua Sthreyt told me that Asher died in combat as a partisan.

From his writings we felt the spirit of a courageous man who didn't want to succumb to his destiny. A year and a half after his family died, he still wanted to fight for his life.

Now that I'm writing these words, it feels as though there is nothing new in them. After the Eichmann trial, the whole world knew what happened.

In Western Europe, they didn't have their brutal methods of people digging their own graves and being buried in them. There they did their awful deeds under the pretense of a "work camp." And the Jews couldn't fathom that it was possible to be so barbaric; they went like sheep to be killed. Unfortunately, the ghetto Warsaw Jews saw the truth too late.

[Pages 338 & 391]

The Soup Kitchen and the Orphanage

by Reuven Prifer

Translated by Dalya Yohai

In my article about the period of the Holocaust in our town, I mentioned the soup kitchen that was established for the Jewish refugees that came from Hungary and stopped in our town. Tuvya Korn and a group of young people from the Zionist Youth movement created this soup kitchen. The first *Yudenrat* approved it. The same group took upon itself to take care of the Jewish orphans that were thrown out of the public orphanage. It is important to know more about this story and to emphasize the devotion and dedication of the group and also to praise the work or a great supporter, Yisrael Kugler.

It was at the beginning of the Holocaust period, at the time of the Hungarian occupation, before the German occupation. Hungary decided to get rid of her Jewish citizens, claiming that they were not authentic Hungarians. The Jews started walking or driving through the former Russian territory. They were allowed in the towns they passed through to ask to for food and clothes from the local Jewish population. Our town responded to them generously; but as the situation in town became worse, we didn't have any more resources to help with.

Then our friend, Tuvya Korn proposed to a youth group in town to open a soup kitchen which would supply one hot meal a day for the refugees. The group consisted of Nina Auerbach, Clara Hartenstien, Berl Hoffman, Nusia Wacher, Savka Friedman, Sara Frankel, Savka Avidor, Munyo Kugler, Yosef Koch, Shlomo Korn, Yosef Reys, Zvi Reys, Munyo Shecter and myself. It was clear that we would volunteer, but the money to buy the equipment and supply the food would have to come from the community. First, it was important to find a place to house the project.

At that time there was already a Yudenrat that represented the Jewish community to the authorities. When the proposal came up, it was positively received. Yisrael Kugler was the one who really was excited about the idea and gave it a lot of support. We solved the problem of a space with the help of Motye Sobel who gave up one of the rooms in his apartment for the project. When he saw that the room was too small he gave us the whole apartment and went to live with his neighbor Asher Shechner. But even the apartment became too small and the entire operation moved to the Kvetshar home near the Polish gymnasium. Finally we got permission to use the home of Michal Kimel. In this house, with its two stories, we could operate properly.

The other problem was trying to get the food. Mr. Kugler did a lot to get the food from the villagers, although this was already very dangerous. He was already 60 years old, but would still go with his friends every day to one of the villages to get fresh produce. He also was very supportive of our Zionist fervor and accepted the idea that we would speak only Hebrew in the kitchen. He also supported speaking Hebrew in the orphanage that opened on the second floor of the house. We had for a short period of time more than 12 children, as all orphans had been kicked out of the public orphanage.

The first "Action" ended all this activity. The first morning of the Action all the children were taken from the orphanage by the Germans; Tuvya Korn was with them. He was warned about the danger and people suggested that he hide. But he couldn't leave the children and went with them to his death.

Israel Kugler lost his wife and daughter in the Action and was terribly lonely. At that time we didn't believe that our destiny would be like those in Michalcze. Kugler invited some of the Zionist youth and gave them his will. He gave all his assets to the Zionist Fund, hoping the world order would return to what it was. There was great innocence in giving his estate away like that but such was his attitude and his devotion to the Zionist cause.

Let his words be a marker and memorial to my young friends – the volunteers – and to Israel Kugler himself.

[Page 339]

Before and After the War

Blumeh Berkover

Translated by Harvey Buchalter

Horodenka was the place of my birth and the place where I was raised. Here I worked and lived until the outbreak of the Second World War. Perhaps this explains why my feelings toward it run so deep and why I believe there is no spot better or more beautiful anywhere on Earth. We had a far-flung family in both Horodenka and in other towns, where we would often visit relatives. But I most recall the happiness that being in my town brought me. Who can put into words the hominess and the joy of celebrating the holidays and *Shabbos*? We had a wonderful and wholesome youth, filled with study and activities. We each had a goal in life. Life became better as each day passed. As the leaves turned green, in my eyes, it was like living in a garden. That is what life was like right before the War.

Ten days before war broke out between Germany and the Soviet Union, on July 1, 1941, we left town. After a strenuous journey, we made it into the interior of the Soviet Union. We came back to Horodenka in November 1945. But what did we find there? Walking from the train station past the sugar factory on the *Goyishe Gass* (the non-Jewish streets) we saw no signs of our family. But as soon as we approached the still-intact*Nikoleskas* Church (as we used to call it) and the street that used to contain row upon row of Jewish houses, we saw flat land. Everything had been razed to the ground. The Ukrainians took apart the Jewish houses to the foundations in search of valuables. Then they dug up the empty lots to plant potatoes and other crops. Only a few of the Jewish homes remained on the main street. The few Jews who had survived the Nazi occupation and the few who had returned from the Soviet Union took over two houses. They all lived together, making ends meet with small-time trading while waiting to be repatriated to Poland. On one Sunday I stood on the threshold and watched as the *goyim* streamed into the church. None had any feeling for me; they regarded me with wonderment as an alien from another planet. But when my eyes left the masses of Ukrainians, I felt the predominating deathly stillness and my heart could feel the emptiness of Jewish life. Words fail me. For someone who remembers each little by-way and path, it was devastating.

Horodenka, which was alive, as were its surrounding villages and towns, was now reduced to a sad spot on the map, no better than the most insignificant hamlet. No former [Jewish] resident took up life anew; only a few Jews from the Soviet Union lived there. This is the ultimate end of our town of Horodenka.

[Page 340]

The town after the destruction

by Mendel Goldberger

On June 6, 1944 I felt like I was hit by lightning when I heard that the Soviet Army had liberated Horodenka. Without knowing that we were very far from Horodenka, my commander, a soldier in the Soviet army, granted my request to go to my hometown for a few days. We knew at that time what the Nazi murderers had done to the Jews. But despite that, all the way home, I was hopeful that even after the great destruction I could find somebody I knew.

As soon as I reached the suburbs near Toliki, I saw the dark and depressing reality. All I saw were the skeletons of the Jewish houses that were destroyed. And everywhere that I looked, I did not see one Jewish face. I felt my hope disappearing minute by minute. I walked on and on and I saw that in all the streets there wasn't one Jewish home left unharmed.

I reached the crossroads of Kolomea, Syniatyn, and Horodenka. It took me a long time to recognize the house of Giter the grain merchant. Everything was destroyed. I went on and got to the marketplace. Even here, everything was dead and empty – like an old cemetery. I couldn't see one Jewish face. I couldn't hear one Jewish voice. And this was the place where most of the Jews used to gather; the place that was alive with the Jewish language of our unforgettable parents, brothers, and sisters. Everything now was dead and silent. The whole town seemed to have been erased from under the skies. I was totally shocked by the misery of this town and the destruction of my family. My feet were walking but I didn't know where they were going. I found myself standing before the big synagogue that was the joy of the town. All that remained were walls; no door, no windows. I walked inside and my eyes saw bits and pieces of clothing, dirty and soiled with blood. I looked through them to see if I could find something familiar, but I found nothing. Not one remnant of the life that was so vivid was left. All I could see in front of my eyes were all the martyrs who died here from hunger, torture, loneliness and misery.

I left the synagogue and went to where the stores used to be but even there, there was nothing. Nothing was left for me to do but go to the grave of my father – but even that wasn't easy. Those murderers and robbers didn't even treat the dead with respect. They had desecrated the graves, breaking the tombstones and uprooting them to use as tiles for the pavement. I wandered in the cemetery, looking for my father's tombstone, feeling my strength leaving me. I was fortunate. His particular tombstone was still there. I stood in front of it complaining and crying bitterly.

With what was left of my strength, and hardly seeing where I was going, I left the cemetery and went back into the town. I reached the house that was supported by two columns. That was the house where the Histadrut Poale Zion (the Union of the Laborers of Zion) met. Of all the clubs in the youth organizations, it was the strongest and most active. It had a large number of members who were always lecturing and discussing with anyone who would listen their theory for developing Palestine.

All I could do was remember dear friends like Itzi Shekhter, the Liser brothers, and others who died so tragically and whom I will never see again. While I was walking like this throughout the town, a Russian soldier approached me and asked me who I was looking for. "If you are looking for Jews, " he said, " you can find them in this house." And he showed me the house of Shmuel Frishling, the watchmaker. I entered the house and I found a very few Jews from Horodenka. From them I learned the whole story of the destruction of the town. Crying and accompanied by the cries of the people I'd left behind, I left the town and went back to my regiment in the army.

[Page 341]

About my Bitter Experience

by Deborah Glazer

Translated by Harvey Buchalter

It lasted three endless months:
Songs from the fields no longer came
When I escaped the Nazi sword
And buried myself deep in the earth.

I exist and I breathe, I eat and drink
I go outside sometimes, even sing
But the thought comes back with horror and fear
How can I sing, when everything is gone?

I feel it's all put-on, all contrived —
My chatting, my speaking, my laughing

The pain lays buried, deep in my heart
I will never take pleasure again in this life.

I ask myself, without end, in sorrow
Why was my own fate not joined with theirs?
Perhaps my destiny was otherwise chosen
To remain, while others perish.

Each one ran frantically off
A wife without her man, an older child
The earth was aflame under their feet
Fear and dread impelled each step they took.

Each searched for his hole in the ground
On streets, on corners, under the enemy's stern face
I became one alone, unwilling
Even today, I know not their fate.

Now anguish engulfs me
I sit, not seeing the world's beauty
Its grandness, the majesty unequaled
I am closed off, I have no doors, no windows.

When I look beyond it, I shudder
They would have murdered me, for being a Jew
Our lives become filthy, unworthy to live
They hunt us down, wherever we may be.

They are criminals without peer
Who judge us as sinners
They await our final day
They are fearless in their pursuit.

Their voices boom from the heights
If we see them, how dare we shoot?
The dreaded commands, which conceal annihilation
Commands to exterminate, from the mouths of murderers.

And so I will live, with patience, I'll live
Until liberation comes, I'll do what I'm able
In misery, alongside my friends
Who are my new brothers and sisters.

Moldy, stinking corners – our resting places
Insects and snakes crawl helter-skelter about
And if one should dare bite us
Blood would erupt from our wounds.

The color from our faces is gone
Our flesh, our skin gnawed and scabbed over
All of our strength has been drained

If only our God would take us from this.

We exist with nothing but hunger and fear
I contemplate death as a choice
I see despair winning the battle with hope
But I will not forfeit my thin claim to life.

And in these desperate and hopeless minutes
As despair, like hail, rains down upon us
Hope lifts me up, gives me courage, and says
"Be brave, my child. Wait … just wait."

Bullets have missed you countless times
Grief has poured from your heart, like blood
Death has searched for you in the cellars, the markets
But you cheated death in his quest.

My body is cold, my limbs feel like ice
Frightening images tore through the forests
When death came to claim my son and me
His voice still comes back, like the howl of the wind.

Like a scarf, his voice covers my ears
"My son, better if you had never been born …"
"Mother, save me … I want to live"
But how can I save you? The murderers are here.

I hold him close to my heart, in dread and fear
His tears seem to choke out his cries
My soul should have fled my body just then
At that moment … when they pushed us into the grave.

Just then, I heard guns being shot
And we plunged, together, into the pit
And my son … a bullet found him!
Another one flew past. It was not meant for me!

And as the moment's sorrow came to pass
I saw what had become of my poor son
My eyes became swollen with tears
And I fell and curled myself up into a ball.

How sweet the moment soon became
I heard nothing, I saw not a thing
But then I awoke from my deathly sleep
To witness the horrendous truth.

All around me lay the dead, I knew them all
They lay in pools of blood, a mockery of life
I myself was soaking in their blood
Sensing my own death was but moments away.

I summoned death to come right now
I pressed my child's hands to my lips
The bullets had swept and skimmed past my head
They didn't touch me; I was still alive!

And twilight, then evening arrived
And with it came the murderers
And I, still stained by the blood of my son
Was touched with the desire to remain alive.

And so how can I tell you what that moment was like?
I cannot; it remains locked within me forever
I imagined myself as a murderous beast
I saw my own heart splitting in two.

I made my way from my dead child
Searching an opening, and a way out
The desire to live was a tug-of-war for my being
But I had already … enough of death.

I did not wail, nor did I ponder the scene
Instead, I made a "staircase" of fallen bodies
Allowing me to climb out of the ground
Stepping with my feet upon the dead.

I saved myself from that grave in the earth
Even though the murderers still lurked about
My pain and my anguish covers me always
My heart breaks with grief and despair.

Yet hope's voice still cries in my soul
She tells me to wait, so that my day of reckoning will come
For our beloved, for neighbors and friends
The enemy's blameless victims.
Horrendous fate became our punishment
Bullets went through us, as lambs to the slaughter
Survival was left for the very few
Deprived of our freedom, exiled from our homes.

So, God, we need your compassion, your help
Have not the corpses been enough for you?
From far or from wide, redemption must come
So that we may exit this bunker as free human beings.

Personalities and Figures

[Pages 343 and 398]

Personalities And Images

Translated by Yehudis Fishman

Rabbis after Teomim

The last rabbi of Horodenka was *Rav* Elimelech Ashkenazi, of blessed memory. However, in our generation, there were some who still remembered the rabbinical genius who preceded *Rav* Ashkenazi, Rabbi Moshe Teomim, of blessed memory, whose name was mentioned frequently, with great admiration. Rabbi Moshe Teomim was from a branch of the rabbinical family that traced its lineage back to the righteous Rabbi Zvi Ashkenazi, who was referred to as the *Chacham* Zvi. *Rav* Moshe Teomim occupied the rabbinical chair in our city until the year 5648 (1888); after his death, his son-in-law Rav Elimelech Ashkenazi was chosen as the rabbi and the head of the *Beit Din*, the rabbinical court. He was considered one of the greatest rabbis in his generation; he understood the spirit of the times and leaned toward Zionism. He served as Rabbi in our city for close to thirty years and passed away during the First World War in 5676 (1916). (The details of the personalities of Rab Moshe Teomim and Rav Ashkenazi are included in the memoirs of Yaacov Halevi Shnitzer, in the section, "Torah Greats in our City.")

*

Until the passing of *Rav* Ashkenazi, the judge *Rav* Menachem Mendel Shapira was the second in leadership. He settled in our city in 1903. Before that, he was a rabbi in Yagelnitsa, where his fathers and grandfathers had occupied the rabbinical chair for six generations. After the passing of *Rav* Ashkenazi, the city was divided into two camps. One camp supported the judge's inheriting the *Rav'*s position; the other camp supported *Rav*Yechiel Rosenberg who was a supreme scholar with a phenomenal memory, who also seemed worthy of the position. The debate about who should take over lasted many years until it was finally decided not to appoint a rabbi at all. The judge remained in his position and received an additional title of "head of the rabbinical court" in addition to his previous one of "judge and righteous teacher." *Rav* Yechiel Rosenberg was appointed official legal codifier and received a modest salary.

The family of the departed *Rav* Ashkenazi also requested continuity to the rabbinical position. After a protracted discussion period, Rabbi

Aryeh Leibish, *Rav* Ashkenazi's son-in-law, was appointed as the second "judge and righteous teacher;" he remained at his post until the days of the holocaust, when he was killed together with the other holy ones of our city.

The *Admorim* (Chassidic *Rebbes*)

To us, the children of this generation, the epoch of the *Rebbe* Shmuel Abba Hager was ancient history. We knew only his young brother, *Reb* Micheleh Hager, who lived in our city from the beginning of this century and left it in 1914, when the First World War broke out, never to return. We remembered the courtyard of the *Rebbe* and the great house that was like a villa, with a broad courtyard by its side that served as a gathering place for the Chassidim on holidays and festivals when the *shul* was too narrow to contain all those who came. A few years before the World War, the *Chassidim* began to erect a large two-story *shul* in the courtyard, but were able only to complete the frame. After the war, the entire courtyard was sold to Meir Frishling and Horodenka ceased to be a city of Chassidic rabbis.

The *Rebbe* was a branch of the dynasty of Vizhnitza and was the brother of the Vizhnitzer Rebbe of Zaleshchiki and Utiniya who was also his father-in-law. He had two daughters and one son, *Reb* Baruch'l. After the war, the *Rebbe* settled in Czernovitz, and there his son *Reb* Baruch'l became one of the leaders of *Mizrachi* in Bokovina. During the years of the Holocaust, *Reb* Boruch'l was exiled to Transendnistria, and there was killed with his family.

The people of the *Rebbe*'s courtyard that were known in the city were the attendants, *Reb* Pinchas, *Reb* Moshe Mendel, and the cantor *Reb* Zalman. The personal attendant of the *Rebbe*, Lubish, was of short stature, had a yellowish beard, and was a well-known member of the community.

Leaders and heads of the community

In general, except in rare cases, the communal leadership was given over to men of action who were trained in public office, and not to men from ultra-religious circles. The communal heads of the last generation were Moshe Pinles, Yosef Bozner, Velvel Zeidman, Shlomo Kramer, Berl Shpierer, Shlomo Shtreyt, and others.

Moshe Pineles stood at the head of the community after the first elections that took place in 1891. The period of his incumbency extended to 1900. After the elections in 1900, Yosef Bozner was chosen as the head of the community. He was an estate owner in the village of Potochishche, but was so involved in the life of the city that he could direct the affairs of the community. He was an enlightened person and was not a member of ultra-orthodox circles.

When Bozner's term was finished, the leadership passed for a few years to the ultra-orthodox circles. In those days the community heads were Jews like Velvel Zeidman and Shlomo Kramer, who were considered among the extremists of the ultra-orthodox. The two of them were among the wealthy, honored and learned scholars in the city, and they placed guards against the incursion of the *maskilim* and the Zionists, whose numbers were growing into leadership roles. Around the year 1910, there were new elections. The Zionists, together with organizations of workers, succeeded in assisting the more modern candidates in the elections, specifically Berl Shpierer, to be chosen as the communal head.

Berl Shpierer joined a youth a group of *maskilim* whose members were also students of Chaim Leib Halpern. After his marriage, he was very successful in business and became somewhat involved in the banking business. He was the communal head for a few years before the First World War and continued leading after the War. He was not counted among the organized Zionists, but was among the friends of the Zionist movement. In his days the Zionists attained a significant influence over communal affairs. Even so, he did not hesitate in holding back support from motions that were presented for the sake of the Zionist causes, in order to acquire the support of the Zionist opponents in 1930.

In 1918, with the return of the first refugees from the western areas of the Austrian monarchy, Reb Shlomo Shtreyt took the mantle of leadership during those first difficult intermediate days. After the majority of citizens returned to their homes, it was possible again to reestablish the central community council that had been elected before the World War. Reb Shlomo Shtreyt was among the greatest scholars of the city and an honored merchant; this position gave him authority for the difficult activity of organizing the life of the community during the period of transition from emergency conditions to normal conditions.

Holy professionals: Ritual slaughterers, cantors, synagogue attendants, and members of the *Chevra Kadisha* (Burial Society)

There were four *shochtim* (ritual slaughterers) in our city in the last generation: Leibele Shochet, Mordechai Shochet, Yidel Shochet, and Yehoshua Hirsh Shochet. It is not necessary to say that they were all G-d-fearing and whole-hearted, knowledgeable in Torah, and exemplary in ethics. Reb Yudel Shochet was, in addition to all the above-mentioned qualities, a good cantor. Even more impressive than him was Reb Yehoshua Hirsh, who prayed with the accompaniment of a children's choir, knew how to play music, and could even transcribe songs that he heard into musical notation.

As was the customary and accepted practice, there were several cantors in the city, since each synagogue had its own cantor. The most notable cantor, the cantor of the the big synagogue, was Yossi *Chazan*, Yossi Shapira. In addition to his position as a cantor, a position that apparently did not provide him with a sufficient livelihood, he had a small olive oil press — called *olinitza* in the local tongue. He knew how to polish the compositions of famous cantors and to give them a traditional Jewish flavor. Without knowledge of musical notes, he organized and conducted a choir of about forty men. After the First World War, he immigrated to America and served as a cantor in one of the synagogues there.

The assistant to the city cantor was Shlomo Chaim whose official title was under-*chazan*. He also needed an additional source of livelihood, and obtained this through a bakery that was established by his wife, Shlomo Chaim'kes. She supported them by baking small loves of bread from wheat flour that was ground together with bran.

A well-known cantor in the city was Reb Shimshele Milnitzer, who was also a teacher of young children. A skinny, weak Jew, he had a pleasant voice, and mesmerized listeners with the sweetness of his prayer. He had an awesome memory for music and a wonderful ear. He collected many tunes that he learned in his visits to the courtyards of neighboring *Rebbes*.

There were two brothers well known for their singing and praying abilities: Yankel and Motti Falafel. The Falafel family came from Russia; when they came to Austria, they changed their name — upon the advice of the *rebbe* — to a Hebrew name, Falafel. They both had joyful temperaments, belonged to the national Jewish troupe, and were experts in Purim *spiels* and presentations like *The Selling of Yosef*. Yankel Falafel was a life-member of the *Chevra Kadisha* and was in charge of the Jewish cemetery records.

Michal Voves (Ivanir), more an amateur than a professional cantor, was a tall man with a pleasant and wide ranging voice; he had a well-developed sense of music. He, too, was from Russia and excelled through the wisdom of experience and love of life. However, economic success seemed beyond his grasp. He was forced to have several different occupations to earn his living; all of them together did not suffice to meet his needs.

Motia Sucher was also an impressive cantor. He was a fine young man who stood out for his good nature and refined manners. He made a living by selling hides in the market square, but generally it was his wife who ran the business while he devoted most of his time to studying in the *kloiz*.

Another special cantor and a pious Jew was Issac Meltzer, who was a carpenter by trade. He devoted a lot of his time to helping the sick through the organizations *Yad Charutzim* (the Hand of the Diligent) and *Bikur Cholim* (Visiting the Sick). In general, he stood out as a person who was good and did well. He was the workers' cantor, and was taken away with them in the first Action.

Other well-known cantors were Zeide Offenberger and Dudia Lazar, both from the new generation, who shortened both their beards and clothes. In his youth, Zeyde Ofenberger was a member of the choir of one the greatest of cantors in his generation, Zalmen Kvartin; he was accustomed to repeating many of the prayers and melodies of his teacher.

*

Two well-known attendants in the city were Dudia Zellner and Dovid Zerach. Dudia Zellner was a soldier in his youth, and, in the course of his service, he acquired many medals of distinction that he would wear at every festive occasion. With the knock of his hammer, he would arouse men from their sleep and call them to wake up for the service of their Creator. Dovid Zerach was the official attendant of the great synagogue. He collected community taxes and would go from door to door of the residents' homes with his notebook under his arm — a notebook that was famous in the city.

A well-known figure in the city was the old attendant known by his nickname, Bundzier. Every Friday, he would walk throughout the city to inspect the *eiruv* (an encircling rope that allows Jews in a city to carry on Shabbat) with his long measuring stick and role of string to repair the parts that came down. He was extremely old. In the cemetery there was a plot of land, which he had bought and prepared with a tombstone. The only thing that was missing was the date of his passing.

The attendant of the great synagogue and its two adjacent rooms was, during the last years, Aaron Palger, who was invited to all the weddings in the city and was an expert regarding the "speech of the dowry." He would exaggerate the praise of every item that was listed, estimating its value at ten percent above its actual worth, and thereby increase the mirth of all the wedding guests.

*

The members of the *Chevra Kadisha* were primarily laborers or small store keepers, who volunteered for the holy work that is referred to as *Chesed Shel Emes*, kindness of truth. They included: Yankel Falafel, Baruch Leib Greidinger, Asher Fetner, Fishel Wasser,

Yehoshua Tzumer (Yehoshua Blume Rachels), and Yisrael Meir Tzumer. Yisrael Meir Tzumer was among those who were designated to be hung as tenth in line, in the year 1915. After the first nine Jews were hung, an order came from the Russian officer that this activity was not proper. He issued a command to release those who were still alive, and even to punish those responsible for the hanging of innocent men. The rope was actually removed from the neck of Yisrael Meir. From that time on, he would arrange a yohrtzeit, every year on the day that he was released from the hanging. At the beginning of the Holocaust, Yisrael Meir revealed an uncanny sense of seeing the future. When the Nazis came to take him from his home, he said: "If this is how they are starting ... terrible and bitter will be our end," and he climbed up to the attic and hung himself.

The man who was involved in bringing the dead to burial, who was an undertaker for many years, was Avrohom Lipe (Frishling). His helper was Mates-Levi Weytsman, the brother of Eli Weytsman. During the final years, the undertakers were Nechemiah Reys and Mekheh Morgenbesser.

Scholars

There were great scholars of the previous generation, who memory did not cease even in our generation. There was *Reb* Meshulem Wagner, who had a sharp mind, an incredible breadth of knowledge, and was an ordained rabbi. His grandson, *Reb* Chaim Shnitser, continued the chain of scholarship in the city. The son-in-law of the Rabbi, *Reb* Elimelech Ashkenazi, like his grandfather, was an ordained rabbi, and together with his brother Simchah'le, had a large store that sold iron equipment and farming machinery. This promised an abundant livelihood for the entire family, and consequently *Reb* Chaim was able to dedicate most of his time to Torah.

There were several other scholars in the city who learned Torah for its own sake, and were experts in Talmudic and *Halachic* authorities, but were not officially ordained as rabbis, and perhaps did not even aspire to become rabbis.

Among the outstanding scholars was *Reb* Shlomo Shtreyt, who was the head of the Talmud Torah Organization. To him the Talmud teachers would bring their students to *fahrher*, to be tested, and to obtain his opinion about their progress in their studies. Velvel Zeidman was also counted among the scholars, and was among the wealthy and honored of our city. So, too, among the scholars was *Reb* Leibele Korn, who also sold iron equipment and was also a man of means. However there were also several scholars who "fulfilled the Torah in a state of poverty", and didn't allow worries of livelihood to distract them from their studies. Among the latter were Nachum Shpund and Vovel Kimel.

Nachum Shpund was the son of Noson Shpund. He was one of those who prayed in the *Bais Medrash* where *Reb* Elimelech Ashkenazi and his son-in-law Reb Chaim Shnitser prayed. There he always found an opportunity to debate *Reb* Chaim Shnitser in matters of Torah and *Halacha.*

Voveh Kimel owned a small grocery store that was next to the house of Dr. Kanapas. He was primarily known in the city as a seller of pure honey, without any suspicion of additives. It was also possible to obtain from him beeswax for candles or the beeswax candles themselves. He was a modest Jew with many children and was considered one of the city scholars.

Another scholar worthy of mention was Zelig Alerhand. He was an old bachelor — an unusual sight in a Jewish section — and a scholar with a brilliant mind. During the days of the second Russian invasion, he was among a group of Jews who were captured and were falsely found guilty of spying against Austria. Among this group that was brought up to the scaffold and hung in the streets of Horodenka were nine men, among whom was Zelig Alerhand, may G-d avenge his blood.

Torah teachers

Until the First World War the education of the young generation was based first and foremost on religion and tradition; attendance at the public high school was considered supplementary to the primary, traditional education. From the age of five, and sometimes even from age of three, a boy was sent to *cheder* to learn his first Hebrew reading, to begin the study of *Chumash,* and to continue learning Talmud, if his abilities allowed him to reach that point. The progression of traditional education was in any case based on the beginning teacher, the *Chumash* teachers — the teachers of Prophets, and Talmud.

One of the beginning-level teachers was Menashe Melamed (his family name was Horn). He brought his pupils to the point of readiness for *Chumash.* He was a successful teacher and had many students. Another teacher like him was Mendele Chanafia, whose family name was Shpigler. Mendele Chanafia was a typical *cheder melamed*; the traditional force of personality completed his *cheder* image.

The teachers, who taught *Chumash* and beyond, even up to the Talmud, were many and varied both in qualities and character. The better-known ones were: Avremeleh Melamed, Mordechai Pupic, Yonah Melamed (Liebman), and Yehudah Bashzor (Tuber).

Yehudah Bashzor was well known as a good teacher from the old generation, but also a strict one, who would "cast bile" into his students and compel them to his will with a stick and a staff. Yonah Liebman was somewhat influenced by the new spirit of the times and introduced recesses between his classes, as well as other innovations. However the most modern was Notah Katz. He also taught *Chumash* with Rashi and the Prophets according to traditional commentaries, with translations into Yiddish. However, he also taught Hebrew language and grammar.

The greatest and most venerable among the children's teachers was *Reb* Kalman Shmuel. He was an outstanding scholar and taught not just Talmud, but the difficult commentary of Tosephos. The best scholars in the city, who continued to learn independently, were Reb Kalman's students. It's as if he had a miniature *yeshiva*, or as was expressed by Dr. Hirsh Blutal, a university course for Talmud.

Teachers

The teachers of public school for Jewish youth established by Baron Hirsh didn't usually mix with the Jewish community in the city, and also didn't interact with the city like the regular citizens. However, there were some exceptions to this. The teacher Zanvil Weiselberg, a relative of Alter Weiselberg, was a teacher of religion and Torah in this school. These subjects were rather limited in scope. Zanvil himself acted like a Jew among Jews; he let grow his beard and prayed every *Shabbos* in a Zionist *minyan*. Similar to him was the teacher Alfred Norad, who married a local woman and remained a resident of the city until the Holocaust. After the Baron Hirsh School closed, he remained in the city as a private teacher; afterward he was a teacher of Jewish religion in public school, in the place of the teacher Dratler, who died in a plague during the First World War. Besides Dratler, there was only one other Jewish teacher in public school was Tsiferblat.

A unique and wonderful chapter is that of my Hebrew schoolteachers. In the period before the First World War, there was for a long time an impressive teacher by the name of Yehuda Goldstein, and the Horodenka-born teacher, Yeshaya Itzik Boker. From his first activities as a teacher in our city, Boker excelled in his pedagogical skills; he had a great charismatic personality. He continued functioning as a Hebrew teacher in Carlsbad, which was in Tchekia, where he remained at the end of the war. Among his students in that period were many important members and leaders of the Zionist movement; he himself was one of the Zionist activists in the city. After the Nazis conquered Czechoslovakia, he succeeded in escaping at the very last minute before the war broke out in 1939. He reached Tel Aviv, though, to our great sorrow, he did not live long. He passed away in Tel Aviv in 1944.

In the era after the First World War, there was a frequent turnover of teachers in the Hebrew school, and only one remained faithful to it, up to the Holocaust. It was the teacher Binyomin Korn. From time to time his destiny declined and he was pushed out of his position as the headmaster of the Hebrew school. However, he kept his standing in the city and in it he raised his sons. His first-born son Tuvya Korn, may G-d avenge his blood, was an active Zionist and communal member. His entire family perished, along with the other sanctified ones of Horodenka.

The second Hebrew teacher, who established a "blood pact" with the city and also perished here during the Holocaust, was the teacher and singer Yitzchak Berger, may G-d avenge his blood. In his days, the school flourished greatly. He awakened in the hearts of his students the will to express their thoughts and feelings in Hebrew, in verse and in prose. A few pages that were a testimony to these activities, reached our hands in the form of a published manual illustrated by the schools' students. So, a few leaves remained from the newspaper dedicated to the concerns of Hebrew education, which was published by Berger in Hebrew and in Yiddish. His wife Reva Berger was snatched from the claws of destruction and she now lives in a country across the sea.

The Yiddish school was actually the youngest educational institution in the city. It was founded soon after the First World War, but during the period of its short existence it became an important institution, whose impact was obvious in the life of the city. Its earliest teachers were members of the Bund in our city — Isaac Fink, Yosef Katz, and Asher Shtreyt — who were conscripted into the holy service of spreading Yiddish culture among the masses. During the last period, the teachers in this school were Weisberg and Boym, who were sent to teach by the Zionist center in Warsaw. There were also two female teachers, Etel Katvan and Kreintze Shteyner, who had been students of this school during the first stage of its existence. They were sent by the administration of the school together with the leaders of the Bund, to complete their Yiddish education in the Yiddish seminar in Vilna. Lastly, we should also mention Yehudah Hirsh Sobel, one of the original Bund members, and one of the founders of the Yiddish school in our city.

Maskilim and Communal Activists

This combination of *maskilim* and communal activists is not an accident at all. The *Haskalah* movement was prominent in the life of the nation, and just as it changed the traditional thinking process, so it changed the approach to communal matters. Therefore, it was natural that the communal activists in the latter generation came primarily from the ranks of the first *maskilim*. In fact, it was very difficult, practically impossible, to distinguish between them.

The first of the *maskilim* in Horodenka to express his liberal views, which opposed the beliefs of most of the community, was Chaim Leib Halpern, who lived and worked in our city at the end of the nineteenth century. He gathered around him the initial group of *maskilim*, who regarded him as their teacher and spiritual leader. Very little is known to us, the children of this generation. It's known only that he struggled to make a living by giving lessons in *Tanach* and the Yiddish language. Groups of *Chassidim* and ultra-orthodox hated and pursued him, until he left the city and settled in the village of Rudol'fodorf, whose residents were *Shvabim* (Germans). There he opened a store to support his family. He died at a young age. Before he died, he was brought to Horodenka, since he wanted to die among Jews; there he died and was buried. In the city various stories circulated about his comments and the various sayings that he would propound on different occasions. He published a book from his own pen according to the spirit of that time, however we presently have nothing definitive about that.

Among the elders of the *maskilim* in the beginning of this century was counted Reb Alter Zilberg. He was a *maskil* of broad background, who walked modestly and lived his whole life as a religious Jew who withheld his liberal ideas. Even though he was like that, he was dedicated to national and Zionist causes, and one of the founders of the group *Bnei* Zion; he sat at the head of this group for many years. He was also among the first to allow his two sons to acquire a broad base of knowledge and to complete formal studies like engineering.

His friend and comrade in the movement, who was slightly younger, was *Reb* Shmuel Yitzchak Lindenburg. In his youth he was a close friend of Chaim Leib Halpern, however that didn't influence the behavior of his daily life, which remained faithful to traditional forms. He was very talented in art and was involved, among other things, in drawing signs. In general, he experimented in a wide variety of fields, and acquired the nickname, "the man of a thousand talents", because of his abilities in all kinds of handicrafts. He was one of the old and respected members and activists of the *B'nei* Zion group, and one of the regular attendants at the Zionist *minyan*. In 1910, he was selected as a member of the community council, as a Zionist representative, and continued in this role for many years. Within the framework of

Zionist activity, he was appointed to the special role of bearing the yoke of concern for the existence of the Hebrew school, which he helped found in 1907. To his children he gave a complete Hebrew education, and his home was one of the few homes in the city where the spirit of Hebrew dominated. In 1926 he went to Israel on the heels of his son and daughter, and lived there through the work of his hands until practically his last years. He passed away in Tel Aviv at the ripe old age of 89, after living to see the founding of the State.

The friend and peer of S. Y. Lindenburg was Hersh Birnboym, both of whom were counted among the group of Chaim Leib Halpern. They both joined the Zionist movement. He was one of the outstanding personalities in the city, due to his personal style and unique approach to many concerns of life — especially his love of nature — that was embedded in him and about which he spoke at every opportunity. One manifestation of his love of nature was his commitment to the healing and preservation of natural resources, which he lectured about to all his friends and acquaintances. At the time of the Holocaust, he lived in Horodenka and was murdered with the other citizens.

One of those most loyal and dedicated to the Zionist ideal and to the Hebrew language was Zvi Preminger. He was ten or more years younger than the elder members of the Zionist organization. However, he towered over all of them in his serious and consistent approach to the question of the revival of the Hebrew language. As mentioned in several places in this book, he audaciously attempted to have the Hebrew language spoken in his house. His boldness is not less daringly expressed by his incorporating a Hebrew title on the packaging of his shoe polish. Because of this he earned the nickname of Zionist. (Ten percent of the profits of the factory were dedicated to the *Keren Kayemet*.) With all this, Zvi was one of the most enthusiastic youth who prayed with the Zionist *minyan*. He was a man of good conversation and abundant humor, who enjoyed the love and friendship of all who knew him. During the First World War he escaped to Vienna and remained there until he went to Israel. In 1925 he visited Israel and tried to find a position as a Hebrew stenographer, according to the approach that he invented, but he didn't succeed and returned to Vienna. In his last years, he lived in Haifa and passed away there in 1957.

The period after the First World War and the Balfour Declaration was the time when Zvi Yiskar, of blessed memory, was a Zionist leader and activist in all areas of communal life in our city. He was born in Horodenka in 1886. At a young age, he joined a Zionist group called *Bnei Zion* and was one of its most active members. In 1912 he joined the young Zionist group *Tz'irei Zion* (youth of Zion), but the war that broke out in 1914 put an end to the activities of this group. In the years after the war, Zvi Yiskar was in the center of the city's Zionist activities and he served alternately as sometimes the leader or the assistant head of the group *Bnei* Zion, until the day that he moved to Israel with his family in 1936. In the last years before his *aliya*, he accomplished a lot in the city. He especially succeeded in establishing the guild of "Professional Zionists," who were formerly under the influence of the Bund. In 1957, he visited America at the invitation of his sisters and brother-in-law. On this occasion, he was enlisted to actualize the plan of publishing a memorial book. About a year before his death, he continued collecting his portion of the memorial book in the form of memories about the Baron Hirsh School, the community council, and other organizations in the city. When he passed away in 1959, his coffin was placed near the grave of his wife in the cemetery in Hertzelia.

Many members of the *Bnei Zion* group joined this group even before the First World War; and some of them continued their activities even after the war. A few of them were: Michael Neyman and Abba Kalmus (both of whom died in their youth during the First World War), Leib Kamil, the brothers Hillel and Beynish Koch, and Ben Tziyon Eyzman.

Leib Kamel was active in the *Keren Hayesod* and *Keren Kayemet* organizations as a fundraiser. In general, he was known as a trustworthy man, in whose hands were entrusted various communal funds. Beynish Koch was also at the center of Zionist activities in the city. After Zvi Yiskar made *aliya*, Beynish took over his place in the Zionist organization. When Zvi Yiskar left, several letters remained from Beynish Koch, in which he described in detail everything that transpired in the Zionist organization and the Hebrew school committee.

Ben Tziyon Eyzman joined the *Bnei Zion* group at a young age, even before the First World War. In 1912, after his marriage with Tzipe Shertzer, he settled in Lvov. However, he returned to Horodenka when the World War was over, and continued living there until the Holocaust. During this long period, he was a member of the Hebrew school committee, and for two years was also the head of the committee. Within the framework of his activities in the Zionist group, he took upon himself to become the assistant to the head of the group and was also one of the Zionist representatives in the community council. In the thirties, together with Dr. Beynish, he helped found the Cooperative Loan Bank. In August of 1942, with the liquidation of the Ghetto in Horodenka, Ben Tzion Eyzman, together with the refugees of the Ghetto, was exiled to the Ghetto in Kolomyja. He remained there a very short time, until he was taken in one of the raids to the extermination camp of Lutz.

Tzipe Eyzman, the daughter of Hertzl Shertzer and husband of Ben Tzion, was also an activist from her childhood, especially in the area of Hebrew education. With the establishment of the first Hebrew school in the city in 1907, she was the first kindergarten teacher, and taught the young ones to converse in Hebrew even before they reached school age. In the period after the World War, she assumed the yoke of responsibility for the existence of the school together with Yaacov Prashel and others, and even volunteered to serve as a teacher without remuneration. At a later time, around 1932, Tziporah Eyzman became a pioneer in the promotion of vocational training for the girls in Horodenka, and together with a group of activists, founded a school for cutting and sewing material. The school was set up under the watch and care of Mrs. Cecilia Clapton from Lvov, one of the most active communal workers in the area of vocational training. The school came to have an outstanding reputation.

Tziporah Eyzman was among the 2500 Jews to be exterminated during the first roundup in Semakovtse, but miraculously she managed to escape from the pit and returned to Horodenka. Like her, another four women escaped. After the destruction of the ghetto in Horodenka, she lived in Kolomyja together with her husband, but she escaped to Lvov and she did hand labor in the Yanovska camp. With the tragic destruction of this camp in November of 1943, all the workers were exterminated, among them also Tziporah Eyzman.

It is fitting to bring up at this point the memory of three people in our city who made *aliya* among the "bourgeoisie" to acclimate themselves to the land. Two of them, Yakov Rat and Note Shechter, did not succeed in their efforts and returned to Horodenka. There they were exterminated with the others of the city. The third one, Yaacov Prashel, succeeded in becoming acclimated, but did not live very long.

The son-in-law of Yudel Ekerling, Yaacov Prashel, came to Horodenka in 1922. He participated in all areas of Jewish Zionist activity for all the years that he lived in our city until moving to Israel.

Yakov Rat and Note Shechter moved to Israel, near Petach Tikva, around 1926. They established a brick-making factory, in which they sunk most of their earnings. For different reasons, their factory did not succeed and they were forced to leave Israel after having lost all the money that they invested.

Here we will mention two citizens of our city who functioned as activists on different and separate stages of Jewish history, both of whom finished their lives in a tragic manner: Yaacov Adlerstein, one of the leaders of the Jewish community in Czechoslovakia, who was exterminated with his family in Auschwitz, and Dov Cohen, one of the commanders of *Etzel, Irgun Tzava Leumi* (Israel defense army), who fell in battle during an invasion.

The movement of Jewish workers known as the Yiddish *Arbeiter Ring*, or, in short, *Der Bund*, took root in the city after the First World War. The members that stood out were: Issac Fink, Yossel Katz, Asher Shtreyt, Ephraim Patner, Sheindel Patner (Podvisaker), Baruch Isaac Shpierer, Yehudah Hirsh Sobel, Hirsh Schecter, Avraham Shneiderman, and others. Among the first activists in this movement, there remained only Isaac Fink and Baruch Isaac Shpierer, who are now living in America. They are very involved in the *Landsmanshaft* organization and the committee to publish the Horodenka book.

The *Bund* accomplished a lot for the proletariat organization of the city It included small businessmen who were not actually proletariats. It awakened in its members an awareness of their position and broadened their horizons through various cultural activities. But the main activity of the *Bund* in our city was the Yiddish School of Avraham Reisin that was established from donations by city members with the assistance of American organizations. Asher Shtreyt and Yossel Katz, who were among the founders of the school, were also the first volunteer teachers. (The foundation and development of this school described in the memoirs of Isaac Fink.)

An uncrowned leader of the Jewish workers' movement in our city was Chaim Tauber — Chaim Baszur — the younger brother of the teacher Yehudah Baszur. He was a tall and broad-shouldered Jew who made a living from selling fish; but he considered himself a proletariat in all matters. He mingled with the poor of the city and he would make a commotion with fiery words about every evil and injustice that affected the impoverished masses or individuals.

*

In our city there were some *maskilim* who did not stand out as activists: Meir Shlam, Nachman Shternhol, and Shlomo Heller. Meir Shlam was a sharp-minded man, both learned and wise. He was an expert accountant and managed the books of one of the wealthiest men in the city. He was at home both among the city's most observant people as well as in Zionist circles. When he was among the Zionists, he would extol the virtues of the ultra-orthodox, and when he came among the latter, he would extol the virtues of the Zionists.

Nachman Shternhol was one of the elders of the city. He had a white beard and an aristocratic face; yet at times he functioned like a *maskil*. Every *Shabbos* afternoon, one could see him in the *Tziyon Farein* reading German newspapers, without wearing the traditional *shtreimel*.

Shlomo Heller was an intellectual Jew who was somewhat scatterbrained. He had no children and it seems like his wife was the primary provider. He himself was involved with giving short-term lessons in *Tanach*, and in managing accounts. During a certain period he was also a correspondent for the *Lemberger Tagblatt* (daily) in our city.

Authors and Performers

Yehudah Cohen, an estate owner in Stetseva, must be counted among the *maskilim* of Horodenka. He was a native of Ozeryany, and he earned a detailed description in the memorial book of that city. His brother, the lawyer David Kohen, lived in our city, and because of this, Yehudah Cohen was well known in our town as a man of letters and a *maskil*. Another native of Horodenka was also the *maskil* and scholar Feivish Meltzer, the *cohen*.

Among the scholars and activists of the last generation who achieved a reputation for their activities outside our city, it is worth mentioning Shmuel Abba Sofer. His youth in Horodenka is broadly covered in this book. His activities as a *sofer* and a journalist in Czernovitz, are treated by Dr. Gelber in the historical journal and in an article by Yitchak Paner, a Yiddish author who lived near him in Czernovitz during the last period of his life.

Horodenka also produced two stage performers with a universal reputation, Rona Pfifer-Laks and Alexander Granach. Rona Pfifer was the daughter of the court accountant Pfeffer and she was an outstanding singer in the state opera in Vienna. In the period between the wars, she visited Horodenka and appeared in concerts in the Sokol auditorium. During a later period, she also visited Israel.

Alexander Granach became famous as an actor on the German and English stage in America in the period between the Wars, and also as a movie actor. He died in New York in 1945, when he was still young, and he left a very literary autobiographical book called *A man and his Journeys*. The chapters that related to the period of his life in our city are transcribed in this book in Yiddish, and so too is mentioned his visit to our city and his influence on the drama circles in Horodenka.

Women Activists

Under the influence of the emancipation movement, a nationalist and socialist women's group called Devorah was founded in 1911. The founders were the Zeyfer and Shpierer (the wives of Berl Zeyfer and Berl Shpierer), Tzivia Herman, Tziporah Eyzman, and Esther Morboym. In the thirties, a women's Zionist organization was established, called *Vayitzav*. Those who participated in its founding were Freide Frishling, of blessed memory, and Dina Rozenboym, of blessed memory, among others. This group developed in a lively and active manner until the very days of the Holocaust. In it were obviously several righteous Jewish women whose lives were dedicated to activities of assisting the weak, the ill, and the poor, or to helping poor and unfortunate brides get married.

From among these righteous women, it's valuable to single out *di bentzioneche*, the wife of the rope maker Ben Tzion Diner, who was well known in the city as a volunteer for charitable matters, especially for the needs of the *Mitzvah* of *Hachnasat Kallah*, attending to the bride.

Doctors

Among the independent professionals in our city, doctors and lawyers were primary; but it was natural that the number of lawyers was much more than the number of doctors. The eldest of all the Jewish doctors was Dr. Oscar (Yehoshua, in Hebrew) Kanapas, who settled in Horodenka right after he graduated, and remained in the city till a ripe old age. Dr. Kanapas was born in Kameka-Strumiloba to the Vashitz family, and was the uncle of Dr. Fischel Vashitz, one of the leaders of the Revisionists in Israel.

During the period of his studies in Lvov, he met Soloma Kurtzer, the daughter of Dr. Kurtzer, and he married her. Dr. Kurtzer settled in Horodenka and after he finished his studies, he established a medical practice. After his father-in-law died, the patients of Dr. Kurtzer transferred to Dr. Kanapas. He established himself as a successful doctor, became the doctor of the Baron, and the doctor appointed by the government to the court, city, and state pharmacy.

To the Kanapas family were born two sons and one daughter, and they all learned medicine. The first born, Gershon-Gustav, who was for some years a doctor in the city of Tluste in east Galicia, was known for his dedication and good heart, his communal and Zionist activities, and his generosity of spirit. Not only did he offer free medical help to the indigent, but also he opened a special account in the local pharmacy, to pay for medicines to the poor. In 1925, a typhus epidemic broke out in Tluste and surrounding areas, which took the lives of many citizens. Many of those who were able, including the city doctors, left the city from fear of the epidemic. Gustav Kanapas provided medical aid to the ill, made his nights like days, until the disease overpowered even him; all the efforts of other doctors who gathered from various places didn't succeed in saving him. The entire city participated in his funeral and the mourning was very great. People of the city said that the only other person to merit such a funeral and such mourning was the beloved rabbi of the city, Rabbi Pinchas Chodorover, of blessed memory.

A peer and "competitor" of Dr. Kanapas was Shimshon, who was a doctor by profession but unlicensed. Shimshon the doctor lived as a Jew from the previous generation, and it was easy to call him, and to ask his advice about any slight ailment. His wife was also involved in the medical profession as a midwife for the women of the city. Shimshon the doctor died by a *Kiddush Hashem* (sanctification of the Name) in 1915, when he tried to rescue a Torah scroll from a synagogue that was enveloped in fire. Russian soldiers, who saw him doing this, threw him into the fire, and he was burned with the Torah scroll in his arms.

In the era before the First World War, there was another Jewish doctor in our city who worked in a special field of veterinary medicine, Dr. Ludvig Bach. Externally, he was no different from other doctors in the city, but his acquaintances said that he was learned and even achieved a level of prominence in scholarship. In the years after the World War, he opened in the center of the city a beautiful clothing store featuring high-class shoes from the Salamander factory. Also, the first pharmacist in our city was a Jew whose name was Meron Luria. The pharmacy was the most impressive building on the main street; the arrangements in the pharmacy were extraordinary.

We should single out two doctors who were in the city during the Holocaust and who were exterminated in the first raid, Dr. Shneyder and Dr. Vassertzveig. Dr. Shneyder was not part of the Zionist group but he happened to visit Israel in 1937 with a group of medical representatives. He was known as a good and kind doctor who healed the poor when they were ill without taking any payment, and even gave them medicine at his own expense, when necessary. As conveyed by the survivors of the Holocaust who got to Israel, his behavior during the Holocaust was exceptional in its ethical level. He and his wife refused to be friends with the *Kreizhoftman*, the enemy Hak, and this prevented his removal from the rows of those judged for death in the great synagogue on the day of the first extermination. When they removed the "useful" Jews, they warned them that they should stay away from the central square according to the order of the Germans. However the doctor refused to leave, and chose to be together with all the other Jews in a situation of danger. In the death camp in Semakovtse, he was the only one who dared to lift his voice to protest against the murderers. As a result he was shot right on the spot, even before they got to the ditch that was prepared as a grave for the victims.

Lawyers and Government Officials

The second group of independent professionals in our city was a group of justice officials. In the period before the First World War there were in our city four Jewish lawyers and one Jewish chief judge named Rothauser. The Jewish lawyers were: Dr. Yitzchak Baron, Dr. Emanuel Werber, Dr. David Kohen, and Dr. Alpert. From among these four, Dr. David Kohen stood out because in addition to his general wisdom and professionalism, he also had a broad command of the Hebrew language. He was similar to his brother Yehudah Kohen from Stotchova, who was one of the foremost *maskilim* with a fluent pen of scholarship.

Dr. Adolf Alpert came to Horodenka as the son in law of Alter Yungeman, a short time before the First World War. In the brief period of the existence of the West Ukrainian Republic in 1918, Dr. Alpert was the head of the national Jewish committee in Horodenka and joined the national gathering in Stanislav, in November of 1918.

In the last ten years before the Holocaust, Dr. Shlomo Zalman (Zunia) Lagshteyn worked in our city as a lawyer and a Zionist activist. He was the son of Nechemia Lagshteyn from the village of Korniv. He was one of the most active and dedicated in all the areas of Zionist activity and was for many years the head of the Zionist group in our city. He was also one of the Zionist representatives in the community council, and he also stood out in his dedication to the Zionist cause. During the reign of the Nazis, he returned to his village and from there he was sent to the concentration camps together with the other Jews in the village.

Just as at the side of the professional Dr. Kanapas, the non-professional Shimshon the doctor had worked, so too non-professional lawyers worked alongside the professional lawyers. The accepted name of this type of lawyer was the *Vinkel Shrieber*, the corner scribe. In the generation before ours, Hirsh Fielder was known as master in this arena; he left for America in beginning of this century.

Similar to the position of lawyers were the court officials and other government offices. This group was not all cut from the same cloth. Among them were those who still kept both feet in the traditional Jewish community, like the court clerk Hirsh Weysberg. Others, however, strove to imitate the world of liberal professionals and distanced themselves from any semblance of traditional life. The best known of this group were: Dovid Zeidman, Yossel Geller, Moshe Nafe and Chalzal.

Dovid Zeidman was a clerk in the central government house, and in addition served for many years as a secretary of the community council. Yossel Geller was a court clerk. He was a member of the *Bikur*

Cholim (visiting of the sick) society and for a certain time was even the head of this group. He was also a member of the community council, and for several years served as a vice president to the head of the council, Berel Shpierer. Moshe Nafe and Chalzal were known in the city as court clerks, but they weren't involved in communal life.

Bankers and Estate Owners

Before the First World War, there were several men in our city who were involved in loans and bill deductions, according to banking principles; they were very successful in their businesses. The top among the bankers in Horodenka was *Reb* Alter Yungerman, who ran his business in partnership with his son Shmuel. The smaller bankers were: Velvel Zeidman, Berel Shpierer, and Yidel Ekerling. The bank did not function independently but rather existed in one of the rooms in the home of the "banker."

A few of these bankers were also estate owners — some small and some large — but they themselves were city dwellers. In contrast, there were some estate owners who actually lived in their estates. Of the latter sort were Yosel Zeidman in Sarafinitz, Yosef Bosner in Potochishche, Yisroel Goldenberg in Strel'cheye, the Baron family in Rakovets, and the Rubal family in Korniv.

The Group of Merchants in our City

As was customary among most of the cities in exile, the composition of the merchants in our city comprised the majority of the Jewish population in our city. Consequently, it is understood that this was a very colorful and divergent group, from an economic perspective, from a personality perspective, and from the perspective of communal affiliation and political activism. We can only mention here the most outstanding representatives of this large group.

The senior member of the Horodenka storekeepers in the beginning of this century was Itzik Reuven Shor, the owner of an upscale grocery store, opposite Luria's pharmacy. Itzik Reuven was a well-to-do Jew and a scholar. In his older age, he transferred the management of the store more and more to his son-in-law Avrohom Yager, who was very popular and an activist in the *Bnei Zion* group. Avrohom Yager, with his wife and one of his sons, Miku Yeger, the head of *beitar* in our city, was exterminated during the holocaust.

The neighbor of Itzik Reuven Shor was Chaim Shuchner, a storekeeper for ready-made clothes for men. Chaim Shuchner was one of the most honored merchants in the city, and was known for his uprightness and honesty. Over the years, he became a member of the committee to evaluate the ability of the city dwellers to pay city taxes, and everyone depended on him and trusted that no one would be short changed through him.

In the market square, there were stores owned by many of the important city merchants. In the square were found the stores of Shlomo Shtreyt and Yanker Haber, who both had high quality grocery stores. However, most of the stores in this row belonged to leather merchants from the families of Berman and Reichman: Moshe Chaim Berman, Hershel Berman and Berel Berman, and the two brothers Anshel and Binyamin Reichman.

Hershel Berman was counted among the honorable young men in the city. (His brother in law, his wife's brother, was professor Fishel Brenner from Czernovitz.) He died in his youth before the First World War. One of his daughters, Dusye, remained in Horodenka and came to her death in the first raid, together with her husband Berish Reichman and their two children. Berel Berman was an active Zionist from his youth. His wife, Miriam from the Shikler house in Gvozdzets, excelled in her deep knowledge of the Hebrew language. Both of them were exterminated in the Holocaust. The brothers Anshel and Binyamin Reichman were considered well-to-do merchants. The sons and daughters of both families actively joined the Zionist groups in our city.

There were in these rows of stores other stores of leather and boots, which did not belong to the Berman and Reichman families. One of them belonged to Chaim Noach Rauchwerger, who died in his youth even before World War One. His widow Yukhbad, her daughter and son-in-law, and their children all perished in the Holocaust. So too did her two sons David and Yehudah perish.

Regarding the significant merchants in the grocery department, Yehuda Wolf

Shuchner should be included. He was primarily involved with selling groceries wholesale to a merchant in one of the nearby villages. His son Milak (nickname for Yerachmiel) was an active Zionist from his youth (even before the World War) and continued to be active throughout his life, until the days of the Holocaust. The oldest son, Boom Shuchner, who was also active in the Zionist organization, moved to Kolomyja after his marriage, opened a wholesale grocery business, and stayed in contact with many of the grocers in our city. The most familiar ones among the storekeepers were: Menashe Bilder, Azriel Fleshner, Yekil Yanekner, Mendel Flohr (before World War I) Feivish Mohler, Yisrael Kramer, Motl Edelstein, Dovid Gluger, Chaim Hirsh Meltzer, Yonah Mayer, and Yonah Kraimer.

A significant number of our citizens obtained their livelihood from hospitality and tourist professions as restaurant, bar and hotel owners. The two best-known inns in our city were that of Shaya Mendel Berg and Shlomo Avraham Shor. The most popular restaurants were owned by Uri Chaim Shartzer, Dudia Shechtal, and Rozenboym, who each had "first rights" in a specific area of entertainment: Shartzer brought to the city the words of the first song; Shechtel, the first gramaphone; and Rozenboym, the first billiard table. Other well-known restaurant owners were Shlomo Avrohom Kramer, Gershon Shpielberg, Chaim Greyf, and Antshel Reichman. There were also several suppliers of cold drinks, for example, Feivel Lichtenthal (also known as Feivele Kvassnik), Melech Marksheid, and Zeide Rindenoy.

Among the clothing merchants were several cloth merchants and shoe salesmen. Chaim Hirsh Zeidman was the owner of a large fabric store. He was very involved in Zionism. Another large fabric storeowner in the period after the First World War was Shimon Pilpel. The fate of the family of his son Moritz is worth special mention. Moritz and his wife succeeded in being rescued, and in a wondrous manner left Europe on the illegal ships that made their way to *Eretz* Israel during the turmoil of the War days. Unfortunately their ship was attacked by Nazi pilots. Many of the travelers were killed, including Moritz and his wife, who was from the Shor family. Their little son was given, at the beginning of the Holocaust, to a Polish family who raised him as their son. A few years after the War was over, the Polish family came out, with the son of Pilpel, in Polish territory. After great difficulty, the boy was taken from the Polish family and brought to the family of Fania Shor-Fishof, his mother's sister.

The best-known shoe store before the First World War was the store of Yonah Kramer. In the last years, another clothing store became well known, that of Elimelech and Feige Salpeter, who succeeded in attracting a large contingent of customers because he offered sales on credit.

In the area of metal merchants was the big store of Mordchele Shnitzer, which was inherited by his sons Chaim and Simcha Shnitzer. Other important iron merchants were: Eliezer Friedler, Leibele Korn, and Zundel Shuchner.

The storehouses of wood merchants were naturally outside the city, where there was appropriate land to store their merchandise. There were two main merchants of this profession; the two lived at the crossroads, practically across from each other. They were Hershel Shartzer and Chaim Wolf Diker. In the middle of the Toliki was the wood storehouse of Yaacov Ofenberger.

The Shartzer family was one of the wealthiest families in the city. Hershel Shartzer was one of the first Zionists in the city. (According to Dr. Gelber, he was the first head of the group *Bnei Zion*.) His daughter Tzipe was the first Hebrew kindergarten teacher.

It's proper to single out the role of women in the economic life of our city. In most of the stores, the women would assist their husbands every day of the week, and of course on market day. However, there were several women who carried the burden of running some big and multi-branched businesses — either alone or with the help of their grown sons. The most important among them were Maltzia Bergman, Paya Grapakh, and Chaya Stark.

Maltzia Bergman was the daughter of Shaul Prashel and the granddaughter of Rabbi Yossel Rozenkrantz. Her husband Moshe Bergman passed away at a young age and she remained a widow with six children. Still, she continued to run the large, all-purpose store in the market square. (There was a saying in the city, "You can buy everything in Maltzia's store, except for wisdom.") She also continued the legacy of her husband, who was famous for giving charity in secret. More than once he would remove the clothes from his own back to give to the destitute. Besides this store, the family owned a brick factory, and when the sons grew up they also got involved in fishing. The second son Yossel went to a school for fishing in Czernovitz, and became known as alicensed fisherman. He and his brother Leibish would lease the rivers in the area, and would sell fish for wholesale. They were also involved in selling crabs to several royal houses in Europe.

Maltzia Bergman passed away in the beginning of the First World War during the period of the Russian conquest. S. Ansky, the author of *The Dybbuk*, happened to be in Horodenka then as a member of the Jewish Assistance in Galicia. He was dressed as a Russian officer, took an interest in her, and sent for a Russian military doctor who cared for her during her illness.

Paya Grapakh also managed a general store, specializing in clothes and knickknacks, with the help of her daughters. Chaya Stark was the owner of a big grocery store in the market square, and was known as an honest and diligent businesswoman.

Workers

Long and colorful is the list of workers and craftsmen in our city, in all their various vocations, so we will mention only those who stand out the most. One of the old workers was Sholom Hirsh Fink, who was involved also in the trade that's considered the "Jewish Vocation." S. H. Fink was a women's tailor, and even though in general the Jews were not really so involved with crafts, compared to the local craftsmen, Fink enjoyed a special relationship because of his personal talents. He was a G-d-fearing Jew, with a handsome face and a long white beard, and was known as an exceptional cantor. In the large synagogue he was the Torah reader all year round, and the cantor for the morning services during the High Holidays. His prayer was known as a pure prayer that pours forth from the heart of a wholehearted and upright man who was loyal to his G-d and his people.

A women's tailor younger than Fink, but no less well known than him, was Moshe Manas Neygiser. He was younger than Fink and known as a modern person. He was one of the first who traveled to America, without their families; but he came back after a few years and remained in our city. In 1907, he was one of the founders of the workers union, *Yad Charutzim* (the hand of the diligent) and was one of its faithful members. In 1929, his daughters immigrated to the United States; his wife also immigrated and remained there. Only Moshe Manas and one of his married daughters remained in Horodenka and were killed in the Holocaust.

Close to the vocation of tailors was Itzy Issy Hecht, who was one of the respected workers in the city. His work was a shoe cobbler, and like Neygiser, he joined *Yad Charutzim*, and remained faithful to it till its dissolution. In the craft of carpentry, the familiar people in the city were from the family of Patner. The father, Asher Patner, was an observant Jew, who was involved in communal activities as a member of the *Chevra Kadisha* and in the group of coffin bearers. His sons Ephraim and Yossel Panter were the heads of the Bundist groups, and were known as activists in the Yiddish school.

Among the best of the furniture builders in the city was Leibele Panter, who also was among the Bundist activists and participated in the movement's drama group in the years 1925-1930. Afterwards he became a member of *Ha'ovaid*, a Zionist union of workers. This union was organized by Lipa Liser and Sholom Yungerman. He was also one of the members of *Tzach*, a city government organization to support trade workers.

Gimpel Patner was also a carpenter, and known in the city as the *Chevra Kaddisha* man, who participated in all funerals, and was also a steady guest at all the happy celebrations in the city. During the Holocaust when deaths were a regular occurrence in the ghetto and there was no one to attend to the burial of the dead, there were two Jews who took upon themselves the responsibility of giving the dead a Jewish burial. The two were Moshe Podvisaker, the father of Abba Podoveh, who was a *brenner* (an expert liquor maker) by profession, and Gimpel Potner. Every day, these two would be involved in this holy activity; quickly would they transport the departed ones to the cemetery, to give them a Jewish burial. At first they did this in secret, in the darkness of night. However, as time passed it reached the point that even the Nazi oppressors valued this activity and saw them as "superior Jews," and therefore didn't harm them until the final raid, when they carried out their "purification" without any discrimination.

Moshe Podvisaker was for all of his life an activist in the group of *Bikur Cholim*, visiting the sick, and in the *Chevra Kaddisha*. He was a very intelligent person and known as a "master of advice," and also very familiar with the laws of healing. He was also one of the founders of *Yad Charitzim*, and also one of the members of the *Konsus*, a cooperative store.

Another outstanding carpenter was Yisrael Shneyderman, who was a furniture maker. He arrived at our city after the First World War, merited the nickname, "the Russian furniture maker," because of his profession, and quickly became famous as a master craftsman of modern, ornate furniture. He employed seven young men, who learned carpentry from him.

Well-known carpenters in the city were also Shikel Kvetsher and his son Shimon. The actor Alexander Granach was the nephew of Shikel Kvetsher. Close to the profession of carpentry were the members of the Kluger family, who thanks to the old patriarch of the family, Yerucham, merited the title *Yerushkes*. Practically the whole family was involved in making burial coffins from wood of the surrounding areas. They also worked in glass making. The best known among the family were Shlomo Ber and his brother Yisroel Kaneh.

Shlomo Ber was the most methodical and respected among the family members. He was a well-to-do householder and he lived near the large synagogue. Sometimes he leased a part of his house to renters; for a period of time Rabbi Ashkenazi lived in his house. He was known as being very hospitable and the poor would continually eat at his table.

Yisrael Kaneh was a man of stormy character and would tend to get involved in every quarrel. He would especially get involved when he saw unjust activities or deprivation of the weak. More than once he risked his life protecting the poor vagrants in the market who were aggravated by the *rekroten*, the young men conscripted to the army who would fall upon them and grab fruit from their stands, as well as other objects. Since he was very bold, his fear fell upon both the Jews and non-Jews together. At the time of the first Action, his family was taken out and brought to the central location, but he himself was not disturbed from his hiding place. When Yisrael Kaneh saw that the house remained empty, despair overwhelmed him and he began running around the city streets, until he was captured and brought to the big *shul*, the place of those who were trapped for slaughter.

Another profession that was prevalent among us was that of furriers; many were involved in it, both in more elegant merchandise for the city dwellers, and also in the preparation of coarse furs for the village and town dwellers. Among the more refined furriers was Avremel Shneur, whose dwelling was opposite the Rutini church, near to the *Zion Farein*. He was also one of the first emigrants to America but he returned from there. Among the other professionals in this line, we should mention

Yankel Prifer, who was known as an observant Jew, and used every moment of his spare time for saying *Tehilim* psalms.

*

There were many butchers in our city. Whole families were involved in this profession, including the Prifer and the Kugelmas families. The Kugelmas family was among the most modern in the city. Aharon Kugelmass and his brother Izzi were both Zionists. In their home was also the headquarters of the *Bnei Zion* organization.

There were many blacksmiths in the city; they were all concentrated in the rows of small stores in the market square. The outstanding personality among them was Yossi Rozenboym, who was generally known as *Yossi Blecher*. In his youth he was friendly with *maskilim*. Eventually he abandoned the profession and was involved primarily in the metal business and with kitchen utensils. He was known for making exaggerated claims and telling fantasies, about what had happened to him in his travels to Lvov and other cities.

The builders of homes and fences in our city were primarily not Jewish. Among those few who were Jews, we should mention Boruch Leib Greidinger, who specialized in installing ovens to warm the dwellings. Boruch Leib participated all his life in the *Chevra Kaddisha*, and was conscientious in the fulfillment of the *mitzvah* of true kindness (attending to the needs of the dead.)

The aristocrats among the professionals in the Jewish quarter were, then and always, the watchmakers. There were four watchmakers in our city during the years before the World War: Shnuel Frishling, Meir Frishling, Avrohom Chaim Bartfeld, and Max Greif. In the last years before the Holocaust, the most well known watchmaker in the city was Hirsh Shechter, who was one of the leaders of the Bund, and a representative of this group in the community council.

Questionable workers and independent professionals were the various wagoners. In the city there were two types of wagoners — carriage drivers who transported passengers like Kopoleh Zankyeh, his son Henach Neyman, Yisrael Yurman, and Dudik Freidman; and wagon drivers for transporting merchandise from other cities, especially from Kolomyja. The best known among them were: Motya Fenster (Motya Shtroi), his brother Todros, and Yisroel Lichtenthal. The eldest of the wagoners was Shmaria Meltzer, the father of Issac Meltzer. Transporting merchandise involved a great measure of trust, since all the merchandise, and at times even its financial equivalent, was entrusted into the hands of these wagon transporters.

Finally, the best of the craftsmen in our city was Velvel Grinberg, who without any formal vocational training, reached a level of expertise in welding machines, a work that demanded great precision. Practically with his ten fingers alone, he put up a mechanical plant activated by steam, with etchings and other modern gadgets. All his sons inherited his skill and continued in the business with much excellence. His son Arzi, who was killed in Horodenka with his family, was an exceptional craftsman and stood out also as a member in the drama group.

*

We shall conclude the list with two Jews, who from the aspect of crafts, knew how to dedicate time to Torah and the fulfillment of the *mitzvah* of "And you shall be involved with them day and night," to the best of their ability. These two were the baker Shlomo Rosenberg and the tailor Yitzchok Aryeh Bumberg. Shlomo Rosenberg was not satisfied with fulfilling the *mitzvot* by himself, but also worked at engaging the masses in this *mitzvah.* Every *Shabbos* in the hours after noon, several Jews would gather in his house and study Torah until the departure of *Shabbos.* Yitchok Aryeh Bumberg would be immersed in Torah even when he was seated in concentration at his work, and he would utilize every opportunity to hear words of Torah while he was working. His youngest son, Meir Bomberg, who was a talented artist and had a natural singing ability, actively joined Gordonia. His second son Dovid reached Israel and died here in his youth.

In this compilation, we wanted to mention and describe several personalities and portraits of people in our city, who stood out in various areas of the life of the community in the last generation. We will not pretend that we satisfactorily handled these descriptions. Without doubt we skipped over people who should have been included in this compilation, and it's almost certain that we have not always succeeded in properly giving credit to those who we have mentioned. Many of the people that we have described here are also described either fully or partially in the last portions of the book, and were also cited here in order to complete the section. We attempted to describe portrayals of those who are not among the living, who were killed in the Holocaust or departed from life in the period afterward. May this section serve as a memorial for their memory and the memory of the community in which they lived and worked.

[Page 355 & 409]

Yakov Edelstein, of blessed memory

Translated by Harvey Buchalter

Yacov Edelstein was born in Horodenka in 1903. His parents were Motl and Mattil Eldelstein. During the years of the First World War, Edelstein and his family found themselves as refugees in Merrin. Following the war, Motl Edelstein and his wife and daughter, Dora, returned to Horodenka; Yaakov remained in Brin and there attended the School of Commerce. From the start he was a firebrand in the *Paole Zion* movement and became involved in the Social Democrat Party. He learned how to be an activist and became one of the most active members of the Party.

In 1927, he left the Social Democrat Party and in next two years he was not involved in any political activity. He was just a member of the "nature-lovers" (*naturfreunde*) Club. In 1929 he left Brin for Teplitz and there joined the Worker's League for *Eretz* Israel. His first work in the League consisted of organizing a referendum on Marxism. In a short time he became one of the most outspoken leader in the Socialist Zionist Movement, which soon took over all of the branches of Socialist Zionism except for *Paole Zion*. In 1931 he married and left immediately for Prague to take over the Zionist movement there. He remained in this position until the office was closed right before the outbreak of the War.

In this renowned era of Zionist activity, he was deeply involved as a great orator in Zionist and Socialist circles in Czechoslovakia. In 1933 he represented the Zionist Socialists and *Paole Zion* in the Zionist Congress. He also was involved in the Zionist Congress in Zurich in August 1939, which was interrupted by the outbreak of the Second World War. In 1937, he was in *Eretz* Israel for barely half a year. He was very active in *Keren Chesud* in Jerusalem.

As the Germans took over Czechoslovakia, Edelstein was forced to cooperate with the Nazis in order to be able to evacuate as many Jews as possible from the occupied zone. In the winter of 1938, he was sent to England along with Dr. Zuker to help facilitate the arrival of Jewish refugees. In the same year, the Nazi authorities allowed him to go to *Eretz* Israel with the same goal in mind (evacuation of Jews) but they then took away his wife's passport, thereby forcing him to return to Czechoslovakia. As late as 1940, during the War, the Nazis permitted him to go to Trieste in order to find ways of evacuating Czech Jews to other lands.

In 1941, the Nazis embarked on making Czechoslovakia *Judenrein*. They concentrated the population in Theresienstadt, and from there the majority were sent to death camps. Edelstein was the leader of the ghetto and was responsible for everything that happened within it. Often he dared to sidestep the Nazi decrees, thereby saving Jews from certain death. Children were not allowed to be born within the ghetto, so he gave the secretly born babies the names of people who had recently perished. Soon the Nazis uncovered his scheme, realizing that this is not the way it was supposed to be. They arrested Edelstein, his wife, and his only son and sent them to Auschwitz. There they let him live from December 1943 until June 1944. On the 18th of June, they permitted the family to reunite, but then murdered his family before his own eyes, and then murdered him.

Many have written about Edelstein's proud and courageous actions in Theresienstadt. They knew him as a Zionist activist and as a leader of the ghetto. This is only a glimpse of the man, taken from the writings of Dr. Max Brod, written in 1947, the third *yahrtzeit* of the death of Yaakov Edelstein.

[Page 356 & 410]

The Heroes of Theresienstadt

Dr. Max Brod

Translated by Harvey Buchalter

The 18th of June 1947 will mark the three-year *yahrzeit* of Yacov Edelstein's death in Auschwitz. Until now, very little has been discussed or written concerning our heroes in Theresienstadt. Generally speaking, the complete history of Theresienstadt has not been thoroughly documented. From 1939 on, Yacov Edelstein was the director of the Zionist movement's branch in Prague; later he took responsibility for everything having to do with the life of Czech Jewry. Some would say he caused Adolph's Eichmann's master plan to be delayed. And if the life of Theresienstadt's Jews contained some reprieve from total misery — they even had a measure of cultural freedom — this was all due to the tireless efforts of Yacov Edelstein and his assistants, Fritz Kahn, the engineer Otto Booker, and to this list of names I can proudly add my brother, Otto Brod. None are still alive. Their brave deeds cost them their lives.

Recently, the news of those days has been updated regarding the blessed work of Yacov Edelstein. He harnessed all of his power to shelter and protect Theresienstadt's Jews from the German oppressors, from the criminals who prevented Jewish women from giving birth in the ghetto. According to the Nazi decree, all pregnant women would have to have abortions performed. But he changed that and created conditions for children to be born in the ghetto. Every day Edelstein and his assistants "changed" the list of the people who were in the ghetto. The newly-born children were given the names of the deceased, or of those who had escaped from the camp. As far as the German bureaucracy was concerned, everything was in order. And the Jewish people lived on!

In September 1943 a change came. Some English soldiers had escaped from a prisoner of war camp and the Jews of Theresienstadt, who lived in misery and fear of death each day, hid the soldiers from the Germans. They might well have used this incident to our advantage with the British Minister Bevens, but as it turned out, it caused the death of leaders of the ghetto. The Germans figured out that the English soldiers had previously escaped; their tracks led to the ghetto. They wasted no time in finding them, and in the process also captured six Jews who had previously escaped. On November 11, 1943, the Germans took a count of all who lived within the ghetto. They took all of them, both young and old, to a meadow outside the ghetto and proceeded to count every one of them, from six in the morning to eleven at night. That is how they found out that Yacov Edelstein, the man responsible for everything that happened in the ghetto, had "betrayed" them. They also accused him of smuggling weapons into the ghetto. They took him to Auschwitz and kept him isolated in a separate bunker. His wife, his son, and his mother in law were sent to Birkenau, close to Auschwitz. On June 18, 1944, the entire family was brought to Auschwitz. As they were brought together, the Germans shot all three before Edelstein's eyes — first his mother-in-law, then his wife, and finally, his son. Then the murderers shot him.

And so a Jewish hero left this world, a man who up to the end did everything he possibly could and never gave up. In his place, they installed as director of the ghetto, a vile personage, a certain Dr. Mermelstein, from Vienna. (He had even once authored a Jewish history.) He soon lived up to the Nazis' expectation of promptness and respectability. This meant as follows: every single day he drew up the requested total of Jewish bodies to be sent off to the gas chambers. (Among them was my brother.) In the time during which Edelstein was director of the ghetto, he obstinately defended the life of every single Jew, and he was successful in saving the lives of hundreds of Jews. Had the war ended half a year earlier, tens of thousands of Jews would have remained alive had not the beast, Dr. Mermelstein, counted them for extermination by the hands of the Nazis.

Tel Aviv, June 1947.

[Pages 357 & 411]

Dov Kohen, of Blessed Memor

Kukeh Yiskar-Greyf

Translated by Harvey Buchalter

Dr. Kohen was born in Horodenka in 1915. His parents were Aaron-Leib and Sophia Kahn. Aaron-Leib Kahn was one of the first Zionists in the town (he even had several letters written to him by Dr. Herzl). All of his children were fervent Zionists. They all had an outstanding character and were all comrades in the *betar* — the youth wing of the revisionist Zionists.

Bertzieh, as his friends and family used to call him, was small and thin, with dreamy blue eyes. But he was extremely stubborn. He completed the *folkeshule* and *mittelschule* in Horodenka and he also graduated with honors from the Hebrew School. He arrived in *Eretz* Israel in 1936 intending to study philosophy at Hebrew University. But he was not able to sit still for long. In the middle of the war, as the first breaking news about the awful fate of Polish Jewry was being revealed, both pain and vengeance impelled him to action. He joined the ranks of the *Irgun Tzvi-Leumi* (the National Defense Organization) and took part in all of their operations in Jerusalem and the surrounding area. But even this did not satisfy his fiery nature, and so he volunteered for service with the British command that fought outstandingly on the African Front.

The Gate into the Grove

Dr. Kahn was exceptionally brave and was in all ways an exemplary soldier. In a very short time he was promoted to sergeant and was recognized and rewarded with a lifetime pension from the

British government. Later he asked to serve and then re-enlisted in the Jewish Brigade and took part in some of the bloodiest battles.

While he was in Europe with the Jewish Brigade, following the defeat of Germany, he witnessed an almost unbelievable accomplishment. His brother, Mark Kohen, had somehow survived and his letters indicated that he knew the name of the Nazi officer who was in charge of the round up and extermination of the Jews of Horodenka. He resolved that he would find him and avenge the revered dead. He roamed throughout Germany. He searched, questioning everyone he encountered, until he found the one he was looking for. He had uncovered the German beast — in human form — and brought upon him the vengeance that he deserved.

After the war he returned to *Eretz* Israel, a famous and well-regarded soldier. Then he made a decision. As much as he wanted to study, he couldn't sit and rock back and forth as *cheder* students, as the rest of the Jewish world was in turmoil and was struggling for the right to absorb the remnants who had been saved. The *Hagganah* had given him important responsibilities in its hierarchy, but this made him all the more nostalgic for his days as a youth in *beitar*. He resolved to enlist in the *Irgun*. He commanded many successful military operations and acquired a new nickname: *Gundir Shimsom*, Brigadier Samson. When the British brought counter-insurgency operation against the *Irgun*, he was already one of the highest in command, as a military planner and chief of operations.

In his last appearance as a commander he directed the demolition of the prison in Acco, May 14, 1947. The operation was considered to be a great success, but he fell as he allowed his men to safely leave the battle zone.

We will always remember him as on of the bravest soldiers in the struggle for freedom for the Jewish people.

[Page 358 & 412]

A Final Tear

by Moishe Fleshner

Translated by Harvey Buchalter

This lament is written for all of you who come from Horodenka, all of you who lived and grew up in our town of Horodenka! Let us all recite a collectively intoned Kaddish as we complete our reading of the *Sefer Horodenka*, whose last chapters read like the Book of Lamentations, a lament on the destruction in Jerusalem. As we recite the prayer of *Kaddish* let the tears fall from our eyes upon the pages of this book which contains all of the details of the crimes that spell out the tragic end of our town and our dear parents, sisters, and brothers. They made a life for themselves with sweat and blood in the centuries they lived there. They used their talents and their skills to build this town into a thriving Jewish community until the murderous hands of the Nazi regime laid claim on it and transformed it into a mass grave for all of these who once called it home.

By having read this *Yizkor* Book each of us has re-lived the years we spent in our old home, in times of happiness, in times of suffering. And in spirit — if nothing else — these memories have taken us one last time around the so-familiar streets, streets which have made such a deep impression on our emotions in the days of our youth. Let it be a final stroll on the *Karzah*, on the wide expanse of the green *Tolliki*, on the *Katikivka* with its abundant cane (pussywillows) in the summer. How these canebrakes instilled fear in our young hearts! And the forests … the smell of which intoxicated all our senses. And *Sobiks Taich* whose flowing waters caressed our bodies as we swam on the hot summer days.

But our pain and suffering did not come to an end with the destruction of the town; there remains not even the smallest trace of Jewish life, even a Jewish grave marker, even if you seek it with tears in your eyes and bloody wounds upon your heart. With beastly cruelty the bloodstained hordes tossed the dead upon the ground — earth that is now literally overgrown with grain and greens for the tables of the new residents, the "inheritors" of what was once Jewish. They are now more than content to be free of their Jewish neighbors once and for all.

Twenty-one years have already passed since we originally planned to erect this monument that has taken the form of *Sefer Horodenka*, the book that will reveal to the world the shameless history of the destruction of this small Jewish community in Eastern Galicia. Almost every chapter of the book reveals the pain of each soul of the murdered Horodenka men, women, and children who would never live on. But even the best description, one that was scripted by the most talented writer, would not be able to express the pain, the anguish, and the wounds that remain in the hearts of those left orphaned in our town. And none of us will ever again have the opportunity to go to the [Horodenka] cemetery, let our hearts unleash the sorrow and pain, and recite *Kaddish* in memory of our dear loved ones.

Therefore, let each of us, as we read our *Sefer Horodenka*, allow a tear to fall in the name of the revered souls of the Jews of Horodenka — many of whom never tasted happiness in their days.

This is how we must fulfill our basic obligation to them, the Souls of Horodenka's Jews, who with their blood illuminated the epochs of Jewish life in Horodenka.

May their souls live forever.

Tel Aviv.

ילדי ישראל שנרצחו בידי הנאצים — 1942

יידישע קינדער, אומגעבראכט דורך די נאציישע מערדער — 1942

Jewish children murdered by the Nazis — 1942

Appendices

List of Holocaust Martyrs

The authors of "Sefer Horodenka" created from memory a list of their family members and neighbors who perished in the Holocaust. We've translated that list from Yiddish to English, and present it to you here.

We used the YIVO style when transliterating names. Due to our inexperience with translating Yiddish, we were sometimes unsure of our translation. In these cases we've included the original Yiddish spelling or our comments [in square brackets] in the text. In some cases, the book's typesetting was incorrect, which led to some confusion in the translation. For example, the typesetters were careless when differentiating between the letters "fey" and "pey." We've translated exactly as printed, except where we could determine with high assurance that the typesetting was at fault.

The names here are listed in the same order as they were in Sefer Horodenka. Because they were originally written in yiddish, using the hebrew alphabet, they were listed in hebrew "alef-beys" order.

The table below lists the Hebrew letters and possible English letters to which they might be transliterated. Use this table as a guide when searching for a surname. For example, if you are looking for the name "Cohen," which in the YIVO style would be transliterated as "Kohen," the name might be listed under

כ , or ק ,

or both.

א	ב	ג	ד	ה	ו	ז	ח
A, E, I, O	B	G	D	H	V, W	Z, S	H
ט	י	כ	ל	מ	נ	ס	ע
T	Y	K, C	L	M	N	S	E
פ ף	צ	ק	ר	ש	ת ת		
F, P	S, Z	K, C	R	SH, S	T, S		

א

ABUSH, Shepsil (Shabsil).

ABTSUG, Shmuel with his wife and their children Leyb and Sara.

ABTSUG, Tuvya, his daughter Sara and his son Yakov (from Korniv).

AGATSHTEYN, Itsik with his mother and two sisters.

AGATSHTEYN, Avraham with his wife; their daughter Gitl; their son Nakhman with his wife Hudl and their children.

AGATSHTEYN, Itsi and his brother Avraham.

AGATSHTEYN, Zeyde with his wife Toybe and their children Manye, Etye and Rukhl.

AGATSHTEYN, Toybe and her daughters Hudye and Kreyndl.

AGATSHTEYN, Mekhl (from Korniv).

ADLER, Khayim-David with his wife Ite and their children, Mendl and Yosef.

ADLER, Moshe and his sister Rivka.

ADLER, Elke and her children, Leyzer and Manye.

ADLER, Fishl and his wife Viltsye

ADELSBERG, Barukh and his wife Pesye ; his two sisters Vitye and Sara.

AVERBUKH, Asher and his wife Feyge.

AVERBUKH, Nina and her parents.

EYZMAN, Ben-Tsion with his wife Tsiupa and their children Ester and Dvora.

EYZMAN, Hershl with his wife and their children Yankl, Itse, Leyzer, and Rukhl.

EYZMAN, Shprintse; her daughter Zisl; her daughter Khaya with her husband; her son Mekhl with wife and children.

EYZMAN, Rivka and her sons Leyzer and Yokl.

IMBERMAN, Beynish with his wife.

IMBERMAN, Mordkhay with his wife; their son Avraham with his family; their son Shmuel with his family.

IMBERMAN, Kofl with his wife Sheyndl and their four children.

ISL, Yosef and his two sisters, Rukhl and Khaya.

ALFERT, Dr. Adolf (attorney) and his son, Mundek (Zigmund or Sigmund) Alfert

OLIVER, Yitskhak with his wife and their children.

AMSTERDAM, Frume; her son Kalman; her son Zakharaya with his wife.

OSTERMAN, Poldek with his wife Fanye and their children.

OSTERN, Binyamin with his wife and their children.

OFENBERGER, Avraham with his wife and their children Khaya and Moshe.

OFENBERGER, Barukh-Leyb and his wife Feyge.

OFENBERGER, Gershon and his wife Zisl.

OFENBERGER, Zeyde with his wife Tsipe and their children Yosl and Feyge.

OFENBERGER, Zeyde and his wife.

OFENBERGER, Khayim-Yisrael.

OFENBERGER, Yenkl and his wife Klara.

OFENBERGER, Leybish with his wife Libe and their children Maks and File.

OFENBERGER, Libke ; her daughter Rivka with her husband (Gilzon).

OFENBERGER, Mikhl with his wife Ester and their daughters Vitsye and Roza.

OFENBERGER, Moshe, his son Leyzer and two daughters.

ORINGER, Mizye.

ORNSHTEYN, Velvl with his wife and their children.

ב

BAKHER, Shamai [shin-mem-alef-yud] and his wife.

BONUS, Shlomo and his children.

BONUS, Meir with his wife and their children.

BOLKHOVER, Frume.

BARTFELD, Avraham and his wife Gizela.

BALAN, [no given name] and his family.

BANDLER, [no given name].

BAKELNIK, Yosef with his wife Elke and their children Minye and Dvora.

BOYMEL, Shlomo with his wife and their children.

BUMBERG, Yitskhak-Arye; his son Eyzik with his family; his son Moshe with his family; his son Meir; his three daughters Blume, Frume and Yehudit.

BUMBERG, two brothers (Akiva Bumberg's sons).

BURG, Shaya-Mendl and his wife Etl.

BIDER, Hersh and his wife Malka.

BIDER, Avigdor.

BIDER, Ester.

BIDER, Henye-Malkha.

BIDER, Moshe.

BIDER, Kune (Alkuna [alef-lamed-kuf-nun-hey]).

BIDER, Rivka.

BIDER, Reyzye.

BILER, Moshe and his wife Frume.

BILDER, Menashe, his wife Ita, their child Risye and their daughter Kheytsye (married name GRINBERG).

BINDER, Eyzik-Shimon and his wife Khana; their son Zeynvl with his wife Rukhl; their daughters Mizye, Brukha and Beyle with their families; their son Yisrael.

BINDER, Golde.

BINDER, Khayim.

BINDER, Frume.

BINDER, Yakov with his wife Dvora and their children Manye and David (from Korniv).

BIRNBOYM, Hersh and his wife Pesye.

BIRNBOYM, Perl.

BISHL, Aharon and his wife Khaya-Hudl.

BLAT, Shimon.

BLAT, Batya.

BLAT, Khonon.

BLAT, Rivka.

BLAT, Menakhem with his wife Sara; their son Yisrael with his wife Pesye; their son Hersh with his wife Pesye.

BLUTAL, Barukh and his wife.

BLAUKOPF, Nakhum with his wife Mintsye; their son Hersh with his wife Babtsye and their children Salo and Ruven (from Korniv).

BLEY, Frume and her children.

BLETERFEYND, Efraim and his wife Kheytsye.

BEKER, Shmuel with his wife and their children.

BEKER, Aharon with his wife Toybe and their children Gitsye and Yosef.

BEKER, Yona and his wife Milke (Milkha).

BERGMAN, Avraham with his wife (from Semakovits).

BERGMAN, Rivka.

BERGMAN, Nekhama.

BERGMAN, Hene.

BERGMAN, Kreyndl.

BERGMAN, Khaya.

BERGMAN, Shifra.

BERGMAN, Feyge.

BERGMAN, Yekhezkeil.

BERGMAN, Mendl and his children.

BERGMAN, Khana.

BERMAN, Berl and his wife Lea.

BERMAN, Berl with his wife Miryam and their daughter Khaya.

BERMAN, Yosl, his son Yehuda and his daughters Kheytsye and Fridzye.

BERNSHTEYN, Avraham, his son Hersh and his daughter.

BERNSHTEYN, Pinye with his wife and their daughter.

BERKOVER, Avraham, his wife Khana and their son Manele.

BRILER, Yosef.

BRILER, Volf.

BRILER, Mantsye.

BRILER, Meir.

BRILER, Frume.

BRILER, Khana.

BRILER, Khaya.

BRILER, Shalom.

BROYNSHTEYN, [no given name] his wife and their children.

BREKHNER, Eydl.

BREKHNER, Shimon.

BREKHNER, Motye.

BREKHER, Iser.

BREKHER, Yitskhak and his wife.

BREKHER, Yehuda (Eydl) with his wife Yehudit and their children Moshe, Yosef and Khana (from Korniv).

BRENER, Aharon, his brother Moshe and their sister Etl.

א

GOLDBERGER, Avraham-Yakov with his wife Rukhl and their children Mendl, Moshe and three daughters.

GOLDBERGER, Shlomo.

GOLDBERGER, Binyamin-Volf with his wife Khana and their children Itsi, Yosl and Moshe-Hersh; their daughter-in-law Reyzl with her daughter Golde.

GOTESMAN, Ester and her children.

GOLDSHTEYN, Antshl and his wife Golde (LAGSHTEYN).

GOLDSHTEYN, Eliyahu, with his wife Hudye and their children Avraham, Yitskhak and Ester.

GOLDSHMID, Moshe-Itsik with his wife and their children

GORFINKL, (the widow); her son Nusye (Natan); her son Yehoshua with his wife and their children.

GUTMAN, Mordkhay-Hersh with his wife Etye; their son Yenkl with his wife and two children; their daughter Reyle with her family; their daughter Kheytsye with her family.

GUTMAN, Aharon with his wife and their children Sabine and Mintsye.

GUTMAN, Yosef-Yitskhak and his wife Beyle.

GUTMAN, Yenkel with his wife and their children.

GUTMAN, Yekl (Yakov) with his wife Khana and their children Rekhamiel [resh-khes-mem-yud-alef-lamed], Zeynvel, Shprintse and Note.

GUTMAN, Leyb with his wife Blume and their daughter Ester.

GUTMAN, Moshe with his wife Sime and their children Mantsye and Yosef.

GUTMAN, Shlomo with his wife Rivke and his son Shmuel.

GUTMAN, Royze.

GUTMAN, Rukhl.

GUTMAN, (the children of Gershon GUTMAN): Leyb; Eyzik; Shmerl with his family.

GITER, Avraham with his children Yitskhak, Aharon and Tsipura.

GITER, Yekhezkeil with his wife Henye and their children Zalman, Tsila, and Tsipura.

GITER, Mendl with his wife.

GITER, Avraham (from Mikhaltshe).

GITER, Yitskhak (Bubi) (from Mikhaltshe).

GITER, Aharon (from Mikhaltshe)

GITER, Dvora (from Mikhaltshe).

GINSBERG, Hersh, his wife Malkha and their daughter Klara.

GINIGER, Hersh-Moshe.

GLOGER, Iser and his wife Golde.

GLOGER, Velvl with his wife Tsirl and their children.

GLOGER, Barukh with his wife Khume (Nekhama) and their daughter Eydl.

GLOGER, Efraim with his wife Freyde; their daughter Golde; their son Moshe-Mendl with his wife Khana and their children; his son Yosl with his wife and children, his daughter Lea'tsye and her children.

GLOGER, Shlomo-Ber with his wife Sara; their son David with his wife Tsharne and their children Fani, Yisrael and Matilde; their son Efraim and his daughter Ester.

GLOGER, Yisrael-Kune with his wife Khana; their son Yirukhem [yud-reysh-vov-khes-mem] with his wife and their children.

GLOGER, Yehuda-Shoel with his wife Tsipe and their children.

GLOGER, Ite; her son Hersh with his wife Sheyndl and children Eydl and Leyzer.

GLATSER, Golde.

GELER, Izye with his wife and children

GELER, Itsi.

GELER, Munye with his wife Hele and their children.

GELER, Munish with his wife Shibe.

GEFNER, Olye with his wife and two children.

GEFNER, Berl with his wife Slove and their children Rutsye, Zalmn and Dvora.

GEFNER, Meir with his wife Yehudit and their children Fride, Kalman, Yona and Dvora.

GERINGER, Mendl with his wife Feyge and their children Sender and Noakh.

GROSKOPF, Shikl with his wife and children.

GRAPAKH, Moshe.

GRAPAKH, Shekhna with his wife Puge [pey(fey?)-vov-giml-ayen] and their children.

GRAPAKH, Aharon with his wife Berta and their children Khana and Gusta.

GRAPAKH, Paye.

GRAPAKH, Eliezer.

GRINBERG, Izak with his wife Malkha and their children Vili, Zusye, and Motl.

GRINBERG, Edzye with his wife Rukhl and their children Aba and Munye.

GRINDLINGER, Hershl with his wife and children.

GRINZEYD, (Dr.) with his wife and children.

GREYF, Hilel with his wife Etke and their children.

ד

DOLINGER, Eliezer with his wife Beyle-Khana; their sons: Alter with his wife and children; Efraim with his wife and children; Moshe with his wife and their children (a son Berl and four daughters).

DOLINGER, Leybele with his wife and children.

DOLINGER, Yosl with his wife and their children.

DOLINGER, Kozil with his wife Mintsye and their daughter Sara.

DOLINGER, Shraka [shin-resh-hey'kuf-eyen] (Sarke).

DORNFELD, Shlomo with his wife Nutsye and their children Meir, Moshe, Menakhem and Feyge.

DANKNER, Lole, his brother Tsale and their sister.

DORF, Yehoshua with his wife and their children.

DORNFELD, Shlomo. [the same one as above?]

DORNFELD, Nutsye. [the same one as above?]

DORNFELD, Feyge. [the same one as above?]

DORNFELD, Aharon-Moshe.

DULBERG, Yosi; his children Khaytsi, Zisl and Blume.

DULBERG, Shlomo with his wife and their children.

DUL, Yekhezkeil and his son Yosl.

DINER, Antshel with his wife Sara; their son Shoel [shin-vov-alef-lamed] with his wife Henye and their children.

DINER, Yosl with his wife Feyge and their children Royze, Khaya and Pile [pey(fey?)-yud-lamed-ayen].

DINER, Ben-Tsion with his wife Sara; their son Yisrael-Mordkhay with his wife and their three daughter; DINER, Shmuel (son of Yisrael-Mordkhay) with his wife and their children.

DINER, Babe (Babe Khaya-Beyles).

DINER, Berl with his wife Beyle and their son Zalman.

DINER, Hersh and his wife Sara.

DINER, ("Yapontshik" [yud-pasekh alef-pey-komets alef-nun-tet-shin-yud-kuf]) with his wife and their children.

DINER, Zalman with his wife and their children Moshe, Beyle and Hudye.

DINER, Lea; her son Yosl with his family; her sons Lipa, Avraham and Meir, and a daughter.

DINER, Malye and her children Shoel and Mendl.

DINER, Peysye (Pesakh) with his wife and their children (Shmuel and others).

DINER, Mendl with his wife Frida and their children Moshe, Yosl, Miryam, Rivka and Gitl.

DINER, Moshe and his children Itsik, Feyge, Shmuel and Matilde.

DINER, Meir with his wife and their children.

DINER, Hersh with his wife Sara and their children.

DIKER, Feyvl with his wife Rukhl and their son Moshe.

DIKER, Herman with his wife and their children Leyzer, Fani and Shlomo.

DIKER, Loti and her son Khayim.

DIKER, Paye and her daughter Royze.

DRAKH, Yitskhak and his wife Perl.

DRANTSH, Khaya.

DERMER, Yakov with his wife and their children Shalom and Kheytsye.

DRUKER, Yitskhak with his wife Ester and their children Shimon, Khayb [khes-yud-yud-beys(veys?)], Ulu [shtumer alef-vov-lamed-vov], Lonye and Manye.

ה

HABER, Yenkl (Yakov) with his wife Royzye; their children Donye, Edzye, Frume and Bela, and their families..

HAHEN, Yakov with his wife Malkha and their son Gershon.

HALPERN, Yona with his wife Khinke and their children.

HALPERN, Beynish with his wife Gitl and their children Moshe and Tsipe.

HAZELNUS, [no given name] with his wife and their children.

HOFMAN, Leybish with his wife and their children.

HOFMAN, Nesye and her children Perets and Gitsye.

HOFMAN, Arye and his daughter Sime.

HOFMAN, Berish with his wife and their children.

HAKER, [no given name] with his wife Babtsye and their children.

HORN, Moshe with his wife and their children Lea'tsye and Velvel.

HORN, Ite-Hentsye and her children Zlate, Moshe, Mikhael and Yosl.

HARTENSHTEYN, Hersh with his wife and their children.

HARTENSHTEYN, Itsi with his wife and their children.

HARTENSHTEYN, Leyb with his wife and their children.

HUT, Yosl with his wife and their children Meshulam, Shlomo and Todres.

HUNDERT, Mikhl and his family.

HUS, Yehoshua with his wife and their children.

HUS, Shlomo with his wife Roza and their children Tsirl, Miryam and Etl.

HUS, Roza and her family.

HUS, Yekl and his family.

HUS, Yitskhak with his wife Rivka and their children Ruven and Hersh.

HUS, Yekl with his wife Maltsye and their children Leybele and Feyge.

HUS, Shaya with his wife and their children; their son Moshe David with his wife Khantsye and their children Note-Hersh, Ite, Milke and Barukh.

HUS, Etl and her family.

HURVITS, Sheyndl.

HURVITS, [no given name] (the brother-in-law of Itsi KORN).

HENIG, Breyntsye (from Korniv).

HERMAN, Toni.

HERMAN, Leyb with his wife Maltsye and their children.

HERMAN, Motl with his wife and their children.

HERMAN, Beyka [beys(veys?)-yud-yud-kuf-pasekh alef] with his wife Maltsye and two daughters.

HERMAN, Yuven with his wife Pesye and their children Roza, Shmerl and Rivtsye.

HESEL, [no given name] (Dr.) with his wife and their children.

ו

VAL, [no given name] with his wife Gitl and their children Pesye and Yekele.

VAKHTEL, Yakov with his wife; their daughter Etl with her family.

VASER, Fishl with his wife Libke and their children Lea and Marlena.

VASER, Feyvl with his wife Maltsye and their children Yehuda and Yekhezkeil.

VASER, Morits with his wife Miryam; their son Beyzye [beys(veys?)-yud-yud-zayn-yud-ayen] with his wife Sara.

VASER, Feliks and his sister Lusye.

VASERMAN, Naftali with his wife and their children.

VAKHER, Yakov with his wife Rivtsye and their children Hersh and Pepi.

VIZER, Bronek, Rozye and Natanya (from Korniv).

VEYKH, Khayim-Yisrael with his wife and their children Maks and Salye; their son Simkha with his wife Iza.

VEYKH, Khayim-Hersh; his son Hertsl and his two children.

VEYKH, Yosl with his wife Roza and their children Khayim, Shalom, David and Yisrael.

VEYNER, Rukhl and her children Yakov, Malkha, Rivka, Ben-Tsion and Hinde.

VEYNROYB, Moshe with his wife Miryam and their children Yukhbad, Yente and Etl.

VEYNROYB, Pinye with his wife; their sons Shimon, Nisan [nun-yud-samekh-nun] and Yisrael, and two daughters.

VEYNSHTEYN, Maks, his son Kamial [kuf-mem-yud-alef-lamed] and his daughters Fantsye and Rosye; his son Peysye (Pesakh) with his wife Ester.

VEYNSHTEYN, Munye with his wife and their children.

VEYNSHTEYN, Eliezer with his wife and their hcildren.

VEYNSHTEYN, Khayim with his wife and their children.

VEYNSHTEYN, Yosef with his wife and their children.

VEYSBERG, Yeti and her daughter Sidonya (Sidzya).

VEYSBERG, Henya and her husband Dr. KORMAN.

VEYSBRAT, Moshe, Lea'tsye, Eyndl and Golde.

VEYTSMAN, Eliyahu with his wife Miryam and their children Sara, Dvora and Elke.

VEYTSMAN, Mates-Loy.

VITSLING, Shaul and his wife Roza.

VITSLING, Ester.

VEBEL, Royze and her children Shmerl, Mendl, Frume, Binyamin and Moshe.

VEBER, [no given name] (Dr.) and his two children.

VERBER, (Dr.) Emanuel and his two children.

VERMUT, Moshe with his wife Tsharne and their daughter Uka (Rukhl).

VERMUT, Mikhl with his wife Yente and their daughter Fridzye.

VERGER, Sheyntsye.

ז

ZALTSINGER, Khayim-Zerakh [zayn-resh-khes] and his wife Tsipura.

ZANKEL, Eydl and her daughters Freyde, Hentsye and Nesye.

ZONENBLUM, Iser with his wife Gindl and their children Eydl and Ite.

ZONENBLUM, Berl and his children Itsi, Leybish and Basye.

ZONENSHEYN, Itskhak-Leyb with his wife Vitye and their children David and Mikhl.

ZEYDMAN, Moshe and his wife Yente.

ZEYDMAN, Khayim-Hersh with his wife Sara and their daughter.

ZEYDMAN, Yulian and his children Natan, Yitl, Zigmund, Lumtsye and Lea.

ZEYDMAN, Adolf and his children David, Klara, Ruzye, Sara-Lea and Rukhl.

ZEYDMAN, Moshe with his wife and their children.

ZEYDMAN, Khana, her son Zigi and her daughter Felo.

ZEYDMAN, Avraham with his wife and their children.

ZEYDMAN, Itsi with his wife Miryam-Bela and their son Yosef.

ZEYDMAN, Efraim.

ZEYDMAN, David with his wife Klara and their daughter Roza.

ZEYDMAN, Zeynvl [zayn-yud-yud-nun-vov-vov-lamed] with his wife Sara and their daughter Rukhl.

ZEYLER, Yosef with his wife Blume and their two children.

ZEYF, [no given name] with his family.

ZEYFER, Berl with his wife and their children.

ZEYFER, Efraim with his wife Lea and their children Gitsye and Shmarya.

ZEYFER, Yosl with his wife Khana and their children Nunye, Freyde, Blume, and Note.

ZEYFER, Yakov with his family.

ZEYFER, Dora with her family.

ZILVER, Leyb with his wife Feyge and their daughter Khaya.

ZILBER, Shmuel (from Pototshiska) with his wife Rukhl and their children.

ZILBER, Shmuel (from Horodnitse) with his wife Libe and their children Lea and Pepi.

ZILBER, Yisrael (from the "Kotikivke" [kuf-komets alef-tes-yud-kuf-yud-vov-vov-kuf-ayen]) with his family.

ZILBER, Moshe and his children.

ZILBERBUSH, Nakhman [nun-khes-mem-nun] with his wife Feyge; his mother and his sister Ester.

ZILBERSHEYN, Zelig with his wife Frida and their children Tsipura-Rukhl and Golde-Mina (from Chernelitse).

ZINGER, Avraham and his wife.

ZEMEL, Eyzik with his wife Bela and their children Berta, Lea and Roza.

ZENENZIV, [no given name] (Dr.) with his wife and two children.

ח

KHARASH, Yeshaya with his wife and their children.

KHALTSEL, [no given name] with his wife Malvina and their son Mietshislav.

ט

TAV, Berl with his wife and their children Zigi, Lilyan, and two daughters.

TAV, Moshe-Zalman with his wife and their two daughters.

TAEYN [tes-pasekh alef-ayen-yud-yud-nun], Berl and his family.

TEYN, Binyamin with his wife Sara and their children Motl and Leytsye.

TOYBER, Avraham with his wife Sheyndl and their children Sender and Khana.

TOYBER, Zalman with his wife Batya and their daughter Khentsye.

TOYBER, Yekhezkeil with his wife and their children.

TOYBER, Meir-Yosl with his wife and their children.

TOYBER, Mordkhay-Yoel with his wife and their children.

TOYBER, Shmuel with his wife and their children.

TOYBER, Khentsye-Rivka and her daughter Manye.

TOYBER, Moshe.

TEYTLBOYM, Zusye and her son Bunye.

TILINGER, Zunye with his wife and their children.

TIKER, Zindl wtih his wife and their children Yoel, Etl, Aharon-Itsik, Shekhna and Nakhum; their son Hersh with his wife and two children.

TIKER, Volf with his wife Libe and their daughter Feyge.

TREYBITSH, Frume and her children Rekhl, Mizye and Freyde.

TREYSTER, Mordkhay; this brother Yosl, his brother Berl and their sister Hentsye.

י

YANKNER, Zelig and his wife Pesye.

YANKNER, Meshulam with his wife and their children.

YANKNER, Yekil with his wife Vitye and their children Davidye, Ruven, Dvora, Yente and Roza; their son Mordkhay-Itskhak with his wife and their children; their son Shepsil (Shabtil) with his wife Etye and their child.

YANKNER, Pinye with his wife Ester and their children Mendl, Yosl and Kheytsye.

YANKNER, Pinye with his wife Rivka and their children.

YANKNER, Moshe-Leyb.

YANKER, Pinye (from Horodnitse) and his children.

YUNGERMAN, Emanuel and his wife Gizela.

YURMAN, Mekhl with his wife and their children Yeshaya, Shlomo and others; their son Moshe with his wife and their children.

YURMAN, Meir-Yoel with his wife and their three children (one of them was named Aharon).

YURMAN, Meir with his wife Rivka and their children Munye and Yenkl.

YURMAN, Gedalya with his wife and their children Yosef and Rukhl.

YURMAN, Yidl with his wife Khaya-Rutsye and their children Kalman, Shmuel, Khaya-Lea, Feyge, Ite and Hersh.

YURMAN, Barukh and his family.

YEGER, Avraham with his wife Rivka and their children Miku (Shmuel) and Mosye.

כ

KOHEN [kof(khof?)-hey-nun], Aharon-David with his wife and their children.

KOHEN, Avraham and his wife.

KATS, Yisrael with his wife and their son Yosef; their son Itsik with his family; their son Hersh with his wife Mantsye and their child; their son Note with his family.

KATS, Yosef with his wife Dora and their daughter Rivka.

KATS, Beyle.

KATS, Pinkhas with his wife Toni and their children Shmarya and Rivka.

KATS, Leybtsye with his wife Batya and their children Feyge, Tsvi and David.

KATS, Berl with his wife and their children.

KATS, Khentsye [khes-nun-tsadek-yud-ayen].

KATS, Naftali with his wife and their children.

KATS, Mordkhay.

KATS, Binyamin ([tes-resh-vov-mem-beys-ayen-resh]).

KATVAN [kof-tof-veys-nun], Rukhl and her sister Etl.

KATVAN, Bela with her husband and their children Aharon and Khaya.

KATVAN, Yakov with his wife and their daughter Doro.

KATVAN, Miryam with her husband and their child Moshele.

ל

LAGSHTEYN, Volf with his wife Roza and their son Aharon (from Korniv).

LAGSHTEYN, Meshulam with his wife Sima and their son Perets [pey-resh-tsadek] (from Korniv).

LAGSHTEYN, Pesakh with his wife Olga and their daughter Eti (from Korniv).

LAGSHTEYN, Shlomo-Zalman (Dr. Zunye LAGSHTEYN) (from Korniv).

LADENHEYM, Yosl with his wife Feyge and their children Hersh, Leyzer, Itsi, and three other children; their son Barukh with his wife and children; their son Shalom with his wife.

LADENHEYM, Yeshaya with his wife and their children.

LOBISH, [no given name] with his wife and his mother.

LAZER, Davidye with his wife Shpira and their children Obadaya and Roza.

LATNER, Joseph, with his wife Hudiye and their children Yente and Yisrael; their son Khayim with his family.

LAM, Arye-Leybush, the thin, and his wife Perl (daughter of Herb Ashkenazi).

LAMPNER, Yisrael and his wife Royzl.

LAMPNER, Akiva with his wife and their children.

LAMPNER, Hersh-Kopl and his family (Kalman, Shprintsye and others).

LAMPNER, Gershon with his wife and children; their son Leyzer with his wife.

LASTER, Itsik with his family.

LASTER, Shmuel with his wife and their children, and his mother Reyzye.

LASTER, David with his family.

LASTER, Yenkl with his wife and their children.

LASTER, Gershon with his wife and their children.

LASTER, Yisrael, Barukh, Shmuel, Reyzl and Malkha.

LASTER, Alte and her children Shmuel, Brurya [beys-resh-vov-resh-yud-hey], Breyne and Toybe.

LASTER, Eydl, Henye, Sara, Freyde and Rukhl.

LOYTMAN, Moshe-Leyb with his wife Miryam and their son Note.

LOYTMAN, Leyb with his wife and their children; his brother Mekhel with his wife; their two sisters Leytsye and Mintsye.

LUFT, Yosl with his family.

LUFT, Freyde and her two daughters.

LIBMAN, Yokhanan with his wife and their children.

LIBMAN, Aba with his wife and their children Meir and Beynish.

LIBSTER, Yisrael and his family.

LIZER, Sabina and her daughter Blanka.

LITMAN, [no given name] and his family.

LIKHTENTAL, Volf and his wife Miryam.

LIKHTENTAL, Pinye and his family.

LIKHTENTAL, Yisrael and his family.

LIKHTENTAL, Etl and Khana-Toybe.

LIN, Shmuel with his wife Ester and their son Yakov.

LISER, Yosl with his wife Breyntsye and their children Mikhal and Dvora.

LISER, Kamial [kuf-mem-yud-alef-lamed] with his wife and their children Itsik-Eli, Yosl and Milek; their son Hersh with his family.

LISER, Breyntsye and her children: Shalom with his family; [yud-resh-khes-mem-yud-alef-lamed] with his family; Rukhl with her family.

LISER, Mendl and his wife Rivka.

LINDNER [no given name], with his wife Rukhl and their son Gershon.

LESTER, Barukh with his wife Feyge and their children David-Volf, Khana and Hilde.

LERER, Note with his family; his son Buzye with his family.

LERER, Meir with his wife Feyge (STAKHEL) and their children David, Volf and Khona.

מ

MAYER, Yona with his wife; their daughter Frume; their son Moshe with his family.

MOLER, Gedalya (death learned of in Bukhenvald).

MASLER, Moshe.

MOSBERG, Aharon and his family.

MOSBERG, Beynish and his family.

MOSBERG, Hersh and his family.

MOSBERG, Moshe and his family.

MOSBERG, Hudye and her daughter Sheyndl.

MOSBERG, Feybish and his family.

MOSBERG, Shmuel and his family.

MORGENBESER, Shlomo and his sons Yisrael and Mekhel.

MARKSHEYD, Khayim with his family.

MOSHKOVITSH, (the Reb) with his family.

MEYTE, the baker with her husband Pinye and their six children.

MEYNHART, Devora and her children Lea, Henye and Mikhael.

MILER, Moshe and his wife Zisl; their son Zerakh [zayn-resh-khes] with his wife Manye; their son Feyvl with his wife Bela and their son Menakhem.

MILER, Kalman with his wife.

MILER, Ite (wedding servant) and her son Obedaya.

MILER, Ruven with his wife.

MINTSER, [no given name] with his wife and their children Shlomo and Berl.

MELTSER, Eyzik with his wife Frume and their children Yeshaya, Shmarya, Rukhl, Etl and Ite; their son Yosl with his family; their son Kalman with his wife Rukhl.

MELTSER, Moshe with his family.

MERBOYM, Yosl with his family.

MERBOYM, Barukh with his family.

MARGOLYOT, Elyakim with his family.

MARGOLYOT, Moshe with his sons Mendl and Avraham.

נ

NAGLER, Yisrael with his wife Tsipura and their two sons.

NAFE, Moshe with his wife and their son Khayim.

NORD, Henrika and her son Yakov.

NUDELMAN, Tsvi-Hersh with his wife Ratse and her children Mendl, Dobrish and Lea; their daughter Yeti with her husband Moshe GRINDLINGER and their children Meir and Milka (from Chernelitse).

NUDELMAN, Etya (wife of Yehoshua NUDELMAN) with her children Ester and Freyde.

NUDELMAN, Barukh with his wife Gitl and their two children (from Chernelitse).

NUDELMAN-HERMAN, Roze with her son Mordkhay (from Chernelitse).

NEYGISER, Moshe-Manes.

NEYMAN, Moshe with his wife and their two children.

NEYMAN, Voltsye with his family.

NEYMAN, Kopl with his wife and two chidren.

NEYMAN, Heynikh with his wife and their three children.

NEYMAN, Zalman with his wife.

NEYMAN, Peysye and his four children.

NEYMAN, Resya.

NEYMAN, Shaul with his wife and their child.

NEYMAN, Shlomo with his wife Nekhe and their two sons.

NIKER, Heynrikh with his wife.

NIKER, Sara and her daughter Gitl.

ס

SOBEL, Motye with his wife Khaya-Rivka and their daughter Manye; their son Volf with his family.

SOBEL, Yehuda-Hersh with his wife Kreyntsye and their children Yisrael and others; his brother Itsik with his family; their sister Babtsye with her family.

SOBEL, Yosef with his family.

SALPETER, Elimelekh with his wife Feygtsye and their children Shalom, David and Khaya.

SHMUEL, [no given name - probably this is the given name and the surname is missing] and his two children Munye and Tsonye [tsadek-vov-yud-ayen].

STRIZOVER, Shmuel and his daughter Etl.

SUKHER, Motye with his wife Rukhl and their children Tsvi and Khana; their daughter Gitl with her husband Meir EYZENKROFT and their child Yosef.

SUKHER, Yisrael with his wife and their child.

SUKHER, Zalman with his family.

SKULER, Aharon-David with his family.

SKULER, Iser.

ע

EDELSHTEYN, Motl and his wife Matl; their daughter Dora with her husban and two children; their son Yakov with his wife Miryam and their son Arye.

EDELSHTEYN, Rivka and her children Teme and Milek.

ELSTER, Avraham-Itsi and his children Ratsye and Shmuel.

EMZIG, Yakov with his wife Nekhe and their daughter Misya.

ENGELBERG, David and his wife Sheyndl.

ESNER, Shmuel with his wife Tsviya and their children Shlomo and Tsvi.

ESENFELD, Shlomo and his family.

EKHOYZ, Gedalya with his wife Khaya and their son Yehuda.

EKHOYZ, Eliyahu with his wife Sara and their children Shlomo, Tsvi and Yisrael.

EKHOYZ, Sara, Yakov and Avraham.

EKHOYZ, Eli with his wife Shlime [shin-lamed-yud-mem-ayen] and two children.

EKERLING, Feyge with her husband and their children.

פ פ

PODVISAKER, Hershl and his wife; his son Itsik-Eli with his family.

PODVISAKER, Moshe and his wife Gitl.

PASVIG, Rukhl.

PALGER, Khayim-Yakov with his wife Hentsye and their son Yekhiel.

PALGER, Aharon with his wife Rukhl and his children Herthye and Yekhiel.

FEYER, Zalman-Hersh and his children Sosye and Motl; his son Rekhamiel [resh-khes-mem-yud-alef-lamed] with his family; his daughter Khana with her family; his son Yenkl with his wife Toybe-Khana and their children.

FEYER, Yosl with his wife and their children.

FEYER, Shlomo with his wife Menye and their children Kalman, Berl and Rukhl.

FEYER, Shmuel and his two sisters.

FEYER, Shalom with his wife and their children.

FEYER, Malkha.

FEYER, Efraim.

FEYER, Yosef and his daughter.

FEYER, Feyvl.

FEYER, Khaya-Henye.

FINK, Mendl.

FINK, Meir with his family.

FINK, Rukhl, FINK Efraim and FINK Libe (Shalom-Hersh FINK's children).

FILFL, Khaya and Blume.

PILFL, Volye with his wife Elke and their children.

PILFL, Khaya and Hudl.

PILFL, Mekhl and his sister Lonye.

PILFL, Shimon and his wife Eydele.

PILFL, Morits and his wife Zshenya.

PILFL, Pesil.

PITSYE, [no given name].

FLOR, Moshe with his family.

FLOR, Fani.

FLIGLER, Yakov with his wife Sheyndl; their son Hertsl with his family; their son Leyzer with his family.

FLIGLER, Itsi and his wife Mizye.

FLIGLER, Natan with his wife Tsipura and their children Binyamin, Khayim, Shmuel and Sara.

FLESHNER, Ezreal with his wife Mantsye; their son Khayim with his wife Lea and their son Eyzik.

FENSTER, Todres with his wife and their children.

FENSTER, Motye with his wife; thier daughter Kheytsye with her family; their son Yidl with his family.

FETNER, Avraham-Aharon with his wife Malkha.

FETNER, Mekhl with his wife and their children.

FETNER, Leyb with his wife Sheyndl (PODVISOKER) and their children.

FETNER, Alter with his wife Etl and their children Brukha and Mizye.

FETNER, Efraim with his family.

FETNER, Gimfl [giml-yud-mem-fey(pey?)-lamed] with his wife and seven children.

FETNER, Avraham with his wife and their children.

FETNER, Mendl with his family.

FETNER, Moshe with his family.

PERLMAN, Lipe with his wife Kheytsye and their children Gimfl [giml-yud-mem-fey(pey?)-lamed] and Shlomo, and another son.

PERLMAN, Yosl with his wife and their children.

PERLMAN, Kamial [kuf-mem-yud-alef-lamed] with his family.

PERLMAN, Kotsye with his family.

FRIKH, Eyzik with his wife Golde and their children Sheyndl and Meir.

FRIKHMAN, Davidik with his wife Gitsye.

FRIKHMAN, Davidik with wis wife and their children Vove and Shmeya [shin-mem-ayen-yud-hey].

FRIKHMAN, Beynish and his children Motye and Shikale.

FRIDMAN, Volf with his wife; their son Moshe with his family.

FRIDMAN, Leybish with his family.

FRIDMAN, Mekhale and his daughter.

FRIDMAN, Mendl and his sisters: Vitye, Mintsye, Elke and Basye (Batya).

FRIDMAN, Nusye (Natan) with his family.

FRIDMAN, Note with his wife Kheytsye and their children.

FRIDMAN, Sime-Khaya; her son Leyb with his family; her daughter Yakhe with her family; her daughter Babtsye with her family.

FRIDMAN, Yenkl (son of Moshe-Leyb, [giml-ayen-hey-resh-giml-ayen-tes] discovered in the Buchenwald camp).

FRIDFERTIG, Shmuel with his wife Ester-Khana and their children Mekhl and Toni.

FRIDFERTIG, Itsi with his family.

FRIDFERTIG, Khayim-Shaul with his family.

FRIDFERTIK, Rive with her family.

FRIMAS, [no given name].

FREYER, Reyzl and her son Itye and daughter.

FREYER, Hersh and his family.

FREYER, Elishe [alef-lamed-yud-shin-ayen] and his family.

FREYER, Khayim and his family.

FREYER, Milek and his family.

FREYER, Breyntsye with her husband and their children Miryam, Etl, Golde, Volf-Moshe and Ester.

PRIFER, Avraham-Leyb with his wife Shprintsye and their children Hersh and Miryam.

PRIFER, Aharon with his family.

PRIFER, Barukh with his wife Reyzye and their children Freyde, Etye, Khana, Rivka and Itsik-Leyb.

PRIFER, Hersh with his wife Freyde and their daughter Nemi.

PRIFER, Hersh-Leyb with his wife Sheyndl and their children Reyzye, Fani and Mendl.

PRIFER, Yosl with his wife Shibe and their children Ruven Leyb [no hyphen or comma], Miryam and Gitl.

PRIFER, Yenkl with his wife Sara and their daughter Golde.

PRIFER, Yisrael and his children Barukh and Yekhezkiel.

PRIFER, Yirukhem [yud-reysh-vov-khes-mem] with his wife Khana.

PRIFER, Mikhael with his wife Kreyntsye and their children Shmuel, Ruven, Lea, Miryam, Rosa and Hinde.

PRIFER, Geyge with her family.

PRIFER, Ruven with his wife Rosa.

PRIFER, Shaya with his wife Sosye and their son Avraham.

PRIFER, Zev (Chernelitse).

FRISHLING, Avraham with his wife Slove.

FRISHLING, David with his wife Rukhl.

FRISHLING, Zalman with his wife Sara.

FRISHLING, Khayim-Volf with his wife Khaya-Tzvia and their son Leyzer.

FRISHLING, Yosl with his wife Frida.

FRISHLING, Yisrael-Itsik with his wife Feyge and their children Mendl, Kune (Alkuna [alef-lamed-kuf-nun-hey]), Munye, and Hersh.

FRISHLING, Meir with his wife Rivka (lost in Buchenwald).

FRISCHLING, Mendl with his wife and their children Schlomo and Etl.

FRISCHLING, Moshe with his wife Rukhl and their children Yisrael and Mizye.

FRISCHLING, Slove and her daughter Rukhl.

FRISCHLING, Shmuel with his wife and their daughter Loti with her husband (GILZON).

FRENKL, Levi [lamed-vov-yud] with his wife and their children (Dusye and others).

FRENKEL, Adolf with his wife Lea and their children Zalka and Yulek.

FRESHL, Kamial [kuf-mem-yud-alef-lamed] and his family.

צ

TSOYDERER, David and his children Geyge, Munye and Bubi.

TSOYDERER, Khana and her children Aharon and David.

TSUMER, Yitskhak Leyb with his wife and their children.

TSUMER, Matl.

TSUMER, Miryam and her son Leyb.

TSUMER, Yisrael Meir; his son Pinye with his wife Sarah'tsye [shin-resh-hey'tsadek-yud-ayen] and three children.

TSUMER, Pinye and Ester.

TSUKEL, Avraham-Ber with his wife Khaya (from Korniv).

TSVENGLER, Meir with his wife and their children Yosef, Etl and Roza.

TSIN, Moshe with his wife Elke and their daughter Sara (Vaser); their son Yitskhak with his wife Tsila.

TSIFERBLAT, Leyzer with his wife and their children.

TSIFERBLAT, Gerl with his wife and their children.

TSIFERBLAT, Mekhl with his wife and their children.

ק

KOHEN, Yosef with his wife.

KOHEN, David (Dr. KOHEN) with his family.

KOVAL, Fishl with his wife Ester; their son Shimon with his wife Freyde and their children.

KOVAL, Meir with his wiefe Khana and their children.

KOVAL, Shmuel-David and his children Roza, Freyde, Sara and Breyntsye.

KOKH, Hilel with his wife Sara and their son Menakhem-Mendl (Emanuel).

KOKH, Beynish with his wife Sheyndl and their son Menakhem-Mendl (Emanuel).

KOKH, Berl with his wife and their children.

KOKH, Yokhanan with his wife Sara; their son Meir with his family; their son Shmerl with his family.

KOKH, Zlate.

KOKH, Moshe with his wife.

KOKH, Nosye (Natan) with his wife and their daughter Miryam; their son Fishl with his family; their son Berl with his family.

KOKH, Shlomo-Yoel with his wife and their children.

KOKH, Shaya with his wife Ratse and their son Yidale; their son Leybele with his family; their son Itsik with his family; their son Nakhman with his family; their son Yosef with his family.

KOKH, Leybele with his wiefe Feyge (from Tshernyatin).

KALMUS, Hersh-Leyb; his son Todres with his family; his son Mekhl with his family.

KALMUS, Moshe with his wife Roza and their daughter Ruzshke.

KALMUS, Yenkl with his family.

KALMUS, Aba-Itsi with his family.

KALMUS, Natan with his family.

KAMIL, Leybke with his wife Sara and their daughter Khana.

KAMIL, Zeyde with his wife Libe and their son Moshe.

KAMIL, Mekhl with his wife Sara.

KAMIL, Moshke with his wife and their children.

KAMIL, Zalman with his wiefe and their children.

KAMIL, Mendl-Noakh with his wife Reyzl and their children Golde, Vitsye and Yetke.

KANAFAS, Gustav.

KANAFAS, Zunye.

KANTOR, Hersh with his wife.

KOSER, Yenkl with his wife and their daughter Nora.

KOSER, Leyb with his wife Gitl and their son Munye; their daughter Nora with her husband Dr. LISER and their child.

KOP, Todres with his family.

KOP, Mendl with his family.

KOP, Shlomo with his family.

KOFLER, Heynikh with his wife Hentsye and their children Malkha, Vitye, Feyge, Yosef, Aharon and Itsik; their son Yakov with his wife and their children; their son Shimon with his wife and their two children.

KARMIN, Feybish, his daughter hanula and his son Yosef (from Korniv).

KORN, Itsi with his wife and their daughter Sosye.

KORN, Binyamin, with his wife and their children: Tuvya, Shlomo, Yedidya, Hilel, and two other children.

KORN, Leybele with his wife.

KORNER, Mendl with his wife and their children.

KARP, Ruven with his wife Etl and their daughter Tsipura; their son Moshe with his family.

KUGLER, Eyzik with his wife and their children Elyokim, Avraham and others.

KUGLER, Yisrael with his wife Masha and their daughter Miryam.

KUGLER, Yosef with his wife Rukhl.

KUGLER, Naftali with his son Leyb.

KUGELMAT, Eyzik with his wife and their children (Yosef and others).

KUGELMAS, Yisrael and his wife Sara; their son Leyzer-Itsik with his family; their son Yehuda with his wife Etye; their daughter (name unknown).

KUGELMAS, Yehuda with wife Etye and their children Meir and Shimon.

KUGELMAS, Leyzer-Itsik with his wife Malkha and their children Yisrael, Eli and Khana.

KUGELMAS, Shmarya with his wife Mintsye; their daughter Tontsye and their son Avraham.

KUGELMAS, Avraham with his wife and their son Mendl.

KUGELMAS, Hersh with his wife Perl and their children Yakov and Yosef; their son Avraham with his family; their son Shikl with his family, their daughter Toybe with her family.

KUGELMAS, Shlomo with his wife Golde and their children Binyamin and Shimon-Avraham; their son Yosi with his family; their daughter Sosye with her family.

KVETSHER, Khano-Itsik with his wife Rivka.

KVETSHER, Shimon with his wife and their children.

KVETSHER, Matl.

KOYFMAN, Fishl with his wife Lea and their children Herman, Lena, Yezshik and Erikh.

KUPFERMAN, Itsi with his wife Khaya.

KUPFERMAN, Berl with his wife Manye and their children Efraim, Zelde, Yehuda, Zime [zayn-yud-alef-mem-ayen], Shlomo and Lea.

KUPFERSHMID, Hersh with his wife.

KUPFERSHMID, Berl with his wiefe; their son Efraim with his family; their son Shlomo with his family.

KIHL, Yidl and his children Khayim, Sara, Manye and Moshe.

KIHL, Pinkhas with his wife Babtsye and their son Motye.

KIHL, Kreyndl; her son Zelig with his family; her son Dolye with his family.

KIMEL, Berl with his family.

KIMEL, Henikh with his family.

KIMEL, Vove and his children: Fishl, Zeyde, and others.

KIMELMAN (the widow); her son Yehuda with his family; her son Yisrael with his family.

KIMERLING, Frume.

KIRSHNER, Yoel with his wife and their children; their son Mendl with his family.

KLIR, Eyber [alef-yud-yud-beys(veys?)-ayen-resh] and his children Yakov, Babtsye and Rukhl.

KLEYNROYKH, Mekhl.

KNOBL, Shimon with his family.

KNOBLER, Hersh and his wife Hentsye.

KNOBLER, Itsi with his family.

KNOBLER, Davidye with his family.

KELMAN, Yehuda.

KRAMER, Itskhak with his wife Khaya and their children Zelig and Pinye.

KRAMER, Yisrael with his wiefe Royze and their children Shlomo and Zelig.

KRON, Ozer [ayen-vov-zayn-resh] with his wife Khana and their children Leyb, Shmuel, Shpira, and Fridzye.

KRON, Royze.

ר

ROZENBOYM, Akiva with his wife Dina and their son Tsvi.

ROZENBOYM, Aharon-Hersh with his wife Tsipura.

ROZENBOYM, Eli-Mekhl with his wife and two children.

ROZENBOYM, Yehoshua with his family.

ROZENBOYM, Shikl with his mother and his sister.

ROZENBOYM, Binyamin with his wife Khana and their children Toybe and Mina.

ROZEBLAT, Yeshaya with his wife Libe and their children Tsvi (Hersh) and Yehuda.

ROSENHEK, Herman with his wife and five children.

ROSENFELD, Avraham with his wife Yente and their son Yosef.

ROSENFELD, Mordkhay-Leyb with his wife and their children Yisrael, Rukhl and others.

ROSENFELD, Yisrael with his wife Yente and their children Yosef and Avraham.

ROZENKRANTS, Itsi with his family.

ROZENKRANTS, Itsik with his wife Khaya and their children Khayim, Gusta, Roza, Yirukhem [yud-reysh-vov-khes-mem], Eftsi [ayen-fey(pey?)-tsadek-yud], and Yekel; their son Mendl with his family; their son Shimon with his family.

ROZENKRANTS, Binyamin with his wife.

ROZENKRANTS, Feyvl with his wife and their children Aharon and Bube.

ROZENKRANTS, Sara.

ROZENKRANTS, Zalman, his sister and his family.

ROZENKRANTS, Leyzer and his mother.

ROZENKRANTS, Yosef and ROZENKRANTS, Blume (relatives of Moshe SHUKHNER).

ROSENROYKH, Dvora.

ROSENROYKH, Rukhl.

ROSENSHTOK, Khana-Miryam.

ROSENSHTOK, Khayim.

RAT, Yakov with his wife Rukhl-Lea and their children.

RAT, Shimon with his wife Toybe and their children.

ROTLEDER, Nekhe.

ROTMAN, Yehoshua and his children Yosef, Noakh, Mendl, Rukhl, Frida and Dvora.

ROTMAN, Etl and her children Khava, Sara and Barukh.

ROTMAN, Reyzye and her children Melekh and Leyb.

RAMER, Yosef with his wife Bronye and their children (Eli and others).

RUBEL, Edvard with his wife Gusta (from Korniv).

RUBEL, Ernestina (from Korniv).

RUGENDARF, Moshe and his children Reyzye and Yente.

RUGENDARF, Yosl and his wife Yeti.

RUGENDARF, Siome with his family.

RUGENDARF, [no given name] with his family: Kheytsye, Yente and Dolye.

RUGENDORF, Mordkhay-Itsik with his family.

ROYKHVERGER, Hersh-Kopl with his family.

ROYKHVERGER, Yukhbad [yud-vov-khes-beys-daled] and her sons David and Yehuda; her daughter Rivka with her husband Tsvi SHERF and their child Nekhe.

ROYKHVERGER, Yakov and his wife Khaya.

ROYKHVERGER, Yisrael with his wife; their son Hersh-Kopl with his family.

ROYKHVERGER, Lea, Zlate, Ite and Yosef (sister and brother).

RUM, Volf with his wife Hudl and their children.

REYTER, Mordkhay-Yoel with his wife and their children.

REYTER, Avraham with his wife and their daughter.

REYTER, Shmuel with his wife and their daughter.

REYTER, Mordkhay with his wife Rivka (from Korniv).

REYKHMAN, Anshl with his wife Hinde; their son Michael with his wife Mintsye; their son Yosef-Hersh with his wife Sime and their children Freyde, Berish and Itsye; their son Berish with his wife Dusye and their children Ronye and Tsvi; their son Aba with his wife.

REYKHMAN, Binyamin with his wife Freyde, their son Berish and their daughter Tsipre; their daughter Kheytsye with her family.

REYKHMAN, Freyde with her family.

REYKHMAN, Samuel (Shmuel) with his children Munye and Sonye.

REYS, Eliyahu with his wife Sheyndl and their children Yakov, Khava and Etl.

REYS, Alter with his wife Frume-Hentsye.

REYS, Zeyde with hi swife Gitl.

REYS, Zigmund with his wife Gizela and their children Yosef, Genia and Aharon.

REYS, Leytsye and her two daughters.

REYS, Mendl with his wife Freyde; their son Fishl with his wife and their children; their son Mekhl with his wife; their son Ruvn with his family.

REYS, Mendl with his wife Khava and their son Shmarya.

REYS, Mendl with his wife Milkha and their children Mekhl, Tsipa, Leyzer and Feyge.

REYS, Nekhamia with his wife and their children.

REYS, Shlomo with his wife Mina and their children Eliezer, Khava, Tsila, Blume and Moshe.

REYS, Shmarya and his children Mendl, Meir, Khaya and Libe.

REYF, Sime and her children Khayim-Hersh, Sara, Rom-Tov and Fishl.

REYF, Ben-Tsion with his wife and their son Maks.

REYF, Heynikh with his wife Golde and their children.

RIKHTER, Yoel with his wife Toybe.

RIKHTER, Moshe with his wife Toybe.

RINDENOY, Zeyde.

RINDENOY, Zelig-Meir with his wife Golde and their children.

RINDENOY, Berl and his sister.

RINDENOY, [no given name] and his family (from Chernelitse).

REGENBOYGEN, Yitskhak-Wolf with his wife.

RESH, Khayim with his family.

ש

SHATSBERGER, Note with his wife Golde.

SHATSBERGER, Gitl and her family.

SHATSBERGER, Ester and her family.

SHOR, Kalman and his children Natan and Dago; his son Aharon wtih his wife.

SHOR, Meir with his family.

SHOR, Miryam (the widow of Sholma-Avraham SHOR).

SHOR, Aharon-Moshe with his wife Roza.

SHOR, Feyge with her husband Advocate [a lawyer's title] HOYZKNEKHT.

SHARPSHTEYN, Shlomo with his wife Babtsye and their children Genya, Izio [alef-yud-zayn-yud-komets alef] and Eliezer.

SHVAKH, Itsi with his family.

SHVAKH, Kopl with his family.

SHVAKH, Leybl with his family.

SHVAKH, Moshe-Mendl and his children Shmuel, Mordkhay, Shikl, Kopl, Gitl, Frume and Shlomo.

SHVARTZ, Elimelkh with his family.

SHVARTZ, Miryam-Beyle with her family.

SHVARTZ, Shmuel with his wife and their son Avraham.

SHVARTSFELD, Yakov with his wife Klara and his two sisters.

SHVARTSKOPF, Shikl with his wife and their six children.

SHVEYGER, Motye with his wife and their daughter Nekhe; their son Yehoshua with his wife and their children.

SHVEYGER, Lea and her son Itzi.

SHVEYGER, Yisrael with his wife and their children.

SHOYDERER, David and his five children.

SHVIMER, David with his wife Feyge (from Korniv).

SHUKHNER, Vove with his wife Yente (daughter of Hadin) and their children Tsvi, Miki and Feybish.

SHUKHNER, Pinye with his wife and their two children.

SHUKHNER, Moshe with his wife and two children.

SHUKHNER-BERGMAN, Khana.

SHUKHNER, Bum and his family.

SHUKHNER, Milek and his family.

SHUKHNER, Zarakh and his family.

SHUKHNER, Aba with his wife and their three children.

SHUKHNER, Zeyde with his family.

SHUKHNER, Zindl with his wife Sarah and their children Yeti and Velvl.

SHUKHNER, Zalman-Leyb with his wife and their children.

SHUKHNER, Yehoshua with his wife.

SHUMER, Yakov with his wife Rosa and their four children (from Chernelitse).

SHTORPER, Yosef with his family.

SHTARK, Munish with his wife and their three children.

SHTIGLITS, Shlomo with his wife and their children; their son Mendl with his family.

SHTEYNER, Mayer.

SHTEYNER, Khana; her son Yehuda with his wife Gitl and their chilfren Itsik and Yirukhem [yud-reysh-vov-khes-mem].

SHTEYNKOYL, Freyde and her children Sara and Simkha.

SHTEYERMAN, Avromtsye with his wife Mintsye and their two children.

SHTENDIG, Avraham with his wife Etl and their sons Obadaya [ayen-vov-beys-daled-yud-hey] and Dolek (from Korniv).

SHTERN, Mayer with his wife; their son Avraham with his family.

SHTERN, Mendl with his wife Alte.

SHTERNHEL, Royze.

SHTRAUCH [shin-tes-reysh-alef-vov-khes], Alter with his wife Batya.

SHTRUM, Moshe.

SHTRUM, Hersh-Leyb with his wife Khava and their children Yosef, Dudye Aharon, Vitye, Zosye and Itsik.

SHTREYT, Shlomo; his son Asher with his wife Bronye and their children Hersh and David; his daughter Sara with her husband Aba NAGLER; his daughter Feyge with her husband Shmuel DINES and their two children Meytale and Khanele.

SHTREYFLER, Shlomo and his two children.

SHEYNBLUM, [no given name] with his family.

SHINDLER, Yente and her children Khana, Yehudit and Lipa.

SHIFTER, Moshe and his family.

SHITS, Hersh-Leyb and his daughter Pepi; his son Eyber with his wife Fridzye and their child.

SHITS, Hersh-Leyb with his wife and their children Ruvn and Fride.

SHITS, Pinye with his wife and their children Yakov, Mendl and Ruvn.

SHIKLER, [no given name] with his family.

SHLAM, Hersh with his wife Khaya and their children Yehoshua, Avraham, Tsipura, Rukhl, Lea and Sosye.

SHLAM, Etl with her husband Yosi VEYSMAN and their children Bina, Yehoshua and Tsipura.

SHLOSER, Moshe with his family.

SHLUMER, Yakov.

SHMERHOLTS, Hersh with his wife Khana-Lea and their daughter Roza; their son Mikhael with his family.

SHMERHOLTS, Zeyde with his wife Zelde and their children Tsharne, Hudl and Pesye.

SHMERHOLTS, Itsi-Mayer with his family.

SHNEYD, Mayer with his wife Gutsa and their children Mina, Yehudit and Batya; Their daughter Pnina with her husband Volf KOD (from Chernelitse).

SHNEYD, Lea (from Chernelitse).

SHNEYD, Shavl [shin-alef-vov-lamed] (from Chernelitse).

SHNEYD, Salomon (from Chernelitse).

SHNEYDER, Leyzer (Dr. SCHNEYDER) with his wife Sabina and their daughter Blanka.

SHNEYDERMAN, Yisrael with his wife Reyzl and their son Hertsl; their daughter Freyde with her family; their son Avraham with his wife Buzye and their children.

SHNITSER, Khayim; his son Meshulam with his wife Rukhl and their children Sara and Ester; his son Moshe with his wife Etl and their children Avraham and Sara; his daughter Kheyke (the widow of Simkha SHNITSER) and her children Mordkhay-Zev, Rivka-Nekhe, Khava, Elimelekh and Yehuda; SHNITSER, Henits (daughter of Simkha SHNITSER).

SHNITSER, Yehoshua-Hersh with his wife Maltsye and their children Toni, Moshe, Pepi, Lea and Aba; their son Leyb with his wife Bronye and their children.

SHNITSER, Avner with his wife; their son Aba with his family.

SHNITSER, Avner with his wife Leytsye and their son Aba and a daughter.

SHEKHTER, Antshl with his wife and their children David, Shimon and Shoshana.

SHEKHTER, Nutsye (Itsi) with his wife Malkha (SHLAM) and their children (Tsipura and two other children).

SHEKHTER, Hersh with his wife Gitl and their children Note and Mordkhay.

SHEKHTER, Velvl with his wife and their three daughters.

SHEKHTER, Mayer with his wife Pepi.

SHEKHTER, Yidl with his wife and their children (Rukhl and others).

SHEKHTER, Note with his wife Yente and their children.

SHEKHTER, Moshe with his wife.

SHEKHTER, Mayer with his wife Eda.

SHEKHTER, Yidl with his wife and their daughter Mintsye.

SHEKHTER, (the Engineer) with his family.

SHEKHTER, (from the lumber-yard) with his family.

SHEKHNER, Asher.

SHEKHNER, Motl with his family.

SHEKHNER, Shmuel.

SHERER, Gaula [giml-alef-vov-lamed-hey] with her son Maks.

SHERF, Hersh with his wife Rivka and their child.

SHERF, Yosef with his wife and their two children; their son Mayer with his wife Hentsye and their two children.

SHERF, Yakov with his wife Malkha and their daughters Ite [alef-yud-tes-ayen] and Rivka.

SHERTSER, Moshe-Hersh with his wife and two children.

SHERTSER, Davidye-Leyzer with his family.

SHERTSER, Shimon with his family.

SHERTSER, Feyge with her family.

SHERTSER, Roza with her family.

SHERTSER, Heytsye with her family.

SHERTSER, Mayer with his family.

SHERTSER, Rivka with her son Meshulam and her daughter Freyde.

SHERTSER, Meshulam with his wife Etl and their children Yosef and Hesye (Hersh).

SHERTSER, Volf.

SHERTSER, Yosef.

SHERTSER, Leyzer with his wife Ite and their children Khana and Leytsye.

SHPAN, Shmuel with his family.

SHPORN, Rukhl (née PODVISOKER) and her two children.

SHPUND, Motye with his family.

SHPUND, Ite with her family.

SHPUND, Hersh with his wife Sara and their children Yisrael, Moshe, Yidl and Vili.

SHPIGLER, Yosef with his wife and their children Tsurtsye and Khava.

SHPIGLER, [no given name] with his family.

SHPIGLER, Yisrael with his family.

SHPIRA, Shmuel with his wife Ite; their daughter Rukhl with her husband Yosef KUGLER and their children Mayer and Feyge.

SHPIRA, Yisrael (son of [hey-daled-yud-yud-nun]).

SHPIRA-TSIMER, Feyge (daughter of [hey-daled-yud-yud-nun]) with her daughter Ester.

SHPIRER, Berl with his wife.

SHPIRER, Ronye with her daughter Khana; her son David with his wife Nekhe and their two children; her son Yosl with his wife Malkha and their children Etl, Aharon, Yitskhak, Dvura and Khana; her son Moshe-Mekhl with his wife Dvura and their son Mendl.

SHPIRER, Aharon.

SHPIRER, Benyamin with his wife Freyde and their son Khayim.

SHPIRER, Davidik with his family.

SHPIRER, Itsik.

SHPIRER, Moshe-Mendl with his family.

SHPIRER, Shmuel with his wife Yente.

SHPIRER, Zalman with his family.

SHPIRER, Leybtsye with his wife and three children.

SHPIRER, Yosl-Itsik with his wife and their daughter Vitye.

SHPIRER, Yenkl.

SHPIRER, Hersh-Mendl with his family.

SHPIRER, David with his wife Yente.

SHPIRER, two sisters.

SHREYER, Todres with his wife Sabina and their son Shikl.

SHREYER, Hersh with his family.

ת ת

TALMUD, Malkha and her children.

**A 10 Crown Note in Theresienstadt Concentration Capm signed by
Jacob Edelstein**

List of Jewish Taxpayers, 1789-1791

Below is a list of Jews who paid taxes in Gorodenka in 1789-1791.
This list is especially significant because it was in 1787 – only two
years earlier than the time period covered by the list – that Austrian
Emperor Joseph II required the Jews of Galicia and Bukovina to adopt
permanent surnames.[1] This list, therefore, may be the earliest existing
record of some of the family names that it contains.

The German text that accompanied the list refers to taxes that were
collected through, and used by, the "Horodenker Jewish Society." A
possible explanation can be found in the book *Shtetl Memoirs*, by
Joachim Schönfeld (1985, Ktav Publishing House, Inc.), who writes
about the town of Sniatyn, not far from Gorodenka.

According to Schöfeld, the interface between the Jewish community
of Sniatyn and the Austrian government was a council called
the *Jüdische Kultusgemeinde* – the Board of Jewish Worship and
Education. Members of the Board were elected by taxpaying members
of the community. Not only did the Board represent the Jewish
community to the government, it also controlled the ritual

---

[1] According to *A Dictionary of Jewish Names and their History* , by Benzion C.
Kaganoff, 1977

slaughterhouses, the mikvah, the main synagogue, the Jewish school, and other community institutions. Most of the income to support these facilities came from taxes imposed by the Board, collected by government tax collectors and returned to the Board. There was probably a similar organization in Gorodenka.

The source of this list is the following document from the Austrian Archiv des Ministerium des Innern (Wien) [Archive of the Ministry of the Interior (Vienna)]:

IV T 11 Galizien Judenwesen 1786-1792 ad 2839 ad 23276 pr 742 Liquidation.

Ihre Aberbach	Koppel Bergbauer	Benjamin
Jankel Aberbach	Saul Berghauer	Dankner
Leib Aberbach	Hersch Bergman	Schapse Dankner
Srol Aberbach	Gerschon Bildner	Chaim Degelman
Wolf Aberbach	Hersch Bildner	Leib Denninger
Moses Aberbachs	Izig Bildner	Maier Diamant
Schaul Aberbachs	Jossel Bildner	Mortko Diamant
Mayer Acker	Hersch Binder	Hersch Diener
Chaim Adler	Isser Bitter	Leib Dolinger
Moses Agatstein	Schmuel Blater	Schlomo Dolinger
Moses Agatstein	Laiser Brait	Hersch Dollinger
Scholem Agatstein	Abraham Brand	Salamon Dolmann
Srol Agatstein	Simon Brauer	Moses Donner
Herschs Ant.	Abraham Braver	Mothie Doppler
Moses Tiger	Jzig Brettler	Moses Dreyer
Herz Armer	Josef Briger	Jankel Eckstein
Hoachim Ast	Berl Briller	Jeruchim
Schlojme Ast	Maier	Edelstein
Abraham Austern	Bruckenstein	Leib Edelstein
Moses Austern	Moses	Mayer Edelstein
Samson Axel	Bruckenstein	Mordko Edelstein
Juda Böhm	Abraham	Kallman Eder
Jacob Balbirer	Bruckner	Moses Edler
Leib Bankner	Jakob Bruckner	Samuel- Eerber
Aaron Barber	Moses Bruckner	Lazar Eisman
Nossen Barth	Abraham Buchner	Chaim Emmer
Hersch Barts	Moses Buchner	Abraham Erdreich
Jone Beerman	Aaron Burger	Jokel Färber
Beril Beermann	Monas Burger	Manele Färber
Gerson Begelman	Berl Dachs	Mayer Färber

Jankel Feihtner
Abraham Feldman
Judas Feldmann
Leib Feldner
Schlome Fessler
Juda Fettner
Dawid Feuer
Hersch Feuer
Leib Feuer
Leib Feuer
Mechel Feuer
Israel Fink
Juda Fink
Schomer Fink
Jossel Fischer
Nochem Fischer
Leiser Flügler
Moses Flügler
Seelig Flaschner
Mayer Fleischer
Karpel Fliegler
Schmuel Fragner
Salamon Frajer
Oscher Freibeck
Moses Freimann
Seinwel Friedman
Jakob Friedmann
Schlome
Frischling
Izig Frohnberger
Koppel Fruchtner
Nussen Fuchs
Srul Fuchs
Simon Gloger
Herschs Gaber
Dawid Geiger
Hersch Geiger
Schlome Geldner
Chaim Gerson
Moses Gettner
Schmul Glas
Abraham
Glasberger
Izig Glasberger
Mordko
Glasberger

Schlome
Glasberger
Kalman Glasser
Mayer Goldberger
Srol Goldschmidt
Izig Gottlieb
Leib Grazer
Abraham Guther
Chaim Guther
Srol Gutman
Aaron Gutser
Mathel Guttman
Leib Guttmann
Schmul Hager
Joachim Halka
Hersch Hallman
Leib Hartenstein
Schmerl
Hartenstein
Seelig Haschel
Schaje Hass
Daniel Hecht
Dawid Heine
Schlome Hengst
Simon Herland
Hersch Herrmann
Abisch Hochman
Tod'res Hoffmann
Elias Hollering
Hersch Hoptasch
Laiser Huber
Mayer Huber
Aaron Huttmann
Hersch Igelman
Schabes
Imberman
Falk Imbermann
Froim Imbermann
Salamon Jäger
Jossel Junker
Leib Jurman
Moses Jurman
Schmul Jurmann
Schmuel Kalker
Simon Kammel
Joachim Kanzler

Hinde Karin.
Berl Katz
Herschls Katz
Israel Katz
Josel Katz
Leiser Katz
Moses Katz
Moses Katz
Moses Katz
Moses Katz
Noa Katz
Nossen Katz
Schmuel Katz
Schoel Katz
Mothie Kaz
Wollf Kaz
Kalman Kellner
Scholem Kiel
Joel Kirschner
Izig Kleinbauer
Moses Knöpfner
Beer Knobler
Beril Koch
Berl Koller
Hinde Koltin
Mayer Korker
Lowisch Korn
Moses Kracher
Isaias Kramer
Moses Kramer
Schlome Kramer
Leib Kramisch
Hersch Kronn
Samuel Krupfbein
Todres Kugelmoss
Abraham Kugelus
Srol Kugler
Srol Lampner
Israel Landmann
Chaim Langer
Jankew Lanpker
Wolf
Latesschneider
Abraham Leihner
Leib Leman
Chaskel Lerner

Aaron Lezter
Juda Libig
Jakob Liderer
Hersch
Liebermann
Godel Lochner
Leib Luster
Mordko Luster
Ihre Lutner
Moses Maas
Srol Mager
Manele Mass
Srol Mass
Maier Mauler
Josias Mayer
Mordko
Meerbaum
Dawid Melzer
Koppel Menschner
Abraham
Neuberger
Israel Neuberger
Kalman
Neuhauser
Hersch Neumeuer
Abraham
Ochsenstern
Chaim
Offenberger
Dawid Offenberger
Hersch
Offenberger
Koppel
Offenberger
Leib Offenberger
Moses Offenberger
Obadia
Offenberger
Schmuel
Offenberger
Wolf Offenberger
Wolf Offenberger
Izig Ohringer
Gerson Oker
Leib Oker
Leiser Ordentlichs

Juda Ordner
Izig Orenstein
Jankel Oringer
Herz Pechert
Markus Pfau
Abraham Pfeffer
Jankel Pfeiffer
Mayer
Pflauminger
Nossen Platzker
Gute Prüffer
Simon Predig
Chaim Prehauser
Josel Prehauser
Hersch Prinz
Michel Propstler
Schaje Puchler
Mendel Pulthman
Abraham
Ragendorf
Moses Rath
Zallel Rats
Jossel Rauchman
Elias Reis
Schije Reis
Jankel
Reismarker
Mortko Reiss
Leib Reither
Yre Reuter
Ruben Richter
Mayer Riegelmann
Hersch Rindner
Leib Rindner
Schmuel Rindner
Wolf Rindner
Fischel
Rittersporn
Abe Rosenbaum
Jankel
Rosenbaum
Dawid Rosenberg
Aaron Rosenkranz
Boruch
Rosenkranz
Feibel Rosenkranz

Hosias Jonas
Rosenkranz
Josel Rosenkranz
Jossel Rosenkranz
Lasar Rosenkranz
Leib Rosenkranz
Maier Rosenkranz
Mendel
Rosenkranz
Wollf Rosenkranz
Leib Rossler
Izig Rubin
Srul Rubin
Taube Rubin
Salamon Ruppert
Mordko Saiffer
Leib Sander
Mothie Saz
Borouch
Schönbrum
Dawid Schaar
Haskel Schaar
Hersch Schaar
Hersch Schaar
Oscher Schaar
Perez Schaar
Dawid Schaffer
Israel Schaffer
Schlome Schaffer
Hersch Schapira
Aaron Schatzberg
Maier
Schatzberger
Gerschon
Schindler
Hosias Schirm
Berl Schleiffer
Hersch Schmidt
Salamon
Schmierer
Chaim Schmitt
Moses Schmukler
Jankel Schnürer
Berl Schneider
Gerschon
Schneider

Leiser Schneider
Schapse
Schneider
Wolf Schneider
Samuel Schneier
Schlome
Schneuer
Baruch Schruber
Jakob Schubert
Monusch
Schubert
Leib Schuhner
Hersch Schutz
Moses
Schwantheil
Hersch
Schwimmer
Nossen Sichig
Jichil Silber
Jzig Silber
Manes Silber
Moses Silber
Nachman Silber
Schlome Silber
Seinwel Silber
Jssak Singer
Chaim Sissler
Wolff Slattner
Hersch Sohar
Jankel Sokeler
Joel Sonnenblum
Hersch
Sonnenfeld
Seelig Spierer
Boruch Splitter

Chaim Stürmer
Salamon Staüber
Izig Steigman
Abraham Stein
Schaje Steinbauer
Peisach Stepner
Leib Stern
Srul Stigliz
Schmul Strisling
Nossen Sturmer
Abraham Sucher
Eisig Sucher
Hersch Sucher
Eeisig Suchner
Juda Sussmann
Moses Töpfner
Schmul
Tannenbein
Hosias Tauber
Moses Tauber
Srol Tauber
Leib Taubl
Herr Thronberger
Jossel Treiber
Litmann
Tuchmacher
Moses Tuchner
Moses Turkner
Izig Walther
Jossel Walther
Berl Wasser
Hersch Wasser
Jankel Wasser
Laiser Wasser
Leib Wasser

Samuel Wasser
Aaron Wechsler
Abel Weidner
Leib Weinberger
Nossen
Weinberger
Abraham Weinreb
Hersch Weinreb
Moses Weinreb
Rifke Weischin
Dawid Weiskern
Kalman Weissman
Leib Wieser
Feibisch Willmann
Rosa Wilmann
Wollf Winkler
Izig Winter
Nochem Winter
Dawid Wisinger
Berl Wohl
Littman Wolf
Hersch
Wolkenstein
Moses Zangel
Srul Zauber
Jossel Ziegler
Izig Zorn
Izig Zuckerman
Nossen
Zuckerman
Wollf Zuckerman
Chaim
Zuckermann
Leib Zuckermann

The Fate of the Thirteen Jewish Orphans Left in the Care of the Zionist Youth Group in the Ghetto of Horodenka 1941-1942

By Reuven Prifer

Translated from Hebrew and donated by Tosia Schneider

One day, the authorities decided to remove the Jewish children from the general orphanage which was established during the Soviet regime. In accordance with their racial laws, they threw out the 13 Jewish orphans, ranging in age from two to five years. The Judenrat asked the Zionist youth group to provide for the care of these children in our homes. We did not know how to begin, we had no experience of taking care of children, but we had to make the necessary arrangements

With the help of Dr. CHARASCH, the son-in-law of Simcha SCHNITZER, the children were housed briefly in his house, until we succeeded in collecting beds and linens and even toys and moved them to the second floor in the house of Mr. KAMIL, where a soup kitchen had already been established by a group of Zionist youth managed by Tovia KORN. Thus, adding to our other duties, we undertook the additional work of caring for these children. We were also helped by a few refugee women. In a few days, we overcame all the difficulties connected with the care of the children, as well as running the kitchen, it simply became a daily routine. It is fitting to note that the operation of the kitchen, as well as the education of the children, were all conducted in Hebrew. All members of our working group were well versed in the Hebrew language (all had completed the "Tarbut" Hebrew School).

We all undertook this difficult and gloomy work voluntarily, without pay, but we found our reward in the progress and the development of the children. Unfortunately, this lasted only a very short time. In the first "AKCIA" on December 4, 1941, the Gestapo captured 2500 Jews in our city, among them the thirteen orphans, together with those of our staff who were on duty at that time. They all found their death in the village of Michalcze-Siemakowcze and lie there in the mass grave of our people.

Among the friends of the Zionist youth group who helped in the orphanage and the soup kitchen were the following people:

Tovia KORN, Shlomo KORN, Joseph KOCH, Minio SCHECHTER, Joseph REIS, Berl HOFMAN, Nin AUERBACH, Klara HARTENSTEIN, Mania KUGLER, Sara FRENKEL, Salka FRIEDMAN. The only survivors of that group are: Savka ZAUDERER, Nusia WACHER, Zvi REIS and Reuven PRIFER.

Considering the age of the people, the task they undertook was, indeed, a very difficult one.

Gorodenka Lists of Victims

Unpublished, undated list of Soviet citizens of Horodenka Region shot by German-Fascist invaders, from documents of a Soviet Commission for the investigation of military crimes 1944 – 46

Transliterated by Alexander Dunai

KEY			
Symbol	Meaning	Symbol	Meaning
-	Not given in original	+	Not given in translation
.	Illegible in original	,	Illegible in translation
[ ]	Unclear in original; possible correct spelling	/	Possible alternative spelling

.toz	-	1887	-	4 December 1942
.toz	Genia	1920	-	4 December 1942
.toz	Klara	1923	-	4 December 1942
.toz	Moses	1885	-	4 December 1942
Abzug	Gitsi	-	-	1942
Abzug	Leiba	-	-	1942
Abzug	Milik	-	-	1942
Abzug	Spi.a	-	-	1942
Abzuk	Bolko	-	-	1942
Abzuk	Feiga	-	-	1942
Abzuk	Isak	-	-	1942

Abzuk	Juda	-	-	1942
Abzuk	Sura	-	-	1942
Balan	Celka	1920	peasant	+
Balan	Chaika	1933	trader	+
Balan	Izio	1923	peasant	+
Balan	Josef N.	1898	trader	+
Balan	Kolnus	1885	furrier	+
Balan	Lebaa	1864	peasant	+
Balan	Leika	1927	baker	+
Balan	Moses	1923	baker	+
Balan	Moses	1928	trader	+
Balan	Munio	1908	peasant	+
Balan	Noeta Mich.	1889	peasant	+
Balan	Rosa	1890	peasant	+
Balan	Schia	1909	trader	+
Balan	Schifka	1918	teacher	+
Balan	Schilan	1912	trader	+
Balan	Schimon	1912	teacher	+
Balan	Sura	1900	trader	+
Balan	Touba	1887	furrier	+
Berman	Chaia	1925	student	4 December 1942
Berman	Hersch	1915	,	4 December 1942
Berman	Maria	1926	student	4 December 1942
Bilder	Brucha	-	-	1942
Bilder	Ita	-	-	1942
Bilder	Perits	-	-	1942
Bilder	Sosi	-	-	1942
Bir	....	1910	......	1942
Blasenstein	-	1900	trader	17 September 1942
Blasenstein	-	1905	housewife	17 September 1942
Blasenstein	-	1932	-	17 September 1942

Blasenstein	-	1940	-	17 September 1942
Bleterfeint	Chaim	1930	student	4 December 1941
Bleterfeint	Jakow	1886	worker	4 December 1941
Bleterfeint	Salda	1888	worker	4 December 1941
Bleterfeint	Sula	1928	worker	4 December 1941
Buch	Schendla	1889	peasant	+
Buch	Selda	1880	peasant	+
Diamant	Abraham	1923	student	17 September 1942
Diamant	Sara	1900	housewife	17 September 1942
Diker	Dawid	1883	worker	11 November 1941
Diker	Frida	1933	student	11 November 1941
Diker	Leicia	1882	housewife	11 November 1941
Diker	Maer	1904	housewife	11 November 1941
Diker	Mortko	1894	worker	11 November 1941
Diker	Weider	....	.	.
[D]iner	Chana	1880	housewife	4 November 1941
[D]iner	Jakub	1935	student	17 September 1942
[D]iner	Josef	1938	student	17 September 1942
[D]iner	Meier	1902	furrier	17 September 1942
[D]iner	Mina	1929	student	17 September 1942
[D]iner	Regina	1912	dressmaker	17 September 1942
Farber	-	-	peasant	1942
Farber	-	-	peasant	1942
Farber	-	-	peasant	1942
Feier	Golda	1920	+	+
Feier	Josel	1885	+	1941
Feier	Malka	1922	+	+
Feier	Rosa	1925	+	+
Fenster	Chaika	1929	student	1941
Fenster	Leon	1895	tailor	1941
Fenster	Mina	1922	student	1941

Fenster	Sara	1890	housewife	1941
Fenster	Todorus	1931	carrier	1941
Fentner	Chaim	1920	dressmaker	1942
Fentner	Lea	1922	dressmaker	1942
Fentner	Matilda	1905	housewife	1942
Fetcher	Abraham	1903	joiner	17 September 1942
Fetcher	Chaia	1936	student	17 September 1942
Fetcher	Estera	1912	housewife	17 September 1942
Fetcher	[K]atan	1932	student	17 September 1942
Fetcher	[K]echa	1929	student	17 September 1942
Findner	Luser	1910	-	4 December 1942
Frenkil	-	-	peasant	1942
Frenkil	-	-	peasant	1942
Frenkil	-	-	peasant	1942
Frenkil	-	-	peasant	1942
Frenkil	-	-	peasant	1942
Frenkil	-	-	peasant	1942
Frig[l]an	Meisel S.	1914	doctor	17 September 1942
Frig[l]an	Rosa	1905	trader	17 September 1942
Frig[l]an	Simon Leib.	1900	trader	17 September 1942
Frischling	Chaia	1885	baker	4 December 1942
Frischling	Ciupa	1921	student	4 December 1942
Frischling	Dawid	1926	student	4 December 1942
Frischling	Etla	1923	baker	4 December 1942
Frischling	Mendel	1885	peasant	4 December 1942
Frischling	Schoina	1920	baker	4 December 1942
Frischling	Srul	1920	baker	4 December 1942
[F]rizgant	-	1887	employee	17 September 1942
[F]rizgant	-	1890	employee	17 September 1942
[F]rizgant	Frida	1900	employee	17 September 1942
[F]rizgant	Klara	1915	employee	17 September 1942

Genedel	Yuremen	1939	baker	1942
Georger	Cila	1915	trader	1941
Georger	Minia	1927	student	1941
Georger	Rachela	1923	student	1941
Georger	Sara	1926	student	1941
Georger	Solon	1910	trader	1941
Gertner	-	1910	-	4 December 1942
Gertner	Nolek	1936	-	4 December 1942
Gertner	Pepi	1920	-	4 December 1942
Gigoger	-	1910	peasant	4 December 1942
Giter	-	1930	student	4 December 1942
Giter	-	1936	student	4 December 1942
Giter	Abraham	1884	-	4 December 1942
Giter	Aron	1929	-	4 December 1942
Giter	Chana	1900	-	4 December 1942
Giter	Maria	1937	-	4 December 1942
Giter	Moses	1880	-	4 December 1942
Gloger	Astla	1926	dressmaker	4 December 1942
Gloger	Chumu	1915	student	4 December 1942
Gloger	Pepi	1923	peasant	4 December 1942
Goldenberg	Chana	-	-	1942
Goldenberg	Moshko	-	-	1942
Goldenberg	Rifka	-	-	1942
Goldenberg	Schloma	-	-	1942
Goldenberg	Sura	-	-	1942
Gorpik	Etka	1907	+	+
Gorpik	Marcus (son of Mendel)	1895	+	+
Gorpik	Mincia	1934	+	+
Grindligner	Chaim	1895	trader	17 September 1942
Grindligner	Loti	1915	milliner	17 September 1942

Grindligner	Mordko	1910	worker	17 September 1942
Grindligner	Rosa	1897	housewife	17 September 1942
Grindligner	[M]isa	1922	student	17 September 1942
Grindner	Chane	1894	housewife	4 December 1941
Grindner	Chesia	1931	student	4 December 1941
Grindner	Lunia	1930	student	4 December 1941
Grindner	Lusia	1932	student	4 December 1941
Grindner	[V]ove	1892	trader	4 December 1941
Gutman	Berko	-	-	1942
Gutman	Blita	1868	housewife	1942
Gutman	Chana	-	-	1942
Gutman	Chana	1905	housewife	17 September 1942
Gutman	Etka	1920	housewife	17 September 1942
Gutman	Jakub	1900	trader	17 September 1942
Gutman	Leon	1938	musician	17 September 1942
Gutman	Leon	1941	-	-
Gutman	Milik (son of Jakub)	1915	trader	17 September 1942
Gutman	Moshko	-	-	1942
Gutman	Natan	1930	student	17 September 1942
Gutman	Rosa	1924	student	17 September 1942
Gutman	Sanbel	1923	student	17 September 1942
Gutman	Schirina	1922	housewife	17 September 1942
Habsknecht	Estera	1895	housewife	17 September 1942
Habsknecht	Genia	1912	tailor	17 September 1942
Habsknecht	Isak	1890	trader	17 September 1942
Habsknecht	Samuel Isak	1920	trader	17 September 1942
Hainer	Jacow	1895	tailor	4 December 1941
Haipern	Ninka	1915	housewife	1941
Halpern	Cila	1928	student	4 December 1941
Halpern	Dawid	1883	trader	4 December 1941

Hauernocht	Barluch	1930	student	1941
Hauernocht	Leon	1885	furrier	1941
Hauernocht	Sara	1910	housewife	1941
Inslicht	+	+	+	+
Inslicht	+	+	+	+
Inslicht	+	+	+	+
Jankner	[Ch]of	1919	teacher	4 December 1941
Kanich	Benzi	1894	worker	4 December 1941
Kanich	Max	19_2	student	4 December 1941
Kanich	Max	1930	student	4 December 1941
Kanich	Roisa	1912	worker	4 December 1941
Kanter	Dawid	1900	,	4 December 1941
Kanter	Dusia	1927	student	4 December 1941
Kanter	Kuba	1932	student	4 December 1941
Kanter	Menia	1915	housewife	4 December 1941
[K]apa	Maria	1899	housewife	4 December 1942
[K]apa	Rosa	1937	housewife	4 December 1942
Karp	-	-	peasant	1942
Karp	-	-	peasant	1942
Karp	-	-	peasant	1942
Karp	-	-	peasant	1942
Karp	-	-	peasant	1942
Karp	Moshko Rubin	-	peasant	1942
Keiman	-	1910	peasant	4 December 1942
Keiman	-	1915	peasant	4 December 1942
Keiman	-	1930	student	4 December 1942
Keitan	Nosia	1885	housewife	1941
Ki[l]	Chaim	1925	tailor	17 September 1942
Ki[l]	Leika	1927	-	17 September 1942
Ki[l]	Malka	1930	-	17 September 1942
Ki[l]	Rosia	1886	housewife	17 September 1942

Kirschner	-	1885	-	4 December 1942
Kirschner	-	1887	-	4 December 1942
Kirschner	-	1921	-	4 December 1942
Kirschner	-	1924	-	4 December 1942
Kirschner	-	1925	-	4 December 1942
Kirschner	Gusia	1926	-	4 December 1942
Kirschner	Peisio	1923	-	4 December 1942
Knobler	Beila	-	-	1942
Knobler	Isak	-	-	1942
Knobler	Malka	-	-	1942
Knobler	Mishlin	-	-	1942
Knobler	Moshko	-	-	1942
Knobler	Tauba	-	-	1942
Koch	-	1888	employee	4 December 1942
Koch	-	1890	peasant	4 December 1942
Koch	-	1926	student	17 September 1942
Koch	-	1927	student	4 December 1942
Koch	Chana	1914	housewife	1942
Koch	Lusio	1936	student	1942
Koch	Mendel	1912	trader	1942
Koch	Sara	1880	trader	17 September 1942
Koch	Yochan	1875	trader	17 September 1942
Kon(Kohn)	-	1910	peasant	4 December 1942
Kon(Kohn)	-	1915	peasant	4 December 1942
Kon(Kohn)	Chaia	1926	student	4 December 1942
Kopelman	Idel	1914	+	+
Korn	-	1885	-	4 December 1942
Korn	-	1887	-	4 December 1942
Korn	Gi.i	1927	-	4 December 1942
Korn	Schlomy	1921	-	4 December 1942
Korn	Tauby	1923	-	4 December 1942

Korn	Uri	1930	-	4 December 1942
Kotelman	Feiga	1921	+	+
Koval	Chana	1916	housewife	17 September 1942
Koval	Simon Filip.	1903	tailor	17 September 1942
Koval	Sosia (daughter of Simon)	1941	-	17 September 1942
Las[p]ner	Chania	1886	housewife	1941
Las[p]ner	Chima	1920	employee	1941
Lautman	Eiar	1929	student	11 November 1941
Lautman	Frida	1900	housewife	11 November 1941
Lautman	Leib	1892	worker	11 November 1941
Lautman	Schlim	1926	student	11 November 1941
Lechner	Chaim	1882	trader	+
Lechner	Cirli	1887	peasant	+
Leiner	Brana	-	-	1942
Leiner	Dawid	-	-	1942
Leiner	Leiser	-	-	1942
Lichtental	Frida	1925	student	1942
Lichtental	Golda	1905	housewife	1942
Lichtental	Maku	1928	student	1942
Lichtental	Moses	1900	trader	1942
Lichtental	Rosa	1924	student	1942
Lichtental	Roza	1938	student	1942
Lichtental	Sanon	1930	trader	1942
Lidman	Leika	1915	housewife	4 December 1941
Lidman	Meier	1910	coachman	4 December 1941
Linn	Rifka	-	-	1942
Linn	Roisa	-	-	1942
Linn	Schmila	-	-	1942
Linn	Sura	-	-	1942
Magles	Abram	1923	student	4 December 1941

Manger	Binda	-	-	1942
Manger	Itli	-	-	1942
Manger	Martin	-	-	1942
Manger	Paldi	-	-	1942
Marguns	Chaim	1901	trader	4 December 1941
Miler	Golda	1936	+	+
Miler	Margulia	1904	+	+
Miler	Rosa	1938	+	+
Miler	Rubin	1898	+	1941
O[r]inger	Hersch(son of Hersch)	1899	+	+
O[r]inger	Moische (son of Hersch)	1927	+	+
O[r]inger	Mona (son of Hersch)	1902	+	+
O[r]inger	Sudko (son of Hersch)	1922	+	+
Ofenberger	-	-	peasant	1942
Ofenberger	-	-	peasant	1942
Ofenberger	-	-	peasant	1942
Ofenberger	-	-	peasant	1942
Ofenberger	-	-	peasant	1942
Ofenberger	-	1885	student	4 December 1942
Ofenberger	-	1935	peasant	4 December 1942
Ofenberger	Schlim	1821	furrier	4 December 1942
Preminger	-	-	+	+
Preminger	-	-	+	+
Preminger	-	-	+	+
Reif	Chaskel	1928	student	1941
Reif	Chawa	1914	housewife	1942
Reif	Josef	1905	worker	1942
Reif	Mina I.	1930	student	1941

Reif	Salamon	1926	student	1941
Reis	-	1897	peasant	4 December 1942
Reis	-	1925	student	4 December 1942
Reis	-	1927	-	4 December 1942
Reis	Broniar (daughter of Leiser)	1892	+	+
Reis	Bronia (daughter of Mendel)	1920	+	+
Reis	Etka (daughter of Emil)	1924	+	+
Reis	Marcus (son of Schimon)	1878	+	+
Reis	Meiorko (son of Leiser)	1912	+	+
Reis	Mendel (son of Leib)	1884	trader	+
Reis	Mendel (son of Leiser)	1910	+	+
Reis	Mendel	1889	trader	4 December 1942
Reis	Mina (daughter of Emil)	1894	+	+
Reis	Mina (daughter of Mendel)	1890	+	+
Reis	Nina (daughter of Leiser)	1918	+	+
Reis	Nisia (daughter of Emil)	1918	+	+
Reis	Nisia (daughter of Leiser)	1914	+	+
Reis	Rosa (daughter of Mendel)	1917	+	+
Reis	Rosa (daughter of Schimon)	19..	+	+
Reis	Ruchla	1902	+	+

	(daughter of Schimon)			
Reisberg	Rosa	1907	+	+
Reiter	+	+	+	+
Reiter	+	+	+	+
Reiter	+	+	+	+
Reiter	+	+	+	+
Reiter	+	+	+	+
Rindner	Lyutti	1915	housewife	4 December 1942
Rindner	Renoti	1910	shoemaker	4 December 1942
Rindner	Renoti	1933	-	4 December 1942
Rindner	Ruti	1929	student	4 December 1942
Roiberg	Blima	1889	+	+
Roiberg	Buniu	1920	+	+
Roiberg	Hesi	1903	+	+
Rosemberg	Blima	1927	+	+
Rosemberg	Chancia	1890	+	+
Rosemberg	Henia	1929	+	+
Rosemberg	Herman	1897	peasant	4 December 1942
Rosemberg	Samila	1900	housewife	4 December 1942
Rosenbaum	-	1885	student	4 December 1942
Rosenbaum	-	1928	student	4 December 1942
Rosenbaum	Amper	1928	student	4 December 1942
Rosenbaum	Benjamin	1891	trader	4 December 1941
Rosenbaum	Chaia	1894	housewife	4 December 1941
Rosenbaum	Lot	1920	housewife	4 December 1941
Rosenbaum	Mina	1930	student	4 December 1942
Rosenbaum	Minka	1925	student	4 December 1941
Rosenbaum	Rachela	1926	student	4 December 1942
Rosenbaum	Seilek	1885	peasant	4 December 1942
Rosenbaum	[B]enuz	1928	student	4 December 1941

Rosenberg	-	1930	-	4 December 1942
Rosenberg	-	1942	-	4 December 1942
Rosenkranz	Hersch	1922	+	+
Rosenkranz	Malka	1925	+	+
Rosenkranz	Moses	1927	+	+
Rosenkranz	Rosa	1889	+	+
Rosenrauch	Isak	1888	-	4 December 1942
Rubinger	Blima	1925	+	+
Rubinger	Hersch	1898	+	+
Rubinger	Malka	1901	+	1941
Schachter	-	1925	peasant	4 November 1941
Schachter	-	1926	peasant	4 November 1941
Schachter	-	1927	peasant	4 November 1941
Schachter	-	1930	peasant	4 November 1941
Schachter	Chana	1890	peasant	4 November 1941
Schachter	Ida	1887	peasant	4 November 1941
Schader	Estera	1910	housewife	17 September 1942
Schader	Lea M.	1928	student	17 September 1942
Schader	Moses Leib.	1907	furrier	17 September 1942
Schader	[M]ina M.	1924	student	17 September 1942
Schafer	+	+	+	+
Schafer	+	+	+	+
Schaiwa	-	-	+	+
Schaiwa	-	-	+	+
Schaiwa	-	-	+	1942
Schauder	Berko	-	-	1942
Schauder	Dawid	1900	peasant	1942
Schauder	Sara	1923	employee	1942
Schauder	Se..ga	1920	employee	1942
Schauder	Yosio	1926	dressmaker	1942
Schmelcer	+	+	+	+

Schmelcer	+	+	+	+
Schmelcer	+	+	+	+
Schmelcer	+	+	+	+
Schmelcer	+	+	+	1942
Schreider	-	1910	peasant	4 December 1942
Schreider	-	1915	student	4 December 1942
Schreider	-	1930	peasant	4 December 1942
Schreider	Mudsio	1926	student	4 December 1942
Schubert	Aron E.	1904	+	+
Schubert	Feiga (daughter of Abraham)	1925	+	+
Schubert	Maria	1901	+	+
Schubert	Moische (son of Abraham)	1928	+	+
Schubert	[L]ida/[D]ida (daughter of Abraham)	1923	+	+
Schuldiner	Babcia	1899	+	+
Schuldiner	Golda	1923	+	+
Schuldiner	Josef	1895	+	+
Schuldiner	Rusia	1920	+	+
Schwarz	-	1910	peasant	4 December 1942
Schwarz	-	1915	peasant	4 December 1942
Schwarz	-	1930	student	4 December 1942
Schwarz	-	1937	student	4 December 1942
Schwarz	Abraham	1920	,	4 December 1942
Schwarz	Aron	1927	student	4 December 1942
Schwarz	Bosia	1920	dressmaker	4 December 1942
Schwarz	Gesio	1900	cooper	4 December 1942
Schwarz	Liba	1929	student	4 December 1942
Seidman	Abram	-	-	1942
Seidman	Klara	-	-	1942

Seidman	Sura	-	-	1942
Seierer	Mendel Sudowich	+	+	+
Seifer	Sara	1874	trader	+
Silber	Benjamen	-	-	1942
Silber	Isaak	-	-	1942
Silber	Itli	-	-	1942
Silberbusch	+	+	+	+
Silberbusch	+	+	+	+
Sirber	Matli	-	peasant	1942
Sirber	Moshko	-	peasant	1942
Sirber	Ruchli	-	peasant	1942
Slosar	-	1927	student	17 September 1942
Slosar	-	1929	student	4 December 1942
Slosar	Beila	1896	housewife	17 September 1942
Slosar	Moilo	1895	employee	17 September 1942
Sobil	Hudi	1880	+	+
Sobil	Josel	1899	+	+
Sobil	Rusia	1901	+	+
Sobil	Wolf	1884	+	+
Solpeter	-	1910	housewife	4 December 1942
Solpeter	Chaia	1929	student	4 December 1942
Solpeter	Dawid	1930	student	4 December 1942
Solpeter	Matler	1910	housewife	4 December 1942
Solpeter	Roida	1939	-	4 December 1942
Spirer	Chaia	1915	housewife	17 September 1942
Spirer	Chaim	1936	-	17 September 1942
Spirer	Gitsi	-	-	1942
Spirer	Golda	1938	-	17 September 1942
Spirer	Isak	1905	trader	1942
Spirer	Moses	1905	furrier	17 September 1942

Spirer	Munio	1935	-	17 September 1942
Spirer	Perla	-	-	1942
Spirer	Rozia	1936	student	1942
Spirer	Schiku	1936	student	1942
Spirer	Selda	1912	housewife	1942
Spunt	-	1910	peasant	4 December 1942
Spunt	-	1915	peasant	4 December 1942
Spunt	Juda	1923	student	4 December 1942
Spunt	Srul	1920	student	4 December 1942
Spunt	Viga	1926	student	4 December 1942
Strisor	Samuel Ab.	1887	worker	17 September 1942
Sucher	-	1885	housewife	4 December 1942
Sucher	-	1885	baker	4 December 1942
Sucher	-	1885	tailor	4 December 1942
Sucher	Chana	1921	student	4 December 1942
Sucher	Jakub	1920	baker	4 December 1942
Sucher	Meier	1923	student	4 December 1942
Ta[u]ber	Chana	1921	-	4 December 1942
Ta[u]ber	Schinder	1884	-	4 December 1942
Ta[u]ber	Sender	1917	-	4 December 1942
[T]echner	-	1895	housewife	17 September 1942
[T]echner	-	1927	student	17 September 1942
[T]echner	-	1932	student	17 September 1942
[T]erner	Dawid	1888	engineer	17 September 1942
Teitler	Blima	1899	+	+
Teitler	Blima	1934	+	+
Teitler	Dudio	1923	+	+
Teitler	Estera	1925	+	+
Teitler	Hersch	1896	+	+
Teitler	Moses	1920	+	+
Teper	Estera	1903	worker	17 September 1942

Teper	Josef Jakub.	1930	student	17 September 1942
Teper	Salia Jakub.	1926	student	17 September 1942
Tiger	Hersch	1905	employee	1942
Tiker	Gesio	1930	student	4 December 1941
Tiker	Golda	1920	employee	4 December 1941
Tiker	Yosio	1930	student	4 December 1941
[T]reibich	Frida	1905	peasant	4 December 1942
[T]reibich	Jacob	1900	peasant	4 December 1942
Vizding	Malka Hersch.	1927	student	17 September 1942
Vizding	Regina Hersh.	1915	employee	17 September 1942
Vizding	Rusia	1940	-	17 September 1942
Vog	Gesio	1936	student	1942
Vog	Gusta	1915	housewife	1942
Vog	Peisio	1930	student	1942
Vog	Samo	1932	student	1942
Weinstein	Chana	1905	housewife	17 September 1942
Weinstein	Chaskel	1925	barber	1942
Weinstein	Froim	1930	-	1942
Weinstein	Sama	1927	student	1942
Weisbrat	Adela	1923	student	1941
Weisbrat	Chana	1930	student	1941
Weisbrat	Golda	1915	housewife	1941
Weisbrat	Kiba	1939	student	1941
Weisbrat	Lotti	1926	student	1941
Weisbrat	Maise	1910	tailor	4 December 1941
Windner	Malka	1887	peasant	1942
Windner	Meier	1930	student	1942
Windner	Seida	1885	peasant	1942
Windner	Seidek	1935	student	1942
Yakhalz	Sulio	1910	peasant	+
Yankner	-	1915	employee	17 September 1942

Yankner	-	1930	student	17 September 1942
Yankner	Basia	1888	housewife	1942
Yankner	Blima	1917	student	1942
Yankner	Burech	1914	baker	1942
Yankner	Chaia	1923	dressmaker	4 December 1942
Yankner	Chaika	1926	student	4 December 1942
Yankner	Cipka	1885	peasant	4 December 1942
Yankner	Deimilen Ya.	1915	employee	17 September 1942
Yankner	Ester	1885	peasant	4 December 1942
Yankner	Frida	1935	student	17 September 1942
Yankner	Ginkas	1910	trader	4 December 1941
Yankner	Jakub	1923	student	4 December 1942
Yankner	Josef	1915	baker	1942
Yankner	Josef	1921	student	4 December 1942
Yankner	Mei.	1880	baker	1942
Yankner	Rifka	1910	housewife	4 December 1942
Yankova	Sara	1915	-	4 December 1942
Yanteno[k]	Chaim	1892	doctor	4 December 1941
Yanteno[k]	Chana	1890	doctor	4 December 1941
Yurman	Chana	-	-	1942
Yurman	Golda	1920	+	+
Yurman	Malka	1924	+	+
Yurman	Marili	1881	+	+
Yurman	Pesch	1922	+	+
Yurman	Rifka	-	-	1942
Yurman	Schangli	-	-	1942
Zaler	Krenci	1900	+	+
Zaler	Mendel	1904	+	+
Zaler	Nusia	1906	+	+
Zaler	Schuluch (son of Josef)	1906	+	+

Zawgerer	-	-	peasant	1942
Zawgerer	-	-	peasant	1942
Zawgerer	-	-	peasant	1942
Zawgerer	-	-	peasant	1942
Zawgerer	Dudio	-	peasant	1942
Zidi.fogin	Leon	1940	-	17 September 1942
Zidi.fogin	Moses	1912	trader	17 September 1942
Zidi.fogin	Sara	1917	housewife	17 September 1942
Ziferblat	+	+	+	+
Ziferblat	+	+	+	+
Ziferblat	+	+	+	+
Ziferblat	+	+	+	+
Ziferblat	+	+	+	+
Ziferblat	+	+	+	+
Ziferblat	Berko	+	+	+
Ziferblat	Bubi	1938	student	11 November 1941
Ziferblat	Chaem	1932	student	11 November 1941
Ziferblat	Dwoira	1929	student	11 November 1941
Ziferblat	Martko	1923	tailor?	11 November 1941
Ziferblat	Mechel	1894	worker	11 November 1941
Ziferblat	Perol	1892	housewife	11 November 1941
Ziferblat	Schmaer	1924	joiner	11 November 1941
Zumer	-	-	+	+
Zumer	-	-	+	+
Zumer	-	-	+	+
Zumer	-	-	+	+
Zumer	-	-	+	+

Some Libraries and Archives that Have *Sefer Horodenka*

Sefer Horodenka is held by libraries all across the United States, and by **Yad Vashem** in Israel. Thanks for much of this list goes to Deborah Dworski and to Sharon Horowitz of the Hebraic section of the Library of Congress.

- California, Sacramento http://www.library.ca.gov/ (California State Library)

- California, Los Angeles http://www.library.ucla.edu/libraries/url/colls/judaica/yizkor.htm (University of California at Los Angeles)

- California, Palo Alto (Stanford University)

- Florida, Boca Raton (Florida Atlantic University)

- Florida, Gainesville http://www.ufl.edu/ (University of Florida)

- Illinois, Chicago http://www.spertus.edu/ (Spertus Institute of Jewish Studies)

- Israel, Jerusalem (Yad Vashem)

- Louisiana, Baton Rouge http://smt.state.lib.la.us/ (Louisiana State Library)

- Massachusetts, Boston (Boston Public Library)

- Massachusetts, Cambridge (Harvard College)

- Massachusetts, Waltham http://www.brandeis.edu/ (Brandeis University)

- Michigan, Ann Arbor (University of Michigan)

- Michigan, West Bloomfield http://www.holocaustcenter.com/ekyiz.shtml (Holocaust Memorial Center)

- Missouri, St. Louis (Washington University)

- New York, Binghamton (State University of New York at Binghamton)

- New York, New York City http://www.baruch.cuny.edu/yivo/ (YIVO)

- New York, New York City
  http://www.nypl.org/research/chss/jws/jewish.html (New York
  City Public Library)

- Ohio, Cleveland (Cleveland Public Library)

- Ohio, Columbus (Ohio State University)

- Pennsylvania, Melrose Park http://www.gratzcollege.edu/ (Gratz
  College)

- Pennsylvania, Philadelphia http://library.cjs.upenn.edu/
  (University of Pennsylvania)

- Texas, Austin (University of Texas)

- Utah, Salt Lake City (LDS Family History Library)

- Utah, Salt Lake City (University of Utah)

- Washington, D.C. http://www.loc.gov/ (Library of Congress)

- Washington, D.C. http://www.ushmm.org/uia-
  bin/uia_query?dl=ushmm_ia&dn=library&qy=Horodenka+or&md=
  250 (United States Holocaust Memorial Museum)

PREFACE

Horodenka is a little town in Eastern Galicia, which was said to be the administrative centre of a region containing forty-eight small villages.

The history of its organised Jewish communal life begins in the year 1743, although Horodenka is mentioned as a small village as early as 1579. According to historical documents it was raised to the rank of a city in the Seventeenth century when it passed into the hands of the famous Polish noble family Potocki, who owned the entire agricultural area. There are certain documents from which it would appear that a number of Jewish families were already living there in the early part of the Seventeenth century, even before it became a town. Reliable sources, however, make it clear that the Jews of Horodenka became significant as a community only in the middle of the Eighteenth century. Jewish merchants from the city are recorded among the visitors to the International Fair at Leipzig, 1739—1748.

Documents of the half-century 1870—1927 show that the average percentage of Jews in the entire population varied between 33% and 40%, against 45%—55% of Ruthenians (or Ukrainians) and barely 10% of Poles.

On the map Horodenka will be found at the point where the one-time Polish frontier touched on the frontiers of Russia to the East and Rumania to the South. As a result of this topographical position the inhabitants of Horodenka, and especially the Jews among them, were always the first to suffer at the outbreak of war between the above countries.

It should also be noted that although the Poles were a small minority, their historical and political aspirations in this region had the result that they were almost always in charge of municipal institutions and life. On the other hand the Ukrainians, who were usually in a numerical majority, were unable to take over municipal institutions and the mayoralty in the absence of properly trained and qualified political leaders. Nevertheless they developed national aspirations, and various official declarations from the neighbouring country encouraged them to attempt to join the Ukraine, which was under the Tzarist regime and part of Russia.

The Jewish Community had to find a way of living together with the other two national groups and their political aspirations which could not always be understood by their two neighbours. In addition, the Jewish leaders of the city often found it very difficult to maintain a single line of policy which at the same time enabled them to live satisfactorily among themselves and with their neighbours.

As a result there were constant disagreements between

מראה הרחוב הראשי בשנת 1915
די הויפט־גאס אין יאר 1915
View on the main street
in 1915.

the various inner Jewish groups regarding the right steps to take as various political problems emerged. It followed that neither of the other national minorities was on friendly terms with the Jews, with results that were clearly felt between 1914 and 1917 during the First World War, when the city was repeatedly occupied and re-occupied by the Russians and the Austrians in turn. In this situation Jewish lives and property were in constant danger, and a virtual pogrom atmosphere was the order of the day.

However, the Jews of Horodenka faced their final tragedy during the Second World War. Horodenka had been occupied by the Russians a few weeks after the German attack on Poland in Autumn 1939. When the Nazis attacked Russia in turn, in June 1941, they occupied Horodenka and remained there until the end of the war. During that period of close on four years they virtually succeeded in their "final solution" by exterminating the whole Jewish population. In this they were gladly assisted by a large number of the local Ukrainians, who as a result have "inherited" all Jewish property in one way or another. According to reliable evidence about 3,000 adults and children were murdered in 1941 and 1942, in the course of three "Actions".

A bare handful of Horodenka Jews succeeded in escaping from the city of their birth and made their way either to Russia or to Rumania. From them it is learnt that no significant resistance was shown by any part of the local population at the commencement of the Nazi occupation. Soon after the first Action, however, Jews ceased to believe Nazi promises and propaganda and began to realise their true position. Several young Jews then joined the partisans who were just beginning to organise resistance activities in the forests on the other side of the River Dniester. Thanks to this handful of men and women, who ultimately reached Israel, U.S.A., U.S.S.R. and Latin America, we know some facts about the destruction and annihilation of Horodenka Jewry and Jewish life.

No matter how much we grieve we cannot bring back our dear and beloved parents, our sisters and brothers and their innocent children, who were deprived of their lives so murderously during the "liquidation" of European Jewry.

In 1945 the first survivors arrived here in Eretz Israel and gave an account of what had happened. Those already in this country who had been born or had lived in Horodenka then organised a Committee with the aims of giving all possible aid and comfort to the newcomers, and establishing a monument for the thousands of Horodenka Jews who had fallen victim to the Nazis between 1941 and 1945. The various suggestions made about the most suitable monument included a proposal for a Memorial Volume to record the story of the Horodenka Jewish community from its beginnings until its end; a history covering a period of 2—4 centuries.

It was decided to adopt this proposal, and so a

התחלת ההדפסה של ספר־הורודנקה
אָנהויב פון דרוקן דעם
„ספר הָארָאדענקע“
The Begin of printing the
"Sefer Horodenka"

beginning was made with "Sefer Horodenka", the Horodenka Book, which has been edited, written and financed by sons and daughters of Horodenka all the world over. Some of the articles, it is true, were written by persons who were not born there; but they either lived in the city for several years or married Horodenka men and women, and can therefore be regarded as residents.

We who have survived are the sole orphans and heirs of what was a flourishing community. We do not set out to produce a volume which is exclusive, nor do we aim at a work of outstanding literary value. What we have tried to produce is a joint co-operative publication made by and speaking for the survivors of this small Jewish town, as part of the history of that remarkable Jewry of Poland which existed for so long, until it was finally obliterated from the map of Jewry throughout the world.

In this brief English preface it is not our purpose to repeat all that is to be found in the Hebrew and Yiddish sections. What we aim to do is to give the children of those who came from our little birthplace some idea of the fate of their grandparents and kinsfolk, in order that they may from time to time remember those thousands who were slaughtered by the Nazis during the Second World War, with all the resources of modern science and organisation. And it goes without saying that this "Sefer Horodenka" could never have come into being if all the children of Horodenka who have survived the

overwhelming catastrophe had not made every effort and assumed the necessary responsibility.

It should be borne in mind that this volume, like others of the same kind, has meant an outlay of about $ 8000, in addition to the difficulties involved in collecting and editing the material itself. It was possible to achieve this result only thanks to an agreement reached between the Horodenka townsfolk in the U.S.A. and Israel. In bringing about this agreement our friends Ruth and Abe Podway of New York played a very important part.

We wish to thank all those who have participated in any form in this volume, and who have helped to bring it into being. Thank you one and all for anything and everything you have done.

We would like all former members of the Horodenka community or from the surrounding villages, and all those who have the names of individual survivors coming from the region, to send their names on to us, in order that we may ensure that all of them have an opportunity of obtaining this volume. For we know that at the proper memorial season each and every one of us will read through the list of Jewish victims who gave up their lives to hallow the Holy Name and the name of the suffering Jewish people.

May their spirits be bound up in the Bundle of Life!

For and on behalf of the Book Committee

M. FLESCHNER

Tel Aviv, Rosh Hashana 5724, September 1963

המסיבה להופעת המחצית הראשונה
של הספר 14.11.1962
צום דערשײנען פון ערשטער העלפט
פון בוך 14.11.1962
The meeting where the completion of the first Part of the Book was announced — Tel-Aviv 14/11/1962.

INDEX

Biderman, 26, 355
Bikel, 142, 292
Biker, 271
Bilder, 121, 127, 143, 144, 237, 241, 242, 243,
253, 270, 312, 389, 455, 473, 515
Bildner, 509
Biler, 473
Binder, 473, 509
Bir, 515
Birenboym, 10
Birnbaum, 6, 86
Birnboy, 417
Birnboym, 109, 123, 142, 143, 152, 153, 235,
241, 247, 251, 257, 258, 270, 446, 473
Bishl, 473
Bitter, 509
Blasenstein, 515, 516
Blat, 473, 474
Blater, 250, 509
Blatt, 227, 346
Blaukopf, 474
Blazenstein, 374
Bleterfeint, 516
Bleterfeynd, 474
Bley, 474
Blukopf, 209
Blum, 385
Blutah, 217
Blutal, 274, 443, 474
Bluthal, 421
Bogan, 110
Böhm, 509
Boikie, 275
Boker, 443
Bolkhover, 472
Bomberg, 81, 461
Bongarten, 416
Bonus, 86, 472
Booker, 464
Boral, 152
Borenstate, 45
Bornstein, 113, 145
Borochov, 237
Bosner, 454
Boulai, 124
Boym, 444
Boymel, 473
Bozner, 209, 437, 438
Brait, 509
Brand, 509
Brash, 388, 392
Brauer, 509
Braver, 509
Breithchess, 331

Brekher, 475
Brekhner, 475
Brener, 114, 475
Brenner, 200, 455
Brettler, 509
Briger, 509
Briler, 248, 474, 475
Briller, 509
Brod, 463, 464
Brontshtein, 79
Broynshteyn, 475
Bruckenstein, 509
Bruckner, 509
Buch, 516
Buchalter, 58, 79, 88, 94, 154, 193, 201, 206,
219, 220, 227, 241, 244, 247, 315, 337, 381,
404, 406, 409, 412, 414, 417, 430, 432, 462,
464, 465, 467
Buchner, 509
Buchovski, 391
Bumberg, 243, 250, 261, 461, 473
Bundzier, 440
Bundzior, 275
Burg, 308, 419, 473
Burger, 509

C

Chaiml, 63
Chalzal, 453, 454
Chamades, 168
Charasch, 340, 513
Chayes, 121
Chayun, 56
Chazan, 296
Chodorover, 452
Clapton, 448
Cohen, 110, 205, 209, 210, 250, 278, 314, 329,
358, 448, 450, 470

D

D]lner, 516
Dachs, 509
Daifek, 81
Dankner, 47, 62, 478, 509
Degelman, 509
Denninger, 509
Dereshinsky, 383
Dermer, 265, 479
Diamant, 509, 516
Dicker, 243, 316
Diener, 509
Diffier, 59

S